THE
ROMANS
DEBATE

THE
ROMANS
DEBATE

REVISED AND EXPANDED EDITION

Karl P. Donfried, *Editor*

Baker Academic
a division of Baker Publishing Group
Grand Rapids, Michigan

© 1977, 1991 by Karl P. Donfried

Published by Baker Academic
a division of Baker Publishing Group
P.O. Box 6287, Grand Rapids, MI 49516-6287
www.bakeracademic.com

Baker Academic edition published 2011
ISBN 978-0-8010-4607-0

Previously published in 1991 by Hendrickson Publishers

Original edition published by Augsburg Publishing House: Minneapolis, 1977

Printed in the United States of America

The Library of Congress has cataloged the Hendrickson edition as follows:
    The Roman debate / edited by Karl P. Donfried.—Rev. and expanded.
        Includes bibliographical references and indexes.
            p.   cm.
        ISBN 1-56563-671-6
        1. Bible. N.T. Romans—Criticism, interpretation, etc. I. Donfried, Karl P.
    BS2665.2.R65 1991
    227'.106—dc20   91-13252

The bas relief on the cover comes from the funeral monument of a rich merchant at Neumagen near Trèves (2nd century CE). The scene depicts a master and his three pupils. The cover art appears courtesy of the Rhineland Museum in Trier, Germany, and is used with permission.

IN MEMORIAM

GÜNTHER BORNKAMM

(October 8, 1905 – February 18, 1990)

TABLE OF CONTENTS

PART II

Section A: Historical and Sociological Factors

Section B: The Structure and Rhetoric of Romans

Section C: The Theology of Romans: Issues in the Current Debate

PREFACE 1977

The essays in this volume are international and ecumenical in scope. Authors from Great Britain, Germany, Scandinavia, and the United States, Roman Catholic and Protestant, are included. The essays by Klein, Jervell, Wiefel, and Stirewalt are printed in English for the first time. The first three of these are translations from the German. My colleague, Jochen Hoffmann of the Smith College German Department, collaborated with me in these translations, and I am much indebted to him. Where possible we have preserved the original writing and footnote style of the individual authors. [These have been conformed to the Short Title List for *Romans Debate: Revised and Expanded Edition*. Ed.] I am also grateful for the consistently good help I have received from my two student assistants, Bitsey Shaw and Amy-Jill Levine.

I wish to acknowledge with thanks the courtesy of the following periodicals, publishers, and individuals for permission to use their copyrighted material in this volume: The John Rylands University Library of Manchester for the article by T. W. Manson; the *Australian Biblical Review* for the article by G. Bornkamm; the Chr. Kaiser Verlag for the article by G. Klein; the *Journal of Biblical Literature* for the article by K. P. Donfried; *Studia Theologica* for the article by J. Jervell; *Judaica* for the article by W. Wiefel; *The Catholic Biblical Quarterly* for the articles by R. J. Karris, K. P. Donfried, and W. Wuellner; and M. L. Stirewalt, Jr., for his permission to publish his typescript.

My deepest gratitude goes to Professor Ernst Käsemann, who, more than any other scholar, has helped me to better understand the complex mind of Paul and who has made me restless with many of the standard presentations of Pauline theology. From him and the other members of the Studiorum Novi Testamenti Societas Paul Seminar, which Professor Karl Kertelge and I were privileged to chair from 1974 to 1977, as well as from my friends in the Paul Seminar of the Society of Biblical Literature, I have learned much. May this small collection make a further contribution to our rethinking of Paul and especially his letter to the Romans.

Karl Paul Donfried
Smith College

PREFACE 1991

The purpose of this volume is both to assess the impact of *The Romans Debate* (1977) on subsequent scholarly discussion and also to assist the student of Romans in understanding the neuralgic issues in the current analyses of this Pauline letter.

An obvious challenge for the editor of a book such as this is that of selection and inclusion. The factors entering into such decisions are several and complex; one can only hope that the essays chosen achieve their intended purpose. I am grateful to several of the contributors in this new volume for their generous assistance and guidance in these matters, as well as to Joseph Fitzmyer, Paul Meyer, and Wilhelm Wuellner. Frank Hughes' critical reading and suggestions with regard to that section of my introductory essay dealing with rhetorical criticism were invaluable. Reginald and Ilse Fuller's translation of Peter Stuhlmacher's article is splendid. The unfailing encouragement and the exeptionally diligent efforts of Patrick Alexander, Academic Editor of Hendrickson Publishers, are deeply appreciated, and I am enormously indebted to my two student assistants, Eleanor Applewhite and Christine Arena, for their excellent assistance in producing indices of authors and ancient texts. To bring some degree of consistency to the latter index, while, simultaneously, not transforming to the point of non-recognizability the individual and unlike ways in which the many international scholars contributing to this volume have cited the ancient texts, was a most complex task. Needless to say, none of these gracious colleagues and friends are responsible for any shortcomings which may still be present.

This volume is dedicated with much gratitude and affection to the late Günther Bornkamm who was both my distinguished teacher and faithful friend. For almost thirty years now I have had the privilege of turning to him as a model and an inspiration in the task of theological exegesis. In a most real sense *The Romans Debate,* as well as this new edition, is deeply indebted to him. Much of my own thinking and scholarship on Romans have had their origin in a respectful tension and dialogue with Bornkamm. Perhaps the greatest tribute to Bornkamm's work on Paul is the fact that hardly an article or book dealing with Romans fails to ac-

knowledge his significant insights. His profound and productive scholarship, his commitment to the church, and his unfailing kindness have left
a profound impression on all who knew him.

Karl P. Donfried
Smith College
Northampton, Massachusetts
1991

ORIGINAL LOCATION OF ARTICLES

T. W. Manson, "St. Paul's Letter to the Romans—and Others," in *Studies in the Gospels and Epistles* (ed. M. Black; Manchester: Manchester University Press, 1962) 225–41.

Günther Bornkamm, "The Letter to the Romans as Paul's Last Will and Testament," *ABR* 11 (1963) 2–14.

Günter Klein, "Paul's Purpose in Writing the Epistle to the Romans." This article appears here in English translation; it was originally published as "Der Abfassungszweck des Römerbriefes" in Klein's volume *Rekonstruktion und Interpretation* (BEvTH 50; Munich: Chr. Kaiser, 1969) 129–44.

Karl Paul Donfried, "A Short Note on Romans 16," *JBL* 89 (1970) 441–49.

Jacob Jervell, "The Letter to Jerusalem," *StTh* 25 (1971) 61–73.

Robert J. Karris, "Romans 14:1–15:13 and the Occasion of Romans," *CBQ* 25 (1973) 155–78.

Wolfgang Wiefel, "The Jewish Community in Ancient Rome and the Origins of Roman Christianity." This article appears here in English translation; it was originally published as "Die jüdische Gemeinschaft im antiken Rom und die Angfänge des römischen Christentums. Bemerkungen zu Anlass und Zweck des Römerbriefs," *Jud* 26 (1970) 65–88.

Karl Paul Donfried, "False Presuppositions in the Study of Romans," *CBQ* 36 (1974) 332–58.

Robert J. Karris, "The Occasion of Romans: A Response to Prof. Donfried," *CBQ* 36 (1974) 356–58.

Wilhelm Wuellner, "Paul's Rhetoric of Argumentation in Romans: An Alternative to the Donfried–Karris Debate Over Romans," *CBQ* 38 (1976) 330–51.

Martin Luther Stirewalt, Jr., "The Form and Function of the Greek Letter-Essay." Previously unpublished.

F. F. Bruce, "The Romans Debate—Continued," *BJRL* 64 (1981–82) 334.

A. J. M. Wedderburn, "Purpose and Occasion of Romans Again," *ExpTim* 90 (1979) 137-41.

Francis Watson, "The Two Roman Congregations: Rom. 14:1–15:13." This essay is from Watson's monograph *Paul, Judaism and the Gentiles: A Sociological Approach* (MSSNTS 56; Cambridge: Cambridge University Press, 1986) 94–105.

Peter Lampe, "The Roman Christians of Romans 16." This essay has not been previously published but it is dependent on his book *Die stadtrömischen Christen in den ersten beiden Jahrhunderten* (WUNT 2/18; Tübingen: Mohr, 1987).

Peter Stuhlmacher, "The Purpose of Romans." This essay appeared originally in German as "Der Abfassungszweck des Römerbriefes," *ZNW* 77 (1986) 180–93 and was translated for this volume by Professors Reginald and Ilse Fuller.

James D. G. Dunn, "The Formal and Theological Coherence of Romans." This essay is from the introduction to Dunn's commentary *Romans 1–8* (WBC 38a; Waco: Word, 1988) lix–lxiii.

William S. Campbell, "Romans III as a Key to the Structure and Thought of the Letter," *NovT* 23 (1981) 22–40.

Robert Jewett, "Following the Argument of Romans." This essay was adapted and expanded by Robert Jewett for this volume from an earlier essay with the same title in *Word and World* 6 (1986) 382–89.

David E. Aune, "Romans as a *Logos Protreptikos.*" This essay is an abbreviation of a more extensive article entitled "Romans as a *Logos Protreptikos* in the Context of Ancient Religious and Philosophical Propaganda," to appear in *Paulus als Missionar und Theologe und das antike Judentum,* ed. Martin Hengel (Tübingen: J. C. B. Mohr, forthcoming).

James D. G. Dunn, "The New Perspective on Paul: Paul and the Law." This essay is from the introduction to Dunn's commentary *Romans 1–8* (WBC 38a; Waco: Word, 1988) lxiv–lxxii.

Lloyd Gaston, "Israel's Misstep in the Eyes of Paul." This essay appears in Gaston's book *Paul and the Torah* (Vancouver: University of British Columbia Press, 1987) 135–50.

J. C. Beker, "The Faithfulness of God and the Priority of Israel in Paul's Letter to the Romans," in *Christians Among Jews and Gentiles* (ed. G. W. E. Nickelsburg with G. W. MacRae; Philadelphia: Fortress, 1986) 10–16.

Peter Stuhlmacher, "The Theme of Romans," *AusBR* 36 (1988) 31–44.

The above are used with the kind permission of the respective publishers.

BIBLIOGRAPHY AND SHORT TITLE LIST

ABD   *Anchor Bible Dictionary*. New York: Doubleday, forthcoming.

Achtemeier, *Romans*   Achtemeier, P. J. *Romans*. Interpretation. Atlanta: John Knox, 1985.

Aland–Aland, *Text*   Aland, K. and B. Aland. *The Text of the New Testament*. Grand Rapids: Eerdmans, 1987.

Aletti, "Incohérence"   Aletti, J.-N. "Rm 1,18–3,20: Incohérence ou cohérence de l'argumentation paulinienne?" *Biblica* 69 (1988) 47–62.

Altaner, *Patrology*   Altaner, B. *Patrology*. Trans. H. C. Graef. Freiburg: Herder; Edinburgh/London: Nelson, 1960.

Amir, "*Ioudaismos*"   Amir, Y. "The Term *Ioudaismos*: A Study in Jewish-Hellenistic Self-Identification." *Immanuel* 14 (1982) 34–41.

AnBib   Analecta biblica

ANRW   *Austief und Niedergang der römischen Welt*

Araud, "Interprétations patristiques"   Araud, R. "Quidquid no est ex fide peccatum est: Quelques interprétations patristiques." *L'homme devant Dieu: Mélanges offerts au Père Henri de Lubac. Théologie*. Etudes publiées sous la direction de la faculté de théologie S. J. de Lyon-Fourvière 56. Paris: Aubier, Editions Montaigne, 1963.

ARW   *Archiv für Religionswissenschaft*

Askowith, *Toleration and Persecution of the Jews*   Askowith, D. *The Toleration and Persecution of the Jews in the Roman Empire*. New York: n.p., 1915.

ATANT   Abhandlung zur Theologie des Alten und Neuen Testaments

Aune, *Logos Protreptikos*   Aune, D. "Romans as a *Logos Protreptikos* in the Context of Ancient Religions and Philosophical Propaganda." In *Paulus als Missionar und Theologe und das antike Judentum*. Ed. M. Hengel. Tübingen: J. C. B. Mohr, forthcoming.

Aune, *Literary Environment*   Aune, D. *The New Testament in Its Literary Environment*. Philadelphia: Westminster, 1987.

Aune, *Prophecy in Early Christianity*   Aune, D. E. *Prophecy in Early Christianity and the Ancient Mediterranean World*. Grand Rapids: Eerdmans, 1983.

Aus, "Paul's Travel Plans"   Aus, R. D. "Paul's Travel Plans and the 'Full Number of Gentiles' of Rom. xi.25." *NovT* 21 (1979) 232–62.

AusBR   *Australian Biblical Review*

AUSS   *Andrews University Seminary Studies*

BA   *Biblical Archaeologist*

Baarda, "Maar de toorn is over hen gekomen"   Baarda, T. "Maar de toorn is over hen gekomen." In *Paulus en de andere joden*. Delft: Meinema, 1984.

BAGD   Bauer, W., W. F. Arndt, W. F. Gingrich, and F. W. Danker. *A Greek-English Lexicon of the New Testament and Other Early Christian Literature*, 2nd edition. Chicago: University of Chicago Press, 1979.

Bammel, "Judenverflogung und Naherwartung"   Bammel, E. "Judenverflogung und Naherwartung." *ZTK* 56 (1959) 294–315.

Bammel, "Pompeius und römisch-jüdische Bündnis" .   Bammel, E. "Pompeius und römisch-jüdische Bündnis." *ZDPV* 75 (1959) 76–82.

Barrett, *Essays*   Barrett, C. K. *Essays on Paul*. London, 1982.

Barrett, "Pauline Controversies"   Barrett, C. K. "Pauline Controversies in the Early Church." *NTS* 20 (1973–74) 229–45.

Barrett, *First Corinthians*   Barrett, C. K. HNTC. *The First Epistle to the Corinthians.* New York: Harper & Row, 1968.

Barrett, "Things Offered to Idols"   Barrett, C. K. "Things Offered to Idols." *NTS* 11 (1964–65) 138–53.

Barrett, *Romans*   Barrett, C. K. *A Commentary on the Epistle to the Romans.* BNTC. London: A. & C. Black, 1957.

Barth, *Shorter Commentary on Romans*   Barth, K. *A Shorter Commentary on Romans.* London: SCM, 1959.

Bartsch, "Die Empfänger des Römerbriefes"   Bartsch, H. W. "Die Empfänger des Römerbriefes." *ST* 25 (1971) 81–89.

Bartsch, "Die antisemitischen Gegner"   Bartsch, H. W. "Die antisemitischen Gegner des Paulus im Römerbrief." In *Antijudaismus im Neuen Testament.* Munich, 1967.

Bartsch, "Paulus und die Juden"   Bartsch, H. W. "Paulus und die Juden. Zur Auslegung des Römerbriefes." *Kirche in der Zeit* 20 (1965) 210ff.

Bartsch, "Die historische Situation"   Bartsch, H. W. "Die historische Situation des Römerbriefes." In *Studia Evangelica* IV, Part 1. (TU 102) 281–91.

Bassler, "Divine Impartiality"   Bassler, J. M. "Divine Impartiality in Paul's Letter to the Romans." *NovT* 26 (1984) 43–58.

Bassler, *Divine Impartiality*   Bassler, J. M. *Divine Impartiality: Paul and a Theological Axiom.* Chico: Scholars Press, 1982.

Bauer, *Orthodoxy and Heresy*   Bauer, W. *Orthodoxy and Heresy in Earliest Christianity.* ET ed. R. A. Kraft and G. Krodel. Philadelphia: Fortress, 1971.

Baur, F. C., "Über Zweck und Gedankengang des Römerbriefes"   Baur, F. C. "Über Zweck und Gedankengang des Römerbriefes." *ThJb* 16 (1957) 66–108; 184–209.

Baur, F. C., *Paul*   Baur, F. C. *Paul: His Life and Works.* ET by A. Menzies. Theological Translation Fund Library, 1876.

Baur, F. C., *Kirchengeschichte*   Baur, F. C. *Kirchengeschichte der drei ersten Jahrhunderte.* 1862 (= Neudruck, 1969).

Baur, F. C., "Römischen Gemeinde"   Baur, F. C. "Über Zweck und Veranlassung des Römerbrief und der damit zusammenhangenden Verhältnisse der römischen Gemeinde." *Tübinger Zeitschrift für Theologie* (1836) 59–178.

BC   *The Beginnings of Christianity.* Ed. Jackson, F. J. F. and K. Lake. 5 vols. Reprint. Grand Rapids: Baker, 1979.

Beale, "Performative Discourse"   Beale, W. H. "Rhetorical Performative Discourse: A New Theory of Epideictic." *Philosophy and Rhetoric* 11 (1978) 221–46.

Beare, *St. Paul and His Letters*   Beare, F. W. *St. Paul and His Letters.* London: A. & C. Black, 1962.

Beare, *Philippians*   Beare, F. W. *A Commentary on the Epistle to the Philippians.* London: Black, 1959.

Beauchamp, "Epouser la Sagesse"   Beauchamp, P. "Epouser la Sagesse—ou n'épouser qu'elle? Une énigme du Livre de la Sagesse." In *La Sagesse de l'Ancien Testament.* Ed. M. Gilbert. Leuven-Gembloux: University Press, 1979.

Beker, *Paul*   Beker, J. C. *Paul the Apostle. The Triumph of God in Life and Thought.* Philadelphia: Fortress, 1984.

Bell, *Juden und Griechen*   Bell, H. I. *Juden und Griechen im römischen Alexandria.* n.p., 1926.

Berger, "Hellenistische Gattungen"   Berger, K. "Hellenistische Gattungen im Neuen Testament." In *ANRW.* Part II, vol. 25/2. Berlin and New York: de Gruyter, 1984.

Berger, *Formgeschichte*   Berger, K. *Formgeschichte des Neuen Testaments.* Heidelberg: Quelle & Meyer, 1984.

Berger, "Almosen für Israel"   Berger, K. "Almosen für Israel: zum historischen Kontext der paulinischen Kollekte." *NTS* 23 (1976–77) 180–204.

Bergmann, *Einleitung zu Ciceros*   Bergmann, A. *Einleitung zu Ciceros Rede für L. Valerius Flaccus.* Programm Schneeberg, 1893.

Berliner, *Geschichte der Juden in Rom.*   Berliner, A. *Geschichte der Juden in Rom.* n.p., 1895.

Bernays, "Juvenal"   Bernays, J. "Die Gottesfurchtigen bei Juvenal." In: *Commentationes philologicae in honorem Theodori Mommseni* (1877). Pages 563–596.

Bertholet, *Die Stelung der Israeliten*   Bertholet, A. *Die Stelung der Israeliten und der Juden zu den Fremden.* n.p., 1896.

BETL   Bibliotheca ephemeridum theologicarum lovaniensium

Betz, H. D., "Literary Composition"   Betz, H. D. "The Literary Composition and Function of Paul's Letter to the Galatians." *NTS* 21 (1975) 353–79.

Betz, H. D., *Sokratische Tradition*   Betz, H. D. *Der Apostel Paulus und die sokratische Tradition.* BHT 45. Tübingen: J. C. B. Mohr, 1972.

Betz, O., "Die Vision des Paulus"   Betz, O. "Die Vision des Paulus im Tempel von Jerusalem." In *Verborum Veritas: Festschrift für G. Stählin.* Ed. O. Böcher and K. Haacker. Wuppertal, 1970.

BEvTh   Beiträge zur evangelischen Theologie

BFCT   Beiträge zur Förderung christlicher Theologie

BHT   Beiträge zur historischen Theologie

BibS(F)   Biblische Studien (Freiburg, 1895–)

Bickermann, "Ritualmord und Eselskult"   Bickermann, E. "Ritualmord und Eselskult." *MGWJ* 71 (1927) 255–64.

Bjerkelund, *Parakalo*   Bjerkelund, C. *Parakalo.* Form, Funktion und Sinn der parakalo-Sätze in den paulinischen Briefen. Oslo: Universitetforlaget, 1967.

BJRL   *Bulletin of the John Rylands University Library of Manchester*

Black, *Romans*   Black, M. *Romans.* NCBC. London: Marshall, Morgan & Scott, 1973.

Blank, *Paulus und Jesus*   Blank, J. *Paulus und Jesus. Eine theologische Grundlegung.* SANT 18. Munich: Kosel, 1968.

Blass–Debrunner–Funk, *Grammar*   Blass, F., A. Debrunner, and R. Funk. *A Greek Grammar of the New Testament and Other Early Christian Literature.* Chicago: University of Chicago Press, 1961.

Blass, *Kunstprosa*   Blass, F. *Die Rhythmen der asianischen und römanischen Kunstprosa.* Hildesheim: Gerstenberg, 1972. Reprint of Leipzig: Teubner, 1909 edition.

Blass, *Hermes*   Blass, F. *Hermes* 30 (1893), 465–70.

BNTC   Black's New Testament Commentary (= HNTC)

Bompaire, *Lucien écrivain*   Bompaire, J. *Lucien écrivain: imitation et création.* Paris: Boccard, 1958.

Bonhöffer, A. *Epiktet*   Bonhöffer, A. *Epiktet und das Neue Testament.* Giessen: Töpelmann, 1911.

Bornkamm, "Last Will and Testament"   Bornkamm, G. "The Letter to the Romans as Paul's Last Will and Testament." In *The Romans Debate: Revised and Expanded Edition.* Ed. K. P. Donfried. Peabody, Mass.: Hendrickson Publishers, 1991.

Bornkamm, "Römerbrief als Testament"   Bornkamm, G. "Der Römerbrief als Testament des Paulus." BEvT 53. Munich: Kaiser Verlag, 1971.

Bornkamm, *Paul*   Bornkamm, G. *Paul.* Trans. D. M. G. Stalker. New York: Harper & Row, 1971.

Bornkamm, *Paulus*   Bornkamm, G. *Paulus*, Stuttgart: W. Kohlhammer, 1969.

Bornkamm, "Baptism and New Life"   Bornkamm, G. "Baptism and New Life in Paul." In *Early Christian Experience.* London: SCM, 1969.

Bornkamm, "Die Offenbarung des Zornes Gottes"   Bornkamm, G. "Die Offenbarung des Zornes Gottes (Röm 1–3)." In *Das Ende des Gesetzes.* Munich: Kaiser Verlag, 1953.

Bouwman, *Paulus*   Bouwman, G. *Paulus an de Romeinen: Een retorische analyse van Rom 1–8.* Abdij-Averbode: Werkgroep voor Levensverdieping, 1980.

Bowers, "Jewish Communities"   Bowers, W. P. "Jewish Communities in Spain in the Time of Paul the Apostle." *JTS* 26 (1975) 395–402.

Brandon, *Fall of Jerusalem*   Brandon, S. G. F. *The Fall of Jerusalem and the Christian Church.* 2nd ed. London: SPCK, 1957.

Brandt, *Rhetoric of Argumentation*   Brandt, W. J. *The Rhetoric of Argumentation.* New York: Bobbs-Merrill, 1970.

Brauch, "Perspectives"   Brauch, M. T. "Perspectives on God's Righteousness in recent German Discussion." In E. P. Sanders, *Paul and Palestinian Judaism.* London: SCM, 1977. Pages 523–42.

Brongers, "Die Zehnzahl"   Brongers, H. A. "Die Zehnzahl in der Bibel und in ihrer Umwelt." In *Studia Biblica et Semitica . . . Festschrift T. C. Vriezen.* Wangeningen: Veenman, 1966. Pages 30–45.

Brooten, "Junia"   Brooten, B. "Junia . . . Outstanding among the Apostles (Romans 16:7)." In *Women Priests.* Ed. L. and A. Swidler. New York, 1977.

Bruce, "Continued"   Bruce, F. F. "The Romans Debate—Continued." *BJRL* 64 (1981–82) 334–59.

Bruce, *Paul*   Bruce, F. F. *Paul: Apostle of the Free Spirit.* Exeter: Paternoster, 1977.

Bruce, "Christianity under Claudius"   Bruce, F. F. "Christianity under Claudius." *BJRL* 44 (1961–62) 316–18.

BS   *Bibliotheca Sacra*

Bujard, *Stilanalytische*   Bujard, W. *Stilanalytische Untersuchungen zum Kolosserbrief als Beitrag zur Methodik von Sprachvergleichen.* SUNT 11. Göttingen: Vandenhoeck & Ruprecht, 1973.

Bullinger, *Figures of Speech*   Bullinger, E. W. *Figures of Speech Used in the Bible Explained and Illustrated.* Grand Rapids: Baker, 1968. Reprint of the 1898 edition by Eyre and Spottiswoode, London.

Bultmann, *Exegetica*   Bultmann, R. *Exegetica, Aufsätze zur Erforschung des Neuen Testaments.* Ed. E. Dinkler. Tübingen: J. C. B. Mohr, 1967.

Bultmann, *Theology of the New Testament*   Bultmann, R. *Theology of the New Testament.* 2 vols. Trans. K. Grobel. New York: Scribner's, 1951, 1955.

Bultmann, *In Memoriam Ernst Lohmeyer*   Bultmann, R. "Die kirchliche Redaktion des ersten Johannesbriefes." *In Memoriam Ernst Lohmeyer.* Tübingen: J. C. B. Mohr, 1951. Pages 381–93.

Bultmann, *Diatribe*   Bultmann, R. *Der Stil der paulinischer Predigt und die kynisch-stoische Diatribe.* Göttingen: Vandenhoeck & Ruprecht, 1910.

Burdick, "*oida* and *ginōskō*"   Burdick, D. W. "*oida* and *ginōskō* in the Pauline Epistles." In *New Dimensions in New Testament Study.* Ed. R. N. Longnecker and M. L. Tenney. Grand Rapids: Zondervan, 1974. Pages 344–56.

Burgess, "Epideictic Literature"   Burgess, T. C. "Epideictic Literature." *University of Chicago Studies in Classical Philology* 3 (1900) 89–261.

BZNW   Beihefte zur ZNW

Cadbury, *Acts in History*   Cadbury, H. J. *The Book of Acts in History.* New York, 1955.

Campbell, "Reaction to Watson"   Campbell, W. S. "Did Paul Advocate Separation from the Synagogue? A Reaction to Francis Watson: *Paul, Judaism, and the Gentiles: A Sociological Approach.*" *SJTh* 42 (1989) 457–67.

Campbell, "Salvation for Jews and Gentile"   Campbell, W. S. "Salvation for Jews and Gentile; Krister Stendahl and Paul's Letter to the Romans." *Studia Biblica* III. Sheffield, 1980.

Campbell, "Why?"   Campbell, W. S. "Why Did Paul Write Romans?" *ExpT* 85 (1973–74) 264–69.

Campbell, D. A., *Rhetoric of Righteousness*   Campbell, D. A. *The Rhetoric of Righteousness in Romans 3:21–26.* Diss., University of Toronto, 1989.

Cancik, *Epistulae Morales*   Cancik, H. *Untersuchungen zu Senecas Epistulae Morales.* Spudasmata 18. Hildesheim: G. Olms, 1967.

CBQ   *Catholic Biblical Quarterly*

Chadwick, "Circle and the Ellipse"   Chadwick, H. "The Circle and the Ellipse." In *Jerusalem and Rome.* Ed. H. Chadwick and H. von Campenhausen. Philadelphia, 1966.

Chase, "Classical Conception of Epideictic"   Chase, J. R. "The Classical Conception of Epideictic." *QJS* 47 (1981) 293–300.

CIJ   *Corpus Inscriptionum Judaicarum.* Ed. J. B. Frey. Vatican City, 1936.

CIL   *Corpus Inscriptionum Latinarum.* 1863–1909.

Clark, *Rhetoric*   Clark, D. L. *Rhetoric in Greco-Roman Education.* New York: Columbia University Press, 1957.

Clarke, "Literary Setting I"   Clarke, G. W. "The Literary Setting of the *Octavius* of Minucius Felix." *JRH* 3 (1964–65) 195–211.

Clarke, "Literary Setting II"   Clarke, G. W. "The Literary Setting of the *Octavius* of Minucius Felix." *JRH* 4 (1966–67) 267–86.

Collange, *Enigmes*   Collange, J.-F. *Enigmes de la deuxième épître de Paul aux Corinthiens.* Cambridge: Cambridge University Press, 1972.

Collins, "Integrity of 1 Thes"   Collins, R. F. "Apropos the Integrity of 1 Thes." In *Studies on the First Letter to the Thessalonians.* BETL 66. Leuven: University Press, 1984.

Collins, *Between Athens and Jerusalem*   Collins, J. J. *Between Athens and Jerusalem: Jewish Identity in the Hellenistic Diaspora.* New York: Crossroad, 1983.

Conley, "General Education"   Conley, T. *"General Education" in Philo of Alexandria.* Fifteenth Colloquy of the Center for Hermeneutical Studies. March 9, 1975. Berkely: Center for Hermeneutical Studies, 1975.

Conzelmann, *Korinther*   Conzelmann, H. *Der erste Brief an die Korinther.* KEK. Göttingen: Vandenhoeck & Ruprecht, 1969.

Conzelmann, *Outline*   Conzelmann, H. *An Outline of the Theology of the New Testament.* ET John Bowden. London: SCM, 1969.

Conzelmann, "Rechtfertingungslehre des Paulus"   Conzelmann, H. "Die Rechtfertingungslehre des Paulus: Theologie oder Anthropologie?" *EvT* 28 (1968).

Conzelmann, *Grundriss der Theologie*   Conzelmann, H. *Grundriss der Theologie des Neuen Testaments.* Munich: Kaiser, 1968.

Conzelmann, "Heutige Probleme"   Conzelmann, H. "Heutige Probleme der Paulus-Forschung." *Der evangelische Erzieher* 18 (1966).

Conzelmann, "Paulus und die Weisheit"   Conzelmann, H. "Paulus und die Weisheit." *NTS* 12 (1965/66) 233f.

Corbett, *Classical Rhetoric*   Corbett, E. P. J. *Classical Rhetoric for the Modern Student.* Oxford: Oxford University, 1965.

Corriveau, *Liturgy of Life*   Corriveau, R. *The Liturgy of Life: A Study of the Ethical Thought of St. Paul in his Letters to the Early Christian Communities.* Studia Travaux de Recherche 25. Brussels: Desclée de Brouwer, 1970.

Corssen, "Überlieferungsgeschichte"   Corssen, P. "Zur Überlieferungsgeschichte des Römerbriefes," *ZNW* 10 (1909), 1–45, 97–102.

Cranfield, *Romans*   Cranfield, C. E. B. *A Critical and Exegetical Commentary on the Epistle to the Romans,* 2 vols. ICC. Edinburgh: T. & T. Clark, 1975–79.

Cranfield, *Romans 12 and 13*   Cranfield, C. E. B. *A Commentary on Romans 12 and 13.* Scottish Journal of Theology Occasional Papers 12. Edinburgh: Oliver & Boyd, 1965.

CSEL   Corpus Scriptorum Ecclesiasticorum Latinorum. Vienna, 1966.

Cumont, *Sabazios et du Judaisme*   Cumont, F. *A propos de Sabazios et du Judaisme.* Musée Belge 14, 1910.

Dahl, *Studies*   Dahl, N. A. *Studies in Paul: Theology for the Early Christian Mission.* Minneapolis: Augsburg, 1977.

Dahl, *Memory*   Dahl, N. A. *Jesus in the Memory of the Early Church.* Minneapolis: Augsburg, 1976.

Dahl, "Future"   Dahl, N. A. "The Future of Israel." In *Studies in Paul.* Minneapolis: Augsburg, 1977.

Dahl, "God"   Dahl, N. A. "The God of Jews and Gentiles." In *Studies in Paul.* Minneapolis: Augsburg, 1977.

Dahl, *Crucified Messiah*   Dahl, N. A. *The Crucified Messiah.* Minneapolis: Augsburg, 1974.

Dahl, "Hovedsak"   Dahl, N. A. "Hovedsak og bisetninger." In *Festschrift for Arne Fjellbu.* Oslo, 1960. Pages 57–66.

Dahl, "Romans v."   Dahl, N. A. "Two Notes on Romans v." *ST* 5 (1951) 37–48.

Dahl, "Anamnesis"   Dahl, N. A. "Anamnesis: Memory and Commemoration in Early Christianity." *ST* 1 (1947) 69–95.

Dahlmann, *Senecas*   Dahlmann. *Untersuchungen zu Senecas epistulae morales.* Hildesheim: Olms, 1967.

Dalbert, *Missionsliteratur*   Dalbert, P. *Die Theologie der hellenistisch-jüdenischen Missionsliteratur unter Ausschluss von Philo und Josephus.* Hamburg: Reich, 1954.

Davies, A. T., *Anti-Semitism*   Davies, A. T. *Anti-Semitism and the Christian Mind.* New York: Herder and Herder, 1969.

Davies, "Paul and Israel"   Davies, W. D. "Paul and the People of Israel." *NTS* 24 (1978) 4–39.

Davies, "Romans 11:13–24"   Davies, W. D. "Romans 11:13–24. A Suggestion." In *Paganisme, Judaïsme, Christianisme.* Paris: Boccard, 1978.

Davies, *Gospel and the Land*   Davies, W. D. *The Gospel and the Land.* Berkeley, 1974.

Davis, *Biblical Numerology*   Davis, J. J. *Biblical Numerology.* Grand Rapids: Baker, 1968.

Dederen, "Esteeming One Day Better"   Dederen, R. "On Esteeming One Day Better Than Another." *AUSS* 9 (1971) 21–23; 29–30.

DeLacy–Einarson, *Plutarch's Moralia*   P. H. De Lacy and B. Einarson, *Plutarch's Moralia.* LCL, VII, 1959.

Dennison, *Greek Particles*   Dennison, J. D. *The Greek Particles.* 2nd ed. Oxford: Oxford Univesity Press, 1959.

Dibelius, *Jakobus*   Dibelius, M. *Der Brief des Jakobus.* 7th rev. ed. MeyerK. Göttingen: Vandenhoeck & Ruprecht, 1921.

Dibelius, *From Tradition to Gospel*   Dibelius, M. *From Tradition to Gospel.* New York: Scribner's, n.d.

Dietzfelbinger, *Berufung*   Dietzfelbinger, C. *Die Berufung des Paulus als Ursprung seiner Theologie.* WMANT 58. Neukirchen-Vluyn: Neukirchener Verlag, 1985.

Dillon, *Iamblichi Chalcidensis*   Dillon, J. *In Platonis Dialogos Commentariorum Fragmenta.* PhAnt 23. Leiden: Brill, 1973.

Dinter, *Remnant of Israel*   Dinter, P. E. *The Remnant of Israel and the Stone of Stumbling in Zion according to Paul (Romans 9–11).* Ph.D. dissertation, Union Theological Seminary, 1980.

Dodd, *Romans*   Dodd, C. H. *The Epistle of Paul to the Romans.* New York: Long & Smith, 1932, 13th ed. 1954.

Donfried, "False Presuppositions"   Donfried, K. P. "False Presuppositions in the Study of Romans." In *The Romans Debate: Revised and Expanded Edition.* Ed. K. P. Donfried. Peabody, Mass.: Hendrickson Publishers, 1991.

Donfried, "Nature and Scope"   Donfried, K. P. "The Nature and Scope of the Romans Debate." In *The Romans Debate: Revised and Expanded Edition.* Ed. K. P. Donfried. Peabody, Mass.: Hendrickson Publishers, 1991.

Donfried, "Short Note on Romans 16"   Donfried, K. P. "A Short Note on Romans 16." In *The Romans Debate: Revised and Expanded Edition.* Ed. K. P. Donfried. Peabody, Mass.: Hendrickson Publishers, 1991.

Donfried, *Romans Debate*   Donfried, K. Ed. *The Romans Debate.* Minneapolis: Augsburg Publishing House, 1977.

Donfried, *Setting of 2 Clement*   Donfried, K. P. *The Setting of 2 Clement in Early Christianity.* Suppl. NT 38. Leiden: Brill, 1974.

Döring, *Exemplum Socratis*   Döring, K. *Exemplum Socratis: Studien zur Sokrates-nachwirkung in der kynisch-stoichen Popularphilosophie der frühen Kaiserzeit und im frühen Christentum.* Hermes-Einzelschriften 42. Wiesbaden: Franz Steiner Verlag, 1979.

Doty, "Review, Aporia, Possible Futures"   Doty, W. G. "Review, Aporia, Possible Futures." Unpublished paper for the SBL Pauline Letters Seminar, 1973.

Doty, *Letters*   Doty, W. G. *Letters in Primitive Christianity.* Philadelphia: Fortress, 1973.

Doty, "Concept of Genre"   Doty, W. G. "The Concept of Genre in Literary Analysis." In *SBL 1972 Proceedings.* Vol. 2, pages 413–48.

Doty, "Classification"   Doty, W. G. "The Classification of Epistolary Literature." *CBQ* 31 (1969) 183–99.

Drane, "Romans"   Drane, J. W. "Why did Paul write Romans? In *Pauline Studies.* Ed. D. A. Hagner and M. J. Harris. Exeter, 1980. Pages 208–27.

Drane, *Paul*   Drane, J. W. *Paul: Libertine or Legalist? A Study of the Major Pauline Epistles.* London, 1975.

Driver, *Aramaic Documents*   Driver, G. R. *Aramaic Documents of the Fifth Century B.C.* Revised ed. Oxford: Oxford University Press, 1965.

Driver, "Sacred Numbers"   Driver, G. R. "Sacred Numbers and Round Figures." In *Promise and Fulfillment: Essays Presented to Professor S. H. Hooke in Celebration of his Nintieth Birthday.* Ed. F. F. Bruce. Edinburgh: T. & T. Clark, 1963.

Dunn, *Romans 1–8*   Dunn, J. D. G. *Romans 1–8.* WBC 38a. Waco: Word, 1988.

Dunn, *Romans 9–16*   Dunn, J. D. G. *Romans 9–16.* WBC 38b. Waco: Word, 1989.

Dunn, "Structure and Argument"   Dunn, J. D. G. "Paul's Epistle to the Romans: An Analysis of Structure and Argument." *ANRW* 2.25.4 (1987) 2842–90.

Dunn, "Works of Law"   Dunn, J. D. G. "Works of the Law and the Curse of the Law (Galatians 3:10–14)." *NTS* 31 (1985) 523–42.

Dunn, *Unity and Diversity*   Dunn, J. D. G. *Unity and Diversity in the New Testament.* Philadelphia: Westminster, 1977.

Dunn, "New Perspective"   Dunn, J. D. G. "The New Perspective on Paul." *BJRL* 65 (1983) 106.

Dupont, "Appel aux faibles"   Dupont, J. "Appel aux faibles et aux forts dans la communauté romaine (Rom. 14,1–15,13)." In *Studiorum Paulinorum Congressus Internationalis Catholicus 1961* . . . AnBib 17. Rome: Biblical Institute Press, 1963.

Dupont, "Structure littéraire"   Dupont, J. "Le problème de la structure littéraire de l'épître aux Romains." *RB* 62 (1955) 365–97.

Düring, *Protreptikos*   Düring, I. *Der Protreptikos des Aristoteles.* Studia Graeca et Latina Gothoburgensia 12. Göteborg/Stockholm, 1961.

Du Toit, "Persuasion"   Du Toit, A. B. "Persuasion in Romans 1:1–17." *Biblische Zeitschrift* 33 (1989) 192–209.

EB   Echter Bibel

Eckardt, *Elder and Younger Brothers*   Eckardt, A. R. *Elder and Younger Brothers.* New York: Scribner's, 1967.

Ehrhardt, *Framework*   Ehrhardt, A. A. T. *The Framework of the New Testament Stories.* Manchester, 1964.

Eichholz, *Theologie*   Eichholz, G. *Die Theologie des Paulus im Umriss.* Neukirchen: Neukirchener Verlag, 1972.

Eisler, *Messiah Jesus*   Eisler, R. *The Messiah Jesus and John the Baptist.* London, 1931.

Erbes, "Zeit und Zeil"   Erbes, K. "Zeit und Zeil der Grüsse Röm. 16,3–15 und der Mitteilungen 2 Tim. 4,9–21." *ZNW* 10 (1909) 128–47, 195–218.

Espy, "Paul's 'Robust Conscience' Re-examined"   Espy, J. M. "Paul's 'Robust Conscience' Re-examined." *NTS* 31 (1985) 161–88.

ET   English Translation

EvT   Evangelische Theologie

Fàbrega, "Junia(s)"   Fàbrega, V. "War Junia(s), der hevorragende Apostel (Röm. 16,7), eine Frau?" *JbAChr* 27/28 (1984/85).

Faw, "First Thessalonians"   Faw, C. E. "On the Writing of First Thessalonians." *JBL* 71 (1952) 217–25.

Festugière, *Les protreptiques de Platon*   Festugière, A. J. *Les protreptiques de Platon: Euthydème, Phédon, Epinomis.* Paris: J. Vrin, 1973.

Feuillet, "Les fondaments"   Feuillet, A. "Les fondaments de la morale chrétienne d'après l'Epître aux Romains." *Revue Thomiste* 70 (1970) 365–66.

Feuillet, "Le Plan salvifique,"   Feuillet, A. "Le Plan salvifique de Dieu d'après l'Epître aux Romains," *Revue Biblique* 57 (1950) 336–87, 489–529.

Fischel, *Rabbinic Literature*   Fischel, H. A. *Rabbinic Literature and Greco-Roman Philosophy.* Leiden: E. J. Brill, 1973.

Fitzmyer, "Letter to the Romans"   Fitzmyer, J. "The Letter to the Romans." In *The New Jerome Biblical Commentary.* Ed. R. E. Brown, J. A. Fitzmyer, and R. E. Murphy. Englewood Cliffs, N.J.: Prentice Hall, 1990.

Focke, *Die Entstehung der Weisheit Salomos*   Focke, F. *Die Entstehung der Weisheit Salomos.* Göttingen: Vandenhoeck & Ruprecht, 1913.

Fraiken, "Rhetorical Function"   Fraiken, D. "The Rhetorical Function of Jews in Romans." In *Anti-Judaism in Early Christianity.* Ed. P. Richardson and D. Granskou. Waterloo, Ontario: Wilfrid Laurier University, 1986. Pages 91–105.

Frankemölle, *Das Taufverständnis des Paulus*   Frankemölle, H. *Das Taufverständnis des Paulus: Taufe, Tod und Auferstehung nach Röm. vi.* SBS 47. Stuttgart: Katholische Bibelwerk, 1970.

Franklin, *Christ the Lord*   Franklin, E. *Christ the Lord: a Study in the Purpose and Theology of Luke–Acts.* Philadelphia: Westminster, 1975.

FRLANT   Forschungen zur Religion und Literatur zum Alten und Neuen Testaments

FS   Festschrift

Fuchs, *Hermeneutik*   Fuchs, E. *Hermeneutik*. Bad Canstatt, 1963.

Fuhrmann, *Lehrbuch*   Furhmann, M. *Das systematische Lehrbuch*. Göttingen: Vandenhoeck & Ruprecht, 1960.

Fuller, *Introduction*   Fuller, R. H. *A Critical Introduction to the New Testament*. London: Duckworth, 1966.

Funk, *Language, Hermeneutic*   Funk, R. W. *Language, Hermeneutic, and the Word of God*. New York: Harper & Row, 1966.

Furnish, *Love Command*   Furnish, V. P. *The Love Command in the New Testament*. Nashville: Abingdon, 1972.

Furnish, *Theology and Ethics*   Furnish, V. P. *Theology and Ethics in Paul*. Nashville: Abingdon, 1968.

Gaiser, *Protreptik und Paräsene bei Platon*   Gaiser, K. *Protreptik und Paräsene bei Platon: Untersuchung zur Form des Platonischen Dialogs*. Stuttgart: Kohlhammer, 1959.

Gale, *Analogy*   Gale, H. M. *The Use of Analogy in the Letters of Paul*. Philadelphia: Westminster, 1964.

Gamble, *NT Canon*   Gamble, H., Jr. *The New Testament Canon*. Philadelphia: Fortress, 1985.

Gamble, *Textual History*   Gamble, H., Jr. *The Textual History of the the Letter to the Romans*. Studies and Documents 42. Grand Rapids: Eerdmans, 1977.

Garlington, D. "Obedience"   Garlington, D. " 'The Obedience of Faith': A Pauline Phrase in Historical Context. Ph.D. Diss. Durham University, 1987.

Gaston, *Torah*   Gaston, L. *Paul and the Torah*. Vancouver, British of Columbia Press, 1987.

Gaston, "Torah"   Gaston, L. "Paul and the Torah." In *Antisemitism and the Foundations of Christianity*. Ed. A. T. Davies. New York: Paulist, 1979. Pages 48–71.

GCS   Griechische christliche Schriftsteller

Georgi, "Religious Propaganda"   Giorgi, D. "Forms of Religious Propaganda." In *Jesus in His Time*. Ed. H. J. Schultz. Philadelphia: Fortress, 1971. Pages 124–31.

Georgi, "Der Kollekte"   Georgi, D. "Die Geschichte der Kollekte des Paulus für Jerusalem." *TF* 38 (1965).

Georgi, *Kollekte*   Georgi, D. *Die Geschichte der Kollekte des Paulus für Jerusalem* Diss. Hamburg, 1965; = Theol. Forschung 38; Hamburg–Bergstedt, 1965.

Georgi, *Die Gegner*   Giorgi, D. *Die Gegner des Paulus im 2 Korintherbrief*. Neukirchen: Neukirchener Verlag, 1964.

Gerhäusser, *Poseidonios*   Gerhäusser, W. *Der Protreptikos des Poseidonios*. Munich: C. Wolf & Sohn, 1912.

Gielen, "Paulinischen Formel"   Gielen, M. "Zur Interpretation der ἡ κατ' οἶκον ἐκκλησία." *ZNW* 77 (1986) 109–25.

Gilbert, "Sagesse de Salomon"   Gilbert, M. "Sagesse de Salomon." *DBS* 60 (1986) 58–119.

Gilbert, "Wisdom Literature"   Gilbert, M. "Wisdom Literature." In *Jewish Writings of the Second Temple Period*. Ed. M. Stone. Philadelphia: Fortress, 1984.

Godet, *Römer*   Godet, F. *Kommentar zum Brief an die Römer*. 2 vols. 1881.

Gommel, *Thukydides*   Gommel, J. *Rhetorisches Argumentieren bei Thukydides*. Spudasmata 10. Hildesheim: Olms, 1966.

Goppelt, *Jesus, Paul, and Judaism*   Goppelt, L. *Jesus, Paul, and Judaism*. New York, 1964.

Grafe, *Veranlassung und Zweck des Römerbriefes*   Grafe, E. *Veranlassung und Zweck des Römerbriefes*, 1881.

Graves and Podro, *Jesus in Rome*   Graves, R. and Podro, J. *Jesus in Rome*. London, 1957.

Grayston, "Not Ashamed"   Grayston, K. " 'I Am Not Ashamed of the Gospel': Romans 1:16a and the Structure of the Epistle," *Studia Evangelica* 2 (1964) 569–73.

Grube, *Greek Critic*   Grube, G. M. A. *A Greek Critic: Demetrius on Style*. Toronto: University of Toronto Press, 1961.

Guerra, *Apologetic Tradition*   Guerra, A. *Romans 3:29–30 and the Apologetic Tradition*. Ann Arbor: University Microfilms, 1986.

Guerrra, "Romans 4"   Guerrra, A. "Romans 4 as Apologetic Theology" *HTR* 81 (1988) 251–70.

Guterman, *Religious Toleration*   Guterman, S. L. *Religious Toleration and Persecution in Ancient Rome*. London, n.p., 1951.

Guthrie, *History of Greek Philosophy*   Guthrie, W. K. C. *History of Greek Philosophy*. 4 vols. Cambridge: University Press, 1975.

Hadot, I. *Seneca*   Hadot, I. *Seneca und die griechisch-römische Tradition der Seelenleitung*. Berlin: de Gruyter, 1969.

Haenchen, *Acts*   Haenchen, E. *The Acts of the Apostles: A Commentary*. Trans. R. McL. Wilson. Oxford: Basil Blackwell, 1971.

Hafemann, "Salvation"   Hafemann, S. "The Salvation of Israel in Romans 11:25–32: A Response to Krister Stendhal," *Ex Auditu* 4 (1988) 38–58.

Hahn, *Der Mission*   Hahn, F. *Das Verständnis der Mission im Neuen Testament*. WMANT 13, 2nd. ed. 1965.

Hahn, *Mission in the New Testament*   Hahn, F. *Mission in the New Testament*. SBT 1/47. London, 1965.

Hahn, "Gesetzeverständnis"   Hahn, F. "Das Gesetzesverständnis im Römer und Galaterbrief." *ZNW* 67 (1976) 29–63.

Hanson, *Paul's Technique*   Hanson, A. T. *Studies in Paul's Technique and Theology*. Grand Rapids: Eerdmans, 1974.

Harder, "Römerbriefes"   Harder, G. "Der konkrete Anlass des Römerbriefes." *Theol. Viat.* 6 (1959) 21.

Harnack, *Marcion*   Harnack, A. v. *Marcion. Das Evangelium vom Fremden Gott. Neue Studien zu Marcion*. 2nd ed., Darmstadt: Wissenschaftliche Buchgesellschaft, 1924.

Harnack, "Chronologische" Harnack, A. "Chronologische Berechnung des Tages von Damaskus." *SBA* (1912) 673–82.

Harnack, *Mission und Ausbreitung*   Harnack, A. von. *Mission und Ausbreitung des Christentums in den ersten drie Jahrhunderten I*. 1924 (reprint, 1959).

Harnack, *Mission and Expansion*   Harnack, A. *The Mission and Expansion of Christianity*. London, 1908.

Harnack, "Verfasser des Hebräerbriefs"   Harnack, A. "Probilia über die Adresse und den Verfasser des Hebräerbriefs." *ZNW* 1 (1900) n.p.

Hartlich, *De exhoratationum*   Hartlich, P. *De exhoratationum a Graecis Romisque scriptarum historia*. Leipzig: Tuebner, 1889.

Heil, *Romans*   Heil, J. P. *Paul's Letter to the Romans; A Reader-Response Commentary*. New York: Paulist, 1987.

Hengel, *Earliest Christianity*   Hengel, M. *Acts and the History of Earliest Christianity*. Trans. J. Bowden. Philadelphia: Fortress, 1980.

Hengel, *Judaism and Hellenism*   Hengel, M. *Judaism and Hellenism*, 2 vols. Philadelphia: Fortress, 1974.

Hester, "Epistolography"   Hester, J. D. "Epistolography in Antiquity and Early Christianity. A Proposal for a Pacific Coast Region SBL Seminar." 1975.

HeyJ   *Heythrop Journal*

Hild, "Les Juifs à Rome"   Hild, A. "Les Juifs à Rome devant l'opinion et dans la littérature." *REJ* 11 (1881) 174–86.

HKNT   Handkommentar zum Neuen Testament

Hock–O'Neil, *Chreia*   Hock R. F. and O'Neil E. N., *The Chreia in Ancient Rhetoric*. Vol. I, *The Progymnasmata*. Atlanta: Scholars Press, 1986.

Hoennicke, *Das Judenchristentum*   Hoennicke, G. *Das Judenchristentum im ersten und zweiten Jahrundert*. n.p., 1908.

Hooker, "Covenantal Nomism"   Hooker, M. D. "Paul and 'Covenantal Nomism.' " In *Paul and Paulinism*. FS C. K. Barrett. Ed M. D. Hooker and S. G. Wilson. London: SPCK, 1982. Pages 47–56.

HNT   Handbuch zum Neuen Testament

HNTC   Harper's New Testament Commentary

HTKNT Herders theologischer Kommentar zum Neuen Testament

HTR   *Harvard Theological Review*

Hübner, *Law in Paul's Thought*   Hübner, H. *Law in Paul's Thought*. SNTW. Edinburgh: T. & T. Clark, 1984.

Hübner, *Gottes Ich und Israel*   Hübner, H. *Gottes Ich und Israel: Zum Schriftgebrauch des Paulus in Römer 9–11*. Göttingen: Vandenhoeck & Ruprecht, 1984.

Hübner, *Das Gesetz bei Paulus*   Hübner, H. *Das Gesetz bei Paulus. Ein Beitrag zum Werden der paulinischen Theologie*. FRLANT 119. Tübingen: J. C. B. Mohr, 1978.

Hughes, *Early Christian Rhetoric*   Hughes, F. *Early Christian Rhetoric and 2 Thessalonians*. JSNTSup 30. Sheffield: JSOT, 1989.

Hunt–Edgar, *Select Papyri II*   Hunt, A. S. and Edgar, C. C. *Select Papyri II. Non-Literary Papyri: Public Documents*. LCL. London, 1977.

Hyldahl, *Philosophie und Christentum*   Hyldahl, N. *Philosophie und Christentum: Eine Interpretation der Einleitung zum Dialog Justins*. AThD 9. Copenhagen: Munksgaard, 1966.

IB   *Interpreter's Bible*

ICC   International Critical Commentary

IDB   *Interpreter's Dictionary of the Bible*

IDBSup   Supplement to the *Interpreter's Dictionary of the Bible*

Int   *Interpretation*

JAAR   *Journal of the American Academy of Religion*

JAARSup   Supplement to the *Journal of the American Academy of Religion*

Jacoby, "Eselskult"   Jacoby, A. "Der angebliche Eselskult der Juden und Christen." *ARW* 25 (1927) 265–82.

Jaeger, *Greek Paideia*   Jaeger, W. *Early Christianity and Greek Paideia*. Cambridge: Haravard University Press, 1961.

Janne, "Impulsore Chresto"   Janne, H. "Impulsore Chresto." In *Mélanges J. Bidez*. n.p. 1934. Pages 531–53.

JAOS   *Journal of the American Oriental Society*

Jaubert, *Alliance*   Jaubert, A. *La notion d'alliance dans le Judaïsme*. Editions du Seuil, 1963.

JBC   *Jerome Biblical Commentary*

JBL   *Journal of Biblical Literature*

Jeremias, "Römer 11,25–36"   Jeremias, J. "Einige vorwiegend sprachliche Beobachatungen zu Römer 11,25–36." In *Die Israelfrage nach Röm 9–11*. Ed. L. DeLorenzi. Rome: Abtei von St. Paul vor den Mauern, 1977.

Jeremias, "Flesh and Blood"   Jeremias, J. "Flesh and Blood Cannot Inherit the Kingdom." *NTS* 2 (1955–56) 151–59.

Jeremias, "Gedankenführung"   Jeremias, J. "Zur Gedankenführung in den paulinischen Briefen." In *Studia Paulina in honorem Johannis de Zwaan*. Haar-
lem, 1953.

Jervell, "Letter to Jerusalem"   Jervell, J. "The Letter to Jerusalem." In *The Romans Debate: Revised and Expanded Edition*. Ed. K. P. Donfried. Peabody, Mass.:
Hendrickson Publishers, 1991.

Jervell, *Luke and the People of God*   Jervell, J. *Luke and the People of God*.
Minneapolis: Augsburg, 1972.

Jervell, "Lehrer Israels"   Jervell, J. "Paulus—der Lehrer Israels." *NovT* 10 (1968)
164–90.

Jervell, "Zur Frage"   Jervell, J. "Zur Frage der Apostelgeschichte." *ST* 16 (1962)
25–41.

Jervell, "Teacher"   Jervell, J. "Paul: The Teacher of Israel." In J. Jervell. *Luke
and the People of God* Minneapolis: Augsburg, 1972. Pages 151–83.

Jewett, "Numerical Sequences"   Jewett, R. "The Rhetorical Function of Numerical Sequences in Romans." In *Festschrift* for George Kenndy. Ed. D. F. Watson. Forthcoming.

Jewett, "Spanish Mission"   Jewett, R. "Paul, Phoebe, and the Spanish Mission."
In *The Social World of Formative Judaism and Christianity: Essays in Tribute
to Howard Clark Kee*. Ed. J. Neusner et al. Philadelphia: Fortress, 1988. Pages
142–61.

Jewett, "Argument of Romans"   Jewett, R. "Following the Argument of Romans." *Word and World* 6 (1986) 382–89.

Jewett, "Ambassadorial Letter"   Jewett, R. "Romans as an Ambassadorial Letter." *Interp* 36 (January 1982) 5–20.

Jewett, *Christian Tolerance*   Jewett, R. *Christian Tolerance. Paul's Message to
the Modern Church*. Philadelphia: Westminster, 1982.

Jewett, *Dating*   Jewett, R. *Dating Paul's Life*. London, 1979.

Jewett, "Redaction of 1 Cor."   Jewett, R. "The Redaction of 1 Corinthians and
the Trajectory of the Pauline School." *JAARSup* 46 (1978) 389–444.

Jewett, "Conflicting Movements"   Jewett, R. "Conflicting Movements in the
Early Church as Reflected in Philippians." *NovT* 12 (1970–71) 362–90.

Jewett, "The Agitators"   Jewett, R. "The Agitators and the Galatian Congregation." *NTS* 17 (1970–71) 198–212.

Jewett, *Anthropological Terms*   Jewett, R. *Paul's Anthropological Terms: A
Study of Their Use in Conflict Settings*. Arbeiten zur Geschichte des antiken
Judentums und des Urchristentums 10. Leiden: Brill, 1971.

Johnson, "Romans 11"   Johnson, D. G. "The Structure and Meaning of Romans 11." *CBQ* 46 (1984) 93–101.

Jordan, "Persuasive Genres"   Jordan, M. D. "Ancient Philosophic Protereptic
and the Problem of Persuasive Genres" *Rhetorica* 4 (1986).

JRH   *Journal of Religious History*

JRS   *Journal of Roman Studies*

JSNT   *Journal for the Study of the New Testament*

JSNTSup   Supplement to the *Journal for the Study of the New Testament*

JTS   *Journal of Theological Studies*

Judge and Thomas, "Church at Rome"   Judge, E. A. and E. R. Thomas. "The
Origin of the Church at Rome." *RTR* 25 (1966) 81–94.

Judge, "Classical Society"   Judge, E. A. "St. Paul and Classical Society." *Jahr-
buch für Antike und Christentum* 15 (1972) 35ff.

Judge, "Scholastic Community"   Judge, E. A. "The Early Christians as a Scholastic Community" *JRH* 1 (1960–61) 4–15, 125–37.

Jülicher–Fascher, *Einleitung*   Jülicher, A. and E. Fascher. *Einleitung in das Neue Testament.* Tübingen, 1931[7].

Juster, *Les Juifs*   Juster, J. *Les Juifs dans l'Empire Romain* II. n.p., 1914.

Karris, "Occasion"   Karris, R. J. "Rom 14:1–15:13 and the Occasion of Romans. In *The Romans Debate: Revised and Expanded Edition.* Ed. K. P. Donfried. Peabody, Mass.: Hendrickson Publishers, 1991.

Karris, "Response"   Karris, R. J. "The Occasion of Romans: A Response to Prof. Donfried." In *The Romans Debate: Revised and Expanded Edition.* Ed. K. P. Donfried. Peabody, Mass.: Hendrickson Publishers, 1991.

Käsemann, *Romans*   Käsemann, E. *Commentary on Romans,* ET Grand Rapids: Eerdmans, 1982.

Käsemann, *Römer*   Käsemann, E. *Der Brief an die Römer,* HNT 8a, 3rd ed. Tübingen: J. C. B. Mohr, 1974.

Käsemann, *Perspectives*   Käsemann, E. *Perspectives on Paul.* Philadelphia: Fortress, 1971.

Käsemann, *Questions*   Käsemann, E. *New Testament Questions of Today.* ET London: SCM, 1969.

Käsemann, "Righteousness"   Käsemann, E. "The Righteousness of Paul." In *New Testament Questions of Today.* ET London: SCM, 1969.

Käsemann, "Konsequente"   Käsemann, E. "Konsequente Traditiongeschichte?" *ZTK* 62 (1965) 137–52.

Käsemann, *Essays*   Käsemann, E. *Essays on New Testament Themes.* SBT 1/41. London: SCM, 1964.

Käsemann, *Paulus*   Käsemann, E. *Paulus und der Frükatholizismus.* Exegetische Versuche und Besinnungen II. n.p. 1964.

Kaylor, *Covenant Community*   Kaylor, R. D. *Paul's Covenant Community: Jew & Gentile in Romans.* Atlanta: John Knox, 1988.

Keck, *Paul and His Letters*   Keck, L. E. *Paul and His Letters.* Proclamation Commentaries. Philadelphia: Fortress, 1979.

KEK   Kritisch-exegetische Kommentar

Kelly, *Pastoral Epistles*   Kelly, J. N. D. *Pastoral Epistles.* New York: Harper & Row, 1963.

Kennedy, *Rhetorical Criticism*   Kennedy, G. A. *New Testament Interpretation through Rhetorical Criticism.* Chapel Hill: University of North Carolina Press, 1984.

Kennedy, *Art of Rhetoric*   Kennedy, G. *The Art of Rhetoric in the Roman World 300 BC to AD 300.* Princeton: Princeton University, 1972.

Kennedy, *Persuasion*   Kennedy, G. *The Art of Persuasion in Greece.* Princeton: Princeton University Press, 1963.

Kertelge, *Romans*   Kertelge, K. *The Epistle to the Romans.* New York: Herder & Herder, 1972.

Kettunen, *Abfassungszweck*   Kettunen, M. *Der Abfassungszweck des Römerbriefes.* AASF 18. Helsinki: Suomalainen Tiedeakatemia, 1979.

Kim, *Familiar Letter*   Kim, C.-H. *The Familiar Letter of Recommendation.* Missoula: Scholars, 1972.

Kinoshita, "Romans"   Kinoshita, J. "Romans—Two Writings Combined. A New Interpretation of the Body of Romans." *NovT* 7 (1964–65) 258–77.

Klappert, "Traktat"   Klappert, B. "Traktat für Israel (Römer 9–11)." In *Jüdische Existenz und die Erneuerung der christlichen Theologie.* Ed. M. Stöhr. Munich: Kaiser, 1981.

Klappert, *Israel und die Kirche*   Klappert, B. *Israel und die Kirche.* Munich: Kaiser, 1980.

Klein, "Paul's Purpose"   Klein, G. "Paul's Purpose in Writing the Epistle to the Romans." In *The Romans Debate: Revised and Expanded Edition*. Ed. K. P. Donfried. Peabody, Mass.: Hendrickson Publishers, 1991.

Klein, "Righteousness"   Klein, G. "Righteousness." In *IDBSup*. Nashville: Abingdon, 1976.

Knibbe, "Neue Inschriften"   Knibbe, D., et al. "Neue Inschriften aus Ephesos IX–X." *Jahreshefte des österreichischen Archäologischen Institutes in Wien* 55 (1984) 107–49.

Knox, "Romans 15:14–33"   Knox, J. "Romans 15:14–33 and Paul's conception of his Apostolic Mission." *JBL* 83 (1964) 1–11.

Knox, "Text of Romans"   Knox, J. "A Note on the Text of Romans." *NTS* (2, 1955/56) 191–93.

Knox, "Romans"   Knox, J. "Romans." *Interpreter's Bible*. Vol. 9. Nashville: Abingdon, 1954.

Koester, "Paul and Hellenism"   Koester, H. "Paul and Hellenism." In *The Bible and Modern Scholarship*. Ed. H. J. P. Hyatt. Nashville: Abingdon, 1965.

Koester, *Einführung*   Koester, H. *Einführung in das Neue Testament*. Berlin and New York: de Gruyter, 1980.

Koester, "Pauline Fragment"   Koester, H. "The Purpose of the Polemic of a Pauline Fragment (Philippians III)." *NTS* 8 (1961–62) 317–32.

König, *Stilistik, Rhetorik, Poetik*   König, E. *Stilistik, Rhetorik, Poetik*. Leipzig: Weicher, 1900.

Koskenniemi, *Griechischen Briefes*   Koskenniemi, H. *Studien zur Idee und Phraseologie des griechischen Briefes bis 400 n. Chr.* Helsinki: n.p., 1956.

Krentz, *Historical-Critical Method*   Krentz, E. *The Historical-Critical Method*. Philadelphia: Fortress, 1975.

Kroll, "Epideiktik"   Kroll, W. "Regeln für Epideiktik." In *PWSup*. Vol. 7, pages 1131–35.

Kümmel, *Introduction*   Kümmel, W. G. *Introduction to the New Testament*. 17th ed. Nashville: Abingdon, 1975.

Kümmel, *Römer 7*   Kümmel, W. G., *Römer 7 und die Bekehrung des Paulus*. Leipzig: Hinrichs'sche Buchhandlung, 1929. Reprinted in *Römer 7 und das Bild des Menschen im Neuen Testament*. Munich: Kaiser, 1974. Pages ix–160.

Kuss, *Der Römerbrief*   Kuss, O. *Der Römerbrief*. Regensburg: Pustet, 1957.

Kuss, "Nomos"   Kuss, O. "Nomos bei Paulus." *MTZ* 17 (1966) 173–266.

Kustas, *Byzantine Rhetoric*   Kustas, G. L. *Studies in Byzantine Rhetoric*. Thessalonica: Patriarchal Institute for Patristic Studies, 1973.

Lamarche–Le Dû, *Epître aux Romains 5–8*   Lamarche, P. and C. Le Dû. *Epître aux Romains 5–8: Structure littéraire et sens*. Paris: Centre National de la Recherche Scientifique, 1980.

Lampe, "Junia"   Lampe, P. "Junia." In *Anchor Bible Dictionary*. New York: Doubleday, forthcoming.

Lampe, *Die stadtrömischen*   Lampe, P. *Die stadtrömischen Christian in den ersten beiden Jahrhunderten: Untersuchen zur Sozialgeschichte*. 2nd edition. Tübingen: J. C. B. Mohr, 1989.

Lampe, "Paulus—Zeltmacher"   Lampe, P. "Paulus—Zeltmacher." *BZ* 31 (1987) 256–61.

Lampe, "Textgeschichte"   Lampe, P. "Zur Textgeschichte des Römerbriefs." *NovT* 27 (1985) 273–77.

Lang, "Gesetz"   Lang, F. "Gesetz und Bund bei Paulus." In *Rechtfertigung*. FS E. Käsemann. Ed. J. Friedrich et al. Tübingen: J. C. B. Mohr, 1976. Pages 305–20.

LaPiana, "Foreign Groups"   LaPiana, G. "Foreign Groups in Rome during the First Century of the Empire." *HTR* 20 (1927) 183–403.

Lapide–Stuhlmacher, *Rabbi*   Lapide, P. and Stuhlmacher, P. *Paul: Rabbi and Apostle.* Minneapolis: Augsburg, 1984.

Larsen, *Jamblique de Chalcis*   Larsen, B. D. *Jamblique de Chalcis, Exégète et Philosophe.* 2 vols. Aarhus: Universitetsforlaget i Aarhus, 1972.

Lausberg, *Elemente*   Lausberg, H. *Elemente der Literarischen Rhetorik.* 3rd ed. Munich: Hueber, 1967.

Lausberg, *Handbuch*   Lausberg, H. *Handbuch der literarischen Rhetorik: Eine Grundlegung der Literaturwissenschaft.* 2nd ed.; Munich: Max Hueber, 1973.

LCL   Loeb Classical Library

Leenhardt, *Romans*   Leenhardt, F. J. *The Epistle to the Romans: A Commentary.* London: Lutterworth, 1961.

Leenhardt, *Romains*   Leenhardt, F. J. *L'Epître de Saint Paul aux Romains.* Neuchâtel: Delachaux et Niestlé, 1957.

Lefay, "Le Sabbat juif"   Lefay, P. "Le Sabbat juif et les poetes latines." *Revue d'histoire et litterature religieuse* 8 (1903) 313–20.

Leipoldt, *Gegenwartsfragen*   Leipoldt, J. *Gegenwartsfragen in der neutestamentlichen Wissenschaft.* n.p. 1935.

Leipoldt–Grundmann, *Umwelt*   Leipoldt, J. and W. Grundmann. *Umwelt des Urchristentums.* 3 vols. Berlin: Evangelische Verlagsanstalt, 1965.

Leitzmann, "Zwei Notizen zu Paulus"   Leitzmann, H. "Zwei Notizen zu Paulus." *SBA* (1930) 8ff.

Leon, *Jews of Ancient Rome*   Leon, H. J. *The Jews of Ancient Rome.* Philadelphia: Jewish Publication Society of America, 1960.

Leon, "Synagogue of the Herodians"   Leon, H. J. "The Synagogue of the Herodians." *JAOS* 49 (1929) 318–22.

Leon, "Greek Inscriptions"   Leon, H. J. "The Language of the Greek Inscriptions of the Jewish Catacombs of Rome." *Transactions and Proceedings of the American Philological Association* 58 (1927) 210–33.

Lichtenberger, "Paulinischen Anthropologie"   Lichtenberger, H. "Studien zur paulinischen Anthropologie in Römer 7." Unpublished Habilitationschrift. Tübingen, 1985.

Lietzmann, *An die Römer*   Lietzmann, H. *An die Römer.* HNT 8. Tübingen: J. C. B. Mohr, 1933 reprint 1971.

Lietzmann, "Zwei Notizen zu Paulus"   Lietzmann, H. "Zwei Notizen zu Paulus." *SBA* (1930) 8ff. = *KZ. Schriften* II (TU 68), 1958, 290ff.

Limbeck, *Ordnung*   Limbeck, M. *Die Ordnung des Heils: Untersuchungen zum Gesetzverständnis des Früjudentums.* Düsseldorf: Patmos, 1971.

Lipsius   Lipsius, R. A. Commentary on Romans in H. J. Holtzmann ed. *Handkommentar zum Neuen Testament* 2, Tübingen, 1892².

Louw, *Analysis of Romans*   Louw, J. P. *A Semantic Discourse Analysis of Romans.* Pretoria: University of Pretoria, 1979.

Louw–Nida, *Greek-English Lexicon*   Louw, J. and E. Nida. *Greek-English Lexicon of the New Testament Based on Semantic Domains.* 2 vols. New York: United Bible Societies, 1988.

LSJ   Liddell, H. G., R. Scott, H. S. Jones, eds. *Greek English Lexicon.* Revised ed. Oxford: Clarendon Press, 1968.

Lüdemann, *Das frühe Christentum*   Lüdemann, G. *Das frühe Christentum nach den Traditionen der Apostelgeschichte.* Göttingen: Vandenhoeck & Ruprecht, 1987.

Lüdemann, *Paul*   Lüdemann, G. *Paul, Apostle to the Gentiles. Studies in Chronology.* ET London: SCM, 1984.

Lüdemann, *Paulus und das Judentum*   Lüdemann, G. *Paulus und das Judentum.* Munich: Kaiser, 1983.

Lührmann, "Freundschaftsbrief"   Lührmann, D. "Freundschaftsbrief trotz Spannungen" *BZNW* (1986) 298–315.

Lundeen, *Risk and Rhetoric*   Lundeen, L. T. *Risk and Rhetoric in Religion. Whitehead's Theory of Language and the Discourse of Faith.* Philadelphia: Fortress, 1972.

Lütgert, *Römerbrief*   Lütgert, W. *Der Römerbrief als historisches Problem.* BFCT 17(2). Gütersloh, 1913.

Luz, "Röm 1–8"   Luz, U. "Zum Aufbau von Röm 1–8." *ThZ* 25 (1969) 161–94.

Luz, *Geschichtsverständnis*   Luz, U. *Das Geschichtsverständnis des Paulus.* BEvTh 49. Munich: Kaiser, 1968.

Lyonnet, "Notes"   Lyonnet, S. "Notes sur le plan de l'épître aux Romains." *RSR* 39 (1951–52).

Mack, *Rhetoric*   Mack, B. L. *Rhetoric and the New Testament.* Minneapolis: Fortress, 1990.

Mack, "Anecdotes"   Mack, B. L. "Anecdotes and Arguments: The Chreia in Antiquity and Early Christianity." *Institute for Antiquity and Christianity Occasional Papers* 10 (1987) 1–48.

Mack–Murphy, "Wisdom Literature"   Mack, B. and R. Murphy. "Wisdom Literature." in *Early Judaism and Its Modern Interpreters.* Ed. R. Kraft and G. Nicklesburg. Philadelphia: Fortress, 1986.

MacMullen, *Christianizing*   MacMullen, R. *Christianizing the Roman Empire, A.D. 100–400.* New Haven: Yale University Press, 1984.

Madden, *Jewish Coinage*   Madden, F. W. *The History of Jewish Coinage.* London, 1864; reprint New York: Ktav, 1967.

Malherbe, "Paraenetic Letter"   Malherbe, A. J. "I Thessalonians as a Paraenetic Letter." unpublished paper presented to the Paul Seminar of the Society of Biblical Literature, annual meeting, 1972.

Malherbe, *Moral Exhortation*   Malherbe, A. J. *Moral Exhortation, a Greco-Roman Sourcebook.* Philadelphia: Westminster, 1986.

Manson, "Letter to the Romans"   Manson, T. W. "St. Paul's Letter to the Romans—and Others." *The Romans Debate: Revised and Expanded Edition.* Ed. K. P. Donfried. Peabody, Mass.: Hendrickson Publishers, 1991.

Manson, *Studies*   Manson, T. W. *Studies in the Gospels and Acts.* Ed. M. Black. Manchester, 1962.

Manson, W. *Hebrews*   Manson, W. *The Epistle to the Hebrews.* London, 1951.

Marmorstein, *Doctrine of Merits*   Marmorstein, A. *The Doctrine of Merits in the Old Rabbinic Literature.* New York: Ktav, 1968.

Martin, "Kerygma of Romans"   Martin, J. P. "The Kerygma of Romans." *Int* 25 (1971) 303–28.

Marxsen, *Introduction*   Marxsen, W. *Introduction to the New Testament.* ET Philadelphia: Fortress, 1968.

Mayer, *Prädestination*   Mayer, B. *Unter Gottes Heilsratschluss; Prädestinationsaussagen bei Paulus.* Würzburg: Echter, 1974.

McDonald, "Separate Letter?"   McDonald, J. I. H., "Was Romans XVI a Separate Letter?" *NTS* 16 (1969/70) 369–72.

Meeks, *First Urban Christians*   Meeks, W. *The First Urban Christians.* New Haven: Yale University Press, 1983.

Merk, *Handeln aus Glauben*   Merk, O. *Handeln aus Glauben: Die Motiverungen der paulinischen Ethik.* Marburger Theologische Studien 5. Marburg: N. G. Elwert Verlag, 1968.

Merril, "Claudius and the Jews"   Merril, E. T. "Claudius and the Jews." In *Essays in Early Christianity.* London: n.p. 1924.

Metzger, *Textual Commentary*   Metzger, B. M. *A Textual Commentary on the Greek New Testament.* London/New York: United Bible Societies, 1971.

Meyer E., *Ursprung und Anfänge*   Meyer, E. *Ursprung und Anfänge des Christentums*. Stuttgart/Berlin: J G. Cotta, 1921–23.

Meyer, "Romans"   Meyer, P. W. "Romans." In *Harper Bible Commentary*. Ed. J. L. Mays. San Francisco: Harper & Row, 1988.

MeyerK   Meyer, H. A. W. Kritisch-exegetischer Kommentar über das Neue Testament

MGWJ   *Monatsschrift für Geschichte und Wissenschaft des Judentums*

Michaelis, *Einleitung*   Michaelis W. *Einleitung in das Neue Testament*, 1954, 1961[3].

Michaelis, "Briefkompositionen"   Michaelis, W. "Teilungshypothesen bei Paulusbriefe: Briefkompositionen und ihr Sitz im Leben." *ThZ* 14 (1958) 321–26.

Michel, *Der Brief an die Römer*   Michel, O. *Der Brief an die Römer*. MeyerK 4. Göttingen: Vandenhoeck & Ruprecht, 1957.

Minear, *Obedience*   Minear, P. S. *The Obedience of Faith: The Purposes of Paul in the Epistle to the Romans*. SBT 2/19; London: SCM, 1971.

Moehring, "Persecution of the Jews"   Moehring, H. "The Persecution of the Jews and the Adherents of the Isis Cult at Rome AD 19." *NovT* 3 (1959) 293–304.

Moffatt, *First Corinthians*   Moffatt, J. *The First Epistle of Paul to the Corinthians*. London: Hodder and Stoughton, 1938.

Moffatt, *Introduction*   Moffatt, J. *An Introduction to the Literature of the New Testament*. New York, 1911.

Momigliano, *Claudio*   Momigliano, A. *L'Opera dell'imperatore Claudio*. Florence: n.p., 1932.

Montefiore, *Judaism and Paul*   Montefiore, C.-G. *Judaism and St. Paul*. 1914. Reprint New York: Arno, 1973.

Morris, *Romans*   Morris, L. *The Epistle of Paul to the Romans*. Grand Rapids: Eerdmans, 1988.

Morris, "Theme of Romans"   Morris, L. "The Theme of Romans." In *Apostolic History and the Gospel: Biblical and Historical Essays Presented to F. F. Bruce on his 60th Birthday*. Ed. W. Ward Gasque and R. P. Martin. Grand Rapids: Eerdmans, 1970. Pages 249–63.

Moule, *Idioim Book*   Moule, C. F. D. *An Idiom Book of New Testament Greek*. Cambridge: Cambridge University Press, 1960.

MTZ   *Münchener theologische Zeitschrift*

Müller, *Römer 9–11*   Müller, C. *Gottes Gerechtigkeit und Gottes Volk. Eine Untersuchung zu Römer ix-xi*. Göttingen, 1964.

Müller, "Luciani dialogorum"   Müller, L. "De Luciani dialogorum rhetoricorum compositione." *Eos* 32 (1929) 574–78.

Müller, *Prophetie und Predigt*   Müller, U. *Prophetie und Predigt im Neuen Testament*. Gutersloh: Mohn, 1975.

Mullins, "Greetings"   Mullins, T. Y. "Greetings as a New Testament Form." *JBL* 87 (1968) 418–26.

Munck, *Christ and Israel*   Munck, J. *Christ and Israel*. Philadelphia, 1967.

Munck, *Paul and the Salvation of Mankind*   Munck, J. *Paul and the Salvation of Mankind*. Richmond: John Knox, 1959.

Munck, *Paulus und die Heilsgeschichte*   Munck, J. *Paulus und die Heilsgeschichte*. 1954.

Munck, "Christus und Israel"   Munck, J. "Christus und Israel. Eine Auslegung von Röm. 9–11." *Acta Jutlandica* 28 3 Teologisk Series 7 (1946).

Mussner, "Ganz Israel"   Mussner, F. " 'Ganz Israel wird gerettet werden' (Röm 11,26)." *Kairos* 18 (1976) 242.

Mussner, *Der Galaterbrief*   Mussner, F. *Der Galaterbrief*. Freiburg: Herder, 1974.

Mussner, "Gesetz—Abraham—Israel"   Mussner, F. "Gesetz—Abraham—Israel." *Kairos* 25 (1983) 200–20.

Mussner, *Tractate*   Mussner, F. *Tractate on the Jews*. London: SPCK, 1984.

Myers, "Romans 5:1–11"   Myers, C. D., Jr., "The Place of Romans 5:1–11 within the Argument of the Epistle." Th.D. diss. Princeton Theological Seminary, 1985.

Nababan, *Römer 14 und 15*   Nababan, A. E. S. *Bekenntnis und Mission in Römer 14 und 15: Eine exegetische Untersuchung*. Diss. University of Heidelberg, 1963.

NCBC   New Century Bible Commentary

Neusner, *Judaism*   Neusner, J. *Judaism: The Evidence of the Mishnah*. University of Chicago, 1981.

Nickle, *Collection*   Nickle, K. F. *The Collection: A Study in the Strategy of Paul.* SBT 1/48. London: SCM, 1966.

Nilsson, *Geschichte der griechischen Religion*   Nilsson, M. P. *Geschichte der griechischen Religion*. II². 1961.

Noack, "Current and Backwater"   Noack, B. "Current and Backwater in the Epistle to the Romans." *Studia Theologica* 19 (1965) 155–66.

Nock, *Conversion*   Nock, A. D. *Conversion*. London: Oxford University Press, 1933.

Nock, *Sallustius*   Nock, A. D. *Sallustius Concerning the Gods and the Universe*. Hildesheim: Olms, 1966.

Nollé, *Die Inschriften von Ephesos*   Nollé, J. *Die Inschriften von Ephesos*, Teil VIII, 2, ed. Kommission für die Archäol. Erforsh. Kleinasiens bei der österr. Akad. d. Wiss., Bonn: Habelt, 1984.

Norden, *Kunstprosa*   Norden, E. *Die antike Kunstprosa vom VI Jahrhundert v. Chr. bis in die Zeit der Renaissance*. Leipzig, Teubner, 1909. Reprint, 2 vols. Darmstadt: Wissenschaftliche Buchgesellschaft, 1958.

NovT   *Novum Testamentum*

NTAbh   Neutestamentliche Abhandlungen

NTD   Das Neue Testament Deutsch

NTS   *New Testament Studies*

Nygren, *Romans*   Nygren, A. *A Commentary on Romans*. Philadelphia: Fortress, 1952.

Nygren, *Romarbrevet*   Nygren, A. *Romarbrevet*. Stockholm: Verbum, 1944.

O'Neill, *Romans*   O'Neill, J. C. *Paul's Letter to the Romans*. Harmondsworth: Penguin, 1975.

Ollrog, "Abfassungsverhältnisse"   Ollrog, W.-H. "Die Abfassungsverhältnisse von Röm 16." In *Kirche*. Ed. Lührmann, D. and G. Strecker. Tübingen: J. C. B. Mohr, 1980.

Park, "Jerusalem Church"   Park, Y. M. "The Effect of Contemporary Conditions in the Jerusalem Church on the Writing of the Epistle to the Romans." Unpublished dissertation, University of Edinburgh, 1979.

Patte, *Power of the Gospel*   Patte, D. *Paul's Faith and the Power of the Gospel*. Philadelphia: Fortress, 1983.

Pavano, *Dionisio*   Pavano, G. *Dionisio D'Alicarnasso. Saggio Su Tucidide*. Palermo, 1958.

Percy, *Kolosser- und Epheserbriefe*   Percy, E. *Die Probleme der Kolosser- und Epheserbriefe*, n.p.

Perelman–Olbrechts-Tyteca, *New Rhetoric*   Perelman, Ch. and Olbrechts-Tyteca, L. *The New Rhetoric: A Treatise on Argumentation*. Notre Dame, Ind.: University of Notre Dame, 1971.

Pesch, *Römerbrief*   Pesch, R. *Römerbrief*. EB 6. Würzburg: Echter, 1983.

Pfleiderer, *Das Urchristentum*   Pfleiderer, O. *Das Urchristentum* 1887, 177f.

PG = Migne, *Patrologica Graeca*

Philippi, *Römer*   Philippi, F. A. *Kommentar über den Brief Pauli an die Römer*. 2nd ed., 1856. Frankfurt a.M. & Erlangen.

PL = Migne, *Patrologica Latinae*

Plag, *Israels Wege zum Heil*   Plag, C. *Israels Wege zum Heil. Eine Untersuchung zu Römer 9 bis 11.* Stuttgart: Calwer, 1969.

Plassart, "L'inscription de Delphes"   Plassart, A. "L'inscription de Delphes mentionnant le Procounsul Gallion." *Revue des Etudes Grecques* 80 (1967) 372ff.

Preisker, "Das historische Problem"   Preisker, H. "Das historische Problem des Römerbriefes." *WZ* (1952–53) 25–30.

Prümm, "Struktur"   Prümm, K. "Zur Struktur des Römerbriefes," *Zeitschrift für Katholische Theologie* 72 (1950) 333–49.

PW   Pauly-Wissowa, *Real-Encyclopädie der classischen Altertumswissenschaft*

PWSup   Supplement to *PW*

Rahn, *Morphologie*   Rahn, H. *Morphologie der antiken Literatur.* Darmstadt: Wissenschaft Buchgesellschaft, 1969.

Räisänen, "Romans 9–11"   Räisänen, H. "Paul, God, and Israel: Romans 9–11 in Recent Research." In *The Social World of Formative Christianity and Judaism.* Ed. J. Neusner, P. Borgen, E. S. Fredrichs, and R. Horsley. Philadelphia: Fortress, 1988. Pages 178–206.

Räisänen, *Torah and Christ*   Räisänen, H. *The Torah and Christ.* Helsinki: Finnish Exegetical Society, 1986.

Räisänen, *Paul and the Law*   Räisänen, H. *Paul and the Law.* WUNT 29. Tübingen: J. C. B. Mohr, 1983.

Räisänen, "Legalism"   Räisänen, H. "Legalism and Salvation by the Law: Paul's Portrayal of the Jewish Religion as a Historical and Theological Problem." In *Die Paulinische Literatur und Theologie.* Ed. S. Pedersen. Aarhus/Göttingen: Aros/Vandenhoeck & Ruprecht, 1980. Pages 63–83.

Räisänen, "Difficulties"   Räisänen, H. "Paul's Theological Difficulties with the Law." In *Studia Biblica 1978.* Pages 25–54.

Ramsay, "Roman Imperial Post"   Ramsay, W. M. "The Speed of the Roman Imperial Post." *JRS* 15 (1925) 60–74.

Rauer, "*Schwachen*"   Rauer, M. *Die "Schwachen" in Korinth und Rom nach den Paulusbriefen.* BSt 21,2/3. Freiburg: Herder, 1923.

RB   *Revue Biblique*

Reese, *Wisdom*   Reese, J. M. *Hellenistic Influence on the Book of Wisdom and Its Consequences.* Rome: Biblical Institute, 1970.

Reifenberg, *Jewish Coins*   Reifenberg, A. *Ancient Jewish Coins*, 2nd ed. Jerusalem, 1947.

Reinach, "La première allusion"   Reinach, S. "La première allusion au christianisme dans l'histoire." *RHR* 90 (1924) 108–22.

Reinach, *Textes*   Reinach, T. *Textes d'auteurs grecs et romains relatifs au judaisme.* n.p., 1895.

REJ   *Revue des études juives*

Rengstorf, "Paulus"   Rengstorf, K. H. "Paulus und die älteste römische Christenheit." *SE* 2 (TU 87, 1964) 447f.

Reumann, *Righteousness*   Reumann, J. *Righteousness in the New Testament.* Philadelphia: Fortress, 1982.

RGG   Religion in Geschichte und Gegenwart

RHPR   Revue de l'histoire et de philosophie religieuses

RHR   Revue de l'historie des religions

Richardson, *Israel*   Richardson, P. *Israel in the Apostolic Church.* Cambridge: Cambridge University Press, 1969.

Ridderbos, *Paul*   Ridderbos, H. N. *Paul: An Outline of His Theology.* Grand Rapids: Eerdmans, 1975.

Roberts, *Demetrius*   Roberts, W. Rhys. *Demetrius On Style.* Cambridge, 1902.

Robinson, "Priesthood of Paul"   Robinson, D. W. B. "The Priesthood of Paul in the Gospel of Hope." In *Reconciliation and Hope. New Testament Essays Presented to Leon Morris on his 60th Birthday.* Ed. R. J. Banks. Exeter: Paternoster, 1974. Pages 231–45.

Roetzel, *Letters of Paul*   Roetzel, C. J. *The Letters of Paul.* Atlanta: John Knox, 1975.

Rolland, *Epître aux Romains*   Rolland, P. *Epître aux Romains: Texte grec structure.* Rome: Biblical Institute, 1980.

Roloff, *Die Apostelgeschichte*   Roloff, J. *Die Apostelgeschichte.* NTD 5. Göttingen: Vandenhoeck & Ruprecht, 1981.

Roosen, "Le genre littérarie"   Roosen, A. "Le genre littérarie de l'Epître aux Romains." In *Studia Evangelica* II. Berlin: Akademie-Verlag, 1964.

Ropes, "Romans"   Ropes, H. H. "The Epistle to the Romans and Jewish Christianity." In *Studies in Early Christianity.* Ed. S. J. Case. (New York/London: n.p., 1928. Pages 353–65.

RSR   Recherches de science religieuse

RTR   Reformed Theological Review

Ruch, *L'Hortensius de Cicéron*   Ruch, M. *L'Hortensius de Cicéron: Historie et Reconstitution.* Paris: Société d'édition "Les Belles Lettres." 1958.

Ruether, *Faith and Fratricide*   Ruether, R. *Faith and Fratricide.* New York: Seabury, 1974.

Ruijs, *Struktuur*   Ruijs, R. C. M. *De struktuur van de brief aen de Romainen. Een stilistische, vormhistorische en thematische analyse van Rom 1,16–3,23.* (With a summary in English) Utrecht-Nijmegan: Dekker & Van de Vogt, 1964.

Sanday–Headlam, *Romans*   Sanday, W. and A. C. Headlam. *A Critical and Exegetical Commentary on the Epistle to the Romans,* 5th ed. ICC. Edinburgh: T. & T. Clark, 1902.

Sanders, *Law*   Sanders, E. P. *Paul, the Law, and the Jewish People.* Philadelphia: Fortress, 1983.

Sanders, *Paul*   Sanders, E. P. *Paul and Palestinian Judaism.* Philadelphia: Fortress, 1977.

Sanders, "Patterns"   Sanders, E. P. "Patterns of Religion in Paul and Rabbinic Judaism." *HTR* 66 (1973) 455–78.

Sanders, J. T., *Ethics*   Sanders, J. T. *Ethics in the New Testament.* Philadelphia: Fortress, 1975.

Sandmel, *Paul*   Sandmel, S. *The Genius of Paul.* Philadelphia: Fortress, 1979.

SANT   Studien zum Alten und Neuen Testament

SBA   Sitzungsberichte d. Akademie der Wissenschaften zu Berlin

SBLDS   Society of Biblical Literature Dissertation Series

SBLMS   Society of Biblical Literature Monograph Series

SBS   Stuttgarter Bibelstudien

SBT   Studies in Biblical Theology

Schäfer, "Rabbi Aqiba"   Schäfer, P. "Rabbi Aqiba and Bar Kokba." In *Approaches to Ancient Judaism II.* Ed. W. S. Green. Brown Judaic Studies 9; Atlanta: Scholar's Press, 1980.

Schäublin, "Konversionen"   Schäublin, C. "Konversionen in antiken Dialogen?" In *Catalepton. Festschrift für Beernhard Wyss.* Ed. idem. Basel: Seminar für Klassische Philologie, 1985.

Schechter, *Rabbinic Theology*   Schechter, S. *Aspects of Rabbinic Theology.* New York: Schocken, 1961 (reprint of 1909 ed.).

Schelkle, "Römische Kirche"   Schelkle, K. H. "Römische Kirche im Römerbrief." *ZKT* 81 (1959) 393–404 = "Wort und Schrift" [1966], 273–81.

Schenke, "Aporien im Römerbrief"   Schenke, H.-M. "Aporien im Römerbrief." *TLZ* 92 (1967) 881–88.

Schlatter, *Gottes Gerechtigkeit*   Schlatter, A. *Gottes Gerechtigkeit. Ein Kommentar zum Römerbrief*. Stuttgart: Calwer Verlag, 1959.

Schlier, *Der Römerbrief*   Schlier, H. *Der Römerbrief*, 2nd edition. HTKNT 6. Freiburg/Basel/Vienna, 1979.

Schlier, "Vom Wesen"   Schlier, H. "Vom Wesen der apostolischen Ermahnung nach Röm. 12, 1–2." In *Die Zeit der Kirche*. Frieburg: Herder, 1966. Pages 74–89.

Schmeller, "*Diatribe*"   Schmeller, T. *Paulus und die "Diatribe": Eine vergleichende Stilinterpretation*. NTA/NF 19. Münster: Aschendorff, 1987.

Schmidt, *Römer*   Schmidt, H. W. *Der Brief des Paulus an die Römer*. THKNT 6. n.p. 1963.

Schmithals, *Der Römerbrief: Ein Kommentar*   Schmithals, *Der Römerbrief: Ein Kommentar*. Gütersloh: Gerd Mohn, 1988.

Schmithals, *Der Römerbrief als historisches Problem*   Schmithals, W. *Der Römerbrief als historisches Problem*. StNT 9. Gütersloh: Gerd Mohn, 1975.

Schmithals, *Paul and the Gnostics*   Schmithals, W. *Paul and the Gnostics*. Trans. John Steely. Nashville: Abingdon, 1972.

Schmithals, *Gnosticism in Corinth*   Schmithals, W. *Gnosticism in Corinth*. Trans. John Steely. Nashville: Abingdon, 1971.

Schmithals, *Paulus und die Gnostiker*   Schmithals, W. *Paulus und die Gnostiker. Untersuchungen zu den Kleinen Paulusbriefen*. TF 36. Hamburg, 1965.

Schneeweiss, *Der Protrepticos*   Schneeweiss, G. *Der Protrepticos des Aristoteles*. Munich: C. Wolf & Son, 1912.

Schneider, *Griechische Poliorketiker III*   Schneider, R. *Griechische Poliorketiker III*. Abhandl. d. königl. Gesellschaft d. Wissensch. zu Göttingen, Philol.-hist. Kl., N. F., 12:5. Berlin, 1912.

Schoeps, *Paul*   Schoeps, H. J. *Paul: The Theology of the Apostle in the Light of Jewish Religious History*. London: Lutterworth, 1961.

Scholem, *Messianic Idea*   Scholem, G. *The Messianic Idea in Judaism*. London: Allen and Unwin, 1971.

Schrage, " 'Ekklesia' und 'Synagoge' "   Schrage, W. " 'Ekklesia' und 'Synagoge.' Zum Ursprung des urchristlichen Kirchenbegriffs." *ZTK* 60 (1963) 187ff.

Schrage, *Ethik*   Schrage, W. *Die konkreten Einzelgebote in der paulinischen Paranese: Ein Beitrag zur neutestamentlichen Ethik*. Gutersloh: Gerd Mohn Verlaghaus, 1961.

Schrenk, "Der Römerbrief"   Schrenk, G. "Der Römerbrief als Missionsdokument." *Studien Z. Paulus*. ATANT 26. Zurich, 1954.

Schulz, *TSK*   Schulz, D. *TSK* 2 (1829) 609–12.

Schumacher, *Kapitel*   Schumacher, R. *Die beiden letzten Kapitel des Römerbriefes*. In *Neutestamentliche Abhandlungen*. Ed. Meinertz. 14 Band, 4 Heft. Münster i. W. 1929.

Schürer, *Die Gemeindeverfassung*   Schürer, E. *Die Gemeindeverfassung in Rom nach den Inschriften dargestellt*. n.p. 1879.

Schürer, *History*   Schürer, E. *The History of the Jewish People in the Age of Jesus Christ*, rev. G. Vermes, F. Millar, and M. Goodman. 4 vols. Edinburgh: T. & T. Clark, 1986.

Scott, *Romans*   Scott, E. F. *Paul's Epistle to the Romans*. London: SCM, 1949.

Scramuzza, *Emperor Claudius*   Scramuzza, V. M. *The Emperor Claudius*. Cambridge, Mass.: n.p., 1940.

Scroggs, "Paul as Rhetorician"   Scroggs, R. "Paul as Rhetorician. Two Homilies in Romans 1–9." In *Jews, Greeks, and Christians: Religious Cultures in Late Antiquity. Essays in Honor of W. D. Davies*. Ed. idem and R. Hamerton-Kelly. Leiden: Brill, 1976. Pages 271–98.

SE   *Studia Evangelica*

Siegert, *Argumentation*   Siegert, F. *Argumentation bei Paulus gezeigt an Römer 9–11*. Tübingen: J. C. B. Mohr, 1985.

SJTh   *Scottish Journal of Theology*

Smallwood, *Jews under Roman Rule*   Smallwood, E. M. *The Jews under Roman Rule*. Leiden: E. J. Brill, 1976.

Smith, "Palestinian Judaism"   Smith, M. "Palestinian Judaism in the First Century." *Essays in Greco-Roman and Related Talmudic Literature*. Ed. H. A. Fischel. New York: Ktav, 1977.

Snodgrass, "Justification"   Snodgrass, K. " 'Justification by Grace' To the Doers: An Analysis of the Place of Romans 2 in the Theology of Paul." *NTS* 32 (1986) 72–93.

SNTSMS   Society for New Testament Studies Monograph Series

SNTW   Studies in the New Testament World

Solin, "Juden und Syrer"   Solin, H. "Juden und Syrer im westlichen Teil der römischen Welt." *ANRW II* 29/2 (1983) 665.

Solin, *Griechischen Personennamen*   Solin, H. *Die Griechischen Personennamen in Rom*. Berlin, 1982.

Souter, *Pelagius's Expositions*   Souter, A. *Pelagius's Expositions of Thirteen Epistles of St. Paul: Text*. Texts and Studies, IX. 2, p. 9.

SR   *Studies in Religion*

ST   *Studia Theologica*

Steck, *Israel*   Steck, O. H. *Israel und das gewaltsame Geschick der Propheten*. Neukirchen: Neukirchener Verlag, 1967.

Stendahl, *Meanings*   Stendahl, K. *Meanings: The Bible as Document and as Guide*. Philadelphia: Fortress, 1984.

Stendahl, *Paul Among Jews and Gentiles*   Stendahl, K. *Paul Among Jews and Gentiles*. Philadelphia: Fortress, 1976.

Stendahl, "Conscience"   Stendahl, K. "The Apostle Paul and the Introspective Conscience of the West." *HTR* 56 (1963) 199–215 = *Paul Among Jews and Gentiles*, 78–96.

Stern   Stern, M. *Greek and Latin Authors of Jews and Judaism*, 3 vols. Jerusalem: Israel Academy of Sciences and Humanities, 1984.

Stirewalt, "Letter Essay"   Stirewalt, L. "The Form and Function of the Greek Letter-Essay." In *The Romans Debate: Revised and Expanded Edition*. Ed. K. P. Donfried. Peabody, Mass.: Hendrickson Publishers, 1991.

StNT Studien zum Neuen Testament

Stoessel, "Romans 13:1–2"   Stoessel, H. E. "Notes on Romans 13:1–2" *Int* 17 (1963) 161–75.

Stowasser–Graubart, "Tricesima sabbata"   Stowasser, I. M., and D. Graubart. "Tricesima sabbata." *Zeitschrift für d. österr. Gymnas.* 40 (1889) 289–95.

Stowers, "Diatribe"   Stowers, S. K. "The Diatribe." In *Greco-Roman Literature and the New Testament*. Ed. D. E. Aune. SBS 21. Atlanta: Scholars Press, 1988. Pages 71–83.

Stowers, *Letter Writing*   Stowers, S. K. *Letter Writing in Greco-Roman Antiquity*. Philadelphia: Westminster, 1986.

Stowers, "Dialogue"   Stowers, S. K. "Paul's Dialogue with a Fellow Jew in Romans 3:1–9." *CBQ* 46 (1984) 707–22.

Stowers, *Diatribe*   Stowers, S. K. *The Diatribe and Paul's Letter to the Romans*. SBLDS 57. Chico: Scholars, 1981.

Strecker, "Das Evangelium Jesu Christi"   Strecker, G. "Das Evangelium Jesu Christi." In *Eschaton und Historie (Gesammelte Aufsätze)*. Göttingen: Vandenhoeck & Ruprecht, 1979. Pages 183–228.

Strobel, *Die Sunde der Wahrheit*   Strobel, A. *Die Sunde der Wahrheit*. Tübingen: J. C. B. Mohr, 1980.

Stuhlmacher, "Romans 3:24–26"   Stuhlmacher, P. "Recent Exegesis on Romans 3:24–26." In *Reconcilation, Law & Righteousness*. Philadelphia: Fortress, 1986. Pages 94–109.

Stuhlmacher, "Der Abfassungszweck"   Stuhlmacher, P. "Der Abfassungszweck des Römerbriefes." *ZNW* 77 (1986) 180–93.

Stuhlmacher, "Jesus Tradition"   Stuhlmacher, P. "Jesus Tradition in Romans?" *TBei* 14 (1983) 240–50.

Stuhlmacher, "Röm. iii 24–26"   Stuhlmacher, P. "Zur neueren Exegese vom Röm. iii 24–26." In *Jesus und Paulus*. Ed. E. E. Ellis and E. Grässer. Göttingen, 1975.

Stuhlmacher "Theologische Probleme"   Stuhlmacher, P. "Theologische Probleme des Römerbrief-praskripts." *EvT* 27 (1967) 374–89.

Stuhlmacher, "Römer 11:25–32"   Stuhlmacher, P. "Zur Interpretation von Römer 11:25–32." In *Probleme biblischer Theologie*. Ed. H. W. Wolff. Munich: Kaiser, 1971.

Suggs, "Romans 10:6–10"   Suggs, M. J. " 'The Word is Near You': Romans 10:6–10 Within the Purpose of the Letter." In *Christian History and Interpretation: Studies Presented to John Knox*, 1967. Pages 289–312.

Suhl, *Paulus*   Suhl, A. *Paulus und sein Briefe: Ein Beitrag zur paulinishcen Chronoligie*. StNT 11. Gütersloh, 1975.

Sundkler, "Contributions"   Sundkler. "Contributions à l'étude de la pensée missionaire dans le Nouveau Testament" *RHPR* 16 (1936) 462–99.

SUNT   Studien zur Umwelt des Neuen Testaments

Talbert, "Tradition"   Talbert, C. H. "Tradition and Redaction in Romans xii. 9–21." *NTS* 16 (1969/70) 85–93.

TBei   *Theologische Beiträge*

Tcherikover, *Hellenistic Civilisation*   Tcherikover, V. *Hellenistic Civilisation and the Jews*. Philadelphia: Jewish Publication Society, 1961.

TDNT   Kittel, G., and G. Friedrich, eds. *Theological Dictionary of the New Testament*, 10 vols. Trans. G. Bromiley. Grand Rapids: Eerdmans, 1964–73.

Teichmann, *Die paulinishcen Vorstellungen*   Teichmann, E. *Die paulinishcen Vorstellungen von Auferstehung und Gericht*. n.p. 1896.

TF   *Theologische Forschung*

Thiaucevert, "Tacit"   Thiaucevert, A. "Ce que Tacit dit des Juifs au commencement du livre V des Histoires." *REJ* 19 (1889) 57–74.

Thiering, *Gospels and Qumran*   Thiering, B. E. *The Gospels and Qumran*. Sydney, 1981.

THJb   *Theologische Jahrbücher*

THKNT   *Theologischer Handkommentar zum Neuen Testament*

Thraede, *Brieftopik*   Thraede, K. *Grundzüge griechisch-römischer Brieftopik*. Munich: C. H. Beck, 1970.

Thüsing, *Per Christum in Deum*   Thüsing, W. *Per Christum in Deum: Studien zum Verhältnis von Christozentrik und Theozentrik in den paulinischen Hauptbriefen*. NTAbh N. F. 1. Münster: Verlag Aschendorff, 1965.

Thyen, "Das Heil"   Thyen, H. "Das Heil kommt von den Juden." In *Kirche*. Ed. D. Lührmann and G. Strecker. Tübingen: J. C. B. Mohr, 1980.

Thyen, *Homilie*   Thyen, H. *Der Stil der jüdische-hellenistischen Homilie*. FRLANT 47. Göttingen: Vandenhoek & Ruprecht, 1955.

TLZ   *Theologische Literaturzeitung*

Trobisch, *Die Entstehung*   Trobisch, D. *Die Entstehung der Paulusbriefsammlung* NTOA 10. Göttingen: Vandenhoeck & Ruprecht, 1989.

Trocmé, "Romains"   Trocmé, E. "L'Epître aux Romains et la méthod missionarie de l'apôtre Paul." *NTS* 7 (1960–61) 148–53.

TRu   *Theologische Rundschau*

TSK   *Theologische Studien und Kritiken*
TU   Texte und Untersuchungen
TWNT   Kittel, G. and G. Friedrich eds. *Theologisches Wörterbuch zum Neuen Testament*
Usher, "Oratory"   Usher, S. "Oratory" in *Greek and Latin Literature*. Ed. J. Higginbotham. London: Methuen, 1969.
van der Minde, *Schrift und Tradition*   van der Minde, H.-J. *Schrift und Tradition bei Paulus*. Paderborn, 1976.
van Unnik, "Literary Culture"   van Unnik, W. C. "First Century A.D. Literary Culture and Early Christian Literature." *Nederlands Theologisch Tijdschrift* 25 (1971) 28–43.
Via, *Kerygma and Comedy*   Via, D. *Kerygma and Comedy in the New Testament*. Philadelphia: Fortress, 1975.
Vielhauer, "Einleitung"   Vielhauer, Ph. "Einleitung in das Neue Testament." *TRu* 31 (1965–66).
Vielhauer, *Oikodome*   Vielhauer, Ph. *Oikodome. Das Bild vom Clemens Alexandrinus*. Diss. Heidelberg, 1940.
Vogels, H. J. *Amicitiae Corolla*. n.p. n.d.
Vogelstein–Reiger, *Geschichte der Juden*   Vogelstein, H., and P. Reiger. *Geschichte der Juden in Rom*. n.p. 1895.
Volkmar, *Römerbrief*   Volkmar, G. *Römerbrief*. n.p. 1875.
von Campenhausen, *Die Entstehung*   von Campenhausen, H. *Die Entstehung der christlichen Bibel*. BHT 390. 1968.
von Weizsacker, "Römische Christengemeinde"   von Weizsacker, C. "Über die älteste römische Christengemeinde." *Jb. f. dt. Theologie* 21, (1876) 248–310
von Wiliamowitz-Moellendorf, "Asianismus und Atticismus"   von Wiliamowitz-Moellendorf, U. "Asianismus und Atticismus." *Hermes* 35 (1900) 1–52; reprinted in *Rhetorika: Schriften zur aristotelischen und hellenistischen Rhetorik*. Ed. R. Stark. Hildesheim: Olms, 1968.
Vouga, "Romains 1,18–3,20 comme *Narratio*"   Vouga, F. "Romains 1,18–3,20 comme *Narratio*." In *La Narration*. Ed. P. Bühler and J.-F. Habermacher. Lieux Théologiques 12. Geneva: Editions Labor et Fides, 1988. Pages 145–61.
Wallach, *History of Diatribe*   Wallach, B. *A History of Diatribe from its Origin up to the First Century B.C. and a Study of the Influence of the Genre upon Lucretius III*. Dissertation. University of Illinois at Urbana, 1974.
Walter, "Jesustradition"   Walter, N. "Paulus und die urchristliche Jesustradition." *NTS* 31 (1985) 498–522.
Walzer, *Galen*   Walzer, R. *Galen on Jews and Christians*. London, 1949.
Watson, *Paul, Judaism, and the Gentiles*   Watson, F. B. *Paul, Judaism, and the Gentiles: A Sociological Approach*. MSSNTS 56. Cambridge: Cambridge University Press, 1986.
Watson, "Painful Letter"   Watson, F. B. "2 Cor. x-xii and Paul's Painful Letter to the Corinthians." *JTS* 35 (1984) 324–46.
Wedderburn, *Reasons for Romans*   Wedderburn, A. J. M. *The Reasons for Romans*. SNTW. Edinburgh: T. & T. Clark, 1988.
Weiss, *Korintherbrief*   Weiss, J. *Der erste Korintherbrief*. Göttingen: Vandenhoeck & Ruprecht, 1910.
Weiss, "Paulinischen Rhetorik"   Weiss, J. "Beiträge zur Paulinischen Rhetorik." in *Theologische Studien: Festschrift für Bernhard Weiss*. Göttingen: Vandenhoeck & Ruprecht, 1897. Pages 165–247.
Welles, *Royal Correspondence*   Welles, C. B. *Royal Correspondence in the Hellenistic Period*. New Haven: Yale University Press, 1934.
Wendland, *Kultur*   Wendland, P. *Die hellenistisch-römische Kultur*. Tübingen: J. C. B. Mohr, 1907.

Werblowsky, "Baptismal Rite"   Werblowsky, R. J. Zwi. "On the Baptismal Rite According to St. Hippolytus." *Studia Patristica 4* = TU. Berlin, 1957.

Werfel, *Paul Among the Jews*   Werfel, F. *Paul Among the Jews (a Tragedy)*. London: Mowbrays, 1928.

Westerholm, *Israel's Law*   Westerholm, S. *Israel's Law and the Church's Faith: Paul and His recent Interpreters*. Grand Rapids: Eerdmans, 1988.

Westerholm, *"Torah"*   Westerholm, S. *"Torah, Nomos,* and *Law*: A Question of 'Meaning,' " *SR* 15 (1986) 327–36.

White, "Epistolary Literature"   White, J. L. "New Testament Epistolary Literature in the Framework of Ancient Epistolography." *ANRW*, forthcoming.

White, *Form and Structure*   White, J. L. *The Form and Structure of the Official Petition*. Missoula: Scholars Press, 1972.

White, *Greek Letter*   White, J. L. *The Form and Function of the Body of the Greek Letter*. SBLDS Series 2. Missoula: Scholars Press, 1972.

Wiefel, "Jewish Community"   Wiefel, W. "The Jewish Community in Ancient Rome and the Origins of Roman Christianty." In *Romans Debate: Revised and Expanded Edition*. Ed. K. P. Donfried. Peabody, Mass.: Hendrickson Publishers, 1991.

Wiefel, "Die jüdische Gemeinschaft"   Wiefel, W. "Die jüdische Gemeinschaft im antiken Rom und die Anfänge des römischen Christentums: Bemerkungen zu Anlass und Zweck des Römerbriefes." *Judaica* 26 (1970) 65–88.

Wifstrand, *Alte Kirche*   Wifstrand, A. *Die alte Kirche und die griechische Bildung*. Bern: Francke, 1967.

Wilckens, *Römer*   Wilckens, U. *Der Brief an die Römer*, 3 vols. EKKNT 6/1–3. Zurich/Neukirchen: Benziger Verlag/ Neukirchener Verlag, 1978–82.

Wilckens, "Abfassungszweck und Aufbau"   Wilckens, U. "Über Abfassungszweck und Aufbau des Römerbriefs." In *Rechtfertigung als Freiheit*. Neukirchen-Vluyn: Neukirchener, 1974. Pages 110–70.

Wiles, *Intercessory Prayers*   Wiles, G. P. *Paul's Intercessory Prayers*. NTSMS 24. New York: Cambridge University, 1974.

Wilke, *Sprachidioms*   Wilke, C. G. *Die neutestamentliche Rhetorik, ein Seitenstück zur Grammatik des neutestamentlichen Sprachidioms*. Dresden and Leipzig: Arnold, 1843.

Williams, J. W. "Romans 3:21–26"   Williams, J. W. "The Interpretation of Romans 3:21–26 and its Place in Pauline Soteriology." Unpublished Ph.D. dissertation, University of Manchester, 1973.

Williams, P. R. "Paul's Purpose"   Williams, P. R. "Paul's Purpose in Writing Romans." *BS* 128 (509, 1971) 62–67.

Williams, S. K. "Righteousness"   Williams, S. K. " 'The Righteousness of God' in Romans." *JBL* 99 (1980) 241–91.

Winston, *Wisdom of Solomon*   Winston, D. *The Wisdom of Solomon*. Garden City: Doubleday, 1979.

WMANT   Wissenschaftliche Monographien zum Alten und Neuen Testament

Wolff, *Jeremia*   Wolff, C. *Jeremia im Frühjudentum und Urchristentum*. Berlin: Akademie, 1976.

Wonnenberger, *Syntax und Exegese*   Wonnenberger, R. *Syntax und Exegese: Eine generative Theorie der griechischen Syntax und ihr Beitrag zur Auslegung des Neuen Testaments, dargestellt an 2. Kor 5.2f and Röm. 3:21–26*. Frankfurt: Lang, 1979.

Wotke, "Octavius"   Wotke, F. "Der 'Octavius' des Minucius Felix ein christlicher *logos protreptikos*." *Commentationes Vindoboneses* 1 (1935) 119–28.

Wright, *Messiah*   Wright, N. T. *The Messiah and the People of God*. Oxford University, 1980.

Wuellner, "Greek Rhetoric"   Wuellner, W. "Greek Rhetoric and Pauline Argumentation." In *Early Christian Literature and the Classical Intellectual Tradition.* Ed. Schoedel, W. R. and R. L. Wilken. Paris: Beauchesne, 1979.

Wuellner, "Paul's Rhetoric"   Wuellner, W. "Paul's Rhetoric of Argumentation in Romans: An Alternative to the Donfried-Karris Debate over Romans." In *The Romans Debate: Revised and Expanded Edition.* Ed. K. P. Donfried. Peabody, Mass.: Hendrickson Publishers, 1991.

WUNT   Wissenschaftliche Untersuchungen zum Neuen Testament

WZ   Wissenschaftliche Zeitschrift

Zahn, *Einleitung*   Zahn, T. *Einleitung in das Neue Testament I,* 2.a., 1900.

Zahn, *Römer*   Zahn, T. *Der Brief des Paulus an die Römer* KNT 6. 1910.

ZDPV   Zeitschrift des deutschen Palätina-Vereins

Zeller, *Römer*   Zeller, D. *Der Brief an die Römer.* RNT 6. Regensburg: Pustet, 1985.

Zeller, *Juden und Heiden*   Zeller, D. *Juden und Heiden in der Mission des Paulus. Studien zum Römerbrief.* Stuttgart: Katholisches Bibelwerk, 1973.

Zeller, "Das odium"   Zeller, E. "Das odium generis humani der Christen." *ZWT* (1891) 356–62.

Ziesler, *Righteousness*   Ziesler, J. A. *The Meaning of Righteousness in Paul.* SNTSMS 20. Cambridge: Cambridge University, 1972.

ZKT   Zeitschrift für katholische Theologie

ZNW   Zeitschrift für die neutestamentliche Wissenschaft

ZTK   Zeitschrift für Theologie und Kirche

ZWT   Zeitschrift für wissenschaftliche Theologie

INTRODUCTION 1977:
THE NATURE AND SCOPE
OF THE ROMANS DEBATE

Karl P. Donfried

The attention which Paul's letter to the Romans is receiving in contemporary biblical scholarship is staggering. Not only is there a plethora of articles, but the number of commentaries and monographs which have been published *since 1970* alone is overwhelming. New commentaries have been written by such prominent scholars as Matthew Black,[1] Charles Cranfield,[2] Karl Kertelge,[3] J. C. O'Neill,[4] Ernst Käsemann[5] and Heinrich Schlier;[6] major new monographs have been authored by Paul Minear,[7] Walther Schmithals,[8] and Dieter Zeller.[9]

The inevitable question arises: why such enormous interest with regard to this particular letter of Paul? Up to the time of F. C. Baur,[10] virtually all scholars would have agreed with Melanchthon's evaluation of Romans as a *christianae religionis compendium*. Although Baur was one of the first major scholars to break with such an understanding of Romans as an abstract theological summary, his insights were quickly overlooked and the situation continued virtually unchanged right to the present. Typical of this understanding of Romans as a "compendium of the Christian religion" is the commentary by Anders Nygren,[11] published as recently as 1944.

The dominant methodological concern and presupposition of twentieth-century biblical scholarship is the historical-critical method.[12] Among the many contributions of this method is the insight that all New Testament

---

[1]Black, *Romans*.
[2]Caird, *Romans*.
[3]Kertelge, *Romans*.
[4]O'Neill, *Romans*.
[5]Käsemann, *Römer*. This commentary is now in its third edition in German and has been translated into English by the Wm. B. Eerdmans Publishing Company of Grand Rapids, Michigan [= Käsemann, *Romans*].
[6]Schlier, *Der Römerbrief*.
[7]Minear, *Obedience*.
[8]Schmithals, *Der Römerbrief als historisches Problem*.
[9]Zeller, *Juden und Heiden*.
[10]Baur, F. C., "Römischen Gemeinde"; idem, *Paulus, der Apostel Jesu Christi* (1845) [ET = *Paul*].
[11]Nygren, *Romans*; original Swedish edition: *Romarbrevet* (Stockholm; Verbum, 1944).
[12]See further Krentz, *Historical-Critical Method*.

documents were written by the early church for its own needs. In other words, the New Testament texts were written to specific audiences who had concrete concerns and problems. Matthew is different from Mark precisely because the needs of his congregation are different from those of Mark's, and thus the gospel must be actualized and conceptualized in a new way. Similarly, Paul's letter to the Galatians is different from that sent to the Corinthians because the actual situations of the two congregations are different: the Corinthians must be warned against an arrogant individualism and the Galatians against reversion to a Spirit-crippling nomism. Different situations call for different responses.

Another contribution of the historical-critical method is the recognition that parallel materials within the same cultural milieu often can be helpful for the understanding of biblical texts. To know that miracle stories occur not only in canonical literature, but also in rabbinic and Hellenistic literature gives the interpreter comparative materials which allow him or her to see more clearly the nuances and intention of each tradition. To know that Paul's letters have certain points of contact with other Hellenistic and literary letters of the period permits one to perceive more clearly both the similarity and the uniqueness of the Pauline letter corpus. The fact, for example, that most Hellenistic letters have a thanksgiving section whereas Galatians alone among the Pauline letters does not, immediately reinforces one's impression of Paul's frustration with and anger toward the Galatians who are apparently quick to abandon the true gospel which Paul had proclaimed to them.

Until the very recent past, the above mentioned advances and contributions of contemporary biblical scholarship have hardly been applied to Romans; for many it just continued to be a *christianae religionis compendium*. Slowly scholars became restless with this state of affairs, and increasingly they began to raise the matter of Paul's intention in writing Romans. And so the question of the concrete *Sitz im Leben* of Romans emerged more frequently. Also the matter of non-canonical literary parallels and general cultural rhetorical influences began to be discussed more seriously. Thus, one possible answer to the question posed concerning the great contemporary interest in Romans appears to be that only now, as the historical-critical methodology is being focused on Romans with intensity, can significant new ground be broken. Such research, still in its infancy, generates much, and often conflicting, literature. That many of the essays which follow move in different directions and, in fact, give differing answers is a sign that there is a Romans debate in process which is far from complete.

Before turning to the contours of the debate, we might ask an even more preliminary question: why is it important to read about and study such a debate if one is not an erudite scholar? The reason is simple: the implications and challenge of the New Testament for the twentieth century can only be made clear when one knows the setting of each New

Testament book in its original context. In other words, if one does not know the original intention of a document one can hardly interpret its contemporary meaning with accuracy and precision. What emerges in the current debate is exactly this question: Why did Paul write Romans? On the one hand, there is a consensus that in all probability Romans was not intended as a timeless compendium of the Christian faith. This fact alone has obvious implications on how *not* to use Romans in contemporary theology and preaching. On the other hand, a consensus as to its actual purpose is still in process. The following essays illustrate the issues at stake and the direction future interpretations of Romans may take.

The first and oldest (1938) essay included in this collection is that by the great British biblical scholar, *T. W. Manson.* He is particularly concerned by the fact that some manuscripts omit the reference to "Rome" in Rom. 1:7 and 15, and, that some manuscripts circulated which apparently ended at 15:23, others at 15:33, and some with a full sixteen-chapter text. Having Manson's study at the beginning of this handbook has the decided advantage of alerting the reader to the significant text-critical problems which must be confronted in finding any solution to the overall situation dealing with the purpose of Romans.

On the basis of his text-critical examination, Manson breaks with a very common interpretation, viz., that Romans was intended as a letter of self-introduction so that the Roman church would give Paul a friendly reception and speed him on his way to Spain. Rather, according to Manson, Romans is a "summing up," a "manifesto" of Paul's deepest convictions. Further, since he would not be able to visit his friends in Ephesus while journeying to Jerusalem, Paul sent them instead a modified copy of this letter to Rome, making it more general and adding a final section of greeting.

The reader will have to ask at least two questions: (1) whether Manson's text-critical hypotheses are plausible,[13] and (2) whether he has persuasively demonstrated the reason why Paul was interested in writing a summary of his positions to the Roman church.

G. Bornkamm is both sympathetic to and critical of T. W. Manson's work. He agrees that Romans was written from the perspective of Paul's previous controversies, and this is documented by a sixteen-point illustration from a variety of Pauline texts. He disagrees with Manson's rejection of Romans as a letter of self-introduction and believes it to be inadequate to understand Romans merely as a report and summary of past controversies. According to Bornkamm, the polemics of the past controversies are now lifted to a new level of generality,[14] and the style of argument in Romans is that of the so-called Hellenistic diatribe.[15] Bornkamm's con-

---

[13]Note especially the criticism of Kümmel, *Introduction,* 314–20.
[14]See the further development in Karris' essay in chapter 6 of this volume.
[15]See further Donfried's reflections on the use of the term "diatribe" in "False Presuppositions," chapter 8 of this volume.

clusion is this: "This great document, which summarizes and develops the most important themes and thoughts of the Pauline message and theology and which elevates his theology above the moment of definite situations and conflicts into the sphere of the eternally and universally valid, this letter to the Romans is the last will and testament of the Apostle Paul."[16]

The student of the New Testament is indebted to Bornkamm for outlining the relationship of the content of Romans to the previous Pauline letters. The reader will wish to consider whether the terms "summary," as well as "last will and testament," are accurate and, particularly, whether the latter phrase gives any new insight as to why Paul wrote this letter to Rome.

G. Klein's review of the many possible interpretations of Romans, including such scholars of previous generations as F. C. Baur and R. A. Lipsius, is especially helpful. Since a purely dogmatic understanding of Romans is not a serious option today, there are, according to Klein, two major contemporary types of interpretations: those which argue that Paul is primarily occupied with his own concerns and those which argue that Paul is primarily occupied with the concerns of the Roman church. For Klein, however, both approaches run into difficulties and therefore leave much to be desired.

Critical for Klein's understanding of Romans is what he refers to as Paul's "non-interference clause," a reference to Rom. 15:20: "thus making it my ambition to preach the gospel, not where Christ has already been named, lest I build on another man's foundation. . . ."[17] Too many scholars, he argues, have not taken Paul seriously at this point. When one does, then there can only be one conclusion: "Paul can consider an apostolic effort in Rome because he does not regard the local Christian community there as having an apostolic foundation."[18]

K. P. Donfried's article on Romans 16 takes issue not only with the interpretations of Marxsen and Bornkamm but also specifically with Klein's contention that "Christianity in Rome still needed an apostolic foundation."[19] Whether right or wrong, Donfried's criticism forces the reader to go back to the text of Romans to see whether Klein's position is justified on the basis of it. The positive force of Donfried's argument, at points indebted to the publication of W. Marxsen,[20] is to show that Romans 16 makes perfectly good sense as an original part of Romans and that it is not a later addition directed to Ephesus as Marxsen and others have suggested. Particularly helpful is the careful linguistic analysis of the names used by Paul in the greetings of chapter 16.

[16]Bornkamm, "Last Will and Testament" (= ch. 2 in this vol.), 27–28.
[17]Note Donfried's criticism of this interpretation, Donfried, "Short Note on Romans 16" (= ch. 4 in this vol.), 44–45.
[18]Klein, "Paul's Purpose" (= ch. 3 in this vol.), 29–43.
[19]Ibid., 42.
[20]Marxsen, *Introduction*, esp. 107.

For *J. Jervell*, Romans can be interpreted only in light of Paul's own existential situation, which is his impending trip to Jerusalem; it is out of this context that Romans is written. Paul is seeking the support of the Roman Christians so that he may represent all the Gentile churches, standing behind him unified, when he arrives in Jerusalem. The major issue in Romans is not the concrete needs of the Roman church about which we know virtually nothing, but that of the relationship between Jewish and Gentile Christians. This is the problem with which Paul will be confronted when he presents the symbolically rich offering of Gentile Christianity in Jerusalem.

Jervell builds an intriguing case for his hypothesis. In testing his argument the reader will have to probe whether the possibility exists that Jervell has overstated the theological differences between Galatians and Romans and whether Romans 9–11 can bear the interpretive weight which Jervell gives to it. One should note, too, how the final pages of this essay stand in sharp contrast with Klein's position that Rome still stands in need of apostolic confirmation. Further, Jervell's entire presupposition about our lack of knowledge concerning the conditions of the Roman church stand in sharp conflict to the position articulated by Wiefel in article seven of this volume. Hopefully this vigorous diversity of perspective will lead the reader directly to the text of Romans and then to some evaluation concerning the merit of these interpretations.

R. J. Karris' position is similar to that of Jervell in denying that Romans was addressed to an actual situation of the church in Rome. He, too, suggests that it is to be viewed in light of Paul's own life situation. Even chapters 14:1–15:13, which appear addressed to concrete problems, are not; they contain only general Pauline paraenesis. Particularly important for the current discussion is Karris' critique of Paul Minear's monograph, *The Obedience of Faith*,[21] which argues that Romans is specifically addressed to the church in Rome, a church comprised of several divergent communities. Karris challenges Minear's identification of "the weak" with Jewish Christians and "the strong" with Gentile Christians on the basis of an often overlooked study by Max Rauer, *Die "Schwachen" in Korinth und Rom nach den Paulusbriefen*.[22] Since chapter 8 in this book discusses Karris' article and Minear's book in detail, we shall proceed to the study by Wolfgang Wiefel.

Weifel's is an article of signal importance, and it appears here for the first time in English translation. It challenges all those who say that we know nothing about the actual historical or sociological situation of the earliest Christian community in Rome. After a detailed review of the ancient sources, Wiefel argues that indeed we know a considerable amount

[21]See note 7 above.
[22]Rauer, "*Schwachen.*"

about Roman Christianity in the first century.[23] Whether Wiefel's portrayal is accurate or not must be judged by future scholarship. Since for the most part Wiefel's work has remained unknown, we can now at least look forward with expectancy to its further evaluation.

M. Stirewalt's work, too, has remained virtually unknown and it appears in print here for the first time. It is presented as an Appendix [now ch. 10, Ed.] to this volume because it does not deal directly with Romans as do the other essays. Yet Stirewalt's essay has enormous relevance for the study of Romans. By probing the form and function of the Greek letter-essay, he presents us with untold parallel and background material which can give us new insights with regard to the background and style of the letter known to us as Romans. The implications of this important study for Romans are drawn out clearly at the end of chapter 8. Stirewalt's is a rich and creative article; yet Stirewalt himself would be the first to admit that it is tentative and awaits a process of further research and testing in this particular specialized area of Greco-Roman backgrounds.[24] Nevertheless, the obvious importance of the material gathered by Stirewalt for the study of Romans and its stimulation for further research should be self-evident.

Donfried's essay, clearly influenced by the work of Wiefel and Stirewalt, and in dialog with Karris, challenges two widely held presuppositions: (1) that Romans is not addressed to the actual situation of the church in Rome, and (2) that chapter 16 is not an original and integral part of Romans. Further, he challenges the imprecise use of the term "diatribe" and also the way that term is used uncritically as a way to discuss the relation of Romans to an actual situation in the church of Rome. In fact, he goes so far as to challenge Bultmann's doctoral dissertation of 1910[25] as being, at points, in error and outdated. A call is made for new studies of ancient rhetoric and its implication for the New Testament in general, and Romans, in particular.

W. Wuellner analyzes Paul's use of rhetoric in Romans. Ancient use of rhetoric and contemporary studies of that subject are thoroughly reviewed. While Wuellner makes a contribution to the Donfried-Karris debate on Romans, the reader will have to ask whether it is in the sense intended by Wuellner, viz., the precedence of rhetorical criticism and the virtual elimination of the theological and historical context of Romans. One wonders whether the real key to unlocking Romans lies rather in a combination of these three factors: historical setting, rhetoric of argumentation, and theological content. Wuellner's work is at the cutting edge of scholarship and one looks forward to its further development and refinement.

[23] A summary of this information can be found in chapter 8 of this volume.
[24] See further, Donfried, *Setting of 2 Clement,* 19–48.
[25] Bultmann, *Diatribe.*

These and other essays concerning the meaning and purpose of Romans are significant, for they show the advance of the historical-critical method in an area which has been hitherto unresolved, and they reveal the issues at stake in the debate. Hopefully as scholars continue their reflections, a greater consensus can be reached. In the meantime both the theologian and preacher need be very cautious in drawing any easy conclusions based on any one thesis concerning its origin. Obviously, Romans will have a very different meaning if it was conceived by Paul as an eternally valid summary of his theological position, or, if he conceived it as a response to an actual, acute problem of the first century, manifesting itself particularly, but not exclusively, in Roman Christianity. Only when one knows the meaning of an early Christian document in its first-century setting can one adequately interpret and proclaim it in the twentieth. It is this fact which encourages us to take seriously the historical-critical method.

Finally, the serious student will want to pursue this topic more thoroughly. One needs to remember that what is presented here is only a representative selection of the current discussion, and that careful attention should be given to the footnotes and the many references to other significant studies in this area. In addition to those referred to in this volume, one should pay especial attention to the well-balanced assessment by Ulrich Wilckens,[26] and, of course, the most important resource of all should not be overlooked: the text of Romans!

[26]Wilckens, "Abfassungszweck und Aufbau," 110–70.

INTRODUCTION 1991:
THE ROMANS DEBATE SINCE 1977

Karl P. Donfried

The Romans Debate, published in 1977, has facilitated an animated discussion with respect to the purpose of Romans. This may be an appropriate time to review the state of the Romans debate since 1977, both to ask whether any consensus has been reached with regard to the neuralgic points in that debate and to examine those issues most current in the present discussions relative to Romans.

F. F. Bruce characterized the Romans debate as one "about the character of the letter (including questions about its literary integrity, the possibility of its having circulated in longer and shorter recensions, the destination of chapter 16) and, above all, Paul's purpose in sending it."[1] One key dimension of the original debate was whether Romans was addressed to a concrete historical situation or was to be considered as an essentially non-historical *christianae religionis compendium*. Section A of *The Romans Debate: Revised and Expanded Edition*, "The Purpose of Romans: Historical and Sociological Factors," takes up this issue and it is to an examination of these five essays that we now turn.

F. F. Bruce's essay, "The Romans Debate—Continued,"[2] is concerned with Paul's primary purpose in sending Romans, which, he suggests, is to prepare the Roman Christians for the apostle's visit. In order to understand how this purpose is related to the main content of the letter it is essential to remember that Paul has three prospective visits in mind as he writes to the Romans: " . . . Rome, the home of the people to whom the letter was addressed; Spain, where he planned shortly to inaugurate the next phase of his apostolic ministry; and Jerusalem, which he was to visit in the immediate future to complete a project very close to his heart."[3]

In discussing the first of these prospective visits, Rome, Bruce affirms what has become the dominant view and one which marks a genuine advance in the Romans debate, viz., that this "document is, in no merely nominal sense, Paul's letter to the Romans—a letter addressed, in all its parts, to a particular Christian community in a particular historical situation."[4] The historical situation described follows in large part that out-

---

[1]Chapter 11 in this volume, p. 175.
[2]Ibid., 177.
[3]Ibid.
[4]Ibid.

lined in Donfried's essay "False Presuppositions in the Study of Romans."[5] Bruce particularly emphasizes the variety present in the house-churches of Rome both "in thought and practice between the firm Jewish retention of the ancestral customs and Gentile remoteness from these customs, with some Jewish Christians, indeed, found on the liberal side of the halfway mark between the two extremes and some Gentile Christians on the 'legalist' side."[6] Undoubtedly the same kind of disputes arose in Rome as they did in other Jewish communities in which Paul's gospel was proclaimed. In addition, the various misrepresentations of the apostle's message and practice abroad found their way to Rome and Paul felt the need to bring clarity to this situation.

The intended visit to Spain permitted the apostle not only to include the Roman Christians in this new missionary project but allowed him an opportunity to express his concern and warmth toward them. The visit to Jerusalem necessitated that Paul explain why he could not come to Rome immediately and also permitted him the opportunity to associate the Roman Christians, through prayer and reflection, with the importance of Jerusalem for the gentile church. Bruce also makes the interesting suggestion that Paul may have considered that if the Jerusalem leaders were aware that Rome was fully informed of his plans, this might influence a favorable reception for Paul and his associates in the very center of Judaism. And, finally, if Paul "could associate with his world vision a whole community like the Roman church," his unfinished task of proclaiming the gospel to the gentile world "might be accomplished the sooner."[7]

Bruce's emphasis on the diversity of the Roman Christian community, especially in terms of "crossovers" (for example, Jews very liberal in their hellenism, Gentiles very conservative in their Judaism), as well as the importance of the collection to the writing of Romans, are topics that are also taken up by *A. J. M. Wedderburn* in his essay on the "Purpose and Occasion of Romans Again."[8] Wedderburn accepts the view that Romans is addressed to a concrete situation in the Roman Christian community. *One of* the significant factors[9] that the apostle has in mind as he writes to them is "that they endorse the Gentile mission and its gospel, whose fruits were being offered in the collection and in the persons of its bearers. . . ."[10] This "endorsement" is far more important than any financial contribution

---

[5]In Donfried, "False Presuppositions," 102–25.

[6]Bruce, "Continued" (= ch. 11 in this vol.), 186. Bruce is sympathetic to Minear, *Obedience*, but he is hesitant to demarcate the distinctions as precisely as Minear.

[7]Bruce, "Continued," 193.

[8]Wedderburn, "Purpose and Occasion" (= ch. 12 in this vol.).

[9]It is important to understand that for Wedderburn this is one of, but not the only, significant factor which Paul has in mind as he writes Romans. See now Wedderburn's useful *Reasons for Romans*.

[10]Wedderburn, "Purpose and Occasion," 202.

to the collection, something which would have been virtually impossible at this final stage of the process. Much of Romans is written to clarify both the nature of the gentile mission and the contents of the gospel which Paul preached.

Wedderburn's essay also provides a competent review for the non-German-speaking reader of Walter Schmithals' *Der Römerbrief als historisches Problem*.[11] Schmithals divides Romans into three letters, Romans A (1:1–11:36 and 15:8–13),[12] Romans B (12:1—15:14–33 and 16:21–23),[13] and (the remainder of) Romans 16. Romans A and B are addressed to Rome; Romans 16 commends Phoebe to Onesiphorus in Ephesus. Romans A was written from Ephesus early in Paul's ministry and was addressed to gentile Christians closely attached to Judaism whom Paul had hoped would come to an understanding of his gospel. Romans B is written some time later to those willing to share his view of the gospel, and it appeals to them to show more consideration to those in their midst who were still attached to the rules of the synagogue. Basic to Schmithals' interpretation of Romans A is the view that Paul is addressing Christian Gentiles at Rome who still had a decided leaning towards Judaism. As Wedderburn puts it, they were "former 'God-fearers' who have received Christ but have not been weaned from their close connection with, and dependence upon, the synagogue; they must be won over to Paul's law-free gospel of grace."[14] Wedderburn correctly asks whether it is really persuasive to imagine that there were *no* Christian Jews (i.e., a Christian who is racially a Jew) in Rome whom Paul is addressing.[15] Schmithals has not to date been followed in this singular view of the Roman Christian community.

That Romans A and B are two different letters with different occasions and purposes is argued primarily on three grounds. (1) The conflict in travel plans as expressed in 1:13 and 15:23–25. In 1:13 Paul states that up to that point he has been hindered from visiting Rome and this hindrance *still remains*. Wedderburn counters this by contending that Schmithals' case would be stronger if in 1:13 one had a present or perfect instead of the aorist. (2) Different policies about the appropriateness of preaching the gospel where Christ is not already named as expressed in 1:13–15 and 15:20. This tension is such that Schmithals cannot conceive of both statements in the same letter. Acknowledging that there is a tension between these verses, which, however, might be explained in various ways short of arguing for two separate letters, Wedderburn concludes that in Rom.

[11](StNT 9; Gütersloh: Mohn, 1975). See now also Schmithals' recent commentary, *Der Römerbrief: Ein Kommentar*.
[12]It is suggested that Rom. 5:1–11 is a fragment from another Pauline letter. See Schmithals, *Der Römerbrief: Ein Kommentar*, 149–65.
[13]It is suggested that Rom. 13:1–7, 11–14 are fragments from another Pauline letter. See Schmithals, *Der Römerbrief: Ein Kommentar*, 456–69 and 479–86.
[14]Wedderburn, "Purpose and Occasion," 196.
[15]Ibid.

15:20 Paul is stating what his goal is but "does not state that he utterly eschews any form of preaching where Christ is already named."[16] (3) In Romans 1 the apostle wishes to visit this Christian community in Rome for its own sake, whereas in Rom. 15:24 the purpose of the visit appears incidental to his trip to Spain. Wedderburn does not find these references incompatible and suggests that it is quite natural for Paul to unfold his further plans with regard to Spain at the end rather than the beginning of his letter.

I am more hesitant than Wedderburn in rejecting the view that some of Paul's letters as we now have them in their canonical form are composite, formed from smaller letters or fragments.[17] On that ground alone one cannot fault Schmithals as Wedderburn does.[18] The question is whether Schmithals' case for a compilation theory of Romans is compelling on its own grounds. Even though Wedderburn has suggested some reasons why the argument is not convincing, one must recognize that Schmithals has with much acumen drawn our attention to a variety of elements in Romans which must be explained and he has made a great contribution in emphasizing the presence of gentile Christians in Rome still closely attached to Judaism. While, undoubtedly, the situation in Rome is broader and more complex than this, the existence of such a dominant group is certainly plausible.

Francis Watson's argument in "The Two Roman Congregations: Romans 14:1–15:13,"[19] that Paul presupposes *two* separate congregations in Rome marked by "mutual hostility and suspicion over the question of the law,"[20] is not that unrelated to Schmithals' position, although markedly different from it at some points. If Schmithals' Romans A were addressed to gentile Christians still attached to Judaism and if Romans B were written to the Paulinist Christians of Rome, that would suggest that there were at least two separate congregations in Rome. Although Watson identifies the initial Christians in Rome as "Jewish Christians,"[21] and Schmithals identifies them as gentile Christians still attached to Judaism, both agree that Paul is attempting to create a single Paulinist congregation in Rome which would hold worship in common, something not currently prac-

---

[16]Ibid., 199.

[17]See, for example, the discussion in Gamble, *New Testament Canon*, 35–46; Jewett, "Redaction of 1 Cor.," 389–444; and Trobisch, *Die Entstehung.*

[18]Wedderburn, "Purpose and Occasion," 198.

[19]Watson, *Paul, Judaism and the Gentiles*, 94–105. For a critical review of this volume see Campbell, "Reaction to Watson."

[20]Watson, "Two Roman Congregations" (= ch. 13 in this vol.), 206.

[21]Here, too, Watson and Schmithals are not as far apart as one might first conclude. In discussing the "weak" and the "strong" in Rom. 14:1–15:13, Watson holds that "one may refer to these two groups as 'Jewish Christians' and 'Gentile Christians', so long as it is remembered that the former group may well have included proselytes, whereas the latter group may well have included Jews who like Paul himself did not observe the law" (Watson, "Two Roman Congregations," 203).

ticed.[22] As a result, both would also have common ground in explaining the absence of the term *ekklēsia* in Romans.

For Watson the founders of Roman Christianity may have been Andronicus and Junias/Junia. Paul greets them in Rom. 16:7 so as to gain the support of these representatives of earliest Jewish Christianity in Rome for his law-free gospel. The apostle intentionally does not greet the individuals named directly but rather urges his readers to greet them, a tactic which presumably will put pressure on both groups to introduce themselves to one another and to respect one another. Thus the gentile Christians are not to despise Andronicus and Junias/Junia, and the Jewish Christians are not to pass judgment on Prisca and Aquila. The Pauline exhortation of 15:7 about welcoming one another is actualized in Romans 16.

The study by *Peter Lampe*, "The Roman Christians of Romans 16,"[23] offers remarkable support for some of the theses proposed by both Watson and Schmithals. Observing that the term *syngenēs* is never used by Paul except in Rom. 16:3–16, where he addresses Andronicus, Junia, and Herodion, Lampe concludes that "Paul has a *special interest* in emphasizing the Jewish origin of Christians (Rom. 16:7, 11, 21)."[24] What is remarkable about this emphasis is that only a small minority (15%) of Jewish Christians are represented among the twenty-six persons referred to in Romans 16, thus indicating that the vast majority of the Christians in the Roman church are Gentiles. Lampe's solution to this paradox is remarkably similar to that of Schmithals: " . . . most people in the Roman church were of Gentile origin but had lived as sympathizers on the margins of the synagogues before they became Christian."[25]

Lampe's detailed analysis of Romans 16 in light of the inscriptions available in Rome, also lends support to some of Watson's observations. Paul never applies the term *ekklēsia* to the entire Roman Christian community[26] because it is a divided community meeting in separate house churches and therefore does not meet together for common worship. While Watson may be correct in asserting "two Roman congregations" in the most general sense of two differing theological positions, Lampe's description of some eight different house-churches may be more descriptive of the actual situation in Rome.[27]

---

[22]It is interesting to note that Watson does not engage Schmithals in dialogue at this point. The only references to Schmithals are with regard to the latter's compilation theory of Romans which Watson rejects.

[23]This essay appears for the first time in *The Romans Debate: Revised and Expanded Edition*. It is based on Lampe's book *Die stadtrömischen Christen in den ersten beiden Jahrhunderten* (WUNT 2/18; Tübingen: Mohr, 1987).

[24]Lampe, "Roman Christians" (= ch. 14 in this vol.), 224.

[25]Ibid., 225.

[26]Note that it is only used in Rom. 16:5 with regard to the house-church gathered around Aquila and Prisca.

[27]Here Lampe builds upon the pioneering work of Wiefel, "Jewish Community" (= ch. 7 in this vol., 85–101).

Lampe's study gives further support to the current consensus[28]—against Schmithals—that Romans 16 is an original and integral part of Paul's letter to Rome. His argument is epigraphical, theological, and sociological. With regard to the first he asks, for example, why such names as "Urbanus," "Phlegon," "Persis," and "Asyncritus" are not found in any of the thousands of Ephesian inscriptions yet are present in ones found in Rome? With regard to the second, he observes that Rom. 16:3–16 is essentially a recommendation for Paul himself and only marginally one for Phoebe. Paul is saying something like " 'Look at these many and honorable personal friends of mine in the midst of your church—and you will find that I, too, am trustworthy.' Here we have the hidden message of the unique and long list of personal greetings."[29] Sociologically, the analysis of Romans 16 indicates that the majority of the Roman Christians were *humiliores* with only a minority of socially elevated members. Lampe cites the illustration of several Roman Christians who, during the first century, had sold themselves into slavery so that they could support their Christian brothers and sisters. He concludes that this "illustrates the necessity for social action—there were many needy among the Roman Christians. And it discloses the lack of enough well-to-do Christians supporting these needy."[30]

The final essay in this section is that of *Peter Stuhlmacher*, "The Purpose of Romans,"[31] in which he views the situation in Rome quite differently than Schmithals.[32] The conflict with Judaizing tendencies is not early but late. The criticisms and objections made against Paul's teaching and person, spread from Asia Minor and Greece to Rome, must be refuted. "The dialogue we are witnessing in Romans is a real one in which Paul is wrestling for the hearts and minds of the Christians in Rome."[33] Given the apostle's desire to proceed to Spain, he must disprove the arguments and slanderous rumors advanced by his opponents before he arrives in Rome.

Given this intention of Romans, Paul does not plan to do missionary work when he arrives in Rome but will attempt to clarify and articulate the substance of his controverted gospel in such a way so that he can gain the support of the Roman Christians for this intended missionary work

---

[28]See, for example, the discussion in Cranfield, *Romans*, 1:1–11 and Pesch, *Römerbrief*, 20–21.

[29]Lampe, "Roman Christians," 218.

[30]Ibid., 229.

[31]This essay appeared originally appeared in German as "Der Abfassungszweck des Römerbriefes," *ZNW* 77 (1986), 180–93 and was translated for this volume by Professor Reginald and Ilse Fuller. See also Stuhlmacher's other essay, chapter 23 in this volume, "The Theme of Romans," as well as his new commentary, *Der Brief an die Römer* (NTD 6; Göttingen: Vandenhoeck & Ruprecht, 1989).

[32]Stuhlmacher's understanding of the Gentiles as closely attached to the synagogue is similar to that of Schmithals, even though he rejects Schmithals' literary hypotheses. See especially page 238 of his present article where Stuhlmacher states that "Paul is by no means exaggerating when he addresses the Gentiles in Rome, e.g., in Romans 7:1, as 'those who know the law' " (p. 240).

[33]Stuhlmacher, "Purpose" (= ch. 15 in this vol.), 240.

in Spain. There is no conflict between what Paul states in Rom. 1:15 and 15:20, when the former is properly translated as a past tense, viz., "Therefore for my part I was prepared to preach the gospel to you in Rome as well." Paul is not at the time he writes this letter planning to do missionary work in Rome. Given the hostility just outlined, coupled with the fragmentation of the Christians in Rome into various house-churches (here Stuhlmacher builds upon the analysis of Lampe), some of which were and some of which were not sympathetic to the apostle, all Paul "hopes for is Christian unity in respect of his gospel."[34]

Also important for Stuhlmacher is that Romans not be viewed as an "abstract dogmatic 'dialogue with the Jews' who reject Paul's gospel, but [as] a didactic and hortatory document with an apologetic accent, to be read and discussed by the Christians in Rome."[35] As a result, careful distinction must be made between the apostle's view of Judaism and the arguments he makes against the provocations of his Jewish Christian opponents. Because of the historical particularity of this letter, "the sum and crown of the Pauline gospel" is not found in any isolated form in Romans but only "when we take Romans together with Paul's other letters and bring them all into relation with one another."[36]

We turn now to consider the essays in *Section B—The Structure and Rhetoric of Romans*. While this theme has obvious overlaps with Sections A and C, it is wise to focus specific attention on the issues of structure and rhetoric.

James Dunn's essay, "The Formal and Theological Coherence of Romans,"[37] correctly notes the increased interest in the literary and rhetorical structure of Romans in the recent literature.[38] Wilhelm Wuellner's article on "Paul's Rhetoric of Argumentation in Romans,"[39] published in 1977, was a bellwether of what was to develop in the field. Yet Dunn is not convinced that this development has made a sustained contribution to the interpretation of Romans. "Thus to label Romans as 'epideictic' or 'deliberative' or 'protreptic' does not actually advance understanding of the letter very far, since the chief force of the letter lies in its *distinctive* Pauline art and content."[40]

While recognizing the problem of the relationship of the epistolary framework of Romans to the main body of the letter, this tension, argues

---

[34]Ibid., 237.

[35]Ibid., 236.

[36]Ibid., 242.

[37]This is part of the introduction to Dunn's commentary *Romans 1–8*, lix–lxiii.

[38]In addition to the essays which follow in this volume and further citations in the notes, one might also wish to consult the following contributions to the literary structure of Romans. From a structuralist perspective, Patte, *Power of the Gospel*, 232–96; from a literary-stylistic perspective, Schmeller, *"Diatribe"*; from a rhetorical perspective, Aletti, "Incohérence," 47–62.

[39]Wuellner, "Paul's Rhetoric," 128–46.

[40]Dunn, "The Formal and Theological Coherence of Romans" (= ch. 16 in this vol.), 246.

Dunn, has never been satisfactorily resolved and simply shows the distinctiveness of the form which Paul created. This tension does not mean that Romans lacks coherence, and Dunn rejects both theological and structural attempts which suggest this. That which integrates Romans is the motif of "Jew first but also Greek," a motif which is intertwined with the primary thematic emphasis on the righteousness of God and the secondary thematic emphasis on the law. Thus, for Dunn the structural coherence of Romans is primarily theological rather than rhetorical. But surely one must ask whether these two dimensions can be so confidently separated as Dunn suggests?

In "Romans III as a Key to the Structure and Thought of Romans," *William S. Campbell*[41] attempts to show that the coherence of Romans is a result of *both* the theology *and* the structure of the letter as it attempts to respond to an actual situation in the Roman church. The key and centerpiece of that theological and structural coherence is Romans 3.

In Rom. 3:21–26 Paul demonstrates that God is righteous and that he rectifies the one who has faith in Jesus. In these verses we have for Campbell "the theological centre and basis of Paul's argument in Rom. 1–11."[42] These twin themes create a strong connection between Romans 1–4 and 9–11, and Romans 5 and 8 should be seen as a "continuation and development" of these themes.

The relationship of Romans 7–8 to the wider context, specifically to Romans 9–11, is not theological but structural. The diatribal pattern of questions and answers illuminates this linkage. Thus, for example, the question asked in Rom. 3:8, "And why not do evil that good may come?" is answered in 6:1–7:6 and may also be the stimulus for Paul's treatment of the law in Rom. 7:7–25. As a result Campbell suggests that the "questions in 3:1–8 link this section with 6–7 and 9–11 whilst those in 3:27–31 link 3:21f. with ch. 4."[43]

Campbell supports the perspective that Romans is addressed to a set of real issues in Roman Christianity. This is suggested by Rom. 3:1–8 and by the fact that Paul is attempting to address such situations in his exposition of the Christ-event in Rom. 3:21–26 and in Romans 8. Romans 4 indicates that Paul's concern centers around the unity of Jewish and gentile Christians; in light of the Christ-event, which allows Gentiles to participate in the fulfilled covenant, Abraham may be regarded as the father of both. Romans 8 makes evident that, in addition, the apostle must refute certain slanderous misinterpretations of his gospel. As a result, this essay views the two main issues in Rome as an "anti-judaism" and an "antinomianism" on the part of the gentile Christians, positions which were further elab-

---

[41]W. S. Campbell, "Romans III as a Key to the Structure and Thought of Romans" (= ch. 17 in this vol.).
[42]Ibid., 254.
[43]Ibid., 259–60.

orated in Marcionism. It is only in connection with this historical perspective that chapters 12–15 are discussed; the theological and structural relationship to the earlier part of the letter are either ignored or touched on in passing. Romans 16 is not discussed. In addition to recognizing the centrality of Romans 16, most of the essays in Section A of this volume would differ from Campbell's analysis by laying greater emphasis on the complexity of the Roman situation as well as on the "pro-Jewish" preference of some gentile Christians in that city.

Recognizing that the elements that scholars like Campbell have brought to our attention—theology, structure, and historical situation—are key to understanding Romans, *Robert Jewett's* "Following the Argument of Romans"[44] offers a rich variety of suggestions concerning the relationship of these three dimensions. The starting point for his analysis is rhetorical criticism and the categories of analysis which it employs. For Jewett, as well as for Wuellner[45] and Kennedy,[46] Romans is an example of "epideictic" (demonstrative) rhetoric which aims at strengthening "some aspect of the ethos of an audience."[47] Rhetoric, according to Kennedy, may be classified as epideictic when it seeks to persuade the audience "to hold or reaffirm some point of view *in the present*," as when the author "celebrates or denounces some person or some quality."[48] For Jewett, the particular direction that Paul's theological argument takes, based on both rhetorical skill and forethought, is an attempt to "unify the competing house-churches in Rome so that they will be willing to cooperate in a mission to Spain."[49]

Following the categories of analysis utilized by the Latin rhetoricians including Cicero and Quintilian,[50] Jewett understands the argument of Romans as being presented in an easy to follow fivefold structure:

Part 1: *Exordium* (Introduction, 1:1–12)

Part 2: *Narratio* (Narration, 1:13–15)

Part 3: *Propositio* (Thesis Statement, 1:16–17)

Part 4: *Probatio* (Proof, 1:18–15:13)

First Proof: *Confirmatio* (Confirmation, 1:18–4:25)

Second Proof: *Exornatio* (Elaboration, 5:1–8:39)

[44]This essay was adapted and expanded by Robert Jewett for this volume from an earlier essay, "Following the Argument of Romans," in *Word and World* 6 (1986), 382–89.
[45]Wuellner, "Paul's Rhetoric," 128–46.
[46]Kennedy, *Rhetorical Criticism*, 152–56.
[47]Jewett, "Argument of Romans" (= ch. 18 in this vol.), 266.
[48]Kennedy, *Rhetorical Criticism*, 19. Italics added. Note, however, that Aristotle adds in the last sentence of *Rhet.* 1.3.4 that the genus of epideictic rhetoric does include the past and future, as well as the present.
[49]Jewett, "Argument of Romans," 266.
[50]It is important to emphasize the continuity among the Greek rhetorical handbook tradition (which Cicero, *De inventione*, brings into Latin), Cicero himself, Quintilian (who contains the fullest statement), as well as others. For a more complete discussion see Hughes, *Early Christian Rhetoric*, 32–43.

Third Proof: *Comparatio* (Comparison, 9:1–11:36)

Fourth Proof: *Exhortatio* (Exhortation, 12:1–15:13)

Part 5: *Peroratio* (Peroration, or conclusion, 15:14–16:27)

This outline[51] provides some clear advances over the initial efforts of Campbell, but also with regard to the pioneering work of Wuellner. With regard to the former, Jewett is able convincingly to integrate Romans 12–15 and 16 into the total structure of Romans; with regard to both he is able to penetrate more deeply into the structure of the letter through the use of various categories of rhetorical proofs such as "confirmation," "elaboration," "comparison," and "exhortation." Thus, the *propositio* (thesis) stated in 1:16–17 is "followed by an initial circle of proof in 1:18–4:25 that confirms the thesis. The next three proofs in Romans provide extensive developments of the thesis, answering relevant theological and ethical questions or ethical objections while amplifying important themes and implications"[52] The basic proof is amplified through ratiocination, which deals with the logical implications of a case already proven, and comparison, which uses "an historical example or an imaginative case to demonstrate the superiority of the argument or case already established."[53] Both *exornatio* and *comparatio* are characteristic of demonstrative rhetoric. The advantages of Jewett's analysis are many. Let us cite two examples. It puts Campbell's correct inclinations with regard to Romans 3 into a broader context and it allows Romans 12–15 to stand in a more integral relationship to Rom. 1:16–17 and 1:18–4:25, thus permitting a far more cohesive relationship between "theology" and "ethics" in Romans. Thus for Jewett the culmination of the argument Paul is making in Romans is to "be found in the peroration in chapters 15–16 rather than in the abstract, doctrinal themes of the earlier part of the letter. If the dynamics of ancient rhetoric are taken into account, the proofs of the earlier chapters of Romans are seen to have a practical purpose developed with powerful emotional appeals at the end of the discourse."[54]

While Romans can be shown to have been influenced by ancient rhetoric and the conventions used by it, the question has still not been answered whether Romans, which is in the form of a letter, can be classified more specifically.[55] This is not an unimportant question, since during the Hellenistic period and before the major concern of rhetoric was the spoken, persuasive word. But the relative uniqueness and creativity of Paul lie precisely in the fact that he applies these rhetorical principles to his letters, and, as we know, he writes different kinds of letters for different kinds

---

[51]For a quite different rhetorical analysis see Vouga, "Romains 1,18–3,20 comme *narratio*."

[52]Jewett, "Argument of Romans," 271.

[53]Ibid., 272.

[54]Ibid., 277.

[55]One should note here Luther Stirewalt's attempt to wrestle with this issue in chapter 10 of this vol., "The Form and Function of the Greek Letter-Essay."

of needs and situations. What needs to come into closer proximity in future studies is the relationship of rhetorical criticism to epistolgraphic studies.[56] A step in this direction is taken in the essay by *David Aune,* "Romans as a *Logos Protreptikos*."[57] Although the essays by Aune and Jewett were written independently of one another, there is a remarkable coherence between them.

Aune's basic thesis is that the central section of Romans (1:16–15:13) can best be understood as a *logos protreptikos* ("speech of exhortation") in an epistolary frame (1:1–15; 15:14–16:27). "Romans is protreptic in the sense that Paul is not only concerned to convince people of the truth of Christianity, but more particularly in the sense that he argues for his version of Christianity over other competing 'schools' of Christian thought."[58] Paul is adapting this inherently flexible genre as a means to persuade Roman Christians about the truth of the gospel which he preaches.

This oral and literary genre is not discussed in the rhetorical handbooks, and Aune suspects that this is due to the well-known hostility between philosophers and rhetoricians. As he points out, the *logos protreptikos* is rooted in both the philosophic and rhetorical traditions, although used in somewhat different ways. Among other features, such an oral discourse included elements of persuasion, intended to lead to conversion, as well as dissuasion (*apotrepein*) or censure (*elenchein*), "aimed at freeing the person from erroneous beliefs and practices."[59]

The fluidity of the form under consideration is evident, and Aune states that there were *logoi protreptikoi* "in the form of oral *discourses* (with both epideictic and deliberative features) as well as written *dialogues, discourses* (i.e., monologues), and *letters*."[60] Following a review of several *protreptikoi* Aune suggests that they all contain three features: (1) a negative section (e.g., criticizing other schools of thought); (2) a positive section (e.g., defending certain schools of thought); and (3) an optional section "consisting of a personal appeal to the hearer inviting the immediate acceptance of the exhortation."[61] Since these *protreptikoi* are essentially epideictic in character, the rhetorical method of *synkrisis* (comparison) is frequently employed.

Aune gives the following analysis of the main part of Romans:

> *Rom. 1:16–4:25*: a major text unit functioning as a protreptic *elenchos* (censure) with three constitutive units: 1:16–2:11; 2:12–3:20 and 3:21–4:25.

[56]See here the excellent review of this matter by Hughes, *Early Christian Rhetoric*, 19–30.

[57]This essay is an abbreviation of a more extensive article entitled "Romans as a *Logos Protreptikos* in the Context of Ancient Religious and Philosophical Propaganda," in *Paulus als Missionar und Theologe und das antike Judentum*, ed. Martin Hengel (Tübingen: J. C. B. Mohr, forthcoming).

[58]Aune, "Romans as a *Logos Protreptikos*" (= ch. 19 in this vol.), 279.

[59]Ibid., 280.

[60]Ibid., 281.

[61]Ibid., 282–83.

Rom. 5:1–8:39: this textual unit functions in a primarily positive manner as an *endeiktikos* (demonstration); it focuses on the life of those who have been justified by faith as well as on the problem of sin. Whereas Rom. 1:16–4:25 focuses on the "outsider," thus the heavy use of the diatribe style, this section is primarily concerned with the "insider." It also has three constitutive units: Rom. 5:1–21; Rom. 6:1–7:25; Rom. 8:1–39.

Rom. 9:1–11:36: this textual unit is concerned with the problem of Jewish unbelief and Gentile belief. For Aune the "focal theological issue is the trustworthiness of God."[62]

Rom. 12:1–15:13: this section is a protreptic appeal to the Roman Christians that they devote themselves totally to God.

Aune concludes that all these originally protreptic sections (except for Rom. 9:1–11:36), were linked by Paul to form the relatively coherent *logos protreptikos* known as Romans. Paul's pattern of argumentation is to move from the "outside" to the "inside," viz., from dialogue with pagans (1:18–2:11), then with Jews (2:12–4:25) and then finally with Christians (5:1–8:39). His intention is to expose error and point out truth so that the Roman Christians may have "concrete examples of the way in which he presents the gospel in a variety of settings to a variety of people."[63] However, with regard to this Pauline intention as well as with regard to Paul's purpose in linking together what may have been originally separate *protreptikoi*, Aune is remarkably ambiguous. He claims that there is "some validity" both to the position that understands the letter as an actual response to a real situation in Rome and to the position that does not see any direct connection with local problems. He then proceeds to suggest that "the significance of the main part of the letter could not be subordinated to any supposedly concrete situation teased out of the concluding paraenetic section (esp. 14:1–15:13)."[64] How this relates to Aune's concluding comments that in each of the sections that he analyzed in Romans, "Paul's purpose is to present to the Roman Christians concrete examples of the way in which he presents the gospel in a variety of settings to a variety of people," is not clear.[65] Why Paul must write to the Roman Christians, why he must present them with concrete examples of how he proclaims the gospel, and why he must expose error and point out truth to them are left ambiguous.[66] Does this not presuppose an actual set of issues in Rome to which Paul addresses himself?

Before moving to a comparison between Aune's and Jewett's analyses of Romans, it is important to note that Aune and many others[67] now sup-

---

[62]Ibid., 294.
[63]Ibid., 296.
[64]Ibid., 289.
[65]Ibid., 296.
[66]Ibid.
[67]For example, Stowers, *Diatribe*. For Stowers' specific indebtedness to *The Romans Debate* see pages 1–5 of his study.

port Donfried's[68] critique of Bultmann's[69] conception of the "Cynic-Stoic diatribe" as a genre employed in popular philosophical preaching. In Aune's suggestion that Paul employed a "diatribe *style*" and that this *style* was used in winning converts to Christianity,[70] one has, in fact, a more modest and correct proposal for penetrating this phenomenon of "diatribe" which has so often been utilized as a way to argue that Romans could not be addressed to a concrete set of historical circumstances in Rome because it made use of such rhetorical features.[71]

But now let us proceed to a more specific comparison between the proposals of Jewett and Aune. First, there is a large measure of agreement that the influence of the rhetorical genus of epideictic can be demonstrated in Romans. Remembering that in the practice of rhetoric the three rhetorical genera could overlap,[72] we need to be free from a rigidity which suggests that in this letter Paul could have been influenced only by *one* of them. A *predominant* influence of epideictic need not rule out occasional contributions of devices and contexts more appropriate to deliberative rhetoric.[73] Particularly if some sections of Romans had a prior *oral* context, it is not surprising that one might find different rhetorical *genera* overlapping in Paul's *written* communication to Rome. Having spoken this cautionary word, there does seem to be agreement among the rhetorical critics that there is a close connection between this letter and epideictic rhetoric.

Second, even though Aune concentrates more on the analysis of the individual parts of Romans and Jewett is more concerned with the rhetorical whole, there is a remarkable agreement between Jewett's four proofs and Aune's four major textual units. The two studies complement each other in such significant ways that hope emerges for the increased congruity of future rhetorical studies of Romans.

The third and final section of this new volume, *The Theology of Romans: Issues in the Current Debate*, probes a few of the key issues in current scholarship concerning the theological intention of Romans. Our

---

[68]Donfried, "False Presuppositions" (= ch. 8 in this vol.), 102–25. Commenting on Bultmann's work, Donfried states that he "never defines precisely or critically what the form of the diatribe is and what justification there is for talking about the diatribe as a Gattung" (p. 113) and, further, that "what he has shown is not that Paul has been influenced by the diatribe, but that he was influenced by rhetorical usages which were common in the Greco-Roman world" (pp. 118–19).

[69]Bultmann, *Diatribe*.

[70]Here Aune's conclusion differs from that of Stowers, *Diatribe*, 175–84.

[71]For example, the position of Bornkamm, "Last Will and Testament," 16–28.

[72]That the three genera of rhetoric overlap is suggested by Aristotle, *Rhetoric* 1.3.4, and can be seen most clearly in speeches given late in the lives of Demosthenes and Cicero, where legal and political issues become practically inseparable. In addition, by the time Paul wrote his letters, judicial rhetoric had grown greatly in importance, so that rhetorical instruction tended to give greater attention to judicial rhetoric, and the other two genera of rhetoric could be defined in terms of it.

[73]See here Aune, "*Logos Protreptikos*," 279–83.

objective is to sample *some* current scholarship, not to give a comprehensive or complete overview of the theology of Romans. As we proceed
it will become clear that there is today little unanimity among exegetes
in their theological analysis of Romans. That, of course, is not a new state
of affairs. However, given the solid progress in the historical and sociological analysis of this last letter of the apostle, and given the newest, although still preliminary, contributions of rhetorical criticism, the question
is posed all the more urgently to this generation of interpreters: Is the stage
now set for a more consistent and unified presentation of the theological
content of Romans than has hitherto been the case?

One of the major points at issue in the contemporary interpretation
of Romans is Paul's perception of Israel's law and of Judaism in general.
In *James Dunn's* overview, "The New Perspective on Paul: Paul and the
Law,"[74] it is made clear that one's understanding of Paul's attitude to the
Jewish law will substantially influence one's interpretation of Paul's theological aims in this letter. It is precisely because the issue of Paul's attitude
to Israel's law in Romans is such a divisive one in the current reading of
the theology of Romans that we begin with Dunn's overview dealing with
Paul and the law. Dunn begins his brief survey by giving attention to the
work of E. P. Sanders, who has attempted to substantiate the perspective
that Judaism's self-understanding was based on the premise of the grace
of the God who entered into covenant relationship with his people.[75] Contrary to the widespread caricature by which the law is understood in terms
of a system in which salvation is earned through the merit of good works,
this "covenant relationship was regulated by the law, not as a way of entering the covenant, or of gaining merit, but as the way of living *within* the
covenant; and that included the provision of sacrifice and atonement for
those who confessed their sins and thus repented."[76] This understanding
of Paul, articulated impressively by Sanders and shared in many details
by Dunn, Gaston, Räisänen,[77] and others, can be descriptively referred to
as the "new perspective" on Paul. At its core lies the conviction that for
first-century Judaism salvation is not based on works; rather "Paul is wholly
at one with his fellow Jews in asserting that justification is *by faith*."[78] As
Dunn acknowledges, the "new perspective" wishes to provide an alternative to "a typically Lutheran emphasis on justification by faith" which
had imposed "a hermeneutical grid on the text of Romans."[79]

In addition, the law, based on God's *hesed* (unmerited mercy), also
takes on certain sociological dimensions which underscore Israel's distinc-

---

[74]Dunn, "New Perspective" (= ch. 20 in this vol.).

[75]Sanders, *Paul*. For a critique of Sanders portrayal of Judaism see the comments by
J. Fitzmyer in Reumann, *Righteousness*, 217–18. Reumann's own more general evaluation of
Sanders is found on pages 120–23 of that volume.

[76]Dunn, "New Perspective," 300.

[77]Räisänen, *Paul and the Law* and *The Torah and Christ*.

[78] Dunn, "The New Perspective on Paul," *BJRL* 65 (1983), 106.

[79]Dunn, "New Perspective" (= ch. 20 in this vol.), 299.

tiveness as a people. As Dunn mentions, the law increasingly functioned as an "identity marker" and "boundary" by which Israel was distinguished from other nations.[80] From the Maccabean period onward circumcision, food laws, and the sabbath gain particular importance as boundary definers. An inevitable consequence of this distinctiveness was the sense of privilege, viz., as a people chosen by God and graced by his bestowal of the covenant and the law, as well as ethnic pride, "pride in the law as the mark of God's special favor to Israel."[81]

According to Dunn, then, Paul in Romans is not reacting to the law as a system of salvation earned through the merit of good works, but, rather, against a covenantal promise and law which "had become too inextricably identified with ethnic Israel as such."[82] In other words, the emphasis on *national distinctiveness* had become too great; what Paul is attempting to do is "to free both promise and law for a wider range of recipients, freed from the ethnic constraints which he saw to be narrowing the grace of God and diverting the saving purpose of God out of its its main channel—Christ."[83] Thus for Dunn, Paul is reacting against the "social function" of the law, "the law misunderstood by a misplaced emphasis on boundary-marking ritual, the law become a tool of sin in its too close identification with matters of the flesh, the law sidetracked into a focus of nationalistic zeal."[84] When this social function of the law is overlooked, one is bound to misunderstand Paul's intentions as well as the theological purpose of Romans. Understood properly, the law "becomes one of the chief integrating strands which binds the whole letter into a cohesive and powerful restatement of Jewish covenant theology in the light of Christ."[85]

Lloyd Gaston's work, "Israel's Misstep in the Eyes of Paul,"[86] also builds on the work of E. P. Sanders. He presents us with a position that is at the other end of the spectrum from what Dunn labels "a typically Lutheran emphasis";[87] characteristic of Gaston's approach is his assertion that "justification is not a central Pauline *doctrine* but language which is used whenever the legitimacy of the status of his gentile converts is being discussed."[88] Important to Gaston's emphasis is that, while Paul is not opposing Judaism as such, "he does have something against his fellow Jews."[89] The fundamental issue between them is Paul's apostolate to the

---

[80]Ibid., 304.
[81]Ibid., 305.
[82]Ibid., 307.
[83]Ibid.
[84]Ibid.
[85]Ibid., 308.
[86]Gaston, *Paul and the Torah*, 135–50. For a critique of Gaston's work see Kaylor, *Covenant Community*, 176–90.
[87]Dunn, "New Perspective," 299.
[88]Gaston, *Paul and the Torah*, 5.
[89]Gaston, "Israel's Misstep" (= ch. 21 in this vol.), 309.

Gentiles. In a manner not dissimilar to the argument of Dunn, Gaston suggests that while being "distracted by works (which of course should be done), Israel was faithful to Torah as it relates to Israel, but with respect to the goal of that Torah as it relates to the Gentiles, they stumbled and were unfaithful."[90] The goal of the Torah was God's righteousness for the Gentiles, which has now been revealed in Jesus, and it is Israel's failure to recognize this which is the object of Paul's irritation. This is, in fact, "Israel's misstep."

Gaston puts his thesis to the test with regard to Rom. 2:17–29, a passage for which there is little consensus among current exegetes, as can be seen, for example, in the different recent interpretations by J. C. O'Neill, H. Räisänen, and E. P. Sanders.[91] This is a text that has nothing to do with Jews as such, with the law or, with soteriology. It is an accusation against some *Jewish missionaries* who, because of their scandalous behavior, cause God's name to be blasphemed among the Gentiles (2:24). Another exegetical decision involves the identity of the remnant, the election, in Rom. 11:5, 7. Are they not to be identified with Jewish Christians? Absolutely not! The remnant refers to "those Jews who like Paul are engaged in the Gentile mission."[92] In no way is he employing this remnant idea as a way of disenfranchising Israel. God's election of Israel has not ceased. The problem is Israel's hostility to the gospel proclaimed to the Gentiles, not Paul's continued certainty of their election.

Gaston summarizes succinctly his thesis in this way: "Because Israel did not accept the task of being 'the light for the Gentiles' that has opened the way for Christ to be that light."[93] Romans, which is explicitly addressed to gentile Christians, communicates to them that, as a result of God's grace which they have experienced in the present, all Israel will be saved. As a result there should be no misunderstanding that the gentile Christians have replaced the Jews in God's favor.

The final two essays in this volume by *J. C. Beker* and *Peter Stuhlmacher* are concerned with a general theological perspective of Romans as a whole. Here a key question in the current literature is whether there is one sustained theological theme in Romans or several. If, for example, Aune is correct that Romans is composed of several originally separate *protreptikoi*, is it perhaps futile to look for a single, coherent theological theme which sustains all of Romans? On the other hand, Robert Jewett's analysis of the *propositio* (Rom. 1:16–17) followed by four proofs would not necessarily make such a position impossible.

In the current discussion Paul Achtemeier, for example, demurs from understanding Romans as an exposition of the doctrine of justification by

[90]Ibid., 316.
[91]Ibid., 312.
[92]Ibid., 317.
[93]Ibid., 322.

faith and prefers to see several important themes in Romans, each demonstrating the course of the history of God's dealing with his creation.[94] In other words, the larger structure of an apocalyptic framework is being articulated in a variety of more specific themes. Paul Meyer also understands Romans in a pluriform way: "the argument of the Letter proceeds by a serial treatment of interlocking and perennial themes, often in sections that stand out as independent literary 'blocks.' "[95] J. C. Beker, in his essay "The Faithfulness of God and the Priority of Israel in Paul's Letter to the Romans,"[96] moves in a similar direction. Paul's hermeneutic is based on the dialectical interaction of the coherence of the gospel and the contingency of the specific historical situation to which the gospel is addressed. As Beker has stated elsewhere, "the *character* of Paul's contingent hermeneutic is shaped by his apocalyptic core in that in nearly all cases the contingent interpretation of the gospel points—whether implicitly or explicitly—to the imminent cosmic triumph of God."[97] Therefore terms like "righteousness," "justification," and "reconciliation" belong to a range of symbols which interpret the gospel to the contingent needs of a specific situation. Thus, while righteousness/justification language is prominent in Romans, it is not the primary theme of the letter. The task of the interpreter of Romans, which is viewed as "a profoundly occasional letter," is to clarify the specific interaction between coherence and contingency.[98] Primary among these challenges is the "Jewish question," viz., the relationship of Romans 9–11 to the entire letter.

For Beker the theme of Romans (1:16–17) revolves around four interrelated issues: "(1) the gospel reveals the righteousness of God; (2) the righteousness of God is apprehended by faith; (3) the gospel is 'the power of God for salvation to everyone who believes, to the Jew first and also to the Greek'; (4) the righteousness of faith in the gospel is the confirmation and fulfillment of the Old Testament promise of Hab 2:4."[99] The basic climax of this theme is reached in 11:32: "For God has consigned all people to disobedience, that he may have mercy on all." Thus, the fundamental question that Paul must address is this: how is he able "to maintain both the priority of Israel and the equality of Jew and Gentile in Christ on the basis of justification by faith alone (cf. Rom. 3:28–31)?"[100]

---

[94]Achtemeier, *Romans*, 9–15. For a review of the newer commentaries and other literature see Fitzmyer, "Letter to the Romans," 830–68, and Meyer, "Romans," 1130–67.

[95]Meyer, "Romans," 1130.

[96]Beker, "The Faithfulness of God" (= ch. 22 in this vol.). These brief remarks must be seen in the wider context of Beker's seminal work, *Paul the Apostle: The Triumph of God in Life and Thought* (Philadelphia: Fortress, 1980). For a criticism of Sanders see especially pages 237–43 in *Paul the Apostle*.

[97]Beker, *Paul the Apostle*, 19.

[98]Beker, "Faithfulness of God," 327.

[99]Ibid., 329.

[100]Ibid.

This query brings to the fore the very matter of God's faithfulness. As a result, Paul wishes to show that the "faithfulness of God" is "an inalienable dimension of the righteousness of God," which is for Beker the "key term for the letter as a whole,"[101] for if it could be demonstrated that God had rejected Israel, "how are the Gentiles to trust the confirmation of these promises to them through God's righteousness in Christ?"[102] Essential for Paul, then, is to argue that an indispensable aspect of the righteousness of God is his faithfulness (Rom. 3:3) and, further, that "the protological election of Israel in the Old Testament will be confirmed by the eschatological priority of Israel at the time of the parousia and the establishment of the triumph of God."[103] Accordingly, the theme of God's faithfulness is able to hold together the tension between Israel's particularity and the universality of the gospel for the Gentiles.

Beker takes issue with both Barth and Käsemann's understanding of the Jew in Romans as the *homo religiosus* in general and with the related exegesis which suggests that Paul's use of *pas* or *anthrōpos* eradicates the ethnic specificity of the two different people, Jews and Gentiles.[104] Precisely because Paul does not blur this difference, it is unnecessary for him to assert in Romans that the church is the "true Israel." Israel has a "priority and separate identity" in the gospel, and it is this gospel which makes evident the nature of Israel's priority. This priority lies not "in Israel's 'boasting,' that is, in its empirical achievement of 'covenant keeping' or in Israel's elitist awareness of its exclusive status before God, but solely in God's faithfulness to his promises, that is, in God's grace."[105]

For Beker Romans is addressed to a concrete situation in Rome— although several other factors converge in this purpose as well[106]—where there is present a divisiveness between a gentile majority and a Jewish minority. In order to correct this situation by emphasizing that there is a unity between these two distinct peoples in the gospel, the apostle stresses both the priority of the Jew in God's plan of salvation as well as the right of the Gentiles to belong to this very people of God. The universality of the gospel for the Gentiles is intimately linked to the people of Israel and, therefore, to the trustworthiness of God's promises made to them. Thus it is simply wrong for gentile Christians to think that because they represent a majority in the Roman church that they have displaced or will displace Israel.

In proposing the "gospel of justification" as the major theme of Romans, *Peter Stuhlmacher* in his "The Theme of Romans"[107] not only claims

---

101Ibid., 331.
102Ibid., 330.
103Ibid.
104Ibid.
105Ibid., 332.
106See here Beker's discussion, ibid., 327–29.
107Stuhlmacher, "Theme of Romans," (= ch. 23 in this vol.).

that there is an identifiable theological motif which lies at the center of Romans but that this motif is characteristic of Paul's theology as a whole. Thus he can state that "the Pauline proclamation of justification was not merely the late fruit of Paul's reflection, but was an initial implication of his understanding of Christ on the way to Damascus."[108] Stuhlmacher agrees with much of the historical and sociological research which stresses the contingent character of Romans,[109] yet he refuses to agree that the theme of justification is itself a result of that contingent situation. Here he clearly disagrees with the "new perspective" as well as with the position of Beker. Against Beker he would argue that justification is *the* master hermeneutic which controls Romans.[110] Believing to be standing in the general tradition of Schlatter,[111] Käsemann,[112] Schlier[113] and Wilckens,[114] he states unequivocally that "the letter to the Romans has as its theme the Pauline gospel of the divine righteousness in Christ or, for short, the righteousness of God (in and through Christ). Finally, the idea that this theme was not first forced upon Paul through the situation of discussion and struggle in Rome, but is the theme of his Christian life as an apostle as such, must still be explicitly dealt with, since this understanding of the focus of Paul's gospel has repeatedly been disputed in recent times."[115]

Building on his earlier essay, "The Purpose of Romans,"[116] Stuhlmacher restates his conviction that Romans is intended to clarify the contents of the Pauline gospel and to convince Christians in Rome about its legitimacy. The apostle's assertion that "I am not ashamed of the gospel" (Rom. 1:16) is a clear indication to the Romans that he plans to remain faithful to the gospel he has proclaimed elsewhere despite severe and sharp criticisms directed against him. This controversial gospel is defined by Stuhlmacher as the *"gospel of the divine righteousness in and through Christ, by virtue of which those who believe from among the Jews and Gentiles (according to the promise of Hab 2:4) obtain life."* [117] The twin themes of "gospel" and the "righteousness of God," together with the related verse "to preach the gospel" and "to justify," are found throughout the letter.

Stuhlmacher agrees with Stendahl, against Käsemann, that Paul's understanding of justification in Romans cannot be described as an

---

[108]Ibid., 345.

[109]See Stuhlmacher's earlier essay in ch. 15 of this volume, "The Purpose of Romans."

[110]The following statement is characteristic of Beker's position: "Although the righteousness of God (and his verdict of justification) constitutes Paul's original hermeneutic of the Christ-event, it is not his only hermeneutic or the master symbol. . . . Each symbol interprets a different aspect of the one lordship of Christ that marks God's imminent triumph over evil and death" (*Paul the Apostle*, 264).

[111]Schlatter, *Gottes Gerechtigkeit*.

[112]Käsemann, *Romans*.

[113]Schlier, *Der Römerbrief*.

[114]Wilckens, *Der Brief an die Römer*.

[115]Stuhlmacher, "Theme of Romans," 342.

[116]Stuhlmacher, "Purpose of Romans" (ch. 15).

[117]Stuhlmacher, "Theme of Romans," 335 (italics are those of author).

"antijudaistische Kampfeslehre" ("anti-Judaic polemical doctrine"). Yet he is concerned lest Stendahl's correct warning be taken as "a ground for diminishing the fundamental meaning of the Pauline gospel of justification!"[118] Stuhlmacher also ponders whether Stendahl[119] goes far enough in his positive description of justification as only a defense of the "rights of the Gentiles to participate in God's promises."[120] Stuhlmacher thinks not and insists that the Pauline gospel "is not simply a message which proclaims the acceptance by God of the Gentiles as well, without having to be circumcised. Instead, the gospel is the only saving revelation of the end-times salvation 'for everyone who believes.' Indeed, according to Rom. 1:16, it even holds true that the gospel of the divine righteousness in Christ is addressed 'first to the Jews,' since God chose Israel and promised his people deliverance through the Messiah."[121] This statement brings to the fore an unresolved issue in the current debate about the theological intention and meaning of Paul's gospel. Does Romans indeed conclude that "there is only one way of salvation and only one single gospel . . ." and " . . . that the heart of this gospel is the divine righteousness in and through Christ available for everyone who believes"?[122]

For Stuhlmacher the event of justification is summarized by Paul in the use of the concept "righteousness of God," a concept which has as its foundation the gracious activity of God and that results in righteousness being granted to the sinner. This gift of righteousness "given to every sinner who believes in Jesus Christ as his redeemer and Lord" is a result of the atonement effected by God "for all sinners" through Jesus' death on the cross.[123] To avoid any individualist misinterpretation of Romans, Stuhlmacher is quick to add that "the righteousness of God" is a phrase that describes the entire redemptive activity of God from creation to redemption, a redemption inaugurated in Christ but only complete when this world must no longer groan under the burden of death and transi-

---

[118]Ibid., 337.

[119]The relevant essays of Krister Stendahl reprinted in his *Paul Among Jews and Gentiles* include: "Paul Among Jews and Gentiles" (pp. 1–77) and "The Apostle Paul and the Introspective Conscience of the West" (pp. 199–215). On should also consult the following essays found in *Meanings*: "Christ's Lordship and Religious Pluralism" (pp. 243–44); "Judaism and Christianity I: Then and Now" (pp. 205–15); "Judaism and Christianity II: A Plea for a New Relationship" (pp. 217–32).

[120]Note the criticism of Stendahl's position by Scott Hafemann, a student of Stuhlmacher, in "Salvation," 38–58. Hafemann argues that it cannot be denied that the parallel between Romans "9:30–33 and 11:5–7 indicates that Paul's doctrine of justification by faith alone through grace is to be applied equally to both Gentiles and Jews. Moreover, justification by faith also occupies a role in the context of the eschatological future for both Jews and Gentiles (cf. 11:30–31). Hence, arguments may differ concerning how close to the center of Paul's theology his doctrine of justification by faith actually is, but Stendahl has moved it too far away" (p. 55).

[121]Stuhlmacher, "Theme of Romans," 337.

[122]Ibid. A strikingly different position is articulated by Gaston when he urges "that one gospel is addressed to Gentiles and one to Israel" (Gaston, *Paul and the Torah*, 115).

[123]Stuhlmacher, "Theme of Romans," 339.

toriness (Rom. 8:18–23) and when God's elect people, Israel, "will have experienced the redemption and fulfillment of the irrevocable promises of God concerning his people in the Parousia of Christ Jesus (cf. Rom. 11:25ff.)"[124] As a result, the theme of the "righteousness of God" holds not only Romans 1 through 11 together, but also the entire letter including Romans 12–16. In these final chapters Paul works out how God's grace claims the believer anew in obedience. "Romans 12–15 are thus the practical test case for the justification which Paul teaches."[125]

Stuhlmacher also tackles the complex issue of Paul and the Jewish law and how fundamentally the apostle distanced himself from it. His answer goes against much of the current tide: it was the revelation of the risen Christ on the Damascus road that "brought about the turning away from his Pharisaic zeal for the law and his embracing of the revealed Christ."[126] Thus, from his call onward, viz., from the *beginning* of his mission, Paul's gospel of justification was critical of the law as a way of salvation for *both* Jews and Gentiles.[127] There can be little doubt that for him faith in Jesus Christ is the way to salvation for both Jews and Gentiles. Although the conflicts in Jerusalem, Antioch, Galatia, Philippi and Corinth did not initiate this critical attitude toward the law, these controversies did force Paul to develop a consistency in his attitude toward the law that was not yet present at the beginning of his missionary career.

Having reviewed some of the representative essays which have appeared since the first edition of *The Romans Debate* in 1977 it is appropriate to ask, on the one hand, in what areas in the interpretation of Romans is there a consensus or at least an emerging consensus, and, on the other hand, in what areas the debate continues.

I. Consensus

1. Without question a consensus has been reached that Romans is addressed to the Christian community in Rome which finds itself in a particular historical situation.[128] How that historical situation is described varies, but many would point to the polarized house-churches as being a key factor leading to turmoil among the Christians in that metropolis. One major component contributing to this polarization are the varying degrees of Christian attachment to Judaism and the attitudes which such dependence/independence fostered among the various groups toward each other.

---

[124]Ibid., 341.

[125]Ibid.

[126]Ibid., 343.

[127]Hafemann, "Salvation," 55, in speaking of Paul's conversion states that "Paul did not just change 'job descriptions,' he changed allegiances, from God's will as revealed in the covenants of the Torah, to God's will as revealed in the new covenant of the Messiah."

[128]This view is also well articulated by Kettunen in his significant contribution, *Der Abfassungszweck des Römerbriefes.*

2. There also appears to be a developing agreement that it is unwise to speak of a single purpose in Paul's writing to Rome. Not only his planned visit to Rome, but also those to Jerusalem and Spain, and all that those prospective visits symbolized, are factors in the composition of this complex and intricate document although the degree of weight which one gives to these different factors still varies in the literature.

3. An especially significant shift has occurred with regard to the understanding of Romans 16, which is now viewed by the majority as being an integral part of Paul's original letter. The most recent and notable exception to this consensus is the commentary of Schmithals. Lampe's monograph and essay on Romans 16 have advanced our understanding of the socio-historical dimensions of the Roman community significantly. Given the diversity and fragmentation of that community there also appears to be an increasing acceptance of the view that Paul's failure to address the Romans as an *ekklēsia* is intentional and due to this fractionalized situation.

4. The so-called diatribe is not a literary genre but rather a series of rhetorical devices. As a result of the most recent studies one can no longer argue against the historical specificity of Romans based on the use of such rhetorical devices.

5. With regard to Romans 9–11 there is today a wide-ranging agreement that these chapters form an integral part of the main argument and that they are not simply a Pauline afterthought as has been argued, in one way or another, by Bultmann, Dodd, Sanday and Headlam, and Scroggs.[129] Further, there is considerable emphasis today that a major concern of Paul as he writes Romans is in defining the relationship between Jew and Gentile in God's plan for salvation.

If these conclusions are plausible, then it can be said that significant advance has been made in resolving some major issues which were dominant in the original edition of *The Romans Debate*.

II. New and Unresolved Issues in the Debate

We are now prepared to ask what issues still need to be resolved with regard to the purpose, structure, and theology of Romans. Some of these questions carry over from the earlier debate, and some have been intensified since then; attention has been called to these topics in this introductory essay. Let us turn to some areas which need further collaborative work among scholars.

1. While both Schmithals' and Watson's analysis of Roman Christianity contain keen insight, do they sufficiently recognize the complexity of the Roman situation? Following the pathbreaking essay of Wiefel,[130] do not the arguments of Lampe and others, for example, concerning the wide-

---

[129]See here Beker, "Faithfulness of God," 327–28.
[130]Wiefel, "Jewish Community," 85–101.

ranging diversity of Roman Christianity contain the greatest plausibility? If one recognizes the complexity of Roman Christianity, divided into a variety of house-churches, should one not henceforth use descriptive categories which are more precise than simply "Jewish Christian" or "gentile Christian,"[131] especially if one accepts the strong Jewish leanings of some "gentile Christians" as Schmithals and Lampe have argued?

2. To what stage in the development of Roman Christianity is Romans addressed? For Schmithals it is to an early and middle stage, and for Stuhlmacher and most others it is a late stage (ca. mid-fifties). If most would agree with Stuhlmacher's sense of timing, to what extent is Paul reacting to uniquely Roman problems, and to what extent is he also attempting to clarify his gospel in light of misrepresentations of it abroad which have also surfaced in Rome? Would there be agreement that these problems are so intertwined that Paul of necessity has to deal with both sets of issues?

3. Can agreement be reached that rhetorical criticism is an indispensable tool in further understanding the structure, methods of argumentation and theological intention of Paul in writing Romans? Will further rhetorical studies confirm the initial inclination to understand Romans in terms in terms of (predominantly) epideictic rhetoric? If rhetorical criticism is to be an exegetical aid, then it would be hoped that future analyses of the letter would develop a commonly accepted outline of the rhetorical structure of Romans. Further, more work will have to be done to clarify the relationship between rhetorical criticism and epistolary theory and between rhetorical criticism and theological intention. In short, the probing efforts of Wuellner and Stirewalt in the original volume have been advanced significantly but we are not yet at the point where it can be shown that a substantial consensus has been reached, although there are clear signs pointing in that direction.

4. What was Paul's *primary* theological intention in writing this letter to Rome? Most will agree that a theological purpose(s) is present, but when one probes for common understandings one will recognize that much effort needs yet to be expended before one can speak of anything approximating consensus. While there is a good deal of commonality in using such terms as "gospel" and "righteousness of God," for example, what is absent is any significant agreement concerning whether there is a master hermeneutical key of Romans, and if so, how it is to be described.

One of the major areas of conflict in assessing Paul's theology in Romans is the issue of the law and, especially, its relationship to the theme of the righteousness of God. Here there is little consensus among contemporary scholars. Should one accept Gaston's distinction between Torah and law, the former relating to Jews and the latter to Gentiles?[132] Or does one follow Dunn in his argumentation that Paul understands only a part of the

---

[131]See here the monograph by Minear, *Obedience*.
[132]Gaston, *Paul and the Torah*, 32.

law as having ceased to function in light of Christ: "it is not the law as such which ceased with the new epoch brought in by Christ, but the law seen as a way of proving righteousness, of documenting God's special regard for Israel, of marking Israel out from the other nations, the law understood in terms of work."[133] Or, with Stuhlmacher, does the gospel of justification totally supersede the law as a way of salvation for both Jew and Gentile?[134] Stuhlmacher's interpretation incorporates much of the recent historical and sociological work on Romans, and he is fully cognizant of the "new perspective" current today; yet he continues to argue for a theological view of Romans that has traditionally had much currency. Will further research demonstrate such an argument to be plausible or inconsistent?

These tensions and conflicting assessments of the theological intention of Romans are the primary issues at stake in the current stage of the Romans debate. What, precisely, is the content of the gospel which Paul is attempting to clarify for the Roman Christians? Now that the historical and sociological background of Romans has come into sharper focus and advances are being achieved in the area of rhetorical criticism, one would hope that meaningful headway will be made in resolving the present impasse concerning the theological hermeneutic of Romans.

[133]Dunn, *Romans 9–16*, 598.

[134]In addition to Dunn's overview in this volume and the bibliography that he provides in *Romans 1–8*, lxiii–lxiv, see the excellent review and critical evaluation of the literature in Westerholm, *Israel's Law and the Church's Faith*.

PART

I

1

ST. PAUL'S LETTER TO THE ROMANS— AND OTHERS

T. W. Manson

The twentieth chapter of the Acts of the Apostles describes the events which followed the termination of St. Paul's Ephesian ministry. We are told that after taking leave of the disciples he set out for Macedonia, where he carried out a preaching tour through the province while making his way to Greece (*Hellas*—the only occurrence of the word in the New Testament). Greece here probably means the Roman province of Achaea, and that in its turn may be taken to mean Corinth. The Apostle stayed in Greece for three months; and it is fairly safe to assume that these were the winter months, which were unsuitable for travel. At the end of the three months he set out for Syria in accordance with plans which he had previously made.[1] It appears from Acts 19:21f. that he had framed a further project: after the visit to Jerusalem he must also see Rome. In Rom. 15:14–33 he gives a fresh statement of his intentions, which confirms the plans already outlined in the Corinthian letters and in Acts, and adds further particulars. The journey to Jerusalem is imminent, if indeed it has not already begun.[2] Paul has serious misgivings, which events later more than justified, about the outcome of the visit. He is doubtful about the reception that he and his gift will have from "the Saints," and he expects to be in danger from "the unbelievers in Judaea," that is, from the active Jewish opponents of Christianity in Palestine, of whom he had formerly been a leader and in whose eyes he was an apostate of the worst kind.[3] He nevertheless hopes that by the prayers of himself and his friends he may come through and be able to carry out his plan of visiting Rome. There is one

[1] 1 Cor. 15:1–9; 2 Cor. 1:15ff.; Acts 19:21ff.
[2] Rom. 15:25. *nyni de poreuomai eis Ierousalēm.* Here *poreuomai* may mean "I am going" or "I am on my way." Cf. Acts 20:22.
[3] Rom. 15:30ff.

new feature: after Rome he proposes to start a missionary campaign in the far west. Spain is to be the scene of these new labors.[4]

All these data combine harmoniously to fix the time and place of the composition of Romans. It clearly belongs to the period of three months in Greece (Acts 20:2f.). The controversies with members of the Corinthian church, which had caused Paul so much anxiety and grief during the Ephesian ministry, were now a thing of the past. The fundamental issues remained, of course, and on these Paul had not changed. But it was now possible to state the issues and set forth the essential truth of the matter without the heat and bitterness that had marked the earlier stages of the dispute. And this in fact is what Romans does. The first eleven chapters are devoted to a full-dress debate on the question which lay at the root of most of the troubles of the Ephesian ministry, the question, Can one be a good Christian without embracing Judaism? To this Paul's answer is that the real question, and the only question for Jews, is, Can one be a good Jew without embracing Christianity? The remainder of the didactic part of the document, 12:1–15:13, is mainly occupied with the discussion of points that had arisen in the Corinthian correspondence. That is to say, Romans is the calm and collected summing-up of Paul's position as it had been hammered out in the heat of controversy during the previous months. It is a positive and constructive statement of his understanding of the gospel.

An absolute dating of Romans is not possible. It involves forward reckoning from the date of Gallio's proconsulship at Corinth and back reckoning from the date of the replacement of Felix by Festus in the procuratorship of Judaea. The former date can be fixed within a year or so; the latter is more doubtful. This much, however, can be said: that the trial of Paul before Gallio is unlikely to have taken place earlier than the summer of A.D. 51. The earliest probable date for the beginning of the Ephesian ministry would then be 52; and this would mean that the three months' stay in Greece could hardly be earlier than the winter of 54–55. The latest date possible for the supersession of Felix would seem to be 61. This is the date defended by Eduard Meyer; but it is far from commanding universal assent.[5] Meyer places the three months' stay in Greece in the winter of 58–59, which is as late as it can well be put. Within those limits, then, late 54– early 59, the composition of Romans must fall. There seems to be a slight balance of probability in favor of the earlier end of this period.

But the real problems concerning Romans have not to do with date or place of origin but with destination. Put in its simplest form the question is this: Is the Epistle to the Romans, in the form in which it appears

---

[4]Rom. 15:23ff., 28.

[5]Meyer, *Ursprung und Anfänge*, 3.51–54. Cf. *BC* 5.464–67, for a statement of the case for the date 55.

in our Bibles, from 1:1 to 16:27, a single composition made by St. Paul expressly for the Christian community in Rome and sent to them entire and complete as it now stands? Of course this general question only arises because a number of particular questions have emerged in the course of detailed study of the text of the document. They are concerned mainly with the first and the last two chapters.

The first seventeen verses of chapter 1 form the longest and most elaborate introduction to any Pauline epistle. We have first the prescript, a single sentence extending over seven verses (1–7) heavily encrusted with doctrinal embellishments, so that it becomes a miniature exposition of the Faith in itself. Then comes a second long passage (8–17) forming the transition from the prescript to the first main theme of the epistle. In both prescript and transition passage we have explicit mention of Rome. In verse 7, which forms the second item of the prescript formula, we read *pasi tois ousin en Rōmē agapētois theou, klētois hagiois.* In verse 15 Paul expresses his readiness *kai hymin tois en Rōmē euangelisasthai.* These clear references to Rome are supported by the great mass of the MSS and other witnesses to the text; but there are a few dissentient voices. In 1:7 we have the variant *pasi tois ousin en agapē theou* offered by the Graeco-Latin MS G. The Latin of G (g) supports this reading in the omission of the reference to Rome, and offers alternative renderings of *agapē: in caritate uel dilectione dei.* The omission of *Rōmē* is also attested by a marginal note in MS 1908 stating: *tou en Rōmē oute en te exēgēsei oute en tō rhētō mnēmoneuei.* That is, somebody who has written a commentary on Romans does not mention the words "in Rome" either in his exposition or in the text which he expounds. This commentator appears to have been Origen. The first stage of the corruption of the text is, then, the substitution of "all who are in the love of God" for "all who are at Rome, beloved of God." The next stage is the attempt to restore the reference to Rome in the corrupted text. This takes two forms: *(a) omnibus qui sunt Romae in caritate dei,* the reading of two Vulgate MSS, Fuldensis and Langobardus, of Pelagius,[6] perhaps also of Ambrosiaster, and of the Latin side (d) of Codex Claromontanus;[7] *(b) omnibus qui sunt Romae in dilectione dei,* the reading of the two Vulgate MSS Amiatinus and Ardmachanus.[8] These are rather obvious attempts to repair the damage that had been done when the refer-

---

[6]Souter, *Pelagius's Expositions,* 9.

[7]On this cf. Vogels, *Amicitiae Corolla,* 283. "Das Wort *romae* ist in einem Vorgänger von d eingefugt worden."

[8]On *dilectio* and *caritas* as renderings of *agapē* see v. Soden, *Das Lat. N.T. Afrika z. Z. Cyprians,* 67ff. He points out that *dilectio* is the regular rendering in Tertullian and probably the earlier of the two in African use. It also seems to be the first choice, *caritas* being used in many cases merely for variety. On the other hand, in the Vulgate *caritas* is the normal rendering in all N.T. books except the Fourth Gospel, which has *dilectio.* In a later study, *Der lat. Paulustext bei Marcion und Tertullian,* in *Festgabe für Adolf Jülicher,* he shows (249) that the Latin version of Marcion's *Apostolikon* translated *agapē* by *dilectio.*

ence to Rome was cut out. In 1:15 G again omits the reference to Rome by dropping *tois en Rōmē*, and in this it is supported by its Latin side (*g*) which omits *qui Romae estis*. In D and *d* we get the following text:

> *kai en hymin en Rōmē euangelisasthai* | *et in uobis in Roma euangelizare.*

Here again we have what appears to be patchwork.[9] These repairs in D*d* go back to the sixth century, which is the date of the MS, and were probably already made in an ancestor of the MS. These and other facts mean, as Corssen[10] showed, that the three bilingual MSS DFG should be regarded as descendants of a common ancestor from which the references to Rome in chapter 1 were absent.

Three conclusions follow from the examination of the text of Rom. 1:1–17: (a) that the omission of the references to Rome is ancient; (b) that it is wrong—the context, particularly verses 8–17, imperatively demands a particular reference to a well-known community not founded by Paul or hitherto visited by him; (c) that we have to do not with accidental loss but with deliberate excision—if "in Rome" were missing in verse 7 or verse 15 it might be accident; but its absence in both places strongly suggests design. But who, it may be asked, would want to cut out the Roman address, and why? One answer, which has received considerable and I think undeserved acceptance is that the object was to turn a particular epistle into a general epistle; by removing the local reference, to make the document more catholic.[11] In support of this view appeal is made to the Muratorian Canon; but that document gives no real support: all it says is that letters addressed to individual churches have a message for the universal church, of which it is said *una tamen per omnem orbem terrae ecclesia diffusa esse dignoscatur* (11.55ff.). Furthermore the theory does not explain why the generalizing process was applied only to Romans, and possibly Ephesians, while all the other Pauline letters are left in their scandalous particularity.

The case of the letter to the Ephesians may or may not be relevant: it should, however, be briefly noticed at this point. Here we have another case where the textual authorities do not agree about the address of the letter. The great mass of the witnesses, including the versions, favor Ephesus as the destination. The minority is divided. On the one side P[46]B*ℵ*, the corrector of 424, Origen, and Basil omit any local reference: on the other the Marcionite *Apostolikon* contains the epistle under the title "To the Laodiceans."[12] Of these three possibilities it may be said that "Ephesus" is probably wrong—the internal evidence of the epistle is against it—and probably

---

[9]See Vogels, *Amicitiae Corolla*, 283f.

[10]Corssen, "Überlieferungsgeschichte," 1–45, 97–102.

[11]See, for example, Wendland, *HBNT, I.* 3, 351 n. 3. Lietzmann, *An die Römer,* 27.

[12]There is a careful discussion of this problem by E. Percy in his *Die Probleme der Kolosser- und Epheserbriefe,* 449–66.

very early, seeing that it appears in all the versions. Secondly the authorities for the omission of a place-name are in the main Alexandrian: the earliest of them, Origen and P[46], take us back to the third century. Thirdly the Marcionite address to the Laodiceans goes back at least to the second century. We are left with questions to which no certain answers can be given. Is the omission of a place-name a piece of higher criticism by someone who saw the objections to "Ephesus" (or "Laodicea"), or is it the primitive text (and so probably evidence that Ephesians was a circular letter)? Is "Ephesians" a very early bad guess or does it reflect the fact that the circular letter ended its travels at Ephesus? What had Marcion before him? Did he displace "Ephesus" in favor of "Laodicea"? Or fill in a blank space with "Laodicea"? Or was "Laodicea" already there?

We do not know, but we may try to guess. My guess, for what it is worth, starts from the fact that these problems of address are peculiar to Romans and Ephesians, and that it is at Rome and Ephesus that Marcion received two great and humiliating rebuffs. It is conceivable that Marcion may have considered that the two churches that had contemptuously rejected the one man who really understood St. Paul had thereby forfeited their status as recipients of a letter from the Apostle. This is no more than a conjecture; and it is time now to turn to the consideration of other factors in the problem of Romans. In view, however, of the fact that so many of the clues lead back to Marcion, it may be worthwhile to keep the conjecture in mind.

The second main group of problems is concerned with the last two chapters of Romans. On these, a very full and careful statement of the progress of research down to 1929 was given by Schumacher.[13] The fact that there is a problem was perceived as early as the eighteenth century by Semler; and the debate has continued ever since. Since Schumacher wrote matters have been further complicated by the discovery of the Chester Beatty Papyrus of the Pauline Epistle (P[46]), and my chief concern is to reconsider the problem of the last two chapters in the light of the new evidence furnished by P[46]. We may begin by setting out the essential facts.

First, the structure of the Epistle. After the prescript (1:1-7) and the transition paragraph (1:8-17), both of which we have already discussed, we come to the first main topic, Judaism and Christianity, which occupies 1:18-11:36 and concludes with a doxology (vv. 33-36). This is followed by the second main section dealing with practical problems of Christian ethics. This extends from 12:1 to 15:13, and is concluded by a benediction (v. 13). The remainder of chapter 15, verses 14-33, is occupied with personal matters, details of Paul's missionary activity in the past and his plans for the future. It is clearly addressed to the Roman community, and it ends with a short benediction (v. 33). Chapter 16 begins with a commendation

---

[13]Schumacher, *Kapitel.*

of one Phoebe, deaconess in the church at Cenchreae near Corinth (vv. 1–2). Verses 3–16 and 21–23 are taken up with greetings to various named persons and greetings from others. The two sets of greetings are separated by a passage in which the recipients are solemnly warned against false teachers. This passage seems to presuppose some personal acquaintance of the Apostle with those to whom it is addressed. It closes with a blessing (v. 20b) whose position is not certain. It appears in the MS tradition in three places: here at the end of the warning passage; as verse 24 after the second list of greetings; and, finally, after the doxology (vv. 25–27). Along with the varying positions go slight differences of wording. Without attempting at the moment to solve the problem of the proper place of this last benediction it may be remarked that these numerous full closes occur in the places where we should expect to find them: 11:33–36; 15:13, 33; and 16:20 or 24 or 27. Whatever views we may hold about the unity of the document, these are the logical places for major pauses.

But this sensible and natural division is crossed by another, which has left its mark in the textual tradition of the epistle. This second system is marked by the position of the final doxology *tō de dynamenō hymas stērizai.* . . . *hō hē doxa eis tous aiōnas amēn.* It is widely held that this doxology is an interpolation originating in Marcionite circles, though not the work of Marcion himself. With this opinion I am inclined to agree. But whether it be genuine or not, it seems to be intended as the concluding word of the text. Now this doxology appears in three different places in the textual tradition of Romans: at the end of chapters 14, 15, and 16. In two of these cases it comes where there is a real full close already in the text, namely after 15:33, at the end of the personal statement to the Roman community; and at the close of the second set of greetings in chapter 16. The position after 15:33 is attested by the Chester Beatty Codex, P[46], the first and, so far, the only witness to this position. The position at the end of 16 is supported by the leading Alexandrian MSS ℵBC as well as by the Sahidic and Bohairic versions, the Vulgate, the Peshitta, the Latin version of Origen's commentary and the Athos MS (1739) based on the Greek Origen, Ambrosiaster, and Pelagius. The position at the end of chapter 14 is supported by the common run of later (Byzantine) MSS along with L, the Harklean Syriac, the Gothic, Chrysostom, and Theodoret. The essence of this position is that it is not one of the natural logical pauses in the epistle. The insertion of the doxology after 14:23 produces a break in the continuity of the text. It is very unlikely that any thinking person with the complete text of Romans as far as 15:13 before him would have thought of putting the doxology at 14:23. The natural inference is that when the doxology was attached to 14:23, it was attached to a form of the text which ended at that point.

This conclusion is confirmed by other pieces of evidence. There is first the table of contents in the Codex Amiatinus of the Vulgate. This divides the epistle into fifty-one sections of which the fiftieth quite clearly refers to the last paragraph of chapter 14 (vv. 13–33), and the fifty-first to the doxology. This capitulation is older than the MS in which it appears; for this MS gives the complete text of Romans with the doxology at the end of chapter 16. Again in the Codex Fuldensis of the Vulgate we have an even more remarkable capitulation, or rather one and a half capitulations. The first one covers chapters 1 to 14 in twenty-three sections: it implies probably a form of the text from which the last two chapters were absent. It tells us nothing about the doxology. Having covered fourteen chapters in this way in twenty-three sections, the capitulation now goes back to the beginning of chapter 9 and gives sections 24 to 51 of the capitulation of Amiatinus. To the evidence of these tables we can add that of three MSS of the Vulgate—in Gregory's notation 1648 and 1792 (both in Munich) and 2089 (of the Monza Chapter Library). In these the text ends at 14:23 and is followed by a short benediction and the doxology. It is to be noted that this is all Latin evidence.[14]

To this we can add some further facts and inferences. It is a fact that the Graeco-Latin MS G does not have the doxology in any of the three places; and it is practically certain from the researches of Corssen that the ancestor from which DFG all descend did not have the doxology anywhere. Corssen has also made it probable that this ancestor of DFG, which he calls Z, had a "Western" text in chapters 1–14, and one with a considerable number of peculiar readings in the last two chapters. From this fact he inferred that behind Z lay a MS which had the short text of Romans (1–14) without the doxology.

How did it come about that a text ending at 14:23 existed? It cannot be the work of the author; for he would not have cut the text in the middle of an argument, and he himself shows that the proper place for a cut would be at 15:13. We must suppose that some other hand was responsible; and we are not left to guess whose hand it was. We have the direct assertion of Origen that it was Marcion who cut the last two chapters of Romans.[15] Tertullian can also be called as a witness that Marcion's text of Romans ended at 14:23 or thereabouts. Origen quotes 14:23 and tells us that Marcion from that point *usque ad finem cuncta dissecuit*. How much is *cuncta*? No doubt for Origen it meant the whole of the last two chapters, for he was acquainted with a text of Romans similar in extent to that in our Bibles. It was natural to assume that the difference between the text known to Origen and the text of Marcion represented the extent of Marcion's cut. But it is not at all certain that the text on which Marcion operated was

---

[14]The Capitulations are printed in full in the great Oxford edition of the Vulgate New Testament, vol. 2, 44–61. For the details regarding the three MSS of the Vulgate see Schumacher, *Kapitel*, 15.

[15]For the text of Origen and a full discussion of its interpretation see Schumacher, *Kapitel*, 3–10.

Origen's text. The fact is that we know what was left when Marcion had finished his work on Romans: we can only guess what was there when he started. Harnack was of the opinion that at this point Marcion had before him a text from which the last two chapters were already absent.[16] This seems to me to be very unlikely.

The whole question is set in a new light by the publication of the third century Codex of the Pauline Epistles (P[46]).[17] Here we have the oldest Greek MS of Paul; and it gives the doxology at the end of chapter 15, that is, at the end of the personal notes addressed to the Roman church. The clear implication is that there was once—at an earlier date than the date of P[46]—a form of the text which omitted chapter 16.

Now more than a century before the discovery of P[46] the hypothesis had been put forward by David Schulz that Rom. 16 is no part of what St. Paul wrote to Rome but is a fragment of a Pauline letter to the Ephesian church.[18] This hypothesis had been accepted on internal grounds by many scholars; but it remained a conjecture unsupported by MS evidence. Now the required testimony was provided by the oldest known MS of the Epistles. The natural inference to be drawn is that we are here in the presence of the form of text that was sent to Rome in the first instance. But, if Harnack is right, "Marcion did not edit his Apostolikon in Pontus or Asia, but in the west. The text that lay before him was thus the text of the Roman community shortly before the middle of the second century."[19] In that case we are justified in supposing that what Marcion removed from the text of Romans was what we now know as chapter 15. Chapter 16 he could not touch, for it was not there; it formed no part of the text known at Rome in the second century. This view is consistent with the evidence from western patristic sources. We have no quotation from Rom. 15–16, in Irenaeus, Tertullian, or Cyprian. There is, however, an indication in the Muratorian Canon which suggests a possible acquaintance with Rom. 15. There an explanation is being offered of the absence of any account in Acts of St. Paul's missionary journey to Spain. The explanation is not that it did not take place, but that Luke was not present when the Apostle set out, and therefore did not report the departure. The point is that the Muratorianum uses the uncommon form Spania instead

---

[16]Harnack, *Marcion*, 145*f.

[17]This MS belongs in part to Mr. Chester Beatty and in part to the University of Michigan. The part of Romans that concerns us is in the Michigan portion. It was published by Professor H. A. Sanders in 1935 (*A Third-century Papyrus Codex of the Epistles of Paul*). Plate III of this edition gives a facsimile of the page containing Rom. 15:30–33; Doxology; 16:1–3. The complete text of the Pauline corpus as given by the Michigan and Chester Beatty leaves was published by Sir Frederic Kenyon in 1936. (*The Chester Beatty Biblical Papyri. Fasc. III Supplement. Pauline Epistles.*)

[18]Schumacher, *Kapitel*, 63. He gives the reference to *Theol. Studien und Kritiken*, 1829, 609ff.

[19]Harnack, *Marcion*, 127*.

of Hispania, and that *Spania* is the word used by Paul in 15:24 and 28 in describing the plans for his future activities.

On the assumption that Marcion removed chapter 15, and that only, we have to attempt to discover some motive for the excision. Here I venture to suggest that the same motive that I have already put forward to explain the removal of local references in Rom. 1:7, 15 and Eph. 1:1, will serve to explain the removal of the personalia in Rom. 15:14–33. It remains to find a reason for breaking off at 14:23 the argument which runs naturally on to 15:13. If we may judge from Marcion's treatment of other parts of Romans, particularly his omission of chapter 4, with its detailed appeal to the Old Testament story of Abraham, and of most of chapters 9–11, with their frequent appeals to the Old Testament, we may perhaps suppose that he found the repeated quotations of Old Testament texts in 15:1–13 uncongenial, as well as the idea (15:4) that "whatsoever things were written aforetime were written for our learning, that through patience and through comfort of the scriptures we might have hope." Moreover, it may be considered that from the Marcionite point of view the statement of 14:23 that "whatever is not of faith is sin" makes a more decisive conclusion to the argument than anything the Pauline continuation can offer.

If the argument up to this point is sound certain conclusions seem to follow, which are not without importance for the textual criticism of the Pauline epistles. First of all we must regard all MSS which present the doxology after 14:23 as at least open to the suspicion of having a Marcionite streak in their ancestry.[20] This may seem to be a surprising conclusion in view of the fact that so many of these MSS belong to the Byzantine or Koine group. We must, however, bear in mind that in many cases the streak in question may be no more than the insertion of the doxology at that point. Further, as the major part of Marcion's activity consisted in excisions, it is quite possible that a text originally Marcionite, in the process of having its omissions supplied, might also be revised in other respects

---

[20]I should add that where, as is probably the case in the ancestor of DFG, we have a text ending at 14:33 without the doxology, we have have a very early form of the text, as it was current in Rome in the second century. In this connexion it is significant that P46, which I regard as the primary witness for the Roman form of the Greek text of Romans in chapters 1–15, shows a far higher degree of agreement with DFG against אABC in Romans than in any other Epistle. The figures as worked out by Sir F. Kenyon are given in the following table:

	P46 with אABC	With DFG
Rom.	89	51
Heb.	79	20
1 Cor.	143	29
2 Cor.	60	11
Eph.	47	5
Gal.	40	5
Phil.	23	6
Col.	20	3

and so brought into closer agreement with a different type of text. It has also to be remembered that at the time when Marcion was active the number of MSS of the Pauline corpus was small, and probably very small. Consequently his Apostolikon may easily have been the source from which many copies were taken simply because there was no other text available.

The second conclusion is that we should regard P^{46} as offering in chapters 1–15 the form in which the epistle was received at Rome; and, what is perhaps more important, its text should be taken as descended from the pre–Marcionite Roman text of the letter. It may not be a very pure example of the text. It has suffered the interpolation of the doxology and the addition of chapter 16. But at any rate it has a pre–Marcionite Roman base. This makes it a very important and valuable witness.

Thirdly we should note that P^{46} has chapter 16 attached after the doxology. In view of the fact that P^{46} comes from Egypt, and that it is the Alexandrian textual witnesses that testify to the longest form of text by having the doxology at the end of chapter 16, and further that our earliest patristic writer to show certain knowledge of chapter 16 is Clement of Alexandria, it may be permissible to guess that this last chapter was added to the pre–Marcionite Roman text underlying P^{46} in Egypt. In favor of such a hypothesis it may be noted that the text of chapter 16 in P^{46} seems to stand nearer to the B type than does the text of other chapters of the epistle.

So much for the text. What can be deduced from these facts about the history of the letter? The first thing that emerges is that in the second half of the second century the document was circulating in three forms: the Marcionite, which had no reference to Rome and ended at 14:23; the Roman, which ended at 15:33; and the full text of sixteen chapters which was in circulation in Egypt and was known to Clement of Alexandria. It is our view that Marcion produced his text from the Roman by the removal of chapter 15 and of the references to Rome in 1:7 and 15. If we eliminate Marcion from the reckoning we are left with two forms of text: a Roman of fifteen chapters and an Egyptian of sixteen. Our problem is to account for the existence of these two types of text. It is here that the hypothesis that chapter 16 is a letter, or part of a letter, to Ephesus comes in.

This hypothesis had been the subject of much debate from its first suggestion by David Schulz in 1829. It is not necessary to go over all the ground again. The arguments are stated in the Introductions to the New Testament and the commentaries on Romans.[21] The major points are that chapter 16 contains a large number of greetings to Paul's friends. It is unlikely that he had so many personal friends—some of them intimate

---

[21]For a clear and fair statement of the case before P^{46} came on the scene, see Dodd, *Romans*, xvii–xxlv.

friends—in the Roman church which he had never visited. Further, those in the list, who are otherwise known, are connected with Asia and Ephesus. Again the exhortations in 16:17–20 read very oddly if they are taken to be addressed to a church to which Paul was a stranger: they are very natural things to say to a community in which he had worked for several years. On the other side comes Lietzmann's acid comment on the theory that Rom. 16 is a letter to Ephesus: "A letter consisting almost entirely of nothing but greetings . . . is a monstrosity."[22] There is further the fact that a detailed study of the names in chapter 16 leads to the conclusion that they *could* have been the names of members of the Roman church in the first century. Professor Dodd concluded (p. xxiv) "It is clear that the arguments for Rome and Ephesus respectively come far short of proof one way or the other. As the burden of proof rests upon those who would set aside the tradition in favor of a conjecture, we may be content to accept chap. xvi (except the doxology) as an integral part of the epistle."

That was certainly a fair summing up of the argument in 1932. In 1935, however, came the new evidence of P[46] to set the whole matter in a new light. The position of the doxology in this MS was a clear enough indication that Romans had once existed in a form which ended where the upholders of the Ephesian theory said it ought to end. They could now buttress their conjecture by the evidence of the earliest known MS of the Pauline corpus. This means that the Ephesian theory now has a stronger claim than ever before to the most serious consideration. Suppose that it is true.

We must then suppose that Paul prepared a letter (Rom. 1–15) and sent it to Rome. At the same time a copy was prepared to be sent to Ephesus. It may be assumed that this Ephesian copy would include the personalia of Rom. 15:14–33; for these, though primarily intended for the Roman church, nevertheless contained information about Paul's plans which would certainly be of interest to the Apostle's friends in Ephesus. As all this was given in 1–15 it was unnecessary to say much more in the added paragraphs. Consequently all that we have in chapter 16 is an introduction to Phoebe, who may be regarded as the bearer of the letter to Ephesus; the greetings to Paul's friends in the province of Asia; and the exhortation of verses 17–20, which has points of contact with Paul's address to the Ephesian elders at Miletus.[23] Any further information that was asked for at Ephesus could doubtless be supplied verbally by the bearer of the letter.[24] Naturally the covering note (16) and the Roman letter (1–15) were associated from the beginning and presumably they formed a single document, which was preserved as such in the archives of the Ephesian

---

[22]Lietzmann, *An die Römer*[3], 29.

[23]Acts 20:17–38. Compare Rom. 16:17f. with Acts 20:29–32.

[24]Such verbal supplements to the written document are contemplated in Col. 4:7ff. and Eph. 6:21ff.

community. From Ephesus copies reached Egypt at an early date, and the sixteen chapters were well-known to Clement of Alexandria as well as to the translators of the Sahidic version.[25]

Meanwhile the Roman letter (1–15) made its way to its destination. It was doubtless preserved in the archives of the Roman church, and a copy of it may have been known to the author of the Muratorian Canon. From this Roman text Marcion, in the first half of the second century, prepared his text ending at 14:23. This became the standard text of the Marcionite communities, which were strongest and survived longest in Syria.[26]

The rest of the history of the text is concerned largely with the intermixture of these types of text. P^{46} itself is one of the earliest examples: a Roman text supplemented from the Ephesian text current in Egypt. Another mixture is represented by AP 533 where the doxology appears in the Marcionite position and the Ephesian.

Returning now to Paul at Corinth, we may ask one final question concerning the motive for the writing of the letter. So long as the letter was thought of as a simple letter to Rome the obvious answer to the question was to the effect that it was a rather elaborate and detailed statement of faith offered by the Apostle as evidence on which the Roman church might give him a friendly reception and set him forward on his Spanish missionary enterprise. But this answer needs reconsideration in the light of the conclusions so far reached in our discussion. It seems to me that we must begin from the facts (a) that the text of Romans was produced at Corinth, and (b) that it was sent both to Rome and to Ephesus.

(a) With regard to the Corinthian origin, we have to note that the document was produced immediately after the close of a period of bitter and violent controversy over matters affecting the church at Corinth and the churches of Galatia, and in all probability the Macedonian churches too. The central issue in this controversy was that of the relation between Judaism and Christianity, law and gospel. This issue is hotly debated in Galatians and in Philippians 3, more calmly in 2 Cor. 3–6 and finally it is discussed at length in a careful and judicial way in the first eleven chapters of Romans. These chapters may fairly be regarded as Paul's considered judgement on the whole issue. Now when we turn to the text of these chapters and study the argument in detail it is difficult to avoid the impression that we have here the report of a real debate. Again and again Paul is answering objections and meeting criticisms of his position. Are

---

[25]For this transmission of Christian material from Asia to Egypt we have striking evidence in the John Rylands Library. The Rylands fragment of John (P. Ryl. Gk. 457) is proof that the Ephesian Gospel had reached Egypt within a few decades of its composition; and this evidence is confirmed by the British Museum papyrus, P. Egerton 2, containing a fragment of an apocryphal gospel, which clearly is dependent on John, and equally clearly was in existence within a few decades of the composition of John.

[26]It may be noted that it is in this area that evidence is strongest for the existence of the doxology in what may be called the Marcionite position, after 14:23.

these imaginary objections and hypothetical criticisms? Or are they points which were actually made in real debate? I am inclined to think that we have here a record made by Paul and his clerical helpers of a real discussion. The order and arrangement of the account is probably Paul's own; but the materials used in putting it together may well have come in large part from the actual debate.

This impression is confirmed when we turn to the sections dealing with Christian practice (12:1–15:13). Chapter 12 takes up the question of unity within the church and stresses afresh the organic conception of the Christian community, a very necessary idea at Corinth where the church had been rent by party divisions. Chapter 13:1–10 deals with the relation of the church to the civil power, a matter that had arisen in another connexion in 1 Cor. 6. Chapter 13:11–14 touches on matters dealt with at greater length in 1 Cor. 15. And finally 14:1–15:13 rediscusses the problems which were earlier considered in 1 Cor. 8–10.

(b) These facts seem to me to lead to the conclusion that we should think of our document primarily as the summing up of the positions reached by Paul and his friends at the end of the long controversy whose beginnings appear in 1 Corinthians and—if the Ephesian dating of Philippians is, as I think it is, right—in Philippians 3. Having got this statement worked out to his own satisfaction, Paul then decided to send a copy of it to his friends in Ephesus, which he did not intend to visit on his way to Jerusalem (Acts 20:16). This copy would be available for the information of all the churches in Asia. At the same time he conceived the idea of sending a copy to Rome with a statement of his future plans. It might be permissible to guess that a written record may have remained in Corinth, though that, I think, is not necessary on the assumption that the substance of what is now in Romans had been gone over in discussion with the members of the Corinthian community. The situation then is that the Corinthian church has had the Apostle's summing up by word of mouth; the church in Syria and Palestine may expect to hear it in the same way in the near future. The church in the province of Asia and the church in Rome will receive it in writing. Looked at in this way Romans ceases to be just a letter of self-introduction from Paul to the Roman church, and becomes a manifesto setting forth his deepest convictions on central issues, a manifesto calling for the widest publicity, which the Apostle did his best—not without success—to give it.

2

THE LETTER TO THE ROMANS AS PAUL'S LAST WILL AND TESTAMENT

Günther Bornkamm

The purpose of this paper is to set forth an answer to the question of the character and peculiarity of the letter to the Romans. First of all, it is necessary to begin with a discussion of the historical situation in which Paul wrote this greatest and most significant of his letters. As is known, the date of this missive can be determined quite accurately—at least within the limits of a relative chronology of Paul's life. More difficult however is the question of the occasion and purpose of the letter. Right up to the present day, there is no widespread agreement on this matter.

I. The Historical Situation

Paul wrote this letter, according to his own declaration in the fifteenth chapter, in that very meaningful moment when he had terminated his missionary enterprise in the eastern half of the Roman Empire (15:19). Now at long last the Apostle was able to set about the task of materializing his long-intended plan to visit Rome and from there to advance even further westward to Spain and the boundaries of the civilized world (15:24–28). First, however, as he himself wrote, it is imperative for him to bear to Jerusalem the offering which was carefully collected in his congregations. For this journey to which he looks forward very hesitatingly and with some concern, he entreats the prayer of the Christians in Rome (15:30ff.). And after a hopefully speedy and happy conclusion to this journey to Jerusalem, he will come to them and they are to send him on his way to Spain (15:24). Since this statement of situation concurs with a brief note found in Acts 20:2f., we can say with certainty that the letter to the Romans was written during Paul's final, three-months stay in Greece, very likely in Corinth in the winter of A.D. 55/56.

Thus, at any rate, even Rome is not supposed to be the final goal of the Apostle, but only a temporary pause and a base for his subsequent work. Therefore Paul prepares the church in Rome for his visit and with his letter engages them in his missionary service. Yet he is not personally acquainted with this congregation; all he knows is that people everywhere are talking about the faith of the Christians in Rome (1:8). This makes it all the more urgent that this church become acquainted with him and that its members participate in his destiny by preparing themselves for the assistance they will have to render him later.

It is behind these few well-known facts that the real questions now appear. Why does the Apostle speak with uneasiness and concern about his forthcoming trip to Jerusalem? In Rom. 15:30f. he states that he fears persecution at the hands of the Jews. And not only that! He is not at all certain that the Jerusalem church is going to accept the offering of the Gentile-Christian congregations. Therefore, he requests the Christians in Rome to join him in praying that he be spared from this threatening danger and that he be not rejected by the "saints" in Jerusalem.

To a certain degree we can conjecture what caused these fears of the Apostle. After his conversion Paul certainly did not remain unknown to the Jews and Jewish-Christians in Jerusalem. The Jews knew him previously as a leading Pharisee and persecutor of the Christian church and had now heard enough about his work among the Gentiles. Thus, at least the Jews regarded him as an apostate, a destroyer of the law and an enemy of God. As we know from the Book of Acts, the impending dangers from the Jews had already shown themselves at the time of his departure from Corinth. From Acts 20:3 we hear that the Jews were plotting against him, so that it became necessary for him to choose for himself and his companions the land route over Macedonia instead of the sea route. Only after he had reached Troas did he embark on a ship.

He had to reckon especially, however, with persecution in Jerusalem by the Jews. Yet if he had to anticipate such difficulties at their hands, why did he expose himself to these dangers? Would he not have done better to let the delegates of his congregations travel to Jerusalem alone while he himself immediately began his western trip to Rome and Spain? Would not the delivery of the collection have been less endangered without Paul's participation in the journey? Certainly the members of the delegation, selected by their congregations, enumerated by name in Acts 20:4, were reliable persons and surely unknown to the Jews. Therefore, it is safe to assume that they would not have aroused the hatred of the Jews in the same degree that Paul would. But Paul did not choose this less dangerous way. He did not want to withdraw himself from the perilous conflicts along the way and at Jerusalem. Why?

Considering these questions we have to realize that Paul could not understand his commission on this journey in terms of the function of a postman. Rather he had to meet the congregation in Jerusalem and its leaders personally. Why, however, had Paul to fear such intense struggles with the Christians there and why just at the occasion of the delivery of his collection? We know from Gal. 2:10 that the collection of the Gentile churches belonged to the agreement of the Apostolic Council in Jerusalem many years before. We know also how carefully Paul carried out this obligation during the later period in his missionary work in Asia, Macedonia and Greece. And the great efforts in Paul's last journey as well as the many delegates prove that the collection must have been quite a large sum. This is surprising! Can you imagine a president of a theological seminary, returning with such a collection, or a minister, fearing and wondering on the way to the General Assembly of his church, whether such a service will be acceptable?

We are to conclude from this that the meaning of this collection was a controversial issue between Paul and the Jewish Christians in Jerusalem. This collection undoubtedly meant more to Paul and his companions than mere material charitable assistance. It was intended to demonstrate the unity of Jews and Gentiles in the church. But at the same time it was to a large degree questionable whether the Jerusalem church under James would let itself become a part of such a demonstration. From that we recognize that this collection was closely associated with the old question contested already at the Apostolic Council in Jerusalem, that is, whether the gospel free from the law can be legitimate and whether the Gentile Christians can be recognized as members of equal rank in the church as a whole. The truth and freedom of the gospel and the unity of the church in the whole world thus led Paul to Jerusalem once again and for the last time. Also, as at the time of the Apostolic Council (Gal. 2:2) Paul by no means wanted to begin his new missionary stage in Rome and Spain on his own account as a freelancer, without the support of the mother church in Jerusalem.

Everything that we have said so far is based on the information contained in the letter to the Romans, chapter 15:14–33 and chapter 1:1–15, and all of it concerns Paul himself. But we are also accustomed to determine the historical context of a letter in consideration of the congregation to which it is addressed. For this reason scholars have wanted to relate the special thematic construction of Romans to particular situations, groups, questions and controversies in Rome. Right up to our own days great effort has been applied to the construction of a most exact picture of the state of affairs in this congregation. In this case, however, the task is especially difficult, because of the well-known fact, that the congregation was not founded by Paul and because its beginnings and conditions at that time remain in the dark.

All that we can say is that the gospel was apparently brought to the capital city at a very early date by unknown Christians and not by any famous apostle. This should not be forgotten because it was precisely the church in Rome which later boasted in a special way of its apostolic tradition. It is possible although not proven, that the new proclamation of Christ caused a disturbance among the Roman Jews and that this fact stands in some sort of relation to the edict of the Emperor Claudius (A.D. 49). According to Acts 18:2, it was as a consequence of this that Aquila and Priscilla were forced to leave Rome and to emigrate to Corinth. Yet the letter to the Romans mentions nothing about this, and at the time of its composition the church had certainly been predominantly Gentile Christian for a long time.

Here, however, our question must be: what did Paul know about the church in Rome and in what degree did he concern himself in his letter with definite circumstances there? Several recent scholars have proposed that there were two factions in Rome, on the one side the Judaizers, who retained the law and circumcision, and on the other side spiritualizing antinomians. It is in view of the former, so it is thought, that Paul in Romans considers so fully his teaching on the law and salvation by faith. In opposition to the other group, according to this opinion, are those sections in the letter, in which the Apostle makes exhortations to a life in obedience, to love, and to subordination to state authorities. A lively discussion has been carried on especially about the "strong" and the "weak," two rival groups in Romans 14 and 15, because these chapters appear to relate themselves most clearly to definite controversies in Rome.

An interesting nuance to the problem has been contributed by H. Lietzmann. He has presented the hypothesis that Peter was already in Rome at an early date and was urging the church there to form an opposition against Paul and his gospel free from the law. Just for this reason Paul had to consider the question of law and justification in this letter. Yet this conjecture is in no way convincing, and for the following reasons. First of all, the assumption of such early activity of Peter in Rome is purely hypothetical. Second, Paul would not have hesitated to use Peter's name publicly as he did in Gal. 2. Third, Peter would clearly then have broken the agreement to which he had consented at the Apostolic Council in Jerusalem (Gal. 2).

We need not here discuss in detail these and similar theories about the condition of the Roman church at that time. For one fact speaks against all such hypotheses. In Romans Paul never mentions a thing about any sort of information which he has received from Rome, and nowhere does he name any informants, as is the case in the other letters. Certainly the Apostle knew something about the Roman church. But it is probable that at the time of his first journey through Asia, Macedonia, and Greece (Acts 16–18) from Galatia via Philippi and Thessalonica some years before, Paul did not know anything about the Christian community in Rome. In his plans to go to Rome, which he was beginning to realize, presumably at that time, he was surely operating on the basis of his own missionary principle not to preach wherever the name of Christ had been previously proclaimed. When Paul did write the letter to the Romans in Corinth some years later, he had surely gained a most general knowledge of the Roman church without details or individual features; for the personal references and allusions to the conditions in this congregation, otherwise so characteristic of Pauline letters, are lacking here.

It is therefore in no way correct to settle on the presence of Judaistic or libertine opponents wherever Paul speaks polemically or in dialog. This belongs to his customary manner and method of argumentation which we also recognize in the so-called Hellenistic Diatribe. Thus Paul handles his hearers and listeners as partners in a conversation and allows himself to be presented with objections and counter-questions from them. Important not only for style but especially for the subject matter is the fact that these objections are always formulated from the standpoint of a commonly accepted, yet perhaps hazardous logic. This, as in Romans, may be from the standpoint of the Jew who must hold the Pauline teaching of law and justification as blasphemous, or also, as in Romans 11, from the standpoint of the Gentile Christian who proudly exalts himself above the non-believing and rejected Jewish people.

But these objections always arise out of the subject, or more accurately, out of a misunderstanding of the subject. In no way do they demand an appeal to particular groups or opponents in Rome. How much this concrete background is really lacking in the letter to the Romans is shown in the section which most readily allows certain inferences about conditions in the Roman church, namely, chapters 14 and 15, and their discussion of the strong and the weak. If one compares these chapters with the similar section in 1 Cor. 8–10, then the difference can be seen immediately. In 1 Corinthians we recognize the historical background most clearly. We hear about spiritualizers who boast of their knowledge and their freedom; we hear also about others whose knowledge and conscience are weak. The concrete problems are clearly named: may a Christian buy meat offered to idols at the market? May he participate in heathen cult festivities?

All of this has no parallel in Romans 14 and 15. Admittedly the quarrelling groups are also characterized here, and we learn that the people either mutually judged or despised each other. Yet, it is not accidental that up to now, unified and exact answers to the identification of these groups have not been given. On the basis of these observations I think we should have reservations about looking to the Roman church as the reason for the exceptional content in the letter to the Romans. What we have established has shown that we are on the wrong track with the questions about the actual conditions of the church in Rome. We shall not find the solution to the problem of the historical context of Romans by following this path. One makes much more progress with other observations and considerations.

The fact is noteworthy that most of the themes and motifs of this letter are found already to a great extent in the earlier letters of Paul, especially in Galatians, the Corinthian correspondence and Philippians (which many scholars today properly consider to have been written in Ephesus). Thus, the letter to the Romans clearly reflects previous questions and perceptions arising out of stirring conflicts in the years directly preceding its composition. From this we can draw the following conclusion about the historical context of Romans. As all other letters of Paul, this letter, too, is thoroughly related to the real historical circumstances out of which it has arisen. It is, thus, not a timeless theological treatise, a textbook of Paul's dogmatics, which accidentally happens to be clothed in the form of a letter. Yet we must not look to the Christians in Rome, whom the Apostle had before him as he wrote, for the individual features of this real history, but rather to the history which lay behind Paul and the churches he had established.

At this point I would like to discuss an interesting and instructive essay by T. W. Manson, entitled "The Letter to the Romans—and Others."[1] In this article Manson presents the hypothesis, that our letter was not at all drafted with only the church of Rome in mind; it was at the same time also written to Ephesus. To establish this Dr. Manson gives the following reasons.

Some manuscripts of Romans demonstrate that originally Romans was not composed in its present form in one piece, destined for the church in Rome. (a) Already in the introduction in Rom. 1:7 and 1:15 the references to Rome are lacking in the Graeco-Latin manuscript G. (b) At the end of Romans some manuscripts differ in a remarkable way. The closing doxology 16:25–27 appears in three different places—at the end of chapter 14, chapter 15 and chapter 16. The first form of the text in chapter 16:33 goes back to Marcion. It cannot be original, for the text is severed here in the middle of an argument. More important is the next form. Since 1935 we have possessed the Chester Beatty Papyrus 46 (3rd century), which is the oldest manuscript of Paul in existence. This codex places the closing doxology after 15:33 and hereby betrays an earlier text of Romans in which chapter 16 did not exist. This chapter appears strange in Romans, for it contains numerous greetings to Paul's friends. It is very unlikely that he had so many intimate personal friends in the Roman church which he had never before visited. Moreover the friends who are otherwise known are connected with Asia and Ephesus. At the same time the exhortation in Rom. 16:17–20 is most peculiar if it is regarded to be addressed to a church to which Paul was a stranger. It is very natural to speak these words to

---

[1]Manson, "Letter to the Romans," reprinted in chapter 1, pp. 3–15 above.

a community which he had founded and in which he had worked for several years. That is precisely why this hypothesis was set forth a long time ago that Rom. 16 was originally a letter or a part of a letter to Ephesus; and this is now supported by Papyrus 46.

Dr. Manson supposed that Paul wrote Rom. 1–15 to the Romans, but at the same time he sent another copy of this letter to Ephesus with the greetings of chapter 16 attached. In this letter he was concerned with questions, debates and controversies that had arisen during the past years prior to the writing of Romans. It was composed in Corinth at the end of a bitter and violent struggle that involved not only the church there but also the Galatian and the Macedonian churches—regarding the relation between Judaism and Christianity, the law and the gospel. In Romans we find Paul's well-considered views on these questions. It is, according to Manson, a report of these very real discussions that had taken place. Therefore, "we should think of our document primarily as the summing up of the positions reached by Paul and his friends . . . worked out to his own satisfaction." Originally it was destined for the churches in Ephesus and Asia, because he did not intend to visit them on his Jerusalem trip (Acts 20:16). Other churches in Greece, Syria, and Palestine might expect to hear all this by word of mouth. It was only to the churches in Asia and Rome that Paul had to write this letter, which is essentially "a manifesto calling for the widest publicity which the Apostle did his best—not without success—to give it" (p. 15).

I agree with Dr. Manson, that Romans was written from the standpoint of the controversies Paul had encountered during his missionary endeavors in the East and that chapter 16 originally belonged to a letter to Ephesus which, however, as I believe, came to be added later to Romans in a different way than Manson conjectures. Nevertheless, the close and original connection of our letter with the church in Rome must not be denied. The name of Rome is engraved too deeply in this letter (chs. 1 and 14) and cannot be contested by the sole testimony of the ninth century codex G. At the same time I cannot follow Dr. Manson in rejecting the old common notion that Romans was a letter of "self-introduction" of Paul to the church in Rome. Indeed, as a matter of fact, this word says too little, for "self-introduction" in this case is intended to mean nothing less than the presentation of Paul's message itself including also the exposition of his deepest convictions in view of the impending discussions at Jerusalem. Yet perhaps most important of all, it seems to me very inadequate to understand Romans as a mere report and record of former controversies. In that case one would have to expect some concrete references to Paul's opponents in the East; and these are completely lacking in our letter. Therefore we shall try to give a different answer to the questions of the peculiarity of Romans, considering more exactly than Dr. Manson did the relationship between Romans and Paul's earlier letters.

II. The Distinctiveness of the Letter to the Romans

We have now come far enough to begin to consider further questions about the character of our letter. We want to do this on the basis of three statements which we have treated already to a certain extent.

1. It is misleading in the letter to the Romans to maintain the presence of very definite Judaistic or fanatical factions at work in the church at that time.

2. In the main theme and in many individual themes of this letter, Paul considers questions with which he had to struggle in Asia, Macedonia, and Achaia before he composed this letter.

3. The third statement is new. Here in Romans, as never before, great themes of Paul's message and theology are coherently discussed in depth and breadth in a carefully considered outline. We read of the wrath and justice of God, justification by faith and by works, Adam and Christ, baptism and the new life, flesh and spirit, Israel's lack of faith and its final deliverance.

The close degree in which Romans is related to the earlier letters can be demonstrated by many examples which we intend to present here in terms of their passages and themes. In so doing we shall simply follow the order of the individual chapters of Romans enumerating them only by key phrases with some occasional explanations.

1. We can begin immediately with the long preface, the longest one in all Pauline letters, because it speaks of Paul's apostolate to the Gentiles (1:1–7). Indeed, although he sees no cause to make a special defence of this apostolate, we should not forget how much Paul had to fight previously for his recognition as an apostle, in Galatians, Philippians (ch. 3), as early as 1 Thessalonians 1 and 2, and especially in the Corinthian correspondence.

2. The main theme of Romans, Paul's doctrine of justification by faith alone, summarized and programmatically announced in Rom. 1:16f., has been previously considered in Galatians and Philippians.

3. We add a special point to this main theme. In Romans Paul develops the teaching of justification by faith alone against the background of the depravity and misery of all men, explained already in Gal. 4:1ff., as slavery under the law, which, according to Paul, means the elemental spirits of the universe. All men know God's will and commandment, and therefore Jews and Greeks alike are guilty before God, as Paul says in Rom. 1–3, for God has revealed himself through the creation. This idea already occurs in a short formulation in 1 Cor. 1:21 and is then extensively developed in Romans.

4. Justification by faith alone is already treated in Gal. 3, in conjunction with Abraham's faith which was accounted to him as justification (Gen. 15:6). The same subject is discussed extensively in the great fourth chapter of Romans.

5. It is noteworthy that the same phrase concerning the power of God as Creator, which occurs in Rom. 4:17 and 1 Cor. 1:28, is adopted and employed in both places for God as Savior, signifying the election of the Corinthians and the justification of Abraham.

6. Rom. 5:1–11 speaks of God's act of reconciliation in Christ, and we hear in this passage an echo of 2 Cor. 5:18f.

7. Even clearer is the antithetical typology of Adam and Christ, Rom. 5:12–21. This is a thought which first appeared in short phrases in 1 Cor. 15:21 and 45 and was then developed into a great, coherent paragraph in Romans.

8. The motif in Rom. 5:20, that the law came in to increase trespasses, already has its parallel in Gal. 3:19, where it is said that the law was added because of transgressions.

9. The theme of Rom. 6 (baptism and the new life) has its antecedent in Gal. 3:27.

10. Another point is Rom. 7:7–25 (man lost under law, sin, and death). What is here explained extensively has its parallel content in 1 Cor. 15:56, "The sting of death is sin and the power of sin is law. But thanks be to God, who gives the victory through our Lord Jesus Christ." In 1 Cor. 15 this sentence appears almost without preparation, so that one could falsely take it as a later, though good Pauline annotation. But actually it is like a one-sentence formulation of the theme which Paul then develops extensively in Rom. 7 (compare the same thanksgiving in Rom. 7:25 and 1 Cor. 15:57).

11. Similar observations can be made on the basis of Rom. 8. What the apostle says here about the spirit of God and adoption of God's children (compare especially Rom. 8:15 and Gal. 4:5f.) has its prelude in Gal. 3 and 4, as do also the expanded statements about death in Christ, life in the spirit and the freedom of God's children in Rom. 8, which are already present in 1 and 2 Corinthians.

12. In 1 Cor. 12–14 we read of the many and various gifts of the spirit and the unity of the church. A similar theme occurs in Rom. 12:4 employing the same image of the one body and its many members. And even as Paul calls the members to love in 1 Cor. 13, so also in Rom. 12.

13. 1 Cor. 14:1ff. also deals with the theme of Rom. 13:1–10 (the Christians and the civil powers).

14. The eschatological sentences of Rom. 12:11–14 have their parallels in 1 Cor. 7:29 and 1 Cor. 15:51ff.

15. The sentence in Rom. 13:14 ("Put on the Lord Jesus Christ") likewise occurs in Gal. 3:27.

16. Yet above all the already mentioned fourteenth and fifteenth chapters of Romans demand a comparison with 1 Cor. 8–10. Here also Paul had to deal with the same problem and a very similar controversy in the church. In both places we hear of those who misused their faith without

consideration for their brother and thus were guilty of offending that brother for whom Christ had died.

If we glance over these themes and subjects and if we compare their treatment in the earlier letters with that in the letter to the Romans, then we very quickly recognize important distinctions between the two. First of all, in the earlier letters we meet, if not all, at least many of these thoughts in definite polemical contexts. As already mentioned, there is the question of Paul's apostleship. There is also the doctrine of justification which in Galatians and Philippians is developed by Paul as a front against the heretical teachings of the Judaizers. In the same way the Adam-Christ theme appears for the first and only time outside of Romans in an argument against the Corinthian fanatics, and it is done in 1 Cor. 15:45ff. with a pronounced polemical application. We can conclude from this that the opponents already operated with these thoughts theologically, but that it was in the sense which Paul himself rejected. For them the first man was Christ, the man of heaven; and Adam was the second, the fallen man. As spiritualizers they apparently considered themselves relatives of the heavenly man and already saved from the fall of Adam. That presupposes Gnostic or, in modern terms, idealistic speculations, which Paul rejects in verses 46ff: "But it is not the spiritual which is first but the physical, and then the spiritual. The first man was from the earth, a man of dust; the second man is from heaven. As was the man of dust, so are those who are of dust; and as is the man of heaven, so are those who are of heaven. Just as we have borne the image of the man of dust, we shall also bear the image of the man of heaven." As a consequence, the image which we should carry with us is one of the future and not one of the past. Also in a polemical, anti-fanatical context are the thoughts in 1 Cor. 8–10 about Christian freedom, which has its limits in responsibility to one's brother. These are only the most important examples.

In Romans, on the contrary, these fronts can no longer be perceived. The previous actual and concrete references have disappeared. The occasional dress, so to speak, has been removed. Instead, all of these ideas are now carefully reconsidered, more profoundly substantiated, and usually placed in a larger context. Above all they have now received a strongly universal meaning, and they bear a sense that is no longer valid just for these or just for those, but for all. It is not by chance that the words "all," "each," or the negative "no one" are used in no other letter of Paul as often as in Romans. Most closely connected with it is the fact that no other letter expresses the world-wide program of the Pauline mission as clearly as Romans. Indeed, even such a specific individual question as that of the strong and the weak in Romans 14 and 15 is placed into the main context of this world mission, and the quarrelling groups are called to unity because all nations should jointly praise and glorify God (Rom. 15:7ff.).

We can also see a second distinction between Romans and the other letters. The observation is important that Romans, too, still remains a polemical letter. But who is the opponent? The answer must be, no longer this or that group in any specific congregation in the East or in Rome, but rather the Jew and his understanding of salvation. What does this mean? Does Paul in this letter addressed to Christians shout out of the window as it were to Jews, to non-Christians? Most certainly not! For Paul, the Jew represents man in general, and indeed man exactly in his highest potential: the pious man who knows God's demands in the law but who has yet failed to meet God's claim and is lost in sin and death. Exactly as antithesis to this man, who exults in his piety before God, Paul develops his doctrine of the law and the message of grace which is now offered to all believers in Christ. This man is indeed not somewhere outside, among unbelievers; he is hidden within each Christian, even in Paul himself, and also in those Gentile Christians, who now want to pride themselves at the expense of Israel. The Apostle can thus never speak of the salvation message without at the same time speaking of this man now freed by Christ for a new life in faith.

But we can also add the following. As no other letter, the letter to the Romans returns to that which Paul himself had experienced in his conversion and call, even though he never once mentions his experience in Damascus. Yet this whole letter is concerned with the original questions and realizations which made him a Christian, the servant of Christ and the Apostle to the nations—the same realizations for which he at one time had to fight in Jerusalem and which later determined his message and his struggles with the Judaizers and fanatics, and the same realizations which in the writing of this letter to the Romans he now wants to defend in Jerusalem for the last time.

Our exposition has shown that behind the letter to the Romans stands the history of the life, work, preachings, and struggles of Paul, and, here it has found its expression. This history is not only an external but more especially an inner history, a history particularly of his theological thinking. Nothing would be more incorrect than the opinion that Romans contains only a loose collection of thoughts which the Apostle had expressed at a much earlier time. No, the letter to the Romans shows how these thoughts have worked further in Paul and how he has worked further on them, until he could give them this great and significant formulation during his last stay in Corinth.

It is very characteristic for Romans, that the questions and realizations which recall earlier controversies have received this new depth and universality. Nothing more is said, as we have seen, about the Judaistic and Gnostic heretics; only the first and last problems which determined the entire message of Paul are still considered here. This enlarged horizon, this process of thinking and this transposition of thought are the peculiarity which distinguishes Romans.

However, at the same time this letter shows how much the Apostle has remained true to the source and beginning of his faith and message. Therefore it is understandable that Paul is concerned here with the problem of Israel as in none of his earlier letters. This question of the unbelief of the Jews and their final deliverance occurs only in Romans, already in chapters 3 and 4, but especially in chapters 9–11. It is most important, however, that Paul treats this question as the question of the justification of all who believe, Jews and Gentiles alike; that is, as the question of God's free grace. Ultimately, who can solve this problem? It is reserved for God alone. Therefore chapter 11:33 concludes with the cry: "O the depth of the riches and wisdom and knowledge of God! How unsearchable are his judgments and how inscrutable his ways!"

III. Conclusion

It was this conclusion that we had in mind when we gave this lecture the title, "The Letter to the Romans as the Last Will and Testament of Paul." In closing it is necessary to add a few short comments about the use of this concept. It is undoubtedly contestable in certain respects. A testament is, strictly speaking, the declaratory act of a man in view of his death. One must not at all understand the letter to the Romans in this sense. The fact is that Paul still hoped to begin a great missionary endeavor in the West and that he prepared for this in his letter. To be sure, he presents clearly enough the concern that the conflict awaiting him in Jerusalem might frustrate his plans. Yet, in spite of this, one must not understand the letter as a testament in a strictly literal sense. For this all stylistic traits are also missing.

Nevertheless this letter, even if unintended, has in fact become the historical testament of the Apostle. This thesis implies several further historical and literary considerations which I do not have the time to present here and establish in detail. Thus, it presupposes that the pastoral letters are deutero-Pauline. Furthermore, our thesis implies that Philippians and Philemon—which I believe to be the only genuine captivity letters—were written by Paul not during his imprisonment in Rome, but during a temporary incarceration in Ephesus. This is supported especially by the lively intercourse between the imprisoned Apostle and the church in Philippi, something which can be recognized in the very letter to Philippians and which the great distance between Philippi and Rome makes difficult to explain. The same is true for the short letter to Philemon.

Even if it is possible to make different judgments about the historical and literary questions, the distinctiveness and character of Romans nevertheless remain undisturbed. We can therefore summarize the results of our investigation in this way: This great document, which summarizes and develops the most important themes and thoughts of the Pauline message and theology and which elevates his theology above the moment of definite situations and conflicts into the sphere of the eternally and universally valid, this letter to the Romans is the last will and testament of the Apostle Paul.

3

PAUL'S PURPOSE IN WRITING
THE EPISTLE TO THE ROMANS

Günter Klein

Problems in the area of New Testament introduction do not, as a rule, immediately manifest their full range of implications. Thus, it is likely that most New Testament scholars will initially react to the topic under investigation in a calm, objective manner. Yet the very urgency of the question concerning Romans is complicated and highlighted by the fact that this document has thus far revealed less of the secret of its occasion than has any other authentic letter of Paul. Therefore, it deserves the utmost attention not only from Pauline specialists, but also from students of the New Testament in general. Some time ago, K. H. Rengstorf characterized the current exegesis of the Epistle to the Romans as having inadequate "insight in the circumstances of its genesis,"[1] and as demonstrating a widespread lag behind F. C. Baur's challenge to consider equally "the situation of the Apostle" as well as the "situation of Roman Christianity at the time when Paul wrote the epistle to them." One can hardly call this assessment of the situation outdated today.

We do not mean to suggest that exegesis in general has ignored the problem. In reviewing the current status of scholarship in this area, one has to agree that it has been a long time since scholars seriously opted for a primarily dogmatic approach as one of two dominant types of exegesis.[2] This being the case, the circumstances surrounding the genesis of the letter provide scholarship on this epistle with one of its most pressing questions. In attempting to answer such unresolved questions, contradictory positions prevail which suggest that the basic methodology is unclear. This has produced a state of affairs where hypotheses of increasingly sharp contours are produced, and at the very time when it appears least likely

[1]See Rengstorf, "Paulus," 447f.
[2]See Sanday–Headlam, *Romans*, xxxlxf.

to produce such hypotheses without forcing the complex intentions of the text into one, single, perspective.

Which positions, then, characterize the present state of scholarship? In the contemporary situation, that timeless dogmatic theory which views the letter to the Romans as an organic part of a consistently developed, systematic concept[3]—as the purest manifestation of the gospel, and thus as something like a common denominator for the remainder of the New Testament[4]—is rarely upheld. Putting aside such positions, two approaches stand out: the first regards the author of the epistle as being more occupied with his own concerns than with those of the Roman community. The second approach suggests that Paul addresses the Romans for their own sake. Both positions, as they are customarily articulated today, contain unsatisfactory elements.

I

One particularly unwieldy variation of the theory—an old insight, by the way—that Paul had pursued his personal objectives in the writing of Romans reads as follows: Paul had been eager to make his way to Rome because he had believed that he would be able to crown his life's efforts "only in the capital of the Roman Empire," and that he had sent this epistle on ahead to insure "a friendly reception."[5] In an era which meanwhile has lost the taste for the religious glorification of the concept of a "Reich" of any kind, it is almost too easy to voice criticism against such psychological-biographical constructions. Before dismissing such a hypothesis, one must respect how a generation of scholars, sensitive to the nuances of the texts, attempted to prove their positions precisely by taking into account obstinate source materials.

Richard Adelbert Lipsius, who assessed the Epistle to the Romans in just this manner, was forced to doubt the integrity of the text towards the end of the Epistle. He eliminates Romans 15:19b, 20b, and 23f., regarding them as interpolations, and in place of v. 28 he offers as the original wording: *eleusomai pros hymas*.[6] By proceeding in this way he allows two major

---

[3]Typical of this is Schlatter, *Gottes Gerechtigkeit*, 10: "At the time of the writing of the Epistle to the Romans, the message of Paul is certain; now it has to be shown which direction this message provides for ethics."

[4]See, for example, Nygren, *Der Römerbrief*, 10: "One becomes acquainted in the Epistle to the Romans as nowhere else in the New Testament with what the gospel actually is, what Christian faith means. The Epistle to the Romans gives to us the gospel in a large context, it gives us the right perspective . . . as to how we are to piece together the fragments from the gospels so that they may give us the right . . . picture." (Editor's translation. ET: *Commentary on Romans*, Philadelphia: Fortress, 1967.)

[5]Lipsius, 75. See also Zahn, *Einleitung*, 1. 2.A., 309: Paul "cannot, as a matter of honor, bypass the imperial capital."

[6]Lipsius, 86. In v. 19ff. the following passages are effected: from *hōste* to the end of v. 19; from *ouch hopou* until *alla* in v. 21a.

arguments to disappear: first, Paul's statement that he regarded Rome as a transit station for his planned trip to Spain; second, Paul's statement that he considered it part of his apostleship to preach only in places where the name of Christ was not yet known so that "I may not build on a foundation laid by others." Obviously, both of these statements are irreconcilable with the argument that Paul was bound for Rome because he romanticized that city. As far as Paul's planned trip to Spain is concerned, no proof is needed. Anyone who would merely want to make a quick stopover in Rome, at best a mere interruption from the larger planned journey to the West, would hardly regard such a stopover as the crowning point of his life's efforts. But also Paul's basic principle, that he did not want to become involved with those Christians who had become such without his assistance, poses insurmountable obstacles to the explanation given, for can we really imagine that Paul, wishing to crown his life's work, would thrust before these Christians in Rome—so intimately involved in his plans yet not converted by him—the fact that a Christian community founded by others was tabu for him?

The suggested textual modifications in Romans 15 were based on too weak an argument. Subsequent scholarship could not quite accept them. Only if one interprets *peplērōkenai* quantitatively[7] and if one ignores that it was characteristic of Paul to be concerned with founding new Christian centers, is it valid to say that in v. 19 "the hitherto described missionary area of Paul was presented in a manner historically unjustifiable."[8] In this context, it matters little whether such limitations regarding the information of representative strong-holds[9] are rooted in his imminent expectations of the parousia or not.[10] The suspicion concerning the planned trip to Spain depends only on the argument from silence: the other Pauline and deutero-Pauline letters do not mention these plans.[11] If one attempts to discredit the principle of non-interference in missionary areas of others as un-Pauline because of its "generality" then one also has to regard 2 Cor. 10:15 as little more than a casual remark, for here too, this same principle is mentioned. Further, it would then be necessary to understand the very guarded evaluation of *epoikodomein* in 1 Cor. 3 as a basic approval of such activity.[12] Both of these interpretations are without support.[13]

---

[7]So Lipsius, 195.

[8]Lipsius, 85.

[9]Compare, for example, Knox, "Romans 15:14–33," 1–11; Hahn, *Der Mission,* 10, 81.

[10]Compare on the one hand, Käsemann, *Paulus,* 244, and, on the other hand, Conzelmann, "Paulus und die Weisheit," 233ff.

[11]Lipsius, 86. We would like to note only in passing that Phil. and Philem., which are the only letters considered from among the authentic Pauline letters, do not, as Lipsius presupposes, have to be of a later date than the Epistle to the Romans.

[12]Compare Lipsius, 196.

[13]Because 2 Cor. 10:15 is meant polemically does not eliminate the fact that Paul considers the principle expressed here as absolutely binding for himself. 1 Cor. 3:10ff. does not lend itself to being considered as a contradiction for the simple reason that Paul rejects the

Yet we should not regard all attempted modifications of the text as the dictates of a preconceived theory. This becomes apparent when, in connection with 15:20, we must acknowledge a contradiction to other statements made in Romans, especially 1:5, 11–15; 15:15.[14] In fact, one cannot possibly overlook the tension resulting from the following: on the one hand, Paul unmistakably makes known to us his intention to preach the gospel to the Romans; on the other hand, he states his principle of non-interference.[15] If we at this point suggest restraint in interfering with the text, the above mentioned difficulty of interpretation will remain a major problem in attempting to clarify the circumstances of the origin of Paul's Epistle to the Romans.

Meanwhile, this question has fallen into oblivion, with the result that the overall problems concerning Romans have been thrown out of focus. This is especially true of the view that Paul sought contact with the Romans primarily for personal reasons. This position is diametrically counter to the heart of Lipsius' theory, although it concurs with his basic premise that Paul established contact with Rome for personal reasons. According to such theorizing, the Epistle to the Romans was primarily, if not exclusively, meant to benefit the planned trip to Spain.

This viewpoint is not always presented with the same clarity as that which characterizes W. G. Kümmel's work.[16] According to Kümmel, Paul regarded the communication established through the Epistle to the Romans as a "demand of missionary politics," because he needed the Roman community to function as a "basis of operation in his further work." Commentators who thus define Paul's purpose in writing the epistle, come to terms with the content of the epistle, which goes far beyond the concrete occasion thus described, on the basis of the following consideration: Paul, in order to introduce himself to the Romans, expounded to them "the basic truths of Christianity." Consequently, the epistle is characterized as "Paul's theological confession resulting from a concrete necessity of his missionary work."

The text of Romans poses considerably more opposition to this kind of interpretation than may seem likely at first glance, despite the allow-

---

ep' alotrion themelion oikodomein as an unfitting interference and as an encroachment upon an alien area of missionary activity only as far as he himself is concerned (Vielhauer, *Oikodome*, 87). Further, Paul's comments with respect to this take a highly critical turn very soon (already at the end of v. 10). Lipsius, 196, therefore only refers to the judgment of Paul "with regard to the *epoikodomein* of Apollos, 1 Cor. 3:6–8," where, however, the key-word is never mentioned.

[14]Compare Lipsuis, 85, 196.

[15]The problem had been recognized as such long before Lipsius. See, for example, Philippi, *Kommentar über den Brief Pauli an die Römer* (2nd ed. 1956), 2, who tries to deal with the problem by resorting to the assumption that the Roman community had been founded by Paul's disciples.

[16]Kümmel, *Introduction*, 305ff. See also G. Friedrich, RGG 5.1138 as well as Dodd, *Romans*, xxv.

ance this perspective makes for a variety of references to actual situations in the Roman church.[17] Already, the far-reaching intention with which Paul's theological deliberations are here credited seems unlikely. Paul could hardly have moved in a more indirect way than to write a letter including his most fundamental ideas and systematic concepts, not because he wanted to deal with these issues directly, but because he had essentially other goals in mind, i.e., the organization of the infra-structure of his missionary strategy.[18] Seldom is it realized what an enormous insinuation actually underlies such a statement, viz., that the intention of the message and its content would no longer be interrelated; in fact, there would be such an irreconcilable contradiction that one would no longer be able to conclude one from the other. Thus, theology would be reduced to merely a means to an end; nothing but grist for his apostolic calling card. As a further consequence, no matter how pure his motives, Paul would have to be viewed as having only ulterior motives, viz., that his theological statements serve primarily as a means to benefit his own prestige. According to such a position, even though the theme of the justification of the godless appears throughout the epistle, Paul does not treat it in a consistently serious manner since he uses it essentially as a suitable medium of communication with the Roman Christians. It has been necessary to state this position so sharply in order to make clear that such a view of the origin of the Epistle to the Romans can only be considered as ultima ratio. There is cause for continued concern when a recent article once again reduced the central chapters 3–8 to the "backwater" of this epistle.[19]

These general reservations are strongly supported by the fact that the relevant remarks in the Epistle to the Romans reveal a motivation totally different from those suggested with regard to Paul's missionary strategy. Apart from the casual remarks in 15:24, 28, there is no mention anywhere of the planned trip to Spain,[20] and in reference to anticipated assistance of the Romans, there is only the ambiguous reference in 15:24: *hyph hymōn propemphthēnai*. In light of this, it is most noteworthy that Paul proclaims his intention *(kai hymin tois en Rōmē euangelisasthai)* in 1:15 in such a prominent place in the epistle. This statement, while evaluated differently by those scholars who uphold the viewpoint under discussion, is not simply

[17]Compare Kümmel, *Introduction,* 309–14.

[18]The fact that this formulation does not exaggerate can already be seen from the concepts borrowed from military language, which are commonly used in the context of the opinions here discussed: "Order of missionary politics" (see above), "Missionary strategy" (Feine–Behm, *Introduction,* 1950[9], 171); "base for all further missions" (Zahn, *Einleitung*); "Operational base for the campaign to the West" (Jülicher–Fascher, *Einleitung in das Neue Testament,* 1931[7], 116); "Bridgehead" (Georgi, "Der Kollekte," 81).

[19]Noack, "Current and Backwater," 159. According to Noack, the Epistle to the Romans is primarily an apology for the preaching of the Gospel to the Jews.

[20]Compare W. Marxsen, *Introduction,* 92: "The strange thing, however, is that Paul speaks of his plans to make the journey only incidentally, and we certainly cannot say that they are the theme of the letter."

discarded by them. But is sufficient justice done to Paul's statement by the assertion that he, although mostly intent on obtaining assistance from the Romans for his trip to Spain, had also "been willing to preach the Gospel to them?"[21] The immediate context of the epistle speaks strongly against such a subordination. Paul, according to 1:14, views the legitimacy of his desire to preach in Rome as a direct result of his mission to the Gentiles. This proclamation of his intended missionary activity in Rome leads directly (5:16f.) to a definition of the gospel and thereby also to the theme of the epistle. One can hardly, therefore, refer to this as a merely "incidental theme."

This impression is strengthened when one pays attention to the function which the theme of proclaiming the gospel has elsewhere in Paul's attempt to clarify his relationship with the Roman Christians. Certainly it is not by accident that the concept *euangelion* occurs already in the first sentence of the epistle and that shortly after this sentence Paul expressly counts the Roman Christians among those to whom he is directed by his apostolic office. And further, when he discusses his hope for the success of his visit to Rome, he introduces in 1:13 a phrase of missionary language: *karpos*. What so decisively shaped the prescript and proem of the letter recurs in the concluding part of the epistle,[22] consciously referring back to the opening sentence: Paul's apostolic responsibility to proclaim the gospel, recited in a solemn, liturgical formulation. It is from the preaching responsibilities outlined here (15:15f.)[23] that Paul derives the preceding contents of the letter.[24] This evidence should suffice to discredit the viewpoint that while Paul regarded Rome primarily as a stage in his missionary plans, he gave it only incidental consideration as a place for his missionary activity. Even more important is this positive insight: if for Paul the content expressed in Romans and his concrete plans for his intended missionary works in Rome are intimately related, Romans 1:15ff. and 15:5ff. are simply two ways of expressing the very same apostolic task and therefore there exists "une équivalence entre cette lettre et la grâce apostolique de l'évangélisation."[25] In light of this, every hypothesis concerned with the intention of the Epistle to the Romans must submit to another

---

[21]So Kümmel, *Introduction*, 312.

[22]The factual connection between the letter opening and 15:14ff. is frequently noted, where by letter opening it is only the proem which is cited, and in the prescript, at best, reference is made to the *charis* theme in 1:5; compare, for example, Sanday–Headlam, 403ff.; Michel, *Römer*, 325; Roosen, "Le genre littéraire," 467. But it is exactly the theme of the gospel and Paul's responsibility for carrying it out in Rome which connect the letter's opening, body, and closing.

[23]This reference is by no means to be confined specifically to 14:1–15:13; compare Roosen, "Le genre littéraire," 466.

[24]Zahn, *Römer*, 21, confuses the issue when he claims that the intention expressed in 1:13ff. "is not again touched upon in ch. 15."

[25]Roosen "Le genre littéraire."

criterion: whether it can succeed in relating the purpose and content of
the letter as closely as both the text and the projected apostolic activity
in Rome call for.

II

This provisional result must be kept in mind as we now deal with a
second type of exegesis, variations of which share a basic presupposition,
viz., that Paul turns to the Romans because he wants something for them,
and not from them. It must be stressed that the hypotheses which fall into
this group are varied and are of different exegetical merit. How difficult
it is to pursue the assumption that Paul directed his letter against a splinter
group in the Roman community is illustrated by two major interpretive
variations in this group: those who hold that Paul is attacking an antinomian group,[26] and those who hold that he is directing his polemics
against an intransigent Jewish Christianity.[27] Both views, however, can-
cel each other out.[28] Much stronger is the assumption that Paul was dealing with division threatening Roman Christianity and that he was
attempting to unify both the Jewish Christians and the Gentile Christians.
This understanding is advocated by H. Preisker,[29] H. W. Bartsch,[30] and
W. Marxsen,[31] who support their opinions in different ways. In support
of this perspective is not only that Paul's concern is directed against the
polarization of the believers into "the strong" and "the weak" (14:1–15:3),
but also the fact, especially stressed by Marxsen,[32] that individual passages in the epistle move in apparently contradictory directions.[33] And

[26]So Lutgert, *Römerbrief.*
[27]So Harder, "Römerbriefes," 21.
[28]Kümmel, *Introduction,* 309.
[29]Preisker, "Das historische Problem," 25–30.
[30]Bartsch, "Paulus und die Juden," 210ff.; idem, "Die antisemitischen Gegner," 27–43, contains a combination regarding missionary strategy. Paul wanted to bring about a united community, of which he had a need as a starting base for his mission to Spain (p. 30).
[31]Marxsen, *Introduction,* 92ff.
[32]Ibid., 96.
[33]At first glance it appears as if this aspect is overstressed by Bartsch. He understands,
for example, the term *hypakoē pisteōs* (1:5) as a provocative combination of the two slo-
gans with which the two reading groups charged each other (Bartsch, "Die antisemitischen
Gegner," 39): *pistis* supposedly refers to "Gentile Christian" and *hypakoē* supposedly to "Jewish
Christian." (38). But *hypakoē hypakouein* is authentically Pauline (compare, for example, Rom.
6:12, 16; 10:16; 2 Cor. 10:5ff.; Phil. 2:12). The phrase *hypakoē eis dikaiosynēn* (Rom. 6:16)
is the equivalent for *pistis.* It is informative to see where this kind of methodological care-
lessness leads, particularly as revealed at this point by Bartsch; he interprets *hypakoē ethnōn*
(Rom. 15:18) as referring to the "obedience demanded of the Gentile Christians with regard
to rules, respecting foods adhered to by the Jewish Christians" ("Die antisemitischen Gegner,"
36). It would be interesting to see how Bartsch would deal with the fact that Paul categorically
rejects the temptation to say anything other than what Christ had effected with regard to
such obedience.

yet, in my opinion, not even this position can hold up under critical investigation for the following reasons:

(1) Paul, when addressing the Romans directly, calls them without qualification "Gentile Christians." Therefore, it is difficult to follow the assumption that Paul considered a mixed community to be the problem (cf. above all, 1:5f.; 13; 15:15f.).[34]

(2) It is still forcing the argument to attempt to derive the contrast between strong and weak dealt with in 14:1–15:13, as arising out of a tension between Gentile Christians and Jewish Christians. Such a grouping might be suggested by the concluding reference concerning the effect of the salvation event upon Jews and Gentiles (15:7f.). Yet one should be cautious in making such assertions,[35] for it is of great significance that the vegetarianism here characterizing the weak is not specifically Jewish.[36] Conversely, Paul refrains from mentioning that the weak should expect the strong to take upon themselves "all that is connected with circumcision."[37] Also, according to 14:1–14ff., not the "weak" but the "strong" seem to be on the offensive. And finally, it is unimaginable how Paul could have called so decisively (14:21) not only for tolerance, but also for adaptation to the practices of the weak if this were to refer to known consequences of circumcision.

(3) There seems hardly enough evidence, even if the classical division of the letter into a dogmatic (chs. 1–11) and a moral (chs. 11ff.) part[38] is much too superficial, to regard Romans 1–11 as the theological foundation of an intended peace settlement between Gentile Christians and Jewish Christians. The decisive statements about the law are meant to shed light on the situation of the non-believing Jews,[39] in fact on non-believers in general, and not on the situation of the Jewish Christians.[40] Especially Romans 9–11 cannot be regarded as a defense of Jewish Christianity[41] in Rome since believing Jews are only mentioned marginally (9:6ff., 24; 11:5ff.); primary reference is made, after all, to unconverted Israel. If then, the preceding passages at no point[42] reflect an antagonism between Jew-

---

[34]In addition, see Kümmel, *Introduction,* 221f.; also Kinoshita, "Romans," 259, whose textual criticism, however, is untenable.

[35]The phrasing of "Accept one another as Christ also has accepted you" appears as a later correction of a statement which, because of the *hymas,* seems to be a much more basic Pauline statement. Thus, we have to consider the possibility that Paul, in order to relativize the existing differences, refers to the fact that Christ, too, allowed for no differences, which does not, of course, mean that it is a question of the same differences in both cases.

[36]Compare Kümmel, *Introduction,* 310–11. One cannot derive from the text the fact that the vegetarianism of the weak results from the fact that after the edict of Claudius concerning the Jews no pure meat could be obtained any longer (Bartsch, 95).

[37]Thus, however, Marxsen, *Introduction,* 102.

[38]Still today, for example, Lyonnet, "Notes," 304ff.

[39]Cf. 2:17f.; 3:1ff.

[40]Cf. 7:1–24.

[41]Against Bartsch, "Die antisemitischen Gegner," 40.

[42]Compare Munck, "Christus und Israel," 15.

ish Christians and Gentile Christians, the passage 14:1–15:13 does not deserve a key heuristic position with respect to an understanding of the epistle as a whole.[43]

(4) One further argument against seeing the theme of community reconciliation as the primary motivation for writing this letter is the fact that the above mentioned coincidence of the letter's purpose with the planned visit is not given full justice in such an interpretation. Paul did not intend to function as an intermediary between two feuding groups during his forthcoming visit to Rome, but to preach the gospel[44] and, according to 1:13ff., he wanted to perform this duty as he had everywhere else thus far. But if the very intention of the Epistle was nothing but to preach the gospel, then we cannot, for this very reason, regard the specific discussion about the strong and the weak as the major emphasis.[45]

(5) Finally, the preceding theory about Paul's purpose in writing the Epistle to the Romans suffers from the same flaws as all its rival interpretations. On the basis of its assumptions, it is impossible to explain the tension resulting from the "noninterference clause" in 15:20 and Paul's determination to visit Rome. This tension was felt by earlier scholars much more acutely than is generally the case today; and one does not come to terms with this discrepancy by simply ignoring it. The following problem still remains: if Paul viewed his apostolic calling as not necessarily involving the entire church, but as a specific, limited mission directed towards the Gentiles and his missionary territory,[46] how do we explain his departure from this controlling perspective with respect to Rome?

III

It has become apparent, then, that any further engagement with the theme of this paper must face up to this problem. It will be helpful to review all the attempts that have been made to dismiss the above described problem particularly after it resisted the literary-critical attempt to eliminate it.

Sanday-Headlam are still among the very few who take this problem seriously. They brought forth all sorts of arguments[47] in an effort to overcome it. Yet their position (which is, by the way, highly hypothetical) suggesting that there was in Rome only a small community of Christians, helps

---

[43]Compare also Vielhauer, "Einleitung," 140.

[44]Roosen, "Le genre littéraire," 467, accurately defines the connection between 1:11–15 and 15:14ff: "Par cette lettre . . . j'ai accompli mon devoir de pretre de l'evangelile."

[45]Characteristically, Bartsch, "Die antisemitischen Gegner," attempts to neutralize certain statements by Paul about his plans to go to Rome by declaring them conventional or rhetorically defined (p. 28).

[46]J. Blank, *Paulus und Jesus,* 203; see this source for further evidence.

[47]Sanday–Headlam, *Romans* 409ff.

little, even if it were accurate. The same is true for their exegetically un-supported assertion that Paul did not intend to stay in Rome for a long time. It makes little difference whether or not one carries out one's ap-ostolic mission in a large or small community as an itinerant or a resi-dential preacher, as long as the counter principles involved in such activity rigorously demand the renunciation of any preaching of the gospel where even the name of Christ is already known. Although the reference to the fact that Paul "specifically says that it is for the sake of mutual grace and encouragement that he wishes to go there" is true (1:12), it also brings forth another facet of the larger problem: how could Paul simultaneously act so unpretentiously and then lay claim to his authority as a proclaimer of the gospel?

These difficulties have been minimized all too readily in the history of scholarship. The point that Paul in this instance alone had become un-faithful to his principle[48] because the capital of the empire was at stake is certainly touching, yet it fails to impress those scholars who consider Paul's fascination with the Imperium Romanum to be insignificant. Also, the speculations of some scholars that Paul, when writing 15:20, was no longer thinking of the fact that in the opening passage of the epistle he had spoken to the Romans about his intent to preach the gospel, charges the apostle with a bit too much forgetfulness, even if such scholars add, in defense of Paul, that the letter after all, was "not finished in one day."[49] Other statements, for example, that Paul's principle of non-interference was "a rule, not a law,"[50] or, that one can only talk of Paul as being self-contradictory "if one twists the words of the Apostle,"[51] come close to abandoning any attempt at serious interpretation. And, finally, the op-posite attempt to solve the problem by denying that Paul had any mis-sionary ambitions with respect to Rome is in violation of Paul's own statements in 1:15.

In contrast to the scholarly positions just discussed, our point of de-parture is the following: the clause of non-interference does not merely relate Paul's conclusive renunciation of any missionary activity in already Christianized areas,[52] but also clarifies his reasoning—*hina mē ep' allo-trion themelion oikodomō*. The manner of reasoning in both parts of the sentence qualifies the invocation of the name of Christ, and it is this which limits Paul's activity: it is a question of an *onomazein* on the basis of an already laid foundation. The meaning of this image is made clear in 1 Cor. 3:1: the distinction between *themelion tithenai* and *epoikodomein* allows

---

[48]Thus Lietzmann, *An die Römer*, 29; H. W. Schmidt, *Römer*, 26.
[49]Thus strangely enough once again Lietzmann, *An die Römer*, 121, apparently without noticing how he has become entangled in a contradiction to his previous explanation.
[50]O. Michel, *TDNT* 5.143. This opinion, by the way, does not blend smoothly with the explanation given in his commentary on the Epistle to the Romans. (See n. 52 below).
[51]Thus Schmidt, *Römer*, 246.
[52]Michel, *Römer*, 330 note 3 (other than n. 42); similarly already Zahn, *Einleitung*, 309.

us to see the former as the first and foremost activity of the apostle, which "stands above all criticism"[53] because it participates in the authority of his God-given calling. These conditions exclude the kind of positivistic misinterpretation of Rom. 15:20 according to which Paul regarded a given geographic area tabu by the mere suggestion that believers already existed there before. But Paul stayed away from only those areas where there was already an established Christian community, i.e., where the apostolicity of the community was an actuality.

The applicability of this principle with regard to Rome is obvious: Paul can consider an apostolic effort in Rome because he does not regard the local Christian community there as having an apostolic foundation. That the Roman community does not owe its existence to a planned missionary endeavor is generally accepted.[54] Yet it has not been so generally acknowledged that Paul was aware of this, that he regarded it as highly significant theologically, and that he looked upon it as a challenge to his apostolic mission. This conclusion, based on complex textual evidence, comes to terms with the tension resulting from the principle of noninterference and Paul's desire to preach the gospel to the Romans. In addition, this conclusion corresponds to a wide diversity of other textual findings.

For the first time it now becomes clear why Paul fluctuates between renouncing and claiming his authority, a phenomenon which is particularly striking in 1:11ff. One cannot overlook the fact that Paul constantly retracts his statements, for he first of all states as the purpose of his intended visit to Rome the mediation of a *charisma pneumatikon*. Thus, he clearly designates its significance. Yet at the same time he restricts this statement in two ways: by inserting the limiting *ti* and by referring with the term *stērizein* to a concept which elsewhere in the New Testament always refers to "believers" and is alien to missionary language.[55] But then he goes on to declare himself satisfied with the expectation of mutual consolation (v. 12), only in order to make a surprising turnabout by stating in distinct missionary terminology that the goal of his efforts in Rome is the "reaping of some harvest."[56] He both limits his apostolic claims with *tina* and at the same time accentuates it significantly by making an anal-

---

[53]Vielhauer, "Oikodome" 84.

[54]Cf. Kümmel, *Introduction*, 310–11; Friedrich, RGG 5.1137.

[55]Compare Luke 22:32; Rom. 16:25; 1 Thess. 3:2,13; 2 Thess. 2:17; 3:3; James 5:8; 1 Peter 5:10; 2 Peter 1:11; Rev. 3:2. On this subject matter see G. Harder, *TDNT* 7.656: "The result . . . of this observation is the indestructibility of Christian faith."

[56]The usage of *karpos* in a missionary theological context is related to the motif of harvest, which was originally used in connection with the eschatological judgment (compare Isa. 27:12; Joel 4:13; 4 Ezra 4:28ff.; Mark 4:29; Matt. 3:12; 13:30, 39), and then was transferred to the Christian mission (see, for example, Matt. 9:37ff.; John 4:35ff.). The biblical character of *karpos* is still present in John 4:36, but has already disappeared with Paul in favor of a more technical usage of the concept; compare also Phil; 1:22 and Michel, *Römer*, 41.

ogy between the Romans and the "other Gentiles." Only in 1:15ff. does
he reveal the reason for his desire to come to Rome by citing the gospel
which cannot be constrained.

This highly conflicting argumentation which regards the Romans both
as Christian brothers and as missionary objects defies all psychological explanation. We cannot view his attitude as an apologetic reaction to reproaches that he had shied away from the hustle and bustle of Rome.[57]
Ouk epaischynesthai in verse 16 does not describe an emotional state, but
stems from confessional language and corresponds to a *homologein*. There
is little convincing quality in the argument that Paul's attempt to obscure
his actual intentions to such a degree is proof of his modesty,[58] pastoral
tact,[59] or delicacy.[60] Such a conclusion[61] is possible if we restrict ourselves
only to v. 12; the remaining elements in Paul's argumentation, however,
remain unintelligible.

In contrast to this, John Knox's approach is an improvement, for he
ignores Paul's subjectivity and attempts a literary explanation of the phenomenon.[62] However, his thesis that behind the present text of Romans
there was a general letter in which Paul supposedly intended to establish
contact with unfamiliar communities is not supported by the text. Even
if this thesis were accurate, it would only multiply the riddles surrounding
the conflicting arguments. These riddles can be solved quite easily, however, if we assume that Paul was in a unique situation, and that he was
dealing with addressees whose faith was beyond question but who still
were lacking the authentic apostolic stamp.

With this fact in mind, several peculiarities of the prescript become
intelligible. While each of them, taken in themselves, can be made more
or less plausible, it is nevertheless peculiar that they should be found together in this brief opening of the letter. The first peculiarity,[63] which has
seldom been regarded as a problem, is that Paul in Romans refers to no
co-sender, a fact for which there is no analogy in the other authentic Pauline letters.[64] This phenomenon can hardly be explained by stating that
here he develops "his very personal theology,"[65] for on the one hand, the
other letters are not inferior to this epistle with regard to their originality;
on the other hand, the programmatic nature of his reference to the pre-
Pauline credo (1:3f.) in defining the gospel as well as the compositional
significance of these confessional phrases incorporated into the corpus of

---

[57]Cf. Noack, "Current and Backwater," 162.
[58]Cf. Michel, *Römer*, 42.
[59]Cf. Schmidt, *Römer*, 25.
[60]Cf. Sanday–Headlam, *Romans*, 21.
[61]Michel, *Römer*, 40.
[62]Knox, "Text of Romans," 191–93.
[63]Noted, but not interpreted in Michel, *Römer*, 26.
[64]Thus only again in Ephesians and the Pastorals.
[65]Thus Friedrich, RGG 5.1139.

the epistle (recognized particularly by H. Conzelmann)[66] suggest how energetically Paul insisted on the binding quality of his theology with regard to the church. The exclusive wording regarding the sender of the epistle becomes clear as soon as one remembers that Paul, wherever the apostolic founding of a community was concerned, claims the authority of a "father," an authority removed from all and beyond all other *paidagōgoi en Christō*, the authority of a "father" who "has created you through the gospel" (1 Cor. 4:15).

This leads us to a second observation: again, contrary to custom, Paul already refers to the concept of the gospel at a place where this concept is otherwise consistently lacking, viz., in the prescript. Being captivated by the implications of this concept in its context, this basic fact is easily overlooked.[67] Yet this fact remains noteworthy as a demonstration of the official claim which the apostle announces to the Roman Christians, and thus it once again throws light on the meaning of his name in the opening sender-formula of the epistle. Wherever the gospel is preached with the objective of founding a church, the apostle stands before his listeners alone and without substitute.

The absence of the concept *ekklēsia* in the context of Romans 1–15, but its striking presence in the prescript, finally proves, in a negative way, that the founding of a church was at stake. Among all the authentic letters of Paul, the only apparently comparable case is the prescript of the letter to the Philippians. But this is not really a parallel[68] usage, since the reference to the *episkopoi* and the *diakonoi* in Philippians attests to its ecclesiastical context,[69] whereas in Romans, Paul is satisfied with individualizing references to the addressees (1:6f.). One cannot relate this to a gradual development of Paul's letter form, viz., that it first stressed the local community, and then went on to single out individual members of the community,[70] because in no other instances is the ecclesiastical horizon scanned with respect to the addressees.[71] Further, one cannot explain this fact with a reference to the organization of Roman Christianity into "house churches."[72] It is unlikely that Paul was guided by empirical consideration in his theological description of the addressees. Since the

---

[66]Conzelmann, "Heutige Probleme," 245ff.: idem, *Grundriss der Theologie,* 187; idem, "Die Rechtfertingungslehre," 395ff.

[67]Characteristic of Stuhlmacher, "Theologische Probleme," 374–89.

[68]Against Michaelis, *Einleitung,* 158.

[69]Schmithals, "Paulus und die Gnostiker," 55 n. 47, considers, and Bartsch, "Die antisemitischen Gegner," 30 n. 13, defends, the fact that the address of the Epistle to the Philippians had been shaped by a redactor. Thus this letter could not be considered.

[70]Thus Sanday–Headlam, *Romans,* 15.

[71]Not even in Philemon! Differently with the deuteroPaulines: compare the prescripts of Colossians and Ephesians.

[72]Thus Michel, *Römer,* 10; Trocmé, "Romains," 152, explains that this concept is missing in the following manner: Paul had criticized the religious individualism of the Roman Christians. However, the text does not reveal this anywhere.

omission of the *ekklēsia* concept corresponds so exactly to the other unusual feature of the prescript, that explanation will be preferable which
can explain all of these phenomena in a consistent way. This is, finally,
also a valid argument against interpretations which evaluate the omission
of *ekklēsia* in favor of the theory that the opposition between the Gentile
Christians and the Jewish Christians had "heretofore prevented the evo-
lution of a united Christian community in Rome."[73] This perspective becomes more and more unacceptable if one considers that Paul does not
even deny to a community such as the Corinthians the designation *ekklēsia*
a community which was, among other things, divided between the weak
and the strong. Paul's refusal to use this term is commensurate with a Pauline ecclesiology which holds that the temple of God exists only where
the apostle has laid its foundation (1 Cor. 3:10–17).[74]

The insight that, for Paul, Christianity in Rome still needed an apostolic foundation allows us not only to understand exegetical details just
discussed, but even beyond that, it allows us to understand the entire problem of Romans so central to scholars concerned with matters of New Testament introduction. Briefly stated, Paul, despite his epistolary habits,
addresses the Romans with a theological treatise which in most parts seems
free of any reference to a concrete situation. "Paul really does write to
the Romans . . . as if they needed a theological treatise."[75] Paul does not
artificially construct the Romans' need; instead, for him it results from their
objective situation, which shows them still lacking the fundamental kerygma. With this in mind, it becomes understandable why the content of
the epistle corresponds so closely to the announced visit, so that the letter
appears in fact, almost as an already accomplished act of that *euangelisasthai* in Rome which Paul personally still has ahead of him (1:15ff.;
15:15ff.).[76] A form-critical distinction between occasional letter and epistle
does not prove to be practicable in this case. The fact that Paul writes to
the Romans in the form of a theological treatise is indicative of an occasion which calls for the normative message of the apostle and demands
that his theological reflections be raised to a new level of general validity.[77]

Even if the total perspective presented here be only remotely related
to the facts, it could not be without theological consequences. On the one
hand, our perspective would confirm from a new angle the fact that the

---

[73]Bartsch, "Die antisemitischen Gegner," 35.

[74]One cannot take the complete absence of *ekklēsia* in Romans 1–15 as proof that the
reception of this concept in primitive Christianity "was not caused by a conscious reference
back to the LXX" (thus Schrage, " 'Ekklesia' and 'Synagoge,' " 187ff., whatever the merit of
this thesis might otherwise be).

[75]Noack, "Current and Backwater," 161.

[76]For the sake of the purity of form-critical categories one should not like Roosen, "Le
genre littéraire," 467, attribute it to the *euangelion* genre.

[77]In this sense the opinion of H. von Campenhausen has to be qualified when he "finds
it difficult to speak of a generally valid apostolic norm or of a canonicity of the Apostle,"
Die Entstehung, 133.

primary content of Romans—the justification of the godless—also constitutes the center of Pauline theology, and that this doctrine must be the exclusive topic wherever it becomes a matter of establishing the correct foundation for the church. On the other hand, Romans, by the very nature of its existence is striking evidence for a shockingly authoritarian understanding of the apostolic office, an understanding which, incidentally, established norms for Christianity contemporary with Paul. Even if one realizes that this is not a matter of hierarchic suppression, but a matter of Paul's apostolic obedience which acknowledges no other foundation for Christian communities than that which has been laid, *hos estin Iēsous Christos* (1 Cor. 3:11), the situation remains sufficiently annoying. This is especially the case at a time in history when the threat exists that bad authority, together with good, is disappearing, at a time when the ecclesiastical ties with theology are characterized as unnatural and foreign, and at a time when in certain minds the so-called latent church is advanced as a partner which should after all be spared the offence of any binding, authoritative teaching. Historical critical research in the field of theology was never meant to find in its texts the favorite dreams of the latest avant-garde scholarship; rather, it has always been committed to rediscovering that word which in contrast to all modernism remains a *verbum alienum* and precisely for that reason makes possible the discovery of faith.

4

A SHORT NOTE ON ROMANS 16

Karl Paul Donfried

There is a growing consensus, especially among continental NT scholars, that Romans 16 was not an original part of Paul's letter to Rome.[1] Most who adhere to this position view the chapter as Pauline, but directed originally to Ephesus and only later attached to Romans 1–15. Curiously, the consensus stops here, and there is little unanimity among these scholars concerning Paul's purpose and intention in writing Romans 1–15. What is perplexing about the present state of affairs is how there can be so little consensus in regard to the original purpose for which Paul wrote Romans, and yet an increasing consensus that Romans 16 was not an original part of this letter. Are not these two problems more closely interrelated than we have been led to believe?[2]

It is not possible to summarize here every position dealing with Paul's purpose in writing Romans; however, for the sake of illustration three current hypotheses will be reviewed, beginning with what must be considered the least likely, that of Günter Klein,[3] and moving to what is the most probable explanation, that of Willi Marxsen.[4]

(1) Günter Klein asserts that the purpose of Paul's visit to Rome and the purpose of the letter are the same: that while there is a Christian church in Rome, it was not founded by an apostle, and thus it is Paul's task to lay the proper apostolic foundation.[5] One of the main arguments in sup-

---

[1]Bultmann, *In Memoriam Ernst Lohmeyer*, 190 (=Exegetica [1967], 382); Bornkamm, *Paulus*, 96; Marxsen, *Introduction*, 107; Knox, "Romans," 365ff.; Manson, "St. Paul's Letter." See also chapter 1 above, pp. 3–15; Suggs, "Romans 10:6–10," 289ff.

[2]This separation of the two problems can be clearly seen in the work of Willi Marxsen. His overall solution for Romans as a whole seems to have no bearing on his interpretation of Romans 16. In an almost axiomatic kind of way he asserts that chapter 16 is not part of the original, even though the reverse position would seem to suit his overall hypothesis better.

[3]Klein, "Paul's Purpose," chapter 3 above, pp. 29–43.

[4]Marxsen, *Introduction*, 95.

[5]Klein, "Paul's Purpose," 39.

port of this interpretation is based on Rom. 15:20, " . . . thus making it my ambition to preach the gospel, not where Christ has already been named, lest I build on another man's foundation. . . . " According to Paul's criterion, Klein claims, it would appear to be a contradiction in terms for him to go to Rome, to an already existing congregation. However, that is not at all the case, Klein goes on, since the proper apostolic foundation was never laid in Rome, and thus Paul is under obligation to go and do this. Unfortunately, Klein's interesting suggestion has little exegetical support. Paul in no way indicates a weakness in the foundation. Quite the contrary, in 15:14 we hear, "I myself am satisfied about you, my brethren, that you yourselves are full of goodness, filled with all knowledge, and able to instruct one another." Then in the next verse he explicitly indicates that what he has just written is "by way of reminder"[6]—hardly a situation which would indicate "that for Paul, Christianity in Rome still needed an apostolic foundation. . . ."[7] Further, one would hardly expect Paul to do such a rebuilding job simply "in passing" (15:24) as he goes to Spain.

Romans 15:20 cannot be used to support Klein's thesis since the context of this pericope moves in another direction. The phrase "thus making it my ambition to preach the gospel, not where Christ has already been named" must be understood as an apology as to why Paul has *not yet* been in Rome—viz., his first responsibility was to preach Christ where he had not yet been preached, in the area "from Jerusalem as far round as Illyricum" (15:19). Paul continues in 15:23–25, "But now, since I no longer have any room for work in these regions, and since I have longed for many years to come to you, I hope to see you in passing as I go to Spain, and to be sped on my journey there by you, once I have enjoyed your company for a little. At present, however, I am going to Jerusalem with aid for the saints." In other words, first things first; now that Paul has finished his work in the east he will come to Rome on his way to Spain, after he has made his last trip to Jerusalem. Thus, he has no hesitation in making a brief stop in Rome, and he can make certain statements in chapter 1 which are quite in harmony with chapter 15. One recalls here his desire to "reap some harvest among you . . ." (1:13) and his eagerness "to preach the gospel to you also who are in Rome" (1:15), "that we may be mutually encouraged by each other's faith, both yours and mine" (1:12). In short, there seems to be little compelling evidence for Klein's interpretation.

(2) A second hypothesis concerning the purpose of Romans has been

---

[6]Note the interesting comment of Michel, *Römer*, 364, on this verse: "Was er geschrieben hat, war nichts anderes als die gelaufige kirchliche Belehrung, die der Gemeinde bekannt sein musste. Die 'Errinnerung' besteht hier in der Einschärfung der katechetischen Tradition. Er lehnt es also ab, in seinem Brief etwas Neues oder der Tradition gegenüber Fremdes vorgetragen zu haben."

[7]Klein, "Paul's Purpose," 42.

presented by Ernst Fuchs. Fuchs argues that while Paul technically addressed his letter to Rome, he really had Jerusalem in mind as the actual addressee. Jerusalem was the "geheime Addressatin des Römerbriefs."[8] What is fascinating about this hypothesis is that it takes account of Paul's itinerary—writing in Corinth, on his way to Jerusalem and then, he hopes, on to Rome—and it takes into account the Jew-Gentile, law-faith dialectic in the letter. But still the troubling question remains, why send such a "secret letter," one which actually has Jerusalem in mind, to Rome?

A variation and expansion of this thesis is found in the work of Günther Bornkamm, who suggests that one must understand Romans as Paul's last will and testament,[9] in which Paul takes up and summarizes some seven major themes from his earlier correspondence.[10] The theology of Romans is understandable in light of Paul's immediately forthcoming trip to Jerusalem and the possible difficulties there, as well as the future mission to Spain. An important consequence of Bornkamm's position is that it is impossible to ascertain any specific information from Romans concerning the concrete life and problems of the church in Rome. As one looks at this thesis in retrospect, one can agree with Bornkamm that in fact Romans did become Paul's last will and testament because of the historical circumstances which led to his death; but this does not help us to understand why Paul should write a letter in the particular manner and style and send it to Rome. Why should the Romans be interested in such a last will and testament? Further, to attribute all polemical, dialogical, and concrete elements in the letter to the diatribe style, as Bornkamm does,[11] is hard to reconcile with Paul's use of the diatribe style elsewhere when he refers to specific and concrete situations.[12]

(3) A third major interpretation concerning the purpose of Romans is that of Willi Marxsen[13] in which he argues that this final letter of Paul was meant to deal with a specific set of problems in the church of Rome. What makes Marxsen's thesis attractive is that he can incorporate the insights inherent in both Bornkamm's and Fuchs's positions, and yet be more precise than they, and also that he can deal with the theology of Romans not abstractly, but in concrete relationship to secular history in the mid-

[8]Fuchs, *Hermeneutik*, 191; and now in a similar manner, Suggs, "Romans 10:6–10," 295; "To employ a metaphor, the letter is a brief drawn up by Paul in anticipation of the renewed necessity of defending his gospel in Jerusalem."

[9]Bornkamm, *Paulus*, 111; this same position is argued by Bornkamm in an earlier article, "Last Will and Testament." See chapter 2 above, pp. 16–28.

[10]Ibid., 108. In chapter 2, pp. 23–25, 16 instances of recurring themes are cited.

[11]pp. 21–23 above.

[12]Cf. esp. Bultmann, *Diatribe*, 1910. Suggs, "Romans 10:6–10," 291, is critical of Bornkamm at this same point.

[13]Marxsen, *Introduction*, 95–109. It is not the intention of this essay to demonstrate the validity of Marxsen's thesis. The purpose is to show the consequence of Marxsen's thesis for Romans 16. A comprehensive argument supporting Marxsen's overall position can be found in Bartsch, "Die historische Situation," 281–91.

50s of the first century. Marxsen's thesis is that the theology of Romans—especially the constant interplay between "Jew" and "Gentile"—reflects a concrete historical problem in the church of Rome. It is no mere summary of his past theology or a preview of his anticipated problems in Jerusalem, though it may—and probably does—include these. What created a problem for the church of Rome was the edict of Emperor Claudius in A.D. 49 by which all Jews were driven out of Rome because they were *impulsore Chresto assidue tumultuantes.*[14] Basic to this argument is that Suetonius's reference to *Chresto* is an alternative reading for *Christo,*[15] and that Claudius's edict did not narrowly refer to Jews alone, but also to Jewish Christians.[16] Marxsen's reference to Acts 18:2 in support of this latter point is justified: "And he [Paul] found [in Corinth] a Jew named Aquila, a native of Pontus, lately come from Italy with his wife Priscilla, because Claudius had commanded all the Jews to leave Rome." The natural way to read the Acts account is that when Paul met them in Corinth they were *already* Christians. Had Paul had any part in their conversion, one might expect mention of this. Thus, one can agree with Marxsen that the phrase "because Claudius had commanded all the Jews to leave Rome" also includes Jewish Christians. That it was not necessary in Acts to make a sharp distinction between "Jews" and "Jewish Christians" is intelligible if we view the earliest stages of the Roman church in a manner similar to that of C. K. Barrett: "It is not impossible that the first Christians in Rome . . . formed a synagogue community with the general framework of the Jewish groups in the city. . . . "[17]

This makes good sense in light of the fragments still left for us to reassemble. Barrett's analysis seems to gain some additional support from a fourth-century writer whom we know only as "Ambrosiaster":

> It is established that there were Jews living in Rome in the times of the apostles, and that those Jews who had believed [in Christ] passed on to the Romans the tradition that they ought to profess Christ but keep the law. . . . One ought not to condemn the Romans, but to praise their faith; because without seeing any signs or miracles and without seeing any of the apostles, they nevertheless accepted faith in Christ, although according to a Jewish rite.[18]

The most that can be asserted in view of the late date of this document is that we have here an interesting hint and indication which again fits what other evidence we have. We would agree with John Knox's analysis that "this account is probable."[19]

---

[14]Sueton., *Claud.,* 25.4, "persisted in rioting at the instigation of Chrestus"; cf. Leon, *Jews of Ancient Rome,* 23.

[15]For a discussion of this matter, see Leon, *Jews of Ancient Rome,* 25f.

[16]See the interesting discussion by Bruce, "Christianity under Claudius," 316–18.

[17]Barrett, *Romans,* 6; also, Bruce, "Christianity under Claudius," 317ff.

[18]Ambrosii, *Works* 3.373, as cited by Knox, *"Romans,"* 362.

[19]Ibid.

Once all the Jewish Christians had to leave Rome in A.D. 49, Marxsen
continues, the Roman church was completely in the hands of Gentile Christians. The dominance of Gentiles continued until the death of Claudius
in A.D. 54; thereafter Jews and Jewish Christians were free to return to
Rome. With this return, a new crisis emerged: how do the long-absent Jewish Christians relate to a church whose theology and internal structure
have substantially changed? The old Galatians 2/Acts 15 problem of Jewish-
Gentile relationships once again reemerged. Thus, the overwhelming concern of the epistle to the Romans with this problem becomes very understandable. In light of this development in Rome, one can see why Paul
would reflect upon and reiterate themes from his previous correspondence
(Bornkamm) and why the themes in the letter to Rome are not dissimilar
to the approaching situation in Jerusalem (Fuchs), where, after all, the problem still existed.

We must now consider the consequences of Marxsen's well-constructed
theory for chapter 16: was it originally part of Paul's letter to the church
at Rome? Given the reference to "Prisca and Aquila" in 16:3, one is likely
to answer the question in the affirmative. Marxsen considers this possibility: "It is conceivable, of course, that as a result of the relaxation of Claudius' edict members of the church who came from Rome and whom Paul
had got to know in the East while the edict was in force, have now returned to Rome."[20] However, this conclusion, rather natural especially in
light of Marxsen's own creative insights into the purpose of Romans, is
dismissed on curious grounds: "But those to whom Paul sends greetings—
apart from a few exceptions—do not have Jewish names."[21] This argument is untenable since it cannot be argued that to be a Jew necessitated
having a Jewish name. On the contrary, we have sufficient evidence from
papyri and inscriptions which indicates that, both in the diaspora as well
as in Palestine, the changing of personal names was a common practice.
The Jews acquired not only Greek, but Latin and Egyptian appellations
as well.

This fact is strikingly confirmed in Harry Leon's 1960 study, *The Jews
of Ancient Rome*. After examining 551 names of Jews in Rome, Leon comes
to this conclusion: "Although the community was fundamentally a Greek-
speaking one, the purely Latin names surprisingly not only outnumber
all the others but are more than equal to the Greek and Semitic names
combined. . . . Apparently, then, the Roman Jews had accepted the Latin
names of their Roman neighbors to a much greater extent than they had
adopted the Latin language."[22] Leon's conclusion establishes the probability
that the names in Romans 16 could easily belong to Roman Jews and thus

[20]Marxsen, *Introduction*, 108.
[21]Ibid.
[22]Leon, *Jews of Ancient Rome*, 107f.; cf. also Tcherikover, *Hellenistic Civilisation*, 346f.;
520, n. 30; 523, n. 3; 524, n. 9.

Marxsen's primary argument against the integrity of Romans 16 falls.

A further and subsidiary argument which Marxsen brings against the integrity of Romans 16 is the reference to Epaenetus, who is described in v. 5 as *aparchē tēs Asias*. Marxsen concludes that Epaenetus "was therefore the first converted Christian of Asia (i.e., from the district of Ephesus)," and asks rhetorically, "Is it just by chance that he also happens to be in Rome?"[23] In response to this question it must be acknowledged that we know so little (in fact nothing) about Epaenetus, that one can hardly expect a final verdict concerning Romans 16 to depend on v. 5. Nevertheless, two considerations can be brought to bear against Marxsen's interpretation: (1) *tēs Asias* does not have to be translated "of Asia," but could be translated "the first convert *in Asia*."[24] (2) Marxsen's doubt expressed in his question, "Is it just by chance that he also happens to be in Rome?" does not take into sufficient account the geographical mobility of the period. Even more justifiably could the same question be asked of Aquila who was Asiatic by birth. Only by chance do we learn from Acts 18:2 that Aquila was in fact in Rome. One should not overlook the fact that Rome was the great political and religious capital of the world. In fact, there was a great movement of peoples precisely from Asia Minor to Rome at this time. In La Piana's study of the foreign groups in Rome we learn that the "Asiatic population was so large in Rome that Athenians could say that entire nations, as the Cappadocians, the Scythians, the people of Pontus, and many others, had settled in Rome."[25] Thus, Marxsen's question, "Is it just by chance that he also happens to be in Rome?" should be answered, "No, not by chance; but given the movements from Asia Minor to Rome it is certainly possible that Epaenetus, as also Aquila, was a participant in this migration."

We have tried to show that if Marxsen's hypothesis concerning the purpose of Romans is correct, as we hold that it is, then it seems to follow quite well that Romans 16 was an original part of the letter to Rome, and the people whom Paul was greeting are persons he has met along his journeys who are now back in Rome after the death of Claudius. Marxsen's basic argument against this logical conclusion of his own thesis, namely, that the names are not Jewish is, as we have seen, fallacious. If Marxsen's general thesis is correct, the burden of proof seems to fall on those who would argue that chapter 16 is a later addition which was originally addressed to Ephesus.

We must briefly deal with three other arguments which are brought against the integrity of Romans 16 by some scholars: (1) that the closing doxology (16:25–27) is not Pauline and that in the textual tradition it is found at the end of Romans 14, 15, 16 and combinations thereof; (2) that

[23]Marxsen, *Introduction*, 108.
[24]BAGD, 80.
[25]LaPiana, "Foreign Groups," 194.

it is without parallel that Paul lists some twenty-six names at the end of a letter; and (3) that the warning in 16:17–20 is not in keeping with the character of the remainder of the letter, the language is "too harsh."

The first objection deals with the doxology. That this doxology is non-Pauline in character is widely held today, and the further suggestion made by some scholars[26] that it is perhaps Marcionite in origin goes a long way in solving the textual difficulties of Romans. We know from Origen[27] that Marcion cut off chapters 15 and 16, and thus Marcion's edition of Romans ended with 14:23. Since that is a rather abrupt note to end on, Marcion perhaps composed this closing doxology. Kümmel[28] and Lietzmann[29] are probably correct in suggesting that Paul's original Romans ended with 16:23 (without the doxology); Marcion then shortened this, so that his edition ended with 14:23, and expanded it with his doxology. All further textual variations are then explained on the basis of a combination of this Marcionite edition of Romans with the primitive Pauline edition which had been preserved elsewhere.[30] Such a solution to this particular complex of text-critical problems in Romans would support our contention that Romans 16 belonged to the original Pauline edition of Romans.

The second objection correctly indicates that Paul's list of names is unusual. But, then, Romans is unusual. Paul is writing to help solve problems in a church which was not founded by him and which he had not yet visited. What is more obvious than that Paul would try to marshal all the support he could by listing persons whom he had met along the way and who were now in Rome? Precisely because of these friendships and despite the fact that he had not yet been in Rome, Paul felt a right and

---

[26]Kümmel, *Introduction,* 310–14; Barrett, *Romans,* 11–13; Manson, chapter 1 above, p. 8.

[27]Origen, *Comm. in ep. ad Rom.,* Lib. x 43 (PG, 14, col. 1290 A-B):
Caput hoc [16:25f.] Marcion, a quo Scripturae evangelicae atque apostolicae interpolatae sunt, de hac Epistola penitus abstulit; et non solum hoc, sed ab eo loco, ubi scriptum est *omne autem quod non est ex fide, peccatum est* [14:23], usque ad finem cuncta dissecuit.
[This chapter {16:25f.} was completely cut by Marcion, who falsified the evangelical and apostolical writings. He cut not only this, but also everything from where it is written: 'anything which does not arise from faith is sin' {14:23} right to the end.].

[28]Kümmel, *Introduction,* 312.

[29]Lietzmann, *An die Römer,* 130f.; cf. Barrett, *Romans,* 13.

[30]Kümmel, *Introduction,* 314–15. Clearly T. W. Manson's argument, p. 10 above, that "there was once—at an earlier date than the date of P[46]—a form of the text which omitted Chapter 16" runs counter to, this conclusion. Yet how probable is Manson's argument? I should suggest that it pays too great deference to the reading of P[46] which, as we know, contains a goodly number of curious readings which cannot be taken too seriously. Thus the reading of P[46] by itself cannot solve the problem of Romans 16. Kümmel, *Introduction,* 317, carefully observes that "the existence of the doxology in P[46] following 15:33 in no way proves that there ever was a manuscript that ended with 15:33, much less that this was the text form that Paul sent to the Romans, especially since P[46] contains Ch. 16!" It is this basic dependence upon Manson which makes the otherwise very suggestive article by Suggs (p. 297) not finally persuasive. Also Suggs's suggestion that Romans is "a pre-Jerusalem brief prepared 'for others–and Rome' " does not take into sufficient account the highly specific references to Rome in chapter 1.

a sense of responsibility to help correct the Roman conflict. His sense of responsibility stems from the fact that *he*, and he alone, is the authorized apostle to the Gentiles (15:15–16). And since it was the Gentiles who were creating some of the difficulty by not readily reaccepting the expelled Roman Jewish Christians, he felt compelled to interfere. This becomes especially clear in Romans 14–15 where the exhortations seem primarily addressed to the Gentile Christians. For example, 15:1 urges that we "who are strong ought to bear with the failings of the weak . . . " and continues by showing how the Gentiles are under perpetual obligation to the Jews. This becomes especially clear in 15:7–8, "Welcome one another, therefore, as Christ has welcomed you, for the glory of God. For I tell you that Christ became a servant to the circumcised to show God's truthfulness, in order to confirm the promises given to the patriarchs. . . . " These verses are followed by four OT quotations, all of which serve the purpose of showing the unity of Gentile and Jew in Christ.[31] In this context Rom. 15:15–16 makes good sense: "But on some points I have written to you very boldly by way of reminder, because of the grace given me by God to be a minister of Christ Jesus to the Gentiles in the priestly service of the gospel of God, so that the offering of the Gentiles may be acceptable, sanctified by the Holy Spirit."

A third objection voiced against the integrity of Romans 16 centers on vv. 17–20. John Knox summarizes the matter well: "This paragraph, in view of the newness of the subject matter and the abrupt change of tone, raises as serious a question as to the original connection of this chapter with the letter to the Romans as does the preceding paragraph of greetings."[32] But is Knox's contention justified that we are here dealing with new subject matter? Two of the key terms, *skandalon* and *didachē* are found elsewhere in Romans, *didachē* in 1:17[33] and *skandalon* in 14:13 (not to mention its use in the Old Testament quotations in 9:33 and 11:9). It is not by accident that *skandalon is* found in Romans 16 and Romans 14, since Rom. 16:17–20 is a concluding summary of the longer discussion in chapter 14. Chapter 14 is the practical application of the *didachē* of chapter 6 and its teaching on baptism; thus, "If your brother is being injured by what you eat, you are no longer walking in love" (14:15), i.e., you are denying the practical implication of your baptism (Rom. 6). A key theme in Romans 14 is that concern for food, for the belly, can be a stumbling block for the weak brother. So we read in 14:20f., "Do not, for the sake of food, destroy the work of God. Everything is indeed clean, but it is wrong for any one to make others fall by what he eats; it is right

---

[31]It is only here (Rom. 14–15) and at Philemon 17 that Paul uses the verb *proslambanesthai*, 14:1,3; 15:7 (bis). Paul, here, is not arguing for the rejection of a certain group (as in Galatians) but for the acceptance of one!

[32]Knox, "Romans," 661.

[33]Rejecting Bultmann's theory of a gloss at 6:17 (*TLZ*, 72 [1947], 202).

not to eat meat or drink wine or do anything that makes your brother stumble." And at the outset of chapter 14 there is the warning to avoid dissension: "As for the man who is weak in faith, welcome him, but not for disputes over opinions. . . . Let not him who eats despise him who abstains, and let not him who abstains pass judgment on him who eats . . . " (14:1–3). It is these themes which Paul is summarizing in the form of a final warning in Romans 16:17–20 and, thus, there is nothing "new" about the subject matter.

But what about Knox's other contention that we have here an "abrupt change of tone"? Certainly there is a shift in v. 17 from the preceding greetings to a brief section of exhortations. But is this unusual for Paul? Is the break in Romans any more "abrupt" than the transition from 1 Cor. 16: 20b, "Greet one another with a holy kiss," to v. 22a, "If any one has no love for the Lord, let him be accursed"? Or to take another example: Gal. 6:11ff., also an autographic postscript, serves to show that Paul is capable of closing his letters with "abrupt," succinct, and pointed summaries of matters which he has discussed previously. In short, then, none of these objections just reviewed compellingly shows that chapter 16 could not have been a part of Paul's original letter to the Romans.

To summarize the major point we have been trying to demonstrate: if one accepts Marxsen's overall thesis concerning the purpose of Romans, then, contrary to Marxsen's conclusion, it is far more probable that chapter 16 was an integral part of Paul's original edition of Romans and not a later addition from some postulated, but unprovable, letter of commendation to Ephesus.

5

THE LETTER TO JERUSALEM

Jacob Jervell

The function of the historical-critical method with regard to the exegesis of Romans was first formulated by F. Chr. Baur in the *Tübinger Theologische Zeitschrift* (1936).[1] Baur stated that a historically unbiased interpretation of this letter had to be based upon knowledge of the circumstances of the apostle as well as knowledge about the Roman community at the time the letter was written.

All contemporary scholars would agree with this intention. Its weakness, however, is that it cannot be carried out and perhaps it would be best if it were not. This is particularly true with the last part of Baur's stated program: that exegesis must be based on knowledge about the Roman congregation at the time Paul wrote this letter. Indeed, many and varied attempts have been made to portray the Roman congregation the way it looked at the time of Paul.[2] There are also numerous attempts to understand Paul's remarks in Romans in light of the internal situation of the congregation.[3] These attempts, however, did not lead to any acceptable or accepted results. After over a century of research, we certainly will not draw any hasty conclusion if we say that we cannot further proceed along a path which has yielded no results to date. It cannot even be determined with any certainty what groups comprised the congregation. Were they Jewish Christians, Gentile Christians, or both?[4] This is not to say, of course, that sociological descriptions of the congregation are unnecessary or a waste of time. To do so is a legitimate historical task in and of itself. But if our knowledge is limited and uncertain, it is a rather daring enterprise to interpret the letter against this uncertain background. Since Baur's pro-

---

[1]Baur, F. C., "Römerbriefes," 59–178.
[2]See Wiefel, "Jewish Community," chapter 7 below, pp. 85–101.
[3]An overview can be found in Kümmel, *Introduction*.
[4]For literature see Wiefel, "Jewish Community," 86 n. 8.

gram cannot be accomplished with success it would be better not to carry it out at all. The attempt to come to a clear understanding about the situation within the Roman congregation during the time Paul wrote the letter is justifiable. However, it is an entirely different matter to see these circumstances as the reason for writing the letter, and to try to interpret it from the situation of the recipients. To do so will lead to defective exegesis. To be sure, this does not happen for lack of information but because the letter itself states clearly that its raison d'être does not stem from the situation of the Roman congregation, but is to be found in Paul himself at the time of writing.

Should this be true, then Romans would have a position different from the other genuine Pauline letters. We know that the other letters are determined, for the most part, by concrete situations in the congregations themselves and by Paul's work on behalf of these congregations. Nevertheless, the difference will not be as great as one would believe at first. At this point we must draw attention to one aspect which is often overlooked whenever Paul's letters are under discussion:[5] Paul writes his letters not only with his congregation, but also with himself and his apostolic work in mind. He is writing for himself. It is beyond question that Paul's letters are written for specific occasions, but how often is the "occasion" Paul himself? The portrayal of Paul in Acts and our traditional image of the apostle leads us to picture Paul more as a theological monument than as a human being. It also leads us to see him more as an invulnerable, superior hero than as an endangered missionary.

But Paul needs the congregation just as much as they need him. Characteristic in this connection are 1 Thess. 2:1–3:10 and Phil. 1:12–26. Paul's further life and work as a missionary is dependent on the congregation (1 Thess. 2:19–20; 3:8–9; Phil. 1:5–19). Paul's reflections about himself, the defense of his apostolate, his request for prayers and intercession, and even his ethical exhortations are written with his own interests in mind. The primary reason is this: a congregation that has achieved the proper degree of life, faith and knowledge is for Paul a "sign of God" which will influence his effectiveness in other geographical locations. In this respect 2 Cor. 10:15ff. is characteristic. One additional important fact is that the apostle together with his congregation will rise or fall on the final day of judgment (1 Thess. 3:6–9). Another passage, 1 Thess. 1:8ff., shows that the faith of a congregation can "precede" the apostle and make his work easier. There is much reason to investigate thoroughly this aspect regarding the occasion of Paul's letters; but in this essay it will only be touched on briefly.

It can be shown that the attempts to understand Romans primarily on the basis of our knowledge of the Roman congregation lead us into

[5]For more details see my "Zur Frage," 29ff.

a dead end. We have then reached the other aspect of Baur's program which says that the exegesis has to be based on the conditions which existed for Paul at the time the letter was written. Of course, there has been no lack of attempted interpretations from this perspective.[6] Some said Paul had a need to reflect on his theology and teaching at this turning point in his life and that he wanted to collect his thoughts. Others have said that the former Jew wanted to reflect further about the relationship between law and faith, or that he was meditating about previous conflicts in which he had been involved. Another theory suggests that Paul was attempting to make contact with Rome in preparation for his visit. To this end he introduced himself to a hitherto unknown congregation in Rome; the apostle of the Gentiles is aiming at the center of that world so as to make Rome the basis for his future work.

We do not wish to dwell on the question of how correct or incorrect these viewpoints are. Those theses of a more psychological nature cannot be verified according to the historical method. However, it is significant to note that many commentators apparently are not satisfied with a justification based on Paul's immediate situation and travel plans. Therefore, scholars like to write that Paul's travel plans and future missionary work are expressions of peripheral or superficial reasons for writing Romans. They run into certain difficulties, however, in attempting to bring explicit theological ideas into agreement with the framework of the letter. Nevertheless, they claim that the casual remarks in the letter about Paul's travel plans can hardly express the actual theme of the letter.[7]

One must ask whether Romans is really a genuine letter. There can be no doubt about that. It is a pastoral letter with an addressee. To be sure, we can be led to see it as a monster of a letter because of the long main part (1:18–11:36) which almost destroys the structure of the letter. And yet, the letter structure is there—with all its characteristics such as opening salutation, expression of thanks, and regret for intercession (1:1–17), with exhortation and conclusion in chapter 12. This makes it mandatory for the interpreter to try to understand the occasion and content of this letter precisely in light of those aspects which have often been characterized as "marginal comments" about Paul's situation and travel plans. The essential content of the letter has to be seen from the perspective of Paul's concrete and immediate concern. Indeed some scholars have offered attempts to make Paul's situation the focal point of their exegesis (e.g., N. A. Dahl,[8] B. Noack[9]). Although I do not share the views of these particular scholars, their methodological advance does yield results. Thus, the major presupposition for an understanding of Romans is that one frees

---

[6]See Kümmel, *Introduction*, 312ff.
[7]For example, Marxsen, *Introduction*, 92f.; Kümmel, *Introduction*, 312f.
[8]Dahl, "Hovedsak," 57–66.
[9]Noack, "Current and Backwater," 155–66.

oneself from the idea that a Pauline letter is primarily determined by the situation of the recipients.

Let me now state my thesis. The essential and primary content of Romans (1:18–11:36) is a reflection upon its major content, the "collection speech," or more precisely, the defense which Paul plans to give before the church in Jerusalem. To put it another way: Paul sets forth and explains what he, as the bearer of the collection given by the Gentiles for the mother congregation in Jerusalem, intends to say so that he as well as the gift will not be rejected. In Jerusalem he expects to be confronted by two parties: non-believing Jews and the Christian congregation (15:30–33). Therefore, Paul has only one objective: to ask the Roman congregation for solidarity, support, and intercession on his behalf. It has been observed long ago that the major content of Romans (chs. 1–11) is more characteristic of a treatise than of a letter. This thesis cannot be dismissed lightly. One additional comment, however, is necessary: major variations in style show that it is a treatise in the sense that it has the markings of an apology together with a concrete addressee. It is primarily directed to Jerusalem, but also to Rome because Paul needs this congregation. But let us not jump ahead.

I

It is easy to reconstruct Paul's own circumstances at the time he wrote the letter. Paul himself informs us about them in 15:25ff. He is about to travel to Jerusalem in order to bring the congregation in that city the collection gathered by the Gentile Christians.

Paul's missionary work in the East is finished (15:23), and he intends to continue his efforts in the West, particularly in Spain (15:24, 28). His intention is to visit Rome on the way (15:24, 29). One notices a degree of uncertainty in his planning of the route to Rome. These feelings are expressed in his prayer (1:10), in his hope of many years (15:23) and in his yearning (15:24). Events in Jerusalem will determine whether he will succeed in getting to Rome (15:31). Two things could prevent this: first, that the Jews would kill him, and second, that the offering for the congregation in Jerusalem would be rejected (15: 31). Should Paul have the opportunity to continue his work and visit Rome, he must avoid trouble with the Jews, and he must receive a favorable reception by the church. We note how Paul himself views his relationship to the Jews. To them he is so well known that, as a result, his very life is in danger; this portrayal is confirmed in Acts 21–28.[10] At the same time it is obvious that Paul cannot proceed with his work without the recognition of the Jerusalem church.

---

[10] Jervell, "Lehrer Israels," 164–90. ET = "Teacher," 153–83.

Why does Paul refer to his trip to Jerusalem at all? He does this not only to inform the Roman congregation where he plans to go, but also because he has a request to make of them with regard to a definite and concrete matter. We know through several studies, especially C. Bjerkelund,[11] that in letters of antiquity and in the Pauline letter a writer's intent and concern is expressed in sentences introduced by a *parakalō* clause, such as "I ask, I request, I beseech." It is also known that these phrases are found primarily at the end of the letter. But these "peripheral" comments cannot be dismissed as insignificant. Three such sentences occur in Romans: 12:1; 14:30 and 16:17. The last one concerns a warning against teachers of false doctrine. This sentence is obviously not part of the letter's essential message[12] since nothing is mentioned about false teaching in chapters 1–15. The first sentence, 12:1, introduces the paraenetic section of the letter. Its very general Christian nature is more noticeable here than in any other letter of Paul, with the exception of Ephesians. In 15:30–32, on the other hand, direct reference is made concerning the Romans and Paul's immediate travel plans: "I appeal to you, brethren, by our Lord Jesus Christ and by the love of the Spirit, to strive together with me in your prayers to God on my behalf, that I may be delivered from the unbelievers in Judea, and that my service for Jerusalem may be acceptable to the saints, so that by God's will I may come to you with joy and be refreshed in your company." Paul is asking the Romans for their prayers, that is, he requests their support and solidarity regarding his impending journey to Jerusalem. He is going there with the collection of the Gentiles and indicates clearly that he is writing to them explicitly as the apostle of the Gentiles (15:15ff.).

The reason for writing Romans is expressed in 15:30–32. Paul is not asking support for his future missionary endeavors in Spain. True, he is expressing hope for some aid—probably in terms of food and lodging—so that he will be able to continue his journey after his stay in Rome (15:24). But he is not specifically requesting such aid. Therefore, that is not the reason for his writing; nor would it explain plausibly his extended remarks in the main section, viz., "first to the Jews and also to the Greeks." Should Paul have been concerned only with financial support for his future efforts, a brief explanation would have sufficed. We have every reason to inquire about the purpose of these detailed remarks if, indeed, his future work in Spain was his only concern. Romans would then, presumably, be a summary of Paul's preaching and teaching designed to inform the congregation in Rome what he intends to say in Spain. But Romans is no such summary. Too much of what we know from other letters to be Paul's teaching is omitted.[13] Everything points to problems which are of

[11]Bjerkelund, *Parakalo.*
[12]For another interpretation see Bjerkelund, *Parakalo,* 156ff.
[13]Cf. Kümmel, *Introduction,* 312f.

particular concern to Jerusalem.[14] We should also ask why, if Paul also plans to do missionary work in Rome (1:15), he presents his gospel in advance and in written form?

There is one other matter we should not overlook: whenever Paul speaks about his work in Rome he himself is uncertain as to what he wants to do there. This fact is often concealed by other critics. He speaks of his intention to preach and do missionary work in Rome (1:13, 15). But he cannot really enter into any such missionary work without violating his own principle never to preach at a place where others already taught before him (15:20). Major exegetical manipulations are necessary to avoid the contradictions contained in these two verses. Further, Paul expresses his desire to visit the congregation in Rome both to strengthen it and to be himself strengthened by it (1:11–12). But he also says that he is merely passing through, he speaks of a "breather," and that he wishes to be helped along on his journey which seems to indicate that no missionary work is intended (15:23–24, 29, 32b). The simplest explanation is that Paul has not come to any decision himself and that there are other, more immediate matters in his relationship with Rome which occupy him aside from the fact that he is simply supposed to go there.[15]

There is not a single mention of the fact that Paul intends to make Rome the base of his missionary work in the West as he did with Ephesus and Corinth for other geographic areas. Therefore the widespread and plausible assumption to this effect remains pure speculation. It is indisputable, however, that he is requesting intercessory prayers for his journey to Jerusalem. Thus, neither his trip to Spain nor his stay in Rome make this letter necessary or explain its content. Only Paul's trip to Jerusalem gives a clue, and it is precisely because of this trip that he needs the help and moral support of the Romans at this time. Paul explains the necessity of this trip and then adds his request.

Not much thought or imagination is required to recognize Paul's critical situation; it is this situation which necessitates Paul's lengthy explanations. He reveals to us (15:30–32) that both his life and his effectiveness as an apostle are at stake. If he and his churches are not recognized in Jerusalem, the unity of the church will be destroyed and Paul's future work would become impossible. This was already true with regard to Paul's earlier visit in Jerusalem (Gal. 2:2). It is unimportant whether we understand the collection historically as a temple tax, as a diaspora donation or something similar to it. In any event it is a sign of the Gentiles' recognition of and respect for Jerusalem as the mother congregation. The collection also acknowledges the close ties of the Gentile Christians to the Jewish Christians and to Israel (15:27; 2 Cor. 9:12–14).

---

[14]Fuchs, *Hermeneutik*, 191, asserts that the "secret address" of Romans is Jerusalem!
[15]See particularly Schrenk, "Der Römerbrief," 192ff.

Acceptance of the collection on the part of Jerusalem can only mean one thing: recognition of Paul's gospel and his churches—that is to say, the "right" of the Gentile world to be saved. It is important to note that Paul points out in 15:31 that he is facing two problems in Jerusalem and that this portrayal corresponds to Acts 21–28. The attitude of the congregation in Jerusalem towards Paul is one of critical aloofness (21:15–26) and the Jews accuse him (21:27–26:32).[16] Both groups act from the same motive: Paul speaks against Israel, the law, and circumcision (21:21, 28; 28:17). Luke describes it as a criticism against Paul which is steadily increasing in intensity and we have no reason to doubt his account. This fact as well as everything else the letters say about continuing opposition on the part of Jewish Christians explains the difference between his earlier visit in Jerusalem and the one which he is planning now. Despite approval and a brotherly welcome (Gal. 2:1ff.), Paul is meeting opposition on the part of church circles in Jerusalem (see already 2:11ff.). The group around James probably never accepted Paul's teaching completely (Gal. 2:12; cf. also Acts 21:18).

The impending trip to Jerusalem and his relationship to the church there are forcing Paul to devote full attention to matters which he only hinted at in earlier letters. Included among these are: Israel's lack of faith and Israel's future as the people of God, the significance of the apostle of the Gentiles for Israel and their conversion, circumcision and the meaning of the law, Jews and Gentiles in their relationship to the final judgment and the righteousness of God, and finally, the role and importance of Jewish Christians in the church. In other words, we have here all those problems which are discussed in Romans 1–11. We have every reason to stress that justification by faith apart from the law is not the theme of Romans. That theme is treated in Galatians. The theme of Romans is this: the righteousness of God is revealed through faith apart from the law, first to the Jews, then to the Greeks, and at the end to all Israel.

Already the relationship between Romans and Galatians shows how decisive the trip to Jerusalem really is. Over and over again it has been stressed that Romans is more thorough, its tone more calm, and that it contains reflections which are more detached with regard to themes which he treated earlier, especially in Galatians but also in Philippians 3 and in 2 Corinthians 3–6.[17] This interpretation can hardly be correct. As far as a comparison between these two letters is concerned, it is the one to the Galatians which is more detached, even if Paul is more excited and temperamental in this letter.

There are significant differences with regard to certain decisive points between the two letters. In Galatians, "Abraham's seed" is Christ. This re-

---

[16]For further detail see: Jervell, "Teacher," 153ff.

[17]Thus, along with others, Munck, *Paulus und die Heilsgeschichte*, 192ff. ET: *Paul and the Salvation of Mankind*.

fers to the faithful among Jews and Gentiles (Gal. 3:16ff.). The promises
of the church are in force: here indeed is a new people and a new creation (3:7ff.; 6:15); in Gal. 6:16 the "Israel of God" refers to the Jewish Christians. In Romans the historical, non-believing Israel continue as the people
of God; Abraham is also the father of the Jews who are faithful to the law,
and salvation is theirs from the beginning. This description does not only
occur in Rom. 9–11 but also in other places (3:1; 4:1, 12, 16; 15:8).

One should also note the many positive statements regarding the law
(2:13, 20ff.; 3:31; 7:12, 14, 16–22, 25; 8:4). In Galatians we find the quote
"neither Jew nor Greek" (3:28). In this context neither circumcision nor
the lack of it is of importance (6:15). This is different from Romans: "to the
Jew first and also to the Greek" (1:16; 2:9–10). The preference of circumcision is maintained (3:1; 9–11; 15:8).

One cannot possibly overlook the noticeable change which has taken
place with regard to Israel between Galatians and Romans. The reason
for this change can only be that Paul, because of his critical situation with
regard to Jerusalem, is now tackling the question regarding Israel's future
thoroughly and in all earnest. He is forced to reconsider his earlier views
in the light of new factors. This is in turn related to the fact that the congregation in Galatia, unlike the one in Jerusalem, is a mission congregation with many Gentile Christians.

The situation in both congregations is different: the Galatians are Gentiles who want to be circumcised; those in Jerusalem are already circumcised. In Galatians Christ is the end of the law and therefore Israel's
termination; in Romans Paul argues that Christ as "the end of the law"
does not mean the termination of Israel. With regard to sin, judgment,
and righteousness there is no difference between Jew and Greek. And yet,
there is the one substantial difference, viz., that the entire non-believing
Israel will find salvation because they are God's people. These are the issues he wishes to explain in Jerusalem.

II

In Romans Paul is absorbed by what he is going to say in Jerusalem.
This fact not only explains the content of the letter but also sheds light
upon its form and structure. Yet only a few stylistic analyses of Romans
are available to date. Only a handful of studies attempt to demonstrate
the significance of style upon the intention and content of this letter. As
a result, we have to be satisfied with some tentative suggestions.

With regard to form, the letter contains considerable variations in style.
Actual letter style can only be found in the introduction and conclusion
of the letter. Only from these elements can it be determined that the letter has concrete recipients to whom Paul is writing. However, between 1:18

and 11:36 the recipients are no longer in focus. Stylistic variations are noticeable in the main part as well. But on the whole, this document is neither consistently written in letter style nor as a didactic monologue serving as an introduction to Paul's preaching. Didactic statements, for example, are partly written in the third person (1:18–32). We find other pericopes in the form of a diatribe, dialogue or discussion (3:1–20). We also find midrashic exegesis (Rom. 4) as well as some sections which are written in a hymnic-liturgical style (e.g., Rom. 11:33–36). Throughout there is a continuous change between first, second, and third person. This is obviously not the way one writes a letter or a didactic treatise. Romans has the characteristics of a speech with marked apologetic, and to a lesser degree, polemic tendencies. In other words, we find here a presentation of Pauline preaching—yet always defensive and intent on clarifying possible misunderstanding. Two things occur simultaneously: vindication and debate. It is quite clear that we are not dealing with a debate Paul is having with the church in Rome, but with objections he is anticipating in Jerusalem.

The commentaries always attempt to present clear and schematic arrangements of the letter and yet it is difficult to recognize such a pattern. The main theme of the letter is found in 1:16–17, and it is carried through until 11:36, and then plays a role again in the treatment of the paraenetic section (e.g. 15:7ff., 15ff.). But this major theme about God's righteousness towards Jews and Greeks is continuously interrupted by digressions, commentaries, excursuses, and parenthetical remarks. Very often questions mark the beginning of these discussions.

Looking at these questions one notices two things. First, Paul himself poses the questions. They are based on the preceding, factual descriptions and not on a concrete situation in the congregation. Second, they are questions and deliberations which have to do with the situation in Jerusalem. Let us look at a few examples: What is the advantage of the Jew? Of what use is circumcision? Chapter 2 necessitates the asking of these questions. In 3:8 Paul asks: Shall we do evil so that good may result? Rom. 3:1–7 forces this question. The reader should look at 3:9ff. when he continues: What did Abraham, our forefather achieve? Romans 7:7 asks "Is the law sin?" This question lurks in the background since 5:20. Romans 9:14 asks: Is there injustice with God? Who can avoid this question after 9:1ff.? We find one more question in 11:1: Has God rejected his people? It is sufficient to look at the questions raised in 1 Corinthians to notice the different function these questions have in Romans. In 1 Corinthians they concern real problems of the congregation. In Romans we are dealing with Paul's own questions. The abruptness and the structure of the letter are explained by the fact that Paul is on the defensive and must be apologetic. He is supposed to both inform Jerusalem and defend himself simultaneously.

The Romans are now being drawn into this defense. This knowledge helps us to move one step further toward a better understanding of Romans.

III

Romans, however, is addressed directly to the congregation in Rome and not to Jerusalem.[18] Now the thought arises whether this long and detailed presentation is really necessary as a presupposition and motivation for the requested intercessory prayers? Without a doubt, certain matters have to be clarified if the Roman congregation is supposed to fight with Paul against Jerusalem, help save him from the Jews, and accept him into their congregation. The Romans must understand that the Jews threaten his life without reason. In reality, he is speaking for Israel and fighting for its salvation (chs. 9–11). The Romans, therefore, must understand the relationship between Jews and Gentiles, how both are sinful and yet equal as far as God's righteousness is concerned. Further, they must understand how, on the one hand, the gospel removes all differences while on the other hand, Israel and Jerusalem still retain a certain priority. They have to affirm the Pauline actualization of the gospel and they have to recognize and agree with him that the accusations against him are wrong. In addition, they have to understand their own situation and their relationship to this apostle of the Gentiles. The request for solidarity in their intercessory prayers can only be made at the end of the letter after Paul has finished his detailed account. No matter what meaning intercessory prayer has for Paul, one thing is obvious: such prayer can only be said on the basis that one knows why and for what purpose one is praying, and that such prayer always takes place in unison.

But why is Paul writing precisely to the Roman church? Why is their support so important? It seems peculiar that Paul is turning to a totally strange congregation—at least it is always asserted that this congregation was unknown to Paul. And yet, there are reasons why one should doubt this. One thing is certain: that Paul did not found the congregation. This does not, however, mean that we should immediately assume that he did not know the congregation, even though we must be cautious and not read too much into the numerous greetings contained in chapter 16 since its authenticity is disputed.

There is clear evidence in Paul's letters that the various congregations were not totally isolated from one another. In any case, the congregations knew one another. One congregation was informed about the other because one aspect of missionary preaching and paraenesis was to report about faith and life in other congregations. In fact, we have evidence that

---

[18]Marxsen, *Introduction*, 95, rejects Fuchs' understanding of the "secret address" of Romans (see n. 14 above).

the faith and life of one congregation was reported to another: 1 Thess. 1:8ff.; 2 Cor. 3:1–3; Col. 1:4; 2 Thess. 3:6; 2 Cor. 8–9.[19] Missionaries and congregations were discussed wherever the gospel was proclaimed. In Rom. 1:8 we even have a direct statement that the faith of the Roman community represents a piece of the gospel "for the world." Regardless of how many or how few people Paul could have known in Rome, there is no doubt that Paul was informed about the condition of the Roman church. This would indicate that other congregations were able to have a share in the knowledge of that which took place between apostle and congregation (1 Thess. 1:8ff.).

It is significant to note how Paul himself viewed the congregation in Rome. He regards the Roman church as a model congregation to which he gives full recognition. Not only is this congregation well-known to him, but also one that he speaks about in the entire world (1:8): it is obedient to the standard of teaching (6:17); its faith is Paul's faith, and this congregation can also edify him (1:12); it is filled with goodness and knowledge, so that every exhortation is superfluous (15:14).

Biblical scholars have attempted to explain this simply as mere courtesy and rhetoric. This is particularly true, they assert, with regard to the many superfluous exhortations (15:14ff.). But certainly this is too simple an exegesis. What is at any rate clear is that Paul unconditionally certifies the genuineness of their Christian life. Even more important, we note that this congregation is recognized within the entire church (1:8; 16:19).

Biblical scholars have tried to show that the importance of the Roman community resulted from the fact that it existed at the center of the Gentile world just as Jerusalem was the center for Israel. Thus, it is important that the apostle to the Gentiles be able to get a foothold in Rome. While this might be true, it does seem strange that Paul only intends to travel through it in passing. Besides, Paul does not mention in his letter that Rome is the center of the Gentile world. He does stress, however, that this Roman congregation has taken on a central position on behalf of the entire church. There is no other congregation which receives a corresponding seal of approval.

We now have an answer to why Paul is writing Romans specifically to the church in Rome. There is still one other matter which must be clarified. In 15:19 Paul asserts that he has proclaimed the gospel to that entire part of the world which stretches all the way from Jerusalem to Illyricum. In the context of the present discussion it is unimportant how the phrase "from Jerusalem to Illyricum" is to be understood. What is clear is that the apostle to the Gentiles is to represent the congregations of the entire East in Jerusalem. He has not yet reached Rome; and yet, this part of the

[19]See Jervell, "Zur Frage," 29ff.

world also belongs to his domain since he is the only apostle to the Gentiles (1:6; 13; 15:15ff.).

This last passage (15:15ff.) is particularly characteristic since it says that Paul is the priest who is supposed to offer this congregation to God as a sacrifice, even though he did not found it. In my view then, the important thing is this: Paul wants to represent the entire Gentile world in Jerusalem, including the West. The entire Gentile world stands behind him. He no longer needs to do missionary work in Rome because the gospel has already been spread there. Paul is telling himself that he ought to have been in Rome earlier to spread the gospel but he was detained (1:13; 15:8ff.). Apparently he means that he ought to have been the first one in Rome. Nonetheless, in a certain sense this congregation, as a part of the Gentile world, does belong to him and he would like to see it on his side. The collection which Paul is carrying with him is a sign that his congregations are closely aligned with him and that they acknowledge his teaching. Rome's support and acknowledgement is to be expressed in its prayers of intercession. Such an influential and recognized congregation is certainly invaluable as a partner in battle and witness to the apostle of the Gentiles.

If these perspectives are valid, our lack of knowledge about the congregation in Rome does not present any great problem. For the purpose of exegesis, we do not need to know more than what Paul is telling us about the situation and status of the congregation. In conclusion, Paul is writing Romans mainly for himself and, thereby, on behalf of the entire Gentile Christian church which he is hoping to present to God as a sacrifice.

6

ROMANS 14:1–15:13 AND
THE OCCASION OF ROMANS

Robert J. Karris

Today there is a growing number of scholars who do not see the situation at Rome as the primary occasion for Romans. In doing so, they do not treat Romans as a theological tractate. Rather they try to locate its occasion in Paul's own life. Franz Leenhardt argues that the occasion for Romans is to be seen in Paul's view of what his missionary work in Spain means for the unity of the church.[1] Günther Bornkamm and Werner G. Kümmel see Romans as Paul's mature articulation of his missionary gospel: Bornkamm terms Romans "Paul's Testament";[2] Kümmel calls Romans "the theological self-confession of Paul."[3] James P. Martin argues that the occasion for Romans is rooted in Paul's missionary vision for the whole world.[4] Jacob Jervell sees Romans as Paul's defense speech in Jerusalem so that his collection and he himself will not be rejected.[5]

[1]*The Epistle to the Romans: A Commentary* (London: Lutterworth, 1961), 12–23.

[2]*Paul* (N.Y.: Harper & Row, 1971) 88–96.

[3]Kümmel, *Introduction,* 312. Bornkamm and Kümmel, however, are troubled by Rom. 14:1–15:13, which prevents them from giving a unified occasion for Romans. Bornkamm, *Paul,* 89, must acknowledge that Rom. 14–15 "are the one exception" to his argument that Paul knows "almost nothing about events, questions, and emergencies in the community." On p. 57 he says that Paul in Rom. 14–15 "has to put an end to a quarrel between two rival groups. . . ." Kümmel, *Introduction,* 312–13, while maintaining that Romans is the "theological self-confession of Paul," which arose out of a "concrete necessity of his missionary work," also holds that there is "no doubt that . . . he joins in the opposition between the vegetarians and their opponents in the Roman community . . ." (pp. 313–14).

[4]Martin, "Kerygma of Romans," 303–28. "In the historical situation out of which Paul wrote (chs. 9–11; 1:5; 14f.; 15:18–25), his kerygma offers the people of God, now reconstituted through Jesus Christ, a world-consciousness and calls them to a world-mission to bring about the obedience of faith among all nations" (p. 328). "The Kerygma in Rom., however, is presented in more elaborate form (than in 1 Cor.) since Paul is not writing to particular difficulties but on questions of the universal faith and mission of the church" (p. 304 n. 1). Martin's view of the paraenesis of Romans (pp. 326–28) takes almost no account of the problems of Rom. 14:1–15:13. This is a weakness in what is otherwise a superb article.

[5]Jervell, "Letter to Jerusalem." See chapter 5 above, pp. 53–64.

Because of Rom. 14:1–15:13, other scholars[6] feel that the occasion for Romans lies in Paul's resolution of the controversy between "the weak" and "the strong" in Rome.[7]

The purpose of this article is to try to break this scholarly impasse by provoking myself and my readers to follow a different road in dealing with the troublesome section, Rom. 14:1–15:13. This article will investigate Rom. 14:1–15:13 from a history of religions perspective, from an exegetical perspective, and from a paraenetic perspective. That is, this paper will argue that Rom. 14:1–15:13 should be analyzed for what it is: general, Pauline paraenesis and not so many pieces of polemic from which a scholar may reconstruct the positions of the parties in Rome who occasioned this letter.

This article has three parts: (1) "The weak" and "the strong" communities in Rome: The bankruptcy of the history of religions approach to Rom. 14:1–15:13; (2) The exegesis of 14:1–15:13; (3) The nature of the paraenesis in Rom. 12–15.

I. "The Weak" and "The Strong" Communities in Rome

The Bankruptcy of the History of Religions Approach to Rom. 14:1–15:13

This section of the article will use as its dialog partner Paul S. Minear's recent monograph, *The Obedience of Faith*. According to Minear the purpose of Romans is to be found in Paul's resolution of the communities' controversies reflected in 14: 1–15:13.[8] Paul is trying to unite "the weak"

---

[6]Fuller, *Introduction*, 53–54; Marxsen, *Introduction*, 92–108; Bartsch, "Empfänger," 81–89, esp. 85–86; Williams, "Paul's Purpose," 62–67; Minear, *Obedience*. The views on "the weak" and "the strong" of Lütgert (*Römerbrief*); Preisker ("Das historische Problem," 25–30), Harder ("Römerbriefes," 13–24), and Marxsen are reviewed and criticized by Jewett, *Anthropological Terms*, 42–47. In Part I below I will have frequent occasion to enter into dialog with Jewett. Cf. also Kümmel, *Introduction*, 313, who criticizes Lütgert, Preisker, and Harder for seeking to have too precise knowledge of the situation at Rome and for reaching out beyond that which can be recognized with certainty. There is no need to spell out all the positions of the authors cited above since Part I below will discuss in detail the somewhat representative view of Minear. Cf. Minear, *Obedience*, 34 n. 2: "Of all recent Introductions, that of Marxsen comes closest to my own position."

[7]Within the recent literature Morris, "Theme of Romans," 249–63 does not address himself to the problematic pursued in this article. Other scholars account for "the Jewish" and "the Gentile" problem in Romans in other ways. Cf. Trocmé, "Romains, 148–53, who maintains that the document underlying Romans is a missionary document which sums up Paul's missionary experience with Judaizers and antinomians; Kinoshita, "Romans," 257–77, who argues that Rom. 1–15 is composed of the original letter to the Romans, addressed to Gentiles, and "the Manual of Instruction on the Jewish Problems." It is significant that neither author sees the primary occasion for Romans in the situation at Rome itself.

[8]Minear speculates that the Roman church was not a unified church: "It is probable that these various cells were brought into existence at diverse times, by diverse leaders, with di-

and "the strong" communities in Rome.[9] In his efforts at reconciliation in 14:1–15:13 Paul employs twelve axioms.[10] It is the purpose of the rest of Romans to explain, support, and defend these twelve axioms,[11] as Paul addresses in the various chapters of Romans one or more of the communities.[12] If Paul can convince the divergent communities in Rome to accept these twelve axioms, then he will have unified the church at Rome.[13] Thus the occasion for Romans and its purpose are to be seen in Paul's attempts to unify the divergent communities in Rome.

Minear's thesis has difficulties. Leaving aside the question of whether chapter 16 is an integral part of Romans and thus indicative that Paul knew the situation at Rome,[14] let me single out some of the inherent weaknesses of Minear's position. His statement that there were many communities in Rome simply goes beyond the facts. The beginnings and early development of the Roman church are obscure.[15] Minear's argument for the equations "the weak" = Jewish Christians[16] and "the strong" = Gentile

---

verse conceptions of the Gospel" (*Obedience*, 7). The Roman church was composed of many communities or house churches: "Instead of visualizing a single Christian congregation, therefore, we should constantly reckon with the possibility that within the urban area were to be found forms of Christian community which were as diverse, and probably also as alien, as the churches of Galatia and those of Judea" (ibid., 8).

[9]Minear's full titles for these communities are: "The 'weak in faith' who condemned the 'strong in faith' "; and "The strong in faith who scorned and despised the weak in faith" (ibid., 8–10). For the sake of brevity I omit allusions to the other three communities that Minear, *Obedience*, pp. 12–16, finds reflected in 14:1–15:13: the doubters; the weak in faith who did not condemn the strong; the strong in faith who did not despise the weak.

[10]Ibid., 17–20. Examples of these axioms are: Axiom 1: "God has welcomed him"; Axiom 9: "If your brother is being injured by what you eat, you are no longer walking in love."

[11]Ibid., 20.

[12]Ibid., 45 n. 8. For example, Rom. 1:1–17 is addressed to all readers, but with distinctions recognized; 1:18–4:15 is addressed to Group One ("the weak"); 6:1–23 to Group Two ("the strong"). Cf. Bartsch, "Empfänger," 85 n. 15, for the suggestion of a venture similar to that of Minear.

[13]Cf. Bartsch, "Empfänger," esp. pp. 83–84, who also maintains that Paul is trying to make "a church" out of the diverse groups in Rome. For a similar view, cf. Michel, *Römer*, 10. For a contrary view, cf. Leenhardt, *Romans*, 15–23, who forcefully argues that although the word *ekklēsia* is not mentioned in Romans, the genesis of the church is the theme of Romans.

[14]Minear, *Obedience*, 22–31, has to argue subtly ("I would grant, however, that these links [between ch. 1–15 and 16] are anything but obvious." [p. 23] and lengthily on this point. Cf. T. W. Manson, "Paul's Letter to the Romans," (ch. 1, above pp. 3–15), who argues that Rom. 16 is not part of the original letter to Rome and that Romans is an encyclical letter. Cf. Kümmel, *Introduction*, 314–20, for the arguments pro and con for viewing ch. 16 as original to Romans.

[15]Cf. the conjectures of Minear, *Obedience*, 38–39, on the situation at Rome: "It is altogether likely that in the development of the dissensions in Rome, the position of Paul had already served as a source of friction, accentuating the existing animosities (cf. 9.1; 10.1f.). To members of Group One ('the weak') he had probably become known as a destroyer of the law and defender of unrestricted licence. Members of Group Two ('the strong') may well have suspected him as a Jew of undue loyalty to his kinsmen. It had been rumored that in other churches he repressed liberty for the sake of expedience. He may thus have been damned by both extremes, but for opposite reasons."

[16]Minear (*Obedience*, 9–10) does not adequately justify how he can identify "the weak" as Jews since there was no law commanding Jews to abstain from meat or wine. On p. 9

Christians[17] is hardly convincing. Furthermore, one can question quite seriously whether Paul really justifies in the rest of Romans the twelve axioms he posited in 14:1–15:13 and whether individual sections of Romans are addressed to one or more of the communities.[18] It seems that Minear's thesis has serious handicaps.[19]

At this point it is advantageous to go back almost fifty years in scholarly research to a monograph[20] which Minear has apparently bypassed. Rauer has made the strongest case for seeing divergent people, not communities or parties in Rome.[21] His argument is that "the weak" are *Gentile* Christians whose practice of abstinence from meat stems from their prior religious background in Gnostic, Hellenistic mystery religions.[22] Paul's mildness of tone indicates that these weak Christians were not heretics or guilty of serious moral lapses.[23] Their weakness in faith consisted in the fact that they preserved their God-pleasing praxis of abstinence from meat when they became Christians and were not convinced that their belief could be supported without this praxis.[24]

Briefly put, Rauer's enduring contributions to current research on Rom. 14:1–15:13 are:

(1) his summary of patristic, medieval, and modern research on the identification of "the weak" is valuable background material for any future study;[25]

---

he does allow that some of "the weak" may have been Gentiles who accepted the yoke of the law and that not all Jewish believers were members of this community.

[17]On p. 11 Minear (*Obedience*) allows that some Jews "who relished this exhilarating 'post-religious' liberty" may belong to the community of "the strong." At times Minear seems to move even further beyond the evidence of Rom. 14:1–15:13 by identifying "the weak" as legalists (p. 19: "tight legalisms") and "the strong" as antinomians (p. 9: "the lawlessness of Gentile believers"; p. 11 quoting W. D. Davies: " 'Among Gentiles, who lacked any deep acquaintance with Judaism, antinomianism was always crouching at the door ready to enter in under the cloak of grace' "; p. 12: "libertarians").

[18]The dialog and polemic in Romans cannot be used to prove that Paul was arguing against "the weak" and "the strong" communities in Rome. Cf. Bornkamm, *Paul*, 90: "In each case, however, the objections arise out of the subject matter, or rather out of a misunderstanding of it, and not an actual historical situation."

[19]For additional arguments against Minear's analysis of Rom. 14:1–15:13, cf. Part II below on the exegesis of the passage and the review by J. C. in *HeyJ* 12 (1971) 460–61: "But Minear's arguments for such clear-cut sections of the letter (too subtle, surely for the recipients themselves), and such clear-cut divisions between communities, are based more on hypotheses than evidence" (p. 461).

[20]Rauer, "*Schwachen.*" This volume is ofttimes paid bibliographical lip service, but few seem to have read it. Cf. the similar complaint in Jewett, *Anthropological Terms*, 43: "A serious shortcoming of the recent discussion is that the unsurpassed study on the problem of the.

[21]Rauer, "*Schwachen,*" 88, 95 insists that "the weak" are individuals and not a community or party.

[22]Ibid., 164–68.

[23]Ibid., 121–69 consistently uses this observation as a criterion against reconstructions of "the weak" community. Cf. Bornkamm, "*Lachanon,*" *TDNT* 4.67 for a similar evaluation.

[24]Rauer, "*Schwachen,*" 166, cf. 89–93.

[25]Ibid., 108–20. For additional material on the history of scholarship, cf. Feuillet, "Les fondements," 365 n. 21; 366; Araud, "Interprétations patristiques," 1.127–45.

(2) his arguments against seeing "the weak" as Jews, Essenes, Pythagorians, or antinomians remain valid to this day;[26]

(3) any explanation of Rom. 14:1–15:13 must take into consideration the mildness of tone that Paul employs;

(4) one can question whether "the weak" abstained from wine; in its context the reference to abstaining from wine flows stylistically from the expression "eating and drinking";[27]

(5) because of the literary integrity of 14:1–12 one can question whether "days" refers to sabbaths or ceremonial holy days; the "days" are fast days.[28]

Rauer has made the strongest case for identifying "the weak" with particular people,[29] ascertainable, imaginable by history of religions research. It is to be observed, however, that even his reconstruction falls short of conviction. When Rauer tries to explain why the converted pagans retained their praxis of abstinence when they became Christians, he has to resort to conjectures not founded in the text of Romans: ascetic tendencies within Christianity, eschatological pre-Noahic vegetarianism, etc.[30]

There is no doubt that history of religions research will continue its attempts to put flesh on Rom. 14:1–15:13's skeletal description of "the weak." Would it be too bold to suggest that Rauer's detailed weighing of all the possible identifications of "the weak" and Minear's recent reconstruction of the situation at Rome have indirectly shown us that such research is moving down a dead-end street and that another approach should be taken to Rom. 14:1–15:13?[31] I would be so audacious as to suggest that the history of religions approach to the origins of the Roman church and to "the

[26]Rauer, "Schwachen," 122–63. Cf. Dederen, "Esteeming One Day Better," 21–23, 29–30, who says that "the weak" were influenced by Essenism. Cf. Michel, Römer, 334, for a cautious evaluation of what groups abstained from certain foods and why. Recall that Minear, Obedience, 9–10, insufficiently accounts for the lack of evidence that the Jews had injunctions to abstain from meat and posits that the abstainers were Jews (cf. n. 16 above).

[27]Rauer, "Schwachen," 97–100. In brief, Rauer's arguments are: (1) abstinence from wine is not mentioned in the programmatic 14:2; (2) the parallelism of eating and drinking in 14:7 stylistically requires eating and drinking in 14:21. Cf. also the parallel between Rom. 14:21 and 1 Cor. 10:31 listed on p. 74 below; (3) if "the weak" abstained from wine, there would be no Eucharist.

[28]Ibid., 182–84. Cf. Dederen, "Esteeming One Day Better," for a similar, independent understanding of "days." His argument is also from context: diet and days are connected in the context; thus "days" is most likely to be referred to "fast days" (p. 31). Cf. Jewett, Anthropological Terms, 43–44, who is also very appreciative of Rauer's contributions to the discussion of Rom. 14:1–15:13.

[29]It is important to keep in mind that Rauer does not argue that a discernible community with distinguishable theological principles/positions existed in Rome. Cf. n. 21 above.

[30]Rauer, "Schwachen," 166–68. Cf. Jewett, Anthropological Terms, 44, for similar disappointment at this part of Rauer's argument.

[31]Cf. Jervell, "Letter to Jerusalem," 53–64, for a similar disquietude with the history of religions approach to ascertaining the situation at Rome. Cf. Jewett, Anthropological Terms, 45, 47, for indications of the frustration he experiences in trying to explain Romans from the situation at Rome: "For all its length, there is insufficient evidence either conclusively to identify the 'Weak' and the rationale of their abstinence or to demonstrate the source of the antinomistic self-consciousness of the 'Strong' " (p. 47). It is significant that even this

weak" and "the strong"[32] communities in Rome is bankrupt. To be sure, such research may yield one word of incontestable truth for every year of research, much as a bankrupt firm may pay one mill per thousand dollars owed. Its bankruptcy, however, challenges us to invest our time and energy elsewhere.

In summary, the first part of this article has indicated the rising tide of opinion that calls for a reconsideration of the question of whether "the weak" and "the strong" communities, reflected in Rom. 14:1–15:13, occasioned Romans. The situation within the Roman community is obscure at best, and mirror-reading from the epistle itself will not dispel that obscurity. Not one of the history of religions identifications of "the weak" or "the strong" communities/parties in Rome can claim more for itself than the designation "conjecture." Is there any other possible path of investigation which may be charted?

II. Exegesis of Romans 14:1–15:13

It is not within the pale of this article to give a comprehensive exegesis of Rom. 14:1–15:13. My procedure will be to isolate those exegetical problems that have been and remain in the center of the discussion.

The Nature of 14:1–15:13

Perhaps one of the few points on which scholars agree is that Rom. 14:1–15:13 falls under the rubric of apostolic admonition.[33] If such be the case, it is a type of paraenesis which is distinct from that contained in Rom. 12–13.[34]

When one asks the question whether this apostolic admonition is ad-

---

accomplished sleuth of the existence and the positions of the opponents in Paul's letters (cf. "Conflicting Movements," 362–90; idem, "The Agitators," 198–212) is mystified by Rom. 14:1–15:13.

[32]Jewett, *Anthropological Terms*, 45–46 summarizes the evidence scholars (cf. n. 6) have gleaned from Romans for the existence and theological positions of "the strong." "They are Gentile Christians with enthusiastic and libertinistic leanings" (p. 45). But as Jewett, 45 is quick to point out, Romans gives us no indication of the reason for this group's proud self-consciousness. Some of this "evidence" can be negated on the basis of Paul's diatribe style in Romans. Cf. n. 18 above. Most of the other items of "evidence" are drawn from the paraenesis of Romans. On this cf. Part III below where it is argued that Rom. 12–15 is not actual paraenesis. Although Jewett argues for the existence of "the strong" at Rome, he admits the difficulty of interpreting Romans on the basis of an actual situation there: " . . . in Romans one not only derives an inadequate picture of the situation in Rome but also is left with the impression that much of the argument is related only tenuously with the concrete.

[33]Cf. Michel, *Römer*, 289. Michel also mentions that apostolic admonition is indebted to tradition. One would have desired that Michel had paid closer attention to Paul's use of the "tradition" of 1 Cor. 8; 9; 10:23–11:1 in Rom. 14:1–15:13. Cf. Part II section B below.

[34]Michel, *Römer*, 289, calls this paranesis ΟΤ and Hellenistic sayings literature. It is to be noted that Minear, *Obedience*, 82–90, experiences grave difficulties when he tries to explain the traditional paranesis of Rom. 12–13 in his interpretation of Romans.

dressed to a specific situation or is general, i.e., not directed to a specific situation, scholars part ways. Let Minear be the spokesman for the group that sees 14:1–15:13 directed to a specific situation within the Roman community(ies):

> It is true that Paul often incorporated into his letters didactic material which was typical of what he taught in all the churches. This catechetical material was often shaped by general practice rather than by particular situations. Chapters 12 and 13 contain material which is probably of this sort (see below, however, for important qualifications, pp. 82–90). There is, however, a change in literary style between ch. 13 and 14. The apostle moves from general injunctions, embodied in traditional oral forms of paraenesis, to the consideration of a specific set of problems. The nearest parallel is 1 Corinthians (8:1–13; 9:19–23; 10:23–11:1). No one doubts that in Corinth he was wrestling directly with a specific situation. Why then should we doubt that this was also true in Rome?[35]

The most recent brief treatment of Rom. 14–15 will serve as an indication of the scholarly view that Rom. 14–15 is general apostolic admonition. In *The Love Command in the New Testament* Victor P. Furnish observes: "Romans is addressed to a church of which Paul has no first-hand knowledge, and his discussion of 'the strong' and 'the weak' in 14:1–15:13 reads like a generalized adaptation of a position he had earlier worked out respecting an actual, known situation in Corinth."[36]

As should be obvious, I share Furnish's view and will offer my exegetical reasons in the sections that follow: Rom. 14:1–15:13 is a generalized adaptation of a position Paul had earlier worked out respecting actual known situations, especially in Corinth.[37]

The Relationship of Rom. 14:1–15:13 to 1 Cor. 8; 9; 10:23–11:1

Most commentators and scholars refer to the relationship between 1 Cor. 8–10 and Rom. 14:1–15:13, but do not go into detail.[38] Rauer[39] and

---

[35]Ibid., 22. Cf. also, e.g., Michel, *Römer,* 9–14: 333–35; Rauer, *"Schwachen,"* 76–78; Barrett, *Romans,* 256–58.

[36]Furnish, *Love Command,* 115. In n. 69 on the same page Furnish has some tentative suggestions on why Rom. 14–15 is a generalized adaptation of a prior situation. During the course of the following discussion I will have occasion to return to his highly provocative suggestions. For similar views on the general character of Rom. 14:1–15:13, cf. Bornkamm, *Paul,* 94; Leenhardt, *Romans,* 344–46; Fitzmyer, "Letter to the Romans," 53, 116, 126; Sanday-Headlam, *Romans,* 399–403; Conzelmann, *Korinther,* 16.

[37]If one follows the hypothesis of T. W. Manson (cf. n. 14 above), one could argue that since Romans is an encyclical letter, Rom. 14:1–15:13 has to be general apostolic admonition addressed to a number of churches; cf. also Jewett, *Anthropological Terms,* 47.

[38]Perhaps the 1963 Heidelberg dissertation by A. E. S. Nababan, *Bekenntnis und Mission in Römer 14 und 15: Eine exegetische Untersuchung,* would provide the most detail. Unfortunately this work is unavailable to me. I am indebted to Merk, *Handeln aus Glauben,* 167 n. 76 for the reference to Nababan's thesis.

[39]Rauer, *"Schwachen,"* 122–25 lists three important parallels between Rom. 14:1–15:13 and 1 Cor. 8–10.

Jacques Dupont[40] have gone into the most detail. When appropriate, I will build upon their suggestions.

Rom. 14:1–15:13 is clearly paraenetic. It contains thirteen imperatives: 14:1, 3*bis*, 5, 13*bis*, 15, 16, 19, 20, 22; 15:2, 7.[41] As Leenhardt has pointed out, most of these imperatives are in the first person plural (14:13, 19) or the third person singular (14:3bis, 5, 16; 15:2). "It is clear from this that Paul is not really addressing a particular group of people, whose concrete circumstances he is considering while pointing out their errors."[42] In comparison 1 Cor. 8 has one imperative: 1 Cor. 8:9. First Corinthians 10:23–11:1 has seven imperatives: 10:24, 25, 27, 28, 31, 32, 11:1. Perhaps no weight should be placed on the fact that 1 Cor. 8 has only one imperative. Yet, that fact becomes more important when one considers another relationship between Rom. 14–15 and 1 Cor. 8–10.

Romans 14:1–15:13 has one circumstantial "if" clause. Romans 14:15 reads: "If your brother is being injured by what you eat, you are no longer walking in love."[43] First Corinthians 8 has two circumstantial "if" clauses: 1 Cor. 8:10, 13.[44] These clauses read: "For if any one sees you, a man of knowledge, at table in an idol's temple, might he not be encouraged, if his conscience is weak, to eat food offered to idols?" (1 Cor. 8:10). "Therefore, if food is a cause of my brother's falling, I will never eat meat, lest I cause my brother to fall" (1 Cor. 8:13).

First Corinthians 10:23–11:1 contains three circumstantial "if" clauses:

> If one of the unbelievers invites you to dinner and you are disposed to go, eat whatever is set before you without raising any question on the ground of conscience. (But if some one says to you, "This has been offered in sacrifice," then out of consideration for the man who informed you, and for conscience' sake—I mean his conscience, not yours—do not eat it.) If I partake with thankfulness, why am I denounced because of that for which I give thanks? (1 Cor. 10:27–30).

The circumstantial "if" clauses in 1 Cor. 8 and 10 serve to make the teaching and principles of Paul concrete and specific. One could argue that since such circumstantial clauses are almost entirely lacking in Rom. 14:1–15:13 Paul is not addressing himself to a concrete situation within the Roman community.[45]

---

[40]Dupont, "Appel aux faibles," 1.357–66 notes the different situations in 1 Cor. and Rom. and argues for a transposing of principles from 1 Cor. to Rom. 14–15 in three instances.

[41]If one takes the *opheilomen* of 15:1 to have imperatival force, there are fourteen imperatives.

[42]Leenhardt, *Romans*, 345. Leenhardt may go beyond the evidence in his evaluation of the meagerness of second person imperatives (six in number), but his observation merits consideration. Second person plural imperatives are used in 14:1, 13; 15:7, second person singular in 14:15, 20, 22.

[43]I omit Rom. 14:8 from the discussion because its "if" clauses are not circumstantial. In this and the following quotations from the NT I employ the Revised Standard Version.

[44]I omit 1 Cor. 8:2, 3 from the discussion because their "if" clauses are not circumstantial.

[45]Confirmation for this argument can be found in Paul's discussion on the application of principles in 1 Cor. 7. 1 Cor. 7:8, 12, 15, 28, 36, 37 ("whoever") contain circumstantial

It must also be observed that it is only Rom. 14:1–15:13 that talks about "the weak" and "the strong." 1 Cor. 8 and 10 do not talk about "the strong." As a matter of fact, 1 Cor. 10:23–11:1 does not mention "the weak." When "weak" does occur in 1 Cor. 8, it refers three times out of five to weak conscience (8:7, 10, 12; cf. 8:9, 11).[46]

It remains to draw out the verbal parallels between Rom. 14:1–15:13 and 1 Cor. 8; 9; 10:23–11:1:[47]

ROMANS

14:1: As for the man who is weak in faith, welcome him, but not for *disputes over opinions.*

1 CORINTHIANS

10:25, 27: Eat whatever is sold in the meat market *without raising any question on the ground of conscience* . . . eat whatever is set before you *without raising any question on the ground of conscience.*[48]

14:6: He also who eats, eats in honor of the Lord, since *he gives thanks to God;* while he who abstains, abstains in honor of the Lord and *gives thanks to God.*

10:30: If I partake *with thankful-*ness, why am I denounced because *of that for which I give thanks?*

14:13: but rather decide never to put *a stumbling block or hindrance in the way of a brother.*

8:9: Only take care lest this liberty of yours *become a stumbling block to the weak.*

14:14, 20: I know and am persuaded in the Lord Jesus that nothing is unclean in itself; . . . everything is indeed clean.

10:26: For 'the earth is the Lord's, and everything in it.'[49]

"if" clauses that apply Paul's teaching on the married and unmarried to concrete situations. One could argue further that Paul's questions in 1 Cor. 7:17–24 (different "states" when called) and 27 (the unmarried) also function as circumstantial "if" clauses. It cannot be argued that 1 Cor. 7:1–7 goes against the position developed here. In 1 Cor. 7:1–7 Paul is not dealing with "indifferent things" or with a moral issue that admits of different applications. The Christian cannot ever commit fornication; thus the imperatives and no circumstantial "if" clauses.

[46]Furnish, *Love Command*, 115 n. 69, argues that Rom. 14–15 is a generalized adaptation of previous positions because "in Romans Paul has crystallized his references to two differing groups into the phrases 'the strong' and 'the weak' . . . whereas in 1 Cor. 8 neither term had been used. . . . " In this connection it is well to recall that Rauer, *"Schwachen,"* 89, admitted the possibility that Paul, in recalling the discussion in 1 Cor., was responsible for calling the vegetarians in Rome "the weak." Cf. Michel, *Römer,* 335, for a different opinion: " 'schwach in bezug auf den Glauben' stammt aus dem Mund ihrer Gegner."

[47]During the discussion of these parallels I presuppose the integrity of 1 Cor. and do not divide it into different letters as does Schmithals, *Gnosticism in Corinth.*

[48]I owe this parallel to the observations of Maurer, "Synoida, synidèsis," *TDNT* 7.915.

[49]Cf. Conzelmann, *Korinther,* 208 n. 16 on 1 Cor. 10:26: "On the matter, cf. Rom. 14:14, 20, a development of the discussion of 1 Cor. Both letters offer here a paradigm for the concrete meaning of belief in a creator for one's relationship to the world, for the grounding of freedom in that world."

14:15: Do not let what you eat
cause *the ruin of one for whom
Christ died.*

8:11: And so by your knowledge
*this weak man is destroyed, the
brother for whom Christ died.*

14:16: So do not let *your good*
be *spoken of as evil (blasphēmeisthō).*

10:29bf.: For why should *my*
liberty be determined by another
man's scruples? If I partake with
thankfulness, why am I *denounced
(blasphēmoumai)* because of that
for which I give thanks?[50]

14:17: For the kingdom of God
does not mean food and drink. . . .

8:8: *Food will not commend us
to* God. We are no worse off
if we do not eat, and no better
off if we do.

14:20b: Everything is indeed
clean, but it is wrong for *any
one to make others fall by what
he eats.*

8:9f.: Only take care lest this
liberty of yours somehow *become
a stumbling block to the weak.*
For if any one sees you, a man
of knowledge, at table in an
idol's temple, might he not be
encouraged, if his conscience
is weak, *to eat food offered to
idols?*

14:21: it is right not *to eat
meat or drink wine or do anything.* . . .

10:31: So, *whether you eat or
drink, or whatever you do,* do
all to the glory of God.

14:21: it is right not to eat
meat or drink wine or do anything that *makes your brother
stumble.*

8:13: Therefore, if food is a
cause of my brother's falling,
I will never eat meat, *lest I
cause my brother to fall.*[51]

15:1: We who are strong *ought
to bear with the failings of
the weak,* and not to please
ourselves.

9:2: *To the weak I became weak,*
that I might win the weak.

---

[50]This is my translation. I believe that the parallel between 1 Cor. 10:29b–30 and Rom.
14:16 clearly establishes the meaning of "your good" as "freedom, liberty." This meaning
is further confirmed by the insight of Sanday–Headlam, *Romans,* 391 on 14:16: "St. Paul is
addressing the strong, as elsewhere in this paragraph and the context seems to point at least
primarily, to opinions within the community, not to the reputation of the community with
the outside world." Cf. Bornkamm, *Paul,* 58 for an opinion different from that of Sanday–
Headlam. Cf. Rauer, "*Schwachen,*" 85 n. 1, for some of the interpretations given to *to agathon*
in Rom. 14:16.

[51]The parallels listed between Rom. 14:14, 15, 21 and 1 Cor. 8:9, 11, 13 respectively are
drawn from Rauer, "*Schwachen,*" 122.

15:2: Let each of us *please his neighbor for his good, to edify him*.	8:1: "Knowledge" puffs up, but love *builds up*. 10:23bf.: but not all things *build up*. Let no one seek his own good, but *the good of the neighbor*.
15:3: *For Christ did not please himself*.	11:1: Be imitators of me as I am *of Christ*.
15:7: Welcome one another, therefore, *as Christ has welcomed you*, for the glory of God.	10:33–11:1 . . . just as I try to please all men in everything I do, *not seeking my own advantage, but that of many, that they may be saved*. Be imitators of me, as I am of Christ.[52]

These parallels clearly indicate to what a great extent Rom. 14:1–15:13 repeats, rephrases, echoes the arguments of 1 Cor. 8; 9; 10:23–11:1. These parallels confirm Hans Conzelmann's observation that Rom. 14:1–15:6 is a theoretic development of the actual treatment of 1 Cor. 8–10.[53] In his treatment of Rom. 14:1–15:13 Paul has excluded personal references, such as are found in 1 Cor. 9; 10:33–11:1. He has eliminated the circumstantial "if" clauses which apply his general principles to particular concrete instances within the community. He has omitted references to the catchwords of the Corinthians: "All of us possess knowledge" (1 Cor. 8:1); "All things are lawful" (1 Cor. 10:23); "liberty, freedom" (1 Cor. 8:9; 10:29b);[54] "conscience" (1 Cor. 8:7, 10, 12; 10:25, 27, 28, 29). He has also omitted references to the concrete situation: the problem of food sacrificed to idols. Paul has given names to two different types of individuals in Rom. 14:1–15:13 whereas in 1 Cor. he mentions "the weak" only and that mainly in reference to their consciences.[55]

Upon closer inspection, however, it must be noted that the parallels between Rom. 14:1–15:13 and 1 Cor. 8; 9; 10:23–11:1 do not seem to account for all the elements within Rom. 14:1–15:13. Quite a number of the parallels are concentrated in Rom. 14:13–23. The question immediately comes to mind: if Paul is dealing with a generalized adaptation of a pre-

[52]1 Cor. 10:33–11:1 clearly indicates the 1 Cor. 8 and 10:23–11:1 cannot be read without ch. 9 where Paul discusses how he "curtails" his freedom for the sake of his missionary work. Cf. the unexpected occurrence of 9:22 after 9:20b–21 ("Those with law" and "Those without law"): "I became weak to the weak so that I might win the weak." Cf. Conzelmann, *Korinther,* 191, and Barrett, *First Corinthians,* 215: "Keep them for the church, instead of driving them out by wounding their consciences." Cf. Part II section D below for additional implications of the parallel between Rom. 15:7 and 1 Cor. 10:33–11:1.

[53]Cf. Conzelmann, *Korinther,* 16.

[54]Cf. Michel, *Römer,* 333, who disposes of these omissions, which are damaging to his view of "the strong" in Romans, by relegating them to a footnote (n. 1).

[55]Cf. Furnish, *Love Command.*

vious position, why does he expand his generalized adaptation? Is the expansion due to an actual situation within the Roman community?

The most noticeable expansion in Rom. 14:1–15:13 occurs in those verses where Paul has introduced quotations from the OT to support and confirm his principles (cf. 14:11; 15:3, 9–12). Michel[56] is absolutely correct when he remarks that these scripture quotations occur in decisive points in the argumentation. One could argue that the addition of these scripture quotations has been made to tighten up, confirm, and solidify Paul's arguments which he made with regard to the situation in 1 Cor. where the catchwords were knowledge, liberty, and conscience. It is Paul's propensity in Rom. 1–4; 9–11 to use scripture quotations to bolster his points.

The argument in Rom. 14:4, 6–9 about the slave-Lord relationship is almost unparalleled in 1 Cor. 8–10, but may stem from Paul's thought elsewhere in Romans. Wilhelm Thüsing[57] has argued quite convincingly: "Rom. 6:10f. probably did not directly influence 14:9 but it together with 7:4 are the presuppositions for the statements about the authority of the Kyrios in 14:9. . . . The point would be that the rule of God through the rule of Christ encompasses all areas of *concrete* life."[58] Rom. 14:4, 6–9 also generalize principles that Paul had fashioned in the conflict in 2 Cor.: "For we must all appear before the judgment seat of Christ, so that each one may receive good or evil, according to what he has done in the body" (5:10). "And he died for all, that those who live might live no longer for themselves, but for him who for their sake died and was raised" (5:15).

Apparently Paul's denoting of "the weak" as "weak in *faith*" (14:1) is almost completely unexplained by the parallels in 1 Cor. 8–10. With this observation should be coupled the two principles of faith contained in Rom. 14:23. Yet one could argue that the idea of conscience has been omitted in Rom. 14 because it seems to have been introduced into the discussion in 1 Cor. 8; 10:23–11:1 by the Corinthians and not by Paul.[59] Faith is Paul's term—a term, idea, reality he is at pains to explain in the rest of Romans.[60]

If Rom. 14:1–15:13 is to be considered a generalized adaptation of Paul's previous theological positions, how does one explain the references to

---

[56]Michel, *Römer*, 335.

[57]Thüsing, *Per Christum in Deum*, 33 n. 88.

[58]Ibid., 38. On p. 34 Thüsing remarks that in the paraenesis of Romans (ch. 14; 12:11 [cf. 16:18]) *douleuein* refers to the Lord Christ whereas in the rest of Romans it refers to God (7:25 6:6; 7:6; 6:18, 22).

[59]Cf. Maurer, *TDNT* 7.914. Cf. also the apropos observation of Koester, "Paul and Hellenism," 193: "In fact, in all Pauline epistles, except Romans (and by all means Philemon), Paul's theological vocabulary is not that of his own theology, but is intimately related to the controversies with his opponents."

[60]Although Paul uses conscience in Rom. 2:15; 13:5, he uses it in a sense different from the eight usages in 1 Cor. 8 and 10. Cf. Maurer, *TDNT* 7.914–917. In 1 Cor. 8:7–13; 10: 25–30 conscience "is man himself aware of himself in perception and acknowledgement, in willing and doing" (Maurer, *TDNT* 7.914). Cf. Part III below for additional reasons for the occurrence of "faith" in Rom. 14:1, 23.

"vegetables" in 14: 2 and to "days" in 14:5?[61] Concurring with Rauer and Dederen,[62] I would argue that "days" refers to fast days. Thus, in both instances there is a question of abstinence from food. Furthermore, I would suggest that Paul is generalizing from his discussion in 1 Cor. 8; 10:23–11:1 which dealt with food sacrificed to idols. That is, "vegetables" is meant to cover all cases of abstinence from food.[63] The reference to "fast days" is also general, typical. Here Paul may be generalizing from the controversy he had with the Galatians (Gal. 4:10).

It may be questioned whether my explanation for all these "unique," elements in the discussion of Rom. 14:1–15:13 is convincing to the last detail. The main question is: Is the addition to Rom. 14:1–15:13 of any one or all these elements, which are not found in 1 Cor. 8–10, of such a specific nature to compel one to view Rom. 14:1–15:13 as being addressed to a specific, concrete situation within the Roman community? My answer is: The evidence from the parallels between 1 Cor. 8; 9; 10:23–11:1 and Rom. 14:1–15:13 favors the view that Rom. 14:1–15:13 is a generalized, expanded adaptation of the position and arguments which Paul developed especially in 1 Cor. 8–10.

Are "The Weak" and "The Strong" Communities in Rome?

In this section I return to a point made in Part I above. The approach is exegetical now. In Rom. 14:1 and 15:1 "the weak" are mentioned. In Rom. 15:1 Paul calls himself one of "the strong."[64] Exegetically we can ask a very simple, direct question: Is there any shred of evidence in the text of Rom. 14 :1–15:13 that "the weak" and "the strong" constituted communities in Rome? By "communities" I follow the interpretation given by Minear and others.[65] A community is a group of people who share the same theological ideas, stances, etc. In this regard I find the observations of Conzelmann on 1 Cor. 8:7 very liberating:

> It should be noted that Paul gives advice neither to the strong nor to the weak on how to strengthen the weak conscience. He practices here the faith in-

[61]I presuppose the validity of Rauer's arguments that whoever "the weak" were, they did not abstain from wine. Cf. n. 27 above.

[62]Cf. n. 28 above.

[63]Cf. Sanday–Headlam, *Romans*, 385: "But St. Paul is writing quite generally, and is merely selecting a typical instance to balance the first (eat everything)."

[64]The fact that Paul joins ranks with "the strong" should be given as much emphasis as possible. If proper emphasis is given to this, then we can lay to rest all those hypotheses that try to see "the strong" as pneumatics, antinomians, etc. Cf. n. 32 above.

[65]Minear, *Obedience*, 7–15; cf. n. 8 above. Although Minear (14 note) cautions against visualizing these groups as being "highly organized and cohesive entities," on p. 8 he states: "The disputes described in ch. 14 are such as to have made common meetings impossible" and habitual ridicule and condemnation had frustrated efforts to combine the several communities." These communities are organized sufficiently so that they can maintain that which separates them. Cf. also Michel, *Römer*, 9–14; Bartsch, "Empfänger."

sight that each one is called and can believe in his concrete situation. . . . The "weak" are neither Jewish Christians nor even a distinct group. They represent no position. They are simply weak.[66]

If "the weak" are simply weak, feeling that freedom to eat everything is dangerous for them, could we not say that "the strong" are simply strong? In other words, "the strong" are not a special community with a distinct theology or *Weltanschauung*. Additional confirmation for this view can be seen in the parallel of 1 Cor. 9:22 (read within its context between 1 Cor. 8 and 10:23–11:1) and Rom. 15:1: we who are strong, i.e., are not afraid of the freedom we have in Christ, should bear with the weaknesses/frailties of the weak; we should become weak to and for the weak.

Supplementary evidence for not seeing "the weak" and "the strong" as distinct communities is found in the fact that within Rom. 14:1–15:13 Paul quite frequently addresses the same imperatives and arguments to the entire community. The following passages in Rom. 14:1–15:7 are addressed to both "groups" or could apply to both "groups":[67]

Rom. 14:3ab: Let not him who eats despise him who abstains, and let not him who abstains pass judgment on him who eats.

14:5c: Let every one be fully convinced in his own mind.

15:6–12: He who observes the day, observes it in honor of the Lord. He also who eats, eats in honor of the Lord, since he gives thanks to God; while he who abstains, abstains in honor of the Lord and gives thanks to God. None of us lives to himself, and none of us dies to himself. If we live, we live to the Lord, and if we die, we die to the Lord; so then, whether we live or whether we die, we are the Lord's. For to this end Christ died and lived again, that he might be Lord both of the dead and of the living. Why do you pass judgment on your brother? Or you, why do you despise your brother? For we shall all stand before the judgment seat of God; for it is written, "As I live, says the Lord, every knee shall bow to me, and every tongue shall give praise to God." So each of us shall give account of himself to God.[68]

14:13a: Then let us no more pass judgment on one another.

14:17–19: For the kingdom of God does not mean food and drink but righteousness and peace and joy in the Holy Spirit; he who thus serves Christ is acceptable to God and approved by men. Let us then pursue what makes for peace and for mutual up-building.[69]

14:22–23: The faith that you have, keep between yourself and God; happy is he who has no reason to judge himself for what he approves. But he who has doubts is condemned, if he eats, because he does not act from faith; for whatever does not proceed from faith is sin.[70]

[66]Conzelmann, *Korinther*, 174–75. Cf. also 174 n. 18: "They show themselves as weak because they maintain that freedom is dangerous, but they are correct because they follow the judgment of their conscience."
[67]Furnish, *Love Command*, 115 n. 69 makes this point *in nuce*.
[68]Rom. 14:6–12 is addressed to both groups as is indicated by the stylistic repetition in 14:10 of "pass judgment" and "despise" from 14:3.
[69]Feuillet, "Fondements," 364, shows that these verses are addressed to all Christians.
[70]These verses are customarily viewed by commentators as addressed solely to "the strong." But Rom. 14:22 clearly picks up the argument of 14:14 addressed to "the weak" and

15:2–7: Let each of us please his neighbor for his good, to edify him. For Christ did not please himself; but, as it is written, "The reproaches of those who reproached thee fell on me." For whatever was written in former days was written for our instruction, that by steadfastness and by the encouragement of the scriptures we might have hope. May the God of steadfastness and encouragement grant you to live in such harmony with one another, in accord with Christ Jesus, that together you may with one voice glorify the God and Father of our Lord Jesus Christ. Welcome one another, therefore, as Christ has welcomed you, for the glory of God.

If Paul's main concern in Rom. 14:1–15:7 is with the communities of "the weak" and "the strong," why does he address only ten out of twenty-eight verses[71] specifically to "the weak" (14:3c, 4, 14) and to "the strong" (14:1, 13bc, 14, 15, 20, 21; 15:1)? I would suggest that Paul's imperatives and arguments to the entire community indicate that he is not trying to create a community out of the disarray of "the weak" and "the strong" communities,[72] but is concerned to show how an established community can maintain its unity despite differences of opinion. Maintenance of unity is rooted in a strong community which in faith and love and concern can tolerate differences of opinion in indifferent matters such as eating or not eating certain types of food. Cf. the preponderance of words denoting community: *adelphos* (14:10*bis*, 13, 15 [cf. Rom. 13:8–10], 21; 15:2 [*tō plēsion*]); *allēlous* (14:13, 19, 15:5, 7); *oikodomē* (14:19; 15:2); "we are the Lord's" (14:9); "with one voice" (15:6).

Rom. 15:7–13: Jews and Gentiles

Those who identify "the weak" with Jewish Christians and "the strong" with Gentile Christians find support for and evidence of their contentions in Rom. 15:7–13 which talks about Jews and Gentiles. Within recent literature this, at times, too facile identification has been challenged.[73] These

---

the argument of 14:20 addressed to "the strong" and specifies its implications for both groups. Rom. 14:23 also applies to both groups, for if "the strong" doubt whether their eating will scandalize "the weak" and nevertheless eat, they condemn themselves. In my analysis of Rom. 14:22–23 I am thankful for the spur to my thought which I received from Feuillet, "Fondements," 364–65. This argument also goes against Minear, *Obedience*, 12–13, who, on the slim basis of Rom. 13:23a, argues to the existence of the third community in Rome, "the doubters."

[71]Rom. 14:2, 5ab are descriptive of possible situations. Cf. pp. 70–77.

[72]It is my contention that Minear's analysis of Rom. 14 in terms of twelve axioms (cf. n. 10 above) masks the fact that relatively little of Rom. 14:1–15:7 is directed specifically to "the weak" and "the strong" communities. In the light of the above exegesis it is more sound to concentrate on the imperatives, which the axioms are supposed to motivate, and to envisage a unified community in Rome.

[73]Dupont, "Appel aux faibles," 364, argues that Rom. 15:9b-12 makes the point: since Christ has accepted the Gentiles who have not received any promise, how can Christians refuse to accept those who do not think exactly as they do? Christ has given us an example of charity that reaches out to all without distinction. Thüsing, *Per Christum in Deum*, 43–44, argues that Rom. 15:8 ("promises given to the patriarchs") does not refer to Jews, but to Gentiles (cf. Rom. 4 and the promise to Abraham, father *of many nations*). Therefore, Rom. 15:8 says nothing (at least not directly) about the acceptance of the Jews. Feuillet, "Fondements,"

challenges are well taken, but do not seem to explain the objection raised by Michel: If the Jews do not mean "weak" and the Gentiles "strong," then how is 15:7–13 related to 15:1–6?[74]

I maintain that the linkage between 15:1–6 and 7–13 can be found in viewing this section in the light of the discussion of 1 Cor. 10:32–11:1. In Rom. 15:1–4 Paul continues the discussion begun in 14:20–21 about the relationship between freedom and love and introduces the example of Christ. Romans 15:5–6 is an elaborate conclusion to these thoughts, and is addressed to the entire community.[75] In Rom. 15:7 Paul introduces the example of Christ again and confirms it solemnly with quotations from all sections of the OT. This example of Christ is a development of the thought of 1 Cor. 11:1: "Be imitators of me as I am of Christ." What example of Christ are the Romans to imitate as they welcome one another? First Corinthians 10:32–33 gives the answer: "Give no offense to Jews or to Greeks or to the church of God, just as I try to please all men in everything I do, not seeking my own advantage, but that of many, that they may be saved." The stress of Rom. 15:7–13, therefore, is on the servant nature of Christ (15:7),[76] who makes the two one. Christ is all things to all men, to Jews and Gentiles,[77] so that he might save them all, so that they might give glory to God. Cf. the perceptive comment of Karl Barth on this passage: Jesus reveals and realizes God's mercy upon earth "in order to make the one nation and the many together into one."[78]

If my interpretation of the connection between Rom. 15:1–6 and 7–13 is correct, then we have no evidence for the view that Rom. 15:1–6 is related to 7–13 via the equation "the weak"= Jewish Christian and "the

---

369, argues for a separation between Rom. 15:1–6, addressed to "the weak" and "the strong," and Rom. 15:7–13, addressed to the question of the relationship between the Jews and Gentiles. In Feuillet's behalf one could quote the remark of Michel, *Römer*, 289: "The third part, Rom. 15:1–13, at first blush, does not appear to be unified."

[74]Michel, *Römer*, 353: " . . . die Heidenchristen und die 'Starken', die Judenchristen und die 'Schwachen' sind bis zu einem gewissen Grade identisch." I accept the solution to the grammatically difficult Rom. 15:8–9 given by Barrett, *Romans*, 271: "The governing sentence is 'Christ has become,' and on this the two other verbs ('to confirm' and 'that they may glorify'—both infinitives in Greek) are dependent. In outline the sentence runs: Christ has become . . . so as to confirm . . . and that the Gentiles. . . . " Following Thüsing, *Per Christum in Deum*, 44 n. 132, I read "you" in Rom. 15:7. Michel, *Römer*, 358 reads "us," but maintains that "us" refers to both groups.

[75]Rom. 15:5: "To think the same thing among yourselves according to Christ Jesus" (my translation) does not mean uniformity in idea, but as the parallel in Phil. 2:2–5 indicates: "to live in self-sacrificing love." On Phil. 2:2–5, cf. Jewett, *Anthropological Terms*, 348–50, and Grundmann, *"Tapeinos, ktl.," TWNT* 8.22: *tapeinophrosynē* means "Selbstlosigkeit."

[76]Cf. Barrett, *Romans*, 271 and n. 74 above.

[77]Jews and Gentiles are an exclusive dichotomy, embracing all mankind. Cf. Gal. 3:28; Rom. 1:16; 9–11. Would it be too risky and without the warrant of evidence to suggest that this passage rounds off the theme of Romans, which began programmatically in 1:16 with: "For I am not ashamed of the gospel: it is the power of God for salvation to every one that has faith, to the Jew first and also to the Greek"?

[78]Barth, *Shorter Commentary on Romans*, 173. Cf. also Leenhardt, *Romans*, 364: "Now Christ had but one thought, which was to disclose the glory of God to men; and He wished to show forth the divine glory by gathering all men together into one single family of brothers."

strong"= Gentile Christian. The link is via the love that should not please itself (Rom. 15:1–3), a love that goes out to save all, to welcome all, despite distinctions of race (Rom. 15:7–13).[79]

In summary of this section on the exegesis of Rom. 14: 1–15:13, enough evidence has been presented to call into serious question the existence at Rome of such configurations of Christians as the communities of "the weak" and "the strong." The exegetical evidence suggests that 14:1–15:13 is a generalized, expanded adaptation of the theological positions Paul arrived at after his discussions in various missionary situations, especially in 1 Cor. 8; 9; 10:23–11:1.[80]

III. The Nature of the Paraenesis in Romans 12–15

For decades the view of Martin Dibelius has dominated the scholarly discussion of paraenesis. In the case at hand, Dibelius would maintain that the paraenesis in Rom. 12–13 has no connection whatsoever with the doctrine Paul has propounded in Rom. 1–11.[81] Paul's paraenesis is general, customary, aimed at the general situation, not the particular situation.

In his *Theology and Ethics in Paul* Victor P. Furnish rightly challenged Dibelius's view. Furnish argued that Paul's ethics are intimately connected with his theology. Paul may have adopted traditional paraenesis for the "exhortatory sections" of his epistles, but he has modified this material by his theological additions, or by the position into which he has inserted the material, or even by the fact that he selected one block of traditional paraenesis rather than another which was available to him.[82]

Furnish himself has shown how Rom. 12:1–2 is connected with the preceding section of Romans, esp. chapter 6.[83] Other studies have questioned

---

[79]Is it too far-fetched to see in Phil. 2:1–11 a structural parallel to this section? The Philippians are asked to love one another with self-effacing love, to look after the needs of the other and not their own needs. They are to have the mind of Christ who emptied himself.

[80]If Romans were written from Corinth (cf. Kümmel *Introduction*, 311), these discussions would still be fresh in his mind. My friend, Prof. Robin Scroggs, has suggested to me that the similarities between Rom. 14–15 and 1 Cor. 8–10 may be based on a common source, *sc.*, Paul's preaching. As an accomplished preacher, Paul progressively hones down his message so that it is applicable to innumerable situations.

[81]Dibelius, *From Tradition to Gospel*, 238: "The hortatory sections of the Pauline letters are clearly differentiated in material from what Paul otherwise wrote. In particular they lack an immediate relation with the circumstances of the letter. The rules and directions are not formulated for special churches and concrete cases, but for the general requirements of earliest Christendom. Their significance is not factual but actual. (The English translation has missed the German here; *usuelle* should be translated with "customary." "Sie haben nicht aktuelle, sondern usuelle Bedeutung." [*Die Formgeschichte des Evangeliums* (3d rev. ed.; Tübingen: J. C. B. Mohr, 1959) 239]—not the momentary need but the universal principle.) Thus we see that the hortatory sections of the Pauline epistles have nothing to do with the theoretic foundation of the ethics of the Apostle, and very little with other ideas peculiar to him. Rather they belong to tradition. . . . What is to be found in these chapters of the epistles arises from didactic habit. For Dibelius' definition of paraenesis, cf. *Jakobus*, 4.

[82]Furnish, *Theology and Ethics*, esp. 68–92.

[83]Ibid., 98–106, esp. 105–6.

Dibelius's position on Romans from other viewpoints. Ernst Käsemann sees Rom. 12:1–2 as the interpretive key for the entire paraenesis of Rom. 12.[84] Raymond Corriveau, building on the work of other scholars,[85] argues that Rom. 12:1–2 is the interpretive introduction to all of Rom. 12:3–15:13.[86] Charles Talbert has made a significant contribution to the separation of tradition and redaction in Rom. 12:14–21 and sees Paul[87] as the redactor of the tradition ascertainable in Rom. 12:16a, 16b, 17a, 19a, 21.[88] Furnish argues that Paul uses "love" as the theme that unifies the disparate materials in Rom. 12–13.[89] Dupont maintains that Paul transposes arguments he developed in 1 Cor. 8–10 to a new situation in Rom. 14:1–15:13.[90] Bornkamm views Rom. 14–15 as a redoing of 1 Cor. 8–10 with the emphasis on "consideration for the other man's conscience and on faith and responsibility for him."[91]

All the above research on the paraenesis of Rom. 12–15 has put 14:1–15:13 in a new light. In Rom. 12–15 Paul is not just giving traditional paraenesis; he is giving paraenesis that has been modified by his own theologizing, by his own solutions to problems which occurred in his former

[84]Käsemann, *Questions*, 188–95. Käsemann's analysis of Rom. 12:3–4 should give pause to those (cf. n. 32 above) who view Rom. 12:3–4 as directed against the antinomian "strong": "An essential element of the authentic worship of God in the world is the right 'measure'. ... the right measure is not the integration of the self-sufficient human being which enables him to adjust socially to his given environment, but participation in faith as the estate of the Christian man, which God has given specifically to each as a grant-in-aid of grace, i.e., as *charisma*" (192). Cf. in addition Cranfield, *Romans 12–13*, 27: "Those who do measure themselves by the standard which God has given them in their faith will not fail to discern the one body." Moreover, the play on words in Rom. 12:3 (*hyperphronein, phronein, phronein, sōphronein*) should have raised the suspicion that Paul is not dealing with the actual situation of "the strong" in the Roman community. Käsemann elsewhere argues that Rom. 12:3–8 functions as the background for the rest of Rom. 12:9–15:13. Cf. *Essays*, 73: "Rom. 12–15 is speaking, as we have already seen in ch. 14 exclusively of charismata and those conditions which are the raw material of charismata. Therefore this whole section ends with a doxology for that Church which is able to praise God's mercy among the Gentiles."

[85]Corriveau, *Liturgy of Life*, 157 n. 7.

[86]Ibid., 155–85. On p. 157 Corriveau observes: "The first two verses of chapter 12 are of special importance because they can be considered as an introduction to the rest of the section 12:3–15:13. These two verses are, as it were, the ground rule, the foundation of Christian ethics. This has the result of placing all of what follows in the light of spiritual worship and transformation of mind. The idea of spiritual worship emerges again explicitly in 14:18 when Paul sums up the whole life of brotherly concern in terms of worship. 'He who thus serves (*douleuōn*) Christ is acceptable (*euarestos*) to God. ... ' " Cf. Martin, "Kerygma," 236: "The ethical section is introduced by an exhortation which summarizes the substance of what follows (12:1f.)."

[87]Talbert, "Tradition," 93 n.5.

[88]Ibid., 91.

[89]Furnish, *Love Command*, 102–3. It might be objected (cf. Talbert, "Tradition," 85) that Furnish cannot sustain his case that Rom. 12:9a ("Let love be genuine") "stands as a sort of introductory heading to the wide-ranging exhortations that follow" (103). It must also be admitted that Furnish too readily omits Rom. 13:1–7 from his discussion: "Whatever be the precise relation of 13:1–7 to the whole of chaps. 12–13. ... " (108). Despite these weaknesses Furnish makes a case worthy of consideration.

[90]Dupont, "Appel aux faibles," 357–66.

[91]Bornkamm, *Paul*, 94.

missionary work. Paul's solution to the problem to unity at Corinth, 1 Cor. 12, is reflected in miniature form in Rom. 12:3–8.[92] If Talbert is correct, then Paul has modified traditional paraenesis in Rom. 12:14–21.[93] The stress on the love command in Gal. 5 is again found in Rom. 13:8–10.[94] Rom. 13:11–14 has parallels in 1 Thess. 5:5–9. The problem of "the weak" at Corinth, 1 Cor. 8–10, is reflected in Rom. 14:1–15:13.[95]

The above research into parallels between Rom. 12–15 and previous Pauline paraenesis and theologizing suggests that Rom. 14:1–15:13 be read as general paraenesis, not in Dibelius's sense that it has nothing to do with Paul's own theology. Rather it is paraenesis that is intimately connected with the theological principles of Paul, but at the same time it is general. It is addressed to possible situations within the Roman community or, if one accepts the hypothesis of Romans as an encyclical letter, within any Christian community. Wherever Christians are, there are bound to be differences of opinion with regard to indifferent items, such as whether to eat certain foods or not. The Christian, in Paul's view, is to judge these indifferent things according to personal faith (Rom. 14:14, 20, 22–23)[96] and

[92]Cf. Talbert, "Tradition," 85: "As has often been observed, the sequence of thought in Rom. xii. 3ff. moves from individual gifts to the Spirit to the greatest gift of all, to *agapē*, just as does the thought of 1 Cor. xii–xiii."

[93]Talbert, ibid., 92–93, fails to answer the questions when and why Paul modified the traditional paraenetic material of Rom. 12:14–21. Perhaps an explanation for the redaction is to be found in the redactional use of the OT in Rom. 12:16c, 17b, 19b, 20 to substantiate the traditional paraenesis (cf. ibid., 90). Such a confirmatory use of the OT would agree with Paul's employment of it in Rom. 14:11; 15:3, 9–12. Cf. p. 76 above.

[94]In the argument being developed here Rom. 13:1–7 seems to stand out like a loud "Yes, but. . . . " Why has Paul included this section here in Romans? If Käsemann's analysis of this pericope (*Questions*, 196–216) is correct, then there is a link between this pericope and Rom. 12:1–6 via discerning what is right and what is in accord with Christian service and what allows Christian service. On pp. 208–10 Käsemann also suggests that Paul may be addressing the Romans in the light of his experience with "enthusiasm" in Corinth. If this point is correct, there is additional confirmation that in Rom. 12–15 Paul is presenting the Romans with generalized adaptations from previous missionary experiences. It is also to be noted that Käsemann's arguments are sufficiently cogent to argue against those who view Rom. 13:1–7 as addressed to a particular, concrete problem in the Roman community. Cf., e.g., Rauer, "Schwachen," 78; Jewett, *Anthropological Terms*, 46.

[95]Feuillet, "Fondements," 366, sees links between Rom. 12:2 and 14:22–23 and thus is able to explain why Paul uses "faith" in Rom. 14 and not "conscience" as he did in 1 Cor. 8 and 10. His explanation is: the word "faith" encompasses Christian faith and conscience, conscience making the application to particular situations of what faith, the universal law of the Christian, prescribes." Thus one returns to the point of departure for the long paraenesis of Rom. 12–15, i.e., the principle affirmed in 12:2: Christian faith united to baptismal grace renews our moral discernment" (366). Cf. also the use of *dokimazein* in both Rom. 12:2 and 14:22. For a similar interpretation of Rom. 12:1–2, cf. Merk, *Handeln*, 158: "Whoever is gifted by the Spirit in baptism is thereby called to use his reason to discern what the will of God is, to discern what, in view of the will of God, are the good pleasing and perfect things of the world."

[96]Cf. Schrage, *Ethik*, 154: "In such peripheral questions, therefore, it is not necessary to have unity and universally binding norms; conscience alone is decisive." "But the Christian conscience is informed and formed by faith (Rom. 14:2, 22f.) and is not autonomous" (p. 153 n. 43)." For the Christian the judgment of conscience coincides with the judgment of faith" (p. 152).

according to personal discernment of what is good, acceptable, and perfect (Rom. 12:2; cf. Phil. 1:9f.; 4:8). Thus, Rom. 14:1–15:13 is a further application of the general principle enunciated in Rom. 12:1–2. Yet since the Christian exists within a community of believers, one's decision cannot be absolute. One must practice charity and try to build up the community, for Christ did not please himself. Christ died for the brother, and Christians are the Lord's.

In summary, this analysis of Rom. 12–15 also indicates that Rom. 14:1–15:13 has no specific referent within the Roman community. It is part of a letter which sums up Paul's missionary theology and paraenesis.

IV. Conclusion

It has been the purpose of this article to challenge scholars to reexamine Rom. 14:1–15:13 before they use its so-called party/community strife to justify their views of the situation obtaining in the Roman community. There is very little history of religions or exegetical evidence that there were communities of "the weak" and "the strong" in Rome. Romans 14:1–15:13 is better explained as general Pauline paraenesis, which is adapted and generalized especially from Paul's discussion in 1 Cor. 8–10 and is addressed to a problem that may arise in any community. Any problem with regard to indifferent things, such as eating or not eating certain foods, should be solved in faith, with love, in the interests of edification because Christ did not please himself and because Christians must accept one another as Christ has accepted them.

7

THE JEWISH COMMUNITY IN ANCIENT ROME AND THE ORIGINS OF ROMAN CHRISTIANITY

Wolfgang Wiefel

Since Ferdinand Christian Baur began the discussion concerning the relationship between the oldest Christian congregation and the Jewish community in the city of Rome, this matter has been raised again and again. For the founder of the Tübingen school, this concern arose out of his attempts to integrate Paul's letter to the Romans into a historical sequence, especially since Romans had hitherto been treated almost exclusively from a dogmatic point of view. It was a decisive step forward in the history of interpretation. Baur emphasized as central the question of the addressees of the letter, making the actual situation of the Roman congregation the focal point of his interpretation. This initial observation was developed gradually. From the outset, he thought the addressees to be Jewish-Christians who had emerged from the Jewish community in Rome.[1] The Jewish tendency toward particularism prevailing in the city is seen by Baur to be in opposition to Paul's own position which is determined by emancipation from Judaism, the nullification of particularism, and an orientation toward a universalism which embraced all peoples without distinction.[2]

It is against such a background that Baur attempts a unified interpretation of Paul's letter to the Romans.[3] In short, then, he places the congregation into a larger historical context, a context resulting from "the frequent intercourse which the rather numerous Jews in Rome maintained with Judea and Jerusalem."[4] Baur's thesis that the Christian community in Rome at the time of Romans was purely a Jewish-Christian one met

---

[1] Baur, F. C.,"Römischen Gemeinde," 59–178.
[2] Baur, F. C., *Paulus* (1845, 1967²) 1.344.
[3] Baur, F. C., "Über Zweck und Gedankengang des Römerbriefes," 184–209.
[4] Baur, F. C., *Kirchengeschichte*, 62f.

with considerable opposition both in his school[5] and beyond,[6] and as a result, it was subsequently modified to a considerable extent.[7]

Since that time it is clear that the problem of the origin of the Christians referred to in Romans and the larger question of the origin of Christianity in Rome cannot be clarified without considering the entire phenomenon of Judaism in Rome. Unfortunately, most discussions do not adequately treat the history of the Jewish community in Rome. This is especially true of the many recent articles concerned with this topic.[8] What follows is an attempt to show how a study of the contemporary history can be beneficial for a proper understanding of this New Testament letter as well as for an elucidation of the historical background against which Paul's reflections on the problem of Judaism can be understood.

I

If one considers the long history of the diaspora in the East, the Jewish community in Rome is comparatively young.[9] It is mentioned for the first time in the year 139 B.C. We know through Valerius Maximus[10] that the Jews had been expelled from Rome by the Praetor Hispaius (Cornelius Hispanus)[11] for the following reason: *Sabazi Iovis cultu Romanos inficere mores conati erant.*[12] One should not conclude from this quote that Judaism had come to Rome in the form of a syncretistic Sabazio cult.[13] One has to keep in mind that the general perception of the Jewish community in Rome was surrounded by misconceptions from the very beginning of its history. The Romans mistook them for followers of the hellenistic-oriental Sabazio cult for one of two good reasons: they misunderstood the Jewish word for God, Sabaoth, the Greek form of Zebaoth,[14] and they might have made the same mistake with the word sabbath, the most conspicuous custom of Judaism.[15] It is important to note that together with the Jews, the Chaldei, the Asiatic astrologers, were expelled as well. Therefore, this action is directed against all religious customs originating in the Orient and thus

---

[5]Weizsäcker, "Römische Christengemeinde," 248–310. Pfleiderer, *Das Urchristentum,* 177f.

[6]Godet, *Römer,* (1881) 1.46–49.

[7]Ed. Grafe, *Veranlassung und Zweck des Römerbriefes,* 1881.

[8]Preisker, "Das historische Problem, 25–30. Harder, "Römerbriefes,"13–24. Schelkle, "Römische Kirche," 393–404. Rengstorf, "Paulus," 450–464. Bartsch, "Die historische Situation," 281–91. Not accessible to me was Judge–Thomas, "Church at Rome,"81–94.

[9]For a discussion of its origin, see Berliner, *Geschichte der Juden,* 1–29. Vogelstein–Rieger, *Geschichte der Juden,* 1.1–21. Leon, *Jews of Ancient Rome,* 2–21.

[10]*Factorum et dictorum memorabilium* 1.3.3.

[11]For this identification see Leon, *Jews of Ancient Rome,* 2f. (n. 3).

[12]With regard to this passage see Cumont, *Sabazios et du Judaisme,* 55–60.

[13]This view is maintained by G. Haufe in: Leipoldt–Grundmann *Umwelt,* 1.116.

[14]Bertholet, *Die Stellung der Israeliten,* 238.

[15]Most recently, following many previous scholars, M. P. Nilsson, *Geschichte der griechischen Religion,* 662f., has opted for this position.

one cannot speak of any specific anti-Semitism. These measures are best viewed in context of a heightened sensitivity of the Roman upper-class towards all things foreign, which is characteristic of the era of the Scipians and the older Cato.

Barely a century later, during the time of Cicero, the Jews made up a significant proportion of the Roman population. Once more, their number increased considerably when Pompeius interceded in the quarrel between the brothers Aristobulus and Hyrcanus, bringing a great number of Jews to Rome as captives.[16] Of these, a large group was freed, and settled on the left bank of the Tiber.[17] As a group which stood out because of its special customs and cohesiveness, they played a considerable role in the internal disputes during the final days of the republic. Cicero, for instance, had to defend his client, Flaccus, who had been dismissed as a praetor of the province of Asia, against the accusation that he had misappropriated funds donated by Asiatic Jews for the temple in Jerusalem.[18] The relationship of diaspora Judaism with this religious center in Jerusalem was an old political problem. Cicero was able to refer to an old senatorial decree against the transfer of funds abroad, a decree which was renewed as late as 63 B.C. It was charged that Flaccus had infringed upon the religious tolerance which had been granted the various religious cults in the provinces. Cicero's arguments are most revealing whenever he counterattacks. He preferred to speak in a low voice so that only the judges could hear him and not the many Jews present, since they were taking advantage of the fact that the trial was open to the public in order to influence the proceedings. Cicero charged the opposition with cooperating with the Jewish groups in the public meeting, considering their good will to be more important than the interests of the state. Already here we encounter a clearly anti-Semitic polemic. This also becomes apparent through the names he gives the Jewish community: manus, turba, corona; they follow a *superstitio barbara;* the worship of their *sacra* is incompatible with the shining Roman names and the customs of the forefathers.

The political aspect of this anti-Semitism is unmistakable. It is hardly the Jews themselves who are supposed to be impressed by such statements; instead Cicero wants to stigmatize the populist party publicly on account of such an alliance. That the Jews are drawn more to that party because of their social and legal situation rather than to the senate party can be seen through their mourning at Caesar's death. Not only did they conduct their own rites, but they also supplied an honor guard at his gravesite for several nights.[19] As we learn from Josephus, the Jews might have

---

[16]Jos., *Ant.* 14.77; *War* 1.155. The historical context is well discussed by Bammel, "Pompeius und römisch-jüdisches Bundnis," 76–82.

[17]Philo, *Embassy to Gaius* 23.

[18]*Pro Flacco* 67–69. A closer examination is offered by Bergmann, *Einleitung zu Ciceros.*

[19]Sueton., *Caes.* 84.

had special reasons for such action considering Caesar's many favors toward them during his term in office[20]—among them the recognition of the synagogue community as a *collegium* present in Rome since ancient times, which therefore did not fall under the restrictions decreed by the senate.[21]

Although Cicero belongs to the century before Christ, we have referred to him extensively because his attitude is representative of future generations of Romans who are conscious of their tradition. This spirit was fostered during the restoration under Augustus in spite of changes in internal conditions. If anything, the Jewish community had increased in number.[22] Although later on the Jews were also able to point to a benevolent toleration under Augustus,[23] their religion appeared to the Romans as a *superstitio barbara* just like the other cults from the Orient which were subject to derision and scorn. Horace, celebrated poet of the Augustan period, is typical of this mood. He describes Jews as a sect whose tenacious efforts to proselytize are difficult to avoid.[24] The most conspicuous customs, the sabbath (misunderstood as new moon[25]) and circumcision, are so well-known that, ironically, Roman playboys suspect each other of adhering to it.[26] The context of the famous *credat Judaeus Apelles* reveals nothing but this: the Jews worship the most incredible superstitions.[27] Such testimony characterizes a social and a psychological situation which of necessity has a bearing upon the legal status of the Jews, viz., the continual shifts between periodic toleration and opposition.[28]

The expulsion of the Jews under Tiberius in A.D. 19 must be seen against this background.[29] Jews, as well as followers of the Egyptian *sacra* (the cult of Isis) were affected by it. The numbers affected must have been considerable. For example, four thousand young men, capable of bearing arms, were sent to Sardinia to fight bandits. It was hoped that many of them would perish there. This episode is interesting for yet another reason: a young woman by the name of Fulvia, wife of a senator, had, in her predilection for Jews, become the victim of an imposter. He had succeeded in obtaining funds from her for a temple in Jerusalem. These funds never arrived in Jerusalem.[30] While the historical reliability of this episode is disputed,[31] it nevertheless illustrates the degree of sympathy upper-class

---

[20]Jos., *Ant.* 14.213–227.

[21]Sueton., *Caes.* 42; Jos., *Ant.* 14.213–216.

[22]According to Jos., *Ant.* 17.61, over 8,000 Roman Jews escorted the legation which arrived in Rome following the death of Herod.

[23]Philo, *Embassy to Gaius* 22; Jos., *Ant.* 16.162–164

[24]Horat., *Serm.* 1.4.143.

[25]Stowasser–Graubart, "Tricesima sabbata," 289–95.

[26]Horat., *Serm.* 1.9.67–72.

[27]Horat., *Serm.* 1.5.100.

[28]Askowith, *Toleration and Persecution of the Jews*; Guterman, *Religious Toleration.*

[29]Tac., *Ann.* 2.85, Sueton., *Tib.* 36.

[30]Jos., *Ant.* 18.81–84

[31]Particularly critical is Moehring, "Persecution of the Jews," 293–304.

women felt for this strange religion. Ovid also must have had this phenomenon in mind when he recommended the Jewish sabbath as a good
day for meeting ladies.[32]

Although the Jewish community in Rome may have been hard hit by
the persecution of A.D. 19, it was not destroyed. It probably benefitted from
the close contacts members of the Herodian family maintained for a time
with the imperial household.[33] In spite of the vacillating policy towards
the Jews in Rome under Tiberius,[34] Caligula,[35] and, initially also under
Claudius,[36] they could nevertheless, to a limited degree, develop and expand without significant hindrance.

We have now reached the point in our story where the birth of Christianity in Rome occurs. As was the case with the expansion of Judaism,
it was the first city in the western Mediterranean where this new religion
took hold. Since the mission of early Christianity was usually started
in synagogues,[37] the existence of a larger Jewish community in Rome
offered the necessary precondition for the creation of a new Christian
congregation.

II

The peculiar legal and organizational position of the Roman Jews
accounts for the fact that Christianity in Rome advanced so rapidly, a phenomenon which entered into the purview of earlier scholarship.[38] However, only because of the extensive discovery, collection, and evaluation
of Jewish inscriptions during the past few decades[39] can this situation now
be perceived with greater clarity.

Many synagogues had sprung up in Rome since, in principle, ten men
capable of worship (a *minyan*) were sufficient to constitute a congregation.[40] That these congregations also had their own individual names can
be gathered from the remaining inscriptions.[41] For example, there is the
synagogue of the Augustesians,[42] probably consisting of the emperor's

[32]Ovid., *Ars am.* 1.76.

[33]Jos., *Ant.* 18.179–194

[34]Philo, *Embassy to Gaius* 24.

[35]Jos., *Ant.* 18.261–304

[36]Jos., *Ant.* 19.286–291.

[37]Act. 13:42ff.; 14:1–6; 17:1–5; 18:4; 19:8f. Luke's somewhat schematic sequence may still,
in principle, be an accurate portrayal of early Christian missionary practice.

[38]Schürer, *Die Gemeindeverfassung.*

[39]The Roman inscriptions here and in the following notes can be found in *CIJ* I (ed. Frey)
1–532.

[40]*Meg.* 3.3, Tos. *Meg.* 4.14.

[41]In our inscriptions the term "synagogue" generally refers to the worshiping congregation. In the non-Roman inscriptions, the term "house of prayer" probably was applied to
the building as such. (*CIJ* 682, 683, 684).

[42]*CIJ* 284, 301, 338, 368, 416, 496.

freedmen or founded by them. Another is named after Agrippa,[43] friend of Herod and general of Augustus, and again another after Volumnius,[44] the procurator of the Syrian province at the time of Herod the Great.[45] Probably also in existence was a synagogue of the Herodians.[46] All these names go back to the first century A.D. In the instances mentioned, Jews seem to have succeeded in winning influential men as protectors of their congregations. But there are also some named after the districts or cities where their members lived. We find synagogue names like Sibura,[47] Campesian[48] and Valkarengian.[49] More fascinating are the designations Synagogue of the Hebrews[50] or of the Vernaculi,[51] since these go back to the time when the Greek-speaking Jews *(vernaculi),* who had settled in Rome a long time ago, lived together with the newer immigrants who still spoke Aramaic. There the connection between immigration and organization of the synagogue becomes apparent. It was natural for larger immigrant groups to form their own synagogues initially. Thus we find among the names of synagogues in Rome also those which point to places outside of Rome. Jews who came from these localities met in congregations from Elea,[52] Tripolis,[53] Skina,[54] and Arca Libanon.[55] We can assume that language assimilation proceeded quickly. Inscriptions are usually in Greek, and seldom, except in later times, in Latin. Hebrew appears only in religious quotations.[56] The legitimate conclusion is that in Jewish congregations Greek was used—the same language in which Paul wrote his letter to the Romans.

In contrast to the many diverse manifestations of the Jewish synagogue in Rome, it is surprising to note how similar the inner structures of the various congregations are. Many designations for institutions and offices appear again and again, indicating an essentially similar organizational structure. At the head of every congregation there is the assembly of elders, the *gerousia.* Consequently, Roman inscriptions often show the title of the *gerousiarch,*[57] whom we can assume to be the principal leader of the congregation. From a variety of references it is fair to assume that

[43]*CIJ* 365, 425, 503.
[44]*CIJ* 343, 502, 517.
[45]Jos., *Ant.* 18.310–317; *War* 1.538–539.
[46]*CIJ* 173. Only fragments of the name can be read. Speaking against a synagogue of the Herodians is Leon, "Synagogue of the Herodians," 318–22.
[47]*CIJ* 18, 22, 37(?), 146(?).
[48]*CIJ* 88, 319, 483(?), 523(?).
[49]*CIJ* 304, 316, 384, 433, 504.
[50]*CIJ* 291, 317, 510, 535.
[51]*CIJ* 318, 383, 398, 494.
[52]*CIJ* 281, 509.
[53]*CIJ* 390, 408.
[54]*CIJ* 7.
[55]*CIJ* 501.
[56]Leon, "Greek Inscriptions," 210–33.
[57]*CIJ* 9, 95, 106, 119, 147, 189(?), 301, 353, 368, 405, 435, 511.

this office exists in every individual congregation.[58] The title *archontes* is found most often in the Roman inscriptions[59] while the title *presbyteros*, with one exception, does not occur.[60] The *archontes* are members of the executive body within the congregation. But it is unclear whether the title refers to all of its members[61] or to a smaller group charged with the business affairs of the congregation.[62] The important fact is that we are dealing again with an office common to individual congregations.[63] Repeated mention of the possibility of serving a second term as *archōn*[64] leads us to think of it as an elected office. In one case, an exception to the rule, a three-term *archōn*[65] is mentioned; in one inscription an *archōn is* referred to as a life-long office-holder.[66] Another congregational officer is called *grammateus*.[67] Since it is occasionally mentioned in connection with a community it probably refers to the position of secretary of the community rather than to a scribe.[68] Jewish congregations also had patrons, just as they existed in other *collegia*. Sometimes, they are referred to as fathers[69] or mothers[70] of a particular synagogue. The inscriptions further establish that descendants of priestly families came to Rome (but probably only after A.D. 70).[71] Also mentioned is the office of *archisynagōgos*,[72] which directly refers to the community at worship. Not mentioned is the synagogue attendant,[73] since such functions were probably too insignificant to be enumerated.

Thus, we have seen that the Jews in Rome are a diverse community of individually structured congregations whose esteemed officials are responsible for their religious and social functions. But we also noticed the absence of a single, controlling organization supervising the individual synagogues. There is no organizational head such as the ethnarch in Alexandria[74] who, together with a council of Jews, represented all other Jews before the authorities.[75] This difference between Jews in Rome and in Al-

---

[58]*CIJ* 301, 425, 504.
[59]*CIJ* 4, 85, 88, 95, 120, 140, 277, 289, 304, 343, 380, 384, 390, 394, 503, 505, 538.
[60]*CIJ* 378.
[61]Frey (=*CIJ*) is of this opinion LXXXVII.
[62]Speaking in favor of this are Schürer, *Die Gemeindeverfassung*, 22, and Askowith, *Toleration and Persecution of the Jews*, 63.
[63]*CIJ* 316, 354.
[64]*CIJ* 289, 316, 335, 354, 391.
[65]*CIJ* 494.
[66]*CIJ* 503.
[67]*CIJ* 7, 18, 24, 36, 67, 99, 102, 122, 125, 142, 148, 149, 180, 221, 284, 351, 433, 456.
[68]*CIJ* 67, 318.
[69]*CIJ* 319, 494.
[70]*CIJ* 166(?), 192(?), 496, 523.
[71]*CIJ* 343, 346, 375.
[72]*CIJ* 265, 287(?), 336, 504.
[73]Apparently the only case is found in *CIJ* 172.
[74]Strabo in Jos., *Ant.* 14.110–118.
[75]*Ep. Arist.* 309f.; Philo, *in Flacc.* 10.

exandria, remarkable in itself, is also of great significance with regard to the origin of Christian congregations in Rome.[76]

The loose structure just described provided an essential prerequisite for the early penetration of Christianity in Rome. The multitude of congregations, their democratic constitutions, and the absence of a central Jewish governing board made it easy for the missionaries of the new faith to talk in the synagogues and to win new supporters. Permission for missionaries to remain in the autonomous congregations could only be revoked if the governing body considered exclusion to be necessary and enforceable.[77] However, since Rome had no supervising body which could forbid any form of Christian propaganda in the city, it was possible to missionize in various synagogues concurrently or to go successively from one to the other. It is likely that the existence of newly converted Christians alongside the traditional members of the synagogue may have led to increased factions and even to tumultuous disputes.

III

Conditions as outlined above cast light on an event which is shared historically by Jewish and Christian congregations in Rome: the edict of Claudius against the Jews.[78] This event is part of the immediate historical background of Romans. The date of this edict allows us to locate more precisely in time the beginnings of Christianity in Rome which were described in the preceding section.

In Suetonius' biography on Caesar Claudius we find this statement: *Judaeos assidue tumultuantes impulsore Chresto Roma expulit.*[79] We can assume that Chrestos is not the name of a Jewish agitator but a careless spelling of the name Christus. Although this is sometimes disputed,[80] F. Blass was able to show that in the common language of the people, Chrestos was used for Christus.[81] Tacitus not only knew the Chrestianoi[82] but also that their name came from the word Christus.[83] *Chrestiani* as a name

---

[76]For these reasons one must agree with Bell's (*Juden und Griechen*, 26f.) rejection of S. Reinach's theses ("La première allusion," 108–22).

[77]This situation is probably presupposed in Acts 18:4–6 (Corinth). In this case, however, Crispus (1 Cor. 1:14–16), the ruler of the synagogue, belongs to the ranks of the converted. In all likelihood Sosthenes (Acts 18:17), Paul's accuser before Gallio, took over this position.

[78]Merril, "Claudius and the Jews," 104–8. Of the many treatments of Claudius' reign, the following specifically discuss questions concerning the edict against the Jews: Momigliano, *Claudio*, 66–77; Scramuzza, *Emperor Claudius*, 140–52.

[79]Janne, "Impulsore Chresto," 531–53.

[80]Citing Reinach, *Textes*, 329; Hoennicke, *Das Judenchristentum*, 159, and later Juster, *Les Juifs*, 199, 2, maintain this position.

[81]Blass, *Hermes*, 465–470.

[82]Tac., *Ann.* 15.44.2: quos per flagitia invisos vulgus Chrestianos (lectio difficilior!) appellabat.

[83]Tac., *Ann.* 15.44.4: auctor nominis eius, Christus.

for Christians appears throughout the first and second centuries.[84] The error of the biographer Suetonius is that he believed the cult-hero to be the leader of a religious group in Rome. If indeed Claudius' edict refers to the followers of this Christus, then it is a dispute within the Roman synagogues about the messiahship of Jesus of Nazareth which led the emperor to act against the Jews. Since there was no central Jewish authority to mediate the dispute, Claudius turned vigorously against all Jews. The unfavorable experiences with earlier Jewish conduct may have played a role as well. Dating these events is made possible through a statement by the early Christian historian Orosius, who writes with regard to the ninth year of Claudius' reign (A.D. 49): *anno eiusdem nono expulsos per Claudium urbe Judaeos Josephus refert.*[85]

The New Testament confirms our interpretation of Claudius' edict. Acts 18:2 speaks of Aquila and Priscilla who came to Corinth because Claudius had decreed that all Jews had to leave Rome. Immediately, they develop a relationship with Paul, which indicates they are already Christians.[86] Further, they are witnesses for the existence of a Christian congregation in Rome at the time of Claudius.

Expulsion of Jews from Rome also meant the end of the first Christian congregation in Rome, which up until then had consisted of Jewish Christians. In Paul's letter to the Romans, written a few years after these events,[87] we meet a new congregation. Although we were able to show that the first Christians in Rome unquestionably originated from the synagogues, all attempts to define the addressees of the Roman letter as Jewish Christians are unconvincing.[88] The real addressee is the "new" Christian congregation in Rome which constitutes itself after the expulsion of the Jews under Claudius.

What has happened during those intervening years with reference to the reign of Claudius? The historian Dio Cassius tells us that the Jews had lost their right to assemble.[89] He does not, however, speak of the expulsion of Jews under Claudius; this seems to contradict Suetonius' report.

[84]Evidence is offered by F. Blass, *Hermes,* 466f., and A. von Harnack, *Mission und Ausbreitung,* 425, 3.

[85]*Hist. contra Pag.* 7, 6, 15 (*CSEL* 5, 451). Harnack, "Chronologische," 673–82, attempts to explain the erroneous reference to Josephus.

[86]Zahn, *Römer,* 635f., who on the basis of his understanding of the edict interprets this passage differently, is criticized by Haenchen, MeyerK III 15, (1968) 476: "To imagine that a Jewish couple expelled from Rome gave employment and room to none other than a Christian missionary is much less probable than that Paul received hospitality from Christians who had been expelled from Rome."

[87]If one presupposes Joach. Jeremias' chronology based on the Sabbath years (*ZNW* 27, [1928] 98–103=Abba, [1965] 233–37), then the year 54 is probable, that is, shortly after the beginning of Nero's reign. Others opt for a much later date: Th. Zahn suggests the spring of 58 (*Einleitung,* 310), and Ed. Meyer the spring of 59 (*Ursprung und Anfänge,* 63).

[88]This latter position is represented by Ropes, "Romans," 353–65, and Lietzmann, "Zwei Notizen zu Paulus," 290ff.

[89]*Historia Romana* 60.6.6.

If, in fact, Dio Cassius' statement was intended to tell us the entire story, we would have to prefer Suetonius because his report agrees with that of Acts 18:2.[90] In an attempt to overcome this conflict, some believed it to be a decree made early during Claudius' reign.[91] Yet this would contradict the emperor's initially cordial attitude towards the Jews.[92] We come to a more fruitful conclusion if we see the denial of free assembly as a first step in moderating the eviction edict. After Jews were again permitted to return to Rome, synagogue assemblies were prohibited for some time since they were seen as seedbeds of dispute. Thus Christians as well had no place to gather. They had to develop new organizational forms to avoid the ban against the Jewish *collegia*. Christians could only assemble in Rome if they, as a group, had broken ties with the synagogue.

By the time Nero came to power, anti-Jewish measures had been repealed.[93] We can assume that it was not until this point that Jews returned to Rome in great numbers. But aside from such growth they also increased in influence as can be seen in the friendly attitude Nero's wife Poppaea showed toward the Jews.[94]

While the Jews were only concerned with the reestablishment of their disbanded synagogues, Christians had an entirely new and different problem. Among the returnees were those Jewish Christians who had been members of the synagogue congregations. But now, as they return, they find Christians who have developed a form of organization independent of the synagogal form. Considering the initial difficulties these Jews had in Rome, the Gentile Christians undoubtedly played an important part at this juncture. It is safe to assume that quite a few of the returning Christians had been influenced by Paul's gospel of freedom from the law.

This impression is confirmed if we look at Romans 16, which, incidentally, is not without consequence for the much debated question about the original relationship of this chapter to Romans as a whole.[95] The chapter is largely a list of salutations,[96] and it appears possible to differentiate between those who are probably Paul's personal acquaintances, whom he describes more fully,[97] and those who are simply referred to

[90]Josephus' obvious silence about these proceedings is noteworthy, but hardly a sufficient basis for Leon, *Jews of Ancient Rome*, 27, to doubt the entire expulsion of the Jews.
[91]Meyer, *Ursprung und Anfänge*, 462; Momigliano, *Claudio*, 66–69.
[92]See Jos., *Ant.* 19.278–291 and *War* 5.214–217; Dio Cass. 60.8.
[93]Leon, *Jews of Ancient Rome*, 27f.
[94]Josephus refers to them as god-fearers (*Ant.* 20.189–196), that is, as half-proselytes, and reports that he himself, through the help of Alityrus, a Jewish actor who knew Poppaea well, effected the freedom of Jewish priests (*Life* 3). Even the manner of their confirmation, which differed from the Roman (Tac., *Ann.* 16.6), is discussed in connection with this.
[95]The discussion since D. Schulz's article *TSK* 2, (1829) 609–612, can be found in such standard introductions to the New Testament as Kümmel, *Introduction*, 314–20 (with a positive evaluation) and Michaelis, *Einleitung*, 160–62 (with a negative evaluation).
[96]The most thorough examination is offered by Erbes, "Zeit und Ziel," 128–47, 195–218.
[97]Rom. 16:3–13.

by name.[98] In any case, Paul has a multitude of connections with this congregation. Of the twenty-five names, only six are Latin: Aquila, Junias, Ampliatus, Urbanus, Rufus, and Julia.[99] Most names are of Greek origin. Even close scrutiny does not allow us to assign them to certain geographical regions. Yet one could refer to Lietzmann's observation that the uncommon names occur in completely different regions of the *Orbis romanus* and conclude with him "that every one wanders to Rome."[100] Also noteworthy is the observation that many names on the list are typical of slaves and freedmen:[101] they either followed their masters to Rome or were there already as freedmen. The only Christians who were known to be victims of Claudius' eviction, Aquila and Prisca, are, according to these greetings, back in Rome. For a short while they had lived in Corinth[102] and probably risked their lives for the apostle[103] while living in Ephesus.[104] That they returned to Rome after several stops is plausible if we think of initially the moderation and then the repeal of the edict by Claudius. They are not the only Jewish Christians greeted by Paul. Junias, Andronicus, and Herodion are referred to as kinsmen, and in the case of Mary the name itself betrays its origin. It is uncertain whether they belonged to the oldest congregation of Jewish Christians in Rome, as did Aquila and Prisca.[105] The latter appear as hosts or leaders of a household.[106] Romans 16 apparently refers to house churches at least twice more.[107]

Presumably these house churches were of particular importance to the Christians in Rome at the time Romans was written. As we pointed out above, the first step in the moderation of the eviction edict was the denial of free assembly to the synagogue congregations, and this necessitated a new organizational structure for the Christians in Rome. House churches provided a setting similar to that of congregations in the East who had also formed them in order to be independent of the synagogue.[108] Creation of these semi-legal house churches eliminated the Jewish element which previously had been rooted in the synagogue assembly. This explains why

[98]Rom. 16:14f.

[99]It is particularly striking that two co-workers of Paul (who had thus far been active only in the East), Ampliatus and Urbanus bear names which are especially frequent in Rome. Did they share the same fate as Aquila and Prisca?

[100]Lietzmann, *An die Römer,* 125. This theme is discussed in a wider context by La-Piana, "Foreign Groups," 183–403.

[101]Lietzmann, *An die Römer,* cites: Ampliatus, Tryphaena, Asynkritos, Phlegon Philologos.

[102]Acts 18:2, 1 Cor. 16:19.

[103]Acts 18:26 (2 Tim. 4:19 refers to this).

[104]One is reminded of the situation described in Acts 19:13ff., and possibly also 1 Cor. 15:32 or 2 Cor. 1:8.

[105]Erbes "Zeit und Ziel," 139f., suggests this for Junias and Andronicus, supplementing Volkmar, *Römerbrief,* 67; for Mary, see Schmidt, *Römer,* 213.

[106]Rom. 16:5.

[107]Rom. 16:14, 15.

[108]1 Cor. 16:19; Philem.; 2 Cor. 4:15. From a later period, Pseudoclem. *Rec.* 10.71 (*GCS* 51, 371).

Jewish Christianity did not regain its dominant position and why Paul, in his letter to the Romans, assumed that his readers were those who lived by the gospel of freedom from the law. Accordingly, the Jewish-Christians, who probably returned in great numbers only after the Claudius edict was finally repealed,[109] found a "new" Christian congregation completely different in organizational structure and spiritual outlook from the old one which had existed in the synagogue. Now they are only a minority in a congregation which previously they had shaped.[110] From this emerges the possibility of specifying the *Sitz im Leben* of Romans: it was written to assist the Gentile Christian majority, who are the primary addressees of the letter, to live together with the Jewish Christians in one congregation, thereby putting an end to their quarrels about status.[111]

IV

Christian Baur recognized the need for a historical perspective in the interpretation of Romans 9–11. In rejecting a purely dogmatic exegesis, he states: "The dogmatic aspect of the letter presents itself primarily in the first eight chapters. . . . The rest, especially, the following three chapters, are of secondary importance." These very chapters, however, disprove Baur's definition of Romans as a missive to a Jewish Christian congregation. Critics recognized this very soon.[112] For the Jewish Christians, a justification of the Gentile mission could have been in order, but not a glorification of Israel's virtues.[113] The same goes for the warning to the Gentile Christians (here seen as a wild olive shoot) that they should not rise self-gloriously against the olive tree, Israel, which supports them.[114] Paul tries to show that the people of Israel have their place within the divine plan and that Christianity does not have to be ashamed of its spiritual descent from Israel. To achieve this, he not only uses all his exegetical skill, but refers to a secret revelation.[115] On the one hand, Paul is concerned that the Gentile Christian majority would welcome the Jewish Christians without any hesitation whatsoever; Paul takes advantage of his authority

---

[109]With the beginning of Nero's reign and therefore shortly before the writing of the epistle.

[110]One might consider whether they are identical with the "weak" referred to in 14:1–15:13. Apparently we are dealing with a minority in both cases who are unable to (and perhaps do not want to) impose their lifestyle upon the congregation as a whole and thus have a claim to toleration and respect.

[111]Baur, F. C., *Paulus*, 1.350, with reference to the exegesis of Tholuck, de Wette, and Olshausen.

[112]Weizsäcker, "Römische Christengemeinde," 256–58. Grafe, *Veranlassung und Zweck des Römerbriefes*, 90.

[113]Rom. 9:4f.

[114]Rom. 11:18.

[115]Paul uses the term *mystērion*, which is used in this sense of revealing apocalyptic events for the first time in the LXX version of Daniel 2:28f.; 4:9, and makes clear that the

among the Gentile Christians to underline this point.[116] On the other hand, he is looking at the future of Israel from the perspective of *Heilsgeschichte,* especially the future of non-Christian Israel.[117]

Paul's judgment of non-Christian Israel must surprise us. Only a few years back, in his earlier letter, 1 Thessalonians, he used a phrase common in anti-Jewish polemics to argue sharply against any interference by Jews against missionary preaching.[118] This represents a change in thinking, which also occurred in his eschatology, which had similar incisive results: from the dominant idea of an imminent parousia in 1 Thessalonians Paul shifted to a conception of individual reunification with Christ after death (2 Cor. 5:1–10 and Phil. 1:21–23).[119] We must consider whether both of these observations are related. If Paul at first considered the persecution of Jews as God's punishment and signal of a near parousia,[120] then a more individualized understanding of eschatology and a lessened expectation of the immediacy of the end will place the question of Israel in a different context.

Romans is the decisive evidence for a new perspective on the part of Paul with regard to the question of Judaism. Certainly Paul's deepened reflections are partially responsible for seeing Israel in a more positive light. But the immediate reason for this new perspective is the special situation of Roman Christianity. Thus, once again, contemporary history provides a key for understanding Romans.

We have shown how anti-Jewish sentiment is part of Jewish history in Rome right from the start. The first Jewish congregation of the Western world was formed in a city which not only became the center of Jewish life but also the center of anti-Semitism. Enmity against Jews seems to have increased further in the second half of the first century. But there are few reliable sources for the time of Nero. The rhetorician Quintilian (A.D. 34–100) speaks about the presence of Jewish *superstitio* as an example of the kind of shame which outlives the time of its originator.[121] The concept of *superstitio is* also the title of a lost text by Seneca from which Augustine quotes.[122] In it he criticizes the Jews for their celebration of the sabbath through which they waste one seventh of their lives. He is even more incensed that this custom—so common among this de-

---

new eschatological role of Judaism is derived from an insight given to Paul in an inspirational way. That inspirational knowledge and reflection do not exclude each other is indicated by the use of the same word in 1 Cor. 15:51.

[116]This demand comes to expression especially in Rom. 15:7f.

[117]Rom. 11:25–32.

[118]1 Thess. 2:15.

[119]The question of a change in Paul's eschatological perspective first raised by Teichmann, *Die paulinischen Vorstellungen,* is discussed among contemporary scholars by Jeremias, "Flesh and Blood," 151–59 = Abba (1966), 298–307; Leipoldt, *Gegenwartsfragen,* 106–8.

[120]Bammel, "Jundenverflogung und Naherwartung," 294–315.

[121]*Instit. Or.* 3.7.

[122]August., *de Civ.* 6.11 (CSEL 39, 298).

generate people—has spread into all regions of the country. The conquered had thus made the laws for the conqueror and yet the great mass of non-Jews did not know what they were doing. In one of his letters, Seneca speaks likewise about the custom of the sabbath light.[123] And for Pliny the Elder, the Jews are a group of magicians.[124]

The picture becomes clearer still if we look at the remarks of authors who came to Rome in those years or who grew up there. Even if these sources are from the end of the first century, they are nevertheless typical of the attitude towards the Jews in Rome at the time of Nero. They are characterized by the disdain with which one often looks at things foreign and by a grotesque ignorance towards everything Jewish: origins, history, and lifestyle. Satirists ridicule obtrusive Jewish beggars[125] and Jewish women who spare no pains to make some money through fortune-telling.[126] Further, they portray Jews as a people of merchants[127] and express anger against Jewish poets[128] and singers.[129] The sabbath, as the most conspicuous sign of Jewish life, has always evoked derision and scorn;[130] it is considered a sign of laziness[131] or of superstition.[132] The Jew is pictured as one who labors over his cooking box (*cophina*) to keep the sabbath meal warm.[133] Indelible in the minds of Romans is the notion that the sabbath is a fast-day for Jews.[134] They may have confused the weekly holiday with the new year, Rosh Hashanah,[135] which also explains Juvenal's assertion that even kings would go barefoot on this day.[136] Persius writes about a *dies Herodis,* but no Jew would have marked the birthday of this king with a special celebration. The context rather points to the consecration of the temple (Hanukkah) celebrated in winter.[137] Next to the sabbath, circumcision stands as the most conspicuous mark of Judaism. Although one spoke of a circumcised man with a certain disdain,[138] real scorn was reserved for him who tried to hide his circumcision because he was ashamed of his descent.[139]

Since Jewish customs were repulsive from a Roman point of view, the Jewish desire to proselytize for their religion was considered even more

---

[123]Seneca, *Ep.* 95.
[124]Plin., *Nat. hist.* 31.11.
[125]Mart., *Epigr.* 10.57.13. Juv., *Sat.* 2.ll.
[126]Juv., *Sat.* 6.541–544.
[127]Mart., *Epigr.* 1.41.3.
[128]Mart., *Epigr.* 11.94.
[129]Mart., *Epigr.* 7.82.
[130]An overview can be found in P. Lefay, "Le Sabbat juif," 313–20.
[131]Juv., *Sat.* 14.105; earlier Seneca (n. 3).
[132]Pers., *Sat.* 5.184.
[133]Juv., *Sat.* 3.14; 6.521.
[134]Mart., *Epigr.* 4.4.7. Sueton., *Octav.* 76.
[135]Askowith, *Toleration and Persecution of the Jews,* 87.
[136]Juv., *Sat.* 6.159.
[137]Pers., *Sat.* 5.179–184.
[138]Pers., *Sat.* 5.184. Mart., *Epigr.* 7.30.5, 9.94. Petr., *Satyricon* 102.
[139]Mart., *Epigr.* 7.82.

objectionable. This tendency toward proselytism, still active in the second half of the century, is described in these words by Juvenal: "If the father starts keeping the sabbath as a God-fearing man, the son proceeds to have himself circumcised, and then the son proceeds to despise the Roman laws so that he may be obedient to the Jewish one."[140] This Roman source alludes for the first time to half-proselytes[141] or the *metuentes*. The word is a Latinized form based on the Greek and is used in gravestone inscriptions.[142] What was otherwise normally respected, the spiritual depth of the Jewish view of God,[143] is also despised. It is seen merely as worship of the heavens and the clouds.[144] A possible reason for this attitude is the Jewish usage of the word *heaven* as a paraphrase for the name of God.

This picture of animosity toward Jews, shaped by ignorance and prejudice, is rounded out if we review the grotesque notions which existed concerning the origin of Jews. Tacitus, for example, leaves the matter completely in obscurity.[145] In the passage that deals with Jews[146] Tacitus stresses the foreign and contradictory nature of the traditions.[147] Already at this point his polemical purpose becomes apparent: obscure origins are for him an indication of an inferior nature.[148] Tacitus follows mostly ancient themes used in polemics against Judaism, particularly those formed in Alexandria. This becomes apparent at the point where he argues that the Jews were expelled from Egypt because of their inherent impurity.[149] This idea which is obviously based on a tendentious misinterpretation of the Exodus event, appears to have been mentioned first by the Egyptian Manetho.[150] But Josephus, in his defense against Apion, mentions three more anti-Semites who use this polemic: Chaeremon,[151] Lysimachus,[152] and Apion himself.[153] This argument is used in the works of other ancient historians as well.[154]

Tacitus replaces the account of these wanderings in the desert with a malicious legend. According to him, the wandering Jews were dying of thirst and were shown their way by a herd of wild asses; this was their reason for a cult-like worship of asses. In this way, another topic of an-

---

[140]Juv., *Sat.* 14.96–102.

[141]Bernays, "Juvenal," 563–596.

[142]*CIJ* 5, 285, 524, 529, 642.

[143]Varro in August., *de Civ.* 6.31.2 (*CSEL* 40, 1, 205), Tac., *Hist.* 5.5.

[144]Juv., *Sat.* 14.97: nihil praeter nubes et coeli numen adorant. Petr., *Frg.* 37.2 (ed. Buecheler). Codex Theodosianus 16, 8, 19 still calls the Jews coelicoli.

[145]Tac., *Hist.* 5.2 cites Crete, Assyria, Ethiopia.

[146]Tac., *Hist.* 5.2–9.

[147]Isid. Levy, *Tacite et l 'origine du peuple juif* (Latomus 1, 1946) 321–40.

[148]Orig., *contra Cels.* 2.4.33–35.

[149]*Hist.* 5.3.

[150]Jos., *Ag. Ap.* 1.227–250.

[151]Jos., *Ag. Ap.* 1.288–292.

[152]Jos., *Ag. Ap.* 1.304–311.

[153]Jos., *Ag. Ap.* 2.8–27.

[154]Diodorus Siculus, *Bibl. hist.* 9, Frg. 28. Just., *Epit.* 36.2 (Pomp. Trogus).

cient polemic is taken up, which claims that Jews worship the donkey[155] and even pray to the head of a donkey in the temple.[156] The point of departure for this interpretation may have been the Hebrew name for God.[157] Tacitus claims,[158] like the Alexandrian Jewish polemic before him,[159] that Jews celebrate the sabbath because they had been saved on the seventh day; but in addition to this he adds the reason stressed by Roman enemies of the Jews, viz., their laziness.[160] Jews had always been mocked for their conspicuous abstention from eating pork.[161] Tacitus connects this practice to the swine pest for which they had been expelled from Egypt.[162] Tacitus also refers bluntly to circumcision as a sign of sexual lust.[163] Satirists before him had suggested such an interpretation but had never used it openly. Critics have sometimes tried to defend Tacitus saying he had used old arguments of Jewish polemic without double-checking his sources.[164] But others have pointed out correctly that Tacitus shared the antipathy of his people, his time, and his own social class against Jews.[165] The rebuke which sums it all up is this: *adversus omnes alios hostile odium.*[166] It was used widely and had such power of attraction[167] that even Paul could not resist it at first. A rather unanimous constellation, it seems, if one considers that an almost similar rebuke was used against Christians only a short time later.[168]

We have shown the existence of a strong anti-Jewish sentiment in Rome at the time of Nero and before. Positive statements regarding all of Israel occur for the first time in Paul's letter to the Romans and must be seen against this background. The Christian congregation in Rome is surrounded by a society marked by its aversion and rejection of everything Jewish. Paul acknowledges the people of his own heritage and develops a theology of history which assigns them an important place at the end of history. Paul's statements not only aim at elevating the stature of Jewish-Christians in the eyes of Gentile-Christians to work against the formers' low esteem on account of their Jewish heritage, but are also written in consideration of that overwhelming majority within the Jewish community which had

[155]Plut., *Sympos.* 4.5.2.
[156]Jos., *Ag. Ap.* 2.79–88. That the same criticism is also made against Christians is evident from Tert., *Apologet.* 16.2 and Minucius Felix, *Oct.* 28.7.
[157]Jacoby, "Eselskult," 265–82. Bickermann, "Ritualmord und Eselskult," 255–64.
[158]*Hist.* 5.3.2.
[159]Jos., *Ag. Ap.* 2.8–27.
[160]Seneca in August., *de Civ.* 6.11 (CSEL 39, 298).
[161]Plut., *Sympos.* 4.5.2. Jos., *Ag. Ap.* 2.135–136. Petr., *Frg.* 37.2.
[162]Tac., *Hist.* 5.4.3.
[163]*Hist.* 5.5.
[164]Hild, "Les Juifs à Rome," 174–86.
[165]Thiaucevert, "Tacit," 57–74.
[166]Tac., *Hist.* 5.1.
[167]Jos., *Ag. Ap.* 2.137–144.
[168]This transfer is discussed by Zeller, "Das odium," 56–362.

closed itself off from the Christian mission. Considering the situation in Rome, Paul makes it a point to resist the temptation of following the trend of anti-Jewish sentiment in this city, and thus turning Christianity into an anti-Jewish movement. The gain might have been missionary success, but that does not outweigh what would have been lost: the message about the universality of God's salvation which is directed especially towards those who have closed themselves off decisively and whose rejection appears most incomprehensible.

8

FALSE PRESUPPOSITIONS IN THE STUDY OF ROMANS

Karl Paul Donfried

Current research concerning the purpose of Romans is in a state of confusion. Almost every recent article or monograph on the subject proposes a different solution. Although the variety of positions is startling, there are basically two major opposing viewpoints: (1) those scholars who believe that Paul directed this letter to deal with a specific, concrete situation in Rome; and (2) those interpreters who hold that it is directed primarily to a situation other than Rome.

I. Part 1

Paul Minear,[1] a representative of the first group, believes Romans deals with the conflict between "the weak" and "the strong" (the Jewish and Gentile Christians, respectively) in Rome. Willi Marxsen,[2] sharing much of this emphasis, specifies the conflict as having arisen when the Jewish Christians, who had been expelled from Rome by the Emperor Claudius in A.D. 49, returned to Rome after Claudius' death in A.D. 54. Wolfgang Wiefel[3] adds even greater specificity to this general approach by suggesting that as Claudius' edict was in the process of being rescinded, a continued ban was imposed on formal synagogue meetings which gave further support to a new developing organizational principle: the formation of house congregations in Rome. This multiplicity of house congregations (reflected in Rom. 16), coupled with a theology dominated by the majority Gentile Christian perspective, led to tensions with the returning Jewish Christians. Wiefel therefore concludes that Romans was written to solve such a crisis.

---

[1]Minear, *Obedience.*
[2]Marxsen, *Introduction,* 92–109.
[3]Wiefel, "Jewish Community." See chapter 7 above.

Also belonging to this historical group, but moving in a different direction, are Klein,[4] who suggests that Romans was written to give proper apostolic authorization to the Roman church, and Schrenk,[5] who views Romans as a "Missionsdokument" which is intended to enable the Roman church to work closely with Paul as he expands the range of his missionary activity.

Bornkamm,[6] a representative of the "non-historical" group, views Romans as Paul's "last will and testament"—a summary of his theology in light of the impending danger in Jerusalem. Fuchs[7] suggests that it is a "secret letter" to Jerusalem. Jervell[8] builds upon and expands Fuchs's thesis: Romans is a draft of the address Paul will give in Jerusalem. Manson[9] and Jewett[10] argue that Romans is a circular letter addressed to several congregations and, therefore, only "tenuously" related to the Roman situation. The most recent representative of this "non-historical" position is Karris[11] who, writing to refute Minear's monograph, urges that Rom. 14:1–15:13 (chapters basic to Minear's treatment) "has no specific referent within the Roman community. It is part of a letter which sums up Paul's missionary theology and paraenesis." [12]

The purpose of this essay, given the present lack of consensus, is to propose two methodological principles and raise selected questions about the current methodologies being used in the study of Romans. In addition, we wish to raise questions about possible false presuppositions implicit in these methodologies which may prohibit an accurate understanding of Paul's intention in writing Romans. Let us begin with two basic methodological principles:

Methodological Principle I

Any study of Romans should proceed on the initial assumption that this letter was written by Paul to deal with a concrete situation in Rome. The support for such an assumption is the fact that every other authentic Pauline writing, *without exception,* is addressed to the specific situations of the churches or persons involved. To argue that Romans is an exception to this Pauline pattern is certainly possible, but the burden of proof rests with those exegetes

[4]Klein, "Paul's Purpose." See chapter 3 above.
[5]Schrenk, "Der Römerbrief," 81–106. The positions just reviewed are intended only to indicate one general direction in Pauline studies and are not intended to be a complete survey of the entire literature.
[6]Bornkamm, *Paul,* 88–96.
[7]Fuchs, *Hermeneutik,* 191.
[8]Jervell, "Letter to Jerusalem". See chapter 5 above.
[9]Manson, "St. Paul's Letter." See chapter 1 above.
[10]Jewett, *Anthropological Terms,* 41–48.
[11]Karris, "Occasion." See chapter 6 above.
[12]Ibid., 98. Further bibliographical information with regard to other studies on Romans may be found in Donfried, "Short Note on Romans 16"; see chapter 4 above. Karris, chapter 6, page 66, notes 6 and 7; see also Noack, "Current and Backwater," 155–66.

who wish to demonstrate that it is impossible, or at least not likely, that Romans addresses a concrete set of problems in the life of Christians in Rome. This methodological principle is of great importance since so many recent studies begin with the opposite assumption and *never* even explore the historical data available concerning Jews and Christians in Rome; on the contrary, one must first begin with a review of the available historical data.

Methodological Principle II

Any study of Romans should proceed on the assumption that Rom. 16 is an integral part of the original letter. The burden of proof rests with those who would wish to argue the contrary, and it would be helpful if they demonstrated their case in the following order of importance: a. why Rom. 16 is incongruous with the intention of Romans *as a whole;* and b. why the textual history of Rom. 16 should be so interpreted as to sever this chapter from that which precedes. This second methodological principle is also of critical importance since the pattern in many recent studies is to proceed without demonstration, on the assumption that Rom. 16 was originally addressed to Ephesus and that it was not an integral part of Paul's letter to the Romans.[13]

We will now examine these two methodological principles as well as some possible false presuppositions found in certain recent studies. Beginning with Principle I, that Paul wrote to a concrete historical situation in Rome, we find that at least three studies are of fundamental importance: Marxsen, Wiefel, and Minear.[14] Since many of Marxsen's suggestions are incorporated by Wiefel and Minear, and because we have discussed Marxsen's position in detail elsewhere,[15] we will proceed directly to the work of Wiefel and Minear, keeping in mind that the intention of such a review is not to suggest that one accept every aspect of their presentation as persuasive, but rather that they must be taken seriously in any study of Romans.

Since Wiefel's article, "The Jewish Community in Ancient Rome and the Origins of Roman Christianity," is one of fundamental importance for a possible reconstruction of the historical background of Romans it is unfortunate that it has received such little attention in the recent discussions.[16] In his careful description of the history of Judaism in Rome, Wiefel makes a number of important observations, including a discussion of the structure and organization of Judaism in that city. We discover that before Claudius' edict in A.D. 49 there were many synagogues with different designations in Rome including, for example, a synagogue of the Hebrews and a synagogue of the Vernaculi; the latter referred to the old established Greek-speaking Jews and the former to more recently arrived Aramaic-speaking Jews. What we find is a large and very diverse Jewish popula-

---

[13]For example, Suggs, "Romans 10:6–10," 294, n. 1.
[14]See notes 1, 2, and 3 above.
[15]See note 12.
[16]It is [was] not even discussed in the newest [1973] commentary by Käsemann, *Römer.*

tion in Rome, highly individual in nature, with no single controlling official or board possessing overall authority. As Christian missionaries moved into this situation some synagogues would be considerably more receptive than others, thus setting the stage for "a series of tumultuous conflicts" between various synagogues in Rome.[17] Such a situation, which probably led to Claudius' edict expelling all Jews from Rome, is the immediate historical background of Romans. Wiefel's analysis further suggests that Claudius had to move against Judaism as a whole precisely because there was no one Jewish leader in Rome having authority over all the synagogues. This edict marks a significant turning point in the development of Judaism in Rome, as well as marking the termination of the distinctly Jewish Christian congregation in that city.

Next Wiefel turns to a remark made by Dio Cassius[18] that about this same time the Jewish right of assembly had been revoked. How does this relate to Claudius' expulsion of the Jews as related in Suetonius[19] and referred to in Acts 18:2? Do we have conflicting accounts? No, argues Wiefel: Dio Cassius reflects that stage in the process (certainly no later than the beginning of Nero's reign) when the Jews and Jewish Christians were permitted to return to Rome, but still forbidden to assemble publicly. This further aided the development of a new organizational form for Christians in Rome: house churches, a phenomenon which Wiefel also finds reflected in Rom. 16. It is easy to perceive that both the new polity involving house churches separate from the synagogue structure and a theological situation heavily dominated by the Gentile Christians who had remained in Rome were bound to be alien to the returning Jewish Christians. The likely result was tension between the two Christian groups. "From this emerges the possibility of specifying the *Sitz im Leben* of Romans: it was written to assist the Gentile Christian majority, who are the primary addressees of the letter, to live together with the Jewish Christians in one congregation, thereby putting an end to their quarrels about status."[20]

Wiefel demonstrates from a wide variety of classical sources the strongly anti-Semitic opinions current in Rome prior to and during the period presently under discussion. It is thus possible that Paul refers to Israel positively in Rom. 9–11,[21] among other important theological reasons,[22] precisely so that the Gentile Christians would resist the temptation to join in the current slanderous anti-Jewish sentiment. Seen in this light the statements made in Rom. 9–11 are quite revolutionary both in their universalism and in their freedom from Roman prejudice. Even though this is one of the few places in which Wiefel makes direct contact with

[17]Wiefel, chapter 7 above.
[18]*Historia Romana* 60.6.6.
[19]*Claud.* 25.4. See discussion in Donfried, "Short Note on Romans 16," 47 above.
[20]Wiefel, chapter 7 above.
[21]Note the different attitude in 1 Thess. 2:15.
[22]See Käsemann, *Römer*, 241ff.

the theology of Romans, his detailed and exacting analysis of Judaism in
Rome is replete with other highly suggestive possibilities for a more comprehensive understanding of Romans. Anyone who disagrees with Methodological Principle I above should show why it is not reasonable to accept
at least part of Wiefel's analysis as helpful in understanding the situation
to which Romans addresses itself.

We turn now to Minear's *The Obedience of Faith*. It accepts the general directions outlined by Wiefel,[23] and proceeds to interpret Romans in
light of a similar historical situation. As we shall see, Wiefel and Minear
complement each other very strikingly; and what is even more significant, they do this independently. Both proceed on the basis of the two
methodological principles noted above.

While Minear is more concerned with the theological purpose of Romans, he reaches similar sociological conclusions as Wiefel, viz., that there
may have been several Christian groups in Rome[24] and that, as a consequence, Rom. 16 can be understood without difficulty as an integral part
of the original letter. For Minear, Paul wrote to Rome for essentially two
reasons: (1) to communicate plans about his future apostolic work, and (2)
to deal with "the difficulties which had been reported *within the congregations in Rome.*"[25] These different groups in Rome can be detected in
14:1–16:27 and include: 1. The weak in faith who condemned the strong
in faith; 2. the strong in faith who scorned and despised the weak in faith;
3. the doubters; 4. the weak in faith who did not condemn the strong; 5.
the strong in faith who did not despise the weak.[26] While the direction
of Minear's general interpretation is persuasive, it is open to question
whether one can determine so precisely that there were five differentiated groups in the Roman churches.[27] Be that as it may, his study attempts
to demonstrate that all of Romans is directed to solve those difficulties
which are found in outline form in 14:1–16:27.

In developing this line of interpretation Minear challenges some standard views concerning the influence of the diatribe on Romans and Paul's
use of paraenesis. 1. In discussing 1:18–4:25 Minear refuses to concede that
Paul is dealing with some fictitious opponent as one finds in the diatribe,

[23]Although he had not seen Wiefel's article.

[24]Minear, *Obedience*, 1–2.

[25]Käsemann, *Römer*, 349, also supports this view: "The following hypothesis is worth
considering: Paul assumes or surmises that there are groups in Rome quarreling with one
another and that this situation is important for understanding the intentionality of Paul's letter."

[25]Minear, *Obedience*, 8ff.

[27]Käsemann's (*Römer* 349) caution is to be preferred: "Apparently Paul does not know
the congregation. However, that does not exclude the possibility that certain information
concerning it was transmitted to him. In fact, it is difficult to deny this possibility especially
since reports from this commercial center would have had to reach Christians of that day
in all parts of the world. For the moment it can remain an open question as to how consistent and self-contained a picture one can derive from the remarks which follow, and/or
how completely one can determine Paul's total intention in writing Romans from them."

but argues instead that "the 'you' which is so prominent in 2:1–6 and 2:17–24 applies more precisely to one of the factions in Rome."[28] At other points as well[29] Minear cautions against the view that Paul is merely setting up "straw men" for the sake of his argument. 2. Despite what many commentators have stated concerning the non-specific, general catechetical thrust of 12:1–13:14 (as well as 14–16), Minear argues for the actuality of the paraenesis in these chapters. Thus, Rom. 13:1–7, for example, is seen as related to the turbulent political conditions which had led Claudius to expel Jews and Jewish Christians from Rome a few years earlier.[30] While we are in general agreement with Minear's direction, viz., that an actual situation in Rome provoked this letter, we are hesitant to concur with Minear in attempting to relate almost every passage to some problem or opponent in Rome. Is it not very possible that Paul can be dealing with actual problems but in so doing employs rhetorical arguments and theological perspectives of a more general nature which will aid in solving them? While acknowledging that all of Romans, including the more general sections, deals with a Roman problem, it is perhaps misleading to suggest an almost point by point correlation.

So far we have stated what appear to us as logical methodological procedures and have reviewed two recent studies which accept such principles. It is evident that this "historical" approach is vulnerable if it can be demonstrated, first, that the diatribe exercised a pervasive and determinative influence upon Paul as he wrote this letter and, secondly, that the majority of the paraenetic material employed by Paul is not directed to a specific situation(s) in Rome. We need to pay attention to these possible objections. A convenient starting point is the question of the purpose of the Pauline paraenesis in Romans, since it is precisely on this issue that Karris rejects the validity of Minear's conclusions.

Karris argues that Rom. 14:1–15:13 should be analyzed for what it is: "general, Pauline paraenesis and not so many pieces of polemic from which a scholar may reconstruct the positions of the parties in Rome who occasioned the letter."[31] Before reviewing Karris' support for this assertion, two methodological questions must be raised at this point. First, can we dissociate chs. 14:1–15:13 from chs. 12–13 quite as easily and sharply as he does?[32] Why should only chs. 14–15 fall under the designation "apostolic

---

[28]Minear, *Obedience* 46.

[29]For example, in his discussion of Rom. 6 on p. 63.

[30]Käsemann (*Römer*, 349) appears to be moving in a similar direction in the following comment where he is relating chs. 14–15 to the two preceding ones: "Similarly, this section is directed concretely to the conditions prevalent in Rome, a process which already began in Rom. 13:1–7. To put it more cautiously: this section is important both for the occasion and the structure of the letter." See also the several discussions on this point in Furnish, *Theology and Ethics*, to which Minear refers at several points as a corroboration of his own views.

[31]Karris, chapter 6 above, p. 66.

[32]Karris, "Occasion," 70–71.

admonition?"[33] While certainly the earlier of these chapters are of a more general paraenetic nature, there is a continuity with that which follows, as Käsemann, for example, suggests.[34] One cannot fully appreciate Paul's intention in Rom. 12–15 without seeing the movement and the heightening specificity, beginning with Rom. 12:1 and moving through Rom. 15:13. Secondly, is it methodologically consistent to criticize Minear's understanding of Rom. 14–15 and simultaneously "leave aside" the question of Rom. 16, as Karris does?[35] That it is not correct should be clear from one fact alone, viz., that Minear devotes ten percent of his monograph to the relationship between chs. 14–15 and 16.

The first step in Karris' analysis of 14:1–15:13 is to make certain grammatical comparisons with 1 Cor. (8; 9; 10:34–11:1). Two observations are made: 1. Rom. 14:1–15:13 contains thirteen imperatives, whereas 1 Cor. 8 and 10:23–11:1 have only eight. Karris cites Leenhardt's conclusion approvingly: "It is clear from this that Paul is not really addressing a particular group of people [in Romans], whose concrete circumstances he is considering while pointing out their errors."[36] Before commenting on this let us turn to his second observation. 2. Rom. 14:1–15:13 has only one circumstantial "if" clause, whereas 1 Cor. 8 and 10 contain five. Karris concludes from this that one "could argue that since such circumstantial clauses are almost entirely lacking in Rom. 14:1–15:13, Paul is not addressing himself to a concrete situation within the Roman community."[37]

It is unfortunate that Karris has not supported the grammatical basis for his conclusions, since our reaction is that he has not been persuasive, for at least two reasons: 1. The observation that Rom. 14:1–15:13 has five more imperatives than 1 Cor. 8 and 1 Cor. 10:23–11:1 does not establish the fact that Romans is not addressed to an actual situation. The fact is that imperatives can serve both specific and general situations, and in 1 Cor. and Romans they can serve both functions. 2. The absence of circumstantial "if" clauses cannot determine that a concrete situation is not being addressed. Is not 2 Cor. 10–13 concretely addressed to a specific Corinthian situation even though there is a paucity of these clauses? Further, the presence of these so-called circumstantial "if" clauses also does not finally establish whether or not a concrete situation is intended. In the last analysis, whether or not an actual situation or circumstance is intended is based solely on Karris' judgment,[38] rather than on an objective grammatical argument, since his circumstantial "if" clauses are composed of

[33]See Schlier, "Vom Wesen," 74–89.
[34]See note 30.
[35]Karris, "Occasion," 67.
[36]Ibid., 72; Leenhardt, *Romans*, 345.
[37]Karris, "Occasion," 72.
[38]Thus where Karris stresses the specificity of the circumstantial "if" clauses in 1 Cor. 8:13, Barrett, *The First Corinthians*, 197, suggests that "Paul simply widens and generalizes the situation."

type one and type two conditions.[39] The very fact that the circumstantial "if" clauses contain the indicative *and* subjunctive mood indicates that they can vary widely in their degree of actuality:[40] from certainty to that which is clearly hypothetical or uncertain. Thus, it is finally the *context* of the circumstantial "if" clauses in the respective letters which must determine what degree of actuality is implied, which means we are right back to the original problem concerning the intention of Romans. In short, the so-called circumstantial "if" clauses by themselves do not support the assertion that 1 Cor. is addressed to a concrete situation and that Romans is not.

Next, Karris attempts to show that Rom. 14:1–15:13 is dependent upon 1 Cor. 8 and 12 by a comparison of vocabulary. No one will dispute that there are similarities including both words and themes between the two. Such similarities, however, in no way prove dependence of one upon the other. What is more likely is that Paul was applying similar principles to two distinct situations. It is not at all unusual that Paul, writing to Rome from Corinth, would be using thoughts and language that he had just applied to a similar (yet in many ways different) situation in Corinth. It is easier to imagine Paul's being flexible in such a way than being woodenly dependent on what he wrote to the Corinthians, excising what was irrelevant and then adding other material.[41]

Before we turn to Karris' discussion of paraenesis, a few other points must be made with reference to his exegesis of Rom. 14:1–15:13. 1. In the sections immediately preceding he discusses the question of "the weak" and "the strong" and "the Jews" and "the Gentiles" in Romans. Essentially he denies identification of "weak" with "Jew" and "strong" with "Gentile." The " 'weak' are simply weak" and " 'the strong' are simply strong."[42] Kar-

---

[39]Moule, *Idiom-Book*, 148–49, gives the following categories of conditional clauses:
1. Past or present conditions, possible or actual.
   The construction is:
   Protasis (if-clause): *ei* with Indic., in appropriate tense.
   Apodosis (result-clause): another Indic. (or its equivalent) in appropriate tense.
2. Recurrent or future conditions, whether real or hypothetical. The construction is:
   Protasis: ei (or *hote*, etc.) with *an* (making *ean, hotan*) with Subj. in appropriate tense.
   Apodosis: Indic. (or its equivalent) in appropriate tense.
3. Past or present conditions, only hypothetical. The construction is:
   Protasis: ei with a past tense of the Indic.
   Apodosis: a past (but not necessarily the same) tense of the Indic., usually with *an*.
I am grateful to my friend and colleague, Prof. Ivan Blazen of Andrews University, for a number of helpful conversations concerning both grammatical and theological dimensions of Romans.

[40]Among those cited by Karris, "Occasion," 10:27 is type one; 10:28, type two 8:13, type one; 8:10, type two.

[41]Karris' entire discussion on pp. 75–77 is very inflexible, failing to entertain seriously other interpretative possibilities. It is difficult to imagine Paul, as he writes Romans, taking 1 Cor. and "exclud(ing) personal references," "eliminat(ing) the circumstantial "if" clauses," "omit(ting) references to the catchword's of the Corinthians," "omit(ting) references to the concrete situation," and then "expand(ing) his generalized adaptation."

[42]Karris, "Occasion," 77–79.

ris is convinced that the history of religions approach in answering this question is "bankrupt."[43] But has he shown this? Minear's suggestions at this point are denied, but hardly refuted. In the case of Rauer,[44] Karris has correctly indicated that he is wrong but that still does not convincingly demonstrate that the history of religions approach is bankrupt.[45] Karris' position that Paul is only "concerned to show how an established community can maintain its unity despite differences of opinion"[46] is difficult to maintain not only because it is based on an assumption of a single community which is challenged by other historical reconstructions of the Roman situation, but also because it fails to take seriously the repeated admonition: *proslambanesthe allēlous* (Rom. 15:7; cf. 14:1,3).[47] Karris argues that Rom. 15:1–6 cannot be related to 7–13 "via the equation 'the weak' = Jewish Christians and 'the strong' = Gentile Christians";[48] rather the linkage is via love. The persuasiveness of this argument is not heightened by the complete absence of *agapē* or its equivalent in the Greek text.

In the final portion of his study dealing with the nature of paraenesis in Rom. 12–15, Karris makes observations that are very important and one

[43]Ibid., 69–70.

[44]Rauer, *"Schwachen."* Even though Rauer's identification of the "weak" and "strong" in Romans is incorrect, his overall perception of the Roman situation is correct: "There existed in the Roman church a lack of unity and a difference of opinion on an issue which both parties believed touched the basis of faith" (p. 79).

[45]Karris, "Occasion," 70, suggests that there is a "rising tide of opinion that calls for a reconsideration of the question of whether 'the weak' and 'the strong' communities, reflected in Rom. 14:1–15:13 occasioned Romans." It is of particular interest to note how the newest commentary on Romans by Käsemann (which was not yet published when Karris wrote his article) deals with this question of 'the weak" and "the strong."
"Most interpreters understand our section [15:7–13] as a continuation and expansion of the dominant theme found in 14:1–15:6: mutual acceptance. This theme also is to be applied to the unity of Christians composed out of Jews and Gentiles, that is, to the unity of the entire church. Vs. 7a actually takes up the central motif once again, while in vs. 7b the thoughts of vs. 3, and with it the scope of the preceding text, are repeated; also, the Christians composed out of Jews and Gentiles now take the place of the weak and the strong. This at least suggests the possibility that the previously described conflict has some relationship to the diverse composition of the Roman church, or put more precisely, this composition determined in a fundamental way the relationship of the Jewish Christian minority to the Gentile Christian majority. The connection, together with the expansion, of this text with what precedes is undeniable" (*Romans*, 368).
After concluding his discussion of Rom. 14:1–15:13 and before entering upon the exegesis of Rom. 15:14ff., Käsemann states:
"Although Romans is almost entirely a summary of Pauline theology, even if within the confines of a somewhat limited perspective, it remains, as is the case with every other writing of the apostle, a document addressed to a specific situation, and therefore one cannot force upon it the designation 'Lehrtraktates' " (*Romans*, 372–73).

[46]Karris, "Occasion," 79.

[47]*proslambanō* is predominantly used to welcome someone who is not already in intimate communion with the one addressed; see Phlm. 17 and Acts 28:2. Further, in indicating words denoting the present existence of a community Karris refers to "with one voice" in Rom. 15:6. Yet the use of the subjunctive, *hina homothymadon en heni stomati doxazēte ton theon* denotes something far less definite; "may with one voice glorify" suggests that Paul is expressing a further hope of what is not now a present reality.

[48]Karris, "Occasion," 80–81.

could only have wished that he would have elaborated them more fully and carried them through more consistently. Karris correctly challenges Dibelius's one-sided view of paraenesis which has so dominated New Testament studies. Contrary to Dibelius's view that paraenesis is general and customary, not addressed to a particular situation, both Karris and Furnish, whose work is cited by Karris, argue that Paul is capable of using and transforming the most traditional paraenesis for the specific needs of his congregations. Both challenge the assumption that to use older paraenetic material from whatever source necessarily means that it cannot be addressed to a specific situation, and both stimulate us to be more precise in distinguishing between different types and functions of paraenesis. Karris applies these reflections to Rom. 12–15 in the following manner: Paul "is giving paraenesis that has been modified by his own theologizing, by his own solutions to problems which occurred in his *former* missionary work."[49] On the basis of our previous comments we would simply challenge Karris' insertion of the adjective "former" since that has not been adequately demonstrated. Nevertheless, the fact that Furnish[50] and Karris have been critical of Dibelius's position is indeed important since it opens up new possibilities of understanding the Pauline paraenetic material. In this warning not to confuse originality or lack of originality with actuality, and not to be led astray in thinking that traditional formulations cannot serve actual and specific situations, these scholars strike a note found in the classical tradition itself. Seneca,[51] for example, while having "a high regard for traditional wisdom, nevertheless realizes that the task of selection, adaptation and application always remains."[52] Seneca himself makes this point most succinctly: "Assume that prescriptions have been handed down to us for the healing of the eyes; there is no need of my searching for others in addition; but for all that, these prescriptions must be adapted to the particular disease and to the particular stage of the disease."[53]

Let us summarize our discussion of Karris' argument that Rom. 12–15 "has no specific referent within the Roman community. It is part of a letter which sums up Paul's missionary theology and paraenesis."[54] It is our contention that Karris has not adequately dealt with the matters which we have for the sake of clarity called Methodological Principles I and II and that the attempted demonstration of his thesis has not been persuasive. He does make an important contribution, however, in challenging Dibelius's understanding that Pauline paraenesis cannot refer to specific situations, although we disagree with Karris' application of this criticism to the concrete case of Rom. 12–15.

[49]Ibid., 82–83.
[50]See especially Furnish, *Theology and Ethics*, 70, 72, 73 and 92.
[51]*Ep.* 84; 64.7ff.
[52]Malherbe, "Paraenetic Letter"; see also Hadot, *Seneca*, esp. 179–90.
[53]*Ep.* 64.8 (LCL).
[54]Karris, "Occasion," 84.

The second major criticism which has been raised against Methodological Principle I is that since Romans is heavily influenced by the diatribe it is not intended to deal with a concrete historical situation in Rome. Thus Karris, for example, states that whatever evidence may be gleaned from Romans which suggests a concrete setting is to be "negated on the basis of Paul's diatribe style in Romans."[55] This is also what Bornkamm has attempted to show in his many influential Pauline studies. In his most recent treatment of Romans he urges that the diatribe influenced Romans more than any other Pauline letter and therefore many of the objections raised by Paul in Romans "arise out of the subject matter, or rather out of a misunderstanding of it, and not an actual historical situation. To take such passages as indications of distinct groups or individuals is therefore not to the point."[56] Bornkamm continues even more boldly: "the idea that the theme of Romans and Paul's reflections on it were dictated by conditions obtaining in the church at Rome gets us nowhere."[57] Since these and other similar treatments of Romans are largely based upon the 1910 doctoral dissertation of Rudolf Bultmann, *Der Stil der paulinischen Predigt und die kynisch-stoische Diatribe*,[58] it will be helpful to turn to that source for further amplification and documentation. As we focus our attention on Bultmann's work, two questions need to be raised, at least in a preliminary manner: (1) Has it been demonstrated that the use of the "diatribe style" automatically excludes reference to real situations or problems? (2) Has there been an adequate form-critical examination of the diatribe to justify our speaking of it as a genre?

Bultmann's primary purpose is to show that a relationship exists between the Pauline letters and the literary *Gattung* known as the diatribe. Yet he is ambivalent throughout his study as to the exact nature of this relationship. At one point in his final conclusion he states "that the impression of differences [between Paul and the diatribe] is greater than the impression of similarity."[59] While there is a difference between the two types of literature, Bultmann adds: "I have no reservation in going one step further. The similarity of expressions of speech *(Ausdrucksweise)* is due to *the dependence of Paul upon the diatribe*."[60] Throughout his study Bultmann repeatedly asserts that Paul's actual preaching also demonstrates this same close relationship to the diatribe since the style of the diatribe is a preaching style, specifically that of the Cynic-Stoic "Volkspredigt."[61]

In order to properly evaluate Bultmann's contribution we need to ex-

---

[55]Ibid., 70, n. 32.
[56]Bornkamm, *Paul*, 90.
[57]Ibid., 93.
[58]Göttingen: Vandenhoeck & Ruprecht, 1910.
[59]Bultmann, *Diatribe*, 107.
[60]Ibid., 108; our italics.
[61]This is true of other treatments of the diatribe as well. For example, Wendland, *Kultur*, 39ff.; Nock, *Sallustius*, xxviiff.; Norden, *Kunstprosa* 2.556ff.

plore two areas: (a) the original sources upon which Bultmann is dependent for his knowledge of the diatribe and, in this connection, the criteria he uses in defining the diatribe genre; and (b) how he analyzes the Pauline letters, specifically for our purposes, Romans, in the light of the original texts which reflect the diatribe genre.

(a) Bultmann cites eight primary sources:[62] 1. Bion (c. 325–255 B.C.), of whom there is almost nothing extant; 2. Teles (active around 235 B.C.), of whom again very little is preserved; 3. Horace (c. 65–8 B.C.), but Bultmann never really shows or specifies how or where the diatribe is revealed in Horace; 4. Seneca (d. A.D. 65), whose *Moral Essays* show the "form of the diatribe," a phrase which is never defined or persuasively demonstrated; 5. Musonius Rufus (d. c. A.D. 100), a Stoic who wrote nothing and whose lectures were written down by Lucian (b. A.D. 120); 6. Epictetus (c. A.D. 55–135), a student of Musonius and also a Stoic, whose lectures are preserved by Arrian; 7. Dio Chrysostomus (A.D. 30–112), from whom about eighty speeches have been preserved; and, 8. Plutarch (A.D. 46–120); here Bultmann makes the simple assertion that the "diatribe style" is found in his *Moralia.*

Several reservations have to be raised at this point. First, Bultmann does not consistently refer to most of these documents since much of the material is not fully extant. He is primarily dependent upon the last three authors, particularly Epictetus. Secondly, he never really gives convincing criteria as to why these eight figures were chosen. This is connected with a third and overriding objection: Bultmann never defines precisely or critically what the form of the diatribe is and what justification there is for talking about the diatribe as a *Gattung.* It will be necessary to explore some of these objections further as soon as we have examined section (b), which contains a brief and rapid overview of how Bultmann attempts to demonstrate the influence of the diatribe upon Romans.

(b) Bultmann divides the influence of the diatribe on Paul into two parts: the dialogical and rhetorical. It is important to observe that Bultmann spends just ten pages in attempting to show the influence of the dialogical elements upon all of the Pauline letters. This is surprising since it is this, rather than the more generally shared rhetorical elements, which are essential to his argument that the Pauline letters are dependent upon a so-called diatribe genre. It will be helpful to review briefly aspects of Bultmann's approach, selecting some examples where Bultmann detects the influence of the diatribe upon Romans.

Dialogical Elements in Romans

Bultmann suggests that several dialogical elements characteristic of the diatribe genre are also found in Romans. These unique dialogical char-

---

[62]Bultmann, *Diatribe,* 6–9.

acteristics shared by the diatribe and Romans would include:

1. Contact or relationship between speaker and hearer:

Rom. 6:16: *ouk oidate . . . hypakouete* (cf. 1 Cor. 9:24; 3:16; 5:6; 6:15)
Rom. 11:2 (cf. 1 Cor. 6:2, 9)
Rom. 6:3; 7:1: *agnoeite*
Rom. 1:13 (cf. 1 Cor. 10:1; 12:1)

2. Characteristic of the diatribe is the address of a teacher to somewhat foolish students:

Rom. 2:1,3; 9:20: *anthrōpe* (*aphrōn*, 1 Cor. 15:36)
Rom. 14:4, 13, 15, 19, 20, 22 (Paul focuses upon the individual)

3. Address and Counteraddress between the speaker and his imaginary counterpart:

Rom. 9:19
     11:19 *ereis oun*
     3:1, 3
     4:2 Zwischenfrage[63]
     7:13

4. Characteristic of the diatribe is a paratactic style which places clauses and phrases together without coordinating and/or subordinating connectives (asyndeton). Examples of this phenomenon in Romans include primarily what Bultmann refers to as "Bedingungsverhaltnissen" (conditional relations):

Rom. 12:8:	*ho metadidous*	*en aplotēti,*
	ho proistamenos	*en spoudē,*
	ho eleōn	*en hilarotēti.*
Rom. 13:3		
Rom. 14:6:	*ho phronōn tēn hēmeran*	*kyrio phronei*
	kai ho esthiōn	*kyriō esthiei*
	kai ho mē esthiōn	*kyriō ouk esthiei.*

(Also Rom. 12:6ff. and 13:7)

Rom. 2:21f.:	*ho oun didaskōn heteron*	*seauton ou didaskeis;*
	ho keryssōn mē kleptein	*klepteis;*
	ho legōn mē moicheuein	*moicheueis;*
	ho bdelyssomenosta eidōla	*ierosyleis;*
	hos en nomō kauchasai, . . .	*ton theon atimazeis.*

Before we proceed to part 2 of Bultmann's argument, viz., the rhetorical devices found in the diatribe and Romans which he acknowledges are not necessarily unique to either, it may be appropriate to raise some further questions. The fundamental question which recurs is whether Bultmann has convincingly demonstrated that the above mentioned elements are sufficiently unique to the diatribe to argue, on the basis of these elements, that it is a unique genre. Is it not in fact the case that the elements isolated by Bultmann are widely shared in both classical and Hellenistic

---

[63]"It is quite clear, however, that this dialogical way of speaking was really part of Paul's flesh and blood. This element of fictitiously creating an opponent for the sake of discussion did not have the same fervor for him as it did for the Greeks" (Bultmann, *Diatribe,* 67).

rhetoric? One should not overlook the fact that the world of Paul was "a rhetorician's world, its ideal an orator; speech became an artistic product to be admired apart from its content or significance."[64]

Some of Bultmann's arguments lose their forcefulness when one finds so-called uniquely diatribal elements elsewhere. Especially Latin rhetoric[65] at this time is characterized by asyndeton, abruptness, failure to achieve clausal balance, and rhetorical questions. The strong influence of Greek rhetoric can be witnessed in this brief selection from the Elder Cato[66] in which we see not only the adaptation of Latin to rhetorical forms, but also a marked similarity with the style of Rom. 2 and 3:

> He said that his provisions had not been satisfactorily attended to by the decemvirs. He ordered them to be stripped and scourged. The Bruttiani scourged the decemvirs; many men saw it done. Who could endure such an insult, such tyranny, such slavery? No king has ever dared to act thus; shall such outrages be inflicted upon good men, born of a good family, and of good intentions? Where is the protection of our allies, where is the honour of our forefathers? To think that you have dared to inflict signal wrongs, blows, lashes, stripes, these pains and tortures, accompanied by disgrace and extreme ignominy, while their fellow-citizens and many other men looked on! But amid how great grief, what groans, what tears, what lamentations have I heard that this was done! Even slaves bitterly resent injustice; what feeling do you think that such men, sprung from good families, endowed with such high character, had and will have so long as they live?

One final comment before moving to part 2, concerning rhetorical devices. Bultmann often refers to the "imaginary opponent or counterpart"[67] in both the diatribe and Romans. This kind of abstraction has often been understood in the secondary literature on Romans to mean that Paul is not dealing with real issues and problems in Rome. When one moves beyond the limitations of the so-called diatribe genre to the more general precepts of rhetoric one gains greater perspective on this matter of "abstraction." Cicero in the *Orator*[68] states: "Whenever he can, the orator will divert the controversy from particular persons and circumstances to universal abstract questions, for he can debate a genus on wider grounds than a species. Whatever is proved of the whole is of necessity proved of the part." Quintilian[69] moves in the same direction as Cicero: "Moreover in inquiries that relate to an individual, though it is not enough to consider the general question, yet we cannot arrive at the decision of the particular point without discussing the general question first. For how will Cato consider whether he himself ought to marry unless it be first settled

[64]Kennedy, *Persuasion*, 22; see also van Unnik, "Literary Culture," 28–43.
[65]Quintilian, *Institutio Oratoria* ix.iii. 66–100; see also Usher, "Oratory," 372; and Clark, *Rhetoric*, 90–91.
[66]*De Agri Cultura*, Usher, "Oratory," 371.
[67]Bultmann, *Diatribe*, 10 and elsewhere.
[68]14.45–46 (LCL).
[69]3.5.5–16 (LCL).

whether men ought to marry at all?" We might well ask, how can Paul
deal with the sensitive question of Jewish-Gentile Christian relations in
Rome without first entertaining the more general question of the relationship between Jew and Gentile in God's plan of history? Such a general
discussion would appear imperative particularly in a letter to Rome, a
church in which Paul could not even presume knowledge of his oral word
as was the case in the other churches to which his letters were addressed.

Rhetorical Devices in Romans

Bultmann discusses rhetorical devices which are found in the diatribe
and in the Pauline letters, fully recognizing that they are not unique to
the diatribe and that the diatribe makes use of "the devices furnished by
the art of rhetoric."[70] It is important to observe that the use of a wide
variety of rhetorical devices by Paul indicates nothing whatsoever about
specific influences from the diatribe; it simply indicates that Paul was
influenced by the widespread rhetorical patterns of his age. It will be
helpful to review Bultmann's selection of rhetorical devices which were
employed by Paul, keeping in mind that they are at home in the rhetoric
of the day[71] and not uniquely "diatribal":

1. Rhetorical Sound Effects (*Klangfiguren*):
   a. Play on words
      Rom. 1:23: *aphthartou/phthartou*
         25: *ktisei/ktisanta*
         27: *arsenes/arsesin*
         28: *edokimasan/adokimon*
         also 2:28; 5:1, 19; 12:3, 15; 13:7; 14:22f.; 3:21; 4:17; 11:36
   b. Parallelism:[72]
      Rom. 12:4–15: *kathaper gar en heni sōmati polla melē echomen, ta
      de melē panta ou tēn autēn echei praxin, houtōs hoi polloi hen
      sōma esmen en Christō, to de kath' eis allēlōn melē.*

   *echontes de charismata kata tēn charin tēn dotheisan hēmin dia-
   phora,*

eite prophēteian	*kata tēn analogian tēs pisteōs*
eite diakonian	*en tē diakonia*
eite ho didaskōn	*en tē didaskalia*
eite ho parakalōn	*en tē paraklēsei*
ho metadidous	*en haplotēti,*
ho proistamenos	*en spoudē,*
ho eleōn	*en hilarotēti,*
hē agapē	*anypokritos,*

   *apostygountes to ponēron, kollōmenoi tō agathō tē philadelphia
   eis allelous philostorgoi tē timē allēlous proēgoumenoi.*

---

[70]Bultmann, *Diatribe*, 20.

[71]See Aristotle, *Rhetoric;* Quintilian, *Institutio Oratoria;* note 65 above; and Donfried, *Setting of Second Clement*, 36ff.

[72]Bultmann is very brief on this subject and largely accepts the previous work of Weiss,
Rhetorik.

tē spoudē mē oknēroi,
tō kyriō douleuontes,
tē thlipsei hypomenontes,
tais chreiais tōn hagiōn
koinōnountes,
eulogeite tous diōkontas,
chairein meta chairontōn,

tō pneumati zeontes,
tē elpidi chairontes,
tē proseuchē proskarterountes,
ten philoxenian diōkontes.

eulogeite kai mē katarasthe.
klaiein meta klaiontōn.

c. Antithesis to synthesis:
   Rom. 14:7f.: oudeis gar
          hēmōn heautō zē,
             kai oudeis heautō apothnēskei;
      ean te gar zōmen, tō kyriō zōmen,
          ean te apothnēskōmen, tō kyriō apothnēskomen.
      ean te oun zōmen, ean te apothnēskomen, tou kyriou
      esmen.
d. Paradox:
   Rom. 7:15, 19.
2. Rhetorical Symbols *(Sinnfiguren)*:
   a. Interjections *(Ausrufungen)*:[73]
      Rom. 11:32–36; 8:31ff.
   b. Comparisons in Paul:
      1. The human body:
         Rom. 12:4f.
      2. Family relations, etc.:
         Rom. 2:20; 13:12, 14; 9:21f.; 14:4; 6:16f.
      3. Sickness and death:
         Rom. 2:19; 6:11, 13; 7:8–11; 8:11.
      4. Nature and man's relation to it:
         Rom. 13:11ff.; 2:19; 1:13; 11:17f.; 8:23; 11:16.
      5. Legal illustrations:
         Rom. 7:14; 7:2f.; 8:17; 11:32; 4:11.
      6. Trades, crafts:
         Rom. 15:20.
      7. Contests:
         Rom. 9:16
      8. War illustrations:[74]
         Rom. 6:13, 23; 7:23.

Has Bultmann established his case for a diatribal influence upon Paul? From 1911, a year after Bultmann's dissertation was published, to the present there has been skepticism. For some this skepticism concerns the effectiveness by which Bultmann has demonstrated the clear influences of the diatribe upon the Pauline corpus for others, whether there is in fact

[73]"Obviously these interjections should not be placed in exact parallel to those of the diatribe. Our only intention is to show that both Paul and the diatribe share analogous elements through which the similarity of the overall characteristics of both is heightened" (Bultmann, *Diatribe*, 87).

[74]"We can come to this conclusion: with reference to his use of illustrations Paul stands in a certain relationship to the diatribe, particularly with reference to the content of such comparisons; this proximity to the diatribe is considerably more distant with reference both to the manner in which these illustrations are composed and in the way in which they are applied . . . " (Bultmann, *Diatribe*, 93).

a genre known as the diatribe. The year after Bultmann's study appeared, Adolf Bonhöffer stated categorically that in his opinion Bultmann "did not produce sufficient evidence which demonstrated that the Apostle, either consciously or unconsciously, is dependent upon either the forms or the thoughts of the Cynic-Stoic diatribe."[75] Further, he is critical of the way Bultmann forces Epictetus into a diatribal mold to which he does not belong.

As one reads the work of contemporary classicists it becomes evident how difficult it is to speak of the diatribe as a genre. Even though full-scale studies are presently lacking, it is possible, nevertheless, to see the directions in which some recent classicists are moving. For example, Hildegard Cancik cites approvingly Dahlmann's book review of E. Kostermann's *Untersuchungen zu den Dialogschriften Senecas* in which Dahlmann rejects the term diatribe as a "Gattungsbezeichnung."[76] Cancik closes her brief remarks concerning the diatribe with the comment that the question of the diatribe "is not yet solved."[77]

More critical of the use of the term diatribe as a description of a specific genre is Helmut Rahn in his masterful little study *Morphologie der antiken Literatur.*[78] For our immediate purposes Rahn makes three important observations: (1) From a morphological perspective the use of the term "diatribe" as a literary-scientific term is difficult to imagine. Since there is no uniform literary *Gattung* known as "the diatribe" no positive results will emerge from its use. It is perhaps more accurate, at best, to speak of something as "Diatribenartiges" which is represented in a variety of genres. (2) The reason there is no "diatribe" genre is because everything we refer to as "Diatribenartiges" is already found in a more complete and perfect form in the literary *Gattung* known as the philosophical dialogue. (3) In addition, Rahn reminds us that many characteristics of the so-called diatribe are also to be found as essay themes given by teachers of rhetoric in the so-called *theseis (proposita)*.

If these classicists are correct then it is still an open question whether there was a genre known as the diatribe in the Greco-Roman world. This leads to the obvious caution that before New Testament scholars can build upon such a questionable genre, it will be necessary for the classicists to explore the whole question in far greater detail than has hitherto been the case. This does not lead to the conclusion that Bultmann's work is irrelevant and can be discarded. Rather, what he has shown is not that Paul has been influenced by the diatribe, but that he was influenced by rhe-

---

[75]Bonhöffer, *Epiktet*, 179, n. 1. I owe this reference, and many helpful discussions to the subject matter, to Prof. A. J. Malherbe of the Yale Divinity School. See also the discussion in Donfried, *Setting of Second Clement*, 25ff.

[76]Dahlman, *Senecas*, 47.

[77]Cancik, *Epistulae Morales* 47, n. 79.

[78]Darmstadt: Wissenschaftliche Buchgesellschaft, 1969.

torical usages which were common in the Greco-Roman world. The use of such rhetorical patterns was so widespread that one cannot deny that Romans was addressed to a specific situation on the ground that it was influenced by such patterns. For example, similar rhetorical influences appear in Galatians and in the Corinthian correspondence, yet Paul, in these letters, is addressing himself to a specific set of problems which he hopes to solve. The point, then, is that one should be most careful in objecting to the "specificity" of Romans in dealing with live issues in Rome on the basis of a supposed influence of the diatribe, not only because it has yet to be established that there is such a genre,[79] but also, because it has not been demonstrated that general theological discussions influenced by the rhetorical patterns of the Greco-Roman world could not be addressed to genuine and actual historical situations.

Thus far we have considered in some detail Methodological Principle I, that any study of Romans should proceed on the initial assumption that this letter was written to deal with concrete situations in Rome, and we reviewed two objections which have been raised against such an assertion:

1. that the Pauline use of paraenesis is so general that it prohibits one from determining any exact situation; and,

2. that since the diatribe had heavily influenced Paul in the writing of Romans he cannot be addressing a real situation in Rome.

Against the first objection we raised serious questions as to the validity of that understanding of paraenesis. Against the second, we argued, among other things, that thus far the existence of a distinct genre known as the diatribe has not been established; all Bultmann has demonstrated is that Paul was influenced by the rhetorical patterns of his day. It is our judgment that since Methodological Principle I has not been convincingly challenged, it must continue to serve as the starting point for an adequate interpretation of Romans.

We must now briefly consider Methodological Principle II, viz., that any study of Romans must proceed on the assumption that Rom. 16 is an integral part of the original letter. Since we have dealt with the problems of Rom. 16 elsewhere it is not our intention to repeat those arguments here,[80] and the following brief comments will be of a summary nature.

1. Any serious study of Rom. 16 should first explore whether Rom. 16 can be understood against the background of the Roman church. We would assert on the basis of our previous study that there is much more probability for the view that Paul is addressing Rom. 16 to friends and house

---

[79]One must avoid, for example, the kind of easy survey and comparison made by Thyen in *Homilie*. Thyen's results are weakened by his initial assumption that there are two fairly specific genres known as the "diatribe" and the "homily." It is our contention that neither has been shown to exist on the basis of form-critical studies. See our criticism of Thyen in *Second Clement*, 27–28.

[80]See Donfried, chapter 4 above, pp. 44–52.

churches in Rome than for the alternative position derived from a faulty understanding of Romans, which argues that it was a separate letter sent to Ephesus. We would repeat what we said before, viz., that Rom. 16 can only be understood in the context of the total intention and theology of Romans and only when this has been proven to be utterly fruitless should one begin to look for other alternatives.[81]

2. The argument that Rom. 16 is a later addition to Rom. 1–15 on the basis of textual evidence alone has steadily weakened in recent years: (a) Harry Gamble persuasively illustrates that the textual evidence is inconclusive and that style and form criticism must be taken into account;[82] (b) the Editorial Committee[83] of the United Bible Societies' Greek New Testament is prepared to allow for either the option that "Marcion, or his followers, circulated a shortened form of the epistle, lacking chapters 15 and 16" or "that Paul himself had dispatched a longer and a shorter form of the epistle (one form with, and one without, chapter 16)." Yet despite the multiplicity of locations at which one finds the doxology, the Committee retained its traditional location at the end of chapter 16 "on the basis of good and diversified evidence" supporting the sequence 1:1–16:23 + doxology;[84] (c) in our 1970 study we also argued that the textual evidence cannot be isolated from the historical intentionality of Romans as a whole.[85]

The view that Rom. 16 is addressed to Ephesus has been repeated so often that many have come to accept it as axiomatic.[86] As we have just observed,[87] this position has been challenged vigorously both on historical and textual grounds; therefore the burden of proof now lies with those who wish to defend a non-Roman destination for Rom. 16.

This first part of our essay has concentrated on work which has already been accomplished and it has tried to reach certain judgments about the validity of this conflicting work on the basis of two methodological principles. In the second half of this study we must ask whether, in addition

[81]Donfried, "Short Note on Romans 16," 44.

[82]Gamble, *Textual History.* Gamble states:
"The only textual evidence to which the Ephesian hypothesis may appeal is that of P[46] with its placement of the doxology between chapters 15 and 16. While no more prestigious witness could be desired, it remains a single witness and cannot carry the case for the originality of the fifteen chapter text form by itself unless compelling internal arguments substantiate the reading. It is natural that the testimony of this MS is brought in by advocates of the Ephesian hypothesis as affording a clear external confirmation of the deduction from internal observations. Yet this has been done rather uncritically, and the real import of this evidence has not been carefully weighed" (96–97).

[83]Kurt Aland, Matthew Black, Carlo M. Martini, Bruce M. Metzger and Allen Wikgren.

[84]Metzger, *TCGNT,* 536.

[85]See n. 12 above. For an elaborate support of our position on this point, see Gamble, *Textual History* 81ff.

[86]See n. 13 above.

[87]In addition to the immediate references just made, see Minear, *Obedience,* 22–35; Kümmel, *Introduction* 314ff.

to a concern for methodological precision, there are other new positive directions in which future studies on Romans might proceed.

II. Part 2

An important advance to be anticipated in forthcoming studies on Romans will be the increased recognition that the Pauline letter corpus includes not one, but several letter types. One of the difficulties in understanding Romans as addressed to a specific situation in the Roman church has undoubtedly been the valid recognition that Romans differs from the more personal style of the other Pauline letters. It is easy to see how interpreters can be tempted to move from this observation to the conclusion that Romans, due to its "theological heaviness," is really a summary of Paul's theology and thus somewhat abstracted from a specific Roman situation. As one surveys ancient epistolography one notes that several of the Pauline letters show similarities with the papyrus letters and one must be especially grateful for the insightful contributions made by a number of recent studies in this area.[88] Yet one must not overlook other types of ancient letters and one must avoid interpreting *all* Pauline letters against the limited types represented in the papyri. New attention needs to be focused on the extant literary letters as well.[89] The recent attempt by Malherbe to view 1 Thessalonians as a paraenetic letter in light of this literary tradition is most welcome and it offers a number of new insights for the interpretation of this perplexing letter.[90]

What epistolographic parallels are there to Romans in the ancient world? This question is hardly entertained in most commentaries. Yet if one could find similar type letters in the non-Christian world it might very well help us in understanding Romans more precisely. Some reflections made by Helmut Rahn, Hildegard Cancik, and Luther Stirewalt are most helpful and suggestive for the future study of Romans. Rahn reminds us of the literary letter which he identifies as the "philosophical Lehr-Epistle" and which presupposes and includes two factors: the impact-producing possibilities of the "diatribenhaften Dialexis" and aspects of the systematic "Lehrbuch-Vortrages."[91] Cancik similarly reminds us that in the Greek world the letter as a literary form could from the very beginning be suited for the communication of *philosophical paraenesis* as well as the more personal aspects of communication. She is correctly impatient with

---

[88]Funk, *Language, Hermeneutic*; Koskenniemi, *Griechischen Briefes*; White, *Greek Letter*; idem, *Form and Structure*; Kim, *Familiar Letter*.

[89]See Thraede, *Brieftopik*.

[90]See n. 52 above.

[91]Rahn, *Morphologie*, 157–58. Further investigations of Romans may do well to give further attention to the ancient "Lehrbuch" and particularly such secondary treatments as Fuhrmann, *Lehrbuch*.

Deissmann's "Brief-Epistle" distinction and vividly draws to our attention the fact that the situation to which a letter is addressed is at least as important for understanding the form and content of the letter as are the facts concerning authorship. She insists, and this is of course quite important for a proper understanding of Romans, that the situation of the addressees determines to a large degree the style and the manner in which the letter is executed.[92] As Käsemann so clearly demonstrates, one cannot understand Paul's style in Romans if one does not comprehend his hesitancy in writing to that congregation.[93]

These observations made by trained classicists are most important for New Testament scholars. However, the terminology "Lehrbrief" or "didactic letter" is a bit vague and perhaps too general; thus it may be that Stirewalt's designation "letter-essay" is the more appropriate. In his study, "The Form and Function of the Greek Letter-Essay,"[94] Stirewalt selects fifteen documents[95] primarily from Epicurus, Dionysius, and Plutarch, and characterizes them as follows: "they are losing some of the form, phraseology, and structure of the letter and are incorporating the more impersonal, objective style of the monograph."[96]

Stirewalt's work is indeed very suggestive and deserves to be well tested by subsequent scholarship. Assuming that it is accurate to designate this type of letter writing with a term something like "letter-essay,"[97] then

[92]Cancik, *Epistulae Morales*, 46ff.

[93]"This permits only one conclusion, viz., that Paul feels very insecure over against the unknown recipients of this letter and is therefore driven into an apologetically defensive position."

[94]See chapter 10 in this volume. References to his work are also made in Doty, *Letters*, esp. 7ff.

[95]1. Epicurus 1 (*Letter I, to Herodotus*, Diogenes Laertius, 10.35–83).
  2. Epicurus 2 (*Letter II, to Pythocles*, Diogenes Laertius, 10.84–116).
  3. Epicurus 3 (*Letter III, to Menoeceus*, Diogenes Laertius, 10.122–35).
  4. Dionysius 1 (*Letter to Ammaeus I*, W. Rhys Roberts, *Dionysius of Halicarnassus. The Three Literary Letters*, Cambridge, 1901).
  5. Dionysius 2 (*Letter to Pompeius*).
  6. Dionysius 3 (*Letter to Ammaeus II*).
  7. Plutarch 1 (*Coniugalia Praecepta. Moralia* 138B–146A).
  8. Plutarch 2 (*Regum et Imperatorum Apophthegmata. Moralia* 172B–208A).
  9. Plutarch 3 (*De Tranquillitate Animi. Moralia* 464E–477F).
  10. Plutarch 4 (*De Animae Procreatione in Timaeo. Moralia* 1012B–1030C).
  11. Plutarch 5 (*De Capienda ex Inimicis Utilitate. Moralia* 86B–92F).
  12. Plutarch 6 (*Consolatio ad Apollonium. Moralia* 101F–122A).
  13. Plutarch 7 (*De Fato. Moralia* 568–575F).
  14. *The Martyrdom of Polycarp*.
  15. 2 Maccabees.

[96]Stirewalt, "Letter-Essay," 148.

[97]See ibid. Concerning the designation "letter-essay," Stirewalt adds: "It has been possible to establish the letter-essay as an epistolary category. It did not become a fixed genre; it was transitory, functioning for communication in highly literate circle . . . (The letter-essay) served a limited, substitutive, instructional function" (pp. 163–65).

perhaps it may be helpful to note at least two significant points at which elements found in the documents selected by Stirewalt may give us further insight into Romans, even though he himself does not make these connections.

1. Stirewalt observes that the letter-essays "are all supplementary in some way to another writing usually by the same author or substitute for a work projected by him, and the idea of instruction is presented in the author's purpose to clarify, abridge, aid in memorizing, defend his thesis, recount history."[98] Plutarch in *De Tranquillitate Animi* makes the statement that " . . . I gathered together from my notebooks those observations on tranquillity of mind; . . . "[99] and in the *Moralia* he writes, "I have therefore drawn up a compendium . . . putting it in the form of a brief comparison that it may be more easily remembered. . . . "[100] Similarly, Epicurus explains, "Therefore, since such a course is useful to all who are engaged with natural science, I . . . have composed for you such a brief compendium of the chief principles of my teaching as a whole."[101]

The summary character of Romans has often been noted and frequently together with it, the incorrect assumption that such a writing cannot refer to a concrete, historical situation.[102] Must, in fact, the only alternative be either "summary" or "historical"? In view of these letter-essays is not the more plausible alternative with regard to Romans a "both-and"—both sharing and repeating insights gained in prior situations *and* addressing a real situation? Stirewalt concludes that in not a single case are these "summarizing" letter-essays fictional. "The letter-setting in each case is authentic." [103] If one reads Dionysius' *Letter to Pompeius*, where the author repeats in one place some pertinent passages from his previous essays as well as supplementing his previous comments, and then looks at Romans, it may not appear so strange that Paul, while dealing with a specific situation in Rome, could without hesitancy refer to earlier thoughts which were employed (albeit with different nuances) in previous church situations. One might also ponder whether Plutarch's reference to gathering things from his notebooks bears any relationship to Paul's compositional technique. For example, how does one explain the midrashic exposition of Rom. 4? What is its "pre-history"? Does Paul create it anew for this letter or did at least parts of it pre-exist its present context in Rom. 4? If the latter option is the correct one, did Paul gather these elements from a notebook? Perhaps the possibly authentic request to Timothy in

---

[98]Stirewalt, "Letter-Essay," 176–77.
[99]*Moralia* 464 (LCL).
[100]*Moralia* 464 (LCL).
[101]Diogenes Laertius 10.35–36 (LCL).
[102]See Käsemann's comments in n. 45 above.
[103]Stirewalt, "Letter Essay," 163.

the deutero-Pauline 2 Tim. 4:13 that "when you come, bring . . . the books and above all the parchments" gives support to the notion of such a Pauline notebook.[104]

2. Another aspect of the letter-essay which Stirewalt draws to our attention is its "public" character. We read the following in Epicurus' letter to Herodotus: "Since this method is useful to *all* studying natural science . . . *I* have made an epitome for *you.*"[105] Stirewalt contributes a valuable insight when he shows that the letter-setting of the letter-essay is triangular: I-thou-they. Since the letter-essay "was a publicly recorded statement, a position paper, issued by an authority" it automatically involves a third party.[106]

Again, this dimension of the letter-essay may shed valuable light upon Romans. Several scholars have argued that Romans is addressed to a much wider audience than just the Roman church. Could it not be argued, on the basis of the letter-essay, that as Paul the authority writes to the Romans ("you") he undoubtedly also has the "they" (all the Christian churches) in mind, as becomes clear from Rom. 15:22–33. Thus, the letter-essay may help us to transcend the "either-or" conflict (Rome *or* elsewhere) in favor of a "both-and" possibility—both to Rome and even beyond. Thus Fuchs,[107] Jervell,[108] and others[109] are partially right when they suggest that Paul also had Jerusalem in his thoughts, as we too have previously indicated;[110] but they are certainly wrong in arguing that Jerusalem was the primary referent. The primary referent was Rome. To assert this does not deny that Paul continued to carry with him the entire burden of the past and present Jewish-Gentile conflict at the particular moment in which he wrote Romans. One cannot divorce Paul's total mind set (past-present-future) from

---

[104]Kelly, *Pastoral Epistles,* 215–16: "The wording, particularly the absence of 'and' with *especially,* indicates that the Apostle is speaking of a particular kind of book, and this is brought out in the translation. As a matter of fact there is abundant evidence that the Latin *membrana* was a technical term, from the first century B.C., for a codex, or leaf-book, made of parchment. Such codices were widely used for note-books, account-books, memoranda, first drafts of literary works, and other writings not meant for the public; it is also likely that they were being used for literary purposes in the first century A.D. We must therefore infer that Paul's reference is to paged note-books of parchment which for some reason he particularly valued. Again we are in the dark about their contents, although the guess that they consisted of O.T. proof-texts is one among other possibilities."

[105]Diogenes Laertius 10.35; see Stirewalt, "Letter Essay," 169.

[106]Stirewalt, "Letter Essay," 169–71.

[107]See n. 7 above.

[108]See n. 8 above. Why was Romans written? The trip to Jerusalem is the answer; precisely because of it Paul needs the help and moral support of the Romans at that moment. Paul points out the necessity of this trip and then adds to this his request for moral support (Jervell, "Letter to Jerusalem," 58). But how are the Romans to provide a "moral support," particularly since he had never been in Rome? If this is an address to Jerusalem how does one explain Paul's responsibility for and frequent address *to the Gentiles?* Still the difficult question remains, why send an address about to be given in Jerusalem to Rome?.

[109]Bornkamm, *Paulus*; Suggs, "Romans 10:6–10."

[110]Donfried, "Short Note on Romans 16," 48.

the specific moment, nor the specific moment (the real historical situation in Rome to which Romans is addressed) from Paul's frame of reference.

This second part of our essay must remain quite tentative until such time when far more research is carried on in the total field of ancient epistolography and particularly into that segment which Stirewalt has identified as the letter-essay. But as the testing goes on one thing remains clear: the increased necessity for New Testament scholarship to delve into the classical literary backgrounds in their study of Romans.[111] While such efforts may throw into question well established hypotheses, they may open up hitherto neglected dimensions of the classical tradition which may offer new insights for understanding Paul's intention in writing Romans.

THE OCCASION OF ROMANS:
A RESPONSE TO PROFESSOR DONFRIED

Robert J. Karris

I am deeply gratified that Professor Donfried has accepted my challenge to rethink the occasion of Romans. His article is masterful in its search for methodological clarity, in its penetrating criticism of the "established fact" of the existence of a diatribe genre, in its provocative proposal to use the paradigm of the "letter-essay" in the study of Romans, and in its sharpening of the question of actual/historical paraenesis.

The purpose of this response is not to defend myself against Donfried's criticism, but to make some observations which have been prompted by his article and which may aid further discussions about the refinement of criteria for determining the occasion of Romans.

Most of my criticisms, questions, and suggestions revolve around one point: Donfried now needs to provide a more detailed delineation of the theological situation in Rome. For example, (pp. 102–3) on the basis of W. Wiefel's article and P. S. Minear's monograph, he argues to the "sociological situation" at Rome, i.e., diverse Jewish synagogues and diverse Christian house churches. But it is a further step to argue from this "sociological situation" to the actuality of the theological situation: "It is easy to perceive that both the new polity involving house churches separate from the synagogue structure and a *theological situation* heavily

[111]See n. 64.

dominated by the Gentile Christians who had remained in Rome were *bound to* be alien to the returning Jewish Christians" (p. 105) [emphases mine]). What was this theological situation? What history of religions background will explain it? What is to be understood by Jewish Christians and Gentile Christians? Are the Jewish Christians legalists, liberals, apocalyptically-oriented, or what? Are the Gentile Christians legalists, antinomians, Gnostic-influenced, or what? What is the specific nature of the conflict between Jewish and Gentile Christians which Paul is supposed to have heard about and is trying to settle by writing Romans?

Put another way, to have stated that there are different synagogues or different house churches in Rome does not necessarily say anything about the religious beliefs and practices of these synagogues or house churches. It seems that one could as easily explain the "sociological situation" of different synagogues and house churches on the basis of the different languages or nationalities involved (pp. 104–5). It is a large step to move from the fact of different synagogues or house churches to the fact of diversity of beliefs and religious practices among these different synagogues or house churches and thus have at hand an interpretive matrix for explaining Romans.

What Donfried says about the letter essay is most provocative for an analysis of Romans. Within the few pages he devotes to this suggestion it was not his intention to give detailed analyses. I would ask the following questions. Granted that the letter-essay can reflect a real situation and therefore is not fictitious, what is that real situation in Rome which Paul addresses? What are the criteria for distinguishing those sections in Romans which are comprised of "sharing" and "repeating insights gained in prior situations" and those which are addressed to "a real situation" (p. 123)? At this point it may be in place to ask Donfried for an explicit formulation of the criteria for his hesitancy in agreeing totally with Minear's analysis of Romans: "While we are in general agreement with Minear's direction, viz., that an actual situation in Rome provoked this letter, we are hesitant to concur with Minear in attempting to relate almost every passage to some problem or opponent in Rome" (p. 107). To summarize the thrust of my questions in the paragraph, the paradigm of the letter-essay suggests that in Romans Paul could have been addressing a real theological situation in Rome, but the paradigm in and of itself does not and cannot tell us what that situation was.

Relative to the existence of the diatribe genre, Donfried has argued forcefully and well that the diatribe is not a genre. The reverse side of Donfried's point must also be emphasized: to have shown that the diatribe is not a genre does not demonstrate that when Paul uses diatribe-like or rhetorical language in Romans he is addressing a real situation in the Roman church(es). The question is open. Whether Paul is addressing a real situation in Romans will have to be shown through careful exegesis of each use of diatribe-like style in Romans.

Concerning the question of general or actual paraenesis, my principal question recurs: *if* Rom. 14:1–15:13 is actual paraenesis, to what concrete situation in the Roman church(es) is it addressed? To say that it refers to the "Jewish-Gentile conflict" (p. 124) is not specific enough. Does such a conflict exist? If so, what are its contours?

I wholeheartedly agree with Methodological Principle I if it states that each authentic Pauline writing is addressed to a particular situation. Why should we make the Pauline letter pattern so rigid that all Paul's letters have to be addressed to the specific situations of the churches or persons addressed? This question is given additional cogency because Donfried suggests that Romans is not like the other authentic Pauline letters, but is a letter-essay. While Stirewalt may be correct in saying that the letter-setting of each "summarizing" letter-essay is authentic (p. 123), it is not clear whether the letter-setting is to be seen exclusively in the situation of the addressees. Could it not be that the quest for the situation of the letter-essay might be more fruitfully centered in the circumstances of the sender whose intent it is to clarify, abridge, etc. (pp. 122–23)? This leads to an additional question: by what criteria do we judge whether the situation behind Romans is a situation in the Roman church(es) or in the life of Paul (his missionary plans, summary of his gospel, journey to Jerusalem) or a combination of both? It is to be recalled that those scholars who argue that Romans is not addressed to a specific situation in the Roman church(es) do not maintain that Romans lacks an occasion or is non-historical.

About Methodological Principle II, until Donfried and others have given a more detailed description of the *theological* situation of the Roman church(es), they have not adequately shown how Rom. 16 can be understood "in the context of the total intention and theology of Romans" (p. 120).

9

PAUL'S RHETORIC OF ARGUMENTATION IN ROMANS: AN ALTERNATIVE TO THE DONFRIED-KARRIS DEBATE OVER ROMANS

Wilhelm Wuellner

My thesis is that the Donfried-Karris debate[1] is unfruitful in its concern over whether or not, or to what degree, the parenetic portion of Romans (12:1–15:13), let alone the letter as a whole, requires a specific or concrete situation. Both Donfried and Karris have some truth on their side, yet neither succeeds in establishing a convincing methodology. The methodological premise of the Donfried-Karris debate reveals one more "false presupposition in the study of Romans," if not in the study of Paul's letters generally.

My proposal is that a study of the rhetorical nature of Paul's argumentation, or a study of the nature of argumentation in Paul's letters, will help us out of the two impasses created by the fixation with form- and genre- criticism on the one hand, and with specific social or political situations on the other hand. I am not proposing that we eliminate literary and historical considerations. Neither am I proposing simply to add rhetorical considerations to an already crowded agenda of exegetical procedures. My proposal is for setting new priorities: I propose to replace the traditional priority on propositional theology and the more recent priority on letters as literature with the new priority on letters as argumentation. Traditional theology, even biblical or Pauline theology, was based on the traditional model of logic and dialectic. The approach to Paul's letters as literature was based on traditional or modern theories of literature or poetics. Instead I am proposing that we consider Paul's letters primarily as argumentative. We understand argumentation as the use of discourse "to influence the intensity of an audience's adherence to certain theses,"[2] the study of which belongs to traditional or "new" rhetoric.[3] I propose

---

[1]Donfried, "False Presuppositions," with a response by Karris. See chapter 8 above.

[2]Perelman–Olbrechts-Tyteca, *New Rhetoric,* 14.

[3]Combining the traditional and modern is Brandt, *Rhetoric of Argumentation.* See also Corbett, *Classical Rhetoric.*

that in the rediscovery of the nature and purpose of argumentation as a basically rhetorical process we will find a more satisfactory way of accounting not only for the dialectical and logical dimensions, and for the literary dimensions in Paul's discourses, but also for the situational and social dimensions presupposed in Paul's letters.

I. The Methodology Issue in the Donfried-Karris Debate

The stated purpose of Donfried's essay was "to propose two methodological principles": (1) Romans, like all other letters of Paul, "addresses a concrete set of problems in the life of Christians . . . ," and (2) Rom. 16 is an integral part of the original letter.[4] Both principles are designed to "aid further discussions about the refinement of criteria for determining the occasion of Romans," which is also the purpose of Fr. Karris' response.[5] Instead of following Karris in his call for "a more detailed delineation of the theological situation in Rome" or of the Roman church(es),[6] which seems to me to be doomed to futility, I would like to explore along another avenue of research intimated in passing by both Donfried and Karris. Donfried agrees on the one hand with Minear's position, shared by W. Marxsen, G. Klein, W. Wiefel, and others, according to which "an actual situation in Rome provoked this letter." But on the other hand Donfried raises the critical question: "Is it not very possible that Paul can be dealing with actual problems but in so doing employs rhetorical arguments and theological perspectives of a more general nature which will aid in solving them?"[7] The domain of rhetoric, to which Donfried points, is indeed where further work needs to be done, but he falls short of the goal when he settles for Bultmann's demonstration "that Paul was influenced by the rhetorical patterns of his day."[8] Karris uses the rhetoric-related argument presented by Donfried concerning the letter-essay observations of Stirewalt[9] in first noting that neither in Stirewalt nor in Donfried is it "clear whether the letter-setting (of the essay) is to be seen exclusively in the situation of the addressees." Karris then asks, "Could it not be that the quest for the situation of the letter-essay might be more fruitfully centered in the circumstances of the sender whose intent it is to clarify, abridge, etc.?"[10] The question is quite to the point. But how is it to be answered? What would be the methodological principles guiding

---

[4]Donfried, "False Presuppositions," 103f.
[5]Karris, "Response," 125.
[6]Ibid., 125, 127.
[7]Donfried, "False Presuppositions," 107.
[8]Ibid., 119.
[9]Ibid., 121–25.
[10]Karris, "Response," 127.

the inquiry? For suggested answers we turn now to a brief review of the efforts from 1970 to 1975 in the seminar of the Society of Biblical Literature on the letters of Paul under the chairmanship of Nils Dahl.

II. The Paul Seminar of the Society of Biblical Literature

In reviewing the history of the SBL Seminar research on Pauline letters, referred to also by Donfried in his treatment of Stirewalt's work on the letter-essay, I rely on the twenty-three page summary by the Seminar's secretary, J. D. Hester.[11] The initial approach to the letters, termed the holistic approach, aiming to go beyond the traditional approach of form criticism, and seeking to interpret each letter as letter, produced a twofold critical reaction. (1) The holistic approach, based on the literary method of the critical study of ancient epistolography,[12] could not account for the variety of Pauline letters. Subsequent efforts, termed by Hester as the "genre" approach, accentuated the dilemma of conflicting methodologies based on models of literary criticism.[13] (2) The critical question arose, and remained a key question throughout the subsequent studies: What dependency, "to a greater or lesser degree," was there in any of Paul's letters "on the situation"?[14]

In 1973 Dahl had raised the issue of the *rhetorical* genre (in contrast to literary genre) in his monograph-sized paper on Galatians. But instead of pursuing the issue that Galatians showed signs of fitting the symbouleutic or deliberative genre of speech, Dahl went on to deal with the apparent variety in the Pauline letter forms in terms of "the situation" which required of Paul that he construct from several models of letters, styles, and rhetorical genres, something new to meet "his need (or the addressees' need!) at the time."[15] By contrast, Betz works with criteria provided by Greco-Roman rhetoric and sticks with them throughout his analysis of Galatians as an "apologetic letter." The evidence for his thesis that the forensic, rather than the symbouleutic, genre informs Galatians is derived from an analysis of the composition of the letter. Betz, too, stresses that the rhetorical genre was modified "to meet the needs of the situation to which it was addressed."[16] But Hester is struck by the fact that, in spite of some

[11]Hester, *Epistolography.*
[12]See Doty, "Classification," 183–99.
[13]See W. G. Doty's 1973 essay for the SBL Pauline Letter Seminar on "Review, Aporia, Possible Futures," and his essay "The Concept of Genre in Literary Analysis" in *SBL 1972 Proceedings*, 2.413–448.
[14]Hester, *Epistolography*, 6. See also the positions of N. Dahl and H. D. Betz in my next paragraph.
[15]Hester, *Epistolography, 14.*
[16]Betz, H. D., "Literary Composition," 353–79.

common points, the result was two different analyses of the letter to the Galatians.[17]

In my contribution to the SBL Seminar discussion in 1974, in which I stressed for the first time publicly the urgent need for a disciplined and differentiated study of both textual and structural rhetoric in interpreting Paul, I, too, with Betz, Dahl, and others, emphasized the need to understand the situation to which the argument is addressed. But unlike Karris, for whom situation here means "theological situation," or Donfried, who means by it something that includes social and political history, I mean by situation something else. With the theoreticians of rhetoric I intend to speak of "the argumentative situation itself, by which is meant the influence of the earlier stages of the discussion of the argumentative possibilities open to the speaker."[18]

Traditional rhetoric offers some very important observations on this "argumentative situation. "The rhetorical textbooks of antiquity discuss this issue in terms of the *intellectio* by the speaker/writer of the nature of the *quaestio, controversia,* or *problēma* as well as the *status* or *stasis*, i.e., the underlying key-issue, before the speaker/writer actually carries out the treatment (*actio*) of the surfacing *causa*.[19] The data collected in Lausberg's monumental study[20] are quite illuminating. Another important discipline of studies that could deal with this "argumentative situation" is modern structuralism in its all-important distinction between the underlying deep-structure (= the *intellectio* of the *quaestio*, and the *status* in traditional rhetoric) and the surface-structure (= the actual treatment, or *actio*, of the *causa* and the resulting structure of the argumentation in rhetoric).[21]

The Donfried-Karris debate over "sociological" versus "theological" situation is methodologically ill-conceived and constitutes a false alternative. It generates yet another "false presupposition" in the study of Romans. Donfried, while taking Bultmann to task over preoccupation with the diatribe genre, ends up in the same trap by remaining preoccupied with the letter-essay genre proposed by Stirewalt. What has been said, and will yet be said, about the letter-essay is likely to be as misleading as that said about the diatribe as models for the interpretation of Romans. Hellenistic-Roman and Near Eastern epistolographic studies, no matter how exactingly

---

[17]Hester, *Epistolography,* 16.

[18]Perelman–Olbrechts-Tyteca, *New Rhetoric,* 491. Brandt, *Rhetoric of Argumentation,* can speak of the "communicative situation," "discoursive situation" or "rhetorical situation" by which the referential possibilities of discourse or argumentation are confined.

[19]Lausberg, *Handbuch,* §§ 66–78 on *quaestio*; §§ 79–138 on *status;* on *actio* and *causa* see vol. 2 *sub vocibus*. On *intellectio* see §7.

[20]A shorter volume is now available in Lausberg's *Elemente*. In his essay on Galatians ("Literary Composition"), H. D. Betz also used Lausberg.

[21]For the application of the methods of modern structuralism to biblical exegesis, see *Linguistica Biblica,* edited by E. Guttgemanns since 1970. For a specific application to Romans, see Via, *Kerygma and Comedy,* 39–69.

they will be executed, cannot solve the problem of Romans or that of any other letter of Paul. Such studies will clarify the letter *frame*, and the conventions of letter frames,[22] but they cannot solve the problem of the letter structure, or the problems connected with the "body" of the Pauline letters.[23]

Far from seeing "the letter-essay (as) most provocative for an analysis of Romans,"[24] I see only new confusion being generated by working with this "genre" as a literary form. The semantic discussion over "didactic letter" *vs* "letter-essay" is irrelevant for Romans. When Stirewalt is quoted as saying that "the letter-essay as an epistolary category . . . did not become a fixed genre; (that) it was transitory, functioning for communication in highly literate circles . . . (and) served a limited, substitutive, instructional function,"[25] he says quite clearly then that the genre *function*, i.e., its rhetorical function, is more important than the nature of the genre as a literary entity. Not theories of literary forms, but theories of rhetorical argumentation, will offer us solutions to the problems of Romans and to the problems we will have with *any* genre, whether it be the letter-essay in Romans, or the apologetic letter genre in Galatians. Betz recognizes this when he points to his own "somewhat different (rhetoric) approach" in contrast to the genre approach.[26]

The difference between my and Betz's procedure is that Betz first states his thesis about the genre and elaborates on the genre. Then he proceeds to derive the evidence for his genre thesis from an analysis of the composition of the Galatian letter. By contrast my procedure is to state first what Betz does later on. I begin with the identification of the epistolary framework. Then, in view of the "interrelations between the epistolary framework and the body,[27] I seek to determine the rhetorical genre by choosing the "best way to approach a piece of argumentation (which is by asking) to what sort of judgment it is ultimately directed."[28]

[22]This applies not only to Pauline letters, but also to the canonical and apocryphal Pauline and other apostolic pseudepigraphical letters, and even to the Apocalypse of John as "letter."

[23]White, *Greek Letter*, 159 comments on the difference between the nonliterary, private, Greek papyri letters and the letters of Paul: "Though the purpose ("idea") of the body-middle (which is the "message" part of the letter, see p. 154) is the same in Paul and in the papyri, the manner of implementation varies considerably." Precisely! For only rhetoric, and not literary form or genre, can account for the variations.

[24]Karris, "Response," 126–27.

[25]Donfried, "False Presuppositions," 122, n. 97.

[26]Betz, H. D., "Literary Composition," 354, n. 4.

[27]Brandt, *Rhetoric of Argumentation*, 14.

[28]Perelman–Olbrechts-Tyteca, *New Rhetoric*, 21.

III. The Exordium of Paul's Argument in Romans 1:1–15

To get an answer to the questions about the "sort of judgment" to which the argument in Romans "is ultimately directed," or what the role is which Paul expected the Romans to perform, or what audience functions Paul gave to the Roman Christians,[29] we turn now to the text of Romans.

The first part of the *exordium* is identical with the letter prescript. Characteristic of the epistolary prescript of Romans are the often noted expansions. They provide us with the same clue for Romans as they do in the prescript to the letter to the Galatians: "It is precisely at the point of expansion where we find close relations between the prescript and various parts of the body of the letter."[30]

These expansions express two major concerns of Paul. On the one hand the expansions are concerned with Paul as agent of the gospel (which is synonymous with agent of Christ, or of faith) for the *nations*. This concern relates to his travels in both directions: to Jerusalem "in the priestly service of the gospel of God" (cf. 1:1–5 and 15:15–22; also chs. 1–4 and 9–11 of the *probatio)* and to the ends of the earth, to Spain. On the other hand the expansions are concerned with Paul as agent of the gospel to the church(es) at Rome (cf. 1:6–15 and 15:23f., 29; also 12:1–15:13 of the *probatio's* exhortation). This concern relates to Paul's claim for support and for authoritative teaching. This, then, is the argumentative situation. Further analysis of the *exordium* section, which is the first of the traditional parts of argumentation, will confirm this.

The *exordium* of Paul's argumentation in Romans includes also the whole of the second part of the "letter opening," commonly referred to as the Thanksgiving section (1:8–15). "The polite form of the disclosure formula: *ou thelō de hymas agnoein, adelphoi"* does not have to function as introduction to the "body opening," for it is recognized that "Paul commonly takes liberties both with the form *and with the function* (italics mine) of these formulae."[31] I want to show instead that rhetorically 1:13–15 is the concluding portion of the *exordium*. In interpreting 1:1–15 rhetorically, rather than epistolographically, we will come to see more clearly (1) what is the nature and scope of the *exordium* for Romans, and (2) what significant connections exist between the opening and the closing portion of the argument, if we take Rom. 15:14–33 as certainly one part of the argumentation's conclusion, leaving aside for the moment the role of chapter 16. The brief section Rom. 1:13–15 shows the speaker in a continuing effort at establishing an *ethos*, that "inescapable dimension in ar-

[29]Brandt, *Rhetoric of Argumentation*, 22.
[30]Betz, H. D., "Literary Composition," 355, n. 5.
[31]White, *Greek Letter*, 156f. and 84f.

gumentation."[32] We see Paul working at what Brandt calls one of the basic functions of the *exordium* which is "chiefly to project a character for the orator, an *ethos*, which would persuade the audience to trust him."[33] The writer can choose whatever *ethos* he likes, just as the reader has the choice of rejecting it. "But *ethos* is a prerequisite to persuasion; it should not be a *means*."[34] One of the argumentative functions of the *ethos* in the *exordium* can be that of "providing implicit premises," such as reminding the reader of the speaker's authority.[35]

One of the "two major necessities" of an argument's introduction is that "the writer must define his problem."[36] Among the various ways of doing this, Brandt mentions the use of a *narratio*[37] "which was defined as a statement of the facts of the case. . . . to serve as a background for the major argument."[38] What are the facts of the case in Romans? With the strongly worded appeal to God as his witness, Paul introduces the facts of his pending visit as God's will in the face of past *and present* obstacles. It is the latter condition which makes the *causa* of Romans look like the *causa* of 2 Corinthians. If, according to traditional rhetorical practice and theory, the *exordium* can vary depending on whether the facts of the case are "noble, confused, paradoxical, or shameful,"[39] then the definition of the problem in the *exordium* of Paul's argument in Romans is something "discreditable," as the *Rhetorica ad Herennium* I,5 would put it.[40]

The apparent judgment, or role, which Paul expects the Romans to perform, is for them not to deliberate (which would require the deliberative or symbouleutic genre, as we have in 1 Corinthians), nor to adjudicate (which would require the legal or forensic genre, as we have in Galatians), but to affirm the communal values which Paul and the Romans share in being agents of faith throughout the world. We expect therefore the use of the epideictic or demonstrative genre.[41]

---

[32]Brandt, *Rhetoric of Argumentation*, 16.
[33]Ibid., Cf. Perelman–Olbrechts-Tyteca, *New Rhetoric*, 319, n. 166.
[34]Brandt, *Rhetoric of Argumentation*, 218.
[35]Ibid., 219.
[36]Ibid., 51.
[37]Ibid., 59. See also Lausberg, *Handbuch*, 1.163ff.
[38]Brandt, *Rhetoric of Argumentation*, 16.
[39]Perelman-Olbrechts-Tyteca *New Rhetoric*, 497, n. 121. See also Lausberg, *Handbuch*, 1.58–60.
[40]Käsemann, *An die Römer*, 17 puts the issue as follows: "Why does Paul see himself forced to even justify his writing to the Romans? Why does this writing in turn acquire the character of a digest of Pauline teaching? Why does the threefold assurance of his long-planned visit sound like an apology or even a defense against the suspicion that he did not take it so seriously or was in any hurry?" Käsemann sees here expressed, "the problem of Paul's apostolate" which "determines almost all his letters and is frequently their crucial point." Käsemann concludes that Romans "also is undoubtedly a document of someone struggling for recognition of his existence and of an apostolic office that has come under question. Without this insight (the letter to the Romans) cannot be interpreted correctly." I disagree with the implication.
[41]The best survey of the epideictic genre still is the monograph-sized article of Burgess, "Epideictic Literature," 89–261. See also Kroll, "Epidektik," 1131–35. For historical comments,

IV. Connections between the Exordium and Peroration

The student of ancient epistolography can only comment on the significant expansions in the "letter opening" and their recurrence in the "body closing." But he cannot account for this unusual feature on purely epistolographic grounds. The student of rhetoric, however, can account for the necessary connections between an argument's *exordium* and peroration.

Besides this concern for structural rhetoric one can discern a stylistic feature in the *exordium* which belongs to textual rhetoric: the chiastic order in which Paul treats the two outstanding issues in the noted expansions.

A Paul's interpretation of the gospel, of Christ, of faith (1:1–5)

  B His apostolic relation to the church(es) in Rome (1:6)

  B' His relation to the church(es) in Rome (1:9–12)

A' The interpretation of his gospel ministry (1:13–15), but with one significant addition: the reference to his having been hindered or frustrated (1:13).

It is this latter point which reappears in 15:22 as past hindrance, and in 15:30–31 as gloomy prospect. Both, the painful remembrance and the dreaded future hindrance, are brought up in the context of his planned visit, i.e., in the context of Paul's relation to the Roman church(es) as apostle. This relation appears in the dual dimension of (1) expecting support for his continuing "priestly service" to (and of!) the nations (on his Spain plans, see 15:24a in the light of 1:5 and 1:13b), and (2) expecting mutual encouragement and refreshment (see 15:24b, 32 in the light of 1:12). And all of this, in turn, is predicated on the common faith (see 15:14 in the light of 1:8).

In examining the postscript of Romans not merely epistolographically as the "body closing," but primarily from a rhetorical perspective as the peroration of Paul's whole argument, we note in Romans, as Betz did in Galatians, "some very interesting structures (which confirm) that we do, in fact, have (such a concluding) part of a speech before us."[42] The difference between Galatians and Romans in their respective postscripts is due to a difference in rhetorical genre or argumentative situation involved in each. While Galatians is forensic, as argued by Betz, I hope to prove my point that Romans is epideictic, as proposed earlier. We will put our

---

see Kennedy, *Art of Rhetoric*, 21–23 and 634–637; and Judge, "Classical Society," 35f. n. 83. For B. Wallach (see below n. 93) the diatribe is quite definitely an epideictic form.

On *dikaiosynē* as one of the traditional "special topics for ceremonial discourse," see Corbett, *Classical Rhetoric* 139–42. See also G. L. Kustas, *Studies in Byzantine Rhetoric* (Thessalonica: Patriarchal Institute for Patristic Studies, 1973), 45f. on the "close association of epistolary literature with the homily, of which panegyric and protreptic are two ingredients." The protreptic is concerned with "the appeal to the faithful to attend the ways of righteousness." Paul's choice of the mode of discourse in Romans could not be better characterized!

[42]Betz, H. D., "Literary Composition," 357.

thesis, that Romans is epideictic, to the test when we return to the issue of the relation between *peroratio* and *exordium*.[43]

The relations between the peroration and the *exordium* are based on the dual goal pursued in both: (1) the stating at the beginning, and restating at the end, of the problem or subject,[44] and (2) some emotional appeal which at the beginning is designed to establish the contact between author and audience, but which at the end is designed to consolidate the practical effects of the argumentation as "a function of the audience addressed," or as paving the way for action.[45] Such emotional appeal, however, must match the nature of the problem which was introduced, then argued over, and is now recapitulated in the conclusion. We shall see that the congruity of the emotional appeal in the peroration of Romans with the *status* of the *causa*, i.e., the "problem," as presented in Romans, will provide us with the solution of the puzzle of Rom. 16.

V. The Peroration or Conclusion of Paul's Argumentation, Romans 15:14–16:23

That the postscript is in itself well composed, and that it can be shown to be fully integrated with the rest of the letter, is as applicable to Romans as it is to Galatians.[46] The very mention of the amanuensis Tertius in 16:22 points to the fact that "the letter itself assumes more and more the character of an official document and less the character of a 'private' letter," as Betz put it.

In his review of the two basic functions of the peroration Brandt observes that there may be three rhetorical functions of an argument's conclusion. We can see all three in Paul's peroration in Romans.

There is, first of all, the function that asserts the credibility of the subject discussed. This is done in two stages: Rom. 15:14–15 and 15:16–29. In 15:14–15 Paul offers the recapitulation, the full statement of the thesis. Käsemann's statement, that "these verses show rhetorical influence" and that 15:14 is "a very artistically composed statement,"[47] lacks precision, or is at best one-sided, for he comments only on textual rhetoric at the total expense of structural rhetoric. The second stage, 15:16–29, is best explained as to structure and sequence by Brandt's observation that "the full statement of the thesis may well be accompanied by a review of the main topics in which the evidence for one's position is maximized,"[48] for

---

[43]See Lausberg, *Handbuch*, 1.432, and Betz, H. D., "Literary Composition," 357.

[44]Lausberg, *Handbuch*, 1.236f.

[45]Perelman–Olbrechts-Tyteca, *New Rhetoric*, 44, 54. Brandt, *Rhetoric of Argumentation*, 69.

[46]See Betz, H. D., "Literary Composition," 356–59. On postscript conventions, see also G. Kennedy, *Art of Rhetoric*, Index s. v. peroration.

[47]*Römer*, 373.

[48]*Rhetoric of Argumentation*, 68.

these verses offer a review of the three main topics which also constituted the *ethos* part of the *exordium.*

(1) Paul's *past* record as apostle (15:19b-20) in accordance with Scripture (15:21) and a general statement of the nature of the apostolic office (15:16–19a) stand at one end, while at the other end of this first topic we find the reference to Paul's frequent delays in visiting Rome which were caused by his past record (15:22). But past is now past!

(2) Paul's *future* plans as apostle (15:23–24a) are related to the two expectations about his Rome visit (15:24b): to be sped on to Spain by them, and to be stilled by them ("enjoying your company" RSV), or, as 15:32 puts it, to be refreshed by them.[49]

(3) Paul's *present* preoccupation (15:25–27) with the collection for Jerusalem, followed by a third reference to his planned Spain campaign but again with strong emphasis on the mutuality between the Roman Christians and Paul (15:28–29). In terms of structural rhetoric, the verses 28–29 restate once more the thesis which was recapitulated in 15:14–15 as the beginning of the peroration, which constitutes the first function of the peroration.

Related to the first function is another one which Brandt identifies as follows: "a peroration will sometimes be found to contain a kind of double conclusion. This occurs when the concrete thesis the writer wishes to argue does not coincide with the point really at issue. . . . The peroration, then, may assert not merely what the essay or oration has argued but also a specific application of that general thesis."[50] This observation is extremely important for the interpretation of Romans, for the assertions in the peroration of Romans are mainly concerned with the specific application of the general thesis (the common cause of Rome's active, world-encompassing faith and Paul's apostolic mission[51]). The specific application appears in the following section which is concerned with the third function of a peroration.

The last of the three rhetorical functions of a peroration is to make "safely (some) overt emotional appeals; (for) the reader, having been convinced intellectually, will not resist incitements to action or confirming arguments of an exaggerated character."[52] The peroration has been specified in Hellenistic rhetoric "as the proper place for *pathos*," i.e., the rousing of emotions for the purpose of stimulating the audience to action. The "only two means to *pathos* available to the writer" are (1) "to lower the level of abstraction of one's discourse," and (2) to stimulate "in ourselves

---

[49]The terms *epipothia* (15:23), *propempesthai* and *plēsthēnai* (15:24), and *synanapauesthai* (15:32) should be studied in their final rhetorical context and function, and should be so noted as to their meaning in context in lexical references, besides being studied historically, or epistolographically (e.g., *epipothia* as letter *topos).*

[50]*Rhetoric of Argumentation,* 69.

[51]Käsemann, *Römer,* 380, points out that Romans was written "at least also with this in view (that) the (Roman) congregation was to support (Paul's) work actively and to shoulder its burdens."

[52]Brandt, *Rhetoric of Argumentation,* 68f.

the emotion we wish from our readers or hearers." What happens in the first instance is based on the knowledge—perhaps ultimately derived from the Sophistic tradition—that "feeling originates in experience, and (that) the more concrete writing is, the closer it is to experience, the more feeling is implicit in it." And in the second instance, "the basis for the pathetic appeal" is "sympathy"; and "seen from this point of view, traditional *pathos* is merely a variety of *ethos*. This fact is apparent in the peroration of almost every traditional speech. The speaker steps forward in a role that is ordinarily a modification of the one assumed to that point, and takes for himself a stance toward the subject which his audience will presumably assume with him."[53]

It is my thesis that the *pathos* section of the peroration in Romans extends from 15:30 to 16:23. It consists of the following parts: 15:30–33 (the appeal to join battle forces in intercessory prayer[54]); 16:1–2 (the recommendation that sister Phoebe receive the treatment which brother Paul expects for himself from them "in the Lord as befits saints"); 16:3–16 (the greetings); and 16:17–18 (the appeal to be on guard against disruptive forces), with 16:19–20 fitting as a summary conclusion not only to vv. 17–18, but also to the *pathos* section as a whole, if not indeed to the whole letter. Käsemann acknowledges this when he comments on the question of the connection of chapter 16 with the rest of Romans on the basis of the reference to the faith obedience of the Roman Christians which is known to all (16:19) as reiteration of the motive first mentioned in 1:8.[55] The argument that 16:19–20 is unrelated to the interests expressed in 15:14–32 can be invented and maintained[56] only by ignoring the rhetorical structure of the concluding peroration. The sixth and final part of the concluding emotional appeal is 16:21–23. The appeal is based on the *syngeneis* character of his associates (all four of the greeters are Jews!), and on Gaius as a model host. By contrast, the first series of greetings was based on

---

[53]Ibid., 224.

[54]For a similar appeal to intercessory prayer in the peroration section of other "epistles," see for Paul 1 Thess. 5:25 and Philem. 22; for Deutero-Paul, Col. 4:18, Eph. 6:18–20, (2 Thess. 3:1–3), Heb. 13:18. In 2 Cor. 1:11 it appears in the exordium, but differently in Phil. 1:19f. According to Wiles, *Intercessory Prayers*, the true significance of appeals to such prayers can be seen only in the light of formal restrictions of Paul's style imposed by epistolographic and liturgical conventions of the one hand, and by reckoning with "the dynamic elements of his positive spontaneity and sincerity" (p. 6) on the other hand. The rhetorical conventions which shape the spontaneity and sincerity are ignored. For the focus on the epideictic genre we note Wiles' comments: Paul's concern is for "an enduring partnership of mutual responsibility, through the medium of their intercessory prayers" (p. 265); he stresses "the note of fellowship that must be the basis of such mutual prayers" (p. 266). Yet, when Wiles comments on "the close parallelism" between 1:7–17 and 15:13–33 which "must reflect a deliberate composition" he makes recourse only to *Literary* genres, (letter conventions, or liturgical patterns), but not to rhetoric, despite the rhetorical connotations of half of his methodological presuppositions when he speaks of "spontaneity," "living function (of a passage)," and the like.

[55]Käsemann, *Römer*, 398.

[56]See ibid., 399.

the recipients' relation to Paul and their common task (16:3–15) and on the addressees' relations to one another and to all Christians everywhere.[57]

To consolidate my point that 15:30–16:23 is the *pathos* section of the peroration I must first clarify one important issue which applies to the *pathos* section no less than to other structural components of Hellenistic rhetoric. It is the issue of the rhetorical genre in contrast to literary genre.[58] Specifically at issue now is the demonstration that Romans belongs to the epideictic genre, and that the *pathos* of the peroration in Romans fits exactly what Lausberg calls the two *Leitaffekte* which are appropriate to the epideictic genre: the emotions of admiring love and of despising hate.[59]

To establish a *rhetorical* genre one begins by clarifying the given relationship—what is called the *aptum*[60]—between the three basic constituents of an argumentation: the relationship between speaker and speech content, the relationship between speaker and audience, and the relationship between speech content and audience.[61] The *aptum* issue is the crucial hermeneutical issue insofar as it concerns the interrelation and interdependence of form and content, the synthesis of *res* and *verba*.[62] The basic distinction between forensic/legal, deliberative/symbouleutic, and demonstrative/epideictic genres is based on the *aptum* of speaker-audience, and the *aptum* of audience-speech content. The forensic genre is concerned with a "right or wrong" judgment about an issue that is rooted in the past. No such judgment is involved in Romans. The deliberative/symbouleutic genre is concerned with a judgment on whether or not something is expedient or harmful about an issue that is emerging in the future. But Paul does not ask the Romans to deliberate on a course of action to be followed. There remains the epideictic genre, which is concerned with judgments about some present situation. The traditional categories for judgment are called "praise or blame"; we might call them today "ok or not-ok" judgments. The significance and importance of epideictic oratory is seen based on its intent to "strengthen the disposition toward action by increasing adherence to the values it lauds."[63]

Yet the epideictic genre has been seriously misunderstood, due to "a false conception of the effects of argumentation."[64] What Paul is after in Romans, as is evidenced so far in the *exordium* and the peroration, is "not limited to obtaining purely intellectual results (or) to a declaration that a

[57]See ibid., 397: "The holy kiss demonstrates the solidarity of all Christendom." Wiles, *Intercessory Prayers*, 264: "this appeal for prayer (15:30) . . . elicits the immediate co-operation of the readers, in the atmosphere of fellowship that would be symbolized by the kiss of peace."
[58]See Lausberg, *Handbuch*, § 53.
[59]See ibid., §§ 241, 258, 437.
[60]See ibid., §§ 54ff., and 258.
[61]Ibid., §§ 54–57.
[62]Ibid., § 45, especially §§ 1055–062.
[63]Perelman–Olbrechts-Tyteca, *New Rhetoric*, 50.
[64]Ibid., 49.

certain thesis seems more probable than another" (e.g., Paul's gospel *vs* somebody else's gospel). What he is after is "an intensity of adherence" which he wants to "reinforce until the desired action is actually performed."[65] Another way of putting it: "the argumentation in (Paul's) epideictic discourse (letter to the Romans) sets out to increase the intensity of adherence to certain values, which might not be contested when considered on their own but may nevertheless not prevail against other values that might come into conflict with them. The speaker (in our case Paul) tries to establish a sense of communion centered around particular values recognized by the audience (in Romans it is the faith stance and faith commitment of speaker and audience), and to this end he uses the whole range of means available to the rhetorician for purposes of amplification and enhancement. In epideictic oratory (as here in Romans) every device of literary art is appropriate, for it is a matter of combining all the factors that can promote this communion of the audience."[66]

Another important clarification brought about by the recognition of Romans as belonging to the epideictic genre is the distinction between education and propaganda, with epideictic oratory serving education, not propaganda. The stalemated discussion over whether or not Romans is a missionary document can be resolved fruitfully only if we pay attention to the rhetorical genre. What is said of epideictic speeches generally, is true also of Romans: in the epideictic mode the writer is "most prone to appeal to a universal order, to a nature, or a god that would vouch for the unquestioned, and supposedly unquestionable, values. In epideictic oratory, the speaker turns educator."[67] With this digression we must now return to the *pathos* section of the peroration in Romans.

Lausberg points out that each of the three rhetorical genres has a *Leitaffekt*, or one overriding emotional appeal *sui generis*. The *Leitmotif* of the epideictic *pathos* is love. That such *Leitaffekt* "dominates the whole argument" can be shown to apply by pointing to the *agapē* references in the main body of Romans,[68] as well as by recognizing the role of *agapē*

---

[65]Ibid.

[66]Ibid., 51 (parentheses are mine). See above on affirmation of communal values. Cf. also Brandt, *Rhetoric of Argumentation* 13: the rhetoric of epideictic argumentation, like the rhetoric of poetry, "performed an important civic function. . . . It was an affirmation of community solidarity."

[67]Perelman–Olbrechts-Tyteca, *New Rhetoric*, 51. See ibid., 51–54 on the difference between education and propaganda. For its application to the interpretation of Philo's works, see Conley, "General Education."

[68]On the role of *agapē* in the *narratio* and *probatio* parts of the argumentation of Rom. 1:18–11:36, and in the parenesis part 12:1–15:13, see E. Stauffer, *agapaō*, in *TDNT* (1964) 1.49–52. Wiles, *Intercessory Prayers*, 389f. comments that Paul in Rom. 12 and 13 "centers his total parenesis around the practice of love as the acceptable will of God (12:2). . . . " See also Furnish, *'Theology and Ethics*, 235: "The Pauline concept of love supplies the key to the apostle's thinking about the discernment of the divine will in the various 'normal crises' of daily conduct."

in 15:30 as the basis for the appeal for intercessory prayer; by recognizing that love again is the implicit key term for the Phoebe recommendation; and by recognizing how often the term *agapētos* appears in the greetings,[69] let alone weighing the significance of the elaborate expansion of the greeting-*topos* in 16:3–16.[70] Even the otherwise abrupt transition from cheerful greetings to stern warnings in 16:17–18 becomes intelligible only when seen in the light of structural rhetoric. To cast the *Leitaffekt* of love (or praise of a common bond) into sharper relief, and to increase the intensity of adherence to that which is to be loved (which is in Romans the intensification of the adherence of the Roman Christians to their faith for the sake of helping Paul to over-come his last obstacle—Jerusalem!—before consummating the faith union in Rome), Paul, the epideictic orator here, contrasts the unloving, the divisive disposition of the self-serving "somebodies,"[71] with the attitude of the audience.

The greetings in 16:21–23 are more than a mere extension of the ones earlier in 16:3–16. Besides emphasizing, as noted earlier, the character of the whole as an official document, by stressing the Jewishness of the associates of the author, and of Tertius the co-author (an emphasis often found in the *exordium* of the argument, rather than in the peroration), we find in 16:23 an *exemplum* or paradigm[72] in the hospitality of Gaius to the "whole church." This further heightens the appeal Paul has been making for Roman hospitality to Phoebe and, not least, to himself. One could also argue that Gaius especially, but also all the other associates listed in 16:21–23, serve as the laudable model over against the vituperative anonymous characters in 16:17–18.[73] Such a view would further stress the rhetorical links in the structural unit of 15:14–16:23.

[69]*Agapētos* appears in 16:5, 8, 9, 12 (cf. 1:7; 12:19). Käsemann, *Römer*, 396, recognizes the "strongly rhetorical character" of the predication used in the greetings, but he believes that they lose in objective credibility (*verlieren an sachlicher Glaubwürdigkeit*)! That one remark is most indicative of the prevailing "false conception of the effects of argumentation" noted earlier (see above to note 64). Mullins, "Greetings," 418–426, comments on Rom. 16: "Perhaps . . . there was such cordiality between the writer and the reader that the former could properly feel that the latter was an extension of his own personality" (p. 424)—apparently without losing in objective credibility!

[70]Mullins, "Greetings," 425f. warns that the elaborate expansion of the greeting form cannot and should not be taken as an expression of Paul trying to introduce himself, nor should the apparent "closeness to the congregation at Rome (be seen as based on) the presence there of the list of friends he was greeting. (The greeting form used suggests) that the *persons* greeted might not be among those who read the letter. The relationship between Paul and the congregation at Rome seems to be other than scholars have assumed . . . something in our usual interpretation of Romans is wrong."

[71]Käsemann, *Römer*, 398 comments only on the anonymous reference as befitting the style of Paul's polemic.

[72]Lausberg, *Handbuch*, §§ 410–426.

[73]On the contrast of "laudantur vel vituperantur homines" as a traditional topic for epideictic argumentation, see Lausberg, *Handbuch*, § 245.

VI. Transitus (1:16–17) and Confirmatio (1:18–15:13)

The evidence for the epideictic form and function of Romans, based on "the argumentative situation"[74] apparent in the *exordium* and the *peroratio* of Paul's argumentation, remains incomplete without at least a brief overview of the other portions of Romans.

I shall bypass the arguments for my claim that Rom. 1:16–17 functions rhetorically as the *transitus*[75] as distinguished from the epistolographic function as "body opening."[76] The verb *epaischynesthai* (1:16) appears to echo the *kalon vs aischron* alternative for subjects treated in the epideictic genre.[77] The rhetorical function of the *transitus* is to signal the end of the *exordium* and to provide a harmonious beginning for the *confirmatio* which lays out the central arguments (1:18–15:13).

In view of the relation of Rom. 12:1–15:13 to 1:18–11:36 Käsemann speaks of "a grand coherency of argumentation which remains hidden only to him who does not spend enough efforts on it."[78] That is a very important observation, but it leaves us without clues or suggestions as to the method by which we can get hold of this coherence of argumentation. Once more I want to argue that the methodological approach here, as in the case earlier when we considered the *exordium* and *peroration* parts of Romans, is to be based on the analysis of the nature and function of argumentations. To understand the rhetorics of argumentation in Rom. 1:18–15:13 will lead to an understanding of the sociological and theological dimensions involved, but not vice versa.

The task of interpreting the argumentative unity of 1:18–15:13 confronts us with two major problems: (1) the general problem of the coherence of argumentation, which was earlier referred to as structural rhetoric, and (2) the relation between parenesis and the "body" of the letter or argument, i.e., the relation between 12:1–15:13 and 1:18–11:36.

To explain the latter leaves the student of ancient epistolography and the student of rhetoric equally puzzled. J. L. White was cited earlier[79] as noting that the message part of Paul's letters varies considerably in the manner of implementation when seen in comparison with papyri letters, and—I may add—also when we compare Paul's letters with each other. In the study of the "body" of Paul's letters White comments on the absence of any "parallels in the principal body-middle conventions of the common letter tradition."[80] Characteristic for all of Paul's letters, except

---

[74]See above n. 18.

[75]Lausberg, *Handbuch,* § 288. Cf. Betz, H. D., "Literary Composition," 361f., on the *transitio* in Gal. 1:10–11.

[76]White, *Greek Letter,* 32–42, 64, 84f.

[77]Lausberg, *Handbuch,* §§ 61.3, and 240. Bultmann's article on *aischynō* in *TDNT* 1.189–191 shows no awareness of the rhetorical traditions. This is true also of his *pisteuō* article.

[78]*Römer,* 309.

[79]See above n. 23.

[80]White, *Greek Letter,* 160.

Philemon, are, according to White, two parts of the argumentation: the first which "is always a tightly organized theological argument; the second . . . less tightly constructed . . . where the principles espoused in the preceding part are concretized."[81]

In his analysis of the parenetic section of Galatians Betz notes with surprise that modern investigations of form and function of epistolary parenesis are rare. He is also puzzled by the fact "that parenesis plays only a marginal role in the ancient rhetorical handbooks, if not in rhetoric itself." The only reason Betz can find for philosophical letters of the Hellenistic period to conclude with a parenetic section is the one expressed by Seneca and his dissatisfaction with mere syllogistic argumentation.[82]

We may have to turn to modern rhetorics to account for the structural unity of the parenesis with the preceding part of the argumentation— a unity commonly referred to as the unity of theology and ethics in Paul.[83] Perelmann and Olbrechts-Tyteca note that "argumentation is essentially adaptation to the audience; in choosing the order in which arguments are to be presented in persuasive discourse, account should be taken of all the factors capable of furthering acceptance of the arguments by the hearers."[84] The basic reason cited for "argumentation involving the practical commitment of those who take part in it" is that argumentation "never develops in a vacuum, but in a situation that is socially and psychologically determined." That is why there is, and has to be "a close connection between argumentative thought and the action it paves the way for or brings about."[85]

Thus, the parenetic part, Rom. 12:1–15:13, spells out the practical commitment of those who took part in the argumentation. Argumentative thought (exordium and probatio in Rom. 1:1–15 and 1:16–11:36) relates to the argumentative appeal to commitment (parenesis in Rom. 12:1–15:13) in the same way that the peroration section has the restatement of the thesis (Rom. 15:14–15 with its concomitant section 15:16–29) related to the pathos section (Rom. 15:30–16:23). Käsemann again senses something to this effect when he asks, "how it would be possible to perceive on the

---

[81]Ibid., 159.

[82]"Literary Composition," 375–76. See also Kustas, *Byzantine Rhetoric*, 43ff. on "the extensive Stoic legacy to the rhetoric of late antiquity," and on the sermon or homily as "the product of a more wholesale assimilation from earlier models." It is "the choice of models" which forms part of the history of the struggle between Asianism and Atticism (p. 17, n. 2).

[83]Furnish, *Theology and Ethics*, 90f. sees the parenetic parts in Paul's letters "assimilated to an evangelical, not a pedagogical, purpose and context" and contrasts this purpose with "Seneca's syllogism about the sufficiency of moral precepts for attaining the happy life." Compare the Seneca reference with Betz's observation to n. 82. On pp. 98–106 Furnish deals with the "difficult" case of Romans, and he concludes that the parenesis (Rom. 12:1–15:13) does "not only presuppose the 'theological' assertions of chaps. 1–11, but supply a further and needed explication of that one gospel (God's power for salvation) which both 'theology' and 'ethics' seek to unfold." See also Sanders, J. T., *Ethics*, 57.

[84]*New Rhetoric*, 491; cf. 19–23 on "The audience as a construction of the speaker."

[85]Ibid., 59; cf. also 59–62 on "Argumentation and Commitment."

basis of this section (referring to the special parenesis Rom. 14:1–15:13) the Pauline intentions for the whole of his letter."[86] Once again, Käsemann shows a keen sense for the rhetorical dimension of Pauline argumentation, but he lacks the methodological tool of structural rhetoric to make his exegetical case plausible.

What happens when one sees the special parenesis in Romans (which forms the basis for Donfried's methodological principle No. 1) in the light of the Pauline intentions stated in the *exordium* and *transitus*, and reiterated in the peroration? We see that the "logical and purposeful thought sequence" of this parenetic section functions as an *exemplum* or paradigm of Paul's basic thesis. Within the argumentation as a whole it functions as a digression.[87] We see Paul emphasizing Christian solidarity in its fulness and its limit (14:1–12); he warns against its loss due to criticism (14:13–23); he points to the model or norm for his *exemplum*, the life and work of Christ, where the traditionally divided Jews and Gentiles found their solidarity (15:1–6); and a concluding appeal for mutual acceptance in the spirit of Christ (15:7–13). Only by ignoring the structural rhetorical function of this whole sequence can one be surprised as Käsemann is by the complete vanishing of all references to the seemingly concrete tensions and controversies at the end when one might expect a climactic resolution.[88] But if we place the special parenesis in its rhetorical structure, then it becomes clear that the *exemplum* of 14:1ff. concretizes in the same way that 13:1–7 concretizes. Both concretize what is expressed in the series of *topoi* or *loci*[89] in 12:3ff. The argumentative quality of these general and special parenetic sections is an extension of the argumentation first introduced in the *exordium*, and carried out in 1:16–11:36, and the case comes to rest not until 15:13, thus making 1:16–15:13 one "coherent" argument.

On the general problem of the coherence of the argumentation in the part preceding the parenesis we have already noted[90] the connections between Rom. 1–4 and 9–11 with parts of the *exordium* (1:1–5) and peroration (15:15–22), and likewise connections between the parenesis (12:1–15:12) and those portions of the *exordium* and peroration in which Paul speaks as agent of the gospel to the church(es) at Rome (1:6–15 and

---

[86]*Römer,* 349.

[87]Lausberg, *Handbuch,* §§ 410–426. On *exemplum* as digression, see § 415. Sanders, *Ethics,* 62, sees Paul's intention in Rom. 14 "to show . . . *paradigmatically* (italics mine) . . . how one moves from the middle axioms given in 12:9–20 to specific parenesis."

[88]*Römer,* 368.

[89]On *topoi* in Rom. see Furnish, *Theology and Ethics,* 99f. Lausberg, *Handbuch* §§ 407–409 refers to the use of *loci communes* for amplification. Fischel, *Rabbinic Literature,* shows the use of *topoi* in rabbinic argumentation (see General Index, s.v. Rhetoric, and Topos). Corbett, *Classical Rhetoric,* 97–132, as well as the "special topics" (pp. 139–142). Of special interest to our case for Romans as epideictic is Corbett's list of the "special topics" of courage, justice, magnanimity, gentleness, and the like, as traditional *topoi for* epideictic argumentation.

[90]See above p. 135f.

15:23f., 29). Furthermore, we had noted[91] that *dikaiosynē* was one of the traditional special topics of epideictic or ceremonial discourse. These observations deserve further exploration which go beyond the limits of this paper.

I want to conclude with references to coherence of argumentation as rhetoricians see the problem. There is E. A. Judge's appeal[92] that we need "to explore adequately the many-sidedness and singularity of Paul's epistolary technique" as part of "a more thorough search of the history of changing fashions in fine speech and self-display in the first century."[93] What is being said here in view of 2 Corinthians applies *mutatis mutandis* to Romans and the changing fashions in epideictic speech.

Brandt's general reflections on argumentation invite application to Paul: "Argumentative thinking is probably always a secondary process, a reduction from some sort of intuited understanding that takes place first."[94] What is more, the ostensible object of an argumentation is, according to Brandt's observation, often not the real one. On the coherence of argumentation as not determined by logic, Brandt notes: "The form (of argumentation) itself requires of (the writer of argumentation) tasks that have no logical or inevitable connection with each other, and that, as a consequence, will never fuse into a whole for him."[95] On the one hand, Brandt sees "no possibility of constructing an argument organically, since judgment, not experience, is the objective. . . . (and) different mental activities must be performed, somehow, into a coherent argument, but regardless of the skill of the writer they remain discrete parts."[96] On the other hand, Brandt notes in view of longer speeches and essays that "one or more of the other parts of the body of an essay will almost always be interwoven into the enthymatic structure."[97] Such coherence of argumentation of the letters of Paul as a whole is to be distinguished from other, smaller units of argumentation.[98]

With guidelines like these I would undertake the detailed analysis of Rom. 1:18–15:13. Mindful of Wilamowitz's point, that any interpretation of

[91]See above n. 41.
[92]"Classical Society," 33 and 36 and n. 75.
[93]See also Kustas's reference to "the choice of models," cited above n. 82. A good example of the kind of study E. A. Judge calls for is Wallach, *History of Diatribe*.
[94]*Rhetoric of Argumentation*, 22.
[95]Ibid., 49f., n. 1.
[96]Ibid., 50.
[97]Ibid., 67.
[98]Bujard, *Stilanalytische*, 78, n. 11, makes only a passing reference to argumentation on the letter as a whole; like most exegetes he concentrates on Paul's thought sequences (*Gedankenführung*) either in terms of the traditional (*textual* rhetoric oriented) "figures of thought" (see Lausberg, *Handbuch*, 1.375–455 on rhetorical *figurae sententiae*) or in terms of rabbinic methods of argumentation. On the latter see now Hanson, *Paul's Technique*, esp. ch. 4, "Motives and Techniques in the Composition of Romans and Galatians."

Paul cannot do without an appreciation of Asianic tradition of rhetoric,[99] I would pay careful attention especially to Paul's handling of proofs (the *pisteis*) in his argumentation. If Wilamowitz is right, we might expect to see in Paul what Gommel sees in Thucydides' rhetorical argumentation: the overshadowing of the traditional primary proofs by the secondary and supplementary proofs.[100]

VII. Conclusion

As a peroration of my own I want to restate my thesis that the study of Paul's letters generally, and of Romans specifically, requires a new orientation in the priority of our methods of study. The argumentative nature of religious literature—traditionally referred to as propaganda literature[101]—calls for a methodology that can account for the nature and effects of argumentation. The various schools of linguistic analysis and of structuralism, all products of this century, provide possible alternatives to old or new rhetorical methods.[102] The rhetorical structure of Romans is coherent with the *status* of its *causa* and its apparent demonstrative genre which requires the inclusion of Rom. 16.

My appeal is: since we are surrounded by a cloud of witnesses of rhetoricians, linguistic analysts, structuralists, and others, let us lay aside every weight imposed by priorities of traditional historical and literary criticism, and by logical and dogmatic preoccupations which cling so closely, and let us run with perseverance the race that is set before us, looking to Paul, the pioneer and perfector of the spirit of faith—the rhetoric of faith argumentation.

[99]U. von Wiliamowtiz-Moellendorf: "Die Atticisten braucht man nicht, um Paulus zu verstehen; die Asianer kann man nicht entbehren" (p. 51), in "Asianismus und Atticismus," 350–401. In this connection the witty warning of classicist A. Wifstrand is worth repeating because exegetes continue ignoring it: "This (Pauline) rhetoric should not be hacked to pieces, least by a Dr. Dry-as-dust or Representative Doodle-Harry from Cunningville who only prove that it is possible to be wrong *without* being rhetorical" (see *Alte Kirche*, 38). See also Kustas's comment in *Byzantine Rhetoric*, 17, n. 2, cited above n. 82; and E. A. Judge's appeal, n. 92.

[100]See Gommel, *Thukydides*, on the traditionally primary *atechnoi pisteis* (quotations from classical literature, or oral tradition; oaths, and oracles; laws and regulations; official documents) as over against the secondary *entechnoi pisteis* (such as: examples, analogies, *topoi*, and the like).

[101]On the distinction between propaganda and education, see above n. 67. Dieter Georgi, "Religious Propaganda," 124–131, makes no such distinction and thereby sows confusion.

[102]As an example of a new rhetorical method informed by process philosophy, see Lundeen, *Risk and Rhetoric*.

10

THE FORM AND FUNCTION OF THE GREEK LETTER-ESSAY

Martin Luther Stirewalt, Jr.

A number of writings with epistolary characteristics remain from Greek authors. They are customarily put with Latin *epistulae* and fictitious letters from the schools in the ill-defined category, literary letters (epistles). The purpose of this study is to show that the selected Greek documents agree in form, function, and theory to the extent of constituting a category in themselves. Fifteen documents are considered: the philosophic Letters of Epicurus, the Letters of Dionysius of Halicarnassus, selections from the works of Plutarch, 2 Maccabees, and the Martyrdom of Polycarp.

The first problem concerns terminology. By what name shall these writings be called? The question will be considered in more detail below. For the present it will suffice to say that "literary epistle" is a misleading designation. The modern English use of "epistle" has a double fault. It imposes a limitation on the Greek cognate which the Greeks never permitted in the use of this broadly generic term, and that limited use is applied to a small field of epistolary activity in reference to which the Greeks rarely applied the term. Also the modifier "literary" (literary epistle or letter) is wholly unsatisfactory. It gives the pieces a dignity which the writers did not claim for them. In fact, they sometimes deny explicitly their literary quality.

This writer is of the opinion that these documents form a category of their own. They were actual written communications with epistolary characteristics, sent between identifiable parties, on particular subjects. Indeed they were intended for others in addition to the ones named as addressees. But this fact does not eliminate the letter-setting in which they were prepared. In addition, they are closely related to another work by the same author; they may supplement one already in circulation or substitute for one projected.

These characteristics distinguish these pieces from the Latin *epistulae* which may be literary compositions in letter-form but are devoid of the initial, genuine letter-setting, or which may be personal letters in form and origin but written with such style and content as to disclose the writer's intention to publish them as a collection.

These pieces are also to be distinguished from school exercises written in letter-form. Such were written for learning and recording information from or about a prominent man of an earlier time. Again there is no genuine letter-setting. Only the form of the letter has been adopted by the schools as a learning exercise.

The term *Lehrbrief* or didactic letter is too general. Such a category might include the school exercises and other instructional types of false letters not written out of a genuine letter-setting.

The pieces collected here were written out of a genuine letter-setting and they retain the formal and structural epistolary characteristics detailed below. On the other hand, they are losing some of the form, phraseology, and structure of the letter and are incorporating the more impersonal, objective style of the monograph. In fact, the writers themselves refer to them most often as *logoi.*

If these findings and this position can be sustained, it is appropriate to choose a distinctive and descriptive term for these documents. This writer uses the term letter-essay.

A short description of each letter-essay included in this study is given in order to introduce the piece and to point out a function common to them all. They are all supplementary in some way to another writing usually by the same author or substitute for a work projected by him, and the idea of instruction is presented in the author's purpose to clarify, abridge, aid in memorizing, defend his thesis, recount history. These similarities in function lead to an inquiry about the similarities in form and content (Part II), and the unity of the category is further determined by the writers' own concept of the function and style of their supplementary, open letter-essays (Part III). A description of the letter-setting completes the study (Part IV).

I. The Examples

Epicurus

Two of the letters of Epicurus are epitomes of longer, technical works. In *Letter I, to Herodotus,*[1] he explains that he has already prepared a "Greater Epitome" of his writings on natural science in order that those who are not able to read his major works might still be able to comprehend the basic principles. But in order to comprehend these principles and

[1] Diogenes Laertius 10.35–38.

memorize them the present work has been prepared as a shorter epitome (X, 35–36). Epicurus continues:

> Hence, since such a course is of service to all who take up natural science, I . . . have prepared for you just such an epitome and manual of the doctrines as a whole. (X, 37. Hicks)

The letter is a short abridgment of the philosopher's works on physics. It is for students already studying in the field. It is not an introduction to the subject. Its purpose is to aid the student to organize and memorize the material.[2]

Letter II, to Pythocles,[3] is also related to other writings of Epicurus. He writes,

> To aid your memory you ask me for a clear and concise statement respecting celestial phenomena; for what we have written on this subject elsewhere is, you tell me, hard to remember, although you have my books constantly with you. (84. Hicks)

This letter was written in answer to a letter from Pythocles, but was in fact, intended for wide distribution both to those who had but recently come under the instruction of Epicurus and for those too busy with their own occupations to spend full time in philosophical pursuits. Pythocles is instructed to study the letter carefully together with the enclosed copy of the epitome to Herodotus (85).

These letters are summaries, condensed statements, of previously written, longer, technical treaties. Since the original works no longer remain, it is not possible to compare the letters with their prototypes for length and style. It is certain, however, that the letters are wholly dependent in content on the originals.

Epicurus' *Letter III, to Menoeceus,*[4] is a summary of the philosopher's ethical doctrine. It is more consistently epistolary and contains no statement concerning its derivation or relation to other works of Epicurus. It is important for our purposes in other respects, and reference will be made to it below.

Dionysius of Halicarnassus[5]

The situation behind the *Letter to Pompeius* is as follows. Pompeius had read some of Dionysius' treatises and had written a scholarly letter to Dionysius in which he expressed dissatisfaction with the critic's treatment of Plato and asked for his views on Herodotus and Xenophon. After

---

[2]See the repeated references to memorizing in Diogenes Laertius 10.35–37, 38; *Letter* 2.10.84, 116; Plutarch, *Coniugalia Praecepta, Moralia* 138C; 2 Macc. 2:25.

[3]Diogenes Laertius 10.84–116.

[4]Diogenes Laertius 10.122–135.

[5]References are made by page and line number to the edition and translation of W. Rhys Roberts, *Demetrius On Style,* (Cambridge, 1902).

the introductory paragraph Dionysius defends his right to criticize the philosopher. Then he quotes a lengthy passage in criticism of Plato's style from his own work, *De Antiquis Oratoribus* (97). In closing this section he compares his approach with that of Pompeius by quoting some passages from his correspondent's letter (103). The rest of the letter-essay deals with the two historians named and with others, this whole latter portion (105ff.) being a passage repeated from Dionysius' work, *De Imitatione*. The letter-essay closes with the end of the quotation.

Letter to Pompeius is an answer to the correspondent's criticism and request. It gives Dionysius opportunity to reprint in one place some pertinent passages from his essays, and to supplement the portion on Plato with additional comments.

In the *Letter to Ammaeus II* we learn that Ammaeus has criticized Dionysius' treatment of the language of Thucydides. Dionysius answers that he thinks that he has sufficiently dealt with the subject. He writes,

> I have in fact previously treated the subject in the essays inscribed with your name, on the Ancient Orators, and a little time before in the treatise on Thucydides himself which I address to Aelius Tubero. . . . (131)

Ammaeus' point is that Dionysius' criticism of Thucydides would be more precise if he would arrange his material by putting the illustrations with each point of criticism as he lists it. Dionysius continues,

> In order that the argument may be easy for you to follow, I will first quote word for word what I have previously said with regard to the historian, and will then cursorily review each several proposition, and will supply the illustrations as you desire. (133)

The body of the letter-essay is composed of a repetition of chapter 24 of the *De Thucydide* which summarizes the characteristics of the historian's style. Then point by point Dionysius repeats the criticism and adds the illustrations.

A similar situation, but one not so fully described, called forth *Letter to Ammaeus I*. A certain peripatetic philosopher had attempted to show that Demosthenes had learned the rules of rhetoric from Artistotle. Dionysius responded, " . . . I did not know what to think; and after careful reflection I felt that the matter needed a more attentive inquiry" (53). This mistaken notion had been communicated to Dionysius presumably by a letter from Ammaeus, and Dionysius would write to correct it. The answer is a series of arguments in refutation of the false statement. It reaffirms the writer's certainty of Demosthenes' independence of Aristotle as he has previously declared it. Now he will offer substantiating proof.

Plutarch

The selection of examples of letter-essays from Plutarch is somewhat complicated by the wide variety of his writings.[6] The characteristics of the letter-essay derived so far from Epicurus and Dionysius are the heading, the epistolary introduction, and the supplementary function.[7] However, in view of the frequency with which scribes omitted the heading on letters that characteristic may be considered expendable.[8] Three of Plutarch's pieces without a heading are therefore included. The epistolary introduction is the invariable criterion. Because of Plutarch's wide range of literary activity the supplementary function may be extended to include the use of the letter-essay as a substitute for another writing which the author has not had time or opportunity to produce.[9] Because of its obvious epistolary character the *Consolatio ad Apollonium* is also included although it is not supplementary or substitutive in any way that can be determined.[10]

Among Plutarch's *Moralia* are four pieces which have as superscriptions the common epistolary greeting. Each one also begins with a short epistolary introduction. The situations behind the letters are as follows:

Pollianus and Eurydice have just been married, and Plutarch would add to their nuptial song by sending them the *Coniugalia Praecepta,*[11] a collection of forty-eight pieces of advice for young married couples. Plutarch himself has made the collection, and he sends it to both as a gift. He writes:

> I have therefore drawn up a compendium of what you, who have been brought up in the atmosphere of philosophy, have often heard, putting it in the form of brief comparisons that it may be more easily remembered, and I am sending it as a gift for you both to possess in common. . . . (Babbitt).

There follows the collection of bits of advice and illustrative anecdotes. There are also personal references at the end (144–145) which are hardly fictional.

---

[6]Among Plutarch's works dialogs, orations, *quaestiones,* table talk, and the simple collections of precepts, are not closely related to the letter-essay. From the broad variety of writings which contribute to the letter-essay or reflect its influence the following should be listed from the *Moralia*:

a letter of consolation to his wife, 608 Bff.; unadorned essays, 93B; 97C; 100B; 164E; 502B; 515B; 523C; 528C; 536E; 599A; 776A; 779D; 827D; et al.; an essay expressedly dedicated, 478A *to syngramma touto . . . anatithēmi* (478B); essays incidentally dedicated (*in honorem*) by the use of the vocative of address in the opening sentence, 351C; 384C; 538A; 548A; 783A; 798A (see 813F); 945F; et al.

[7]The epistolary characteristics in body and closing will be listed below.

[8]The absence of a heading may be an accident of manuscript transmission. It is missing from numerous letters. See Hercher's edition passim.

[9]As will be noted later the letter-essay as supplement to another published work is more common in academic circles.

[10]The *consolatio* may be a genre in its own right. However, there is a marked difference between the *Consolatio ad Appollonium (Mor.* 101F) and the *Consolatio ad Uxorem* (608B). The latter is epistolary throughout and thus is not included in this chapter; the former is a collection of quotations strung together in an impersonal manner. In this way it is similar to the *Coniugalia Praecepta* and other of Plutarch's letter-essays, and thus it too may substitute for a more polished composition. See the discussion below on the style of the letter-essay.

[11]*Mor.* 138B–146A.

The second piece in the *Moralia*[12] which begins with a letter-heading sends greetings to the Emperor Trajan after which the writer continues, " . . . I beg that you will be good enough to accept . . . the utility which may be found in these brief notes . . . " (Babbitt). The "notes" are a collection of sayings gathered from the *Vitae* of Plutarch. By gleaning the sayings from the larger work in which they are interspersed with narratives and action, the writer hopes that the separate collection will make the sayings available, and " . . . serving, so to speak, as samples and primal elements of the men's lives, will not, I think, be any serious tax on your time, and you will get in brief compass an opportunity to pass in review many men who have proved themselves worthy of being remembered" (172 E, Babbitt).[13]

The *De Tranquillitate Animi*[14] is the third piece in this classification and was prepared after Plutarch received from Paccius a letter in which the correspondent requested Plutarch to write to him something on that subject. A mutual friend was about to leave for Rome. Plutarch did not have time to comply fully with the request, nor did he want the friend to return to Paccius empty-handed. Therefore, he wrote,

> I gathered together from my notebooks those observations on tranquillity of mind which I happened to have made for my own use, believing that you on your part requested this discourse, not for the sake of hearing a work which would aim at elegance of style, but for the practical use in living it might afford. . . . (Helmbold)

The fourth piece to which Plutarch added epistolary heading and introduction is entitled *De Animae Procreatione in Timaeo.*[15] It was prepared for his sons to whom he wrote:

> Since you think it necessary for me to gather together the things I have said and written at many times and places and in various articles explaining Plato's opinion about the soul as I understand it, and since you think this discourse ought to have its own write-up . . . I shall begin by quoting the lines from the *Timaeus. (Moralia* 1012 B)

The rather involved and lengthy compilation follows.[16]

Three other writings in the *Moralia* lack the formality of a letter heading, but since they have other characteristics of letter-essays they are in-

---

[12]*Regum et Imperatorum Apophthegmata Mor.* 172B–208A. The authenticity of this piece is not beyond question, but it adds its evidence to the study of the letter-essay regardless of authorship.

[13]After the epistolary introduction the sayings follow immediately without any transitional sentence or closing. The *Moralia* includes other collections of sayings, but none has a heading or introduction: 194Eff. (of Romans), 208Bff. (of Spartans), 240Cff. (of Spartan Women).

[14]*Mor.* 464E–477.

[15]*Mor.* 1012B–1030C.

[16]See the appended "epitome" 1030C–1032.

cluded here. The *De Capienda ex Inimicis Utilitate*[17] is a supplement to another essay by Plutarch. He says:[18]

> Some thoughts, therefore, on this subject, which I recently had occasion to express, I have put together in practically the same words, and now send them to you, with the omission, so far as possible, of matters contained in my *Advice to Statesmen,* since I observe that you have that book close at hand. (86 C, Babbitt).

Plutarch is saying that the content of the letter had recently been delivered perhaps as an oral address, but it is now recorded for Cornelius Pulcher as a supplement to the writer's essay, *Praecepta Gerendae Reipublicae,*[19] which Cornelius has admired.

The *Consolatio ad Apollonium*[20] is a lengthy collection of quotations gathered and sent to comfort the recipient after the death of a son. It has the formal epistolary introduction and closing. It is a collection of *praecepta* sent as a gift very much like the *Coniugalia Praecepta,* and like that piece may be thought of as substituting under the immediate circumstance for a writing of higher literary quality.

The letter-essay *De Fato*[21] is substitutive in the sense that it is a preliminary outline of the subject, the fuller treatment of which must wait for a later time. The author, who was not Plutarch,[22] states in the epistolary introduction that he will try to send to Piso his views on fate in as clear and concise a form as possible. And in closing he says:

> I have dealt with these matters thus briefly in order to present the main headings of the topic of fate in a compendium form; these we must investigate when we subject the two arguments to exact scrutiny. The details that come under these headings we shall enter into at some later time. (574 F, De Lacy and Einarson)

The Old Testament Apocrypha

2 Maccabees. The original epistolary introduction to 2 Maccabees is obscured by the fact that the beginning has been removed in part, and two introductory letters of uncertain origin have been prefixed to the work. However, a portion of the writer's preface remains in 2:19–32.

The work is an epitome (2:26, 28). The epitomist explains that from the five books of the historian Jason of Cyrene he has abridged the

---

[17]*Mor.* 86B–92F.

[18]The Greek text is quoted in Part II, B, 3 below.

[19]*Mor.* 798A–825F. This essay is itself a collection of *Praecepta* dedicated by means of the simple vocative of address.

[20]*Mor.* 101 F–122A.

[21]*Mor.* 568B–574F.

[22]"The writer, evidently a Platonist, is apparently either a teacher or fellow student of the unknown Piso to whom the treatise is addressed. . . . Our treatise, then, was probably not written before the first decades of the second century," De Lacy–Einarson, *Plutarch's Moralia,* 303f.

account of the Maccabean revolt. One of his expressed purposes is
to ease the task for those who desire to memorize the facts (2:25).
The rest of the work is the story of the revolt, broken once by an address to the readers (6:12ff.), and ending with a short closing statement.

The Apostolic Fathers

The Martyrdom of Polycarp. This work is a contemporary account
of the martyrdom of Polycarp, and the first of its kind remaining to
us from the early church. It is addressed from the church at Smyrna
to the church at Philomelium. It begins with an epistolary heading
and introduction, after which the death of the bishop is told as a
straight narrative account. The epistolary mode is resumed in the
closing (ch. 20).
    The letter is an instruction and an example in the way of the
martyr.

> For one might almost say that all that had gone before happened in order
> that the Lord might show us from above a martyrdom in accordance with
> the Gospel. For he waited to be betrayed as also the Lord had done, that we
> too might become his imitators. . . . (1, 1–2. Lake)

The closing gives the only information of the substitutive role of this
piece as the writer conceived it. He wrote: "You, indeed, asked that the
events should be explained to you at length, but we have for the present
explained them in summary by our brother Marcion: therefore when you
have heard these things, send the letter to the brethren further on . . ."
(20, 1. Lake). The church had asked for a full account, but the writer has
supplied what he calls a short one. He gives no explicit reason, but the
sentence which follows implies that he has prepared this condensed account at a length suitable for reading in the churches. It is in this sense
a substitute for the whole story; it also is an epitome.
    Fifteen pieces have been gathered to represent the letter-essay. They
come from writers in varying fields of interest and living in different centuries and centers of Hellenistic culture. They have a common functional
character. They are all in some manner or degree instructional, and they
are supplementary to another writing, or they substitute for one projected
but not completed. Other examples might be included,[23] but these form

---

[23]For writings of Plutarch related to the letter-essay see n. 6 above. No true letter-essay
is found in the works of Lucian, though its influence is observable. He appears to have further
developed the personal essay out of the letter-essay. Two of his pieces begin with short introductory letters, and another is designated for a friend. The epistolary confrontation, the
challenge and response resulting from a genuine request, is missing. And none of the pieces
is supplementary to another writing. The three pieces are: *Nigrinus*, a dialog beginning with
a short introductory letter; *The Passing of Peregrinus*, a short opening letter, Lucian to Cronius, passes without a closing (3) into the account. Cronius is again recognized at the end
(45); *Alexander the False Prophet*, more closely approximates the letter-essay; it includes:
dedicatory introduction to Celsus giving reason for writing and plan of the work (1–2); *men*

a fair sampling and are sufficient to represent the field. Further observations must be made concerning the function of the letter-essay, but first it is necessary to inquire into the more basic questions about its form, content, and style. If some consistency is found also in the characteristics, then the letter-essay may be classified as a distinct form.

For the sake of ease in reference in the rest of this article, the letter-essays are designated by author and number as follows:

Epicurus	1. *Letter I, to Herodotus.* Diogenes Laertius 10.35–83. R. D. Hicks, *Diogenes Laertius. The Lives of Eminent Philosophers* (LCL, Vol. II, 1950).
Epicurus	2. *Letter II, to Pythocles.* ibid. 10.84–116.
Epicurus	3. *Letter III, to Menoeceus.* ibid. 10.122–135.
Dionysius	1. *Letter to Ammaeus* I. W. Rhys Roberts, *Dionysius of Halicarnassus. The Three Literary Letters* (Cambridge, 1901). References are given to page and line.
Dionysius	2. *Letter to Pompeius.*
Dionysius	3. *Letter to Ammaeus II.*
Plutarch	1. *Coniugalia Praecepta. Moralia* 138 B–146 A. F. C. Babbitt, *Plutarch's Moralia* (LCL, Vol. II, 1928).
Plutarch	2. *Regum et Imperatorum Apophthegmata. Moralia* 172 B–208 A. F. C. Babbitt, op. cit. Vol. III.
Plutarch	3. *De Tranquillitate Animi. Moralia* 464 E–477 F. W. C. Helmbold, *Plutarch's Moralia* (LCL, Vol. VI. 1939).
Plutarch	4. *De Animae Procreatione in Timaeo. Moralia* 1012 B–1030 C. C. Herbert, *Plutarchi Moralia.* Vol. VI, 1 (Leipzig: Teubner, 1954).
Plutarch	5. *De Capienda ex Inimicis Utilitate. Moralia* 86 B–92 A. F. C. Babbitt, op. cit. Vol. II.
Plutarch	6. *Consolation ad Appolonium. Moralia* 101 F–122 A. ibid.
Plutarch	7. *De Fato. Moralia* 568 B–574 F. P. H. DeLacy and B. Einarson, *Plutarch's Moralia* (LCL, Vol. VII, 1959).
Mar. Polycarp	*The Martyrdom of St. Polycarp, Bishop of Smyrna.* Kirsopp Lake, *The Apostolic Fathers* (LCL, Vol. II, 1950).
2 Macc.	2 Maccabees. Alfred Rahlfs (ed.), *Septuaginta*, Vol. I (Stuttgart, 1935). *The Apocrypha of the Old Testament* (Revised Standard Version, New York, 1957).

---

oun (2) . . . *proteron* (3); direct address (17, 21, 32f.); conclusion including direct address and expression of hope that the work will be pleasant and helpful to Celsus and other readers (61). However, this tale was not written in response to a request nor was it in any way dependent on another writing. The letter-essay has become a personal essay written for a friend. For other writings approximating letter-essays see: Hipparchus Astronomus. C. Manitius (ed.) *In Arati et Eudoxi Phaenomena commentariorum libri tres* (Leipzig, 1894 [T]); Jos., *Ag. Ap.* (1.320; 2.296); Athenaeus Mechanicus. Schneider, *Griechische Poliorketiker III*; Apollodorus, *Poliorc.* 137.1. Schneider, 11:1 (Berlin, 1908). The Letter of Aristeas.

II. Form and Content

The analysis of the form and content of the letter-essays falls into the following divisions:

A. Heading

B. Epistolary introduction

C. Transition from introduction to body

D. Body

E. Closing.

The subdivisions under these headings have been determined from the pieces themselves, and the appropriate phrasing or cross reference thereto has been supplied for each piece. English translations have been quoted except where the Greek text is necessary in part or in whole.

A. Heading

The customary epistolary form is used: "Writer to reader chairein (eu pratten)." It has been removed from the epitomist's introduction to 2 Macc., and replaced by a Christian greeting on Mar. Polycarp. Several pieces by Plutarch which do not have the heading are included because they have the other epistolary characteristics, and the heading seems to have been often expendable in the gathering and editing of letters. (See the numerous examples in Hercher, *Epistolographi Graeci.*)

B. Epistolary Introduction

1. A statement of the theme of the letter and an acknowledgment of the request or need which called it forth.

a. Request received by letter: Epicurus 2; Dionysius 2; Plutarch 3. e.g. "It was only very recently that I received your letter in which you urged me to write you something on tranquillity of mind . . . " (Plutarch 3. Helmbold).

b. Request received by means not disclosed: Dionysius 1 and 3; Plutarch 4 and 7; Mar. Polycarp (see 20,1). e.g. "Our age has produced many strange paradoxes; and among them I was inclined to class the following proposition when I first heard it from yourself" (Dionysius 1. Roberts).

c. The theme selected on the author's own initiative and prepared for the benefit of the recipient: Epicurus 1 and 3; Plutarch 1, 2, 5, and 6; e.g. Epicurus 1. See quotation in section 2 below.

d. No statement in the remnant of the introduction to 2 Macc.

2. The writer's response to the request or need including a statement of cause or purpose and often the presupposition of his work:

Epicurus 1. Epicurus discusses in detail purpose and principle (Diogenes Laertius 10.35–36), and ends the introduction: "Therefore, since such a course is useful to all who are engaged with natural science, I . . . have composed for you such a brief compendium of the chief principles of my teaching as a whole" (ibid., 10.37. Geer).

Epicurus 2. "We will then complete our writings and grant all you ask. Many others beside you will find these reasonings useful. . . . So you will do well to take and learn them . . . " (ibid., 10.85. Hicks).

Epicurus 3. "For no age is too early or too late for the health of the soul. . . . Therefore, both old and young ought to seek wisdom. . . . So we must exercise ourselves in the things which bring happiness . . . " (ibid., 10.122. Hicks).

Dionysius 1. "Our age produced many paradoxes; and among them I was inclined to class the following proposition when I first heard it from yourself." The proposition was that Demosthenes learned the rules of rhetoric from Aristotle, "and after careful reflection I felt that the matter needed a more attentive inquiry." . . . "This I have done, my dear Ammaeus, out of regard not only for the truth, which I think ought to be fully sifted in every issue, but for the satisfaction of all who are interested in civil oratory" (53, 55. Roberts).

Dionysius 2. A correspondent has expressed dissatisfaction with Dionysius' criticism of Plato. Dionysius discusses the principles of criticism and states the one especially applicable to his answer. He says, a writer "ought to apply the most rigorous investigation and to take account of every quality whether good or bad. For this is the surest way of discovering truth . . . " (91. Roberts).

Dionysius 3. "Desiring, therefore, to meet every criticism, I have taken this course, and have followed the didactic method in place of the epideictic" (133. Roberts).

Plutarch 1. "Of the many admirable themes contained in philosophy, that which deals with marriage deserves no less serious attention than any other. . . . I have therefore drawn up a compendium . . . putting it in the form of brief comparisons that it may be more easily remembered, and I am sending it as a gift . . . " (138 C. Babbitt).

Plutarch 2. " . . . I beg that you will be good enough to accept . . . the utility which may be found in these brief notes. . . . [The sayings] will not, I think, be any serious tax on your time, and you will get in brief compass an opportunity to pass in review many men who have proved themselves worthy of being remembered" (172 C. E. Babbitt).

Plutarch 3. The writer makes a long statement, rhetorically patterned including the citing of authority and analogy (465 A-C).

Plutarch 4. On his sons' suggestion Plutarch will gather in one monograph his studies on Plato's opinion about the soul (1012 B).

Plutarch 5. Cornelius Pulcher has assumed a political office, and Plutarch sends him advice (86 B).

Plutarch 6. "I shall endeavor to send you my views on fate in as clear and concise a form as possible, dear Piso, since you have asked this of me although not unaware of my scruple about writing" (568 C.; De Lacy and Einarson. See 574 F in part I).

2 Macc. "For, in view of the flood of statistics and the difficulties presented by the mass of material to those who desire to go into the narratives of the history, we have aimed at attracting those who are fond of reading, at smoothing the path for those who like to memorize their facts, and at being of some service to our readers in general" (2:24–25). "Still, to reap the gratitude of many, we will cheerfully undertake this toilsome labour; leaving the historian to investigate details, we will exert ourselves to prepare an epitome upon the usual lines" (2:28. Charles).

Mar. Polycarp. "You, indeed, asked that the events should be explained to you at length, but we have for the present explained them in summary by our brother Marcion. . . . " (20, 1. Lake).

3. The writer's statement of the method or manner of presentation:

Epicurus 1. "I have prepared for you such an epitome and a manual of my whole exposition." (Diogenes Laertius 10.37).

Epicurus 2. "You request a short, well arranged statement," (ibid., 10.84. See the paragraph on the "scientific method," 87–88. The careful arrangement is effected by an index listing. See D, 2 below.)

Epicurus 3. The method or manner of presentation is not explicitly described. It is implied in the sentence, "Observe and cherish the things I have constantly set before you and consider them the basic elements of the good life. First of all . . . " (ibid., 10.123).

Dionysius 1. fully discussed, p. 54, 4–56, 18. (See part I above.)

Dionysius 2. fully discussed 88–96. (See part I above.)

Dionysius 3. p. 130, 14–132, 5. See quotation in section B, 2 above.

Plutarch 1. See quotation in B, 2 above.

Plutarch 2. The compilation of sayings has been gleaned from the *Vitae*, (172 C), and "the sayings have been gathered into a separate collection to serve as examples and nuggets of the lives." (172 E)

Plutarch 3. "I selected from the note-books which I happen to have made for myself these notes on tranquillity." (464 F)

Plutarch 4. "First therefore I shall set forth the opinion I hold about these matters relying on the reasonable, and reconciling, as far as I am able, the unusual and the paradoxical; then I shall quote the words of the text and combine exegesis and proof." (1014 A)

Plutarch 5. "I have complied and sent to you in almost the same words some things I recently had occasion to say on this subject. I have omitted as far as possible the things I wrote in my *Advice to Statesmen* since I often see you with that book in hand." (86 C-D)

Plutarch 6. "[Since time has passed] I have thought it proper to share with you words of comfort. . . . " (102 B, see 121 E)

Plutarch 7. See quotation in section B, 2 above.

2 Macc. See quotation in section B, 2 above and the continued discussion in 2, 29–32.

Mar. Polycarp. See quotation in section B, 2 above.

4. The direct address

a. The second person singular personal pronoun or finite verb form (pl. Plutarch 1,4):

In all pieces the pronoun is found in the introduction with one exception. The exception is the lone verb, *oiesthe*, in Plutarch 4 (1012 B). The expendable nature of this verb shows how much of a formality the personal reference may become.

b. The vocative:

The vocative case used in reference to the recipient is found in: Epicurus 1; Dionysius 1, 2; Plutarch 2, 5, 6, 7; Mar. Polycarp 1,1. For evidence of its use in marking the terminus of the body of a letter-essay, see below.

c. The second singular imperative:

Epicurus 2, 3, Plutarch 7, (Epicurus 1, *dei* + infinitive).

d. See the prefixed letters on 2 Macc. 1:2–9; 2:16.

C. Transition from Introduction to Body.

A formal pattern is observable. It is built on the phrase, *prōton men oun*, or some variation thereof.

prōton men oun: Epicurus 1 (Diogenes Laertius 10.37), Epicurus 2 (ibid., 10.85), Plutarch 5 (87 B), Plutarch 7 (568 C).

prōton oun: Plutarch 4 (1014 A).

prōton men: Epicurus 3 (Diogenes Laertius 10.123).

men oun . . . prōton men: Plutarch 3 (465 C).

prōton: Dionysius 1 (p. 56 15).

men oun: Dionysius 3 (p. 136, 18), Mar. Polycarp 2, 1 (cf. 20, 1).

oun: Dionysius 2 (p. 88, 18), see *men oun . . . loipon d'* p. 96 11, 14.

tote men oun . . . epeidē oun kai . . . kai: Plutarch 6 (102 A).

enteuthen oun: 2 Macc. 2, 32

The phrase is, of course, not exclusively epistolary. Plutarch, for example, uses it for the transition to the "body" of an essay, *Moralia* 16 A; 93 E; 798 C; 855 B. For its use see J. D. Dennison, *The Greek Particles* (Oxford, [2]1959), 470ff. See the similar use of WK'th "and now," in the letters collected in, G. R. Driver, *Aramaic Documents of the Fifth Century B.C.* (rev. ed. Oxford, 1965); Yohanan Aharoni, "Arad: Its Inscriptions and Temple," *BA.* 31 (1968), 2ff.; see pp. 11–13.

D. Body

1. The use of person in the composition of the body of the letter-essay:

a. Composition in the third person uninterrupted by parentheses of a personal nature or by personal reference to the recipient:

Epicurus 1, 2, Dionysius 3, Plutarch 1 (but see 145 Aff.), Plutarch 2, 4, 5 (the second person in 88 C–D is influenced by the construction in the quotation in 88 C), Mar. Polycarp.

b. Composition in first and third persons interrupted by personal references:

Dionysius 1, Plutarch 7.

After the introductions (long in Dionysius 1, p. 52–56, 18; a few lines in Plutarch 7) the writers vary the third person with the first person singular and plural including the hortatory subjunctive or its equivalent. Even in the short closings neither writer reverts to the second person of the introduction. (See the exception and the parenthesis acknowledging Piso in Plutarch 7, 569 A-C.)

c. Other patterns in the use of person inducing a more epistolary-personal, "I-thou" reference:

Dionysius 2 intermingles epistolary-personal references with the impersonal attitude necessitated by the incorporation of previously written essays into the body of the letter-essay. In Part I (pp. 88–96) Dionysius counters, person to person the attack by his correspondent. In Part II (pp. 96–104) the writer quotes a long section from another work, at the end of which he again confronts his critic by repeated references to the letter which he had received from him (p. 102). Part III begins with an acknowledgment of Pompeius' request for the critic's views regarding Herodotus and Thucydides (p. 104), and the rest of the letter (pp. 104–26) is consistently impersonal. There is not even a pause when the writer adds his views of other historians (but see p. 104, 16–19), nor does he acknowledge Pompeius in the short closing.

In Plutarch 3 the otherwise unbroken accumulation of quotations, gnomes, and anecdotes is once interrupted by what is almost a digression. The second person singular appears in 467 Dff., but its first appearance is rhetorical, because the questions used for illustration of misfortune (Are you childless? Has your wife been unfaithful?) are hardly the type which Plutarch would use publicly to quiz a friend. It does, however, lead to a specific reference to Paccius marked by the intensive pronoun (. . . *ouch hēkista moi dokeis kai autos epitarattomenos . . .* 468 B) and finally to the vocative—almost as if marking the close of the letter-essay *(all' hora, phile Pakkie . . .* 468 E). (See the use of the vocative in closing below.)

After this Plutarch resumes to the end of the piece the withdrawn position with the remark: *hothen ekeinon authis ton peri tōn pragmatōn logon analabōmen.* (468 E). In Plutarch 6, similarly, the quotations from literature sent for consolation to Apollonius are generally treated in an impersonal manner. Within the body once the recipient is acknowledged by name (119 E). Otherwise the few appearances of the first and second person singulars are hardly more than stylistic reliefs from the wearisome third person (107 A; 109 D). One might expect a *consolatio* to be more personal, as is the case with Plutarch's letter of consolation to his wife *(Moralia* 608 A), pseudo-Plato, *Axiochus,* and Seneca.

In Epicurus 3 the body of the letter is more epistolary-personal than in any other of the examples. The second person of the introduction is continued through the use of the imperative into the body of the letter-essay (Diogenes Laertius 10.124). Then the writer changes to the first person plural including the hortatory subjunctive or equivalent (127–132). A rhetorical question in the second person singular (133) focuses attention again on the addressee and leads to the closing admonition, again in the imperative second person singular (135).

The body of material in 2 Maccabees as is fitting for a historical account is written in the third person. However the epitomist himself at one point breaks the abridged narrative by an address to the reader (third person): "Now I beseech those who read this book . . . " (6.12). This singular occurs again in the conclusion. In both places it contrasts strangely with the first person plural of the various letters which serve as introduction (1:1 and 10; cf. 1:18; 2:16–18; 2:15f. and 32. These plurals are presumably used because of the multiple senders named in the letters. (See also 6:15–16.)

2. Arrangement of material

In Epicurus 2 each subject is announced by the noun at the beginning of the paragraph (indexed listing):

kosmos (Diogenes Laertius 10.88)

hēlios te kai selēnē kai ta loipa astra (90)

to de megethos hēliou (91)

tropas hēliou kai selēnēs (93)

kenōsis te selēnēs kai palin plērōsis (94)

ekleipsis hēliou kai selēnēs (96)

Plutarch's *Coniugalia Praecepta* is similarly arranged for easy reference but not so regularly nor unimaginatively as Epicurus' scientific letter. A catch word or phrase begins each paragraph. For example:

hoi philomousio tōn basileōn (140 C)

Lakaina paidiskē (140 C)

idious ou dei philous ktasthai tēn gynaika (140 D)

ho Platōn phēsin (140 D)

philoploutos hē Helenē (140 E)

ho Rōmaios (141 A)

ho basileus philippos (141 B)

palin hē Olympias (141 C)

The admonitions and anecdotes of this piece are reportedly arranged *en tisin homoiotēsi bracheiais* (138 C), but of what these "short comparisons" consist is not clear, nor is any suggestion which presents itself consistently carried through (viz. one to bride, one to groom; see 145 A and B). Plutarch's *Apophthegmata Laconica (Moralia* 207 Aff.) is arranged alphabetically by personal names.

A different type of listing is effected in Epicurus 1 by a repetitious use of introductory particles dominated by *alla mēn kai* (8 times), and *kai mēn kai* (10 times).

The informality of accumulations of quotations, proverbs, anecdotes and the like is found in Plutarch's *De Tranquillitate Animi,* and *Consolatio ad Apollonium.* (See Isocrates, *Ad Demonicum* and *Ad Nicoclem.)*

Order is imposed by the parent work when the letter-essay is a commentary thereon (Dionysius 2) or an abridgment thereof (Epicurus 1, 2; 2 Macc.; Mar. Polycarp).

E. Closing

1. The following have no closing: Plutarch 2, 3, 4, 5.

2. The following have non-epistolary closings: Dionysius 1, 2; Plutarch 7; 2 Macc.

3. Epistolary closings (resumption of the direct address):

a. Second person singular personal pronoun or finite verb form:

Epicurus 1, 2, 3, Dionysius 3; Plutarch 1, 6; Mar. Polycarp (pl.). See Epicurus 1 for the extent of formalization. The pronoun and imperative formally introduce a comparatively long recapitulation of the introduction.

b. Vocative marking the beginning of the closing: Epicurus 1 (also in the transition); Epicurus 2: Dionysius 3; Plutarch 1, 6 (also at the beginning of the introduction).

c. Second person singular imperative: Epicurus 2, 3; Plutarch 6.

4. Other characteristics:

a. Admonition concerning profitable use of the material presented: Epicurus 1, 2, 3; Dionysius 2; Plutarch 6, 7 (for use in future treatment of the subject); Mar. Polycarp. 20, 1.

b. Recapitulation of introduction (even repetitious) and ending in rhetorical question: Plutarch 1.

c. Laconic: Plutarch 7.

d. *Q.E.D.:* Dionysius 1.

e. *Finis:* Dionysius 3; 2 Macc.

f. Note *tauta* in reference to body: Epicurus 1, 2, 3; Dionysius 2 (*houtoi . . . hoi syngrapheis*); Plutarch 6, 7.

Summary

The letter-essay usually begins with the letter-heading, though it is too often omitted in collecting and editing to be expected as a regular feature.

The distinguishing feature is the epistolary introduction. It regularly includes:

1. a statement of the theme of the letter, and

2. an acknowledgement of the request or need which called it forth;

3. the writer's response to the request including a fuller statement of purpose, and often the basis or presupposition of his work;

4. a description of the method or manner by which the work is presented.

The introduction is written in the grammatical forms based on the second person singular which acknowledge a correspondent and respond to him.

The transition from introduction to body is marked by a conventional use of *prōton men oun* or a variation thereof. The omission of a transition in Plutarch 1 and 2 causes an abrupt break and indicates how closely the introduction is approximating a "covering letter." The omission of a closing at the end of a letter-essay also reveals the same tendency (Plutarch 2, 3, 4, 5).

Thereafter the body of the letter is almost rigidly cast in the objective third person or editorial first person. The one full exception is Epicurus' *Letter III, to Menoeceus*. The partial exceptions emphasize by the awkward results the writers' preference for the objective position. For example, in *Letter to Pompeius*, Dionysius met the charges of his critic which had been sent by letter. This method of response required the I-thou setting which, however, is dropped as soon as possible, and the last portion of the work is altogether impersonal including even the formal closing. Another exception is in the *De Tranquillitate Animi;* Plutarch introduced the second person apparently incautiously. He made an epistolary digression out of it and almost apologetically remarked at its close, "But let us take up again the subject of the logos." (See D.1.c. above)

The arrangement of content in the letter-essay reflects the freedom customary in a letter. It varies from rubric listings to chance accumulations, and from order imposed by commentary on another document (see below) to a thematic development of subject matter.

The closings reveal no consistent pattern. Four writers in seven pieces add admonitions concerning the profitable use of the material. In half of the pieces the writers returned to some acknowledgement of the recipient of the letter. There is a noticeable tendency to use the vocative addressing the recipient to mark the transition from body to closing. But the closing may be omitted or reduced to a literary formality, stylistically non-epistolary and short. It is as if the writers felt little inclination to reestablish the I-thou letter-setting once it had been discontinued in the body of the letter.

It should be emphasized that there is not one bit of evidence which indicates that the letter-setting behind any one of these pieces is fictional. The letter-setting in each case is authentic. It is only minimized, after the introduction, in the progress of the author's thought.

III. Function and Style of the Letter-essay

A. The Supplementary or Substitutive Function

The supplementary function of the letter-essay was the characteristic which first led to the gathering of the fifteen examples. The letters have been more closely associated by the fact that they fall into a formal pattern consistent enough to distinguish the letter-essay as a distinct form in ancient epistolary literature. It is appropriate now to consider the writers' concept of the function and theory of these pieces, beginning with a fuller statement of their supplementary nature.

Both in regard to the supplementary character of the letter-essay and in regard to the writers' consideration of their style, Isocrates had already set the precedent.

Letter I of Isocrates is addressed to Dionysius of Syracuse (368 B.C.); *Letter IX* is addressed to Archidamus III shortly after that prince succeeded his father as one of the kings of Sparta (ca. 356 B.C.). Both letters state their theme: to persuade the ones addressed to lead a united Hellas against the Persians; both are incomplete. They were written in the period between the *Panegyricus,* 380 B.C. and the *Philippus,* 346 B.C., the two grand orations also on the subject of unification. Their fragmentary nature makes it impossible to determine their exact relationship to the *Panegyricus.* However, enough remains to show that they are thematically closely related to the oration. They presuppose the oration. They are directed toward the solution of a single, basic problem in Isocrates' whole plan and work. They address the problem of leadership in a move for unification specifically to Dionysius and Archidamus.

Following the *Philippus* Isocrates addressed two letters to Philip. They are short but complete. *Letter II* (342 B.C.) is a plea to the king not to risk his life in battle, and it contains a summary of the situation at Athens. Philip's leadership of a united Hellas is treated only indirectly. Nevertheless, the letter is rather too obviously supplementary to the *Philippus* of two years earlier. The writer acknowledges the relation by indirect reference to the oration at the beginning of the letter and by allusions throughout.

Letter III, the second one to Philip, was written in 338 B.C., shortly before Isocrates' death at the age of ninety-eight. It is openly a plea to Philip to assume the pan-Hellenic leadership. Isocrates specifically states at the beginning of the letter:

> I wanted to write to you about the things I think must be done after the peace. What I say is similar to what I have written in the oration but much shorter than that.

Isocrates refers both to the *Philippus* and to the *Panegyricus* at the close of this letter (III, 6).

Each one of these four letters of Isocrates is in its own way supplementary to one of the orations. Generally speaking, each serves to revive the subject and to direct its appeal to a particular recipient.

The idea of supplementation is explicitly expressed by Dionysius in his *Letter I to Ammaeus.* He argues that Demosthenes did not learn rhetoric from Aristotle. The orator's speeches were the product of instruction in other schools. "On this matter," says Dionysius, "I shall publish my views in a separate article for a study on that subject would be a major one which could not well be made a supplement to another publication. In the present work I shall try to make this fact clear, namely that . . . [Demosthenes had delivered most of his speeches before Aristotle wrote his Rhetoric]" (p. 56, 8–10). Dionysius denies the necessity of modifying or retracting his views concerning Demosthenes' independence of Aristotle. The reaffirmation and proofs merit only a supplement, an appendix, to his published studies. Such a *parergon* is the letter-essay.

In the same manner the other two letter-essays of Dionysius are appendices to published essays. In *Letter to Pompeius* the writer responds to a criticism of his treatment of Plato in *De Antiquis Oratoribus*, and he answers a request for his views on certain historians. The criticism is met by commentary on a quotation from the essay; the request is met by quotations from *De Imitatione*. In *Letter II to Ammaeus*, Dionysius also responds to a criticism concerning his methodology in the essay, *De Thucydide*. He repeats a chapter from that essay and experiments with his critic's suggestion for rearranging the commentary on it.

In a more formal academic circle, *Letter I* of Epicurus was to be used for aid in mastering the writings of Epicurus on the physical universe, and *Letter II* explicitly states that the letter-essay is a course prospectus supplementary to the text books on celestial phenomena and specifically intended for aid in memorization.[24] Second Maccabees is an abridged account of a longer work by another author and was intended to facilitate learning the facts about the historical event. The Martyrdom of Polycarp is a shorter account than that requested. It was prepared for reading in church and as a model for martyrdom.

Other pieces are supplementary in the sense of being subsidiary or substitutive. The *De Fato is* a preliminary outline prepared in anticipation of fuller treatment in the future (574 F). For a busy emperor a digest made up only of sayings gathered from the *Lives* will supply the best portion and still save time for one too busy to find leisure for reading (172 E). Plutarch could well use his notes on tranquillity of mind for a finished essay, but since his own tranquillity has been interrupted by the request from Paccius and by the pressure of time for using the service of a mutual friend as a letter-carrier, he collects his notes on the subject from his notebooks and sends them on (464 F).[25]

The fact is that all these letter-essays are related to another work, and, with the exception of the notebooks of Plutarch, the parent works are all of a higher literary order. In the case of those made up of collections of notes or preliminary studies like the *De Fato* the letter-essays substitute

[24]The source of *Letter III* of Epicurus is not disclosed. It is a summary of his teaching on ethics and likely drawn from other works (Diogenes Laertius 10.135).

[25]In Plutarch's *Coniugalia Praecepta* and *Consolatio ad Apollonium* nothing is said about sources nor the reason for using the letter-essay. In the former the collecting of advice to be sent as a wedding gift (138C) suggests a hurried preparation. See also *Mor.* 172C, Isoc. *Ad Demonicum* 2 and *Ad Nicolem* 7.

for the more polished essay which, were it completed, would also be written in a higher style.

B. Style

The writers of letter-essays themselves were aware that the plain style was appropriate for these works. This fact is disclosed by their own remarks and by the terms used in reference to the letter-essay.

Again reference is made first to a type of writing of Isocrates—the *protrepticus*. The type is represented by the *Ad Nicoclem*.[26] The recipient was the young king of Cyprus. The writings are nothing more than collections of ethical advice, the individual units being strung together in a formless series of quoted maxims and personal observations. In content and style, therefore, they are closely related to the letter-essay.

Fortunately Isocrates left his own description of these works. In the *Antidosis* he quotes at length from his other writings. He repeats portions of the *Panegyricus* and *On the Peace* (59, 66). The third quotation is from his advice *Ad Nicoclem,* and he introduces it by contrasting its composition with that of the orations which he had just quoted. He says:

> The one which is about to be produced before you is addressed to Nicocles of Cyprus, who at that time was kind, and is made up of advice to him as to how to rule over his people. It is not, however, composed in the same style as the extracts which have been read. For in them each part is always in accord and in logical connection with that which goes before; but in this, on the contrary, I detach one part from another, and breaking up the discourse, as it were, into what we called general heads, I strive to express in a few words each bit of counsel which I have to offer. But my reason for writing on this subject was that I thought my advice would be the best means of aiding his understanding and at the same time the readiest means of publishing my own principles. *(Antidosis* 67–69; Norlin)

The disjointed composition of a collection of precepts does not permit stylistic niceties in the manner of a sustained composition.

Dionysius and Plutarch are also aware that the regularizing of a formal pattern demands a plain style.[27] Dionysius concedes to his critic's suggestion and rearranges a portion of his essay on Thucydides by following each point of criticism with an illustration. This results in a highly regularized pattern concerning which Dionysius remarks, "I have taken this course, and have followed the didactic method rather than the epideitic."

---

[26]See also the *Ad Demonicum* (mistakenly ascribed to Isocrates). For the general background and the contention with Aristotle see, Düring, *Protreptikos,* 19–24, 33–35, 173–175.

[27]Epicurus is notoriously indifferent to stylistic refinements and would hardly trouble himself about such matters. However, he suggests the need for the plain style in several phrases dealing primarily with form. *Letter* I consists of *kephalaiōdestata . . . epitetmēmena* (Diogenes Laertius 10.82); and *Letter II* is an *euperigraphon dialogismon* (84). The latter refers to the topics well marked and serially arranged. For *kephalaia* see Plu. *Mor.* 138C and 574F (supplied by Wyttenbach); Mar. Polycarp, 20, 1.

(*Letter to Ammaeus II*, p. 132, 3ff. Roberts). Plutarch apologizes for the condition of his notes, *De Tranquillitate Animi*. He has compiled them hastily from his notebooks and sent them on, as he says, "not for the sake of hearing a work which would aim at elegance of style, but for the practical use in living it might afford . . . "(464 F, Helmbold). The literary quality of a letter-essay is reduced by the use of a form and style which are suitable to the purpose at hand but which minimize the literary and aesthetic value.

The imposition of a regularized order and the resulting demand for a plain style is further evidenced by a linguistic study of the terminology used by the writers in reference to the letter-essays and to the parent works to which they are related.

Within the letters themselves[28] the word *epistolē is* used only once in reference to the letter-essay itself. The writer of the Martyrdom of Polycarp requested his readers to send the "letter" on to another congregation (20,1). His phrasing is likely influenced by the similar request made by Paul to the Colossians (4:16). Epicurus used the descriptive terms *epitomē, dialogismos;*[29] 2 Maccabees, *epitome.*[30] The compiler of the collection of sayings sent to Trajan called them *apomnēmoneumata,*[31] and Plutarch called *Coniugalia Praecepta* a collection, *kephalaia*, and sent it as a gift.[32] Otherwise the only word used with any consistency by the writers themselves in reference to their letter-essays is the neutral word *logos*. It is found in the following places:

> Isocrates, *Ad Demonicum* 2; see *protreptikous logous* 3; and *parainesis* 5.
>
> Plutarch, *Coniugalia Praecepta. Moralia* 138 B. *De Tranquillitate Animi. Moralia* 464 F. *Consolatio ad Apollonium. Moralia* 121 E. *(paramythētikos logos)*.
>
> Dionysius, *Letter to Ammaeus I, en tō paronti* (sc. *logō*) p. 56, 9f.
>
> Dionysius, *Letter to Ammaeus II*, p. 132, 6.
>
> 2 Maccabees 15:37

The word *epistolē is* avoided; preference is given to the generic and widely applied word, *logos*.

The writers also used descriptive terms for those writings to which their letters are related. These terms imply contrasts and similarities between the parent work and the letter which aid in further determining the author's intention in the employment of the letter-essay.

In *Letter to Ammaeus II*, Dionysius implies a differentiation between the letter-essay *(logos)* which he is writing and the previously published

---

[28]Occasionally other writers call one of these pieces an *epistolē* Diogenes Laertius 10.34, 83, 121.
[29]Diogenes Laertius 10.35, 37, 84, 85.
[30]2 Macc. 2:26 and 28.
[31]*Mor.* 172C.
[32]*Mor.* 138.

hypomnēmatismoi (De Antiquis Oratoribus)[33] and the *graphē (De Thucydide)* to both of which the letter-essay is related. *Hypomnēmatismoi* are written memoranda, anything from a shopping list, minutes, diary, class notes, to decrees and commentaries. That is, the idea of order or arrangement is uppermost, and the order is imposed by external factors but little subject to the writer's control. Here the word is best translated "commentary." The idea of following Thucydides' text and of listing characteristics of his style, and the order thereby imposed upon the essay, *De Antiquis Oratoribus*, account for its use.

Plutarch used the form *hypomnēmata* in referring to the notes (notebooks) from which he compiled the letter-essay, *De Tranquillitate Animi.* It too is a term for written memoranda, a little more general and common than *hypomnēmatismoi.* Plutarch apologized to Paccius. He wrote that he had gathered the notes " . . . believing that you on your part requested this discourse, not for the sake of hearing a work which would aim at elegance of style, but for the practical use in living it might afford" (*Moralia* 464 F, Helmbold).

Both Dionysius and Plutarch were referring to the larger work from which the letter-essays were drawn. The terms used for the parent work show that both writers were conscious of a restraint upon the arrangement and style of these parent works as compared with the free composition and originality of writings of another type. If this realization of limitation was felt for the works with which the letter-essays were closely related, it was also felt for the letter-essays themselves. This is what Dionysius meant in the last sentence of his introduction to *Letter to Ammaeus II.* He conceded to the request of his critic for the rearrangement of the composition with the words, "Desiring, therefore, to meet every criticism, I have taken this course [you suggested], and have followed the didactic method in place of the epideictic" (p. 132, 4f. Roberts). That is, what little freedom of style and form the writer had in making his commentary on Thucydides has now been curtailed by the demand for a further regularizing of a formal pattern.[34] Dionysius is to make of it a *didaskalikon schēma* a classroom lecture, arranged schematically. In this case the letter-essay is a degree more regularized than the *hypomnēmatismoi.*[35]

---

[33]Or, if it was a separate work, the reference should be to, *De Admiranda vi dicendi in Demosthene.* See chaps. 1, 9, 10; Roberts, *Demetrius*, pp. 6, 7, 31, 32. In *De Thucydide 1*, Dionysius refers to *De Imitatione* as *hypomnēmatismoi.* See, Pavano, *Dionisio.*

[34]The idea of the imposition of an order is seen also in the other two letters of Dionysius. In the manner of 1 Cor. they comply with a request or demand communicated to the writer from another person. The form of response is governed by the demand, and any declamatory style (epideictic) would be incongruous. Notice also the transitional phrase, *peri men . . . peri de,* in Letter to Pompeius *fin.* and Letter to Ammaeus II *init.;* cf. 1 Cor. 7:1, 25; 8:1; 12:1; and Faw, "First Thessalonians," 217–25. See also *Letter to Ammaeus* I, VII *init.,* VI *init.* In Isoc. *Philippus* 30, *peri d' autōn tōn pragmatōn,* marks the transition from the introduction to the presentation of the subject of the oration.

[35]In *Letter to Ammaeus II* (Roberts, *Demetrius,* p. 130, 15,) Dionysius also implies a contrast between his letter-essay and a *graphē (De Thucydide, De Antiquis Oratoribus).* The word

The writers of letter-essays recognized both in theory and in practice the subsidiary or substitutive function of the work. It was ancillary to other existing or projected writings. It served to correct mistaken conclusions drawn by others from previously written monographs, to experiment with the arrangement of the content of another work, to provide an epitome of a major study or a draft of one planned by the writer, to substitute for a more finished piece which the writer has not had time or occasion to produce. The subject of the letter is limited by its function in relation to its parent piece.

The writers also recognized the necessity for a restrained style. The style suitable to the letter-essay was the plain style, and it was often even more "plain" than that recommended by Demetrius for personal letter-writing.[36] In fact the author of the essay *De Elocutione* would applaud the restraint practiced both in subject matter and in style by the writers of the letter-essays. According to Demetrius the letter should be a little more studied in style than the dialog, and there are subjects suitable to personal letter-writing. On the other hand the letter should not be written in an elevated style, nor should its content be too lofty for this humble literary form. If the letter is so used, the results are rather *syngrammata* with *chairein* attached; and for illustration Demetrius offered the letter of Nicias in Thucydides' history and the philosophical portions of Plato's correspondence. The one is rhetorically stylized beyond suitable epistolary limits, and the others are philosophical speculations that should be recorded in an instrument better fitted for such writings.

IV. The Letter-setting

The letter-setting behind the letter-essay is triangular, I-thou-they. The triangle of persons is illustrated in Epicurus, *Letter I to Herodotus*, the introduction of which concludes with the triangular perspective: "Since this

---

graphē is customarily used in a general way for published writings, for works that are available for reference. Thus one speaks of "the writings of the philosophers" (LSJ). The word may refer to the division of a work, e.g., "the first book of Homer"; in Jewish circles, "the Scriptures." Thus Dionysius distinguished his letter-essay from the earlier treatments of the same subject now known and available for consultation and to which the letter-essay is closely related.

[36]See Grube, *Greek Critic,* 29. The more restrained style for letter-writing was recommended also by Apollonius (Hercher, 113f.).

In *ep.* 19 he named in fifth place the *hypomnēmatikos* (*sc. charaktēr*) as one of the *charaktēres tou logou*. The other four are the philosophic, historic, forensic, epistolary. They appear to be arranged in descending order according to the writer's idea of their literary merit. If so, he rated the letter between the primary classical forms and systematic reports. There appears to have been no consistent use of terms to distinguish systematic reports whose order was logical (scientific treatise, commentary) and those whose order was chronological (diary, minutes). Apollonius seems to have used *hypomnēmatikos* inclusively. Galen (16.532) defined *syngrammata* as systematic works as opposed to *hypomnēmata*. For *syngrammata* see in addition to LSJ, both the noun and the verb in Soc., *ep.* 15.2–3; *ep.* 22. To what kind of writing *hypomnēma* refers to in Archytas, *ep.* 1 cannot be determined.

method is useful to *all* studying natural science . . . *I* have made an epitome for *you*." The vocative addressing Herodotus follows in the transitional sentence. Thus the writer of the letter-essay holds both the "thou" and the "they" in mind.[37]

Not only is the content of the letter-essay made comprehensible to a third party, but it must also be made accessible to him. It must be made public. Publishing a letter-essay is especially important when it supplements a previously published work and when the writer must defend a position he has taken. So, for example, Ammaeus has informed Dionysius about the views of a certain peripatetic on the relationship between the works of Demosthenes and Aristotle. They are contrary to the published views of Dionysius. The latter must, therefore, either change his mind or, "induce the person who has adopted this view, and is prepared to put it in writing, to change it before giving his treatise to the world." And Dionysius will prove his own position, "not only for the truth . . . but for the satisfaction of all who are interested in civil oratory."[38]

Something of the official letter-setting influenced the setting of the letter-essay. The forthright inclusion of the third party in the triangular relationship underlying the letter-essay makes explicit in academic circles that characteristic which was often only implicit in public circles which formed the letter-setting of official communication. Public reading and the inscribing of official letters had long before made provision for the inclusion of the third person in the letter-setting. Like the official letter, the letter-essay was a publicly recorded statement, a position paper, issued by an authority. The publicizing of the letter-essay was much more academic; it was an article for a professional journal, a monograph written on request and dedicated *in honorem*. The letter-essay was developed and used in highly literate communities. It was instruction and argument *in writing;*[39] it was often supplementary to a previously *published* work. It was a supplement or substitute to other writing; the official letter and the personal letter were, on the other hand, extensions of oral communication.

In some ways the letter-essay is related to the personal letter. There is evidence that correspondence of a personal nature had previously existed between the writers and the recipients of some of the letter-essays. (See above Part II, B, a and b.) The relation between writer and recipient

___

[37]In Epicurus *Letter II, to Pythocles* the three person perspective is also found. The writer acknowledged the request from Pythocles, expressed his pleasure in complying, and added, "to many others also this work will be useful." The many others are neophytes and those wishing to pursue further the study of celestial phenomena.

[38]*Letter to Ammaeus I* (Roberts, *Demetrius*, p. 55). See Isoc., *Antidosis* 69, quoted above p. 200.

[39]"Epistles became not merely the ties knitting like-minded scholars together, but means of instruction, defence, and debate. In the treatment of scientific questions the epistle thus acquired a new role of its own. It accompanied and promoted the popularizing of knowledge" (Moffatt, *Introduction,* 48ff.).

behind each piece gives the impression of authenticity.[40] A real challenge to Dionysius caused him to rearrange his study of Thucydides' language. Plutarch sent the *Coniugalia Praecepta* as a wedding present to a newly married couple. In all the pieces the whole tenor of the introductions, greetings, personal references, as well as the freedom in organizing the content, indicate relationship to personal letter-writing. Also the restraint in style and content is in accord with that prescribed in the *De Elocutione*.

In the letter-essay the author acknowledges the relation to the recipient. But the subject of the letter-essay involves a third party. The content must be made clear and available to the third party. It is readily made available by publication as an "open letter." It is made clear by dropping the intimacies of private correspondence and by including in the introduction such items as were found above to be characteristic of the letter-essay: the reason for writing, the purpose and presuppositions of the work, the method or manner of presentation. In this way the third party is informed and drawn into the letter-setting.

It has been possible to establish the letter-essay as an epistolary category. It did not become a fixed genre; it was transitory, functioning for communication in highly literate circles. However, it was not considered as a type of writing worthy of such a designation as is implied by the English word "epistle," nor did its authors deem it worthy of the designation "literary." To the contrary it served a limited, substitutive, instructional function.

The isolation of the letter-essay leaves the designation, "literary letter," free for application to the letter of entertainment, to other fictional letters such as Lucian's "Correspondence with Cronus," and to the Latin *Epistulae*. In the literary letter the writers retained the I-thou letter-setting of the personal letter but wrote in such a manner as to make the content generally intelligible and anticipated preservation and publication, trusting in the literary merit of their writings.

---

[40]It should be noted that in the case of the *De Fato (Mor.* 568Bff.) the author and setting are unknown. It is generally thought not to have been written by Plutarch; it does not claim to be; it has no letter-heading. I find no cause to question the authorship of the letters of Epicurus.

PART

II

Section A
Historical and Sociological Factors

11

THE ROMANS DEBATE—CONTINUED

F. F. Bruce

The title of this lecture[1] was suggested by the title of a symposium edited by Karl Paul Donfried and published in 1977 as *The Romans Debate*.[2] This symposium brings together ten essays composed and published over the previous thirty years. The first of these essays originated as a lecture delivered by Professor T. W. Manson in the John Rylands Library in February 1948 and published in the Library's *Bulletin*, later in the same year, under the title "St. Paul's Letter to the Romans—and Others."[3] It seems, therefore, specially appropriate to devote this twenty-first Manson Memorial Lecture to the continuation of the debate.

The "Romans debate" is the debate about the character of the letter (including questions about its literary integrity, the possibility of its having circulated in longer and shorter recensions, the destination of chapter 16) and, above all, Paul's purpose in sending it. This lecture confines itself mainly to the last of these issues. With regard to other questions, suffice it to say that the lecture presupposes the literary integrity of the document (from Romans 1:1 to at least 16:23) as a letter addressed to the Christians of Rome, and the probability that a later editor (Marcion, it appears) issued a shorter recension of it which has influenced the textual tradition but has no relevance for our understanding of the original work or for the destination of chapter 16.

Since that symposium was published, further contributions have been made to the debate. A few distinguished new commentaries on Romans have appeared;[4] among them, in relation to our present subject, special

---

[1]The Manson Memorial Lecture delivered in the University of Manchester on 19 November 1981.

[2]Donfried, *Romans Debate*.

[3]Manson, "Letter to the Romans"; reprinted in T. W. Manson, *Studies in the Gospels and Epistles*, ed. M. Black (Manchester, 1962), 225–41.

[4]Cf. Cranfield, *Romans*; Käsemann, *Romans*; Schlier, *Der Römerbrief*; Wilckens, *Römer*.

mention should be made of Ulrich Wilckens's work in the Evangelisch-Katholischer Kommentar zum Neuen Testament. Apart from commentaries, there is an important monograph by Dr. Harry Gamble on *The Textual History of the Letter to the Romans*.[5] Here the various textual phenomena which Professor Manson discussed in his lecture of 1948 are reviewed afresh; the problem of chapter 16 is dealt with among others and answered—conclusively, in my judgement—in favour of a Roman destination. In fact I think that C. H. Dodd said as much as needed to be said on this subject in his Moffatt Commentary on Romans in 1932,[6] but Dr. Gamble has dotted the i's and crossed the t's of the case for Rome.

On several aspects of the Romans debate there is widespread agreement. When Paul dictated the letter he had completed ten years of apostolic activity both east and west of the Aegean Sea. In the great cities of South Galatia, Macedonia, Achaia and proconsular Asia the gospel had been preached and churches had been founded. Most recently Illyricum also had been visited. Paul now reckoned that his work in the eastern Mediterranean area was at an end: "I no longer have any room for work in these regions," he said (Rom. 15:23). He was essentially a pioneer, making it his ambition to preach the gospel where the name of Christ had never been heard before. But where around the Mediterranean shores could he find such a place in the later fifties of the first century? Paul was not the only Christian missionary in the Gentile world, though he was the greatest, and several Mediterranean lands which he had not visited had probably been evangelized by others. But Spain, the oldest Roman province after Sicily, Sardinia and Corsica,[7] remained unevangelized; Paul resolved that he would be the first to take the gospel there. To Spain, then, he turned his eyes.

A journey to Spain would give him the opportunity of gratifying a long-cherished desire to visit Rome. He had no thought of settling down in Rome: it was no part of his policy to build, as he said, on someone else's foundation[8] (we know what he thought about certain people who invaded his mission-field and tried to build on *his* foundation[9]). But a stay in Rome would enable him to enjoy the company of Christians in the capital and to renew acquaintance with a number of friends whom he had met elsewhere and who were now resident there. After his missionary exertions in the east, and before he embarked on a fresh campaign in the west, it

[5]Gamble, *Textual History*.

[6]Dodd, *Romans*, xvii–xxiv, 236–40.

[7]Spain was annexed and organized as two Roman provinces (Hispania Citerior and Hispania Ulterior) in 197 B.C., soon after the Second Punic War. Sicily was the first Roman province, annexed in 241 B.C., at the end of the First Punic War; Sardinia and Corsica were annexed shortly afterwards (238 B.C.), and were administered as one province from 231 B.C. to the beginning of the fourth century A.D.

[8]Rom. 15:20.

[9]Cf. 1 Cor. 3:10–15; 2 Cor. 10:12–16.

would be a refreshing experience to spend some time in Rome. No doubt there would be an opportunity, during such a visit, to exercise his ministry as apostle to the Gentiles.[10] But any converts that he made by preaching the gospel in Rome would be added to the Christian community already existing in the city: there was no question of his forming them into a separate Pauline church.

One thing only remained on his programme before he could fulfil this plan. He had to go to Jerusalem with the delegates of churches in his Gentile mission-field who were to hand over to the leaders of the mother-church their churches' contributions to a relief fund which Paul had been organizing among them for some years. When this business had been attended to, then, said Paul to the Roman Christians, "I shall go on by way of you to Spain" (Rom. 15:28).

This, then, as may be gathered from information given in the letter, was the occasion of Paul's writing to the Christians of Rome. The letter was sent from Corinth, early in (probably) A.D. 57.

But if the primary purpose of the letter was to prepare the Roman Christians for Paul's visit to them, how is that purpose related to its main content? This question, indeed, is the crux of the Roman debate, and an attempt will be made to answer it. In trying to answer it, we shall bear in mind that Paul, while dictating the letter, had three places specially in mind—Rome, the home of the people to whom the letter was addressed; Spain, where he planned shortly to inaugurate the next phase of his apostolic ministry; and Jerusalem, which he was to visit in the immediate future to complete a project very close to his heart. A consideration of these three places, one by one, should help us to come to terms with some important aspects of the Roman debate.

I. Three Prospective Visits

Rome

This document is, in no merely nominal sense, Paul's letter to the Romans—a letter addressed, in all its parts, to a particular Christian community in a particular historical situation. Communications between Rome and the main centres of Paul's mission-field were good, and Paul was able to keep himself informed, through friends who visited Rome or were now resident there, of what was happening among the Christians of the capital.

It is plain from Paul's language that the Christian community in Rome was large and active, enjoying a good reputation among churches elsewhere in the Mediterranean world.[11]

[10]Rom. 1:13–15.
[11]Rom. 1:8; 15:14.

The origins of Christianity in Rome are obscure. The words of the fourth-century commentator called Ambrosiaster are frequently quoted in this regard: "The Romans had embraced the faith of Christ, albeit according to the Jewish rite, although they saw no sign of mighty works nor any of the apostles."[12] We know too little about Ambrosiaster's sources of information to accept this as an authoritative statement, but it certainly agrees with such other evidence as we have, not least in relation to the Jewish base of early Roman Christianity.[13]

It is probable that Christianity reached Rome within a few years of its inception, given the degree of social mobility in the Roman Empire in those days. The people most likely to take it to Rome were Hellenistic Jewish Christians, members of the group in which Stephen and Philip played a leading part. The name of the Synagogue of the Freedmen in Jerusalem, with which Stephen was associated,[14] suggests a link with Rome (if the *libertini* in question were the descendants of Jews who were taken as captives to Rome by Pompey to grace his triumph in 61 B.C. and subsequently emancipated). The introduction of Christianity into the Jewish community of Rome was bound to lead to the same kind of disputes as its introduction into other Jewish communities; and if such disputes played their part in the constant tumults in which, according to Suetonius, the Jews of Rome were indulging (*adsidue tumultuantes*) in the principate of Claudius, we can understand his further remark that these tumults were stirred up by "Chrestus" (*impulsore Chresto*).[15]

We have ample evidence for the use of *Chrestus / Chrēstos* and *Chrestiani / Chrēstianoi*, in Latin and Greek alike, as misspellings for *Christus / Christos*, and *Christiani / Christianoi*.[16] It is about as certain as can be with such an allusion that the person referred to is Jesus Christ. Had he been another, otherwise unknown, bearer of the name Chrestus, Suetonius would probably have said *impulsore Chresto quodam*. It is not at all likely that

[12]Ambrosiaster, *Ad Romanos*, ed. H. J. Vogels (*CSEL* 81.1; Vindobonae, 1966) 6.

[13]This appears from non-literary (as well as literary) evidence, such as the indebtedness of early Christian catacombs to the Jewish catacombs of Rome (like that on Monteverde). As for literary evidence, the surviving influence of Jewish lustral practice in the Christian worship of Rome has been traced in Hippolytus, *Apostolic Tradition* 20.5, where a purificatory bath on Maundy Thursday is prescribed for those preparing to be baptized on Easter Day; cf. Werblowsky, "Baptismal Rite," 93ff.

[14]Acts 6:9.

[15]Suetonius, *Claudius* 25.4.

[16]Chrestus was as common a slave-name as its near-synonym Onesimus. For the incidence of Chrestus in Rome cf. *CIL* VI: 668, 880, 975, 1929, 3555, 7460, 7846, 11707, 14058, 14433, 14805, 20770, 21531, 22837, 26157, 28324, 28659, 37672, 38735. While Suetonius has the spelling *Chresto* here, he has *Christiani* in *Nero* 16.2. But in Tacitus, *Ann.* 15.44.3 the MS Mediceus 68.2 had originally (it appears) *Chrestianos*, which was corrected to *Christianos* by a later hand. Tacitus himself, however, may have spelled the word *Christianos*, since he links it closely with Christus ("auctor nominis eius"). In the NT the first hand in Vaticanus consistently shows the spelling *Chrēstianos*. The apologists exploit the confusion between the two forms: "We are accused of being *Christianoi* but it is unjust that one should be hated for being *chrēstos*" (Justin, *Apol.* 1.4.5).

the reference is to another messianic claimant, a rival Christ—e.g. Simon Magus (whose presence in Rome under Claudius is attested elsewhere).[17] There is no evidence that Simon Magus claimed to be the Messiah, and in any case a pagan writer would not have said *impulsore Chresto* if he had meant "at the instigation of a Messiah"—Chrestus for Suetonius was a personal name, as it was for pagans in general.

True, Jesus Christ was not in Rome during the principate of Claudius.[18] But Suetonius may well have understood his sources (wrongly) to mean that he was. Tacitus knew that Christ was executed under Tiberius,[19] but Suetonius had not the same concern for historical precision. If his sources told him that the rioting among the Jews of Rome was caused by disagreement about the claims of Christ, it was a natural, if mistaken, inference that Christ himself was in Rome at the time.

It was because of these riots, says Suetonius, that Claudius expelled the Jews from Rome. He does not date the expulsion edict: Orosius, early in the fifth century, says that it was issued in A.D. 49.[20] Orosius's inaccuracy in the very act of supplying this information does not inspire confidence, but the record of Acts makes A.D. 49 a probable date.[21] Luke says that, when Paul first visited Corinth, he met a Jew named Aquila, "lately come from Italy with his wife Priscilla, because Claudius had commanded all the Jews to leave Rome" (Acts 18:2). The reference in Acts 18:12 to Gallio as proconsul of Achaia during Paul's stay in Corinth enables us to date Paul's arrival in that city in the late summer of A.D. 50; it is therefore quite probable that Priscilla and Aquila left Rome the previous year.[22]

Since Paul, in his references to Priscilla and Aquila, never implies that they were converts of his own, the likelihood is that they were Christians before they left Rome—perhaps, as Harnack suggested, foundation-members of the Roman church.[23]

[17]Cf. Eisler, *Messiah Jesus*, 581. Judge–Thomas, "Church at Rome," 87, refer to Simon as "the most suggestive example" of the type of agitator in question. Simon's presence in Rome in the time of Claudius is mentioned by Justin (*Apol.*, 1. 26.2). An even more improbable identification of Chrestus than that with Simon Magus—namely, with James the Just—has recently been proposed by Thiering, *Gospels and Qumran*, 271.

[18]That he was indeed there at that time is argued by Graves–Podro, *Jesus in Rome*.

[19]Tacitus, *Ann.* 15.44.4. See n. 36 below.

[20]Orosius (writing A.D. 417–18) quotes Suetonius on the expulsion and says that Josephus dates the incident in A.D. 49 (*Hist.* 7.6.15f.). But there is no reference to the incident in the extant writings of Josephus.

[21]The question arises of the relation of the expulsion recorded by Suetonius to an action of Claudius dated by Dio Cassius (*Hist.* 60.6) to the first year of his principate: "When the Jews [sc. of Rome] had again multiplied to a point where their numbers made it difficult to expel them from the city without a riot, he did not banish them outright but forbade them to meet in accordance with their ancestral way of life." If this ban on meetings was later lifted, then perhaps Claudius, "annoyed that his relaxation . . . had led to a repetition of disorder, reacted more severely than before, this time with an expulsion" (Smallwood, *Jews under Roman Rule*, 215f.)

[22]Gallio's entry on the proconsulship is dated to A.D. 51 (if not earlier) by Claudius's rescript to the Delphians of A.D. 52 (*Sig* 2³, 801). Cf. Plassart, "L'inscription de Delphes," 372ff.

[23]Cf. Harnack, "Verfasser des Hebräerbriefs," 16ff.

In Claudius's expulsion of Jews, no distinction would be made between those among them who were Christians and the majority who were not. The expulsion could have gone far to wipe out the Roman church. But perhaps it did not wipe it out altogether. If in A.D. 49 there were some Gentile Christians in Rome, they would not be affected by the edict of expulsion. By A.D. 49 Gentile Christianity was firmly rooted in several cities of the eastern Mediterranean, and if in the eastern Mediterranean, why not also in Rome, to which all roads led from the imperial frontiers? We do not know this for certain: what we can say is that by the beginning of A.D. 57, when Paul sent his letter to the Roman Christians, the majority of them were apparently Gentiles.[24]

After the expulsion of Jews from Rome, if the course of events may be so reconstructed, the small group or groups of Gentile Christians in the city had to fend for themselves. But they continued to receive accessions of strength in the years that followed. They were probably not organized as a single city church, but existed as a number of separate house-churches, conscious nevertheless of the bond which united them in faith and love. Some of these house-churches, indeed, may have been associated with the imperial establishment. It is at a later date that Paul refers to "saints . . . of Caesar's household" (Phil. 4:22).[25] But the evidence of Romans 16:10f. suggests that there were Christians in some of the groups that made up "Caesar's household" of slaves and freedmen—among the *Aristobuliani*, for instance, and the *Narcissiani*.[26]

When, around the time that Nero succeeded Claudius in the principate (A.D. 54), the expulsion edict became a dead letter (like earlier expulsion edicts of the same kind),[27] Jews began to return to Rome, and Jewish Christians among them. Priscilla and Aquila seem to have returned soon after the end of Paul's Ephesian ministry (A.D. 55); their residence in Rome served as the headquarters of a house-church (Rom. 16:5) as their residence in Ephesus had done (1 Cor. 16:19). There were no doubt other Jewish house-churches added to the Gentile house-churches already existing. What kind of reception did these returning Jewish Christians meet with from their Gentile brethren? It is implied in Romans 11:13–24 that the Gentile Christians tended to look down on their Jewish brethren as poor relations. Paul, discussing the place of Jews and Gentiles in the divine purpose, warns his Gentile readers not to give themselves airs: even if they are now in the majority, they should bear in mind that the base of the church—of the Roman church as well as of the church universal—is Jewish.

[24]This is a reasonable inference from Rom. 1:13; 11:13.
[25]See *Bulletin* 62 (1980–81) 265.
[26]Cf. Dodd, *Romans,* xxii; Bruce, *Paul,* 386f.
[27]E.g., the expulsion under Tiberius in A.D. 19 (Josephus, *Ant.* 18.65, 81ff.; Tacitus, *Ann.* 2.85; Suetonius, *Tiberius* 36), ascribed by Philo (*Embassy to Gaius* 159ff.) to the malignity of Sejanus.

Caution must be exercised when evidence is sought in this letter for the state of the Roman church at the time of writing, lest we find ourselves arguing in a circle. It is all too easy to draw inferences from the letter about the state of the church, and then use those inferences to help us in understanding the letter.

Here, however, we have a letter from Paul explicitly addressed to the Christians of Rome: "to all God's beloved in Rome" (Rom. 1:7). True, there is one textual tradition which omits the phrase "in Rome" both here and in verse 15, but this omission cannot be original. The sense requires a place-name, and no other place-name than Rome will fit the context (this is no circular letter in which a variety of place-names might be inserted in a blank space left for the address). The omission of the reference to Rome can best be explained, as T. W. Manson explained it, by the supposition that Marcion struck it out, after his rejection by the Christian leaders in Rome, to show that in his judgement such a church did not deserve the honour of being addressed in a letter from the only true apostle of Christ.[28]

Paul writes to the Roman Christians, he says, because he hopes to pay them a visit soon. He had planned to visit their city on earlier occasions but had not been able to put those plans into action. One of the occasions he has in mind may have been the time when he first set foot in Europe. Having crossed the Aegean to Macedonia in A.D. 49, he found himself travelling from east to west along the Egnatian Way, evangelizing first Philippi and then Thessalonica. Had nothing interfered with his programme he might have continued his westward journey until he reached one of the Adriatic termini of the Egnatian Way, after which the natural course would have been to cross the Straits of Otranto to Brindisi and proceed along the Appian Way to Rome.[29] He was prevented from doing this by the riots which broke out in Thessalonica while he was there—*impulsore Chresto*, it might have been said there also, for he and his colleagues were charged with proclaiming "another emperor, namely, Jesus" (Acts 17:7). Paul was not only forced to leave Thessalonica and proceed no farther along the Egnatian Way; as he turned south he found that there was no place for him anywhere in Macedonia, and he was unable to settle until he reached Corinth, where he stayed for eighteen months.

But even if he had been left in peace to continue along the Egnatian Way, it would have been an inopportune time for him to visit Rome: it was just then that Claudius issued his expulsion edict. A visit to Rome must await a more convenient season, and early in A.D. 57 the way seemed more propitious for such a visit than ever it had been before.[30] The situation

[28]Manson, "Letter to the Romans," 226–29 (*Studies*, 227–30); see, however, Gamble, *Textual History*, 29–33, 100ff.

[29]Cf. Harnack, *Mission and Expansion*, 1:74f.; Cadbury, *Acts in History*, 60f.; Bornkamm, *Paul*, 51ff.; Judge–Thomas, "Church at Rome," 90.

[30]The date A.D. 57 is indicated by forward (from Gallio) and backward (from Festus) dating. By Pentecost of the year in which Romans was written Paul had arrived in Judaea; not

had changed: Nero was now on the imperial throne, halfway through his
first quinquennium, which was greeted, especially in the eastern provinces,
as a kind of golden age.

This, then, is the background to the letter, and there is general agreement that Paul sent it to prepare the Roman Christians for his prospective
visit. But why, it may be asked, did he send a letter with these particular
contents? He mentions his visit only at the beginning and at the end; what
is the relevance to the Roman Christians of the main body of the letter?

After his preliminary remarks about his occasion for writing, Paul
launches into a sustained and coherent statement of the gospel as he understood it, with special emphasis on the justifying grace of God, available
on equal terms to Jews and Gentiles (1:16–8:40). Then comes a careful inquiry into God's purpose in history, with particular reference to the place
of Jews and Gentiles in that purpose (9:1–11:36). Various ethical admonitions (12:1–13:14), including a problematic paragraph on the Christian's
relation to the state (13:1–7), are then followed by a particular paraenesis
on the mutual responsibilities of the "strong" and the "weak in faith" within
the Christian community (14:1–15:13). Next, Paul makes a short statement
about his activity as apostle to the Gentiles thus far (15:14–21), together
with an account of his plans for the immediate and subsequent future
(15:22–33). The letter comes to an end with the commendation of Phoebe,
who is taking it to its destination (16:1f.), and a series of greetings to twenty-
six individuals, who belong to at least five groups or house-churches (16:3–
15). Greetings are sent from "all the churches of Christ," presumably those
of the Pauline mission-field (16:16). A final admonition (16:17–20) is followed
by greetings from named individuals among Paul's present companions
(16:21–3), and by a benediction (16:24) and doxology (16:25–7) of disputed
authenticity.[31]

If we knew more about the current situation in the church of Rome,
it might be seen that the detailed contents of the letter are more relevant
to that situation than can now be established. But it will be rewarding to
look at the contents section by section.

As regards his lengthy statement of the gospel (1:16–8:40), it was in
any case expedient that Paul should communicate to the Roman Christians an outline of the message which he proclaimed. Misrepresentations
of his preaching and his apostolic procedure were current and must have
found their way to Rome. It was plainly undesirable that these should be
accepted in default of anything more reliable. Paul does not, for the most
part, refute those misrepresentations directly (there are a few incidental

---

long after his arrival he was detained in custody in Caesarea, and remained there for two
years, until Festus became procurator (Acts 24:27). There is numismatic evidence for dating
the accession of Festus in A.D. 59 (cf. Madden, *Jewish Coinage*, 153; Reifenberg, *Jewish Coins*,
27; see also Schürer, *History* 1:465, n. 42).

[31]See Metzger, *TCGNT*, 539–41; Gamble, *Textual History*, 121–24, 129–32.

allusions to them, as in Romans 3:8, *kathōs blasphēmoumetha*) but gives a systematic exposition, showing how, if the contemporary plight of mankind, Gentile and Jewish, is to be cured, God's justifying grace, without discrimination among its beneficiaries, is alone competent to cure it.

This exposition is carried on largely in terms of a debate or dialogue with the synagogue. Paul must have engaged in this kind of exchange repeatedly in the course of his preaching—what, for example, were the terms in which some members of the synagogue in Pisidian Antioch "contradicted what was spoken by Paul" (Acts 13:45)?—but it was probably relevant to the state of affairs in Rome. The rioting which attended the introduction of Christianity into the Jewish community of the capital some years previously was sparked off by arguments not dissimilar, perhaps, to those voiced in the Jerusalem synagogue where Stephen's teaching was first heard.[32] Paul's exposition of the new faith had different emphases from Stephen's, but was sufficiently like it to provoke the same kind of violent reaction, as indeed it did from one city to another.

Paul's gospel, we know, was charged with promoting moral indifferentism, if not with actively encouraging sin, and the form of his argument in this letter implies his awareness that this charge was not unknown in Rome: "Are we to continue in sin that grace may abound?" (Rom. 6:1). He makes it plain, therefore, that the gospel which he preaches is not only the way of righteousness, in the sense of the righteous status which God by his grace bestows on believers in Christ, but also the way of holiness, in which "the righteous requirements of the law are fulfilled in us who walk not according to the flesh but according to the Spirit" (Rom. 8:4).

The relation of chapters 9–11 to the plan of the letter as a whole has been much debated. It has been said that, if Paul had moved from the end of chapter 8, with its celebration of the glory which consummates God's saving work in his people, to the beginning of chapter 12, with its practical application of that saving work to the daily life of Christians, we should have been conscious of no hiatus. Yet Paul judged it fitting to grapple at this point with a problem which, as he confesses, caused him great personal pain.

Israel, the nation which God had chosen to be the vehicle of his purpose of grace in the world, had as a whole failed to respond to the fulfillment of that purpose in Jesus Christ. Paul was conscious of this as a problem for himself both on the personal and on the apostolic level. If in Israel's failure to respond he saw writ large his own earlier unbelief, that very fact brought hope with it; as his eyes had been opened, so his people's eyes would surely be opened. For this he prayed incessantly.[33] Indeed, if Israel's salvation could be won at the price of his own dam-

---

[32]Acts 6:9f.; see p. 178 above.
[33]Rom. 10:1.

nation, he would readily pay that price.[34] He would gladly have devoted his life and strength to the evangelizing of his people,[35] but he was specifically called to be Christ's apostle to the Gentile world. Yet he trusted that even by the evangelization of Gentiles he would indirectly do something for the advantage of his own people: they would be stimulated to jealousy as they saw increasing numbers of Gentiles enjoying the gospel blessings which were the fruit of God's promises to the patriarchs, and would wake up to the realization that these blessings were for them too— that in fact they should properly have been for them first, since they were the descendants of the patriarchs and the inheritors of those promises. This prospect enhanced the prestige of his apostleship as he contemplated it: "inasmuch as I am the Gentiles' apostle, I glorify my ministry in order to make my kinsfolk jealous and thus save some of them" (Rom. 11:13f.).

But it is not simply to share with the Roman Christians his concern for Israel and his appreciation of the significance of his apostleship that he writes like this. His theme is relevant to the situation in Rome. It is in this context that he warns the Gentiles among his readers not to despise the Jews, whether the Jews in general or Jewish Christians in particular, because God has not written them off. They continue to have a place in his purpose, and his purpose will not be completed until, with the ingathering of the full tale of Gentile converts, "all Israel will be saved" (Rom. 11:25f.). Gentile Christians must not pride themselves on the superiority of their faith, but remember that they are what they are only by the kindness of God. This will induce in them a proper sense of humility, and respect and understanding for their fellow-believers of Jewish stock.

The paragraph about the Christian's relation to the secular authorities (Rom. 13:1–7) is best understood in the light of the Roman destination of the letter. This is not a universal statement of political principle. The injunction to "render (apodote) to all their dues" (13:7) may indeed be viewed as a generalization of Jesus' precept: "render (apodote) to Caesar what belongs to Caesar" (Mark 12:17). That precept was addressed to a particular situation in Judaea, in face of a firmly held and violently defended doctrine that for Jews of Judaea to pay tribute to a pagan overlord was to take from God the things that were his and hand them over to another. That situation, of course, did not exist in Rome. But in generalizing the dominical precept Paul has in mind the situation which did exist in Rome and in other cities throughout the empire.

Eight years previously, it appears, the introduction of Christianity into Rome had led to riots. About the same time, according to Luke, the arrival of Paul and his fellow-preachers in Thessalonica provoked the charge that they were the men who had subverted the whole world and kept on

---

[34]Rom. 9:1–3.
[35]Cf. Acts 22:17–21, on which see Betz, O., "Die Vision des Paulus," 113ff.

"acting against the decrees of Caesar" (Acts 17:6f.). The name of "Christian" had subversive associations in Rome and elsewhere: some at least remembered that the founder of the movement had been executed by sentence of a Roman judge on a charge of sedition.[36] It was most important that Christians in the imperial capital should recognize their responsibility not to give any support by their way of life to this widespread imputation of disloyalty, but rather refute it by punctilious obedience to the authorities and payment of all lawful dues. Thus far the representatives of imperial law had, in Paul's experience, shown at least a benevolent neutrality to the prosecution of his mission.[37] The time was to come, and that in Rome itself, when this would no longer be so. When Caesar demanded the allegiance which belonged to God, his demand had to be refused. But Caesar had not yet done so, and Paul does not mention this eventuality. His approach to the matter is relevant to the situation of Roman Christians at the time and in the circumstances of their receiving the letter.

Equally relevant to the Roman situation is the practical section in Romans 14:1–15:7 in which Paul deals with the relation between the "strong" and the "weak" in the Christian fellowship—the "weak" being those who scrupulously abstained from certain kinds of food and paid religious respect to certain holy days, while the "strong" (like Paul himself) had a more robust conscience with regard to such externalities.

There is a degree of resemblance between what Paul says here and what he says to the Corinthian church on the issue of eating or avoiding the flesh of animals offered in sacrifice to a pagan deity (1 Cor. 8:1–13; 10:14–30). But in this section of the letter to the Romans there is no direct word about eating eidōlothyta (an issue bound to be acute in a mainly Gentile church like that of Corinth). The distinction here is rather between the believer who can, with a good conscience, eat food of any kind and treat all days alike, and the believer whose conscience forbids the eating of any but vegetable food and the doing of ordinary work (however normally legitimate) on a holy day. The principle of mutual considerateness which Paul inculcates in this section would, of course, cover the issue of eidōlothyta, but if Paul has one particular situation in mind here, it is a situation in which Jewish and Gentile Christians have to live together in fellowship. It was to such a situation, indeed, that the Jerusalem decree was addressed a few years before, but Paul takes a different line from the decree. The decree urged abstention from eidōlothyta and flesh from which the blood had not been completely drained;[38] Paul urges his readers to consider one another.

---

[36]Cf. the only mention of the trial of Jesus by a pagan author: "Christus Tiberio imperitante per procuratorem Pontium Pilatum supplicio adfectus erat" (Tacitus, Ann. 15.44.4).
    [37]Notably Gallio, who refused to take up a complaint against him at Corinth (Acts 18:12–16).
    [38]Acts 15:28f. Cf. Barrett, "Things Offered to Idols," 138ff.

It was not simply that Jewish Christians continued to confine themselves to kosher food and to observe the sabbath and other holy days, while Gentile Christians practised complete liberty in both respects. The situation was probably more complex. Many Jewish Christians had become more or less emancipated from legal obligations in religion, even if few were so totally emancipated as Paul was. On the other hand, some Gentiles were more than willing to judaize, to take over the Jewish food restrictions and Jewish regard for holy days, even if they stopped short at circumcision.[39] We have examples of this tendency to judaize in our own day, even if it is not expressly called judaizing; and in the apostolic age we have only to think of Paul's Gentile converts in Galatia, who were not only beginning to keep the Jewish sacred calendar but even to accept circumcision.

Among the house-churches of Rome, then, we should probably envisage a broad and continuous spectrum of varieties in thought and practice between the firm Jewish retention of the ancestral customs and Gentile remoteness from these customs, with some Jewish Christians, indeed, found on the liberal side of the halfway mark between the two extremes and some Gentile Christians on the "legalist" side.[40] Variety of this kind can very easily promote a spirit of division, and Paul wished to safeguard the Roman Christians against this, encouraging them rather to regard the variety as an occasion for charity, forbearance and understanding.

Instead of laying down rules which would restrict Christian freedom, Paul makes it plain that, religiously speaking, one kind of food is no worse than another, one day no better than another. It is human beings that matter, not food or the calendar. Christian charity, on the one hand, will impose no limitations on another's freedom; Christian charity, on the other hand, will not force liberty on the conscience of someone who is not yet ready for it. The scrupulous Christian must not criticize his more emancipated brother or sister; the emancipated must not look down on the over-scrupulous. The only limitation that can properly be imposed on Christian liberty is that imposed by Christian charity, and it can only be self-imposed. No Christian was more thoroughly emancipated than Paul, but none was readier to limit his own liberty in the interests of his fellow-Christians.[41] In such matters as abstention from food or observance of days he conformed to the company in which he found himself: in themselves they were matters of utter indifference.[42] This example he recommends to others. For the rest, they should do what they believe to be right without forcing their convictions on others or thinking the worse of others if they do not see eye to eye with them.

---

[39]Cf. Juvenal, *Sat.* 14.96ff.

[40]The varieties need not be demarcated so distinctly as in Minear, *Obedience,* 8ff., where five different outlooks are identified.

[41]Cf. 1 Cor. 8:13; 10:33; Rom. 14:14.

[42]Cf. 1 Cor. 9:19–23.

Spain

If Spain plays a less crucial role in the letter than either Rome or Jerusalem does, it is no merely peripheral one. Not only did Paul's plan to visit Spain provide him with an opportunity to gratify his long-cherished desire to see Rome, but it enabled him to invite the Roman Christians' collaboration in the next phase of his apostolic enterprise. It meant, moreover, that he could tell the Roman Christians of his plan to visit them without giving them cause to suspect that he was coming to put down his roots among them or assert apostolic authority over them. At the same time, by assuring them of his ardent longing to make their acquaintance he makes it plain that he does not simply see in their city a convenient stopping-off place on his way to Spain. Rome probably lay no less close to his heart at this time than Spain did.[43]

But why should he think of evangelizing Spain? If he judged his task in the Aegean world to be complete and wished to adhere to his policy of confining his ministry to virgin soil, his range of choice in the Mediterranean world, as has been said, was limited. By A.D. 57 the gospel had certainly been carried to Alexandria and Cyrene, if not farther west along the African coast. The close association between proconsular Asia and Gallia Narbonensis would suggest that the evangelization of the former territory in A.D. 52–55 led quickly to the evangelization of the latter. But Spain, for long the chief bastion of Roman power in the west, beckoned Paul as his next mission-field.

We have no idea what contact, if any, Paul may have had with people from Spain who could have told him something of conditions in that land.[44] One thing is certain: the language which had served him so well in his ministry hitherto, and served him equally well in his present communication with Rome, would not be adequate for the evangelizing of Spain. Spain was a Latin-speaking area. Paul was probably not entirely ignorant of Latin, but he would require to speak it fluently if he was to do effective work in Spain. It was perhaps in order to spend some time in a Latin-speaking environment that he had recently paid a visit to Illyricum. We should not, in fact, have known about his visit to Illyricum but for his mentioning it in Romans 15:19 as the westernmost limit of his apostolic activity thus far.

If Illyricum provided him with some linguistic preparation, there were other kinds of preparation required for such an enterprise as he contemplated in Spain. In earlier days the church of Syrian Antioch had provided Paul and Barnabas with a base for the evangelization of Cyprus and South Galatia. Later, when Christianity had been established in Corinth and Ephe-

---

[43]Chrysostom goes farther: "he mentions Spain in order to show his eagerness and warmth towards them [the Roman Christians]" (*Homilies on Romans* 30 [on 15:28]).
[44]Cf. Bowers, "Jewish Communities," 395–402.

sus, these two cities provided Paul with bases for the evangelization respectively of the provinces of Achaia and Asia. But where would he find a base for the evangelization of Spain if not in Rome? He does not in so many words ask the Roman Christians to provide him with such a base, but he sets the situation before them in such a way that they would see his need of one and could, if they were so minded, spontaneously offer to supply what was needed. "I hope to see you in passing as I go to Spain," he says, "and to be sped on my journey there by you (*hyph' hymōn propemphthēnai ekei*), when first I have enjoyed your company for a little" (Rom. 15:24). Here certainly is one facet of his purpose in writing—not, of course, the only one. What the sequel was—whether or not he did go to Spain, and whether or not the Roman church did provide him with a base—is quite unclear, and is in any case irrelevant to our investigation of the purpose of the letter.

Jerusalem

Towards the end of his personal remarks in Romans 15, Paul tells the Roman Christians that, before he can come to their city and spend some time with them on his way to Spain, he must for the present go to Jerusalem "with aid for the saints" (Rom. 15:25). This is a reference to his involvement in the Jerusalem relief fund, which we know from his Corinthian correspondence to have been very much on his mind for some time back.[45]

One obvious reason for mentioning the relief fund to the Roman Christians was to explain why he could not set out for Rome immediately: this business of delivering the collected money to Jerusalem must be completed first. Therefore he could not give them even an approximate date for his arrival in Rome—as things turned out, it was just as well that he did not try to give them one! Even if nothing untoward happened, there was no way of knowing how long the business would take. According to Luke's record, he hoped to be in Jerusalem in time for Pentecost (which in A.D. 57 fell on May 29).

But evidently Paul is not merely advising his friends in Rome that there may be some delay in his setting out to see them: he tries, tactfully, to involve them in his Jerusalem enterprise. He does not, either expressly or by implication, invite them to contribute to the fund. It had been raised among the churches of Paul's own planting, in which the Roman church had no place. Indeed, just because the Roman Christians were not involved in the fund in this sense, Paul could tell them about it in a more relaxed manner than was possible in writing to people whom he wished to make a generous contribution. The Gentile churches, he says, are debtors in Jerusalem in respect of spiritual blessings; it is but fitting that they should

---

[45]Cf. 1 Cor. 16:1-4; 2 Cor. 8:1-9:15.

acknowledge that debt by imparting to Jerusalem such blessings as they could impart—material blessings, monetary gifts.

It is plain from his Galatian and Corinthian letters that Paul was greatly concerned to preserve his churches' independence of Jerusalem. Yet here he himself acknowledges their dependence on Jerusalem for the gospel itself. Indeed, we learn more here than anywhere else of Paul's real attitude to Jerusalem. Throughout his letters there is an ambivalence in his relation to the Jerusalem church and its leaders: on the one hand, they must not be allowed to dictate to his churches or himself; on the other, he must at all costs prevent his apostolic ministry and the Gentile mission from having the ties of fellowship with Jerusalem severed. This appears clearly enough in Galatians: in the very context in which he asserts his independence of Jerusalem he tells how he went up to Jerusalem on one occasion and laid his gospel before the leaders of the church there.[46] Happily, they appear to have recognized the validity of Paul's gospel and his authority to communicate it to the Gentiles. What if they had withheld such recognition? Paul was under orders higher than theirs, but his work would be largely frustrated if he had to carry it on in isolation from Jerusalem. Luke does not always tell his readers why Paul's apostolic ministry was punctuated by the successive visits to Jerusalem which he records (Acts 9:26; 11:30; 15:2; 18:22; 19:21), but in the light of Paul's letters we can see why he was so careful to maintain contact with Jerusalem, and we can accept Luke's account in this regard as being true to the facts.

The place which Jerusalem occupied in Paul's thinking is emphasized by his statement in Romans 15:19 about the range of his apostolic activity to the time of writing: "from Jerusalem and as far round as Illyricum I have fully preached the gospel of Christ." It is evident from Acts and from Paul's own testimony that it was not in Jerusalem that he first preached the gospel. Why then does he give Jerusalem pride of place in this statement? Perhaps because Jerusalem is the place where, by divine decree, the preaching of the gospel is initiated:

> out of Zion shall go forth the law, and the word of the LORD from Jerusalem (Isa. 2:3).

This primacy of Jerusalem is recognized in the Lucan tradition—for example, in the direction "beginning from Jerusalem" in the risen Lord's charge to his disciples (Luke 24:47; cf. Acts 1:8). Paul appears to acknowledge this primacy not only in Romans 15:19 but elsewhere in his letters. He had, in fact, a greater regard for the Jerusalem church and its leaders than they evidently had for him, and was indeed, as the late Arnold Ehrhardt put it, "one of the greatest assets for the Jerusalem church" because, either by his personal action or under his influence, versions of the gospel

[46]Gal. 2:2–10.

which were defective by the standards of Jerusalem were brought into conformity with the line maintained in common by Paul and the leaders of the mother-church.[47] And it is a matter of plain history as well as a "theological presupposition" that, from the inception of the church until at least A.D. 60, "Christendom" (in the words of Henry Chadwick) "has a geographical centre and this is Jerusalem. Gentile Christians might be free from Judaism; they remained debtors to Zion."[48]

Jerusalem also played a central part in Paul's understanding of the consummation of God's purpose in the world. He himself, as apostle to the Gentiles, had a key place in that purpose as he understood it—not only directly, as the progress of the gospel prospered under his hand among the Gentiles, but also indirectly, when (as he hoped) the large-scale participation of Gentiles in the blessings of the gospel would stimulate the Jewish people to jealousy and move them to claim their own proper share in those blessings. This development would mark the climax of gospel witness in the world and precipitate the parousia. This seems to be the point of Paul's quotation of Isaiah 59:20f. in this context (Rom. 11:26f.). He quotes it in the form: "The Deliverer will come from Zion, he will banish ungodliness from Jacob." The Hebrew text says "to Zion"; the Septuagint version says "for Zion's sake." Paul has apparently derived "from Zion" from Psalm 14:7//53:6, "O that salvation for Israel would come out of Zion!" The implication is that the climax of salvation is closely associated with Jerusalem. Not only did the gospel first go out into all the world from Jerusalem; Jerusalem (if we interpret Paul aright) would be the scene of its consummation. And Paul's own ministry, as he saw it, had a crucial role in speeding this consummation.[49]

No wonder, then, that Paul related his ministry closely to Jerusalem. This adds a further dimension of meaning to Paul's organizing of the Jerusalem relief fund and to his resolve to be personally present in Jerusalem with the messengers of the Gentile churches who were to hand it over. It was not only his response to the request of the Jerusalem leaders at an earlier date that he should "remember the poor" (Gal. 2:10); it was not only an acknowledgment on the part of the Gentile churches of their indebtedness to Jerusalem and a means of promoting a more binding fellowship of love between them and the church of Jerusalem. It was all that, but it was at the same time the outward and visible sign of Paul's achievement thus far, the occasion of his rendering to the Lord who commissioned him an account of his discharge of that commission. It was also, in his eyes, a fulfillment of prophecy.

One of the prophets of Israel had foreseen the day when "the wealth of nations" would come to Jerusalem, when foreigners would "bring gold

---

[47]Ehrhardt, *Framework*, 94.
[48]Chadwick, "The Circle and the Ellipse," 25.
[49]On this see Munck, *Paul and the Salvation of Mankind*, passim.

and frankincense and proclaim the praise of the LORD." "They shall come up with acceptance on my altar," said the God of Israel, "and I will glorify my glorious name" (Isa. 60:5–7). A careful study of Romans 15 leads to the conclusion that Paul sees this promise being fulfilled in the impending visit of Gentile believers to Jerusalem, carrying their churches' gifts and prepared to join their fellow-believers of Jerusalem in thanksgiving to God. It was this vision that prompted his earnest prayer that "the offering of the Gentiles (*prosphora tōn ethnōn*) might be acceptable, being sanctified by the Holy Spirit" (Rom. 15:16). This language echoes that of Isaiah 66:20, where the brethren of the Jerusalemites will be brought "from all the nations as an offering to the LORD." In the Old Testament context the "brethren" in question are Jews of the dispersion; for Paul they are fellow-members of that extended family which embraces believing Gentiles and believing Jews—together children of Abraham.

The Gentile Christians brought their monetary offering, but they themselves constituted Paul's living offering, the fruit of his own *hierourgia*. Paul would not have thought of presenting this offering anywhere other than in Jerusalem. Hence his decision to accompany the Gentile delegates as they travelled there to hand over their churches' gifts to the mother-church. He may have had it in mind to render an account of his stewardship thus far and to re-dedicate himself for the next phase of his ministry in those very temple precincts where, more than twenty years before, the Lord had appeared to him and confirmed his commission to preach to the Gentiles (Acts 22:17–21).[50] His Gentile companions could not accompany him into the temple, but there in spirit he could discharge his *hierourgia* and present as a "pure offering" the faith of his converts through which the name of the God of Israel was now "great among the Gentiles" (Mal. 1:11).

He may indeed have hoped that on a later occasion, when his contemplated evangelization of Spain was completed, he might pay a further visit to Jerusalem with a fresh offering of Gentiles from "the limit of the west"[51] and render a further, perhaps the final, account of his stewardship.[52]

But at the moment his visit to Jerusalem with the fruit of his Aegean ministry had to be paid, and he could not foresee how it would turn out. He lets his Roman readers fully into his motives for paying the visit, and shares with them his misgivings about the outcome. That the "unbelievers in Judaea" would stir up trouble for him as on previous occasions was only to be expected; but would the gift-bearing Greeks (*Danaos et dona ferentes*)[53] be "acceptable to the saints" (Rom. 15:31)? Paul could not feel sure on this score, and he invites the Roman Christians to join him in earnest

---

[50]See p. 184 above, with n. 35.

[51]Cf. 1 Clem. 5:7 (*to terma tēs dyseōs*).

[52]For the argument that the "full number of the Gentiles" (Romans 11:25) will not "come in" until Paul "has brought Christian representatives from *Spain* to Jerusalem as part of his collection enterprise" see Aus, "Paul's Travel Plans," 232–62.

[53]Virgil, *Aeneid* 2.49.

prayer that his hopes and plans would be fulfilled. If things turned out
otherwise, then all the care which had gone into the organization of the
fund, all the high hopes which Paul cherished for the forging of a firmer
bond of affection between the mother-church and the Gentile mission,
would be frustrated. Whether or not the leaders of the Jerusalem church
did in fact accept the gifts in the spirit in which they were brought is disputed, but it does not affect our understanding of Romans.[54] One thing
is clear: Paul was anxious that they should so accept them, and he seeks
the prayers of the Roman Christians to this end.

Did he seek more than their prayers? Their prayers were all that he
explicitly asked for, but did he hope that they would read between the
lines and do even more than he asked?

We may certainly dismiss the view that the letter is addressed only
ostensibly to Rome but is essentially directed to the Jerusalem church—
that Paul throughout the letter really develops the argument which he
hoped would be effective in Jerusalem.[55] There is nothing in the letter
to suggest that its contents are not primarily intended for Roman con-
sumption; we have argued indeed that its contents are as a whole suited
to the Roman situation, as they are for the most part unsuited to the Jerusalem situation.

But might Paul be hinting that the Roman Christians could do something to pave the way for a favourable reception in Jerusalem?[56] We have
no direct information on such contact as may have existed at this date
between the Christians of Rome and the church of Jerusalem, but it would
be surprising if there were no communication between them. There would,
however, be no time for the Roman Christians to get in touch with Jerusalem between their receiving this letter and Paul's arrival in Jerusalem.
Paul was evidently on the point of setting out for Jerusalem when he sent
the letter (*poreuomai*, "I am on my way," he says in Rom. 15:25). If the
year was A.D. 57, he left Philippi about 15 April—"after the days of Unleav-
ened Bread" (Acts 20:6)—and reached Caesarea with his companions about
14 May. Even if Phoebe left Cenchreae a month before Paul set out for
Jerusalem (mid-March was the earliest date for the resumption of sailing
after winter),[57] she would not have reached Rome much earlier than mid-
April, and there was no way that messengers from Rome could reach Ju-

---

[54]J. D. G. Dunn thinks it most likely that "the Jerusalem church refused to accept the
collection" (*Unity and Diversity,* 257). (For my part, I think it more likely that they did accept it.)

[55]Amplifying the suggestion of E. Fuchs that the "secret address" of the letter is Jerusalem (*Hemeneutik,* 191), J. Jervell argues that "the essential and primary content of Romans (1:18–11:36) is a reflection upon its major content, the 'collection speech,' or more precisely,
the defense which Paul plans to give before the church in Jerusalem" ("Letter to Jerusalem,"
56).

[56]So Park, "Jerusalem Church."

[57]Vegetius, *De re militari* 4.39. Even a journey by land could not have begun much
earlier.

daea before Paul did, even if they had set out as soon as the letter was received.[58]

But Paul certainly did wish to involve the Roman Christians as closely as possible with his Jerusalem enterprise, and if the Jerusalem leaders could be given to understand (tactfully) that Rome was being kept in the picture, this might have influenced their reception of Paul and his Gentile friends.

II. Conclusion

In short, not only in his impending visit to Jerusalem to discharge the relief fund and not only in his subsequent Spanish project, but in all the aspects of his apostleship Paul was eager to involve the Roman Christians as his partners and to involve them as a united body. He did not know how much longer time he had to devote to the evangelization of the Gentile world. He may have believed himself to be immortal till his work was done (he never explicitly says so), but for one so constantly exposed to the risk of death it would have been irresponsible to make no provision against the time when death or some other hazard would prevent him from continuing his work. He had his younger associates, we know—men like Timothy and Titus—who could bear the torch after his departure. But if he could associate with his world vision a whole community like the Roman church, the unfinished task might be accomplished the sooner. The influence of that church sprang not only from the centrality of the imperial capital and its unrivalled means of communication with distant regions, but even more (he had reason to believe) from the outstanding faith and spiritual maturity of which the Roman Christians gave evidence. An individual might suffer death or imprisonment, but a church would go on living. Therefore in all the parts of his letter to the Romans he instructs them, he exhorts them, he shares with them his own concerns and ambitions in the hope that they may make these their own. These hopes and ambitions embraced not only the advance of the Gentile mission but also the ingathering of Israel which, he was persuaded, would follow the completion of the Gentile mission. Because of its history and composition, the church of Rome was uniquely fitted for this ministry. That its members might see the vision and respond to it Paul sent them this letter.

Did the Roman Christians rise to the occasion? The witness of history is that they did. From now on, and especially after A.D. 70, Christendom,

---

[58]It would not have made much difference to the timing if Phoebe went to Rome by the Via Egnatia rather than all the way by sea. The promptest journey from Rome to Judaea took nearly five weeks; for example, news of the death of Tiberius on 16 March A.D. 37 (Tacitus, *Ann.* 6.50), reached Jerusalem on the eve of Passover (Josephus, *Ant.* 18.122–124), which in that year coincided with the full moon of April 17 or 18. Cf. Ramsay, "Roman Imperial Post," 60–74.

which could hitherto be represented by a circle with its centre at Jerusalem, became rather (in Henry Chadwick's figure) an ellipse with two foci—
Jerusalem and Rome.[59] The influential part played henceforth by the Christians of Rome in the life of the ecumenical church is due not so much
to their city's imperial status as to the encouragement given them by Paul
in this letter.[60]

[59]Chadwick, "Circle and the Ellipse," 29.

[60]And later, no doubt, during his two years' residence among them. This much may be
said with confidence, even if we do not go so far as to say with Henry Chadwick that, "if
there is one man who more than any other man may be regarded as founder of the papacy,
that man is surely St. Paul" ("Circle and the Ellipse," 36).

12

THE PURPOSE AND OCCASION OF ROMANS AGAIN

A. J. M. Wedderburn

In an admirably succinct survey of recent views on the purpose and occasion of the letter to the Romans in *ExpT* 85 (1974), 264–69, Dr. W. S. Campbell set out his answer to the question "Why Did Paul Write Romans?" Rightly he argued that any view which saw in Romans a letter directed rather to the Jerusalem church failed to explain why it was ever sent to Rome. Rightly he criticized those who saw the letter as a general statement of Paul's views or as a circular letter; chs. 12–15 are too specific for that. Rightly he was skeptical of the assertion that Paul saw the Roman Christians as somehow deficient; after all, their faith was proclaimed in all the world (Rom. 1:8). He was prepared to grant that Paul's desire to seek support for his Spanish mission was one reason among others for the writing of Romans, but, equally, prayerful support for the safe delivery of the collection from the Gentile churches could be another. But more important, he felt, was the fact that Paul was writing to a church divided between a liberal Gentile Christian majority, the "strong," and a conservative Jewish Christian minority, the "weak"; primarily Paul was writing to the former, stressing the equality of Jew and Gentile Christians, but also that God's gifts to Israel are not to be lightly dismissed; such a conceited attitude on the part of Gentile Christians could have had an adverse effect upon the outcome of Paul's journey to Jerusalem and thus upon the unity of the whole church. Because Paul's letter touches on themes of such magnitude it is hardly surprising that parts of his letter are less directly related to the Roman situation than others, but the whole should nevertheless be seen in the light of that situation.

This article takes up this much-debated theme again for two reasons; the first is the appearance of W. Schmithals' monograph, *Der Römerbrief als historisches Problem (Studien zum Neuen Testament* ix, Gütersloh [1975]), which demands a fresh look at the problem in the light of the important questions which it raises and the thoroughness and erudition with which it supports its conclusions. The second is to underline a further factor in the historical setting of Romans which has gone relatively unnoticed.

Schmithals points to a basic tension in Romans between the fact that its recipients are Gentiles and the argument of the first eleven chapters which has the character of a debate with the Jewish synagogue. Paul plainly writes to Gentiles (1:5, 13ff.; 11:13; 15:15ff.); Schmithals did not have access to the recent commentary of J. C. O'Neill (Harmondsworth [1975]), who would delete such references as glosses and holds that Romans was written to Jews, but it is hardly likely that so arbitrary a treatment of the text would have persuaded him to change his mind. But the arguments of chs. 1–11, concerned as they are with the universality of salvation in Christ,[1] with the direct access of the Gentiles to God's kingdom and with the abrogation of the law in favour of faith, have their place in an argument with Jews. There is in fact, he argues, nothing in Romans to indicate an argument with Jewish Christians.

At this point the first difference between the positions of Schmithals and Campbell emerges: are the Christians at Rome Gentiles or Jews? Schmithals argues that they are Gentiles, but Gentiles with a decided leaning towards Judaism, former "God-fearers" who have received Christ but have not been weaned from their close connection with, and dependence upon, the synagogue; they must be won over to Paul's law-free gospel of grace. But here it must be asked, against Schmithals, whether it is likely that there would be *no* Christian Jews in Rome? There was there a large Jewish population and, however diminished their community may have been by Claudius' expulsion of the Jews, there seems little reason to suppose that Rome was for long cleared of all Jews, especially once Claudius was dead.[2] But here it is as well to note an ambiguity in the phrase "Jewish Christian"; does this mean a Christian who is racially a Jew or a Christian who observes Jewish customs and seeks to make his Christianity conform to Judaism? In denying the presence of Jewish Christians at Rome Schmithals obviously uses it in the first sense, but does Campbell? It seems that his argument would be compatible with either sense, and it is the stronger for that.

But now a second point of difference arises: for Campbell Paul was writing primarily to the liberal Gentile Christian majority in Rome, whereas for Schmithals he initially wrote to the Gentile Christians at Rome who are still attached to Judaism, influenced by it and *au fait* with its problems, its literature and its beliefs. There is much to be said for Schmithals' view, since it does make more sense of the contents of chs. 1–11 and of the reference in 7:1, "for I speak to you as ones who know the law" (it is easiest

---

[1]Cf. Cranfield, *Romans*, 1.90.

[2]Cf. Marxsen, *Introduction*, 98–100; Wiefel, "Die jüdische Gemeinschaft," 171–84 = "Jewish Community," 85–100.

to take this as a reference to the Jewish law).[3] Not only is it exegetically preferable, but it does justice to the fact that a considerable proportion of the Gentile converts to Christianity in those early days would have come to Christ via Judaism; in this respect the Book of Acts probably reflects very accurately the manner of the gospel's progress, as it depicts Paul's Gentile mission as winning the majority of its recruits from amongst the Gentile adherents of the synagogues in the various cities of the Graeco-Roman world. But is it necessary to hold that all the Christians at Rome, or even the majority of them, were Judaizing Gentile Christians? Had none migrated thither from the Pauline churches, bringing with them a Pauline understanding of the law-free gospel? It seems gratuitous to assume that they had not, particularly in view of the presence of the "strong" in the Roman church (chs. 14 and 15).

But Schmithals holds that Paul wrote only *initially* to Gentile Christians attached to Judaism. It will come as little surprise to those familiar with Schmithals' treatment of other Pauline epistles that he discovers in Romans a composite letter made up from two letters to Rome and other fragments of Pauline and non-Pauline origin (e.g., he surmises that 5:(1)2–11 and 13:11–14 belong to the Thessalonian correspondence). Letter A to the Romans (1:1–4:25; 5:12–11:36; 15:8–13) was written from Ephesus early on in Paul's ministry there, before the enthusiasts at Corinth had started troubling him, but in the light of the problems in Galatia; in this Paul, who was still hindered from visiting Rome in person, sought to secure these Gentile Christians for his understanding of the gospel. He succeeded, at least with some of them, and to these he wrote some time later, urging them to show more consideration for their fellows who still clung to the rules of the synagogue; this is his letter B (12:1–21; 13:8–10; 14:1–15:4a, 5f., 7, 14–32; 16:21–23; 15:33). 16:1–20 commends Phoebe to Onesiphorus in Ephesus.

This thesis is important for our purpose since, on the one hand, it means that the purposes and occasions of the two Roman letters were different, and, on the other, Schmithals' argument is quite largely based on evidence of these different purposes and occasions. The weightiest arguments seem to be that (a) in 15:23–25 Paul announces quite definite travel plans, whereas in 1:13 he says that up till then he has been hindered from coming to them, "and one can only understand this to mean that the hindrance still remains" (p. 167); (b) in 15:20 Paul states that it is his policy not to preach the gospel where Christ is already named, lest he should build on another's foundation, but in ch. 1 he speaks of desiring to win some fruit in Rome, where there already were Christians; Schmithals says of 15:20 that "this basic principle is in such tension with the proem, where Paul contends for the right to preach in the Roman church, that it is im-

---

[3]So, e.g., Cranfield, *Romans*, 1.333.

possible to hold both passages together within the same letter" (p. 169); (c) in 15:24 he merely proposes to visit Rome *en route* to Spain, but in ch. 1 he seeks to visit the Roman Christians for their own sake, and there is no mention of further activity in regions beyond Rome.

Schmithals has done a valuable service in pointing once again to these difficulties, and any account of the purpose of Romans must henceforth do justice to his arguments. It needs to be said first that there is a fundamental difficulty about his various proposals for reconstructing the original form of Paul's letters before they were fitted together by an editor or editors to form the conflate letters which we know today. In each case the argument points to tensions and untidy sequences of thought as signs of this editorial activity and seeks to produce more coherent letters, free from internal contradictions; paradoxically the more successful this argument is the less plausible it becomes, since one then has to explain why anyone should take these tidy, coherent letters and fit them together in such untidy, incoherent ways;[4] in other words the text-critical principle of giving preference to the more difficult reading applies here too on a larger scale.

When that is said, how are we to circumvent Schmithals' arguments? The first argument, (a) above, depends upon a particular interpretation of 1:13, *ekōlythēn achri tou deuro*, "I was prevented up till now"; Schmithals contends that this means that he is still prevented, but his case would be stronger if, instead of the aorist, the present or perfect were read here (cf., e.g., Jos., *Ant.* 11.93, Dittenberger, *Sylloge*[3] II. 821E §§*2, 3*); 15:22 uses the imperfect *enekoptomēn* (lit. "I was often being hindered from coming to you"), but here the hindrance has clearly ceased.

Schmithals does, however, further support his claim by appealing to 1:10: Paul asks that "somehow by God's will I may now at last succeed in coming to you" (RSV). It is, Schmithals claims, uncertain whether he will succeed (p. 167 n. 58). But in ch. 15 Paul does no more than say that he hopes to see them (v. 24) and evidently is aware of the considerable risks that he is taking in this trip to Jerusalem (v. 31). Moreover it can be argued that the words "now at last" (*ēdē pote*) indicate that circumstances have now changed, and there is a possibility that the hindrance has ceased.

Schmithals' second argument is, he concedes, not enough by itself: "if 1:14f. and 15:20 are . . . quite inconceivable within *one* letter, then assigning the writing of both letters to two different occasions may make the explanation of the contradiction easier, but it still does not eliminate the contradiction as such" (p. 172). His own explanation is that Paul is not saying that he will not preach where there are Christians already—he had done that in Corinth—but Roman Christianity at the time of his writing

---

[4]Cf. Michaelis, "Briefkompositionen," 321–26. This argument would also apply to the proposal of Schenke, "Aporien im Römerbrief," cols. 881–888, that 14:1–15:13 are also part of a letter to Ephesus.

lacked a founder, an organized mission, and a constitution as a church; hence he writes to them as a group of individual Christians rather than as a church. By the time of his second letter, as the result of his long-range efforts, he could write to them as one of his churches.

But the tension remains: Christ is certainly already named in Rome, and yet Paul proposes to preach the gospel there (1:15). Either Paul is using *euangelizesthai* in two different senses in ch. 1 and ch. 15 or he is guilty, not just of ambiguity, but also of inconsistency. That time has passed and circumstances have changed makes the inconsistency more intelligible, but, as Schmithals rightly saw, it does not remove it. Schmithals criticizes Jervell for his explanation of the tension between chs. 1 and 15, that Paul did not yet know what he wanted, on the grounds that this saves the epistle's integrity at the expense of the apostle's integrity (p. 170), but it is doubtful whether Schmithals finally rescues Paul, however many extenuating circumstances he can adduce. Yet must the apostle's integrity, let alone his consistency, be preserved at all costs?

But is Paul using *euangelizesthai* in the same sense in both passages? Insofar as the "you" of 1:15 means the Christians at Rome it is clear that Paul must be speaking of a proclamation of the gospel to those already converted (so, e.g., Cranfield *ad loc.*) The context of 15:20, however, is clearly concerned with initial pioneering work, with the laying of the foundations of churches (cf. 1 Cor. 3:10ff.). This is the more usual sense of *euangelizesthai* (the parallels to Rom. 1:15 cited by G. Friedrich in *TDNT* II, p. 720, can quite easily be taken of this initial preaching). What must be noted is that in his introductory remarks Paul is handling, it is widely admitted, a situation of some delicacy, in which he seeks to avoid giving the impression of overbearing authority and superiority; hence in vv. 11f. he speaks circumspectly of the fruits which he has sought from a visit to them. Yet, if Schmithals' analysis of the constitution of the Christian community at Rome is at all correct, Paul all the same needs to correct the understanding of the gospel held by at least some of them (yet, *pace* Schmithals, probably not all of them, not even initially).[5] It may be that Paul is guilty of an indiscretion in using this word in Rom. 1:15 and that he is not sticking to the letter of his principle laid down in 15:20; however, in all fairness it must be noted that he merely states what his ambition is in the latter verse and does not state that he utterly eschews any form of preaching where Christ is already named.

The third argument, (c) above, is less problematic; there is no reason why Paul should mention his detailed plans early in the letter and indeed to mention his Spanish plans might call into question the extent of his interest in the Romans (1:10f.); moreover his wish for the Romans and him-

---

[5]Paul, in Gal. 1:8f., recognizes that some may come into his churches and do the same thing to his gospel, replacing it with another.

self to be "mutually encouraged" by their faith (1:12) is quite compatible with his desire to be refreshed in their company (15:32 RSV).

But if Paul's reasons for writing to the Romans are several—winning over those still thralled to Judaism, moderating the zeal and curbing the conceit of those who despised the Jews and all things Jewish, seeking their prayers for his forthcoming journey and their support for his Spanish mission—why then does he choose this moment to do so? The need for prayer and for support for the Spanish mission would perhaps be sufficient cause if none other were detectable. But perhaps there is.

When Paul wrote Rom. 15 he was on the point of setting out for Jerusalem with a collection for the church there; the churches of Macedonia and Achaea had contributed for the poor of that church (15:26); the Galatian churches had also been called upon to contribute (1 Cor. 16:1). In his brief explanation in ch. 15 Paul notes the willingness of the Macedonian and Achaean churches to do this, since they were under a debt to them; "for if the Gentiles have come to share in their spiritual blessings, they ought also to be of service to them in material blessings" (v. 27 RSV). What is striking here is that Paul draws from this no implications for the Roman Christians; they were among "the Gentiles" (1:13), they had shared in the spiritual blessings of the Jewish Christians at Jerusalem, perhaps even more directly than many in churches founded by Paul; they too should be under debt, owing it to the Jerusalem Christians to share their material blessings with them. They were in fact one of the very few major Gentile Christian churches in existence at this date which was not represented in the collection. (Antioch would be another.)

This problem is accentuated, not diminished, if the collection was not merely concerned with the relief of the needy Christians in Jerusalem, but had a symbolic significance too. For Dieter Georgi, for instance, the collection demonstrated the complete transformation of the eschatological hopes of Judaism. The salvation of the Gentiles had become the preliminary to the salvation of Israel. By the collection, as a "sign" of the former, Paul hoped to "provoke" Israel (cf., e.g., 11:14). The arrival of Paul with not only the collection but also a delegation of uncircumcised Gentiles would recall the eschatological hope of the pilgrimage of the Gentiles to Jerusalem.[6]

More recently Klaus Berger, starting from Paul's statement in Acts 24:17 that he brought "alms and offerings" to Israel, has argued that the Jewish understanding of the role of almsgiving in the relationship between "God-fearers," uncircumcised adherents to the Jewish faith, and Judaism pro-

---

[6]Georgi, *Kollekte*, 84–86; cf. Munck, *Paul and the Salvation of Mankind*, ch. 10, esp. 303f.; Hahn, *Mission in the New Testament*, 108–10. However, Nickle (*Collection*, 129–42, esp. 139) argues that what was symbolized was that the Gentiles were coming "as the true Israel of God," in the place of Israel; he also argues that the delegation and its significance were not mentioned lest Paul should seem to be criticizing the Jerusalem church's efforts to convert the Jews and to be taking over this task from them contrary to the agreement of Gal. 2:9.

vides a more satisfactory explanation of the collection; the giving of alms demonstrated the reality of a Gentile's conversion and his attachment to Israel. So for Paul the collection meant that the Gentile Christians had stepped into the place of the "God-fearers," independent and yet united. Of course Gentile Christians and some Jewish Christians would see it differently; the latter, for instance, might regard it as meaning that these uncircumcised Gentile Christians were second-rate members of the community, and the inability of the former to appreciate this background of ideas may explain the different explanations of the collection which Paul gives to them, like that of Rom. 15:27.[7] Whether or not Berger is right—and if Luke was a converted former "God-fearer" himself,[8] the language of Acts 24:17 may well reflect *his* view of the collection rather than Paul's—yet the collection remains a symbol of something that held good for all uncircumcised Gentile Christians.

But there were Gentile Christians at Rome, unrepresented in this delegation. Should they not have had a part in it?[9] But Paul asks them neither to contribute money nor to send delegates. Why? In the first place, if the letter is largely a unity and is Paul's first contact with the Roman church, it would have been a tactical error, suggesting an overbearing authority which would have been only too open to criticism. However, if Schmithals were correct in assigning the part of ch. 15 which mentions the collection to a later letter to a group of Paul's supporters, it would have been more appropriate for Paul to ask them to take part. His failure to do so could only be explained by another reason, that by this stage the gathering of the collection was far advanced and to have waited for the Romans would have delayed Paul's plans too much.

What Paul could do very appropriately and did do was to let the Roman Christians know of the collection and ask them to support it with their prayers. Yet could they thus support it? With this question we come nearer an understanding of the contents of the preceding parts of the letter, for we have seen that it is likely that the Roman church contained both Gentiles with a leaning towards Judaism and Gentiles believing in a law-free gospel (as well as probably some Jews of both persuasions). To the former, Paul and his mission were an object of suspicion; that suspicion would also apply to the collection and delegation which symbolized this mission and what it stood for. They suspected it because of the doubtful ethical implications of Paul's message as well as what seemed an unduly cavalier attitude to the lofty claims of Judaism.[10] The latter group might

[7]Berger, "Almosen für Israel," 180–204.

[8]Cf. Franklin, *Christ the Lord,* esp. 178f.

[9]Others too, like the Christians at Antioch, should have been there; is this evidence that Paul lost the argument of Gal. 2:11ff.? (Cf. Barrett, "Pauline Controversies," 229–45, esp. 230).

[10]Yet, unless Georgi is correct in seeing the collection as a provocative act (see above) and unless the Judaizing Christians at Rome saw it as such, the collection itself and its purpose would not arouse their suspicion, only the movement which sponsored it.

often hold a more extreme view than Paul himself, as the attitudes of the "strong" in the Corinthian church seem to indicate, and for them anything which smacked of a recognition of the superior position of Jewish Christianity thralled to Judaism seemed to be a denial of the freedom and liberty proclaimed in the gospel (and we should recall that some modern scholars have compared the collection to the Jewish temple tax). To this extent it is appropriate to think of Paul addressing himself, if not to two distinct groups of readers, at least to a broad spectrum of different views of the relationship between the Christian gospel and Judaism: at one end of the spectrum were those, both Judaizing Gentiles and, we may infer, at least a few ethnic Jews who had been converted to Christianity, who attended the gatherings of the synagogue and clung to its ways; at the other were those Gentile Christians who had flung off whatever ties to Judaism they had had before, if any, and had espoused a law-free gospel like Paul's (a view perhaps also held by some Christian Jews in Rome) or who had gone even further in severing all connections with Judaism. To this extent Paul S. Minear may be correct in assuming that different viewpoints and groups of readers are addressed at different points in the letter, although it is questionable whether so detailed a reconstruction as he offers is either plausible or desirable.[11] Nor is it clear that these groups formed completely distinct house-churches; Schmithals' argument seems to suggest that the Judaizing Gentile Christians at least would still be attending the synagogue, and it may be that they would have felt no need to group themselves into a distinct house-church as well. (And here may lie the reason for Paul's failure—often noted—to address the Roman Christians as *ekklēsia*, since that name would only be applicable to at most some of the Roman Christians, those who were aware of their distinctive existence over against ethnic Israel.)

There is still, of course, the objection that, if the collection and the purpose behind it were so important for the writing of Romans, it is very odd that it should be mentioned so late in the letter and so little emphasized. But if it is borne in mind that it was impracticable for the Romans to contribute to it at this late stage and that it would have been impolitic of Paul to suggest this and that it was far more important that they endorse the Gentile mission and its gospel, whose fruits were being offered in the collection and in the persons of its bearers, then the manner of Paul's approach to Romans is the more intelligible.

[11]Minear, *Obedience*; cf. Donfried, "False Presuppositions," 106f.: note too that Paul often addresses an opponent in the second person *singular*, hardly the natural way to address a specific group in the congregation.

13

THE TWO ROMAN CONGREGATIONS: ROMANS 14:1–15:13

Francis Watson

The legitimacy of using Rom. 14:1–15:13 as evidence about the situation of the Roman church has been strongly disputed by R. J. Karris. He argues that the identification of the "weak" and "strong" parties has been conjectural and unproductive ("Occasion," 70–71), and that this section is rather to be interpreted as a generalized rewriting of 1 Cor. 8–10 (71ff.), eliminating everything which has reference only to a concrete situation (i.e., food offered to idols).[1] The present argument aims to show that Rom. 14:1–15:13 should not be understood as mere general paraenesis, but gives clear evidence of the situation in the Roman church.[2] First, it must be shown that there is no real problem identifying the "weak" and the "strong": the former are Christians who observe the Mosaic law, while the latter are Christians who do not.[3] For convenience, one may refer to these two groups as "Jewish Christians" and "Gentile Christians," so long as it is remembered that the former group may well have included proselytes,[4] whereas the latter group may well have included Jews who like Paul himself did not observe the law.

The main difficulty in identifying the "weak" with straightforward Jewish Christians who observed the law is that according to 14:2 they abstained not simply from pork, from the meat of animals that had been incorrectly slaughtered and from meat offered to idols, but from meat in general: "The

---

[1]So also Bornkamm, "Last Will and Testament," 28; Furnish, *Love Command*, 115f.; Bassler, "Impartiality," 57 note. Drane, "Romans," 212, describes the whole of Rom. 12–15 as "vague and general." This is probably true of Rom. 12–13, but 14:1–15:13 seems considerably more specific.

[2]Käsemann, *Romans*, 366; Wilckens, *Römer*, 3.79.

[3]Against Klein, "Paul's Purpose," 36f.; Räisänen, *Paul and the Law*, 48.

[4]Proselytes were actually called "Jews": according to Dio Cassius, the name "Jew" "applies also to all the rest of mankind, although of alien race, who affect their customs" (*Hist. Rom.* 37.16.5–17.1; Stern, II, 351); cf. Epictetus, *Diss.* 2.9.20 (Stern, I, 543).

weak man eats only vegetables."[5] The difficulty is increased when Paul refers to abstention from wine as well as meat (14:21; cf. 14:17).[6] Some scholars have concluded from these statements that the "weak" have been influenced by syncretistic ascetic ideas.[7] But Jewish abstention from meat and wine is mentioned several times in other texts. In Dan. 1:8–16, Daniel and his companions obtain permission to abstain from meat and wine, which would defile them (v. 8), and to live off vegetables and water. Judith refuses to eat and drink the food and wine provided by Holofernes (Jud. 12:1–4). Esther tells how she has not eaten at Haman's table or at the king's feast, and how she has not drunk "the wine of the libations" (Esth. 14:17, LXX). Josephus commends the priests who were taken captive to Rome in A.D. 61, and who did not forget their religion and so "supported themselves on figs and nuts" (Life 14).[8] In all these examples, Jews are in a Gentile environment, cut off from their community, in which ceremonially pure meat and wine might be obtained, and this suggests a plausible interpretation of the "weak" in Rom. 14. Suetonius tells us that there was constant unrest in the Jewish quarter of Rome[9] because of Christian preaching, and even before the expulsion of A.D. 49 it must have been hard for the Jewish Christian minority to live alongside the non-Christian Jewish majority. The situation would have been exacerbated by the expulsion. Non-Christian Jews would blame the Christians for what had happened, and the ill-feeling might well have been sufficient to prevent the Christians resettling in the Jewish quarter when the return to Rome took place. They would therefore be forced to live in another part of Rome, where they would be unable to obtain the ceremonially pure meat and wine which was available only in the Jewish quarter.[10] They therefore did what Daniel, Judith, Esther and the priests did when in a Gentile environment: they abstained from meat and wine.[11] The fact that they did so is therefore not evidence of syncretistic or ascetic tendencies, but is fully compatible with the situation of Jewish Christians who wished to remain faithful to the law in difficult circumstances.[12]

[5]Minear claims that the weak were only vegetarians when eating with Gentile Christians (Obedience, 10). This is possible, but Rom. 14 does not indicate that the problem was concerned only with table-fellowship.

[6]Thus Käsemann claims that "Jewish orthodoxy can be ruled out as a source," since "general abstinence from meat and wine is not found there" (Romans, 367).

[7]So Barrett, Romans, 257f.; Schlier, Der Römerbrief, 405f. Käsemann, Romans, 368.

[8]Schlier's survey of the historical background to Rom. 14 (Der Römerbrief, 403ff.) surprisingly does not mention most of these texts.

[9]Philo, Embassy to Gaius 155, indicates the existence of a definite "Jewish quarter" in Rome.

[10]Cf. Cranfield, Romans, 2.695.

[11]Cf. Barrett, who thinks that Rom. 14:2 is speaking of the Jew who has been expelled from the synagogue (Essays, 42).

[12]There is no need to suppose that abstinence from wine is mentioned only hypothetically (against Cranfield, Romans, 2.696).

There are several further indications in Rom. 14:1–15:13 that show that the weak are to be identified as Jewish Christians.[13] First, in 14:14 Paul mentions the belief of the weak that certain food is *koinon*, and elsewhere in the New Testament this term refers to food which is unclean according to the Jewish law (Acts 10:14, 28; 11:8). In Rom. 14:20, *panta men kathara* is equivalent to *ouden koinon* in v. 14,[14] and this recalls Acts 10:15 and 11:9, *ha ho theos ekatharisen, sy mē koinou*; cf. Mk. 7:19, *katharizōn panta ta brōmata*. Secondly, Rom. 14:5 tells us that "one man esteems one day as better than another," and Rom. 14:6 speaks of "he who observes the day." This seems to refer to Jewish Sabbaths, feasts and fasts.[15] Thirdly, 15:7–13 speaks unambiguously of the duty of Jews and Gentiles to welcome one another as Christ has welcomed them. There is no break between 14:1–15:6 and this passage, and it is therefore natural to conclude that the whole passage concerns the relationship between Jewish and Gentile Christians. Indeed, this final point puts this identification virtually beyond doubt.

The purpose of Rom. 14:1–15:13 is indicated in 14:1: "As for the man who is weak in the faith, welcome him, but not for disputes over opinions." We have here two separable injunctions: (i) Welcome him; (ii) Do not argue with him. In 14:1, Paul adopts the standpoint of the strong, but elsewhere he is more even-handed. Thus, the second injunction is applied both to the strong and to the weak in 14:3–9: those who eat and who esteem all days alike are not to despise those who abstain and who esteem one day as better than another, but nor are the latter to pass judgment on the former. For Gentile and Jewish Christians to be able to meet together in harmony, both sides must make concessions. Gentiles must not regard observance of the Jewish law as incompatible with Christian faith (indeed, according to 14:13ff., it may be wise for them to make concessions as regards what they eat),[16] and Jews must not regard it as essential to Christian faith. By far the greater concession is demanded of the Jews. They are required to abandon the idea that the law is the authoritative, binding law of God, to which all must submit, and to regard it in-

[13]Cf. Cranfield, *Romans*, 2.695f.

[14]Käsemann's claim that 14:14 abolishes the age-old boundary between the sacred and the profane (*Romans*, 375) is —to say the least— exaggerated, as the most cursory look at the contents of, for example 1 Cor. 5–11 indicates. The boundary is shifted (in some cases), but by no means abolished. Käsemann's view is accepted by Hübner, *Paul and the Law*, 84.

[15]So Schlier, *Der Römerbrief*, 407; Barrett, *Romans*, 259; Cranfield, *Romans*, 2.695; Wilckens, *Römer*, 3.83. Käsemann's claim that "Christians are in view who are convinced that days stand under lucky or unlucky stars" (p. 370) seems unwarranted.

[16]The apparent implication in 14:13ff. that Gentile Christians should submit to food-laws for the sake of "peace and mutual upbuilding" (v. 19) does not seem consistent with the exhortation to the weak in v. 3 not to "pass judgment on him who eats," which implies that Gentile Christians will continue to ignore food-laws. In vv. 13ff., Paul is perhaps more concerned with explaining the standpoint of the weak to the strong, so as to avoid "disputes over opinions" (v. 1) than with persuading the strong to adopt the food-laws of the weak.

stead as purely optional, a matter of individual choice and of private piety.
In the light of this, it is not surprising that their present tendency is to
"pass judgment" on Gentile Christians who ignore important aspects of
the Mosaic law.

The fact that the two sides differed so fundamentally about the law
makes it extremely unlikely that they shared common worship. *Paul's argument does not presuppose a single congregation in which members disagree about the law; it presupposes two congregations, separated by mutual
hostility and suspicion over the question of the law, which he wishes to
bring together into one congregation.* This is the significance of the injunction of 14:1, "Welcome him," or, applying it to both sides impartially,
"Welcome one another, therefore, as Christ has welcomed you" (15:7).[17]
The purpose of welcoming or receiving one another is common worship:
"that *together* you may *with one voice* glorify the God and Father of our
Lord Jesus Christ" (15:6).[18] Because Christ came to save both Jews and
Gentiles, Jews are exhorted to join with the Gentiles in common worship:
"Therefore I will praise thee *among the Gentiles*" (15:8f.).[19] Likewise, Gentiles are exhorted to join with Jews for worship: "Rejoice, O Gentiles, *with
his people*" (15:10). Then the Jews are again reminded that Scripture speaks
of the Gentiles praising God (15:11) and of the salvation which the "root
of Jesse" will bring to the Gentiles (15:12). There is therefore no need for
them to continue to separate themselves from the life and worship of the
Gentile Christian community.[20]

Thus, Rom. 14:1–15:13 addresses itself not to tensions between Jewish
and Gentile Christians within a single congregation (the usual view), but
to the problem of two separate congregations who regard each other with
suspicion and who hold no common worship. 15:7–13 seems to put this
interpretation beyond doubt: why should Paul exhort Jewish and Gentile
Christians to worship together if they are already doing so? It is probable
that the Jewish Christian congregation is the remnant of the first Roman
congregation which was dispersed in A.D. 49; Rom. 14:1–15:13 thus confirms the essentially Jewish nature of that congregation.[21] Paul exhorts

[17]According to 15:7, "Both groups are to recognize and accept one another (Cranfield,
Romans, 2.739). But this suggests that at the time of writing, the two groups do *not* recognize and accept each other, i.e., that they are separated. Käsemann's understanding of the
imperative in 14:1 as a call for "everyday recognition of brotherhood, in the broad sense
of solidarity" (*Romans*, 366), or as "leaving space for growth and communication (ibid., 367),
is thus too vague.

[18]Rom. 15:6 indicates not that "conflicts are disturbing worship" (Käsemann, *Romans*,
366), but that common worship does not yet take place at all.

[19]Cranfield rightly notes that for Paul the quotation concerned "the combination of Jews
and Gentiles in the believing community" (Cranfield, *Romans*, 2.745).

[20]It is therefore not the case that in 15:7ff. the tensions of 14:1–15:6 "vanish completely
from view" (Käsemann, *Romans*, 384).

[21]There is no evidence that these Jewish Christians were in the minority (against Käsemann, *Romans*, 366).

them to recognize the legitimacy of a Gentile Christianity which does not require submission to the law. They are to regard the law, and especially its commandments about food, sabbaths and feast days, as purely optional, matters between the individual and God rather than authoritative divine commands. Conversely, Gentile Christians are to regard these practices as permissible, and are not to despise those who observe them; but in their case nothing of fundamental importance has been sacrificed, whereas for the Jewish Christians a radical change of outlook is required. Paul's aim is thus to create a single "Paulinist" congregation in Rome—"Paulinist" in the sense that the Pauline principle of freedom from the law is accepted. To put it another way, he wishes to convert the Jewish Christian congregation to Paulinism—to the theory of freedom from the law, if not to the practice.

If this view of the purpose of Rom. 14:1–15:13 is correct, it has considerable importance for the interpretation of the rest of Romans, which may be interpreted in a similar way: Paul's purpose in writing Romans was to defend and explain his view of freedom from the law (i.e., separation from the Jewish community and its way of life), with the aim of converting Jewish Christians to his point of view so as to create a single "Pauline" congregation in Rome.[22] At the same time, he encourages Gentiles to be conciliatory towards their Jewish fellow-Christians, since the union for which Paul hopes will not be possible without a degree of tact and understanding on the part of the Gentile Christians. But before attempting to interpret Rom. 1–11 in the light of these conclusions, a discussion of Rom. 16 is necessary. This will confirm the conclusions already reached and provide a possible answer to the historical riddle of the origins of Gentile Christianity in Rome.

I. Gentile Christianity in Rome: Romans 16

It has often been suggested that Rom. 16 is addressed not to the church of Rome but of Ephesus, and that it is either an independent letter (in whole or in part)[23] or an appendix to a copy of Romans which was sent to Ephesus.[24] The main reason for this hypothesis is that it is thought unlikely that Paul should have known as many individuals in the Roman church as are mentioned in vv. 3–16. Ephesus is suggested because Prisca

---

[22]Schmithals, *Der Römerbrief als historische Problem,* 106f., notes that despite the prominence of the strong in 14:1–15:6, nothing is said about these people in Rom. 1–11. He deduces from this that Romans combines two letters sent by Paul to the Roman congregation. On the present hypothesis, however, 14:1–15:6 fits in well with chs. 1–11, as my *Paul, Judaism and the Gentiles,* chs. 6 and following attempt to demonstrate. For a discussion of Schmithals' thesis, see Hübner, *Law,* 65ff.

[23]Käsemann, *Romans,* 419; Bornkamm, *Paul,* 246; Georgi, *Kollekte,* 79f.

[24]Manson, "Letter to the Romans," 12ff., opposed by Cranfield, *Romans,* 1.11.

and Aquila were last heard of in connection with that city (Acts 18:19, 26), and because of the reference in v. 5 to "my beloved Epaenetus, who was the first convert in Asia for Christ." But Prisca and Aquila were only ever in Corinth (Acts 18:2f.; cf. 1 Cor. 16:19) and Ephesus (Acts 18:18f., 26; 1 Cor. 16:19) because they had been expelled from Rome along with other Jews by Claudius (Acts 18:2). It is therefore by no means unlikely that they should have returned to Rome by the time Romans was written. Some of the others who are named in Rom. 16 may also have been refugees from Rome, whom Paul met in the East as he had met Prisca and Aquila, and who have also now been able to return to Rome.[25] Even if one still finds it surprising that Paul should have known so many individuals in the Roman church, the view that Rom. 16 like Rom. 1–15 is addressed to Rome is preferable to the cumbersome theory that without any break or explanation Paul suddenly addresses not Rome but Ephesus, and to the view that an entirely unrelated letter-fragment has unaccountably been attached by a later editor to the letter to the Romans.[26] If Rom. 16 can be satisfactorily explained as an integral part of the letter to the Romans, the Ephesian theory collapses automatically.

It is in fact by no means certain that Paul knew personally all the individuals who are named in Rom. 16.[27] He clearly knew Prisca, Aquila, and Epaenetus (vv. 3–5), and he must also have known those who are described as "beloved": Ampliatus (v. 8), Stachys (v. 9) and Persis (v. 12). The fact that he describes Rufus' mother in v. 13 as "his mother and mine" suggests that he knew them both. Urbanus is described as "our fellow-worker in Christ" (v. 9, cf. v. 3); but Mary, whose work only in the Roman congregation (and not alongside Paul) is mentioned (v. 6), may never have met him personally. It is not certain whether "those workers in the Lord, Tryphaena and Tryphosa" (v. 12) have worked alongside Paul or solely in Rome. Paul refers to Andronicus and Junias as "fellow-prisoners"(v. 7), but he also describes them as "fellow-countrymen," and it may be that in both expressions he is simply wishing to assert his solidarity with people he has never met;[28] like him, they are Jews, and like him, they have suffered imprisonment for the sake of Christ.[29] Paul may or may not have known "Apelles, who is approved in Christ" (v. 10). There is nothing in vv. 10f. to show that Paul knew personally the family of Aristobulus, or Herodion, or the family of Narcissus, and this is true also of the ten individuals who are listed in vv. 14f., about whom nothing is said other than the instruc-

[25]So Wilckens, *Römer*, 1.25.

[26]The Roman destination of Rom. 16 is asserted by Wilckens, *Römer*, 1.24ff.; Cranfield, *Romans*, 1.5ff.; Donfried, "Short Note on Romans 16," passim, Lüdemann, *Paul*, 174f.; Meeks, *First Urban Christians*, 16; and Kettunen, *Abfassungszweck*, 64ff.

[27]So Meeks, *First Urban Christians*, 56.

[28]So Sanday–Headlam, *Romans*, 1.423. Cranfield, *Romans*, 2.788f. Others assume that imprisonment with Paul is meant (Barrett, *Romans*, 283; Käsemann, *Romans*, 414; Wilckens, *Römer*, 3.135; Schlier, *Der Römerbrief*, 444, leaves both possibilities open).

[29]Literal imprisonment is presumably meant (against Kittel, *TDNT*, 1.196f.).

tion that they are to be greeted. This leaves only nine people who are certain to have been known personally by Paul: Prisca, Aquila, Epaenetus, Ampliatus, Urbanus, Stachys, Persis, and Rufus and his mother.[30] Some of the others were no doubt also known to him; but when one bears in mind the possibility that some may have come from Rome in the first place, as Prisca and Aquila had done, the evidence of Rom. 16 is hardly sufficient to suggest that it must have been sent to Ephesus. In answer to the obvious question of why Paul should have bothered to greet people who were known to him by name and reputation only, one may point out that Romans as a whole is addressed to such people. Having written at great length to people most of whom he has never met, it is not at all surprising that he should send individual greetings to some of the more eminent of them.

In discussing Rom. 14:1–15:13, it was suggested that this section gives evidence of two separate groups within the Roman church: Gentile Christians, who like Paul himself had abandoned many of the ceremonial prescriptions of the law of Moses, and Jewish Christians for whom the whole law was still in force. Paul exhorts them to worship God *together* (15:7ff.), and this suggests that at the time of writing the two groups did not share common worship. Rom. 16 sheds further light on these two groups. We may assume that most or all of the people named there whom Paul knew personally were associated with the Gentile group. This is certainly the case with Prisca and Aquila, who are mentioned in connection with "the churches of the Gentiles" (v. 4). Since they had once been members of the original Roman congregation (for Acts 18 never suggests that they were converted by Paul) their association with "the churches of the Gentiles" who did not observe the law must have been due to Paul's influence.[31] If our interpretation of Rom. 14:1–15:13 is correct, they would have been regarded with great suspicion by other Jewish Christian members of the original congregation. As regards the others, Epaenetus and probably Ampliatus were Paul's own converts, Urbanus and perhaps Persis had worked alongside him, and Rufus and his mother had shown him hospitality (hence "his mother and mine")—these people too were perhaps Paul's converts. Such people may be described as "Paulinists"—i.e., Christians who shared Paul's practice of freedom from the law and separation from the Jewish community. The fact that they were known to Paul personally suggests a solution to the riddle of the origin of Gentile Christianity in Rome: the Gentile group addressed especially in Rom. 14:1–15:13 and in 11:13ff. may well have been founded by Paul's own converts and associates: *Gentile Christianity at Rome is therefore Pauline Christianity*. In encouraging Jewish Christians to worship together with Gentiles, Paul is encouraging them

---

[30]Cf. Meeks, *First Urban Christians*, 56.

[31]Acceptance of Paul's doctrine of freedom from the law by Jewish Christians cannot have been common; Col. 4:11 seems to reflect this fact.

to recognize the legitimacy of his own work.[32] He wishes to convert the
Jewish Christian congregation in Rome to Paulinism.[33] They are to regard observance or non-observance of the law as a matter of purely private piety, and the obstacle to worshipping together with Paul's Gentile
Christian friends (and Paul himself, when he comes to Rome) is thus to
be removed.

Rom. 16 also seems to confirm the existence of a (separate) Jewish
Christian congregation at Rome. In v. 7, Paul writes: "Greet Andronicus
and Junias, my fellow-countrymen and my fellow-prisoners; they are men
of note among the apostles, and they were in Christ before me." Andronicus and Junias (or Junia)[34] are thus linked with earliest Jewish Christianity.
As apostles, they will therefore have shared in the Jewish church's mission "to the circumcision" (cf. Gal. 2:7–9), for Paul knows of no apostle
other than himself (and perhaps Barnabas) who is sent to the Gentiles.[35]
We may therefore assume that Andronicus and Junias shared the Jerusalem church's deep suspicion of Pauline "freedom from the law"—a suspicion to which Paul alludes in Rom. 15:31, and which is evident above
all from Gal. 2. For Paul, being an apostle implies first that one has seen
the risen Lord, and secondly that one has founded a congregation (cf. 1 Cor.
9:1f.), and it is therefore probable that these two people were the founders
of the Roman congregation.[36] In any case, their status as apostles must
have made them the most important and influential members of the Jewish Christian congregation, whose favour Paul had to gain if he was to persuade that congregation to unite with the Paulinists.

Another member of that congregation may have been "my fellow-
countryman Herodion" (v. 11). As with Andronicus and Junias, Paul stresses
the link of Jewish birth between himself and the recipient of the greeting,

---

[32]According to Hübner, "The polemical thrust of his argument is directed against those
Jewish Christians who were making life difficult for the Pauline Gentile Christians" (*Law*, 68).
However, he also considers possible the view that the conflict in the Roman congregation
was between Gentile Christians and proselytes.

[33]Brandon notes that Paul is trying to do in Romans what the Judaizers had tried to in
Galatia: convert the respective congregations to a new understanding of the gospel (*Fall
of Jerusalem*, 148f.). In Rom. 15:15, Paul claims that he has sought merely to "remind" them
of what they already know, but this claim does not carry conviction (so Käsemann, *Romans*, 392).

[34]Cranfield thinks it more likely that a woman, presumably Andronicus' wife, is here referred to, on the grounds that there is no evidence elsewhere for "Junias" as a man's name
(*Romans*, 2.788). This receives some support from Paul's statement in 1 Cor. 9:5 that the other
apostles were accompanied by their wives. Cf. also Wilckens, *Römer*, 3.135f.

[35]Against Wilckens, *Römer*, 3.136, who thinks that Andronicus and Junia were "Paul's
fellow-workers in the Gentile mission."

[36]Kettunen thinks that they may have been sent there from Jerusalem (*Abfassungszweck*,
77). However, he regards them as members of the "Hellenist" group there (p. 76), for whom
circumcision was "in principle meaningless"; despite this, they were welcomed by many in
the synagogue (p. 80). The very existence of a Hellenistic group with views such as these
is more than doubtful, and it is hard to see why Roman Jews should have welcomed people
for whom the sign of the covenant had become meaningless.

and in this way tries to bridge the gap between himself and Jewish Christianity; cf. Rom. 9:3; 11:1. (In the case of Prisca and Aquila, who were also Jews, according to Acts 18:2, this was not necessary, since they were already Paulinists.) If it is correct to identify Aristobulus in v. 10 with the member of the Jewish royal family who had died in Rome probably between A.D. 45 and 48,[37] then the members of his family whom Paul greets in v. 10 may also have been prominent members of the Jewish Christian congregation.

Thus, Rom. 16 confirms the hypothesis about the purpose of Romans derived from 14:1–15:13. The purpose of Romans is to encourage Jewish and Gentile Christians in Rome, divided over the question of the law, to set aside their differences and to worship together. The latter group are Paulinists, and it is converts and associates of Paul who have brought his message of freedom from the law and separation from the Jewish community to Rome, and established a congregation there. The former group represents the remnants of the original Roman Jewish Christian congregation, which regards Paulinism with deep suspicion.[38] The chief purpose of Romans is to overcome this suspicion. One of the means by which Paul attempts to do this is to include greetings for members of both congregations in the final part of his letter.

Two other features of Rom. 16 support this interpretation. First, in vv. 3ff. Paul does not greet the individuals named directly; rather, he commands his readers to greet them, for the verbs are all in the imperative. Paul is in effect requesting his readers in both groups to introduce themselves to one another.[39] Thus, Gentile Christians are not to "despise" (cf. 14:3) Andronicus and Junias, the most important members of the Jewish Christian group. They are to regard them as "men of note among the apostles," and to bring them their greetings. Conversely, Jewish Christians are not to "pass judgment" (cf. 14:3) on Prisca and Aquila; they are to be greeted as people who have greatly assisted the spread of the gospel. The function of these commands to greet the individuals named is thus similar to the general command to Jewish and Gentile Christians to welcome one another (15:7).

Secondly, the reason for Paul's polemic in 16:17–20 becomes clear. On the whole, Paul has tried to keep his letter to the Romans as tactful as possible, and until 16:17–20 it is free of the violent polemic that characterizes Galatians and Phil. 3.[40] In Rom. 16:17, Paul writes: "I appeal to you,

---

[37]So Sanday–Headlam, *Romans*, 1.425; Cranfield, *Romans*, 2.791f. Aristobulus is mentioned by Josephus (*War* 2.221–222; *Ant.* 18.273–276; 20.13).

[38]It is therefore not the case that "the characteristic and peculiar thing about Romans" is "the fact that it was not, or was only in slight degree, aimed at circumstances within a certain congregation" (Nygren, *Romans*, 4).

[39]According to Schlier, *Der Römerbrief*, 442f., the imperatives make the Roman congregation the "Übermittlerin" of Paul's greetings.

[40]Käsemann gives the contrast between the violence of 16:17–20 and the rest of the letter as an additional reason for separating ch. 16 (*Romans*, 419). But Kettunen points out that it fits just as badly into ch. 16 itself (*Abfassungszweck*, 67).

brethren, to take note of those who create dissensions and difficulties, in opposition to the doctrine which you have been taught; avoid them."[41] The best explanation for this is that Paul knows that there will be opposition to his attempt to persuade Jewish Christians to accept the legitimacy of the Paulinists and to join with them for worship. Not all of the Jewish Christians will be convinced even by Romans that observance of the law is a matter of personal taste, and Paul here anticipates their objections and denounces them in advance for creating, or rather perpetuating, "divisions." As in the case of Gal. 6:13 and Phil. 3:19, the view that Paul's language implies that his opponents were antinomians[42] takes his violent polemic much too literally. When Paul denounces people, he does not do so with scrupulous fairness; the idea that one should be fair to one's opponents was not widespread in antiquity.

II. The Evidence of Romans 1:1–17 and 15:14–33

The hypothesis developed above has suggested that there were two main groups in Rome: Jewish Christians, who comprised the remnants of the original Roman congregation, and Gentile Christians who were Paulinists—converts and associates of Paul. The former observed the law, whereas the latter did not, and for this reason the two groups were separated from each other. Paul is writing chiefly to persuade the Jewish group to recognize the legitimacy of the Gentile group, and thus of his own Gentile mission; this would mean in effect a final break with the Jewish community. The real test for this hypothesis is whether or not it sheds light on the doctrinal core of Romans (1:18–11:36); that is the subject of my *Paul, Judaism, and the Gentiles*. But it is important to ask whether the hypothesis is consistent with the two passages in which Paul speaks directly of the Roman Christians and of his aim in writing to them, 1:1–17 and 15:14–33. If it is not, then there is little point in trying to apply it to 1:18–11:36. But in fact, it does appear to be consistent with 1:1–17 and 15:14–33, and indeed suggests possible solutions to one or two of the exegetical problems of those passages. Rom. 1:1–17 and 15:14–33 provide support for the following three aspects of the hypothesis developed above: (i) Romans was addressed primarily to Jewish Christians; (ii) Gentile Christianity in Rome was Pauline in origin; (iii) Paul wrote Romans to persuade the former group to accept the legitimacy of the latter.

---

[41]Kettunen, *Abfassungszweck*, 67, identifies "the doctrine you have been taught" with "the pattern of faith delivered to you" (6:17). If so, then Paul is maintaining the fiction of 15:15 that he is merely "reminding" them of things with which they are already familiar. Those who dissent from his teaching are thus seen as dissenting from "the pattern of faith delivered to you."

[42]Schmithals, *Paul and the Gnostics*, 222ff.; Dodd, *Romans*, 244f.; Käsemann, *Romans*, 418.

(i) 1:5f. is a crucial passage for determining whether or not the primary addressees of Romans were Jewish Christians.[43] Apostleship has been entrusted to Paul *eis hypakoēn pisteōs en pasin tois ethnesin hyper tou onomatos autou, en hois este kai hymeis klētoi Iēsou Christou.* Here, *en hois* must mean "among whom" either in the sense that the addressees are themselves Gentiles,[44] or in the sense that they live in the midst of Gentiles.[45] If the former is the meaning, the Roman Gentile Christians are being seen as the objects of Paul's missionary activity, just like any other Gentiles. But this seems unlikely, for the addressees are *already* "called by Jesus Christ" (1:6). The key to the verse is the phrase, *kai hymeis*: "among whom *you too* are called by Jesus Christ."[46] "You too" probably means "you as well as me," for Paul has spoken of himself in 1:1 as having been "called," and in 1:5 he states that his call has taken him among the Gentiles. Paul is saying: "You too are called by Jesus Christ in the midst of Gentiles, just as I am." Already a hint is given that the relationship of Jewish Christian addressees to the Gentiles is to be the main theme of the letter.[47]

(ii) In 1:13–15, Paul expresses his desire to undertake a mission to the Gentiles in Rome. He wishes to come to Rome "so that I may reap some fruit among you just as among the rest of the Gentiles" (1:13; cf. 1:15). In 1:13 and 1:15, *kai en hymin* and *kai hymin* are used somewhat loosely; Paul does not mean that his readers are themselves to be the objects of his missionary activity (cf. 1:8), [48] but is simply addressing them as inhabitants of Rome—hence, "to you who are in Rome" (1:15). But the real problem of 1:13–15 is that Paul announces his intention of conducting a Gentile mission in a place where there are already Gentile Christians (cf. 14:1–15:13; 11:13), thus apparently contradicting the principle expressed in 15:20, not to build on another man's foundation (cf. also 2 Cor. 10:13ff.).[49] The problem is solved if the Roman Gentile Christians are con-

[43]According to Kettunen, 1:5f., 13–15; 11:13; 15:16, 18, clearly indicate that the readers were Gentiles (*Abfassungszweck*, 27). But in no case is this certain. Even 11:13 could easily imply that elsewhere Paul has been speaking primarily to Jews—otherwise he would not have to single out the Gentiles for special mention.

[44]So Sanday–Headlam, *Romans*, 1.12; Barrett, *Romans*, 22; Käsemann, *Romans*, 15; Schlier, *Der Römerbrief*, 30.

[45]So Cranfield, *Romans*, 1.20; Wilckens, *Römer*, 1.67.

[46]Cf. Cranfield, *Romans*, 1.67f.

[47]If the primary addressees were Jewish, this resolves the problem posed by Zeller, *Juden und Heiden*, 38f.; Schmithals, *Der Römerbrief als historische Problem*, 24; and Kettunen, *Abfassungszweck*, 22, that a letter supposedly written to Gentile readers is concerned with Jewish problems. Schmithals' solution is that the readers were former God-fearers (*Römerbrief* 83, 90, 93).

[48]Against Klein, "Paul's Purpose," 39–40.

[49]Cf. Klein, "Paul's Purpose," 32; Wilckens, "Abfassungszweck," 114ff. Schmithals, *Der Römerbrief als historische Problem*, 167ff., tries to solve this problem by means of source criticism.

verts and fellow-workers of Paul;[50] his Gentile mission in Rome will therefore not involve building on another man's foundation.

(iii) Romans was not addressed exclusively to Jewish Christians, even though its content suggests that they are the primary addressees.[51] 1:6 does not exclude Gentile Christians, and 1:7 addresses the letter "to *all* in Rome who are beloved by God, called to be saints." It may be significant that, contrary to his normal practice at the beginning of his letters, Paul does not address the recipients as an *ekklēsia*.[52] This need not be of any great importance, since the same is true of Phil. 1:1.[53] But Rom. 1:7 is at least consistent with the view that there was no single Roman congregation, but two opposing groups. This is apparently confirmed by 1:16. Paul has just spoken of his own apostleship in 1:13–15: he is apostle to the Gentiles, so he wishes to preach the gospel in Rome. But in 1:16, he unexpectedly states that the gospel is "for the Jew first, and also for the Greek." This sudden reference to the Jews is comprehensible if 1:16 is still referring to the Roman situation, like 1:8–15: "For the Jew first" expresses Paul's acknowledgment of the priority and the pre-eminence of the Roman Jewish Christian congregation,[54] whereas "and also for the Greek" asserts the legitimacy of the group of Pauline Gentile Christians in Rome. Paul wishes to persuade the Roman Jewish Christians that salvation is not for them alone but "for *everyone* who believes"—including Gentiles.

If Paul is primarily addressing Jewish Christians, why does he do this so explicitly as apostle to the Gentiles (1:4; 15:15–21)? The situation is perhaps somewhat similar to Gal. 2:2, where Paul tells how he "set forth the gospel which I preach among the Gentiles" to Jewish Christians, in an attempt to secure recognition of the legitimacy of his work. This is also the case in Romans, whose primary aim is that the Roman Jewish Christians should unite with the Roman Paulinists.

Rom. 1:11ff. and 15:23ff. also provide hints of a longer-term aim: having won over the Roman Jewish Christians by means of this letter, he would be able to use the Roman church as a base for mission in Rome (1:13ff.) and in Spain (15:24, 28). The collection (15:25ff.) is to be seen as another attempt to secure recognition from Jerusalem of the legitimacy of his Gen-

[50]Cf. Hübner, *Law,* 69: despite Rom. 15:20, Paul still sees Rome as his mission field "as his Paulinist followers live there."

[51]Most commentators hold that Romans is addressed to a predominantly Gentile readership: so Sanday–Headlam, *Romans,* xxxiii; Barrett, *Romans,* 22; Schlier, *Der Römerbrief,* 5; Käsemann, *Romans,* 15. Cranfield argues that both Jewish and Gentile Christians were numerous in the Roman church (*Romans* 1.21ff.) Baur, *Paul,* 1.321ff., and W. Manson, *Hebrews,* 172ff., argue for a Jewish Christian readership.

[52]Cf. Klein, "Paul's Purpose," 41.

[53]So Wilckens, "Abfassungszweck und Aufbau," 115.

[54]This seems more likely than Käsemann's theological interpretation: "Paul gives Judaism precedence for the sake of the continuity of the plan of salvation" (*Romans,* 23). The context suggests that the historical reality of the Roman church is in view.

tile Christian congregations in Asia Minor and Greece (see the Excursus to chapter 9, *Paul, Judaism, and the Gentiles*). This would then stop the Judaizing interference he had experienced in the Galatian churches and which he feared would take place at Philippi, and free him for a new stage of his universal mission, using Rome as a base. The conversion of the churches of Jerusalem and of Rome to his way of thinking was essential to the accomplishment of these grandiose plans, and Paul sought to secure the former through the collection and the latter through the letter to the Romans.

It is possible to speculate further. Had these plans been devised in consultation with Prisca and Aquila, who knew the Roman church and who had a particularly close relationship with Paul (cf. Rom. 16:3f.)? Had they, and others to whom greetings are sent in Rom. 16, volunteered to go to Rome to prepare the way for Paul? But at this point, we can only guess.

Contrary to the picture given in Acts (cf. 20:22–5, 37; 21:4, 10–14), Paul did not go up to Jerusalem with the sombre sense that the end of his apostolic labours was near. In Romans, he manifests an extraordinary self-confidence, a sense that he stands on the threshold of new worlds to conquer.[55] The desire to do so was present some months before at the time of the "severe letter" to the Corinthians (2 Cor. 10–13),[56] in which Paul complains that unnecessary problems are holding him back from breaking new ground (2 Cor. 10:15f.). By the time of Romans, he feels that such obstacles have at last been overcome; now at last he can bring to fruition his plans in connection with the Roman Christians (Rom. 1:9f.; 15:22f.). The letter itself was an essential part of these plans. Its function was preliminary: to persuade the Roman Jewish Christians to accept the Paulinists, in preparation for Paul's longer-term plans.

Yet this view of the function of Romans must be regarded as a mere hypothesis until it can be shown that it makes sense of the letter as a whole.

[55]Cf. Georgi, *Kollekte,* 90.
[56]For this identification, cf. Watson, "Painful Letter."

14

THE ROMAN CHRISTIANS OF ROMANS 16[1]

Peter Lampe

Was Romans 16 originally addressed to Rome, or was it a separate letter to Ephesus, as has been proposed?[2] I do not want to discuss in detail the problems to which the Ephesus hypothesis leads us, such as:[3] (a) Why does Paul greet only his co-workers Urbanus, Aquila, and Prisca in "Ephesus" (Rom. 16:3, 9), when many others have been staying there?[4] Has the whole group moved? Does Paul forget to greet them? (b) Why was a letter to the Ephesians added to a letter to the Romans? This would be without parallel. It is true, 2 Cor. was comprised of several letters, but these separate letters were not addressed to different churches. (c) We know letters that consisted mainly of greetings.[5] But can we picture *Paul* writing such a letter? (d) Why do the Romans 16 names "Urbanus," "Phlegon," "Persis," and "Asyncritus" not occur in any of the thousands of Ephesian inscriptions, while they do show up on epigraphs in the city of Rome?[6]

---

[1]A more comprehensive study will be forthcoming in one chapter of the English translation of my book, *Die stadtrömischen Christen in den ersten beiden Jahrhunderten: Untersuchungen zur Sozialgeschichte* (Tübingen: Mohr 1989) 2nd edition, pp. 124–53, 301–2, 358; ET by Fortress Press, translated by Dr. L. Holland (Dr. Holland, unfortunately, did not translate this article into English).

[2]Cf. for one example: Scott, *Romans*, 24.

[3]Cf. the discussion in Ollrog, "Abfassungsverhältnisse," 221–24.

[4]Epaphras, Mark, Luke, Aristarchus, Demas (Phlm. 23–24; cf. Col 4:7–14); Sosthenes (1 Cor. 1:1); Apollos, Stephanas, Fortunatus, Achaicus (1 Cor. 16:12, 17); Jesus Justus (Col. 4:7–14) and others.

[5]See McDonald, "Separate Letter?" 369–72.

[6]For Rome see below. For Ephesus see the concordance by Nollé, *Die Inschriften von Ephesos*, and Knibbe, "Neue Inschriften," 107–49. "Olympas," "Patrobas," and "Herodion" cannot be found in the epigraphs of either of the two cities. The remaining names of Rom. 16:3–16 are represented in both cities.

I. Romans 16 as an Original Part of the Letter to the Romans

I want to discuss positively the reasons why Romans 16 has to be considered an integral part of the original letter to the Romans.

1. Paul would never have ended a letter with Romans 15:33. Formulations like "the God of peace [with you]" never conclude a letter but precede requests to greet—greetings like the ones in Romans 16![7] The *de* in Romans 16:1, on the other hand, presupposes a *previous* text. That means: Romans 15 and 16 mutually presuppose each other. Why separate them?

2. Textual criticism teaches that no Romans manuscript ever ends with chapter 15. The manuscripts either omit both chapters (15:1–33 and 16:1–23), or they have them both in one block.[8] Therefore, 15:1–16:23 have to be treated as one unit by the textual critic—one block which is addressed to Rome, as 15:22–29 assures.

There are only two exceptions from this rule. (a) The minuscule 1506 from the year 1320 has chapter 15, but omits 16:1–23. The medieval scribe copied Romans 1–14; 16:25–27; chapter 15, and again 16:25–27. How can this strange arrangement be explained? The genealogical trees (*stemmas*), which have been proposed for the manuscripts of the letter to the Romans agree that the text of minuscule 1506 is a descendant of Marcion's Romans text (Rom. 1–14) and of texts that offer chapters 15 and 16:1–23 as one block *together*.[9] Thus, minuscule 1506 only *seems* to be an exception to the rule. The ancestors of minuscule 1506 assure that Romans 15 and 16:1–23 belong together once we come to the older strata of textual history. (b) P[46] from the year ca. 200 reads chapters 1–14; 15; 16:25–27; 16:1–23. It presents both chapter 15 and 16:1–23, but this time they do not appear in one block. Did P[46] therefore descend from a text which consisted only of 1–14; 15? In other words, Does P[46] suggest this textual history: 1–14; 15 → 1–14; 15; 16:25–27 → 1–14; 15; 16:25–27; 16:1–23 (=P[46])? No. Again, we have to look at the possible *stemmas* that put all manuscripts into a genealogical relation. We know fourteen text types for the letter to the Romans, having the task to put them together into a family tree. If we wanted to put 1–14; 15 at the root of the genealogical tree, an organic plant would not grow. The *stemma* would have several missing pieces, representing the weakest hypothesis.[10] P[46] therefore cannot support the hypothesis that Paul's original letter included only chapters 1–15.

3. Romans 16 shows several unique features when compared to the rest of the Pauline letters. Romans 1–15, on the other hand, offer the unparalleled quality that Paul writes to a church which he has never visited in person, a church which does not belong to his missionary area, but one with which he wants to get acquainted and from which he hopes to start a new missionary project in Spain. In other words, the uncharacteristic

---

[7]Phil. 4:9; 2 Cor. 13:11; 1 Thess. 5:23; 2 Thess. 3:16; Heb. 13:20; 3 John 15. Neither do Gal. 6:16; Eph. 6:23 end a letter. The only exception in the New Testament is not Pauline: 1 Pet 5:14. *amēn* does not conclude letters: Rom. 1:25; 9:5; 11:36; Gal. 1:5; 1 Thess. 3:13, etc.

[8]See the material in Lampe, "Textgeschichte," 273–77.

[9]Ibid.

[10]Ibid.

features of Romans 16 can be explained *by* the unusual situation of Romans 1–15. Thus, Romans 1–15 and 16 should not be separated.

What do I mean specifically? (a) The ecumenical greeting in Romans 16:16 is unusual for Paul: "All the churches of Christ greet you." This global perspective can be easily explained by the unique situation of Romans 1–15. Paul stands on the door step between east and west. He looks back at his missionary work in the east, leaving behind and summing up (15:19, 23). Making this survey, his eye easily catches "all churches of Christ" in the east. Furthermore, Paul looks ahead (15:22–32). Planning to do missionary work in Spain, he wants the Romans to support him (15:24, 30). But they do not even know him personally. Paul therefore first has to gain their confidence.[11] "All churches" sending greetings through Paul are the best recommendation for Paul himself and for his trustworthiness!

(b) Romans 16:3–16 as a whole is a text of recommendation for Paul himself—and only marginally also for Phoebe (16:1–2). The greetings of Romans 16:3–16 present two peculiarities compared to the other Pauline letters: greetings are sent to individual persons, and the list of greetings is unusually long. Both irregularities can be explained in light of Romans 1–15. Not knowing the Roman church as a whole personally, Paul sends greetings to individuals whom he does know in person.[12] Common friends build a first bridge of confidence between people who do not know each other. Paul wants to signal: See, I already know many of you personally (therefore the long list). And some of these common friends to whom I am connected with love (*agapētos*) have merits (e.g., 16:4, 6) and authority (16:7). They cast some light on myself. Look at these many and honorable personal friends of mine in the midst of your church—and you will find that I, too, am trustworthy. Here we have the hidden message of the unique and long list of personal greetings. The list is a reference for Paul himself! And Paul certainly needed all the recommendations he could get after he and his law-free gospel had become so controversial in the east.

Our interpretation attributes some sense also to the fact that Paul does not greet his personal friends directly but makes the Romans deliver his greetings to them (*aspasasthe*). The greetings send a message to the Roman church as a whole; they are not merely communication between Paul and these individuals.

(c) A last oddity is Timothy's introduction as "my co-worker" (16:21). The eastern churches to which the rest of Paul's letters were addressed

---

[11]The whole letter has this purpose. Paul assures that he has been mentally and emotionally connected with the Romans for a long time (1:9–11, 13, 15). He explains the contents of his gospel in order to introduce himself. He uses *captationes benevolentiae* (e.g., 1:8; 15:14; 16:19a), etc.

[12]The same pattern is imitated in the deutero-Pauline letter to the Colossians: Not knowing the church in Colossae personally, "Paul" uses personal relations (4:7ff.) and greetings to individuals (4:15; cf. 4:17).

knew Timothy. For them this introduction was not necessary, while it makes sense in a letter to the Romans.

4. According to Romans 15:19–29, chapters 1–15 were written in Greece at the end of the so-called third mission journey (Acts 20:1–5). This co-incides perfectly with the situation of Romans 16: (a) Romans 16 also was written in Greece; Paul sends off Phoebe from the Corinthian harbor Cen-chreae (16:1). (b) The people whom we would expect in Paul's surround-ings at the end of the "third mission journey" (Acts 20:4) are exactly those who send greetings in Romans 16:21–23: Timothy, So(si)pater, and Gaius.[13] Both lists, Romans 16:21–23 and Acts 20:4, coincide surprisingly well, al-though they are source-critically independent from each other.[14]

5. The following material is often quoted in favor of Ephesus as the addressee of Romans 16. I will try to show that it can be understood in a letter to Rome as well. In other words, this material is neutral—it should be left out of the discussion of Rome or Ephesus.

(a) According to Romans 16, Paul knows 26 Christian persons in Rome.[15] Is this strange in a letter to a city where he never has been? Have all these 26 people been in the east? Is 26 an outrageous number? In view of mobility in the Roman Empire, this number is not surprising. Many fa-mous Roman Christians had immigrated to Rome from the east: Aquila, Hermas, Marcion, Valentinus, Justin, many of his students in the Acta Ius-tini, Tatian, Hippolytus, and the presbyter Anicetus.[16] The fact that the Roman church still spoke predominantly Greek even during the whole sec-ond century indicates how high the percentage of eastern immigrants must have been. The Jews, too, were busy travelling back and forth between Rome and the east.[17] On the inscription CIG 3920, the craftsman Flavius Zeuxis brags that he sailed 72 times (!) from the east to Italy. Of course, this was exceptional, because it is proudly mentioned on an epitaph. But it shows how vast the possibilities for travel were. Furthermore, many jour-neys between the east and Rome may even have been forced upon the Christians. It is possible that many of the 26 persons had been expelled from Rome under Claudius and had returned after Claudius' death—just like Aquila and Prisca (Acts 18:2; Rom. 16:3).

No, a number of 26 is not surprising. And for those who still have doubts it may be stated that 26 is only a maximum number. Nothing forces

[13]*So(si)patros*: Both forms stand for the same name. See the later textual history of Acts 20:4 and cf. BAGD, 800. If *Gaius* (Rom. 16:23) were the Gaius of 1 Cor. 1:14, this would fit as well into the situation of Rom. 1–15. This Gaius lived in Greece (Corinth) where Rom. 1–15 was written.

[14](a) Both lists name people whom the other list does not have. (b) So(si)pater's name is reproduced in the two different versions.

[15]I exclude Narcissus and Aristobulus, both not being Christian as will be shown below.

[16]According to the Liber Pontificalis (s.v.) Anicetus was "natione Syrus."

[17]E.g., Acts 2:10. Rabbis who visited Rome: Joshua ben Hananiah, Akiba, Eleazar b. Azar-iah, Rabban Gamaliel (m. *Erub.* 4.1; cf. also m. *Abodah Zarah* 4.7, and Schäfer, "Rabbi Aqiba," 113–30).

us to assume that Paul actually knew *all* of the 26 personally and that consequently all of them had been in the east for a while. The names of the last ten individuals in verses 14–15 *may* have come to Paul's attention only through narratives told by third persons.[18] Mentioning only the names and no other individual information (vv. 14–15), the greetings for these ten pale in comparison to the ones in verses 3–13. Not even Mary (Maria, 16:6) needs to be personally acquainted with Paul. The information "she has worked hard among you" presupposes that Paul was told things about her he had not witnessed himself. The same may be true about Tryphaena and Tryphosa (16:12) and about Herodion, (16:11) whose Jewish "kinship" may have been reported to Paul by third persons too. Only for the remaining twelve people do we *have* to assume that they saw Paul in person in the east; the comments added to their names leave hardly any room for another interpretation: Prisca, Aquila, Epaenetus, Andronicus, Junia, Urbanus, Rufus and his mother, Ampliatus, Stachys, Persis, and probably also Apelles.[19] Whether 26 or 12 mobile people, a basis for Ephesus as destination can hardly be found in these figures.

(b) The presence of Aquila and Prisca among the addressees has already been explained: After having been expelled from Rome by Claudius (Acts 18:2), they returned to Rome between the times that 1 Corinthians 16:19 and Romans 16:3 were written. In other words, they returned around the year 55/56. This date fits well. Claudius died in the fall of the year 54, which was reason enough to give up finally any remaining timidity to return to Rome.

The craftsman[20] Aquila had already moved at least three times in his life: Pontus—Rome—Corinth—Ephesus (1 Cor. 16:19; the tradition in Acts 18:1–2, cf. 18:18, 26). Why could he not have moved a fourth time? The Christian Aberkios[21] in the second century stayed in Phrygia, in Rome, in Syria, and in Nisibis across the Euphrates. Again, mobility was no problem, especially since Aquila and Prisca were apostolic co-workers (Romans 16:3). It is easy to imagine that Paul had sent them back to Rome as a "vanguard" for himself, as he had already done with them in Ephesus (Acts 18:18–21, 24–26; 19:1). It is possible (nothing more) that their return to Rome had been "strategically" planned by Paul. In Rome, they indeed were active again as Paul's "co-workers," assembling even a house-church around them (Rom. 16:3–5). Epaenetus, "the first convert in Asia," may have moved

18Aquila and Prisca could easily have informed Paul about the Roman church and its details. They knew it in person, as the tradition in Acts 18:2 assures.

19I tend to believe that also Paul's appraisal of Apelles as "approved in Christ" (16:10) could hardly be said without a personal acquaintance: According to the context (14:18), *dokimos* is defined as "serving Christ" in the everyday love and care of interhuman relations (14:15–21).

20Concerning Aquila's tentmaking, see Lampe, "Paulus—Zeltmacher," 256–61. Aquila did not produce leather tents for the military, but linen tents and awnings for private clients in the cities—which allowed mobility for the craftsman.

21See the famous Aberkios-Inscription, e.g., in Altaner, *Patrology,* 95–96.

from Ephesus to Rome together with Prisca and Aquila. He is named right after them (Rom. 16:5).

These are only conjectures as to how it could have been. But in our argumentation, they have the function of showing that the Roman addressee of Romans 16 is as conceivable as an Ephesian. In other words, the fact that, for example, the "first convert of Asia" is greeted does not prove anything in favor of an Ephesian addressee. This Asian may easily have moved to Rome together with the people who most likely had converted him: Prisca and Aquila.

Only 2 Timothy 4:19 could be the last branch to hold on to for the defenders of the Ephesus hypothesis: The Pastoral Letters place Paul in Rome while Aquila and Prisca still dwell in Ephesus. Is this a proof for Ephesus? No. It is likely that 2 Timothy 4:19 only presents another example of the historical flaws in the Pastoral Letters; also the next verse (4:20) is historically untenable.[22] Why did the Pastoral Letters place Prisca and Aquila in Ephesus? The author needed some prominent names in Ephesus to support the portrayal of Paul writing from Rome (1:16–17) to Ephesus (1:16–18; 4:13, 19) and sending greetings to people there. In 1 Corinthians 16:19 and Acts 18:26 the author found what he or she wanted: two prominent Christians in Ephesus—Prisca and Aquila. Similarly the Ephesian Tychicus (Acts 20:4; Col. 4:7; Eph. 6:21) was placed fictitiously in Ephesus (2 Tim. 4:12), as was even Mark (2 Tim. 4:11), who had been known to have visited Ephesus (Phlm. 24; Col. 4:10).

(c) Commentators often wonder about the changing of tone in the anti-heretical section of Romans 16:17–20a.[23] Contrary to the rest of the letter, Paul suddenly sounds a sharp note. Is Romans 16 therefore not part of the original letter to the Romans? No. The harsh tone is not directed against the Roman church, which is even praised (16:19) like it is in the rest of the letter (1:8; 15:14).[24] The sharp polemic is directed against third persons: against possible heretics not belonging to the Roman church but maybe planning to infiltrate it. Paul may think of his opponents in the east, fearing that they could reach out and influence the Romans' opinion of him. In the rest of the letter, these outside "heretics" were not mentioned directly (except for maybe 15:31). We therefore cannot expect the angry tone in the other Romans passages.[25]

[22](a) 2 Tim. (1:16–18; 4:13, 16–20) tries to reflect the situation of Acts 28:16–31 and the collection trip of Acts 20:2–3, 5ff., 15ff. But contrary to 2 Tim. (4:20), Timothy was *present* at least in Corinth (Acts 20:4; Rom. 16:21). Thus 2 Tim. 4:20a is superfluous. It tells Timothy that Erastus stayed in Corinth. The historical Timothy already knew it! (b) Trophimus was not left behind sick in Miletus (2 Tim. 4:20), he gladly accompanied Paul to Jerusalem (Acts 21:29; 20:4). (c) Another example would be 1 Tim. 1:3. Contrary to this verse, Timothy was not left behind when Paul moved from Ephesus to Macedonia (Acts 19:22; 20:1–4; Rom. 16:21).

[23]E.g., Käsemann, *Römer,* 399–400.

[24]*parakalō* (16:17), on the other hand, occurs also in Rom. 12:1, 15:30.

[25]For other arguments in favor of Rome as the destination of Rom. 16, see my *Die stadtrömischen* 124ff. Pages 131–35, e.g., furnish *linguistic data* which indicate that Rom. 16 was dictated together with the rest of the letter to the Romans.

II. The Households of Aristobulus and Narcissus (16:10b, 11b)

Aristobulus and Narcissus are non-Christians: (a) Paul does not send greetings to them but to people in their households. If they were Christians, Paul would also greet these heads of households themselves—similarly to 16:3–5 and probably 16:14, 15. (b) Only a *part* of their households is Christian. Otherwise Paul would have formulated *hoi Aristoboulou* instead of *hoi ek tōn Aristoboulou*. The attribute *tous ontas en kyriō* points in the same direction: those who are Christian—contrary to the others in this household. These Christians were slaves, freedmen, or freedwomen of Aristobulus and Narcissus. There is no means to define their social status more concretely.[26]

Was Aristobulus a member of the royal Herodian family? The least we can say is that he seems to have immigrated to Rome: His name occurs very rarely in the city of Rome.[27] In the event that he had brought his Christian slaves with him from the east, we would be able to identify one channel through which Christianity entered into the capital city of the empire.

III. Women—Men

Romans 16:3–16 name 26 Christian individuals in Rome: 9 women and 17 men. But who is praised for being especially active in the church? More women than men!

* Seven (or six) women:

— Prisca 16:3–4, *synergos* etc.
— Mary 16:6, *polla ekopiasen eis hymas*
— Junia (see below) 16:7, *synaichmalōtoi mou, episēmoi en tois apostolois*
— Tryphaena and
— Tryphosa 16:12, *kopiōsas en kyriō*
— Persis 16:12, *polla ekopiasen en kyriō*
— perhaps also: Rufus' mother 16:13, *mētēr kai emou*

* Five (or three) men:

— Aquila 16:3–4, *synergos* etc.
— Andronicus 16:7, *synaichmalōtoi mou, episēmoi en tois apostolois*
— Urbanus 16:9, *synergos hēmōn*
— perhaps: Apelles 16:10, *dokimos en Christō*
— perhaps: Rufus 16:13, *eklektos en kyriō*[28]

---

[26]Slaves could live in the house of the patron even after being freed: cf. e.g., Pliny, *Ep.* 2:17:9.

[27]In the thousands of inscriptions of *CIL* VI only twice: 17577 and 29104.

[28]Epainetos is *aparchē tēs Asias* and *agapētos mou*, but this does not express a special activity in the Roman church. The same is true about the *agapētoi mou* Ampliatus and Stachys. *agapētos* is not an indication of special activity as Persis shows. She is "beloved." but her activity has to be mentioned separately: she "has worked hard in the Lord" (16:12).

If we were especially picky, we could even state that Andronicus' and Urbanus' activities mentioned took place in the east and not in Rome (*synaichmalōtoi mou, hēmōn*). Mary on the contrary earned special merits in the Roman church (*eis hymas*).

The active part the women took can also be observed in two other instances: (a) *kopiaō* is a technical term describing the labors of a missionary. Paul uses it for himself in Galatians 4:11 and 1 Corinthians 15:10. In Romans 16:3–16 it is used·four times—exclusively for women, not for men. (b) Prisca is mentioned *before* her husband Aquila in Romans 16:3; Acts 18:18, 26; and 2 Timothy 4:19. Only 1 Corinthians 16:19 (cf. Acts 18:2) presents the opposite order. Apparently Prisca was even more outstanding in her work for the church than was Aquila.[29]

One woman in our list deserves special attention since she has been mistaken for a man for centuries: Junia. In the majuscules, we cannot distinguish between *Iounian*, an accusative of a feminine "Junia," and *Iounian*, the accusative of a masculine "Junias." Therefore we have to move on to the minuscules. According to Aland's textual critical apparatus, the feminine "Junia" does not appear in the manuscripts. Indeed, most of the medieval scribes of minuscules made Junias a man. But not all, as I discovered recently: Minuscule 33 (9th century) reads the feminine *iounian*. Which reading is to be preferred? Clearly "Junia." "Junia" was a common name in the Roman Empire, while "Junias" did not exist. The modern grammars[30] support a masculine reading by theorizing that "Junias" was a short form of "Junianus," without being able to quote evidence for this assumption. The fathers and mothers of the early church knew better, always identifying Andronicus' companion as the woman Junia.[31] The very first church father coming up with the masculine version was Aegidius of Rome (A.D. 1245–1316).[32] For medieval authors and scribes "Junia" was the *"lectio difficilior."* They could not picture a woman as an active missionary.

Andronicus and Junia may have travelled together as a married mis-

---

[29]Meeks, *First Urban Christians*, 59, assumes that Prisca occupied a higher social position than Aquila and was therefore mentioned before him. Our source (Rom. 16), however, is not secular but Christian. It stands in the wider context of Gal. 3:28 and hardly cares about a person's significance in the Roman society. It cares about a person's significance for the church: see e.g., Rom. 16:3b, 4, 5a. Also the passage Rom. 16:21–23 does not list the socially elevated first (Erastus with his municipal office and Gaius with his spacious habitation). It first mentions five other Christians. One of them is a missionary co-worker, another functions as Paul's secretary. If Luke had known anything about a socially elevated status of Prisca, he would have loved to mention it, distinguished women being a preferred subject for him: e.g., Luke 8:3; Acts 17:4, 12; cf. 16:14; 17:34.

[30]E.g., Blass–Debrunner–Funk, *Grammar*, 68.

[31]Some also as a woman Julia—like P[46].

[32]See the history of interpretation of Rom. 16:7 by Brooten, "Junia," 141–44. Fàbrega, "Junia(s)," 59, erroneously relies on Migne's reading "Junias" in Origen's commentary (Migne, PG 14, 1281B and 1289A), although all other textual witnesses to this commentary (including the quotation by Hraban of Fulda in PL 111,1608D) offer "Junia."

sionary couple, as 1 Corinthians 9:5 reports about other apostles too. The most natural understanding of *episēmoi en tois apostolois* is that they both were outstanding apostles—and not only splendid *in the eyes* of the apostles. Why would they have been famous only in *their* eyes? The *en* has to be translated as "among" (the apostles) like in 1 Corinthians 15:12 and James 5:13–14, 19.

After having analyzed the women's role in Romans 16, we unfortunately cannot generalize these results. A group of 26 people hardly allows any generalization about the Roman church as a whole. On the contrary, the data that I analyzed in my book about Rome[33] suggest that the women's influence in the Roman church was reduced to a minimum at the latest by the end of the first century. While the 50s of the first century still saw influential church women like Prisca, Junia, Persis, Phoebe, and others, this female influence later survived only in marginal Christian groups which soon were viewed as having the taint of heresy. In 1 Clement 21:7; 1:3, at the end of the first century, the voices of the women were already silenced—otherwise these verses could not have been formulated.

IV. Jewish Christians—Gentile Christians

The names by themselves do not release any information about the persons' Jewish or pagan background.[34] But luckily Paul calls three Roman persons in Romans 16:3–16 "my kins(wo)men": Andronicus, Junia, and Herodion. The term *syngenēs* never occurs in the other Pauline letters. In Romans, however, after chapters 9–11 and especially 9:3,[35] Paul has a *special interest* in emphasizing the Jewish origin of Christians (Rom. 16:7, 11, 21). Why? Paul prays for the salvation of the Jews (10:1). "I ask, has God rejected his people? By no means! I myself am an Israelite" (11:1), and he thus offers a proof that God did not reject the Jews. The "kins(wo)men" in Romans 16 are living proofs of the same grace towards Israel. They and Paul himself are the "remnant at the present time, chosen by grace" (11:5). "Israel failed to obtain what it sought. But the elect (i.e., Paul and his Christian kins[wo]men) obtained it" (11:7). They are signs of hope that Israel is not yet lost. On the contrary, Israel will be fully included in the salvation one time in the future (11:12, 23, 24, 26, 29, 31, 32).

Having this kind of special theological interest in emphasizing the Jewish kinship of Christians in Romans—and only in Romans—Paul probably applies the term "kins(wo)man" rather consistently to all Jewish Christians

---

[33]See Lampe, *Die stadtrömischen.* See pages 119–23, 297–99, 73, 78, 82, 96–102, 104, 106–7, 112, 115, 161, 180, 200–203, 207, 229, 238–39, 263, 269, 284–87, 305 about the women in Roman Christianity.

[34]See also Solin, "Juden und Syrer," 665. Concerning "Maria" as a pagan name see below.

[35]*hyper tōn adelphōn mou tōn syngenōn mou kata sarka.*

he can identify in the group of Romans 16.[36] The list, then, shows that only a small minority of Jewish Christians existed among the 26 persons of this Roman group (15%).

This result is affirmed by two other observations. (a) Several times in Romans Paul presumes that the vast majority in the Roman church is Gentile.[37] These clear and direct statements seem to contradict the impression that much of the contents of Romans could be understood only by people who were trained in Jewish culture. The solution of the paradox is at hand if we assume that most people in the Roman church were of Gentile origin but had lived as sympathizers on the margins of the synagogues before they became Christian.[38]

(b) Only three names of the Romans 16 list occur also in the Jewish inscriptions (CIJ) of Rome: "Maria" (=Mary) and the typically Latin names "Rufus" and "Julia."[39] Besides these two Latin names, even "Maria" cannot be considered especially Jewish. It is often taken for granted that "Maria/Mary" equals the semitic *mirjam*. The following epigraphical data, however, suggest that "Maria" in Romans 16 represents the pagan name of a Roman *gens*. "Marius," in the feminine form "Maria," was a Latin *nomen gentile* by which a woman was sufficiently characterized without having to carry a *cognomen*. This Latin-pagan "Maria" occurs approximately 108 times in the city of Rome inscriptions of CIL VI. The semitic "Maria" cannot be counted even 20 times in Rome.[40] Thus, chances are good that our Christian Maria was a Gentile—Paul in fact does not call her a "kinswoman," as we saw.[41]

[36]The only exception seems to be Aquila, a Jewish Christian according to Acts 18:2. Paul reports so many other things about him and his wife that the ethnic attribute is understandably left unremarked.

[37]1:5–6, 13–15; 11:13, 17–18, 24, 28, 30–31; 15:15–16, 18; 9:3ff. Cf. also 15:9ff., 6:17–21 in connection with 1:18ff., further Acts 28:24–31.

[38]See a more elaborate discussion of the problem and materials in my *Die stadtrömischen*, 53–63; ET forthcoming. There the issue is also put into the broader perspective of the first two centuries. A strong flow of originally Jewish materials prevailed in the Roman church during both centuries. Gentile Christians being bearers of Jewish traditions, etc. The *sy Ioudaios* in Rom. 2:17 is rhetorical and cannot be used for the identification of the addressee: 2:17ff. are an example for the rhetorical *dialogus cum Iudaeis* that Paul leads in front of a predominantly Gentile audience.

[39]"*Maria*" CIJ 251, 252, 457, 459, 1, 137, 374, 375, 511, 96, 12. Outside of Rome also Josephus, *War* 6.201; *CPJ* II 223, 227. "*Julia*" e.g., *CIJ* 123, 124, 34, 35, 352. "*Rufus*" CIJ 145, 146. Outside of Rome also Josephus, *War* 2.52, 2.74; *Ant.* 17.266, 17.294. Josephus and *CPJ* only attribute two other names of our list to Jews *outside* of Rome: "Andronikos," Jos. *Ant.* 13.75ff., *CPJ* I 18, III 470, and "Tryphaina" *CPJ* II 421:183, III 453:20. The remaining 19 names of our list are not mentioned in Josephus or *CPJ.*

[40]See the epigraphical material in *Die stadtrömischen*, 146–47.

[41]Fàbrega, "Junia(s),"49–50 (see above note 32) translates *syngenēs* as "friend" instead of "kins(wo)man." His decision is weakly based. (a) According to Fàbrega, Jason and Sosipater in Rom. 16:21 were not Jewish Christians (Acts 17:5; 20:4). But Jason could have easily been a Jew in Luke's eyes (see Acts 17:4a). The same is true about Sopater (see Acts 17:10–12). (b) The context is decisive for the semantical definition: Rom. 9–11, especially 9:3, clearly suggest the meaning "kins(wo)man" in Rom. 16. (c) Fàbrega notes that the "Jewish Christians" Mary, Rufus, his mother, Prisca, and Aquila are not called *syngeneis* in Rom. 16. The

V. Immigrants—Natives of Rome

We already saw that *at least* Prisca, Aquila, Epaenetus, Andronicus, Junia, Urbanus, Rufus, his mother, Ampliatus, Stachys, Persis, and Apelles had travelled between the east and Rome. But who was actually of oriental origin? Many of the twelve persons mentioned may have been Romans, having been expelled by Claudius and returning to Rome later. Only four were visibly of oriental birth: Aquila (Pontus), Epaenetus (first convert in Asia), Andronicus, and Junia, who belonged to the first Palestinian apostles and had been Christians already before Paul.

Do we have to give up on our question? A second approach is possible on the basis of the inscriptions in CIL VI (computerized concordance) and of Solin's book about Greek names in Rome.[42] Which names of our list were rare in the city of Rome, which occurred frequently?[43]

Julia	+ 1400 times
Hermes	640
Rufus	ca. 374
*Junia	+ 250
Prisca/Priscilla	+ 200
Maria	ca. 108
Urbanus	ca. 95
Ampliatus	ca. 80
Tryphaena	47
Tryphosa	29
Nereus	28
*Aquila	ca. 28
*Andronicus	19
Philologus	18
Apelles	15
Stachys	11
Phlegon	7
Persis	3
Hermas	3
*Epaenetus	3
Asynkritos	1
Olympas	0
Patrobas	0, but the name is a shortened version of Patrobius
Patrobius	4
Herodion	0

---

reason is easy: Not only Mary, but also Rufus and his mother were not Jewish Christians. Nothing tells us that Rufus and his mother belonged to the Jewish Christian family of Mark 15:21 (Simon of Cyrene and his sons Rufus and Alexander). The connection is not even likely: Why didn't Paul mention Rufus' famous father in Rom. 16:13? Concerning Aquila see above note 35. About Prisca's background we know nothing.

[42]Solin, *Griechischen Personennamen*. Note that I shall deduct the Rom. 16 examples from Solin's figures in order to obtain a picture of the environment.

[43]The figures in the table are already a result of subtractions. Many inscriptions being clearly not contemporary to Rom. 16 are already subtracted from the total number of oc-

How does this list coincide with our previous findings? The four oriental persons we found earlier are marked with an asterisk. Three of them, Aquila, Andronicus, and Epaenetus, indeed appear in the lower section (< 29) of the table. Only the oriental Junia ranks high—for good reasons: Her name is not a *cognomen* but a Latin *nomen gentile*, by which a woman was sufficiently identified. Prominent Roman *gentes* included a lot of orientals among their slaves. Being freed, they obtained the name of the *gens*, in this case "Junius/Junia." Our oriental Junia is indeed most likely a freed slave or a descendant of a freed(wo)man of the *gens Junia*.[44]

With three factual orientals occurring in the lower section of the table, chances are good that also the other rare names in the lower section belong to immigrants. Indeed, earlier we had already identified three of them as names of individuals who had at least travelled between the east and Rome: Apelles, Stachys, and Persis.

Thus, about 14 people out of 26 were presumably not born in Rome itself. An oriental origin of the remaining 12 cannot be excluded—but neither can it be indicated. We do not even get a clue about Prisca: Did Aquila meet and start seeing her in Pontus—or in Rome?

Looking at the Roman church of the first and second centuries as a whole, the proportion 14:26 seems a minimal figure. Other data suggest that the proportion of immigrants in the Roman church was much higher than just 54% during this period. The influx of *peregrini* to the church of the capital city was immense—and also had its theological impact.[45]

VI. Juridical and Social Position

Which juridical position did the 26 people obtain? Do their *names* release any information about *free birth* or *slave origins*? I am not going to repeat the methodological state of affairs, the five criteria I used, or the many epigraphical data.[46] I just quote the results of my analysis:

1. The names "Urbanus," "Prisca," "Aquila," and "Rufus" do not indicate any affinity to people born into slavery. Surprisingly, this result co-

---

currences in Rome. See the more comprehensive list in my *Die stadtrömischen*, 139–40. This does not mean, however, that all the inscriptions counted in the table talk about first-century people. The dating of the inscriptions is often uncertain.

[44]A more elaborate discussion of Junia's social position in *Die stadtrömischen*, 146, 147, and see Lampe, "Junia" in the *Anchor Bible Dictionary* (forthcoming). "Junia" and "Aquila" are only examples for the general rule that Latin names do not indicate a western origin of a person. See my *Die stadtrömischen*, 140 note 47.

[45]For the whole see *Die stadtrömischen*, 117–19, 296–97, 347; specific material 26, 34, 36, 42, 44, 46, 48, 52, 64, 66, 68, 79, 95–96, 110–11, 128, 136–42, 146, 148–49, 152–53, 156, 159, 182–200, 202, 208, 219–21, 230–31, 238–39, 242, 246–50, 253–70, 284–87, 289–90, 294–95; theological impact pp. 320–34.

[46]See *Die stadtrömischen*, 141–53. Prosopographical information about most of the Rom. 16 individuals can also be found in the corresponding articles I wrote for the *Anchor Bible Dictionary* (forthcoming).

incides with three other independent observations. And the reader may decide whether this is mere coincidence or whether a causal relation plays a role: (a) Two of the persons mentioned are married: Aquila and Prisca— apparently both free born. They are also the only ones about whom we have more detailed prosopographical information.[47] (b) Only Aquila, Prisca, and Urbanus are called Paul's "co-workers" in Romans 16—nobody else! (c) Rufus' mother was a mother also to Paul (16:13). This fits well to a free matron of a household being hospitable to an apostle.

2. The following people were most probably slaves or freed(wo)men: Nereus, Hermes, Persis, Herodion, Tryphosa, Tryphaena, Ampliatus. Freed- women or descendants of freed(wo)men were Julia, Junia, and most likely Maria.

3. For the remaining twelve persons, we are not able to make a proba- bility statement (Asyncritus, Patrobas, Philologus, Andronicus, Olympas, Apelles, Phlegon, Hermas, Stachys, Epaenetus, also Nereus' sister and Rufus' mother).[48]

4. Thus, more than two thirds of the people for whom we can make a probability statement have an affinity to slave origins. The slaves or freed(wo)men of Narcissus and Aristobulus were not alone in the Romans 16 group. And looking at the first two centuries as a whole, we discover indeed plenty of Christian slaves and freed(wo)men in Rome.[49]

But to what extent is the two-thirds proportion representative for the Roman church? Interestingly enough, a similar proportion between free- born people and persons born into slavery occurs in a variant Roman data pool;[50] although it is difficult to know whether this is mere coincidence or not. We do not even know for sure how high the percentage of slaves and freed(wo)men was in the entire society. The estimations vary between 20% and 40% slaves. The freed(wo)men counted at least as many on top of the slave figure, which leaves 20–60% to the freeborn people.[51] How- ever, if we take the mean average of these figures (30% slaves, 30% freed[wo]men, 40% freeborn), we end up with proportions comparable to the aforementioned two data pools of the Roman church (63–67% slave-

---

[47]See the chapter about the couple in *Die stadtrömischen*, 156–64.

[48]While Rufus most likely was freeborn, the same is not necessarily true about his mother who could have been a freedwoman. While Nereus' most likely was born a slave, the same is not necessarily true about his sister.

[49]Named and anonymous; see *Die stadtrömischen*, 68ff., 71ff., 80, 98ff., 104ff., 153ff., 182ff., 278ff., etc.

[50]Looking at the list on pp. 422–24 in my *Die stadtrömischen*, we discover a similar per- centage of slaves and freed slaves as in Rom. 16: out of the remaining 74 Christians whom we know by name in the first two centuries in Rome (I subtracted the 26 people of Rom. 16), 18–19 were slaves or freed slaves, 10–12 were freeborn, while we cannot state anything about the juridical status of the remaining 43. This means that ca. 63% of the people about whom we can make a statement were of slave origins, and only ca. 37% were freeborn.

[51]See *Die stadtrömischen*, 143.

born, 33–37% freeborn). At some points, the social profile of the church indeed seems to mirror the profile of the entire society.[52]

To what extent is the juridical status an indicator for the social position? Many freed(wo)men were rich business people and in a better economic position than many freeborn. Therefore the juridical status—free birth, slave, or freed slave—does not necessarily say much about the socioeconomic position of an individual. Only a general direction can be given for the Romans 16 persons by asking: How did the proportions between socially elevated persons and lower strata people look in the Roman church during the first two centuries? The *humiliores* represented the vast majority in the Roman church—and socially elevated people formed only a minority.[53] This is especially true for the first century. Referring the reader to the materials in my book, I only select one significant example here: Several Roman Christians during the first century sold themselves into slavery in order to finance the support of Christian brothers and sisters.[54] This illustrates the necessity for social action—there were many needy among the Roman Christians. And it discloses the lack of enough well-to-do Christians supporting these needy.

VII. Divided Nature of the Roman Christianity— House Congregations

During the two first centuries the Christians of the city of Rome met separately in privately owned locations scattered around the capital city. Forming a number of house-churches, they had no central worship facility— a lack of central coordination that matched the profile of the separated synagogues in Rome.[55]

With separate pockets of Christians in the city of Rome being prevalent throughout the first two centuries and even beyond them, Romans 16 must be read in this light. Indicating the divided nature of Roman Christianity, Paul does not call it *ekklēsia* anywhere in Romans, not even in 1:7 where we would expect it according to the other Pauline letters. Only a part is called *ekklēsia*: the house-church around Aquila and Prisca (Rom. 16:5).[56]

Besides this first one, four other pockets of Christians in the city of Rome are identified by Romans 16:

[52]See ibid., 113, 451 with other examples.

[53]See ibid., 112ff.

[54]See ibid., 68–69 where these cases are further analyzed.

[55]See ibid., 301–45, 367–68. In a topographical study on pp. 10–52 I also try to indicate the quarters in Rome where early Christians lived.

[56]I do not agree with Gielen, "Paulinischen Formel," 109–25, who suggests that this formula meant the whole church in one city. (a) She admits herself (note 70) that this view can only be maintained if Rom. 16 was a separate letter. (b) Only in Corinth we know of a central meeting place for all Christians in the city (Rom. 16:23 e.g.). But for Corinth this formula is never used!

— The Christians around Asyncritus, Phlegon, Hermes, Patrobas, and Hermas (16:14).

— The Christians around Philologus, Julia, Olympas, Nereus, and his sister (16:15).

— The Christians in Aristobulus' household (16:10).

— The Christians in Narcissus' household (16:11).

If we assume that the other fourteen individuals in the Romans 16 list belonged to none of these five crystallization points, and that they hardly have belonged to only *one* further circle, the result is at least seven separate groups. The number grew to at least eight when Paul himself started to assemble Christians in his Roman rented lodging (Acts 28:30–31).[57]

Looking at the lack of a central worship place in Rome throughout the centuries, we can hardly avoid the conclusion that these (at least) eight circles also worshipped separately—in separate dwellings somewhere in the different quarters of the city. Thus, probably all eight can be identified as worshipping "house-congregations" or "house-churches." This does not exclude that some of them were also held together by kinship or household-ties.[58]

In the later history of the Roman church, this divided nature helped "heresies" to survive in the capital city for decades. It also prevented the institution of a Roman monarchical bishop until the second half of the second century.[59] Although we are already far beyond Romans 16 with this, it shows again the broader perspectives in which the data of Romans 16 can be integrated.

---

[57]Verse 30 is pre–Lukan, as Lüdemann affirms (*Das frühe Christentum,* 275). I do not agree, however, that *en idiō misthōma* could be translated "at his own expense" (see also the RSV). This is too general: *misthōma* always means specifically the contract price, the rent you pay. *en idiō misthōma* therefore indicates that Paul lived "at his own *rental* expense." But what did he rent? Certainly not a horse and buggy. Also the context (v. 30b) assures that Luke talks about a dwelling place.

[58]See, at least, the worshipping communities of the slaves and freed(wo)men in Aristobulus' and Narcissus' households. Their "house-churches" are not without parallel: we know of several households in which the slaves and freed(wo)men cultivated their own religion—independently from the patron. Also Jewish slaves and freedmen of one and the same households constituted their own synagogues. See the materials in *Die stadtrömischen,* 319.

[59]See *Die stadtrömischen,* 320–45.

15

THE PURPOSE OF ROMANS

Peter Stuhlmacher

In most editions of the Bible the Pauline collection begins with the letter to the Romans. This is no accident. Of all the Pauline letters we possess Romans is without doubt the most important. From Origen through Augustine, Luther, and John Wesley down to Karl Barth, the letter to the Romans has made history both in theology and in the church, and that because of its contents. Anyone who wants to become acquainted with Paul's gospel must above all study Romans. It is this letter which has attracted ever new attention to Paul's gospel right down to the present day. That explains why Romans has been read by the church as the *doctrinae Christianae compendium* (Melanchthon) and is still regarded as such.

Within the framework of Christian theology the exegesis of the Old and New Testaments has the task of confronting the other theological disciplines and the church itself with the primary testimony of Holy Scripture. The original witness of the Bible is the gospel as it was formulated in the historical situation in which it arose. The task of biblical exegesis is to reconstruct that message in such a way that church history, dogmatics, ethics, practical theology, and the church as whole may be sustained and challenged by that message.

Confronted by this task, the New Testament exegete cannot simply take for granted or merely assert the importance of Romans for theology and the church. Rather, he or she must try to show how this letter came into being and why it has proved so important. The more clearly the exegete can demonstrate why Paul wrote Romans and what his purpose was, the better modern readers will be able to come to grips with it. They can then see what it means for them today and where there are reasons for dissenting from Paul. Thus our topic, the purpose of Romans, is not merely a problem of New Testament introduction. It also involves an attempt to develop an understanding of the text in such a way as to facilitate a confrontation with the arguments Paul uses. In this way we shall serve theology and the church today.[1]

I

It is more difficult to come up with a precise definition of the purpose of Romans than would appear at first sight. In part I of *The Romans Debate* (1977) Karl P. Donfried has shown how many different answers have been given to this question in contemporary scholarship. At the same time, he has tried to suggest a way out of the controversy which has a sound methodological basis and makes historical sense.

In the course of history there have been three major ways of understanding Romans: (1) Romans can be understood as a letter addressed particularly to the church in Rome. In that case it must be shown what Paul's objective for the church in Rome was and what made him give such a detailed and comprehensive account of his gospel to a community he had never visited personally. (2) If this solution proves impossible we may ask whether the letter may have been intended not for Rome at all but for some other destination. In 1977 Jacob Jervell published an essay with the suggestive title: "The Letter to Jerusalem: The Origin and Destination of Romans."[2] In Rom. 15:25–33 Paul tells us that before coming to Rome he is going up to Jerusalem with the collection he had made in Galatia(?), Macedonia, and Achaia. He is afraid he will encounter resistance there from the Jews and from his Jewish Christian opponents. So he asks the Christians in Rome to pray for him and for the success of this difficult project. Beginning with Romans 15:25–33 Jervell argues that the core of the letter (i.e., 1:18–11:36) is this: "Paul sets forth and explains what he, as the bearer of the collection given by the Gentiles for the mother congregation in Jerusalem, intends to say so that he as well as the gift will not be rejected. In Jerusalem he expects to be confronted by two parties: non-believing Jews and the Christian congregation (15:30–33)."[3] (3) Finally, it is possible to combine these two suggestions and argue that the message Paul intends to defend at Jerusalem is identical with the gospel he plans to preach at Rome, and from Rome all the way to Spain. Thus Romans is a synopsis of Paul's gospel as a whole, and in the course of history it became for subsequent generations his "testament." This is the view

---

[1]The first draft of this article was delivered in October, 1983, at Fuller Theological Seminary at Pasadena, California, where I was invited to give the Payton Lecture. It is dedicated to my teacher, Ernst Käsemann, in gratitude for his introducing me to Paul's gospel and for the way in which he did it.

[2]Jervell, "Letter to Jerusalem," 53–64.

[3]Ibid., 56.

which Günther Bornkamm developed in an impressive essay.[4] Ulrich Wilckens took the same view in his own great commentary.[5]

If we are to enter the debate with full understanding we must first recognize the reasons which have led to such different answers as to the purpose of Romans. Only when we have achieved this can we propose a plausible solution of our own.

II

The main reasons why the debate about the purpose of Romans has so far remained unresolved are as follows: Paul himself appears to give contradictory reasons for writing this letter and for his intended visit to Rome. (The text of Romans has come down to us in three different versions.) We have only meager information about the beginnings of Christianity in Rome and about the state of the church there at the time the letter was written.

Turning to the first issue, we learn from Romans 1:11–17 that Paul would like to have been the first Christian missionary in Rome but had been prevented for various reasons from being so. Now when he arrives in Rome he will find Christians there already who are praised all over the world for their faith and loyalty. Paul would like to strengthen them in their faith. In Romans 1:11–12 he says he wants to impart to them "some spiritual gift to strengthen you, that is, that we may be mutually encouraged by each other's faith, both yours and mine." At the end of the letter in 15:14–33, Paul goes over his plans again, but this time he expresses himself more clearly. He regards the preaching that had been entrusted to him in the eastern Mediterranean as completed. All that remains is to bring the collection to Jerusalem. After this he plans to press on from Rome to the western part of the Mediterranean. Thus he hopes Rome will serve as a base for his mission to the West. Meanwhile his letter to the Romans would prepare the way for his visit to Rome. A close examination of the text shows that there are both consistencies and seemingly also discrepancies with 1:11–12. It is quite consistent with 1:11–12 when Paul emphasizes in 15:15–16 that he is writing "very boldly by way of reminder because of the grace given" to him by God. He wants to remind them of the essential points of the gospel with which he has been entrusted. According to verse 24 he expects to see the Christians in Rome only in passing on his way to Spain and hopes to receive their support for the new phase of his missionary activity. Meanwhile the Romans can pray for the success and friendly acceptance of the collection in Jerusalem (vv. 30–32). Up to this

[4]Bornkamm, "Last Will and Testament," 16–28. See also Bornkamm's discussion in his *Paul*, 88–96.
[5]Wilckens, *Römer*, 41–48.

point there is no discrepancy between chapters 1 and 15. But as is generally known, things become difficult when we compare what Paul writes in 15:20 (that he makes it his "ambition to preach the gospel, not where Christ has already been named, lest [he] build on another man's foundation") with the usual translation of 1:15 as given in the commentaries of Wilckens, Michel, Schlier, Cranfield, and others (which reads, "So I am eager to preach the gospel to you also who are in Rome").[6] According to 1:15, Paul seems to want to preach his gospel in a community he had not himself founded, whereas in 15:20 he takes pride in preaching the gospel only where no one else had preached it before. So it looks as though Paul is being unfaithful in this very letter to the principle he enunciates in 15:20 (and 2 Cor. 10:13–15). Any answer to the question as to the purpose of Romans must come up with a satisfactory explanation of the relation between 1:15 and 15:20.[7] Does Paul really intend to do missionary work and preach the gospel in Rome himself, or is he trying only to clarify and present that gospel in such a way that the Christians in Rome can agree with him and give him practical support in his further missionary work which has Spain as its goal?

With regard to the second issue the interpreter of Romans is faced with a further problem, this time in connection with the Greek text. At 1:7, 15 the superscription "in Rome" is omitted in Codex Boernerianus (G; 9th century A.D.). Was Romans perhaps not meant as a letter to Rome at all, at least initially? Was it rather a general letter to Christian communities at large? The question becomes acute when we remember that there are three competing versions of the text of Romans. First and foremost there is the familiar long version in our Bibles consisting of chapters 1–16. This is represented by the best texts, Sinaiticus, Vaticanus, etc. Then there is a short version consisting of chapters 1–14. Origen (*Commentary on Romans* X, 43; VII, 453) attributes this shorter form to Marcion, but it was undoubtedly more widespread than the Marcionite communities. Finally, there is the version attested uniquely by P[46], which is dated as early as the second century A.D. This famous manuscript contains only Romans 1–15 + 16:25–27. Chapter 16 has been added as an appendix only. Those who are familiar with the epistle will be aware that Paul takes a strong line in chapters 14–16 over the conflict between "the strong and the weak" in the Roman community.[8] He also gives a clearer picture of his own mis-

---

[6]Wilckens, *Römer* 76; Michel, *Römer*, 79, translates it: "so bin ich bereit, auch euch in Rom das Evangelium zu verkündigen"; Schlier, *Der Römerbrief*, 34, also chooses to translate: "So bin ich bereit, auch euch in Rom das Evangelium zu verkündigen"; Cranfield, *Romans*, 1.74, opts for the following rendering: "so my eager desire is to preach the gospel to you also who are in Rome."

[7]In pregnant fashion Klein, "Paul's Purpose," 29–43: "The solution of this difficulty is the touchstone for every attempt to clarify the circumstances of the origin of Romans" (32, translation revised).

[8]Marxsen, *Introduction*, 95–104, starts, correctly in my opinion, with the assumption that Romans must be taken primarily as addressed to Rome. He also recognizes that after the

sionary strategies and intentions in chapter 15 than he does at the beginning of the letter (see above). Again, chapter 16 contains a surprising number of greetings to friends and acquaintances in Rome. If chapters 15 and 16, or perhaps just chapter 16, are omitted from the original letter it looks very different from what it does with the inclusion of the long list of personal greetings. Hence the question of the purpose of Romans cannot be answered unless we solve the textual problems of chapters 15 and 16.

The third issue concerns our historical knowledge about the origin and development of Roman Christianity in the time of Paul.[9] Given the paucity of evidence we can only surmise that the gospel was brought to Rome from Antioch or Jerusalem by anonymous missionaries, merchants, or artisans, and took root there among the large Jewish population and the so-called God-fearers. Christian missionary activity in the Roman synagogues led to tumults, and the emperor Claudius banished the protagonists, both Jews and Christians, from the city, including the married couple Aquila and Prisca (cf. Acts 18:2). The so-called Claudius edict reported by Suetonius (*Vita Claudii* 25,4) is probably to be dated A.D. 49 (see the entirely credible dating by the Roman historian Orosius, *Hist.* 7,6,15). Only after the death of Claudius, when Nero succeeded him in A.D. 54, were the Jews allowed to return.[10] In Romans 16:3–4 it is assumed that Aquila and Prisca are back in Rome. This is basically all we know. But it should be recalled that in Romans 1:5–6 Paul reckons the Roman Christians as Gentiles. This means that he assumes that by the time he wrote Romans the majority of the community was of Gentile origin. Any answer to the problem of the purpose of Romans must be consistent with the data just mentioned.

This covers the historical situation and the issues relevant to our theme. We must now take up these questions in detail.

III

In his earlier essay in *The Romans Debate* Donfried lays down two principles of vital importance for the interpretation of Romans. First, "any study of Romans should proceed on the initial assumption that this letter

---

Claudius edict the Jews and Christians in Rome split up. When the edict was rescinded, the tension between these two groups, far from diminishing, became more acute. In his opinion Romans was written to strengthen the Christian community and to enable it to stand on its own feet. The question of the "strong" and "weak" living together, which Paul discusses in concrete terms, leads Marxsen to assume that it was the prevailing situation in Rome that was responsible, at least in part, for the lengthy exposition at the beginning of the letter. What this situation was he unfortunately does not specify in detail.

[9]On these issues see Lampe, *Die stadtrömischen.*

[10]On the resulting division between the synagogue and the Christian community see n. 8 above and Lampe, *Die Stadtrömischen,* 8–9: "Hat Loslösung des Christentums von der Syn-

was written by Paul to deal with a concrete situation at Rome. . . . "; and
second, "any study of Romans should proceed on the assumption that Romans 16 is an integral part of the original letter. . . . "[11] Both principles
are methodologically sound and lead to an interesting and consistent view
of the letter. Let us start by stating this view in the form of a thesis. Paul
writes Romans, probably from Corinth, shortly before setting off for Jerusalem with the collection. In writing it he is preparing for his intended
visit to Rome and requests the Roman Christians' help in his plan to carry
his mission as far as Spain. Paul knows from friends and acquaintances
such as Aquila and Prisca, however, that there is not only agreement with
his gospel in Rome but also some doubt about it. This doubt calls into question his whole missionary preaching, aimed as it was primarily at the Gentiles. Doubts arose in the main from Jewish Christian criticism. In this letter
he attempts to convince the Roman Christians of the substance of his controverted gospel. The letter is an exposition and clarification of that gospel vis-à-vis the criticism Paul knows to be rampant in Rome. It is very
likely that Paul intends to defend himself before the Christians in Jerusalem with arguments similar to those presented in Romans. But Jerusalem
is not the letter's principal destination. The Apostle's main intention was
to achieve a consensus with the Christians in the metropolis. That is why
he engages in chapters 1–16 in a detailed discussion of problems and questions which the Christians at Rome are asking about the Pauline gospel—
as Paul himself knows from the reports of his friends. This being so, Romans is not an abstract dogmatic "dialogue with the Jews" who reject Paul's
gospel, but a didactic and hortatory document with an apologetic accent,
to be read and discussed by the Christians in Rome. In the course of history
this document came to be regarded by the church as Paul's testament. After
all, it does bring out the Pauline gospel in all clarity. Now that we have
the thesis before us let us present the reasons which lead to this view.

IV

The three main questions which arise when we try to define the purpose of Romans are answered most simply and clearly when we take the
view of Romans we have just presented.

First, as regards the discrepancy between 1:15 and 15:20, which has
been so much discussed, it should be noted that it does not exist at all

---

agoge etwas mit Auseinandersetzung und Streit zu tun und suchen wir in Rom etwas derartiges,
dann kennen wir nichts anderes als die Ereignisse rund um das 'Claudiusedikt.' [If the de-
tachment of Christianity from the synagogue has anything to do with confrontation and conflict, and if we look for something like this in Rome, we know of nothing other than the
events surrounding the edict of Claudius.]

[11]Both quotations from Donfried, "False Presuppositions," 103–4.

in the Greek text![12] If 1:13–15 is read in context, these verses state that the Apostle had often wanted to visit Rome but up to now had always been prevented from "bearing fruit" as a missionary there as he had elsewhere among the Gentiles. As the Apostle to the Gentiles he is equally indebted to Greeks and barbarians, cultured and uncultured—hence his long-standing readiness to preach the gospel in Rome as he had done elsewhere. Verse 15 refers back to verse 13 and explains Paul's original plan, not what he means to do at the time of writing. Käsemann and Zeller are right in their commentaries when they take verse 15 as the conclusion of verses 13–15 and translate it in the past tense: "Therefore for my part I was prepared to preach the gospel to you in Rome as well."[13] Thus this verse in no way indicates that Paul is still intending to come as a missionary to preach his gospel in Rome. What he hopes to achieve there he has already told them in verses 11–12, and he repeats it in unambiguous terms in 15:15, 23–24. He intends to visit the Christians in Rome, reach a consensus with them, and enlist their support for the missionary work he was planning in the West. He has no intention of engaging in such activity in somebody else's area. All he hopes for is Christian unity in respect of his gospel, such as would help him in the evangelization of still unconverted Gentiles in northern Italy, southern Gaul, and the Iberian Peninsula.

As regards the textual problems in Romans, there can be no doubt that the omission of "in Rome" in 1:7 and 15 in Codex Boernerianus is a later corruption rather than a secondary addition in all the other MSS. It is what is called an "ecumenical correction," "made in order to show that the letter is of general rather than of local application."[14] The simplest explanation for the three different textual traditions about the length of Romans[15] is to suppose that the longest version, Romans 1–16, is the original. It was then reduced to the short version consisting of chapters 1–14, as attested by Marcion and other witnesses. This reduction was done for various reasons. It was then successively expanded to include chapters 1–15 and 1–16. The textual peculiarity of P[46] marks an intermediate stage on the road to restoration and had no effect on the subsequent history of the text. Historically superior, and therefore the most authentic version of Romans, is the Alexandrian text, which includes all sixteen chapters. But if we start with chapters 1–16 as the original text of Romans, the widespread opinion that Paul wrote his letter to a community unknown to him becomes considerably less probable. Mail from Corinth to Rome by sea under favorable sailing conditions took about seven to eight days

[12]Thus, M. Kettunen in his dissertation written under my direction, *Abfassungszweck*, 119ff., has worked it out very admirably.

[13]Käsemann, *Römer*, 14. The ET *Commentary on Romans*, 16 misses the point by translating the verb "bestand" in the perfect instead of the past tense. Zeller, *Römer*, 39, translates: " . . . So (bestand) meinerseits Bereitschaft, auch euch, den Römern, das Evangelium zu verkünden."

[14]Metzger, *TCGNT*, 505.

[15]For the following argument I am indebted to my colleague, Walter Thiele of Sigmaringen.

(cf. Pliny, *Natural History* 19,1, 3–4).[16] Thus Paul could easily and frequently have been informed by his friends in Rome mentioned in chapter 16 about conditions prevailing there.

Coming finally to the few data we have regarding Christianity in Rome prior to and contemporary with Paul, we discover some really interesting facts. If it is true that Christianity reached Rome through Gentile missionaries from Jerusalem or Antioch, they must have brought a type of Christian faith which had many affinities with the gospel preached by Paul. Paul, of course, had used Antioch as a base for his missionary work for several years (cf. Acts 11–15). And the local Christian tradition in that city was derived from the "Hellenists" who were driven out from Jerusalem. It was this tradition that Paul himself adopted and shared with the Hellenists. Paul is therefore not being merely rhetorical when he expresses his gratitude for the "standard of teaching" which was current in Rome (6:17). He really means it. Above all, this phrase is not the "stupid interpolation" of a later copyist as Bultmann suggested.[17] Paul is quite sure that the Romans and he would be able to agree unreservedly about the original gospel. Now there is a further consideration. The Christian mission in Rome as in other cities of the diaspora attracted primarily the "God-fearers" who congregated around the synagogue.[18] These God-fearers were profoundly influenced by the teaching and preaching of the synagogue. They lived in obedience to the commandments but were reluctant to accept circumcision. Hence from a legalistic Jewish point of view they were still pagans. When Paul speaks of the Christians in Rome as former "Gentiles" this does not mean that from a religious point of view they were no better than pagan idolators, incapable of understanding the gospel of Jesus as the Christ. The "Holy Scriptures," in the form of the Septuagint, the Decalogue, the prayers of the synagogue, the Jewish messianic hope, etc. were familiar to many of them. Therefore Paul is by no means exaggerating when he addresses the Gentiles in Rome, e.g., in Romans 7:1, as "those who know the law."

Paul probably wrote his letter in the spring of 56 while at Corinth and sent it to Rome with Phoebe, the deaconess mentioned in 16:1. At this time not only Aquila and Prisca had returned to Rome with other Jewish

[16]My attention was called to this passage by Dr. Rainer Riesner of Tübingen.

[17]"Glossen im Römerbrief" in Bultmann, *Exegetica*, esp. 278–84.

[18]On the Godfearers see Schmithals, *Der Römerbrief als historisches Problem*, 69–91. I do not subscribe to Schmithals' literary hypotheses about the composition of Romans because it unnecessarily transgresses the clearly defined limitations laid down most recently by Aland–Aland, *Text*, 291–92: "None of the composition theories advanced today in various forms with regard to the Pauline letters, for example, has any support in the manuscript tradition, whether in Greek, in the early versions, or in the patristic quotations from the New Testament. At no place where a break has been posited in the Pauline letters does the critical apparatus show even a suspicion of any interference with the inevitable deposit of telltale variants. In other words, from the beginning of their history as a manuscript tradition the Pauline letters have always had the same form that they have today."

Christian friends and acquaintances of Paul who had been banished by Claudius, but other Jewish Christians who had lived through or at least had heard about Paul's conflicts in Galatia, Philippi, and Corinth also returned. They had also encountered the criticisms of Paul's enemies against the Apostle's person and gospel. This means that by the year 56 there were living at Rome Christian opponents as well as friends of Paul. His critics included members of those Jewish circles who were angry (with some justification) at the "apostate" Paul because of his preaching and missionary methods (cf. 15:31). But first and foremost there were those, mainly from Jewish Christian circles, who since the Apostolic Council and especially since the fracas at Antioch (cf. Gal. 2:11–14) did not agree any longer with Paul's mission and preaching. It would appear that the conflicts Paul had faced in Galatia, Philippi, and Corinth with Jewish Christian "counter missionaries" now threatened to spread to Rome, thus making it impossible for him to set foot in the metropolis.

How do we know all this? From Romans itself. According to 3:8 Paul is embittered over the "slanderous charge" which "some people" are leveling at him: "Let us do evil that good may come" (KJV). Only Christians can speak like that of "us." The Apostle is so infuriated by the slanderers who are saying this sort of thing behind his back that he declares them worthy of God's judgment (just as harshly as he does in Galatians, Philippians, and 2 Corinthians).[19] Romans 3:8, "their condemnation is just," is not the only instance of this. In 16:17–18 Paul advises his correspondents in Rome to beware of those who "cause dissensions and difficulties in opposition to the doctrine which you have been taught." This final warning is certainly not the gloss of a later copyist interrupting and disturbing the greetings. Rather it is the well-grounded advice of the Apostle. The Romans should pay no attention to the insinuations of those in Rome who oppose the gospel planted there, for Paul is entirely in agreement with it. Romans 16:17–18 points back to 6:7 and draws the consequences of the laudatory remarks Paul had made there about the "standard of doctrine" which was maintained in Rome.

Once these connections have been recognized, the various assertions and enquiries Paul makes in the course of this letter fall easily into place. When the Apostle emphasizes in 1:16 that he is not ashamed of the gospel, he is signaling to friend and foe alike among his recipients that he intends to stick to his embattled cause in Rome as elsewhere.[20] In 2:16 he proceeds to defend the gospel against the charge of preaching cheap

[19]It is sufficient to compare Gal. 1:9; Phil. 3:7, 18–19; 2 Cor. 11:13–15.

[20]Schmithals, *Der Römerbrief als historisches Problem*, 92, has rightly pointed to the fact that v. 16 is clearly to be understood as a reference to Rome: "Ich scheue mich nicht, *dies* Evangelium auch in Rom zu predigen . . . ich fürchte mich nicht vor der Auseinandersetzung, die meine Predigt auch in Rom mit sich bringen wird" [I am not hesitant to preach *this* gospel in Rome. . . . I am not afraid of the confrontation that my gospel will also call forth in Rome] (author's italics).

grace. In preaching the gospel Paul teaches that Christ is to be seen not only as Savior but as Lord and Judge. Instead of dismissing this as a "foreign body in the text"[21] it would be better to speak of it as a pointed argument necessitated by the situation in Rome and by Paul's need to defend his proclamation. Nor are the rhetorical questions which punctuate the argument merely matters of style. They are more than that. Take for example Romans 3:31. Here the Apostle asks, "Do we overthrow the law by this faith?" Or 4:1, "what then shall we say about Abraham, our forefather according to the flesh?"[22] Or 6:1, "Are we to continue in sin that grace may abound?" Or 6:15 "What then? Are we to sin because we are not under the law but under grace? By no means!" Or finally 7:7, 12, 14, "What shall we say then? That the law is sin? By no means! . . . the law is holy, and the commandment is holy and just and good." And a little later, "We know that the law is spiritual."[23] In every case the Apostle is alluding to criticisms and challenges from his Jewish Christian opponents as they spread from Asia Minor and Greece to Rome. His intention is to refute and answer them. The dialogue we are witnessing in Romans is a real one in which Paul is wrestling for the hearts and minds of the Christians in Rome. In doing so he has in view the criticisms and objections which have been raised against his teaching and person mainly by his Jewish Christian opponents. If we accept an early date for the letter of James we are in my opinion led to the plausible view that this document was written to encourage Paul's opponents—as far away as Rome.

The reason for the astonishing detail of Paul's arguments in Romans is that he wants to allay the arguments of his opponents and the slanderous rumors before he arrives. He feels free to omit some topics, such as the Lord's Supper, because there is no controversy over such matters in Rome. But he does have to contend about justification, the law, Israel's election, and Christian obedience in view of the last judgment. He must prevent the Roman Christians from rejecting him and his cause.

There is one quite simple historical fact which supports our dialogical interpretation of Romans. The text of Romans, i.e., the long form consisting of chapters 1–16 and all the familiar historical details about Paul and the Roman Christians as they are reported in the letter can be explained without resorting to any complicated supplementary hypotheses.

[21]So Bultmann, "Glossen," *Exegetica,* 283.
[22]In this interpretation of Rom 4:1 I follow Luz, *Geschichtsverständnis,* 174.
[23]Lichtenberger has shown in his inaugural dissertation, *Paulinischen Anthropologie,* xeroxed, 150–51, that the positive affirmation about the law which reaches its climax in Rom. 7:14 is without analogy. This means that it is a slogan of Paul, deliberately formulated to exclude any antinomianism on his part.

V

As early as 2 Peter 3:15–16 we read: "There are some things in them (sc. Paul's letters) hard to understand which the ignorant and unstable twist to their own destruction." Since that time people have continually complained that Paul's letters, and particularly Romans, are too demanding and that it would be better to stick to the simple message of Jesus rather than bother with Paul, who is so difficult to understand. If Romans is really aimed at Rome and seeks to engage the Christians there in a dialogue, it opens up tempting possibilities as we come to grips with the letter and seek to identify ourselves with the various groups of listeners and readers in Rome.

Peter Lampe's study of the social history of "urban Christianity in Rome during the first two centuries"[24] has at last thrown light on the mystery of the address of the letter (1:1–7). He explains why Paul wrote not "to the church at Rome" but "to all God's beloved in Rome, who are called to be saints." In A.D. 56 there was not as yet a consolidated Christian community in Rome with a single large center for its assemblies. Rather, the Christians lived in Jewish or working-class quarters of the metropolis and met in small cells or house-churches.[25] This meant that the letter to the Romans had to be passed around from one group to another. It would be read aloud and discussed in the individual house-churches meeting, for example, at the home of Aquila and Prisca or in any of the other notorious blocks of apartments in the city. In these small groups, friends and enemies of Paul, skeptics and enquirers, gathered together; but they had one thing in common. From the day of their baptism they had accepted the Christian creed, and from the synagogue and Christian assemblies they were familiar with the Psalms, the Law, and the Prophets. Moreover their Christian preachers and teachers, whose identities are unknown to us, must surely have told them as well of Jesus and his story.[26] They had also heard

[24]Cf. note 9 above.

[25]Cf. Lampe, *Die stadrömischen,* 332 (in the original in italics): "The Christians in Rome—fractionalized—met in facilities provided by private persons which were scattered throughout the metropolis." Klein, "Paul's Purpose," 41, "the absence of the concept *ekklēsia*" in the prescript of Romans and "the context of Romans 1–15" falls nicely into place historically. Also the reference to the house churches of Aquila and Prisca and of others in Rom. 16:1–16 is explained very clearly by Lampe. Klein's main thesis, that Paul "can consider an apostolic effort in Rome because he does not regard the local Christian community there as having an apostolic foundation" ("Paul's Purpose," 39), I no longer regard as probable in view of Rom. 6:17 and 16:17. On both these passages see above in the text.

[26]From the citations and allusions in 1 Clement (which also emanates from Rome) this can be substantiated with some degree of certainty. See, e.g., 1 Clem. 13:1–4; 16:16–17; 46:7–13; 49:1. From this it seems to me highly probable that the Christians in Rome would have been able to recognize and appreciate the various allusions to Jesus tradition which occur in Romans. On this compare my sketch: "Jesus Tradition" 240–50. N. Walter is more skeptical on this point in his fine article: "Jesustradition," 498–522, esp. 502. He draws no comparisons between Rom. and 1 Clem.

of Paul. At least they knew the legendary story of his conversion from having been the persecutor of the Christians to becoming an apostle of Christ.[27] Aquila and Prisca could tell them about Paul's preaching and mission, for they had worked and lived with him in Corinth and Ephesus (cf. Acts 18:1–4, 26; 19:1–7). But there were also disturbing rumors about Paul's teaching and his permissive morality. It was easy for his opponents to deduce such notions from, for example, the letter to the Galatians. And now there was even talk of this famous man's coming to Rome. How should they react? Cautiously? Should they welcome him? Or simply ignore him?[28] That is the situation to which Romans was directed. The reader who asks these questions is involved willy-nilly in a dialogue which pinpoints in every sentence the very core of the gospel and of our faith in Jesus Christ. Since Romans is an apologetic dialogue arising from such a precise historical situation, we should be careful not to regard it only as the sum and crown of the Pauline gospel. That gospel becomes clear only when we take Romans together with Paul's other letters and bring them all into relation with one another.

If our view of Romans is correct it will be necessary to draw a careful distinction between the arguments Paul chooses when discussing the challenges and provocations of his Jewish Christian opponents and his view of Judaism and the Jewish tradition. There was no contradiction to the gospel of justification when Paul spoke of Israel's continuing special status, based as it was on Israel's election and the promises! As the gospel shows preference for the Jews but by a miracle is open to the Gentiles as well (1 Cor. 1:21–24; Rom. 1:16; 3:28–29), so God's promise which goes beyond the salvation of the "fullness of the Gentiles" holds good for the people of God through Jesus Christ. Israel will be saved by the messianic redeemer who will return from Zion as the universal Savior (Rom. 11:25–26). Finally, among the various points we have made in our analysis it must be remembered that Romans is not simply a faithful reflection of Paul's preaching, which by exposing the sinfulness of Gentile and Jew, i.e., by preaching the law, opens up the way for the gospel. Rather, we have before our eyes in Romans 1–15, and again in 16:17–20 the arguments Paul employed vis-à-vis mature Christians.[29] How he preached and taught as a missionary cannot be simply inferred from the outline of Romans. It has to be deduced from an analysis of the Pauline literature as a whole and from the tradition of Acts which deals with Paul.

[27] Dietzfelbinger, *Berufung*, 80, starts from the fact "that the church in Damascus, already during the lifetime of Paul, produced this [Acts 9:1–19a] undiminished pro-Pauline story."

[28] In this connection we should take note of the striking circumstance that in Acts 28:11–16 there is initially mention of a friendly welcome for Paul by the Christians in Rome, whereas later Luke is silent about the Roman community. As Roloff comments, "It is as if an enormous triumphal arch is erected but to no avail. Apparently Luke had good reasons for his silence, reasons which undoubtedly are related to the history of this, his own church. . . ." See Roloff, *Die Apostelgeschichte*, 368–69.

[29] On Paul's arguments as an instrument of style and communication see Siegert, *Argumentation*.

PART

II

Section B
The Structure and Rhetoric of Romans

16

THE FORMAL AND THEOLOGICAL COHERENCE OF ROMANS

James D. G. Dunn

The increasing emphasis of the last two decades on the importance of the historical situation addressed for an understanding of Romans has been matched by an increasing interest in its literary structure and rhetorical features (Donfried, *Romans Debate*; cf. Beker, *Paul*, 61–63).

I. The Literary Form of Romans

The key issue here is the relation of the epistolary framework of the letter (1:1–15; 15:14–16:23) to the main body of the letter (1:16–15:13). On the one hand, it is generally recognized that the introduction and conclusion are essentially variations on the familiar pattern of letter writing in the ancient world (Doty, *Letters,* 13–14); this greatly strengthens the impression that however else Romans may be categorized, it was intended at least in part as a personal letter to a particular group of people in Rome in the middle of the first century A.D. On the other hand, the body of the letter is highly distinctive in content and character. It seems to share little if anything of the personal letter form and would more accurately be described as a "treatise" or "literary dialogue" or "letter essay" (Stirewalt, "Letter Essay"). The tension between these two different literary forms in Romans has never been resolved with complete satisfaction—which simply underlines the distinctiveness of the form Paul created. Certainly any attempt to determine the letter's character solely in terms of literary parallels to introduction and conclusion is self-evidently defective; just as it is self-evidently essential that the character of the document be seen in the relation of the body of the letter to its introduction and conclusion.

The key fact here is that the distinctiveness of the letter far outweighs the significance of its conformity with current literary or rhetorical custom. Parallels show chiefly how others wrote at that period; they provide no prescription for Paul's practice and no clear criterion by which to assess Paul; and the fact that no particular suggestion has commanded wide-spread assent in the current discussion suggests that Paul's style was as much or more eclectic and instinctive than conventional and conformist. Thus to label Romans as "epideictic" (demonstrative; Wuellner, "Paul's Rhetoric"; Fraiken, "Rhetorical Function") or "deliberative" or "protreptic" (persuasive; Stowers, *Letter Writing*, 114) does not actually advance under-standing of the letter very far (Aune, *Literary Environment*, 219), since the chief force of the letter lies in its *distinctive* Pauline art and content. At most we can speak comfortably of formal features which were part of the idiom of the age (what every well-educated schoolboy learned as part of his basic equipment for social intercourse) and through which Paul nat-urally expressed himself in an unselfconscious way. This is probably true even of the most impressive suggestion, that Romans was written on the model of an "ambassadorial" letter (Jewett, "Ambassadorial Letter") which sheds occasional light on specific features of the introduction and con-clusion. Similarly we may assume that the letter's familiar forms and idioms made it more readily hearable and assimilable for the recipients. But the reason they retained the letter and recognized its authority was the dis-tinctively Pauline use made of these, including the myriad idiosyncratic variations and embellishments, and above all, of course, the fact that they heard the word of God addressing them through both the more familiar and the less familiar content of Paul's words and sentences (Barth, *Romans*, preface[2]).

In terms of the document's coherence as between framework and body, however, the most important feature is the way in which the body of the letter (1:16–15:13) has been neatly sandwiched between two statements of Paul's future plans which are strikingly parallel (see 15:14–33; Dunn, *Romans 1–8*, "Form and Structure"). The second statement, however, is markedly fuller and more explicit, particularly about Paul's purpose in com-ing to Rome. The most obvious deduction to draw from this is that Paul thought it necessary to elaborate his understanding of the gospel at length before he made his specific requests to the Roman Christians, on the as-sumption that they needed to have this fuller insight before they could be expected to give him the support he sought. This deduction seems to gain strength from the care with which Paul has meshed introduction and peroration into the body of the letter: 1:16–17 serves both as the climax to what has preceded and as the thematic statement for what follows (see 1:16–17; Dunn, *Romans 1–8*, "Form and Structure"), with the overarching Christology already carefully embedded in the introduction (1:2–6); and 15:14–15 is a polite way of saying that the whole of the preceding treatise was an expression of Paul's grace as apostle, that is, an example of the charism to strengthen faith and of the gospel he had been given to preach (1:11, 15), with which he would hope to repay their support for his future missionary work (cf. 1:12 with 15:24, 27–29).

The other main problem regarding literary framework is whether ch. 16 was part of the original letter. The arguments have been reviewed repeatedly and most recent commentators accept that Romans 16 was part of the letter to Rome, even though the suggestion that it was originally directed to Ephesus continues to command a surprising amount of support. The case for its being part of the original letter is briefly outlined in Dunn, *Romans 9–16, Introduction* to 16:1–23. The textual history is complex (Dunn, *Romans 1–8*, lx), but it requires no detailed analysis to argue the greater likelihood of Paul's letter to Rome being copied in an abbreviated form (to omit the more explicitly personal references, perhaps including the specific mention of "Rome" in 1:7 and 15, as in some texts), than of Paul himself writing more than one version with ch. 16 appended to the version to Ephesus. A collector and distributor of Paul's letters would see no difficulty in circulating the letter with its introduction and conclusion largely intact; whereas Paul himself would be less likely to leave the introduction and peroration unchanged when they were so much less fitted to churches of his own foundation. The fact that the letter was not subjected to greater abbreviation (apart from the Marcionite elimination of all of ch. 15 as well as of ch. 16) is some indication that the coherence of framework and body was recognized by most copyists.

For other matters regarding language and style of the letter, reference may be made to Sanday-Headlam, *Romans*, lii–lxiii, and Cranfield, *Romans*, 1.24–27.

II. The Theological Coherence of Romans

In a review of Romans research one impression which could easily be given is that Romans *lacks* coherence. Sanders, *Law*, 123–35, and Räisänen, *Law*, 101–9, find key points in ch. 2 at odds with what Paul says elsewhere. The function of ch. 5 within the development of the overall argument is greatly disputed (see 5:1–21; Dunn, *Romans 1–8, Introduction*). Kinoshita ("Romans") suggests that Romans is a combination of two separate letters; Scroggs ("Paul as Rhetorician") likewise argues that the letter is an amalgamation of two distinct homilies (chs. 5–8, and chs. 1–4, 9–11); and Noack ("Current and Backwater," 164) describes chs. 5–8 as a "backwater." Chapters 9–11 are sometimes regarded as an excursus or appendix to the main argument, or indeed a completely preformed unit incorporated as it stood (Dodd, *Romans*). And several have found chs. 12–15 completely unrelated to what has gone before, an application simply of standard parenetic tradition (Dibelius, *From Tradition to Gospel*, 238–39).

Most radical in such denials of the integration and coherence of the letter as a whole have been Schmithals (*Der Römerbrief als historisches Problem*), arguing for two separate letters (A—1:1–4:25 + 5:12–11:36 + 15:8–

13; B—12:1–21 + 13:8–10 + 14:1–15 + 15:14–32 + 16:21–23 + 15:33), and O'Neill (*Romans*), arguing for a much redacted and expanded original with major interpolations (consisting of 1:18–2:29; 5:12–21; 7:14–25; 9:11–24; 10:7–15:13). Less radical have been the suggestions of Bultmann ("Glossen") of a number of glosses added to the letter at some stage subsequent to its composition by Paul (2:1, 16; 5:6–7; 6:17b; 7:25b; 8:1; 10:17; 13:5), and of Schenke ("Aporien," 882–84) that 14:1–15:13 + 16:3–20 were originally addressed to Ephesus.

A close study of the text, however, shows that all of these and similar suggestions are in greater or less degree unjustified. As for Schmithals in particular: since his letter A lacks a conclusion, and his letter B an introduction, and since the two fit together quite coherently, his surgery is unnecessary (on Schmithals and Schenke see also Wilckens, *Der Brief an die Römer*, 1.27–29). O'Neill's reconstruction proceeds on the wholly unrealistic assumption that Paul was a paragon of literary and theological consistency, and by taking only one aspect of his complex treatment of such key motifs as "law" and "flesh" as genuine, he leaves a mutilated and monochrome Paul far less impressive than the author of Romans. Other individual claims are dealt with in more detail chiefly in the introduction to each main section in Dunn, *Romans 1–8, 9–16*. For the rest we may confine ourselves here to more general observations.

2.1 In the first place, we can illustrate the coherence of the letter from the integration of the various purposes Paul evidently had in writing the letter (see Dunn, *Romans 1–8*, §3). Paul's missionary purpose (*Romans 1–8*, §3.1) is hardly to be held quite apart from his apologetic purpose (*Romans 1–8*, §3.2). On the contrary, it was precisely his theological conviction regarding the eschatological fulfillment of the purpose of God in Christ for Gentile as well as Jew which provided Paul's motivation as a missionary. The christological emphasis throughout ties together not only the main body of the letter (e.g., 3:21–26; 5:14–21; 8:1–4; 9:32–10:13; 12:5; 14:8–9; 15:1–9), but also the introduction and conclusion in which Paul attests that his commissioning for this gospel came from this Jesus (1:1–6, 9; 15:16–20). So also the personal note interjected at 11:13–14 is in no way erratic or out of character, but confirms that Paul saw the theological exposition climaxing in chs. 9–11 as a necessary or essential explanation if his readers were to understand and sympathize with his powerful compulsion to take the gospel to Spain. Likewise, it is by recognizing the mixed (Jew/Gentile) character of the congregations in Rome (Dunn, *Romans 1–8*, §2) that the tie-in between apologetic and pastoral (Dunn, *Romans 1–8*, §3.3) purposes becomes clear: the Roman congregations were something of a test case for Paul's apostolic vision of the body of Christ consisting in each place of Jewish and Gentile believers functioning in harmony (15:7–13). Paul's theological exposition of chs. 1–11 is the ideological foundation for the particular parenesis of chs. 12–15 (so also Wilckens, *Der Brief an die Römer*, 1.39–42; cf. Wuellner, "Paul's Rhetoric," 144–45).

Not least do we need to recall the integration provided by Paul's own personal and spiritual pilgrimage and by his commission as Jewish apostle to Gentiles, taking to the non-Jewish world the message of God's promises to Abraham as fulfilled in and through Messiah Jesus. It is precisely the tension between "Jew first but also Greek" (1:16), which Paul experienced in his own person and faith and mission (Dunn, *Romans 1–8*, §1), which also provides an integrating motif for the whole letter. First he argues that Jew as much as Greek is in need of God's eschatological grace (1:18–3:20). Then he spells out the means by which Jew as well as Gentile, the "many," the "all," are brought within the experience of that grace (3:21–5:21), and explains how these blessings, characteristically understood as belonging to Israel, work out in the present for each of the "many," the "all" (chs. 6–8). The question which has long pressed, "If Israel's blessings are freely open to Gentiles, what then of the promises to Israel itself?," at last commands center stage in the climax of the theological exposition (chs. 9–11). Finally, with the character of the people of promise thus redefined (Jew *and* Gentile), traditional Jewish ethnic and social mores can no longer simply be assumed as the obvious ethical outworking for the people of the promise. Consequently, Paul spells out a fresh set of guidelines, inspired by a new model (the body of Christ), and made up of a discreet mix of older Jewish wisdom which still applies and the newer guidelines of the love of neighbor commended and lived out all the way to the cross by Jesus himself (12:1–15:6).

This is no doubt the fullest exposition Paul had attempted of a theological, apologetic, missionary, pastoral explanation for his work. That he had used and rehearsed elements of it in previous discussions and expositions to Jews, Jewish Christians, God-worshipping Gentiles and Gentile Christians, need not be doubted. It is very likely, too, that he had an eye to the defense he would almost certainly have to offer in Judea and Jerusalem (if he had the chance to do so—15:31). But in the event, the exposition transcends the immediacy of its several purposes and provides a coherent and integrated vision of the eschatological people of God (Gentile *and* Jew) which is of lasting value.

2.2 The importance of "Jew first but also Greek" as the integrating motif is also demonstrated by other features in Romans.

One feature of the treatise section is the repeated use of diatribe style (dialogue with an imagined interlocutor)—particularly 2:1–5, 17–29; 3:27–4:2; 9:19–21; 11:17–24. Here Paul certainly shows familiarity with this contemporary style of philosophic discourse. Characteristic of the diatribe is the attempt to criticize and correct pretension and arrogance. Stowers (*Diatribe*, 75–78) has also made the important observation that the typical function of diatribe was not as polemic against an opponent but, in a school context, as a critical questioning of a fellow student designed to lead him to the truth (so also Aune, *Literary Environment*, 200–201, 219). Consequently, in Romans, Paul's use of diatribe, particularly in chs. 2 and 3, should not be seen as outright opposition to "the Jew" or to Judaism as such, but rather as a critical dialogue which Paul conducts with his fellow pupils within the school of Judaism, in which the aim is to understand aright the Jewish heritage common to both. This helps us to recognize, moreover, that a consistent concern of Paul's throughout the letter is to puncture presumption, wherever he finds it, and to prevent arrogance from raising its head. Thus we can see that the warning of 11:17–25 against Gentile boasting is an attempt to prevent Gentile believers from falling into the trap which had caught his fellow Jews (2:17, 23; 3:27; 4:2); and at the same time it ties the concern of the treatise section into that of the parenesis (particularly 12:3, 16 and 14:3).

Intertwined with the theme of "Jew first and also Greek" is the integrated thematic emphasis on the righteousness of God, on righteousness through faith, and on the faithfulness of God (1:17). Here it is important to give full weight to the insight of Stendahl ("Conscience" and *Paul Among Jews and Gentiles*, 2–3) that Paul's treatment of the righteousness of God is primarily an exposition of the same Jew/Gentile theme, Paul's way of arguing that Gentiles are full recipients of the righteousness (= saving grace) of God, fully heirs of the promises to Abraham and Jacob as much as Jews are. The repeated emphasis on "all" — "all who believe" (1:16; 3:22; 4:11; 10:4, 11–13), "all injustice" (1:18, 29), "all who judge" (2:1), all who bring about evil/good (2:9–10), all under sin (3:9, 12, 19–20, 23; 5:12), "all the seed" (4:11, 16), "all Israel" (11:26), and so on—means primarily all Jews as well as Greeks, all Gentiles as well as Jews. So, too, the emphasis on God's faithfulness as an integral part of the same exposition comes to expression not just in key assertions like 3:3, 9:6, and 11:29, but also in the stress on "the truth" (= faithfulness) of God, which has the effect of setting the concept of God's covenant faithfulness within the larger consideration of God's faithfulness as Creator and Judge (1:18, 25; 2:2, 8, 20; 3:7). Not least of significance is the way in which Paul uses 15:7–13 both to integrate the parenetic section more fully into the overall theme and to underscore his claim that God's truth and faithfulness to the promises made to the fathers had in view all nations and all peoples united in a praise to the one God. The importance of this stress on God's faithfulness *as part of* the theme enunciated in 1:16–17 has not been given sufficient recognition in exposition of Romans.

Equally important is it to recognize the significance of the law as the chief secondary theme running through the letter. This has probably caused more confusion than any other aspect of the whole letter and to deal with it adequately we will have to step back a little to gain a fuller view of the issues.

17

ROMANS III AS A KEY TO THE STRUCTURE AND THOUGHT OF THE LETTER

William S. Campbell

Numerous and varied suggestions have been proposed by scholars in recent years concerning the occasion and purpose of Paul's letter to the Romans.[1] Though not all are sceptical as to the outcome, some scholars feel that the varying conclusions witness to an increasing confusion rather than clarity in the interpretation of the letter.[2]

One reason for this diversity of opinion may be the actual structure and content of Romans itself. Chapters 1:1–17 and 15:14f. function as brackets around the "body" of the letter.[3] Since these chapters deal with Paul's travel plans and his concern for the Roman Christians, it is inevitable that they will be at the centre of any discussion concerning the situation to which the letter is addressed or out of which it emerged. Consequently these passages tend to receive undue attention from scholars concerned with the occasion and purpose of the letter.[4] Other scholars, however, who lay more stress on the theological significance of Romans, tend to con-

---

[1]Cf. the most recent discussion in Cranfield, *Romans*, 2.814–23, and Wilckens, *Römer*, 33–52; cf. also Part 1 above and my critique of some of these essays in "Why?" 264–69.

[2]Luz's verdict, after a survey of the literature, sums up the reaction of some scholars: "Eine eindeutige Lösung drängt sich aus dem Studium der Sekundärliteratur nich auf" ("Röm 1–8," 165).

[3]"Body" is used loosely in this instance only—normally we take it to refer to chs. 1–11; cf. Roetzel, *Letters of Paul*, 28. Cranfield warns of the danger of regarding the introduction and conclusion, i.e., 1:8–16a and 15:14f. as detachable from the rest of the letter (*Romans*, 2.818f.). Although he takes the view that Paul sends to the Romans a summary of the gospel as he understood it, Cranfield rejects as "quite unacceptable" the view "that the structure and contents of 1.16b–15.13 were determined simply and solely by the logic of the gospel" (*Romans*, 2.818f.; i.e., entirely without reference to the situation at Rome).

[4]E.g., Minear, *Obedience*. Only half of the contents of Minear's study is devoted to the body of the letter; cf. also Cranfield's criticisms, *Romans* 2.820–21.

centrate on the body of the letter—usually chs. 1–8, sometimes 1–11,[5] and, less frequently, 9–11.[6]

The way to a comprehensive and more generally acceptable interpretation of the letter must lie, therefore, in a proper combination or unification of these two emphases; i.e., in seeking an explanation of the occasion and purpose of Romans which is consistent with, and adequately related to, the content of 1:18–11:36. Any interpretation which makes good sense of only part of the letter is automatically, by definition, excluded. A coherence must be established also between 1:18–11:36 and 12–15(16).[7] In the search for a comprehensive interpretation of the letter, some light, we believe, may emerge from a closer study of ch. 3.

Scholars have frequently drawn attention to the great extent to which ch. 3 is composed of questions which are answered at a later point in the letter.[8] The chapter begins with a series of questions in vv. 1–8 and ends with another series in vv. 27–31. The remainder consists of a summary-conclusion (to 1:18–2:29) in v. 9a—also introduced by a question—and supported by a catena of Old Testament citations demonstrating the utter sinfulness of all men whether Jew or Gentile (vv. 10–18), Paul's commentary upon these (vv. 19–20), and a statement concerning his understanding of the revelation of God's righteousness in Jesus Christ (vv. 21–26). Since the latter passage is generally regarded as being of crucial significance both in the letter and in Paul's theology, it is to it that we will give first consideration.

I. Chapter 3:21–26 as the Centre of Paul's Theology in Romans

This section differs from the diatribe[9] style of the question-answer sections (such as 3:1–8); it differs also in content. It is characterized by a kerygmatic or declaratory style similar to that of ch. 5 and, to a lesser extent,

---

[5]In his review of Bultmann's *Theologie des Neuen Testaments* (*Theologische Rundschau* 22 [1954] 21–43, = Dahl, *Crucified Messiah*, 90–128), N. A. Dahl criticized Bultmann for his gross neglect of Rom. 9–11; this tendency in the Bultmann school has not yet been entirely overcome, cf. Müller, *Römer 9–11*, 5–27.

[6]Stendahl, *Paul among Jews and Gentiles*, 4, represents what might loosely be termed a Scandinavian interest in Rom. 9–11 which comes to full expression in Munck, *Christ and Israel*. Cf. also Noack, "Current and Backwater," 155–66. Goppelt, *Jesus, Paul, and Judaism*, 153, sees Rom. 9–11 as the keystone of Paul's theology and F. C. Baur regarded these chapters as the kernel out of which the entire letter emerged (*Paul*, 315).

[7]The most recent research supports the view that ch. 16 was a part of the original letter, see Gamble, *Textual History*, and Wilckens, *Römer*, 24–27. For a contrary opinion see Käsemann, *Römer*, 400f. The view taken here is that ch. 16 should not be used as a basis for any interpretation of the letter, but only as supporting evidence for interpretations arrived at on the basis of chs. 1–15.

[8]Cf. Lietzmann, *An die Römer*, 89. Schlatter, *Gottes Gerechtigkeit*, 122; Luz, "Röm 1–8," 169.

[9]The reference here is only to a dialogical or diatribe style. Thyen maintains that Paul's letters are closer in style to the synagogue homily than the diatribe, *Homilie*, 59f. On the

of ch. 8.[10] In contrast to the diatribe style sections, punctuated by frequent questions and interjections, here Paul is not asking questions or addressing real or imagined opponents, but expounding the meaning of the Christ-event as he understands it in the light of earlier Christian traditions.[11] Already in the statement of the theme of the letter in 1:16f., Paul has stressed three elements in his gospel: (i) the gospel is not something of which he is ashamed but that which puts Paul in debt to all men and which therefore demands universal proclamation; (ii) in the gospel the righteousness of God has now been revealed as a power which through faith in Christ leads to salvation; and (iii) the gospel is to the Jew first but also to the Gentile.

In 1:18–2:29 Paul has shown that, in the light of the Christ-event, the former distinctions among men whether as Jews or Gentiles, have now (cf. *nyni de* in 3:21 and *en tō nyn chairō* in 3:26) been rendered obsolete by the new aeon that has dawned with the gospel.[12] The only distinctions that are now valid are those which God the judge of all the earth, makes on the basis of the gospel. The unbelieving Jew in the old aeon is now no better than the unbelieving Gentile.[13]

In 3:21f. Paul interprets the meaning of the Christ-event as the present eschatological activity of God which has transformed the relationship between Jew and Gentile. We note the emphasis on the eschatological present in 3:21 and 3:26 and again in 5:9, 11 and 8:1. The similarity in style and content between these sections suggests that the latter sections are a development and a continuation of the former. It is significant that in 3:24–26, as already in 1:3–4, Paul uses a Jewish-Christian credal formula to expound his gospel.[14] His intention, it would appear, is to demonstrate that

---

diatribe style see also Dahl, *Studies*, 188–89; Donfried, "False Presuppositions," 112f., and Scroggs, "Paul as Rhetorician," 270f.

[10]O. Michel notes that vv. 21–26 are distinguished from their immediate context by "einen proklamatorischen Stil," whereas vv. 27–31 have "einen aufgelockerten, dialogisch-rhetorischen charakter," *Römer*, 146–47. Stoessel, "Romans 13:1–2," 168, by charting the number of questions, divides Rom. 1–11 into two types of passages, those in declarative and those in an argumentative style.

[11]We take the view here that Paul is deliberately using earlier traditions to show that he recognizes the Jewish origin of his gospel and the (temporal) priority of Jewish-Christianity; where he quotes or uses the tradition we presume that he does so with approval; the argument in this paper is not dependent on whether certain verses are pre-Pauline. On Paul's use of credal formulations see Conzelmann, *Outline*, 166f.; Eichholz, *Theologie*, 123f. and 189f.; cf. also van der Minde, *Schrift und Tradition*, 38f. and 190. Käsemann, "Konsequente," 143, argues that while Paul's theology is based upon tradition generally it is not based on credal formulations in particular.

[12]See Barrett's excellent treatment of the theme of judgment in 1:18–3:20 (*Romans*, 31–71). On the contrast between the old and new aeon, see Käsemann, *Römer*, 85f.; Luz, "Röm 1–8," 171–72. Müller, *Röm 9–11*, 50.

[13]Marxsen, *Introduction*, 105.

[14]According to Käsemann, Paul here cites "ein hymnisches Fragment" (*Römer*, 88). See also van der Minde, *Schrift und Tradition*, 58–67. For a fuller discussion of righteousness, see Käsemann, *Questions*, 168–82, and Brauch, "Perspectives," included in Sanders, *Paul*, 523–42; Klein's "Righteousness," 750–52, and several essays on this theme in *Rechtfertigung: Festschrift für Ernst Käsemann zum 70 Geburtstag* (Tübingen/Göttingen, 1976).

the gospel which he preaches, which Gentiles believe, is none other than the good news of the fulfilment of God's promises to Israel.[15] Paul's gospel did not originate in a vacuum, it has a pre-history. Although it proclaims the power of God as "creatio ex nihilo,"[16] it is not itself of this nature. It is based on the redemption that has now taken place in Christ, the Christ-event being understood as the explanation, revelation and culmination of the divine purpose in the world for which God first entered into covenant with Israel.

If Käsemann is correct in his understanding of Paul's additions to, and modification of, the Jewish Christian formula in 3:21f.,[17] it is legitimate to take v. 26 (b and c) as indicative of Paul's own theology. To a certain extent this is also true of vv. 24–26a, in that we presume that what Paul quotes he intends to endorse and that v. 26b–c modifies rather than corrects vv. 24–26a.[18] According to 3:26, Paul considers that the Christ-event has a twofold outcome: (a) to demonstrate that God is righteous and (b) to demonstrate that he rectifies[19] him who has faith in Jesus. Here we have what may, with some justice, be termed the theological centre and basis of Paul's argument in Rom. 1–11. We stress that there are two emphases.[20] It has been the tradition in Protestant, particularly Lutheran, theology to concentrate on the second of these, i.e., the justification or rectification of the ungodly. But both must be stressed simultaneously and the one certainly not at the expense of the other.

That God in Christ has revealed himself as righteous and self-consistent means that he keeps faith with his people, that he keeps his promises to Israel. It follows that any consideration of righteousness as the rectification of the ungodly must also necessarily involve a consideration of righteousness in relation to God's promises to Israel—his faithfulness to the covenant. This is in fact demanded by the scope of Paul's gospel which is universal not in opposition to Jewish particularism, as has often mistakenly been believed,[21] but precisely on the basis of that Jewish particu-

---

[15]"The aim of Romans is to show the Gentiles how their hope rests on Israel's Messiah" (Robinson, "Priesthood of Paul," 232).

[16]See Käsemann, *Römer,* 114–17. See also Käsemann's essay, "The Faith of Abraham in Romans 4," in *Perspectives,* 91–93.

[17]Käsemann regards 3:26b and c as Paul's commentary upon an earlier Jewish-Christian fragment (*Römer,* 92). See also Williams, J. W., "Romans 3:21–26," 251f.

[18]Contra Käsemann, *Römer,* 94. Cf. Stuhlmacher, "Röm. 3:24–26," 331. Kuss, *Der Römerbrief,* 160, and Cranfield, *Romans* 1.199. Müller, like Käsemann, claims that Paul thinks in terms of God's faithfulness to the whole creation rather than to the covenant people, but he acknowledges that God's acts are still oriented towards Israel since Israel remains the secret center of history (*Römer 9–11,* 112–13).

[19]Keck, *Paul and His Letters,* 120, suggests the term "rectification" instead of the traditional "justification."

[20]See Barrett: "Righteousness . . . has two aspects represented by the two clauses in v. 26" (*Romans,* 73), and Müller's criticism that Bultmann identified *dikaiosynē* and *dikaiosynē theou* with *dikaiosynē ek pisteōs* (*Römer 9–11,* 25).

[21]See Sundkler, "Contributions," 462–99, and Munck's discussion of the same in *Paul and the Salvation of Mankind,* 258f. See also Dahl's criticisms of Käsemann on this point (*Studies,* 191).

larism which, through the fulfilment in Christ of the promises to Israel, is now opened up to include Gentiles also.[22]

This means that Rom. 1–8 should not be considered in isolation from 9–11. The history of post-Reformation interpretation reveals that the contrary has in fact been the case.[23] In the discussion of the righteousness of God there has been a consistent failure to take into account chs. 9–11 with the result that in Bultmann's exegesis, justification has tended to deteriorate into a theory concerning the rescue or the new self-understanding of the individual.[24] This could have been avoided by a more consistent interpretation of Rom. 1–11 where the rectification of the individual is set in the context of the promises and the people of God. Michel rightly emphasizes that chs. 9–11 are the criterion by which one may judge whether 3:21f. has been rightly understood.[25] Only when the rectification of the ungodly is viewed in relation to the historic people of God is there any compelling necessity for chs. 9–11 to succeed chs. 1–8, but when the motif of the constitution and continuity of the people of God is seen as central, then it is the theme of "Rechfertigungslehre" which provides a unified interpretation of chs. 1–11.[26] This demands that due regard must be paid to both chs. 1–8 and 9–11; neither may be considered as either supplementary to, or simply an elaboration or illustration of the other, otherwise a one-sided interpretation will result. As Marxsen notes, "Taken out of context, passages (in Romans) could be interpreted in an anti-Jewish sense; but taken out of context, chs. 9–11 could be interpreted in a pro-Jewish sense. But Paul's concern is neither with the one nor the other but with peace in the new aeon."[27]

It is noteworthy that when the twin themes of the righteousness of God as self-consistent and as rectifying the ungodly, are emphasized together, then a strong connection is established between chs. 1–4 and 9–11. Chapters 5–8 then become the problem[28] or to use terminology suggested by Noack, what used to be regarded as the "current" turns out to be the "backwater."[29] The theme of Jews, Gentiles, and the gospel prevalent throughout chs. 1–4 and 9–11 points to a similar conclusion.[30] But,

---

[22]See Richardson, *Israel*, 133.

[23]See Müller, *Römer 9–11*, 14–18. Müller here follows Käsemann contra Bultmann; cf. Käsemann's comments in this respect in several essays in *Questions*, 14–15, 131f., 181, 191.

[24]See Müller, *Römer 9–11*, 21–27. Müller praises Lohmeyer's attempt to avoid an individualistic view of justification—"Gottesvolkfrage und Rechtfertigungslehre gehören für ihn zusammen. Wenn die Auslegung beide Voneinander isoliert, erfasst sie beide falsch" (*Römer 9–11*, 15).

[25]Michel, *Römer*, 307.

[26]Käsemann includes the term "Gerechtigkeit" in the title of each of the five main sections of his commentary on Romans. In this emphasis he has followed Schlatter, *Gottesgerechtigkeit*, 292, 302, 329.

[27]Marxsen, *Introduction*, 103.

[28]See Luz, "Röm 1–8," 163.

[29]Noack, "Current and Backwater," 155f.

[30]This is well argued by Scroggs, who concludes that "Romans 1–4 and 9–11 are united in theme, structure and use of scripture" ("Paul as Rhetorician," 281).

as we shall see later, different patterns may be discerned in the letter when it is viewed from different perspectives. What is significant is that throughout chs. 3:21–26, 5 and 8, the theme is the eschatological present viewed as the time of fulfilment in Jesus, the son of David, of the messianic promises. In a synopsis of 5:1–11 and 8:1–39 Dahl has demonstrated a parallelism between these two sections of the letter; almost all the major themes of 5:1–11 reappear in ch. 8. The vocabulary of 5:1–11 however, differs from that of ch. 8 in that in it the vocabulary is that of chs. 1–4 whereas that of ch. 8 is set against the background of 5:12–7:25.[31] Thus chs. 5 and 8 are a continuation and development of the themes of 3:21–26.[32]

In a high point of his argument in ch. 8, Paul reminds the Roman Christians that they have not received the Spirit to fall back into fear but the spirit of sonship whereby they can call "Abba," Father (v. 15). This, in turn, means that they are children and heirs of God, joint-heirs with Christ (v. 17) and, provided they share in Christ's sufferings, God will deliver his elect to their full redemption in the consummation of the new creation (vv. 18–31).[33]

It is not surprising that post-Reformation exegesis has stressed the centrality of justification by faith in Romans (and therefore also in Paul's theology). But Paul's emphasis in ch. 8 is not simply on the safe conduct of believing (or elect) individuals to their eventual glorification. What prompted Paul in the first instance is more likely to have been a concern to stress the actualization in the church composed of both Jews and Gentiles[34] of the promises given to Abraham. God's word or promise has not failed in that the eschatological blessings are now being realized among believers. This part of ch. 8 is already a partial answer to the problem of Jewish unbelief with which Paul will deal in 9:6f. In spite of the sin of the Jews, God has vindicated Jesus as Messiah, the heir and fulfiller of the promises to Abraham which are thereby guaranteed to be fully realized in the revelation of the sons of God in the consummation of the new creation. Paul's interest here is primarily in the promise and its realization, whereas Protestant interest has centred on the recipients of the promise and has therefore showed little concern for the Jews who through disobedience have excluded themselves.

[31]Dahl, "A Synopsis of Romans 5:1–11 and 8:1–39," in *Studies*, 88–90.

[32]See Jeremias, "Gedankenführung," 148, and Michel's illuminating discussion of the structure and content of the letter (*Römer*, 43–54).

[33]Since *ti eroumen?* in Romans usually introduces Paul's answer to an objection, as in 3:5, 4:1, 6:1, 7:7, 8:31, 9:14, 30, Jeremias considers that the section 8:18f. may be the answer to an objection that suffering contradicts the assurance of salvation claimed in 8:1–17 ("Gedankenführung," 45).

[34]Robinson claims that the theme of ch. 8 is "the liberty of the Jew who has entered his inheritance in Christ and his hope of glory according to promise and election"; the positive Christian experience and the expectation of final glory are "set forth deliberately as the experience of the justified Jew, indeed, of Israel itself in the person of the servant and apostle of the Lord" ("Priesthood of Paul," 244–45).

Thus the doctrine of justification by faith is the presupposition and basis on which Paul approaches the failure of his fellow Jews to accept the gospel.[35] We will find also that Rom. 8 is not his only or last word on the subject.[36] He has yet to deal with the faithfulness of God which demonstrates that he himself is righteous, even in his relation to disobedient Jews. What he has to say on this in chs. 9–11 runs a great risk of being misunderstood if the emphasis of 3:21f., ch. 5, and ch. 8 is not kept in view.[37] In order to clarify further the relationship between chs. 1–8 and 9–11, we must look again at ch. 3 in order to get a clearer picture of the structure of the letter.

II. Chapter 3 as the Structural Centre of the Letter

In search for clues to the organization of the letter, the question-answer sections especially 3:1–8, offer useful guidelines for discerning the structural centre out of which the entire letter is developed.

The quest for a fresh understanding of Romans which has recently culminated in what we may term "The Romans Debate" was inaugurated by T. W. Manson in 1948.[38] Manson viewed Romans primarily as a summing up of Paul's missionary controversies, a circular letter which set forth his deepest convictions on central issues. Munck took up Manson's suggestions claiming that the new approach had invalidated the widespread assumption that Romans is a theological presentation unaffected by time and history. The letter may now be regarded as "a missionary's contribution to a discussion."[39]

[35]We do not mean to imply that Rom. 9–11 is simply an illustration of Paul's application of this doctrine. Dahl asserts in this respect, "we express ourselves more correctly when we say that from the beginning Paul's view of the relation of Israel to the Gentiles profoundly shaped his doctrine of justification. Only later, especially in the thought of Augustine and Luther, did the doctrine of justification become fundamentally important apart from the problem of Israel and the Gentiles" (*Studies*, 156). See also the essay "The Doctrine of Justification" in the same volume (*Studies* 95–120). Stendahl, *Paul among Jews and Gentiles*, 129–32, expresses similar views but disagrees with both Dahl and Käsemann that it is polemical. "It has *not* grown out of his struggles with the Judaistic interpretation of the law—it is not a 'fighting doctrine, directed against Judaism'" (p. 130)—as Käsemann has asserted; cf. "Justification and Salvation History" in *Perspectives*, 63–78, for Käsemann's defense of the centrality of the doctrine in Paul's theology. Recently Sanders has also claimed that justification is part of Paul's polemics and not the center of his theology, which he describes (following Schweizer) as "participationist eschatology" (*Paul*, 434–47, 483–96, 502–8).

[36]We must also take into account 11:29, "The gift and call of God are irrevocable," in determining the meaning of justification in Romans. This, rather than 8:39 represents the climax of Paul's argument.

[37]Stendahl's view that Rom. 11 is non-christological and that there is a God-willed separate existence for unbelieving Jews fails to take into account 3:21–4:25 (*Paul among Jews and Gentiles*, 4 and 129f. See also Davies, "Paul and Israel," 15–16, 33, n. 1. and my article, "Salvation for Jews and Gentiles."

[38]Manson, "St. Paul's Letter," above pp. 3–15, and earlier, idem, *Studies*, 225–41.

[39]See Munck, *Paul and the Salvation of Mankind*, 200.

One result of relating Romans to Paul's missionary context was that a "Sitz im Leben" was thereby provided for the questions and objections in the letter. Jeremias, rejecting the view that Romans is a dogmatic treatise, viewed it as an epistle which had developed from Paul's frequent dialogues with Jews.[40] The dialogue style of the letter has been a subject of debate in much subsequent research. In one of the more recent commentaries, M. Black describes the letter as a Jewish-style rhetorical discourse which owes much to the rhetorical practices of the Stoic diatribe of the period, especially as adapted by Jewish controversialists.[41]

It would seem preferable in view of the deliberate literary style of the letter to modify Jeremias' view by stressing that the objections need not always or necessarily be of Jewish origin. Paul may simply be speaking as a Jewish Christian, or asking a rhetorical question to further the progress of his argument or even taking up positions adopted by the Roman Gentile Christians.[42] If, as seems likely, the letter is the written equivalent of the oral presentation which Paul would have delivered to the congregation had he himself been present,[43] then in the majority of cases he would have been addressing a predominantly Gentile congregation and this ought to be reflected in his letters; this does not however preclude the possibility of Paul speaking personally and apologetically either as an apostle or as a representative of believing Jews.[44]

Jeremias provided a useful insight in his observation that the thought sequence of Rom. 1–11 is determined largely by these questions and objections. The answers to them occupy the greater part of these chapters.[45] Again, the fact that the interruptions have the effect of making some sections of the letter appear as digressions[46] must not be allowed to mislead us as to Paul's real intention. Since the questions-objections frequently serve as the heading for a new section, as in 6:1, 15; 7:7; 9:14, 30; 11:1, 2, or as the conclusion of one section and the commencement of another, as in 3:31–4:1, it is clear that these introduce major issues which Paul wishes to discuss in the letter.

It is significant that the common diatribe style provides a link between 6–7 and 9–11. We have already noted how the theme of Jews, Gentiles, and the gospel links 1–4 and 9–11, thereby somewhat isolating 5–8.[47] But

---

[40]Jeremias, "Gedankenführung," 147.

[41]Black, *Romans*, 29–30.

[42]See Robinson, "Priesthood of Paul," 245. Lütgert maintained that in 6:1f. Paul is addressing antinomian Gentile Christians and not protesting self-defense against the views of Jews or Jewish-Christians who criticize him (*Römerbrief*, 76–79).

[43]White, "Epistolary Literature," *ANRW*, forthcoming.

[44]On this see Robinson, "Priesthood of Paul," 147. Wilckens, *Römer*, 18, still regards the objections as Jewish in origin.

[45]Jeremias "Gedankenführung," 147. See also Dupont, "Structure littéraire," 365–97.

[46]See Dahl, "Two Notes," 41.

[47]Scroggs holds that the material in chs. 1–4 and 9–11 is completely self-consistent and demonstrates a continuous development of thought and use of scripture, chs. 5–8 being so

when stylistic considerations are uppermost then we find that chs. 5 and 8 share a common kerygmatic declaratory style with 3:21–26 whereas 6–7 and 9–11 are linked by that of the diatribe.[48] The structure of the letter will become clearer when we observe the relationship between the questions Paul asks and the answers he gives to them.

The first question with which ch. 3 commences is not in fact really answered here—the answer is not fully developed until 9:4f. It is only then that Paul continues the list of the advantages of the Jew, the first of which is given in 3:2—"they were entrusted with the word (promises) of God."[49] Following this initial question comes a list of questions extending to 3:8. In 3:3 the question is put, "What if some (Jews) were unfaithful? Does their faithlessness nullify the faithfulness of God?" The answer to this—that God's word has not failed—is provided in 9:6f. Again in 3:5 the question is put that if the unbelief of the Jews serves God's good purpose (in allowing the gospel to go to the Gentiles) is God not in fact unjust in judging the wicked (Jews)? The answer to this question is likewise provided in ch. 9 in vv. 14f. in terms of God's freedom to use nations as he wills for his own glory. God is committed to Israel but his commitment is in keeping with the glory of his great name so that his covenant faithfulness may mean the salvation of only a remnant of Israel at the present time.[50]

One unanswered question remains. "Why not do evil that good may come?" (3:8).[51] This is in fact answered in 6:1–7:6 and may also account for Paul's discussion of the law in 7:7f. The second series of questions in 3:27–31 arise out of Paul's exposition of the Christ-event in 3:21–26 and provide an outline for Paul's treatment of the Abraham tradition in ch. 4.[52] From this survey of Paul's questions and of his answers to them in subsequent chapters, we have arrived at a conclusion similar to that in the discussion of the diatribe style. The questions in 3:1–8 link this section

---

different that they cannot be said originally to have belonged to that homily. Scroggs argues that Rom. 1–11 comprises two homilies—an exegetical homily in 1–4 and 9–11 having as its model the narrative of "Heilsgeschichte" found in Jewish homiletic tradition, whereas in chs. 5–8 Paul "speaks out of a diatribe structure perhaps remoulded by the Hellenistic Synagogue" ("Paul as Rhetorician," 297).

[48]This is a strong argument against Scroggs's view that Rom. 5–8 is a different homily from that in 1–4 and 9–11.

[49]The plural *ta logia* in 3:2 may also be taken in the wider sense of God's self-revelation; cf. Cranfield, *Romans,* 2.178–79. Despite the use of the singular in 9:6, the recurrence of the same term denotes the connection between the two chapters; cf. Luz, "Röm 1–8," 169.

[50]Israel is not a title that belongs indiscriminately or inalienably to all the descendants of Abraham; cf. Richardson, *Israel,* 126–46.

[51]Whether 3:7–8 should be regarded as one objection or two in unclear. Dahl, "Two Notes," and Jeremias, "Gedankenführung," 148, take them as one objection. If v. 7 is taken separately from v. 8, then the content of v. 7 relates back to the objection in v. 5 and provides a transition to the objection in v. 8; cf. Cranfield's discussion, *Romans,* 2.183–87.

[52]Dupont, "Structure littéraire," 372, n. 3. Wilckens, *Römer,* relates the objection in 3:31 to 7:1–8:11 following Käsemann in stressing the unity of 7–8, but differing from him in that he sees 8:12–30 as two sections separated from 8:1–11, which take up again themes from vv. 3–5.

with 6–7 and 9–11, whilst those in 3:27–31 link 3:21f. with ch. 4. The issue which must now be considered is whether the diatribe style sections, in spite of their appearance as digressions, do not, in fact, constitute the real theme of the letter and, if so, then how do they relate to the kerygmatic, declaratory sections.

III. Romans 3 as Witness to the Historical Situation to which the Letter is Addressed.

The fact that the questions in 3:1–8 precede Paul's exposition of the Christ-event in 3:21f. is significant. This indicates that Paul looks to the Cross for an understanding of and solution to the problems he faces. It could reasonably be argued that the questions in Romans are purely rhetorical, literary devices to draw out the practical consequences of doctrines such as baptism. The sequence in ch. 3 points, we submit, in the contrary direction. Our suggestion is that Paul faces real issues in Rome as outlined in 3:1–8 and that his exposition of the Christ-event in chs. 3:21–26, 5 and 8 is particularly designed to answer these problems.[53] The latter chapters deal with the eschatological present whereas the questions put may sometimes refer to the pre-Christian era—the place of the law or the election of Israel, i.e., items in Heilsgeschichte, the significance of which have been radically transformed by the coming of Christ. The question of continuity between Judaism and Christianity was a real issue among the Roman Christians.[54]

Our contention is therefore, that Rom. 3 provides an insight into the existential centre or focus of the letter. F. C. Baur rightly claimed that "it certainly appears that he (Paul) cannot have devoted so large a part of his epistle to answering this question (the relation of Judaism and heathenism to each other, and the relation of both to Christianity) without some special reason prompting him to do so, such as might have arisen out of the circumstances of the church at Rome."[55] Our contention is that the issues with which Paul deals in Romans are not simply the outcome or development of previous missionary disputes, not hypothetical questions to draw out the significance of Christian doctrines, but problems within the Roman Christian community about which Paul is informed and with which he intends to deal. If we take the example of Paul's use of the Abraham tradition in ch. 4, this will illustrate our thesis.

---

[53]See Michel's suggestion that it might be possible to reconstruct a simple outline of Paul's message from chs. 1–2, 3:21–30, 5 and 7:1–17, *Römer*, 45. See also Luz, "Röm 1–8," 225f., on kerygmatic formulations in Romans.

[54]W. D. Davies claims that "throughout his treatment of circumcision and the Law . . . Paul was concerned with a central question: the nature or constitution of the people of God—its continuity and discontinuity with the Jewish people of history" (*Gospel and Land*, 171).

[55]Baur, *Paul*, 316.

The outcome of Paul's discussion of Abraham is found in 4:16f..[56] "That is why it depends on faith, in order that the promise may rest on grace and be guaranteed to all his descendants—not only to the adherents of the law but also to those who share the faith of Abraham, for he is the father of us all. . . . " The grammatical structure here with its concentration on the purpose and intention of God's dealings with Abraham—particularly the reference to Abraham being intended to be "the father of us all,"[57] i.e., of Jewish and Gentile Christians, shows us that Paul intends to use Abraham as a uniting figure in the church composed of Jewish and Gentile Christians, and probably also as a model of "the strong in faith."[58] Not only this, but it is presupposed in 4:1 that what Abraham found was grace. Thus the concern in Rom. 4 is not merely with Abraham as an example of a man of faith, the prototype of the believer, or simply as scriptural proof of what is already asserted in ch. 3. David or Moses could not have served Paul's purpose here. Abraham is chosen as the one who found grace, the bearer of the promise who is replaceable by no other figure, the one with whom God first entered into covenant to bless the nations.[59] In the time of fulfilment the covenant is opened up to include Gentiles also so that Jewish and Gentile Christians may both regard Abraham as father.

Chapter 6:1f. is an even better example to show that Paul's questions are not merely rhetorical and that the objector is not necessarily Jewish. According to 3:8 some people slanderously report that Paul preaches the doing of evil that good may ensue and grace abound. In 6:1f., Paul repudiates such suggestions with a strongly ethically orientated exposition of the Christian's union with Christ's death and resurrection in baptism.[60] The catechetical teaching associated with baptism is continually evoked in Paul's reply, e.g., 6:3, 9, 16; 7:1.[61] It is significant that in 6:3f. Paul addresses directly the Roman Christians using the second person plural and in 6:11–13 he becomes even more precise in his use of the imperative. This is clear proof that the suggestion—that continuing in sin in order that grace may abound represents a Jewish parody of Paul's gospel—is a mistaken opinion. Paul is addressing baptized Christians and exhorting and commanding them not to live an antinomian existence. This suggests that those

[56]Dodd, *Romans,* 69.

[57]Despite his useful discussion of Abrahamskindschaft in ch. 4, Michel, *Römer,* 170, claims that Paul's aim is to show that Abraham is primarily father of Gentile Christians; contrast Barrett, *Romans,* 96.

[58]Minear, *Obedience,* 53–56.

[59]See Käsemann, "The Faith of Abraham in Romans 4," *Perspectives,* 98, and Wilckens, *Römer,* 261–85, esp. 283.

[60]See Frankemölle, *Das Taufverständnis des Paulus,* 24.

[61]When Paul uses *oidamen de* he is referring to commonly accepted traditions; cf. Bornkamm, "Baptism and New Life," 85, n. 5; see also Michel, *Römer,* 200, 268, n. 13; Dahl, "Anamnesis," 69–95 = *Memory,* 11–29; Burdick, "*oida* and *ginōskō,*" 344–56.

who slanderously reported Paul in 3:8 may be Gentile Christians who mistakenly attributed their own antinomianism to Paul's gospel of grace.[62]

Further support for the view that Paul's questions represent real issues in the church at Rome is found in 9–11. In 11:13f. Paul after a long discussion begun in 9:1, addresses himself pointedly to the Gentile Christians and specifically warns them not to boast over the fate of the unbelieving Jews. "If you do boast remember it is not you that support the root, but the root that supports you"(v. 18). Again he warns "do not become proud, but stand in awe" (v. 20). This is no hypothetical situation, and the dialogue style gives no reason to believe that Paul does not address himself to a real situation in Rome where current anti-judaism was threatening the unity of the church.[63] Paul's carefully constructed conclusion in 11:30–32 and his exhortations in 12:1f. and in 14–15 support this interpretation of ch. 11.[64]

An even clearer indication in support of the above is the concluding, scripturally substantiated imperative in 15:7f., "Welcome one another, therefore, as Christ has welcomed you, for the glory of God." Here is clear evidence that Paul commands two groups to accept each other as equal and full members of Christ and his church. The succeeding twofold emphasis upon Christ's ministry—(i) "He became a servant to the circumcised to show God's faithfulness, in order to confirm the promises given to the patriarchs and (ii) in order that the Gentiles might glorify God for his mercy," shows that Paul wishes to demonstrate that the gospel concerns both Jews and Gentiles. This is further substantiated by a number of Old Testament citations which speak of Israel and the Gentiles respectively enjoying the salvation of God.

In view of the direct connection of 15:7f. with 14:1f., it is clear that the division between the weak and strong is one along Jew-Gentile lines, and it is then easy to read back via 12:3 and to relate chs. 9–11 with 4:16f. and 6:11f. to a particular set of circumstances in the Christian community at Rome.

IV. Conclusion

In the letter to the Romans, differences in style and content are indications of the manner in which Paul addresses himself to the situation of the Roman Christians. The source of his answers to the problems of Christian life or doctrine is his "Kreuzestheologie" in which the doctrine of justification by faith is central. In Romans the Christ-event is depicted as the inbreaking of the new aeon in which the righteousness of God is

[62]Lütgert, *Römerbrief,* 78–79.
[63]Davies, "Paul and Israel," 13f., 36.
[64]Bartsch, "Die antisemitischen Gegner," 27–43.

revealed. In the letter Paul's gospel is presented as the fulfilment in Christ of the promises made to Abraham and his descendants. This form of presentation is to be expected in view of Paul's reminder to the Gentile Christians, "it is not you that supports the root but the root that supports you" (11:18). The emphasis upon Jewish-Christian tradition, the fulfilment of the promises, the goodness of the law, and the advantage of the Jew indicates that the question of the constitution and continuity of the people of God was a crucial issue among the Christians at Rome. Without appearing to be unduly specific we maintain that Paul faced two main issues in Rome (i) anti-judaism on the part of Gentile Christians, which was a cause of division among the Christian groups, and (ii) antinomianism—also on the part of Gentile Christians—some of whom were possibly former proselytes.[65] The latter problem may in fact, through the issue of the place of the law, have been related to the first and major problem. The outlook of the Roman Gentile Christians had marked similarities with that which later came to expression in Marcionism.

If Robinson is correct in his claim that Christian experience in Romans is deliberately depicted in terms of the justified Jew who has entered on his inheritance in Christ,[66] then the reason for this form of presentation could be that Paul wished to oppose "Marcionite" tendencies in the Roman Christians. It might also have the aim of assuring the Jewish Christian minority that God's promises to Israel had not failed. If one of Paul's aims in the letter is to show Gentile Christians how their hope rests on Israel's Messiah, in order to achieve this it was necessary for Paul to demonstrate the righteousness or faithfulness of God to Israel. As a compromise with Cranfield's view that the logic of the gospel partially determines the structure and argument of the letter,[67] we would suggest that it was because of the needs of the Christians in Rome that Paul felt compelled to demonstrate the fulfilment in Christ of the promises to Abraham.

It was not simply that Paul prepared a summary of his gospel because for various reasons he wished the Roman Christians to be better informed as to its content. Paul's interest is in the divine activity that derives from the covenant with Abraham and culminates in the saving event of Jesus Christ and the proclamation of the gospel to both Jews and Gentiles. But where the gospel is too individualistically interpreted Romans has sometimes been understood mainly as depicting the progress of the gospel in the lives of individual Christians, i.e., in terms of justification, sanctification, and glorification. But in Paul's theology, justification and the people of God are themes which belong inseparably together.

For Paul it is the logic of the gospel as the outcome and fulfilment of the hope of Israel that he presents to the Romans, because this is for

[65]Marxsen, *Introduction,* 98, and Schmithals, *Der Römerbrief als historische Problem,* 83f.
[66]See note 15.
[67]See note 3.

him the only adequate response to an incipient Marcionism. Our thesis is, however, that the raison d'être of Romans is the needs of the Roman Christian community and that it was the nature of these that incidentally caused Paul to write a letter which, in some respects at least, reads like an abstract summary of his gospel or theology. The centre of Paul's argument in the letter is 3:21–26 and its climax is chs. 9–11; but the actual situation that determines both how he argues and the themes of his arguments is the circumstances of the Roman Christians. Paul's own situation as he heads for Jerusalem and his commission as apostle to the Gentiles are also relevant for a full understanding of Romans, but these play a secondary role.[68]

We conclude that despite its careful structure and the length of its sustained arguments, Romans must still be regarded as a letter addressed to a specific situation in Rome. There is also evidence in the letter that Paul is acquainted, in outline at least, with the circumstances of the Roman Christians. The fact that he had not yet visited Rome cannot be regarded as an adequate reason for viewing the letter simply as an outline of his theology or as a summary of his gospel unrelated to any particular issues in Rome. The onus rests on those who disregard Paul's specific exhortations and commands in the body of the letter and in chs. 12–16 to explain why these should not be interpreted in the same way as those in Galatians or Corinthians.

The fact that the doctrinal sections in Romans were written for the sake of a particular historical situation in no wise denigrates them as witness to Paul's gospel or theology. But we must be careful to distinguish between what is central in Romans and what is central to Paul's theology. It may be that by a fortunate coincidence, these may actually be similar, possibly even identical, but it would be difficult to prove this is in fact the case. This means that Romans must play its part in helping us to construct the theology of Paul; but until we are clear what that theology is, we must be cautious and not give way to the tendency to use this letter alone as the measuring line for all that constitutes genuine Pauline theology. However it may be interpreted, there is no doubt that this letter will continue to play a major role in the development of Christian theology. We have no need to defend its position even for the best of those dogmatic reasons which F. C. Baur deplored in his day. "The dogmatic view is not to yield one step to the historical, lest the position of an epistle such as that to the Romans should be impaired, and the Lutheran forensic process of justification, which is of such moment to maintain in its integrity, suffer from the shaking of its great buttress."[69]

[68]On this see my article listed in note 1.
[69]Baur, *Paul*, 313.

18

FOLLOWING THE ARGUMENT OF ROMANS[1]

Robert Jewett

While I was working on this article in May of 1986, I happened by the bulletin board of Immanuel Lutheran Church in Evanston. It announced Professor Emeritus Joseph Sittler as the guest preacher. A flood of memories arose concerning classes with him in Chicago and on one memorable occasion, a trip together to an ecumenical meeting. It was the spring of 1957, if my memory serves me well, and Sittler was to preach on Romans. To my amazement, he embarked on a summary of the argument of the entire letter. It was a tour de force that started with Romans 1:16 and got as far as 5:21 when he ran out of time. As I reflect on that engrossing experience in the light of subsequent years of study of Romans, I am struck by how very Protestant, indeed quintessentially Lutheran, that sermon was. Following the leading commentaries, this masterful exposition bypassed the introduction in the first 15 verses of Romans, and hence the situational purpose of Paul's writing, perceiving the climax of the argument in doctrinal statements in chapters 3 and 5. Both the fascination and the dilemma of this approach are captured by J. Christiaan Beker: "The presupposition that Romans is a 'theological confession' or a 'dogmatics in outline' is the real reason for the immense interest in the letter's architectonic structure and the neglect of its 'frame.' "[2] These words describe the challenge we face in approaching the question of the argumentative structure of Romans.

Since I share Beker's conviction that Romans is a situational letter rather than a doctrinal treatise, and since previous analyses of the letter have tended to reflect the thematic and theological interests of scholars,[3]

---

[1]Adapted and expanded by Robert Jewett from *Word and World* 6 (1986) 382–89.
[2]Beker, *Paul,* 62.
[3]Classic studies are Feuillet, "Le Plan salvifique," 336–87, 489–529; Prümm, "Struktur," 333–49; Lyonnet, "Notes," 301–16; Jeremias, "Gedankenführung," 146–54; Dupont, "Structure

it seems apparent that we need a more impartial approach to following Paul's argument. The rhetorical method is our most promising resource. It allows us to grasp the structure of the argument within the context of the peculiar purpose of the letter, which stands in a communicative context with a specific audience. This may allow us to counterbalance the tendency to follow the argument primarily from the viewpoint of contemporary theology.

I took a preliminary step toward applying this method in "Romans as an Ambassadorial Letter,"[4] an effort to refine the rhetorical genre of this highly abstract letter. As suggested by Wuellner,[5] Romans conforms to demonstrative rhetoric, whose aim is to reinforce some aspect of the ethos of an audience.[6] The investigation of this genre by Theodore C. Burgess identifies several types of demonstrative rhetoric that fit well with Romans: the "speech on disembarking," the "paranetic speech," the "hortatory speech," and most distinctively, the "ambassador's speech."[7] An ambassador arrives in an alien court, states his credentials, and then advocates the interest of his sovereign or constituency.[8] Similarly Paul introduces himself to the Roman churches he has not founded and then proceeds in a diplomatic fashion to provide a rationale for his forthcoming visit. As evident in the introduction and conclusion of the letter, Paul aims to provide a theological argument that will unify the competing house-churches in Rome[9] so that they will be willing to cooperate in a mission to Spain, to be mounted from Rome. The continuation of conflicts between the "weak" and the "strong" (Rom. 14:1–15:7), involving tensions between Jewish Christians and Gentile Christians, conservatives and liberals, would jeopardize this mission.[10] The cautious manner in which Paul refers to his intended visit (Rom. 1:9–15) and to the help he needs from the Roman churches (Rom. 15:22–29) is consistently ambassadorial, aimed at appealing to various sides in Rome. The thesis of Romans concerning the gospel as the "power of God" to achieve the triumph of divine righteousness (Rom. 1:16–17) is integrally related to the scheme of world mission (Rom. 15:8–13),

---

littéraire," 365–97; Grayston, "I Am Not Ashamed," 569–73; Ruijs, *Struktuur*; Luz, "Röm 1–8," 161–81; Morris, "Theme of Romans," 249–63.

Significant recent studies include Dunn, "Structure and Argument," 2842–90; Lamarche-Le Dû, *Epître aux Romains*; and Rolland, *Epître aux Romains*; unfortunately the last item remained unavailable to me at the time of final revision of this article.

[4]Jewett, "Ambassadorial Letter," 5–20.

[5]Wuellner, "Paul's Rhetoric," 128–46.

[6]Wuellner was primarily dependent on Perelman–Olbrechts-Tyteca, *New Rhetoric*, for the understanding of the demonstrative / epideictic genre as reinforcing communal values. Beale, "Performative Discourse," 221–46, offers a significant refinement of this understanding.

[7]Burgess, "Epideictic Literature," 110–13; for a more recent discussion of the epideictic or demonstratic genre, see Chase, "Classical Conception of Epideictic," 293–300.

[8]See the classic study of diplomatic correspondence, Welles, *Royal Correspondence*.

[9]For a discussion of the splintered house-churches in Rome, see Lampe, *Die stadtrömischen*, 301–45 (pagination from first edition).

[10]Cf. Jewett, *Christian Tolerance*, 23–36.

which Paul now hopes to extend to the traditional end of the world, Spain. A recent article elaborates this final motif,[11] working out the implications of W. P. Bowers's discovery of the absence of Jewish communities in Spain at the time of Paul's letter,[12] and exploring the cultural and linguistic situation that necessitated the missional preparation of translating the gospel and its related Old Testament foundations into Latin and the Celt-Iberian dialects. The paucity of Greek speakers in Spain provided a barrier almost as large as the absence of Jewish synagogues. Up to this point of course, the Christian mission in the Roman Empire had been articulated in Greek rather than in Latin. The diplomatic argument in Romans was designed to encourage the cooperation of the house-churches in organizing this daunting project to extend the circle of the mission (Rom. 15:19) to the "barbarians" (Rom. 1:14) in Spain.

I. Romans and Rhetoric

It has long been recognized that the arrangement and invention of the argument of Romans reflect some of the principles promoted by the rhetorical handbooks of antiquity.[13] Aristotle refers to the arrangement of four parts in a typical discourse as containing an introduction, a statement or narrative of the issue, the proof, and an epilogue.[14] Cicero advises the rhetor to organize his discourse in five sections, an *exordium* or introduction, a *narratio* or narration of the case, a *confirmatio* or proof of the thesis, a *reprehensio* or rebuttal of opposing views, and finally a *conclusio* or conclusion.[15] The Latin rhetorician Quintilian refers to similar categories whose nomenclature is quite useful in understanding Romans.[16] The letter begins with an *exordium*, an introduction (Rom. 1:1–12), which is followed by a brief *narratio*, a narration of the background of Paul's intended visit to Rome (Rom. 1:13–15). Quintilian then refers to the main portion of the discourse, the *probatio* or proof of the case being argued, which in the case of Romans is divided into four distinct proofs (Rom. 1:18–4:25; 5:1–8:39; 9:1–11:36; and 12:1–15:13). The next section according to Quintilian is the *refutatio*, the rebuttal of opposing views. However, since

[11]Jewett, "Spanish Mission," 142–61.

[12]Bowers, "Jewish Communities," 395–402.

[13]See the history of research beginning with the church fathers in Siegert, *Argumentation*, 5–15. Particularly interesting is his observation on p. 114 that Bengel's *Gnomon* contains an analysis of the disposition of Romans that sounds quite contemporary: *exordium* (1:1–15); *propositio* 1:16–17); *tractatio* (1:18–11:36); *paraclesis* (12:1–15:13) and *conclusio* (15:14–16:27). A broad orientation to this history in English is available in Mack, *Rhetoric*, 9–17.

[14]Cf. the chart in Lausberg, *Handbuch*, 148–49. Aristotle's scheme is found in *Ars rhetorica* 3.13.4.

[15]Cicero, *De inventione* 1.19. In *De partitione oratoria* 27, Cicero consolidates the *reprehensio* and *confirmatio*, drops the category of *partitio*, and calls the conclusion *peroratio*.

[16]Quintilian, *Institio oratoria*, 3.9.1.

Romans is not a forensic letter requiring a rebuttal of charges, this section is replaced, as it were, by diatribal components within the several proofs that refute alternative views and false inferences. Finally there is a *peroratio*, the conclusion of the letter that provides the practical appeal (Rom. 15:14–16:27). Several Latin rhetoricians add a *propositio* or *partitio*, a brief statement of the thesis or enumeration of the issues placed between the narration and the proof, a detail that is matched in Rom. 1:16–17.[17] Paul's letter therefore has a fivefold outline that would have been easily followed by the Roman audience conditioned to understand classical rhetoric.

George A. Kennedy has provided a methodical application of such rhetorical categories to New Testament material.[18] He follows the suggestion of Wilhelm Wuellner[19] and myself in viewing Romans as a demonstrative letter but organizes the arrangement somewhat differently than suggested above. Here is an outline reconstructed from his discussion in which I have attempted by the material in parenthesis to supply some of the missing details:

1:1–15	I	(Address) and Proem
1:16–17	II	Proposition
1:18–11:36	III	Headings: Doctrinal Message and Refutation of Objections
1:18–2:16		A Narration on the Power of God for Damnation
2:17–4:25		B The Situation of the Jew
5:1–6:23		C The Situation of the Gentile
7:1–25		D Address to Jews on the Nature of Faith
8:1–39		E (Life in Spirit) without Separation from Christ
9:1–11:36		F Address to Gentiles on the Situation of the Jews
12:1–15:13	IV	Pastoral Headings: Application of the Doctrine Developed in the Doctrinal Headings
15:14–33	V	Epilogue
16:1–23	VI	Postscript and Letter Closure

Several points in Kennedy's analysis deserve discussion. He sees a kind of narration in the beginning of Paul's theological argument (Rom. 1:18–2:16), but both the content and location of Rom. 1:13–15 serve this purpose more precisely. Here Paul provides the background of his intended visit, placing it in the context of his previous missionary activities. Consequently I would argue that the introduction proper, identified by Kennedy with a Greek rhetorical term, the proem, is completed by Rom. 1:10–12, the statement of the *causa* of the letter, i.e., the main purpose of writing—to prepare the way for Paul's intended visit. I am closer to agreement with Kennedy in identifying Rom. 1:16–17 as the "proposition" of

---

[17]Cicero, *De inventione* 1.31–33; Quintilian, *Institio oratoria* 4.5.1ff.; Martianus Capella, *Liber de arte rhetorica*, 44 (544); 45–53 (545–65); C. Iulii Victoris, *Ars Rhetorica*, 1 p. 373, 27.

[18]Kennedy, *Rhetorical Criticism*, 152–56.

[19]In "Paul's Rhetoric," cited in note 5 above, Wuellner provides a rhetorical analysis of Romans as consisting of *exordium* (1:1–15), *propositio* (1:16–17), *confirmatio* (1:18–15:13) and *peroratio* (15:14–16:23). See also Wuellner, "Greek Rhetoric," 177–88.

the letter that acts as a "partition underlying the structure of 1:18–11:36."[20] As commentators have frequently observed, these verses contain the thesis of the letter as a whole. I would contend, however, that the formal argument of the letter reaches beyond Rom. 11:36 to chapters 12–15 as well. In contrast to previous commentators, I would favor a more integral connection of these final chapters to the theological thesis in Rom. 1:16–17, and I would like to avoid non-rhetorical categories like "pastoral headings" or the terms frequently employed in Romans commentaries such as "ethical teaching"[21] or "Christian Living."[22] The use of the Greek term *paraklēsis* is more adequate. [23] Another problem in the Kennedy analysis is that the term "headings" employed to describe the argument of the letter does not convey a sense of logical development that moves from the thesis right through to Rom. 15:13. The final question is whether the material in chapter 16 should be viewed as a "postscript." Kennedy observes how important these details are in "establishing a personal tie with those he [Paul] addresses: these are, as it were, his witnesses,"[24] which would seem to bring this material in line with the category I prefer, "peroration," in which the emotional ties between writer and audience are adduced in the appeal for the particular values or actions promoted in the argument.

Despite minor differences, I feel that the work of Kennedy represents a step in the right direction in using rhetorical categories to understand the entirety of Romans as an expression of demonstrative rhetoric. Parallel efforts to understand the persuasive impact of the argumentation of Romans have been made recently by Siegert, Wonnenberger, Bouwman, Rolland, and du Toit.[25] I prefer to build on the foundation of rhetorical theory to gain a more coherent grasp of the argument as a whole. Resources in classical and modern rhetoric in addition to the insights of generations of commentaries on Romans can be employed to analyze the individual proofs in Paul's argument.

II. A Rhetorical Approach to the Proofs in Romans

The remarkable coherence of Paul's argument may be most easily grasped by using the argumentative categories taught by ancient rheto-

---

[20]Kennedy, *Rhetorical Criticism*, 153.

[21]Knox, *Romans*, 578. Dunn categorizes 12:1–15:13 as "The Outworking of the Gospel for the Redefined People of God in Everyday Terms" in *Romans 9–16*, 705.

[22]Morris, *Romans*, 431, categorizes 12:1–15:13 as "Christian Living," which seems to follow Dodd, *Romans*, 188: "The Righteousness of God in Christian Living." Heil, *Romans*, 12, describes 12:1–15:13 as "Paul exhorts his audience to live the new life God has given them."

[23]Wilckens, *Römer*, 1.

[24]Kennedy, *Rhetorical Criticism*, 152.

[25]Siegert uses syntactic rather than rhetorical categories in his analysis of the first twelve chapters of the letter in *Argumentation*, 112–19, following the example of Wonnenberger, *Syntax und Exegese*. According to Siegert, a complete syntactic analysis of the letter is avail-

ricians. The terms "confirmation," "amplification," "ratiocination," "elaboration," "example," "rationale," "opposition," and "comparison" were used in classical rhetoric to describe typical components in the development of proofs. As Burton Mack and his colleagues in the Chreia Project at Claremont have recently pointed out, the student exercise handbooks of ancient rhetoricians beginning in the second century B.C.E. contained lists of standard components in the development of a "theme" or "thesis."[26] In the *Rhetorica ad Herennium*, the "complete argumentation" of a thesis contains:

1. *propositio* (proposition),
2. *ratio* (rationale, reason),
3. *confirmatio* (confirmation),
4. *exornatio* (elaboration) consisting of a simile, an example, an amplification, and an evaluation, and finally,
5. *conplexio* (concluding recapitulation).[27]

In another location, the *ad Herennium* provides a sevenfold outline for developing a thesis:

1. *res* (the statement of the theme),
2. *ratio* (reason),
3. *pronuntio* (paraphrase of the theme),
4. *contrario* (statement of the opposite of the thesis),
5. *simile* (analogy),
6. *exemplum* (example), and
7. *conclusio* (conclusion).[28]

Hermogenes provides eight components in the "elaboration" of a thesis based on a familiar quotation, the chreia:

1. praise of the author of the quotation
2. quotation of the chreia
3. rationale
4. opposite
5. analogy
6. example
7. judgment
8. exhortation[29]

There is a broad similarity in these school exercises, suggesting a widespread tradition of instructing students in the development of arguments.

---

able in Rolland, *Epître aux Romains*. A less readily accessible analysis of the first eight chapters of Romans using traditional categories informed by the new rhetoric may be found in Bouwman, *Paulus*. A. B. du Toit remains critical about the use of rhetorical categories for analyzing the disposition of Paul's argument, preferring epistolary categories in "Persuasion," 192–209.

[26]Mack, *Rhetoric*, 42–47; idem, "Anecdotes and Arguments," 1–48; Hock–O'Neil, *Chreia*.
[27]*Rhetorica ad Herennium* 2.18.28.
[28]*Rhetorica ad Herennium* 4.43.56.
[29]Hermogenes, "On the Chreia," 7,10–8,10; see also the chart on p. 21 of Mack, "Anecdotes and Arguments."

While these categories are ordinarily applied to shorter blocks of material, some of them seem quite descriptive of the proofs in Romans. The application of such categories would help to clarify the relation between Rom. 1:18–4:25 and the subsequent sections of the letter, a subject that has been intensively debated by Romans commentators. The main argument is stated in the first four chapters; yet themes, questions, and implications from that discussion are taken up in subsequent arguments in the letter. I would contend that these later sections are all part of the proof of the letter, elaborating the basic thesis that has been developed in what I would identify as the *confirmatio* section of Rom. 1:18–4:25. The confirmation of the thesis concerning the righteousness of God begins with the sin of Jews and Greeks alike, moves on to proclaim the gift of righteousness through faith in Christ, and climaxes with the example of Abraham as the parent of all who are set right by faith. One might visualize the structure of the argument as a thesis in 1:16–17 followed by an initial circle of proof in 1:18–4:25 that confirms the thesis. The next three proofs in Romans provide extensive developments of this thesis, answering relevant theological and ethical objections while amplifying important themes and implications.

A useful descriptive term for the second proof in Romans is the one used by *Rhetorica ad Herennium*, "elaboration" (*exornatio*). It is closely associated with "amplification" (*auxēsis*) the term preferred by Hermogenes. Another closely associated term is "ratiocination," which deals with the logical implications of an already proven case, often proceeding with a series of arguments dealing with the consequences of the intended circumstance, according to Heinrich Lausberg.[30] This type of argument is particularly typical for writings in the demonstrative genre.[31] The use of these categories under the general heading of "elaboration" for Rom. 5:1–8:39 helps to clarify the logical connections with the confirmation section of 1:18–4:25. Chapters 5–8 deal with a series of objections raised against the doctrine of righteousness through faith. The effect of Nils Dahl's appraisal of the pivotal role of Rom. 5:1–11 can be taken into account in this analysis.[32] This pericope summarizes major themes of the first proof that are to be developed in the second proof, thereby introducing the themes of what I identify as the *exornatio* section of the letter.

The form of proof called *comparatio* uses a historical example or an imaginative case to demonstrate the superiority of the argument or case already established. It is also a favored argumentative form in demonstrative rhetoric, says Lausberg.[33] I believe that this category fits the peculiar content of Rom. 9–11 very nicely. Here Paul takes up the problem of Israel's

---

[30]Lausberg, *Handbuch*, 223. The argumentative form of *ratiocinatio* is discussed in Quintilian 8.4.15.

[31]Ibid.

[32]Dahl, *Studies*, 82–91.

[33]Lausberg, *Handbuch*, 222f. *Comparatio* is discussed in Quintilian 8.4.9.

unbelief, examining whether it disproves the thesis concerning the triumph of divine righteousness through the gospel. Far from being a somewhat irrelevant appendix or a "separate treatise,"[34] Rom. 9–11 is fully integrated as an essential argument in Paul's extended proof of God's righteousness. Paul does not have to be "ashamed of the gospel" (1:16) because the "word of God" has not failed (9:6), even in the case of a disobedient Israel. The fourth proof in 12:1–15:13 sets forth the ethical implications of the main thesis in 1:16–17, providing guidelines for living out the righteousness of God. Since none of the classical rhetoricians used the term *exhortatio* in describing the arrangement of a speech or a letter, it has been difficult to justify its use for this section despite the congruity in content. Hermogenes' use of the term "exhortation" to describe a phase in the elaboration of a thesis opens the door to its employment in the analysis of Romans. In this instance, the exhortation section is an essential portion of the proof concerning the righteousness of God manifest in the gospel as stated in the thesis of 1:16–17. The use of this category defined in this way may help to resolve one of the major problems in the interpretation of Romans, namely the relation between theology and ethics. The ethical theories and admonitions in these chapters do not comprise a secondary and inferior dimension of the argument, but rather are the climactic proof of the main thesis of the letter.

III. Sketching the Argument

I would now like to sketch the argument of Romans, using these rhetorical terms along with other categories descriptive of the argumentative material that Paul develops. Only in the case of the major components in the arrangement are the technical Latin terms employed. Topical sentences are used to describe the content of the argument in each section.

Part One: Exordium (Introduction, 1:1–12). Here Paul introduces himself to the divided Roman audience, stressing his apostolic authority, defining his gospel in a preliminary way, and thanking God for their faith. He concludes with the main purpose of his letter: his forthcoming visit to Rome for the sake of the world mission.

Part Two: Narratio (Narration, 1:13–15). Paul describes the background of his missionary project to come to Rome, which has thus far been frustrated.

Part Three: Propositio (Thesis Statement, 1:16–17). Paul states the major contention of the letter concerning the gospel as the powerful embodiment of the righteousness of God.

Part Four: Probatio (Proof, 1:18–15:13). Paul proves that the righteousness of God, rightly understood, has transforming and unifying implica-

---

[34]Sanday–Headlam, *Romans,* 225f.; Dodd, *Romans,* 148.

tions for the Roman house-churches and their participation in world mission. There are four elaborate proofs in Romans: an extensive confirmation of the thesis followed by three wide-ranging amplifications. Though couched in the generalities typical for demonstrative discourse, each proof has an important bearing on the situation in the house-churches and the issue of the mission to Spain.

The First Proof: *Confirmatio* (Confirmation, 1:18–4:25). Paul confirms the basic thesis of 1:16–17 by showing that the impartial righteousness of God provides righteousness for Jews and Gentiles alike, by faith. This argument contains five major sections, each with two pericopes: (1) The revelation of divine wrath (1:18–32), including (a) the thesis and rationale of the exposure of human suppression of the truth about God (1:18–23) and (b) the elaboration of human distortion as a current indication of wrath (1:24–32); (2) the righteous judgment of Gentiles and Jews (2:1–29), consisting of (a) a diatribe concerning impartial judgment according to works (2:1–16) and (b) a diatribe concerning the non-exemption of Jews from impartial judgment (2:17–29); (3) Jewish involvement in universal sin (3:1–20), with (a) a diatribe refuting objections to impartial judgment (3:1–8) and (b) a diatribe and catena of quotations showing the universal condemnation of sin (3:9–20); (4) the righteousness of God that makes right all persons of faith (3:21–31), consisting of (a) the thesis and rationale concerning the triumph of righteousness in Christ (3:21–26) and (b) a diatribe showing the one God of Jews and Gentiles (3:27–31); (5) Abraham as the example of righteousness that comes through faith (4:1–25), with (a) a diatribe and midrash showing Abraham received righteousness by faith before he was circumcised (4:1–12) and (b) a midrash showing that Abraham's promise comes to the righteous through faith (4:13–25).

The Second Proof: *Exornatio* (Elaboration, 5:1–8:39). Here Paul deals with a series of implications and objections to the doctrine of the righteousness of God conveyed by Christ. This elaboration consists of ten pericopes: (1) introduction (5:1–11) stating and explaining the theme of righteousness as peace with God and hope in the midst of afflictions; (2) ratiocination about the contrasting realms of Adam and Christ (5:12–21); (3) diatribe that refutes an objection on the basis of baptism, with concluding exhortation (6:1–14); (4) diatribe refuting an objection on the basis of the exchange of lordship (6:15–23); (5) enthymeme concerning life in Christ as freedom from the law (7:1–6); (6) refutation of an objection concerning the moral status of the law (7:7–12); (7) refutation of an objection concerning the effect of the law (7:13–25); (8) thesis and rationale concerning the cosmic struggle between flesh and Spirit (8:1–17); (9) thesis and rationale concerning the hopeful suffering of the children of God (8:18–30); and (10) the conclusion showing that nothing can separate believers from the love of Christ (8:31–39).

The Third Proof: *Comparatio* (Comparison, 9:1–11:36). Paul takes up the case of unbelieving Israel to demonstrate that the righteousness of God will still be triumphant, that the gospel in the end will not fail. This necessary elaboration of the argument is developed with ten pericopes that match the structure of the preceding proof, with a formal introduction and conclusion as follows: (1) introduction: the tragic riddle of Israel's unbelief (9:1–5); (2) thesis and midrash on Israel and the righteousness of divine election (9:6–18); (3) diatribe and midrash refuting an objection by scriptural proofs (9:19–29); (4) diatribe responding to a question about righteousness by a doctrine of unenlightened zeal (9:30–10:4); (5) ratiocination showing that righteousness by faith is confirmed in scripture (10:5–13); (6) diatribal syllogism concerning the gospel preached but rejected (10:14–21); (7) diatribe answering a question about the status of Israel in relation to the remnant chosen by grace (11:1–10); (8) diatribe, thesis, and simile dealing with the missional purpose of Israel's trespass (11:11–24); (9) oracular disclosure and rationale of the mystery of Israel's salvation (11:25–32); and (10) conclusion, a hymn concerning the mysterious mind of God (11:33–36).

The Fourth Proof: *Exhortatio* (Exhortation, 12:1–15:13). Here Paul lays out ethical guidelines for living in righteousness, thus developing the final proof of the thesis in 1:17 that the righteous shall *live* by faith. Like the preceding two proofs, this argument consists of ten pericopes with a formal introduction and conclusion. The argument develops as follows: (1) introduction: the thesis concerning the motivation and assessment of praiseworthy behavior (12:1–2); (2) the elaboration of sober self-appraisal and the exercise of charismatic gifts (12:3–8); (3) the elaboration of guidelines for genuine love (12:9–21); (4) the elaboration of guidelines for relations to the government (13:1–7); (5) the definition of love in relation to the neighbor (13:8–10); (6) the admonition to moral alertness in the last days (13:11–14); (7) exemplary guidelines and rationale for the weak and the strong (14:1–12); (8) exemplary guidelines and rationale for mutual upbuilding in pluralistic congregations (14:13–23); (9) admonition to follow Christ's example in edifying each other (15:1–6); and (10) recapitulation of the motivational horizon of world mission and unification (15:7–13).

Part Five: Peroratio (Peroration, or conclusion, 15:14–16:27). This consists of an appeal for the cooperation of the Roman house-churches in missionary activities in Jerusalem, Rome, and Spain. With the elimination of two interpolations identified by a number of contemporary exegetes, the warning against heretics in 16:17–20a and the concluding doxology in 16:25–27, this peroration is organized in five distinct sections: (a) The recapitulation of Paul's missionary calling and strategy (15:14–21); (b) an appeal to participate in Paul's present and future missionary plans (15:22–33); (c) a recommendation of Phoebe as the patron of the Spanish mission (16:1–2); (d) greetings and commendations between potentially cooperating missionary leaders (16:3–16, 21–23); and (e) the epistolary benediction (16:20b).

The identification of the pericopes in this analysis follows for the most part the semantic discourse structure suggested by J. P. Louw.[35] He provides a colon analysis of the Greek text and then organizes the cola into closely associated pericopes. I have altered his scheme by consolidating several pericopes into the five double units in the first proof, following the perceptions of a number of commentators about the major divisions in 1:18–4:25. I followed his analysis exactly in discerning the ten pericopes of second and third proofs.[36] Since Louw does not use rhetorical categories to identify the large units of the argument, the tenfold scheme was not recognizable in his study. I have altered his outline at one point to produce the ten units of the fourth proof: I divided the first unit into the thesis statement of 12:1–2 and the material in 12:3–8, following commentaries by Käsemann, Harrisville, Dodd, Michel, Knox, Wilckens, and others at this point. I have also altered Louw's outline to produce the five pericopes in part five, separating the recommendation of Phoebe in 16:1–2 from the greetings and commendations of 16:3–16, 21–23.[37]

There now appears to be a remarkable symmetry in ten pericopes of the second, third, and fourth proofs, each beginning with a formal introduction and ending with a formal, often liturgical conclusion. The correspondences between the five double pericopes of the first proof and the ten pericopes of the succeeding proofs as well as the five pericopes of part five are also noteworthy. My impression is that this formal prominence of fives and tens places Romans firmly within the arena of a culture shaped by the Jewish Torah.[38] Series of fives and tens are distinctive indications

[35]Louw, *Analysis of Romans.*

[36]The parallel analysis of the Greek text using a grammatical and literary methodology by Lamarche and Le Dû, *Epître aux Romains,* 91–109, agrees with Louw's organization of the pericopes in Rom. 5:1 through 6:14 but joins the seven pericopes of 6:15–8:39 into three larger units.

[37]Louw, *Analysis of Romans,* 2.141 provides support for this division of 16:1–16 into two pericopes.

[38]The Hebraic preferences are not only visible in the organization of the pericopes in Romans, but also in the series of quotations and the stylistic flourishes throughout the letter in which fives, sevens, and tens are particularly prominent. See my forthcoming article, "Numerical Sequences." For instance the description of Jewish boasting in 2:17–25 is artfully constructed of three strophes with five lines each, while 2:26–29 contains five pairs of somewhat unbalanced lines ending with the clausula of 29c. In 8:24–25 there are five successive lines in which the terms "hope" or "to hope" are repeated five times; the next strophe in vv. 26–27 also contains five lines; the pericope concludes with a sevenfold climax in which the stages of the glory manifest in Christians are described in vv. 28–30. In 8:31–37 there are seven rhetorical questions arranged in three strophes of which the last contains seven forms of suffering in a rhetorically effective series linked with "or" (8:35). The next strophe contains ten forms of demonic power linked with "nor" (8:38–39c). In 9:4–5 there is a listing of seven attributes of Paul's Jewish kinfolk, followed by two further attributes introduced by relative pronouns, the second of which is defined by a further relative clause, making a formal series of ten. In 9:19–39 we find an artful series of ten texts proving the propriety of divine election, while in 10:5–13 there are seven quotations proving that righteousness through faith derives from scripture. The material in 11:33–36 has been structured into a hymn of ten lines, with triple structuring within verses 33 and 36. In 12:6–8 we find a series of seven graces, while in 12:10–13 there are five pairs of neatly balanced exhortative phrases that elaborate the meaning of the love command in 12:9. In 13:9 we find five quotations from the law while

of Jewish rhetorical preferences.[39] The oral effectiveness of the public reading of Romans to the original churches would have been further enhanced
by the brilliantly varied poetic style that begins in 1:13 and continues to
the end of the formal proofs in 15:13. Johannes Weiss provided the pathbreaking investigation of Paul's flexible use of Hebraic and Hellenistic parallelism, often enhanced by anaphora, antistrophe, chiasm, homoioptoton,
homoioteleuton, parechesis, paronamasia, climax, and clausula.[40] The audience would have been carried inexorably forward through the theological
proofs to the peroration, where the appeals for missional cooperation and
mutual acceptance are expressed, forming the intended climax of the letter.

IV. Concluding Reflections

Some preliminary, concluding reflections may now be in order. The
structure of Romans not only shows rhetorical skill and forethought, but
also the intent to find common ground between Jewish Christian and Gentile Christian factions in the Roman house-churches. Nowhere else in Paul's
writing are the concerns of Jewish Christians taken up in so systematic
and friendly a manner, thus counterbalancing the prejudices of the Gentile majority of Roman Christians. The unparalleled density of citations
from the Jewish scriptures appears to be matched by the use of Hebrew
rhetorical series in the disposition of the argument. Yet Paul abandons
neither his critique of the Torah as a means of salvation nor his commitment to a gospel that transcends cultural barriers, including Jewish ones.
The goal of the entire argument, in fact, is to sustain the ethos favoring
world unification through the gospel, as the conclusion of the theological
and ethical argument in 15:7–13 reveals.

If one were to pose the traditional question of the "high point" or
"climax" of Romans, it is surely to be found in the peroration in chapters
15–16 rather than in the abstract, doctrinal themes of the earlier part of

---

15:7–13 concludes the formal argument of the letter with quotations from five different passages drawn from all three divisions of the Hebrew scriptures.

[39]For general orientation see Driver, "Sacred Numbers," 62–90, and Davis, *Biblical Numerology.* While ten was an important number in the Greco-Roman world, it attained crucial
significance in Judaism with the ten commandments, the tithe, and the requirement of ten
males to make a synagogue quorum, according to Brongers, "Die Zehnzahl," 30–45. Although
there is no particular interest in series of five in the Hebrew scriptures, this number becomes
rhetorically important as symbolic of the Torah and the Megillot for later Judaism. Early
Christianity reflects this preference as one can see from Luke 12:52; 14:19; 16:28; John 4:18;
1 Cor. 14:19, etc.

[40]Weiss, "Paulinischen Rhetorik," 165–247. Important parallel contributions were made
by Wilke, *Sprachidioms;* Bullinger, *Figures of Speech;* König, *Stilistik, Rhetorik, Poetik;* Blass,
Kunstprosa (Hildesheim: Gerstenberg, 1972 reprint of 1905 edition); Norden, *Kunstprosa.* I
have extended these preliminary studies by identifying the stylistic features of each pericope
in Romans in preparation for a commentary in the Hermeneia series, and have been aided
recently by Campbell, D. A., *Rhetoric of Righteousness.*

the letter. If the dynamics of ancient rhetoric are taken into account, the proofs of the earlier chapters of Romans are seen to have a practical purpose developed with powerful emotional appeals at the end of the discourse. This purpose was to elicit the cooperation of the Roman house-churches in Paul's missionary activities, thus serving the ultimate purpose of divine righteousness in regaining control of a lost and disobedient world. The doctrines that theologians have struggled so long and so divisively to define and defend were originally intended to advance a larger goal—the unification of God's world. The passionate squabbles over each detail in chapters 1–11 without regard for the thrust of the argument as a whole, driven by the presumption of conforming to dogmatic systems, have turned the humane and unifying argument of Romans into its ethnocentric opposite. The rhetorical analysis of Romans allows us to understand that salvation is inextricably joined with cosmic transformation, theology with ethics, faith with tolerance. If Paul's grand argument were better understood, it might still provide a basis for achieving its original vision: to bring "all the peoples" (Rom. 15:11) to praise the One whose gospel can still restore our eroded and fractured world to its intended wholeness.

ROMANS AS A *LOGOS PROTREPTIKOS*

David E. Aune

The *logos protreptikos*,[1] or "speech of exhortation," is a lecture intended to win converts and attract young people to a particular way of
life. The primary setting of the *logos protreptikos* was the philosophical
school, where it was used to attract adherents by exposing the errors of
alternative ways of living by demonstrating the truth claims of a particular
philosophical tradition over its competitors. During the Hellenistic period
many Jewish intellectuals conceptualized Judaism as a philosophy and
presented it in philosophical categories to outsiders. Christianity inherited
this conception and, in the words of Werner Jaeger,

> Thus it was the early Christian mission that forced the missionaries or apostles
> to use Greek forms of literature and speech in addressing the Hellenized Jews
> to whom they turned first and whom they met in all the great cities of the
> Mediterranean world. This became all the more necessary when Paul ap-
> proached the gentiles and began to make converts among them. This pro-
> treptic activity itself was a characteristic feature of Greek philosophy in
> Hellenistic times.[2]

I. Introduction

In this paper I wish to propose that in its present form the central section of Romans (1:16–15:13) is a *logos protreptikos* in an epistolary frame
(1:1–15; 15:14–16:27). That is, Romans is a speech of exhortation in written
form which Paul addressed to Roman Christians to convince them (or re-

---

[1]This is an abbreviated version of a more extensive article entitled "Romans as a *Logos
Protreptikos* in the Context of Ancient Religious and Philosophical Propaganda," *Paulus als
Missionar und Theologe und das antike Judentum*, ed. Martin Hengel (Tübingen: J. C. B.
Mohr, forthcoming).

[2]Jaeger, *Greek Paideia*, 9–10.

mind them) of the truth of *his* version of the gospel (Rom. 2:16; cf. 16:25; Gal. 1:6–9; 2:1) and to encourage a commitment to the kind of lifestyle which Paul considered consistent with his gospel. Thus Romans is protreptic not only in the sense that Paul is concerned to convince people of the truth of Christianity, but more particularly in the sense that he argues for his version of Christianity over other competing "schools" of Christian thought.

While several scholars have identified Romans (in whole or in part) as a *logos protreptikos*,[3] they have not supported this with a description of the essential features of the genre and have not provided an analysis of Romans to support their contentions. If it can be demonstrated that Paul's letter to the Romans is in fact a *logos protreptikos* in an epistolary frame, there are then two important implications which invite exploration. *First,* a recognition of the appropriate generic category to which Romans belongs will affect the exegesis of the letter in whole and in part. *Second,* if Paul has adapted the generic conventions of Greco-Roman philosophical propaganda for the purpose of proclaiming the Christian gospel, a number of subsidiary questions arise: (a) Was Paul himself primarily responsible for enlisting the *logos protreptikos* into service as a tool for Christian evangelization, or is there evidence for previous Jewish or Christian adaptation of this oral and literary genre? (b) If Paul's adaptation of the *logos protreptikos* is connected with his own Jewish background and education, what are the implications for our knowledge of Jewish proselytism? (c) Since Romans is very probably the only example in the New Testament of a *logos protreptikos*, in what context(s) did Paul develop this form of argumentation? (d) Since the primary setting of the *logos protreptikos* was the Hellenistic philosophical school, does this have any implications for Paul's conception of Christianity and his role as a Christian leader? (e) Is Paul's use of the *logos protreptikos* an isolated occurrence in early Christianity, or did others make use of the same literary form with similar intentions? The complexity of these questions indicates that in the present context only an initial foray into some of the more important of these issues can be undertaken.

II. Generic Features of the *logos protreptikos*

On the one hand, in *rhetorical* contexts the terms *to protreptikos* ("persuasion") and *to apotreptikos* ("dissuasion") refer to two different aspects of deliberative speech. In *philosophical* contexts, *protreptikos* is paired

---

[3]This view is by no means widespread among New Testament scholars. It is held by Klaus Berger, *Formgeschichte*, 217; cf. Berger, "Hellenistische Gattungen," 1140, who finds protreptic elements in Rom. 1:17–11:36; Matt. 11:25–30; 7:13–27; John 3:1–21; 1 Tim. 4:7b-10; 1 Cor. 13. A less qualified appraisal is found in Stowers, *Letter Writing*, 114: "In both form and function, Paul's letter to the Romans is a protreptic letter."

with *elenchos* ("censure") and refers to a single method comprised of both encouragement and rebuke intended to bring a person to the truth. The *logos protreptikos*, on the other hand, is an oral or literary genre used by philosophers for outsiders. It is rooted in both the rhetorical and philosophical protreptic traditions but must be distinguished from both.

The central function of *logoi protreptikoi*, within a philosophical context, was to encourage *conversion*. Conversion is possible only when a belief system is considered ultimately true and excludes alternative or competitive traditions. Yet the term "conversion" is not fully appropriate, since there were several levels of acceptance involved in adopting the philosophical way of life, and these involved both cognitive and behavioral commitment: (1) the love of wisdom (*philosophia*) generally, (2) the selection of a particular philosophical school superior to the others, and (3) the discipline to persevere in advanced study in that school.[4] However, *logoi protreptikoi* also characteristically included a strong element of dissuasion (*apotrepein*) or censure (*elenchein*) aimed at freeing the person from erroneous beliefs and practices. Lucian has created just such a protreptic confrontation between Nigrinus the Platonist and (presumably) himself (*Nigrinus* 4; trans. LCL):

> For he [Nigrinus] went on to praise philosophy and the freedom that it gives, and to ridicule the things that are popularly considered blessings—wealth and reputation, dominion and honour, yes and purple and gold—things accounted very desirable by most men, and till then by me also.

While religious conversion to Judaism, Christianity, and Islam has always been possible, philosophical conversion to the exclusive cognitive and behavioral claims of particular philosophical schools was also possible in the Hellenistic world.[5] In his parody of the protreptic genre, Lucian claims that adherents to particular philosophical traditions "persuade as many as they can to the same situation" (*Hermotimus* 75). Few philosophers, claims Lucian's character Lycinus, realize the error of their ways and try (like the skeptic Lycinus himself) to dissuade (*apotrepein*) others from such errors (*Hermotimus* 75).

The fact that the *logos protreptikos* is not discussed in any of the extant rhetorical handbooks makes it necessary that our knowledge of the content and sequence of argumentation used in such speeches must be discovered inductively. The silence of rhetorical theorists probably reflects the long-standing hostility which existed between philosophers and rhetoricians. The inductive analysis of the genre, however, is impeded by the fact that few examples have survived from the Hellenistic period, most are known by name only, and others survive only in fragmentary form

---

[4]Jordan, "Ancient Philosophic Protreptic," 309.
[5]Nock, *Conversion*, 164–86; Nock's anachronistic view of "true religion" is critiqued in MacMullen, *Christianizing*, 3–5.

(Aristotle's *Protrepticus*; Cicero's *Hortensius*). Those which have survived come from the period of the Empire (Iamblichus' *Protrepticus*). There are, however, general or theoretical statements in ancient literature which indicate the character of protreptic speech.[6]

There were *logoi protreptikoi* in the form of oral *discourses* (with both epideictic and deliberative features) as well as written *dialogues, discourses* (i.e., monologues), and *letters*.[7] This variety makes it difficult to claim generic status for the *logos protreptikos* only if an artificially rigid view of the nature of oral and literary genres is maintained. There is an element of fluidity between these forms, since many late dialogues (particularly those of Plutarch and Lucian) are frequently dominated by lengthy speeches for which the dialogical framework is relatively superficial, and dialogical elements frequently characterize discourses and letters. Further, Plato's *Euthydemus*, the earliest extant *logos protreptikos*, is a dialogue, while Aristotle's *Protrepticus* (dependent on the *Euthydemus*), was written in the form of a discourse,[8] probably using diatribe style.[9]

According to Philo of Larissa (Stobaeus, *Anth.* 2.7.2): "All protreptic consists of two parts, of which one is the demonstration of the value and profit of philosophy, whereas the other refutes the views of those adversaries who misrepresent or condemn this activity." Inductive analysis suggests that *endeiktikos* ("demonstration"), and *apelegmos* ("refutation") are indeed characteristic of *logoi protreptikoi*. For Philo of Larissa, protreptic is defined as "urging on to virtue." W. Gerhäusser, who accepts the protreptic structure proposed by Philo, has outlined the negative and positive arguments used in protreptic.[10] Ways of responding to adverse arguments take the form of responses to the following questions: (1) Is philosophy possible? (2) Is philosophy necessary? (3) Did not people at the dawn of civilization live without philosophy? (4) Does philosophy have value though lacking practical utility? (5) Is there not a contradiction between the theory and practice of philosophers? The positive arguments emphasize the fact that philosophy is the only road to happiness by (1) making a comparison (*synkrisis*) with other goods, (2) defining philosophy and the tasks included, (3) establishing its connections with other arts and sciences, (4) demonstrating that philosophy derives from the true nature of humanity, and (5) ultimately affirming philosophy by the divinization of the philosopher.

In a discussion of the generic characteristics of philosophical protreptic, M. D. Jordan analyzes the structure of several *logoi protreptikoi*, including Plato's *Euthydemus* and Aristotle's *Protrepticus*.[11] Jordan finds three

---

[6]In *Ep.* 7.340b–c, for example, Plato outlines a "protreptic" program.

[7]Letters which have a protreptic character include Seneca, *Ep.* 90 and the *Letter to Menoeceus* by Epicurus (Diogenes Laertius 10.122–35).

[8]Düring, *Protreptikos*, 29–32.

[9]Schneeweiss, *Der Protrepticos*, 238.

[10]Gerhäusser, *Poseidonios*, 11ff.

[11]Jordan, "Ancient Philosophic Protreptic," 314–27.

stages in protreptic sections of *Euthydemus*: (1) desire for good as a choice based on knowledge; (2) critique of rival sources of knowledge; (3) exhortation to choose philosophy, the only valid source of knowledge (307c). This structure, according to Jordan, is typical of later protreptic.[12]

Konrad Gaiser, following Werner Jaeger, found evidence to suggest the threefold structure of Aristotle's *Protrepticus* may be preserved in the way Iamblichus arranged his excerpts (Iamblichus, *Protrepticus* 6, 7–8, 9–12).[13] The threefold structural analysis of the *Protrepticus* by Gerhart Schneeweiss supports Gaiser's suggestion:[14] (1) Epideictic Section, (2) Apelenktic Section (the opponents are not actual; Aristotle has attributed objections to fictional opponents), (3) Summary Epideictic Section.

Lucian of Samosata (ca. 120–180 C.E.) wrote four dialogues which focus on conversion, one of which is a *logos protreptikos* (*Nigrinus*), while the other three are parodies of *logoi protreptikoi* (*Hermotimus*, *De parasito*, *De saltatione*).[15] Each concludes with a "conversion." In the adaptation of protreptic to the dialogue form, the speeches of the participants first focus on dissuasion, then on persuasion. The *Nigrinus*, for example, is structured as a *synkrisis* comparing praiseworthy Athens with despicable Rome in light of the virtues appropriate for the philosophical life and vices inappropriate for the philosophical life.[16] Lucian's *Hermotimus* is an example of a *logos apotreptikos*, i.e., a discourse intended to result in "aversion" or "deprogramming," rather than "conversion."

Finally, in the protreptic section which provides the introduction to the *Dialogus cum Tryphon*, Justin recounts his philosophical journey (through Stoicism, Aristotelianism, Pythagoreanism, and Platonism) and then recounts his discussion with an old man (a literary figure personifying wisdom, in this case Christianity). The old man first tries to demonstrate the errors of Platonism (*Dial.* 3.1–6.2), then attempts to persuade Justin that Christianity is the true philosophy, and concludes with an appeal for a response that eventually resulted in Justin's conversion (*Dial.* 7.1–9.3).

This survey of the basic structure of a number of *protreptikoi* indicates that they characteristically consist of three features: (1) a negative section centering on the critique of rival sources of knowledge, ways of living, or schools of thought which reject philosophy; (2) a positive section in which the truth claims of philosophical knowledge, schools of thought and ways of living are presented, praised, and defended; followed by (3) an optional section, consisting of a personal appeal to the hearer,

---

[12]Ibid., 321.

[13]Gaiser, *Protreptik und Paräsene bei Platon*, 219f.

[14]Schneeweiss, *Der Protreptikos*, 231–35. For a brief sympathetic critique of Schneeweiss, see Düring, *Protreptikos*, 17–20.

[15]Schäublin, "Konversionen," 117–31.

[16]Cf. L. Müller, "Luciani dialogorum," 574–78; Bompaire, *Lucien écrivain*, 277.

inviting the immediate acceptance of the exhortation. In view of the basic epideictic character of the *logos protreptikos*, it is natural that the rhetorical strategy of *synkrisis* is frequently employed. Further, the essentially propaedeutic character of the genre meant that the diatribe *style* (the terms genre or *Gattung* are no longer appropriate) was eminently suited for use in *logoi protreptikoi*. Stowers has recently argued that the older conception of the "Cynic-Stoic" diatribe as a form of popular philosophical preaching is inadequate and that the term diatribe should be reserved for "teaching activity in the schools, literary imitations of that activity, or for writings which employ the rhetorical and pedagogical type typical of diatribes in the schools."[17] Yet while Stowers' proposal that the philosophical school was the primary social setting for the diatribe works for Musonius Rufus, Epictetus, and perhaps Teles, it does not fit the activities of Maximus of Tyre, Plutarch, Dio Chrysostom, and Bion, who were concerned with mass propaganda.[18]

III. The History of the *logos protreptikos*

The Pseudo-Isocratean *Ad Demonicum*, perhaps a response by a student of Isocrates to the threat posed by Aristotle's *Protrepticus*, indicates that the *logos protreptikos* was a widely used genre. By the first century C.E., competition between philosophical schools for attracting and retaining adherents meant that the oral and written dissemination of *logoi protreptikoi* became a growth industry. Their popularity is suggested by the fact that Lucian parodied the genre in four dialogues (*Hermotimus, De parasito, De saltatione, Vitarum auctio*), though in the *Nigrinus* he produced a largely serious account. The successes of philosophical propaganda were celebrated in stories of philosophical conversions (Diogenes Laertius 2.113–14, 125; 4.16).

As noted, the earliest extant example of a *logos protreptikos*, a form developed by the sophists, is Plato's *Euthydemus* (two protreptic discourses, or one interrupted discourse, are embedded in 278e-282d, and 288b-307c).[19] The first discourse is explicitly described as a *logos protreptikos* in 282d. In addition to the *Euthydemus*, two other Platonic dialogues have frequently been considered *logoi protreptikoi, Phaedo* and *Epinomis*.[20] Aristotle's lost *Protrepticus* (referred to in Diogenes Laertius 5.1.22 and Stobaeus 4.32.21) became an influential literary model for the genre. Aristotle's *Protrepticus* found many imitators including Cicero, whose *Hortensius* (in which the ideas found in Aristotle's *Protrepticus* are synthesized in dia-

[17]Stowers, "Diatribe," 73; Stowers, *Diatribe*, 76.

[18]Schmeller, *"Diatribe,"* 41–53.

[19]Guthrie, *History of Greek Philosophy,* 4.266–83; Jordan, "Ancient Philosophic Protreptic," 319–21.

[20]Festugière, *Les protreptiques de Platon.*

logue form) was instrumental in Augustine's first conversion (Augustine, *Conf.* 3.4.7–5.9). Cynics who wrote protreptic treatises include Antisthenes (Diogenes Laertius 6.16) and Monimus, a student of Diogenes (Diogenes Laertius 7.83). Epicurus is credited with a lost work entitled *Protrepticus* (Diogenes Laertius 10.28). Among the Peripatetics *protreptikoi* are attributed to Theophrastus, Demetrius of Phaleron, and Ariston of Ceos (Diogenes Laertius 5.49; 5.81; 7.163). Stoic authors of *protreptikoi* include Persaeus (Diogenes Laertius 7.36), Cleanthes (Diogenes Laertius 7.175), Chrysippus, whose work was entitled *Protreptika*,[21] and Posidonius of Apamea, who was the author of a lost work entitled *Protreptikoi* (Diogenes Laertius 7.91, 129). Though a *Protrepticus* is not ascribed to Epictetus, the whole of his *Dissertationes* (recorded and arranged by Arrian) belongs to the *genus protrepticus*.[22]

The Neoplatonic philosopher Iamblichus of Chalcis (ca. 250–325 C.E.) wrote *Protrepticus* as the second book of a comprehensive ten book work entitled "Encyclopedia of Pythagorean Doctrine"; the first book was *De vita Pythagorica* ("On the Pythagorean Life").[23] The *Protrepticus* itself is a catena of material drawn from Plato's *Euthydemus* and Aristotle's lost *Protrepticus*. Iamblichus' *Protrepticus* appears to have been intended to introduce Neoplatonic philosophy generally, rather than Neopythagoreanism. Because of the largely technical nature of the *Synagōgē* within which the *Protrepticus* was buried, it does not seem to have been directed to outsiders, but rather to confirm insiders of the choice of Neoplatonism which they had already made. A collection of Pythagorean maxims (which Iamblichus calls *protreptika*, *Protrepticus* 21) is found in the final two chapters. In sum, Iamblichus' *Protrepticus* is an example of a late scholastic development of protreptic which departs in significant ways from the earlier use of the genre.

Did the *logos protreptikos* as a literary genre exert any influence on Hellenistic Judaism? One important Jewish work, the Wisdom of Solomon (written before the middle of the first cent. B.C.E.), is arguably an example of a *logos protreptikos*. This view was first suggested by F. Focke, who was much more concerned to argue for the presence of a *synkrisis* ("comparison") in Wisdom 11–19.[24] More recently, J. M. Reese has argued convincingly that Wisdom is a *logos protreptikos* containing shorter literary units of various types, including *diatribes* (1:1–6:11; 6:16–20; 11:15–15:19), *aporiai* (6:12–16; 6:21–10:21), *sorites* (6:17–20), and *synkriseis* (11:1–14; 16:1–

[21]Plutarch, *De Stoicorum repugnantiis* 17 [1041E]; Arnim, *Stoicorum Veterum Fragmenta*, III, 203.
[22]Hartlich, *De exhortationum*, 310.
[23]For what follows, see Larsen, *Jamblique de Chalcis*, and the introduction to Dillon, *Iamblichi Chalcidensis*, in revised form in "Iamblichus of Chalcis (c. 240–325 A.D.)," *ANRW*, 36.2, pp. 862–909.
[24]Focke, *Die Entstehung der Weisheit Salomos*, 86.

19:22).[25] This view has since been accepted by a number of scholars,[26] though others regard Wisdom as an encomium (which has close generic connections with protreptic).[27]

In second-century Christianity, the *logos protreptikos* strongly influenced the Christian adaptation of the dialogue. The first extant literary dialogue is that of Justin Martyr. Though no Jewish dialogues from the late Hellenistic period have survived, they probably existed (cf. *Arist.* 181–294, where a dialogue is set in a symposium framework). Several dialogues of Philo with dogmatic presuppositions are known, including the fragments of *De providentia* (cf. Eusebius *Praep. evang.* 7.21.336b–337a; 8.14.386–99). In Justin's *Dialogus cum Tryphon,* chapters 1–9 form an introductory protreptic unit which concludes with Justin's conversion to Christianity, the "true philosophy" (*Dial.* 8.1). Justin's views on the origin and history of philosophy may have been derived from the *Protrepticus* of Posidonius of Apamea.[28] A later and more sophisticated adaptation of the dialogue form is found in the early third-century *Octavius,* by Minucius Felix. This dialogue too is a *logos protreptikos.* It begins with a set speech by the pagan Caecilius (5–13), which is followed by a lengthy speech by the Christian Octavius (16–38); the dialogue concludes with the abrupt conversion of Caecilius.[29] The use of the *logos protreptikos* in discourse form continued to be adapted by Christian writers such as Clement of Alexandria (*Protrepticus*), the *Epistle to Diognetus,* a protreptic letter, and Augustine's *Contra academicos.*[30]

IV. Judaism and Christianity as "Philosophies"

Paul's missionary activity took place in a world filled with the competing claims of numerous religious sects and popular philosophical traditions. Many of these groups had developed a variety of communication strategies for defending themselves against the hostile criticism of outsiders, for attracting new members into their ranks, and for encouraging the continued loyalty of insiders by reiterating traditional values and norms. In the written expression of these literary categories, defense took the form

[25]Reese, *Wisdom,* 117–21.

[26]Winston, *Wisdom of Solomon,* 18–20; Collins, *Between Athens and Jerusalem,* 182; Mack–Murphy, "Wisdom Literature," 380f. This view is hesitantly subscribed to in the new Schürer, *History of the Jewish People,* III/1, p. 570, though the encomium genre is suggested as another possibility (see the next note).

[27]Gilbert, "Wisdom Literature," 2.306; idem, "Sagesse de Salomon," 58–119, esp. 72–87. Gilbert follows P. Beauchamp, "Epouser la Sagesse," 347–69.

[28]Hyldahl, *Philosophie und Christentum,* 112–40.

[29]Wotke, "Octavius," 110–28; Schäublin, "Konversionen" 119–22; Clarke, "Literary Setting I," 195–211; "Literary Setting II," 267–86.

[30]This last composition is explicitly dependent on Cicero's *Hortensius* (Augustine, *Contra acad.* 1.4); cf. Hartlich, *De exhortationum,* 296; Voss, *Der Dialog,* 199–208.

of apologetic writings, attempts to win adherents took the form of missionary literature, and efforts to maintain values took the form of novellas, novels, didactic, and apocalypses.

In many respects Judaism both presented itself and appeared to outsiders as a philosophy.[31] Several Greek intellectuals of the late fourth and early third century B.C.E. so understood Judaism, including Theophrastus, the student and successor of Aristotle, who reportedly described Judaism as "a race of philosophers," as did Megasthenes.[32] Clearchus of Soli claimed that the Jews were descendants of Indian philosophers (Josephus, *Ag. Ap.* 1.176–82). Aristobulus of Alexandria proposed that Greek philosophers learned from Moses, an argument used frequently by later Jewish and Christian apologists. Philo described the central activity of Jewish synagogues as the study of philosophy (*Life of Moses* 2.215–16). Josephus presented the various Jewish sects as philosophical schools (Josephus, *War* 2.119; *Ant.* 18.11) and ancient Israelite worthies as philosophers. Josephus described his eventual selection of Pharisaism (which he regards as very similar to Stoicism) as an enlightened choice resulting from his having sampled the three Jewish sects, the Pharisees, Sadducees, and Essenes (*Life* 9–12). This quest is presented as a conventional literary form modeled after the stylized Hellenistic accounts of philosophical pilgrimages and of philosophical conversions (parodied by Lucian, *Icaromenippus* 4–5 and *Necyomantia* 4–6).

First-century Christianity presented its contemporaries with an ambiguous phenomenon. In a world which understood religion in terms of ritual and experience, and philosophy in terms of ultimate truth claims matched by appropriate living, ancient perceptions of Christianity wavered between these two alternatives. Was Christianity, a diasporic religious cult with its spiritual and national center in Palestine (like Judaism, with which it was closely identified), the celebration of distinctive ritual? From this perspective outsiders characterized Christianity as a *superstitio*, a Roman term for a foreign cult (Pliny, *Ep.* 10.96.10), or more neutrally as a *thiasos* (cf. Lucian, *Peregrinus* 11), or (in view of its proximity to Judaism), a *synagōgē* (cf. Lucian, *Peregrinus* 11). Neither Greek nor Latin had a term corresponding to the modern English word "religion."

Or was Christianity a philosophical school with a system of esoteric doctrines defining what is ultimately real and true with a corresponding emphasis on exclusivity?[33] By the second quarter of the first century C.E., some educated Christians (particularly the Christian apologists) used the intellectual framework of the major Greek philosophical traditions to fashion both their own understanding of Christianity and the ways in which they communicated their faith to Jews and Greeks. Some, such as Justin

---

[31]Nock, *Conversion*, 78; Smith, "Palestinian Judaism," 195f.; Hengel, *Judaism and Hellenism*, 1.255–61; Collins, *Between Athens and Jerusalem*, 8; Collins discusses "Philosophical Judaism" on pp. 175–94.

[32]*Fragmente der griechischen Historiker*, 737F6, F8.

[33]Judge, "Scholastic Community," 4–15, 125–37.

and Tatian, turned from philosophy to Christianity as the true philosophy; Justin continued to dress like a philosopher (Justin *Dial.* 1; Eusebius, *Hist. eccl.* 4.11.8). In the 160s Miltiades wrote an apology in which he apparently referred to Christianity as a philosophy (Eusebius, *Hist. eccl.* 5.17.5), and in 172 C.E. Melito of Sardis addressed an apology to Marcus Aurelius in which he referred to Christianity as a philosophy of barbarian origin (Eusebius, *Hist. eccl.* 4.26.7). The infamous Peregrinus (ca. 100–165 C.E.), lampooned by Lucian, moved from Cynicism to Christianity but then returned to Cynicism. During his Christian period, Peregrinus was called the "new Socrates" because some Christians saw parallels between the innocent suffering of Socrates and Jesus.[34] The physician and medical writer Galen, writing in the mid-second century C.E., categorized both Judaism and Christianity as "the philosophical school [i.e., "way of life"] of Moses and of Christ" (*De puls. diff.* 2.4), and attacked them, like adherents to the Greek philosophical schools, for the dogmatic basis of their views and their discussion of undemonstrated laws.[35] The rivalry among the Hellenistic philosophical schools is paralleled in the rivalry between Christians and Jews and the rivalry between different Christian sects (Origen, *Contra Celsum* 5.61f.)

V. The Problem of the Genre of Romans

Despite extensive scholarly research on Romans and the recent emphasis on analyzing NT letters in accordance with the categories of Greco-Roman rhetoric and epistolography,[36] the problem of the literary genre of Romans has attracted surprisingly little attention. Various scholars have proposed that Romans is (1) a "testament" (Bornkamm), though Bornkamm does not mean this in a literary or generic sense; (2) an *euangelion*, or "gospel" (Roosen); (3) a "letter-essay" (Stirewalt); (4) an epideictic speech (Wuellner, Kennedy); (5) an ambassadorial letter (Jewett); (6) a letter of self-recommendation (Koester); and (7) a letter of friendship (Lührmann).[37]

Though the presence in Rom. 1–3 of many motifs recurring also in the apologetic and missionary literature of Hellenistic Judaism has long been recognized, the question of just how those motifs should be evaluated remains problematic. There have been several attempts to understand

---

[34]Döring, *Exemplum Socratis*, 143–61.

[35]Walzer, *Galen*, 10–16 (texts) and pp. 37–48 (discussion).

[36]Cf. Kennedy, *Rhetorical Criticism.*

[37]*Testament*: Bornkamm, "Römerbrief als Testament," 2.120–39; idem, "Last Will and Testament," 16–28; *Euangelion*: Roosen, "Le genre littéraire," 2.465–71; *Letter-essay*: Stirewalt, "Form and Function," 147–71; *Epideictic speech*: Wuellner, "Paul's Rhetoric," 128–46; Kennedy, *Rhetorical Criticism*, 152–56; *Ambassadorial letter*: Jewett, "Ambassadorial Letter," 5–20; *Letter of recommendation*: Koester, *Einführung*, 575; *Friendship letter*: Lührmann, "Freundschaftsbrief," 298–315, esp. 304.

Romans, in part or in whole, as a Pauline adaptation of Hellenistic Jewish apologetic literature. Günther Bornkamm proposed that even though Rom. 1:18–3:20 reflects such adaptations, they are used in a radically different way.[38] Bornkamm's central concern, however, was not simply the identification of Rom. 1:18–3:20 as a "missionary-apologetic" sermon with a Hellenistic Jewish character, but rather Paul's Christian theological transformation of themes from Hellenistic Jewish apologetics.

Though Helmut Koester has suggested that Romans is a *letter of recommendation*, that epistolary category not only is so general that it is not helpful, but it also plays no role in his analysis of the letter. The general outline of the letter (especially 1:18–3:31), he claims, follows the traditional schema of Jewish apologetics: while the Gentiles have a partial knowledge of God and the law, acquaintance with biblical revelation would provide them with complete knowledge of God and the law.[39] Had Paul followed the "protreptic interests of traditional apologetics," he would have elaborated on the proper conduct consistent with his message; but since he has put all human achievement in question, he must shift to explain how freedom from sin and death (i.e., justification) is a gift of God through faith.

In a 1986 Harvard dissertation, Anthony J. Guerra amplified the arguments of Bornkamm by proposing that the apology for the gospel preached by Paul extends from 1:18 beyond 3:20 to 4:25.[40] Though Guerra claims that he is raising the question of the "literary genre" of Romans,[41] he does not really do that, since he does not use the term "apology" or "apologetic writing" in a specifically generic sense, but rather as a broad designation for Hellenistic Jewish literature written for Jewish insiders as well as Gentile outsiders.[42] He uses the term "apologetics" so comprehensively that it is effectively drained of any generic significance. "Apologetic literature" must be distinguished from "missionary propaganda," even though these terms describe only general types of literature, not literary genres. A potential strength of Guerra's approach is that he isolates several "apologetic" motifs in Rom. 1:18–4:25, which he identifies through parallels in Hellenistic Jewish compositions as Pauline adaptations of Jewish apologetics. He claims that a comparison of the apologetic motifs of Rom. 1:18–3:31 with *Arist.* 121–71 indicates a common schema and demonstrates Paul's dependence on Jewish apologetics, though some of his comparisons are unconvincing.[43] Even if these two compositions do share a similar sequence of motifs, that does not demonstrate the presence of a *generic* structure. As a rhetorical genre, the term "apology" should be re-

[38]Bornkamm, "Die Offenbarung des Zornes Gottes."
[39]This paragraph summarizes the arguments in Koester, *Einführung*, 575–77.
[40]Guerra, *Apologetic Tradition*; idem, "Romans 4," 251–70.
[41]Guerra, *Apologetic Tradition*, 2f.
[42]Ibid., 42, n. 16.
[43]Ibid., 51.

stricted to that type of forensic rhetoric concerned with defense rather than prosecution.

VI. The Protreptic Character of Romans

Romans is the most distinctive of the letters of Paul. It is the only genuine letter of Paul addressed to Christian groups (i.e., several house-churches) in an urban area which he himself had neither visited nor founded. The main section of the letter (1:16–11:36) consists of a chain of interconnected theological arguments and positions for which little if any connection can be found with the specific situation of the Christian communities in Rome. This fact demands an explanation. One of the central issues in current Romans research is therefore whether Paul wrote the letter in response to an actual situation in Rome, or whether his primary purpose was to present his views on important issues without any direct connection with local issues and problems.[44] While there is some validity in both positions, the significance of the main part of the letter should not be subordinated to any supposedly concrete situation teased out of the concluding paraenetic section (esp. 14:1–15:13).[45]

Though the social setting of Paul's mission remains imperfectly understood, there have been a number of proposals regarding the specific social context within which Paul developed this material: (1) synagogues (Acts 9:20; 13:5, 14–43; 14:1–2; 17:1–3; 18:4; 19:8), (2) private homes (Acts 18:7f.; 20:7–11; 28:30–31; cf. Lucian, *Hermotimus* 11, where a sophist reportedly hung this sign on his gate: "No philosophizing today"); (3) rented lecture halls (like the *scholē* of Tyrannus, Acts 19:9f., where Paul reportedly taught for two years; here Luke depicts Paul as an itinerant philosopher, cf. Epictetus 3.23.30); (4) Paul's own "school," i.e., the way he taught the Christian faith to actual or potential students; (5) the workshops in which he plied his trade and engaged in discussion; (6) in public places (Acts 17:16–34; cf. Dio Chrysostom, *Or.* 13.12–13); and perhaps even (7) in prison (cf. 2 Cor. 11:23–33). There is no reason, however, why any of these settings should be considered inappropriate for Paul's teaching ministry.

In many respects the description of Paul's activity in several passages in Acts coheres well with the protreptic character of Romans. According to Acts 18:4, "And he argued [*dielegeto*] in the synagogue every sabbath, and persuaded [*epeithen*] Jews and Greeks." Here *dialegesthai* can mean

---

[44]These issues are discussed in Donfried, *Romans Debate*. A recent comprehensive discussion of the complex purpose of Romans is found in Wedderburn, *Reasons for Romans*. Attempts to reconstruct the epistolary situation of Romans usually appeal to the section dealing with the "weak" and the "strong" (14:1–15:13). For arguments that Rom. 14:1–15:13 does not reflect a specific occasion, see Karris, "Occasion," 65–84.

[45]Luz, "Röm. 1–8," 162f. An unsuccessful attempt to connect the whole of Romans with the specific circumstances of the Roman Christians is elaborated in Wedderburn, *Reasons for Romans*, 66–139.

either "to argue" (about differences of opinion), or "to speak in a somewhat formal setting" (probably implying a more formal use of language).[46]
Both definitions cohere well with the dialogical and rhetorical features of
Romans. Acts 28:23b constitutes Luke's concluding vignette of Paul's missionary activity: "And he expounded the matter to them from morning
till evening, testifying to the kingdom of God and trying to convince
[*peithein*] them about Jesus both from the law of Moses and from the
prophets." Here *peithein* means "to convince someone to believe something and to act on the basis of what is recommended" and belongs to
the same semantic subdomain as *protrepein*, "to urge a particular course
of action."[47] Finally *dialegesthai* and *peithein* are both used of Paul's three-
month ministry in the synagogue at Ephesus according to Acts 19:9: "And
he entered the synagogue and for three months spoke boldly lecturing
[*dialegomenos*] and pleading [*peithein*] about the kingdom of God." After
Paul was forced to shift the venue of his missionary activity, Acts reports
that he "lectured [*dialegomenos*] in the hall of Tyrannus" for two years
(v. 9), with the result that "all the residents of Asia heard the word of the
Lord, both Jews and Greeks" (v. 10). Acts often depicts Paul as attempting
to persuade both Jews and Greeks together, a feature which characterizes
much of the argument in Rom. 1:18–11:36. At the very least these passages suggest that Luke is trying to present Paul as one who used persuasive speech in attempting to convince both Jews and Greeks to accept
the truth of the gospel.

The central section of Romans (1:16–15:13) is set within an epistolary
framework (1:1–15 and 15:14–16:27). The theological complexity of the central section suggests that Paul had worked and reworked this material over
a period of several years. Though the sophistication of Paul's discussion
is recognized, the length of time it must have taken to develop his arguments is seldom appreciated. The following analysis of Romans focuses
on aspects which cohere with its character as a *logos protreptikos*.

Romans 1:16–4:25

Romans 1:16–4:25 constitutes a major text unit which functions as a
protreptic *elenchos*, consisting of three constitutive units: 1:16–2:11, 2:12–
3:20, and 3:21–4:25. In the first section Paul begins with a condemnation
of humanity due to the impartiality of God. Using the diatribe style, Paul
debates with a fictional Jewish interlocutor in the next two sections and
by the process of indictment and protreptic brings him to the conclusion
that justification is possible only through faith. That Paul is arguing with
an unconverted Jew indicates the propaedeutic character of 1:16–4:25. This
section with its use of indictment, censure, and correction is appropriate

[46]Louw–Nida, *Greek-English Lexicon*, 1.33.446, 1.33.26.

for a *logos protreptikos*. Each of the three shorter units must now be examined.

(1) Rom. 1:16–2:11: *Universal sinfulness and divine impartiality.*[48] This section is delimited by a formal *inclusio* consisting of references to "the Jew first and also the Greek" in 1:16 and 2:10, and is distinctive in Paul in that it exhibits no Jewish or Christian features and therefore provides a rare glimpse of how Paul argued with pagans. It consists of three shorter units. (a) Rom. 1:16–32 is a narrative describing how primitive people knew God but did not properly honor him and became idolaters (vv. 18–23), and therefore God gave them over to all the vices they lusted after (vv. 24–32). This section has a distinctive style identifying it as a text-unit delimited from what precedes and follows. It is cast as a third-person narrative, all dialogical elements are lacking, it exhibits no specifically Christian features, and it has well-known parallels to the Hellenistic Jewish tradition found in Wisd. 12–14 and several passages in Philo (*Decalogue* 52–81; *Special Laws* 1.13–35; *Contemplative Life* 3ff.; *Preliminary Studies* 133). (b) Rom. 2:1–5 is in diatribe style, with a characteristic sudden shift addressing the interlocutor (in the vocative and the second-person singular) as an arrogant and pretentious man; this functions to focus and sharpen the indictment in 1:18–32.[49] (c) Rom. 2:6–11 switches back to a third-person discourse where, for the first time, the author uses a *synkrisis* to contrast the reward of the good and the punishment of the wicked. The rhetorical technique of *synkrisis*, "comparison," is often found in *logoi protreptikoi*.[50] A *synkrisis* is a comparison of good and bad people or things to demonstrate the superiority of the one and the inferiority of the other. Usually the inferior is presented before the superior, often in the form of antitheses. This form is particularly suited to *protreptic*, in which the superiority of one way of life is argued by emphasizing the inferiority of the alternate ways.

(2) Rom. 2:12–3:20: *God impartially condemns those who do not obey the law/Torah.* This section introduces and focuses on the term *nomos* (used 23 times in this section with several meanings) and consists of five shorter constitutive units: (a) Rom. 2:12–16 is a third-person discourse which includes a *synkrisis* comparing those who have lived without law to those who have lived with law. (b) Rom. 2:17–24 is a section in diatribe style in the form of an apostrophe addressed to an imaginary Jewish interlocutor (in the second-person singular) who is indicted as a pretentious re-

---

[47]Ibid., 1.33.301, 1.33.300.
[48]Schmeller, *Paulus*, 232–35; Bassler, *Divine Impartiality.*
[49]Stowers, *Diatribe*, 93–96, 110–12.
[50]Aristotle, *Rhet.* 1.9 (1368A); Isocrates, *Panath.* 39–40; Theon, *Progym.* 2.112; Hermogenes, *Progym.* 8; cf. Focke, "Synkrisis," 335–39. On the use of *synkrisis* in *logoi protreptikoi*, see Gerhäusser, *Der Protreptikos des Poseidonios*, 34–42, with references to ancient sources on p. 34, and Ruch, *L'Hortensius de Cicéron*, 18.

ligious teacher.[51] (c) Rom. 2:25–29 again reverts to third-person discourse style with a *synkrisis* on the deeper meaning of circumcision and uncircumcision. (d) Rom. 3:1–18 is a diatribal dialogue in which the fictitious Jewish interlocutor addressed by Paul in 2:17–24 introduces an objection; Paul censures his opponent by repeatedly correcting him.[52] OT texts from Ps. 14:1–2, 53:1–2, and 5:9 conclude the section. (e) Rom. 3:19–20 is again in discourse style and draws the conclusion that justification cannot be achieved through obeying the law, for the law is the means for revealing sin.

(3) Rom. 3:21–4:25: *Justification by faith, not the works of the law.* The term *pistis* is introduced in this section, where it is found eighteen times. This section consists of three shorter units. (a) Rom. 3:21–26 is in third-person discourse form and emphasizes that true righteousness is not available through the law but through faith in Jesus Christ alone. This section sets up the *synkrisis* between law and faith which dominates 3:21–4:25. (b) Rom. 3:27–4:2 is in the form of a diatribal dialogue, is framed by the boasting motif in 3:27 and 4:2, and is designed to indict and censure the views of Paul's fictional Jewish interlocutor, who appeared in 2:17–24 and vanishes after 4:25 (Jewish issues are taken up again in Rom. 9–11).[53] (c) Rom. 4:3–25 uses the *paradeigma* or *exemplum* of Abraham, who was justified by faith not works, concluding with an admonition in 4:23–25.[54]

Romans 5:1–8:39

Romans 5:1–8:39 is a unified textual unit which takes a new turn by focusing on the life of the insider (the Christian who has been justified by faith) and the problem of sin. The features of diatribe style in this section are limited to a series of objections and false conclusions raised from the standpoint of a Christian with erroneous views (6:1, 15; 7:7, 13). The concentration of diatribe style in Rom. 1:16–4:25, where the erroneous views of *outsiders* are corrected, in contrast with the meager traces of diatribe style in Rom. 5:1–8:39, suggests that it was a style Paul used in winning converts to Christianity.[55] In light of comparable *logoi protreptikoi*, the section functions in largely a positive manner as an *endeiktikos*. The level of discussion is more abstract than that found in typical Pauline paraenesis (e.g., Rom. 12:3–15:13) but is similar to that found in protreptic discourses. This section consists of several constituent units of text:

(1) Rom. 5:1–21, which consists of two subsections: (a) Rom. 5:1–11, a brief introductory discourse on the Christian's undeserved justification and reconciliation achieved by Christ; and (b) Rom. 5:12–21, a *synkrisis* in which

---

[51]Stowers, *Diatribe*, 96–99, 112–13.
[52]Stowers, "Dialogue," 707–22.
[53]Stowers, *Diatribe*, 155–67.
[54]Ibid., 168–73.
[55]This runs counter to Stowers' conclusions in *Diatribe*, 175–84.

the disobedience that produces death and came through Adam is contrasted with the obedience of Christ which produces life.

(2) Rom. 6:1–7:25: *The conflict between sin and obedience to God* consists of several subsections, each marked by the fact that they are introduced with various objections and false conclusions: (a) Rom. 6:1–14: we cannot live in sin because we have died to it through identification with Christ in baptism. (b) Rom. 6:15–23: we who are under grace and not the law are not free to sin because we have been liberated from bondage to sin. (c) Rom. 7:1–6: Christians have died to the law through Christ and are now free. (d) Rom. 7:7–12: the law is not sinful but rather reveals sin. (e) Rom. 7:13–25: Christians who desire to be obedient to God in their inner selves find this desire in conflict with the flesh.

(3) Rom. 8:1–39: *Life in the Spirit and its rewards* consists of two shorter sections: (a) Rom. 8:1–17 is a *synkrisis* contrasting the obligation of Christians to live according to the Spirit because they have been liberated from bondage to the flesh. (b) Rom. 8:18–39 is a first-person plural discourse focusing on the eschatological hope which cannot be denied to Christians.

The distinctive subject matter of Rom. 5:1–8:39, the problem of sin and the struggle between the flesh and the Spirit, requires a brief excursus at this point to discuss analogous problems treated in Greek philosophical protreptic. In spite of the theological distance, there is a striking structural and phenomenological similarity between the anthropological dualism of popular Greek tradition and that of Paul. According to ancient Greek popular psychology (Stoic and Epicurean materialism are partial exceptions), human beings are understood in terms of a *sōma-psychē* dichotomy, i.e., a body-soul, material-immaterial, irrational-rational, dualism (Aristotle, *Prot.* frag. B34, Düring). The *psychē* was considered immortal (hence divine), was regarded as the seat of the intellectual and spiritual faculties, and was temporarily united with the material body. Aristotle and later the Middle Platonists understood the *psychē* in terms of higher and lower elements, rational and irrational parts, i.e., the *nous* and the *psychē*. The *nous*, "mind" or "reason," is the divine part of the *psychē* and is in irreconcilable conflict with the irrational part of the *psychē*, which is closely linked to the irrationality and materiality of the *sōma*. The philosophical pursuit of *phronēsis*, an activity of the *nous*, is the highest good (Aristotle, *Prot.* frag. B38, Düring). If we could be carried in spirit (*tē dianoia*) to the Islands of the Blessed, suggests Aristotle, there we would need nothing except the life of the mind, a condition called the truly free life in this world (Aristotle, *Prot.* frag. B43, Düring), for the conflict between the somatic and noetic modes of existence would be resolved in favor of the latter. Would we not be ashamed, he continues in the same fragment, if we were given the opportunity to live in the Islands of the Blessed and failed to do so? (In effect this is a type of realized eschatology, i.e., the

challenge to live in this world in a way approximating post-mortem conditions as far as possible).

Mutatis mutandis, the ethical dualism reflected in Paul's view of the
dilemma of the Christian, expressed in Rom. 7:25 (with his *nous* he serves
the law of God but with his *sarx* the law of sin), is structurally similar to
the situation of Greeks to whom a philosopher would direct his *logos
protreptikos,* offering freedom from the material bondage of wealth and
reputation (e.g., Lucian, *Nigrinus* 4). On the one hand, for the Greek philosophers, human beings possessed the potential to turn from material en-
cumbrances to embrace the philosophic life. For Paul, on the other hand,
freedom from sin and death is impossible for the natural person and is
a possibility only for those who have been justified by faith (Rom. 8:1–2).
For Paul the central anthropological terms are *sarx* (which occurs 16 times
in Rom. 7:5–8:13; 26 times in all of Rom.) and *pneuma,* and Christians can
"set their minds" (*phronein, phronēma*) on either, with negative or positive consequences (Rom. 8:5–6). Christians are exhorted to live according
to the Spirit rather than the flesh with the goal of eschatological triumph
(Rom. 8:12–17).

Romans 9–11

Romans 9–11 is a unit of text in which Paul deals with the problem
of Jewish unbelief and Gentile belief, arguing that the former is simply
a temporary measure which is part of God's overall plan. The focal theological issue is the trustworthiness of God. If the gospel is "the *power* of
God for salvation to everyone who has faith, to the Jew first and also to
the Greek" (Rom. 1:16), how then can the failure of the Jews to be converted be explained? While the structural relationship of Rom. 9–11 to the
rest of the letter continues to be debated, there is general recognition that
Rom. 9–11 constitutes a formally delimited textual unit, though the consistency of Paul's argument presents a problem.[56] The section is introduced
by a solemn oath (9:1) attesting Paul's anguish over the fact that Jews have
not responded to the gospel (9:1–3), followed by a list of Jewish privileges
(9:4–5a), and concluded by a doxology (9:5b). Romans 9–11 is just as obviously concluded with 11:33–36, which begins with a hymn and concludes
with a doxology. Romans 9–11 is distinguished from other sections of Romans by virtue of the fact that it consists of the exegesis of about thirty
OT passages. C. H. Dodd proposed that the unity which Rom. 9–11 exhibits suggests that it was a sermon previously delivered by Paul.[57] Although this proposal cannot be proven, it is likely that the main arguments
and the exegetical supports for those arguments had been carefully worked
out by Paul in earlier and perhaps different contexts. The very coherence

[56]Räisänen, "Romans 9–11," 178–206.
[57]Dodd, *Romans,* 148f.

of this section, combined with the fact that it is difficult to account for its placement after Rom. 5:1–8:39, suggests that it is a kind of excursus or digression. That Paul turns again to the use of the diatribe style in 9:14–33, 10:18–21, and 11:1–24[58] (within which is set an exegetical discourse in 10:1–17) suggests that Paul is again picking up the threads of an earlier argument which now requires further elaboration (cf. 3:1–18); i.e., Rom. 9–11 constitutes a delayed answer to an earlier objection to Paul's gospel.

Romans 12:1–15:13

Romans 12:1–15:13 is an extensive paraenetic section, delimited by an introductory statement in 12:1–2 (which also functions as a conclusion to 1:16–11:36), and a meta-textual statement in 15:14–16 (i.e., a statement by the author commenting on the text he has just written) closing the entire central section of the letter. When he says *tolmēroteron de egrapsa hymin apo merous hōs epanamimnēskōn* (15:15), he probably means "I have written to you boldly [in part of this letter] to remind you," i.e., he is referring to the paraenetic section (12:1–15:13) which he has just concluded.[59] The term "remind" (*epanamimnēskōn*) is a term typically used in paraenesis, emphasizing the traditional character of the moral exhortation and admonition in view.[60] In addition 12:1–15:13 is distinctive in that it contains none of the features of the diatribe style used so frequently in many sections within 1:16–11:36. The section is introduced with the verb *parakalein*, which in this instance is not simply an epistolary formula but is used with the meaning "exhort" (synonymous with *protrepein*). This protreptic appeal to the Romans that they dedicate themselves completely to God (12:1–2) provides a fitting conclusion to his presentation of his gospel in 1:16–8:39, only slightly interrupted by the digression in Rom. 9–11. Paul has brought the reader through the problems confronted by outsiders in the Christian gospel, whether Gentiles or Jews (Rom. 1:18–4:25), and he has further presented with great clarity his view of the nature of the Christian life as a life lived from the perspective of the Spirit rather than the flesh. He now appeals to the readers (12:1–2), no matter what their status, to devote themselves fully to God. The paraenesis that follows in 12:3–15:13 describes precisely how Paul understands the abstract implications of Rom. 6:1–8:39 in terms of the duties and obligations of Christians living in community.

[58]On 9:19–21, see Stowers, *Diatribe*, 98f., 113f.; on 11:17–24, see Stowers, *Diatribe*, 99f., 114f.; on 11:1–24, see Schmeller, *Paulus*, 286–332.

[59]Cranfield, *Romans*, 2.753; Dunn, *Romans 9–16*, 858f. (though he suggests that "it may be better" to take *apo merous* as a reference to the entire letter).

[60]Malherbe, *Moral Exhortation*, 125; Stowers, *Letter Writing*, 128.

VII. Conclusions

The proposal that Romans is a *logos protreptikos* provides a reasonable explanation for the distinctive form and content of Rom. 1:16–15:13. Although the main section of Romans is not precisely similar to other surviving examples of the *logos protreptikos,* that is not only because of the inherent flexibility of the genre, but also because Paul has Christianized it by adapting it as a means for persuading people of the truth of the gospel. Further, in Romans as in his other letters, Paul used and combined genres and forms in distinctive ways.

Romans is protreptic on *two* levels. First, sizable sections of text (1:16–2:11; 2:12–4:25; 5:1–8:39; 9:1–11:36) show signs of having been developed orally during many years of Paul's preaching and teaching. In their original setting three of the four sections (all but 9:1–11:36) appear to have had a protreptic character and function. Second, these originally protreptic sections have been linked together to form a relatively coherent *logos protreptikos* in their present context in Romans. Paul's argument moves gradually from the "outside" to the "inside"; he first argues with pagans (1:18–2:11), then with Jews (2:12–4:25), and finally with Christians (5:1–8:39). In each of these sections he exposes error and points out truth. Paul's purpose is to present to the Roman Christians concrete examples of the way in which he presents the gospel in a variety of settings to a variety of people. In so doing he is also presenting his gospel to *them,* i.e., he is imparting to them a spiritual gift (Rom. 1:11). Romans 9–11, though it has some links with what precedes, functions as a digression which focuses on the problem of Jewish unbelief and makes an uncharacteristically concentrated used of OT exegesis. Since the exegesis of authoritative texts was an important feature of Hellenistic school activity, this section exhibits another aspect of the Pauline curriculum. The complex paraenetic sections in 12:1–15:13 form an appropriate conclusion to the main protreptic section (cf. Iamblichus, *Protrepticus,* 21–22), for they provide examples of the kind of concrete moral behavior expected of Christians.

PART II

Section C
The Theology of Romans:
Issues in the Current Debate

20

THE NEW PERSPECTIVE ON PAUL: PAUL AND THE LAW

J. D. G. Dunn

A fresh assessment of Paul and of Romans in particular has been made possible and necessary by the new perspective on Paul provided by E. P. Sanders, *Paul*, 1–12, and pt. 1 (though Limbeck's [*Ordnung*] earlier critique of the negative depiction of the law in OT and "intertestamental" scholarship should also be mentioned; see also particularly Gaston, "Torah," 48–54, and Watson, *Paul, Judaism and the Gentiles*, 2–18; for examples of discussion in terms of older categories see Kuss, "Nomos," with review of earlier literature; Lang, "Gesetz"; and Hübner, *Paul and the Law*). Sanders has been successful in getting across a point which others had made before him (e.g., Stendahl, "Conscience," and Dahl, on justification, *Studies*, particularly 110–11, 117–18), but which had been too little "heard" within the community of NT scholarship. The point is that Protestant exegesis has for too long allowed a typically Lutheran emphasis on justification by faith to impose a hermeneutical grid on the text of Romans (see, e.g., the way in which Bornkamm, *Paul*, 137, sets up his discussion of the subject). The emphasis is important, that God is the one who justifies the ungodly (4:5), and understandably this insight has become an integrating focus in Lutheran theology with tremendous power. The problem, however, lay in what that emphasis was set in opposition to. The antithesis to "justification by faith"—what Paul speaks of as "justification by works"—was understood in terms of a system whereby salvation is *earned* through the *merit of good works*. This was based partly on the comparison suggested in the same passage (4:4–5), and partly on the Reformation rejection of a system where indulgences could be bought and merits accumulated. The latter protest was certainly necessary and justified, and of lasting importance, but the hermeneutical mistake was made of reading this antithesis back into the NT period, of assuming that Paul was protesting against in Pharisaic Judaism precisely what Luther protested against in the pre-Reformation church—the mistake, in other words, of assuming that the Judaism of Paul's

day was coldly legalistic, teaching a system of earning salvation by the
merit of good works, with little or no room for the free forgiveness and
grace of God ("the imaginary Rabbinic Judaism, created by Christian
scholars, in order to form a suitably lurid background for the Epistles of
St. Paul"—Montefiore, *Judaism and Paul*, 65; in addition to the examples
cited by Sanders, *Paul*, and Watson, *Paul, Judaism and the Gentiles*, see,
e.g., Leenhardt, *Romans*, passim, and Ridderbos, *Paul*, 130–35).

It was this depiction of first-century Judaism which Sanders showed
up for what it was—a gross caricature, which, regrettably, has played its
part in feeding an evil strain of Christian antisemitism. On the contrary,
however, as Sanders demonstrated clearly enough, Judaism's whole religious self-understanding was based on the premise of grace—that God had
freely chosen Israel and made his covenant with Israel to be their God
and they his people. This covenant relationship was regulated by the law,
not as a way of entering the covenant, or of gaining merit, but as the way
of living *within* the covenant; and that included the provision of sacrifice
and atonement for those who confessed their sins and thus repented. Paul
himself indicates the attitude clearly by his citation of Lev. 18:5 in Rom.
10:5—"the person who does these things [what the law requires] shall live
by them." This attitude Sanders characterized by the now well-known
phrase "covenantal nomism"—that is, "the maintenance of status" among
the chosen people of God by observing the law given by God as part of
that covenant relationship (e.g., *Paul*, 544; see further Dunn, "New Perspective"; similarly Limbeck, *Ordnung*, 29–35; cf. Ziesler's earlier phrase
"covenant-keeping righteousness"—*Righteousness*, 95). Sanders' review had
not encompassed all the available Jewish literature of the period, but it
has been confirmed by the work of one of my own postgraduates, D. Garlington ("Obedience"), who has demonstrated the consistency of the
"covenantal nomism'" pattern throughout the Jewish writings contained
in "the Apocrypha." See also Collins, *Between Athens and Jerusalem*, who
notes, however, that the pattern is not so consistent through all diaspora
literature (pp. 14–15, 29, 48, 77, 141, 167, 178–81, 236–37). For the importance of the covenant in Judaism leading up to and at the time of Paul,
see also particularly Jaubert (*Alliance*).

Unfortunately Sanders did not follow through this insight far enough
or with sufficient consistency. Instead of setting Paul more fully against
and within this context of Judaism so understood, he advanced the thesis
that Paul had jumped in arbitrary fashion (as a result of his Damascus road
encounter) from one system (covenantal nomism) into another (Christianity;
Paul, 550–52), leaving his theology, particularly in reference to the law,
incoherent and contradictory (*Law*). On this last point he has been given
strong support by Räisänen (*Law*), who also argues that Paul "intended
to portray Judaism as a religion of merit and achievement" ("Conversion,"
411) and that he thus "gives a totally distorted picture of the Jewish re-

ligion" ("Legalism," 72 [in agreement with Schoeps, *Paul*, 200]; though with an important concession in Räisänen, *Torah*, 183). Just as puzzling from a different angle is the fact that the "covenantal nomism" of Palestinian Judaism as described by Sanders bears a striking similarity to what has been commonly understood as the religion of Paul himself (good works as the fruit of God's prior acceptance by grace; Hooker, "Covenantal Nomism")! What, then, can it be to which Paul is objecting?

I. Exegetical Questions

The exegetical questions exposed here focus very largely on the issue of Paul and the law (hence, not surprisingly, the titles of the books by Sanders and Räisänen, as also by Hübner). This is important since the law actually forms a major secondary theme of the letter, to an extent not usually appreciated ("an indispensable accompanying motif"—Hahn, "Gesetzeverständnis," 30). Rather striking is the way in which Paul regularly in Romans develops part of his discussion before bringing in the law (2:12ff.; 3:27ff.; 4:13ff.; 5:20; ch. 7), while in other key sections it is the role of the law which provides a crucial hinge in the argument (3:19–21; 8:2–4; 9:31–10:5). Since these references taken together span the complete argument of chs. 1–11 in all its stages, there can be little doubt that the tension between his gospel and the law and his concern to resolve that tension provide one of Paul's chief motivations in penning the letter.

Moreover, it is hardly a coincidence that several of the most recalcitrant exegetical problems in Romans are bound up with this central secondary theme of the letter. Thus it is significant once again that Sanders and Räisänen are unable to integrate Paul's treatment of the law in ch. 2 into the rest of his theology (Sanders, *Law*, 147—"true self-contradiction"; Räisänen, "Difficulties," 307—"contradictory lines of thought"; also *Law*). The use of *nomos* in 3:27–31 has caused unending puzzlement: should we take *nomos* in v. 27 as a reference to the law or translate "principle"? And how can Paul claim in v. 31 to be "establishing the law"? The centrality of the law in ch. 7 has been recognized, but how and whether that insight facilitates the exegesis of 7:14–25 in particular is a matter of unresolved controversy, with the meaning of *nomos* in 7:23 and 8:2 disputed in the same way as in 3:27. In the obviously crucial resumptive section, 9:30–10:4, there is equal controversy over the meaning of *nomos dikaiosynēs*, "law of righteousness" (9:31), and *telos nomou*, "end of the law" (10:4). And in the parenetic section the claim that love of neighbor is a fulfillment of the law (13:8–10) causes further puzzlement to those who think that Paul has turned his back on Judaism and its law. As Räisänen's withering critique has underlined (*Law*, 23–28, 42–83), the problem of holding together in an integrated whole both the positive and the negative

statements regarding the law in Romans has not reached a satisfactory
solution; though Räisänen's own atomistic treatment of the texts is itself
a critical hindrance to an integrated and coherent overview of the theme.

Clearly, then, this major secondary motif in the letter presents problems of central importance for our understanding of the letter. It may be,
indeed, that they all hang together, and a correct resolution of one may
carry with it resolution of the others. At all events it will be necessary
to gain a clearer view of the role of the law in first-century Judaism before
we venture into the letter itself. Only when we can take for granted what
Paul and his readers took for granted with regard to the law and its function will we be able to hear the allusions he was making and understand
the argument he was offering. The confusion and disagreement still remaining with regard to the passages listed above strongly suggest that the
role of the law, both within the Judaism against which Paul was reacting
and within the new perspective on Paul, has not as yet been properly perceived. In what follows I will therefore attempt briefly to "set the scene"
for an understanding of this important integrating strand of the letter.

II. Nomos as Equivalent of Torah

First of all, we should clarify a point that has occasioned some misunderstanding and confusion, namely, the appropriateness of *nomos*/law
as the translation equivalent or "meaning" of *torah*/Torah. Since Schechter (*Rabbinic Theology*) and Dodd ("Law") it has frequently been claimed
that *torah* does not mean *nomos* or "law"; rather, *torah* means simply
"instruction" or "teaching," and the Torah (the Pentateuch, or indeed the
whole of the scriptures) includes more than law. According to an influential body of opinion, this equation of *torah*/Torah with (the) law as given
by the LXX translation of *torah* using the narrower word *nomos*, subsequently contributed to Paul's "distorted" understanding of his ancestral faith,
and lies at the root of the modern characterization of Judaism as "legalistic"
(e.g., Dodd, "Law," 34; Schoeps, *Paul*, 29; Sandmel, *Paul*, 47–48; cited by
Westerholm, "*Torah*," 330–31; also Lapide–Stuhlmacher, *Rabbi*, 39). However, Westerholm has now shown clearly (1) that *nomos* can be an appropriate rendering of *torah* (e.g., Gen. 26:5; Exod. 12:49; Lev. 26:46); (2)
that the technical use of "*torah* to refer to a collection which spells out
Israel's covenantal obligations" goes back to Deuteronomy, which provides
the basis for Torah = *nomos* = law as an appropriate title for the Pentateuch (e.g., Deut. 4:8; 30:10; 32:46); and (3) that Paul's use of *nomos* to
sum up Israel's obligations as set out by Moses is "fully in line with Hebrew usage of *torah*" (cf. e.g., Rom. 2:12, 17–18; 7:12; and 10:5 with 1 Kings
2:3; Ezra 7:6, 10, 12, 14, 26; Neh. 8:14; 9:14, 34; and Jer. 32:23).

In particular, the basic understanding of "covenantal nomism" is more
or less self-evident in the central foundation act of Israel as a nation—the

exodus from Egypt and the giving of the law at Sinai. As quintessentially expressed in Exod. 20 and Deut. 5, the law (here the ten commandments— cf. Deut. 4:8 with 5:1) follows upon the prior act of divine initiative ("I am the Lord your God, who brought you out of the land of Egypt . . . "); obedience to this law is Israel's response to divine grace, not an attempt to gain God's favor conceived as grudgingly given and calculatingly dispensed. As already implied, the fullest and most sustained expression of this basic Jewish theologoumenon is Deuteronomy, the classic statement of Israel's covenant theology: the statutes and ordinances of the law (chs. 5–28) set out explicitly as God's covenant made with Israel (5:2–3; 29:1); the promise (and warning) repeatedly reaffirmed in numerous variations, "This do and live" (e.g., 4:1, 10, 40; 5:29–33; 6:1–2, 18, 24; 7:12–13; etc.; see also Dunn, *Romans 1–8, 9–16*, on 2:13 and 10:5). Not surprisingly, in Romans Paul interacts more frequently with Deuteronomy than with any other section of the Pentateuch; and his exposition of Deut. 30:12–14 is at the center of his attempt to expound the continuing and wider significance of the law in a way which retrieves the law from a too narrowly defined understanding of "This do and live" (10:5–13).

It is unnecessary to enter the debate about how deeply rooted this understanding of covenant and law was in pre-Exilic Israelite religion (see, e.g., Nicholson). Whatever the actual facts in that case, the attitude of covenantal nomism was certainly given determinative shape by Ezra's reforms in the post-Exilic period, with their deliberate policy of national and cultic segregation as dictated by the law (Ezra 9–10). This trend was massively reinforced by the Maccabean crisis, where it was precisely Israel's identity as the covenant people, the people of the law, which was at stake (1 Macc. 1:57; 2:27, 50; 2 Macc. 1:2–4; 2:21–22; 5:15; 13:14), and where "zeal for the law" became the watchword of national resistance (1 Macc. 2:26–27, 50, 58; 2 Macc. 4:2; 7:2, 9, 11, 37; 8:21; 13:14; see further Dunn, *Romans 9–16*, on 10:2). So, too, in the period following the Maccabean crisis the tie-in between election, covenant, and law remains a fundamental and persistent theme of Jewish self-understanding, as illustrated by ben Sira (Sir. 17:11–17; 24:23; 28:7; 39:8; 42:2; 44:19–20; 45:5, 7, 15, 17, 24–25), *Jubilees* (1:4–5, 9–10, 12, 14, 29; 2:21; 6:4–16; 14:17–20; 15:4–16, 19–21, 25–29, 34; 16:14; 19:29; 20:3; etc.), the Damascus document (CD 1.4–5, 15–18, 20; 3.2–4, 10–16; 4.7–10; 6.2–5; etc.) and Pseudo-Philo (*LAB* 4.5, 11; 7.4; 8.3; 9.3–4, 7–8, 13, 15; 10.2; 11.1–5; etc.). In particular we may note the outworking of all this in two of the main groups in Palestinian Judaism at the time of Jesus and Paul. The Qumran community defined membership of the covenant of grace in terms of observing God's precepts and clinging to God's commandments (1QS 1.7–8; 5.1–3), and commitment to the law had to be total and to be examined every year, with any breach severely punished (1QS 5.24; 8.16–9.2). And the Pharisees were known for their *akribeia*, "strictness," in observing the law (see Dunn, *Romans 1–8*, §1.1), and evidently also for their concern to maintain a level of purity in their daily lives which the law required only for the temple cult itself (see also idem, *Romans 9–16*, on 14:14). For rabbinic traditions on Israel's special relationship with the law see Str-B, 3:126–33. We may confine ourselves to two quotations provided by Schoeps, *Paul*, 195 and 216: *Sifre Deut.* 53b–75b— God addresses Israel in the words "Let it be clear from the keeping of the commandments that you are a people holy to me"; and *Mek. Exod.* 20:6— "By covenant is meant nothing other than the Torah."

3.1 The law thus became a basic expression of Israel's *distinctiveness* as the people specially chosen by (the one) God to be his people. In sociological terms the law functioned as an "identity marker" and "boundary," reinforcing Israel's sense of distinctiveness and distinguishing Israel from the surrounding nations (Neusner, *Judaism*, 72–75; Meeks, *First Urban Christians*, 97; Dunn, "Works of Law," 524–27). This sense of separateness was deeply rooted in Israel's national consciousness (e.g., Lev. 20:24–26; Ezra 10:11; Neh 13:3; *Pss. Sol.* 17.28; *3 Macc.* 3.4) and comes to powerful expression in *Jub.* 22.16:

> Separate yourself from the Gentiles,
>   and do not eat with them,
>   and do not perform deeds like theirs.
> And do not become associates of theirs.
> Because their deeds are defiled,
>   and all of their ways are contaminated,
>   and despicable, and abominable.

The letter of Aristeas expresses the same conviction in terms which reinforce the sociological insight.

> In his wisdom the legislator . . . surrounded us with unbroken palisades and iron walls to prevent our mixing with any of the other peoples in any matter. . . . So, to prevent our being perverted by contact with others or by mixing with bad influences, he hedged us in on all sides with strict observances connected with meat and drink and touch and hearing and sight, after the manner of the Law (*Ep. Arist.* 139, 142).

Similarly Philo, *Mos.* 1.278—a people "which shall dwell alone, not reckoned among other nations . . . because in virtue of the distinction of their peculiar customs they do not mix with others to depart from the ways of their fathers." And a funerary inscription from Italy praises a woman "who lived a gracious life inside Judaism [*kalōs biōsasa en tō Ioudaismō*]"— Judaism understood as "a sort of fenced off area in which Jewish lives are led" (Amir, *Ioudaismos*, 35–36, 39–40).

Consistent with this is the characterization of Gentiles as *anomos* and their works as *anomia*: by definition they were "without the law, outside the law," that is, outside the area (Israel) coterminous with the law, marked out by the law; so already in the Psalms (28:3; 37:28; 55:3; 73:3; 92:7; 104:35; 125:3), in 1 Maccabees (Gentiles and apostates—3:5–6; 7:5; 9:23,

58, 69; 11:25; 14:14), and in the self-evident equation, Gentile = "sinner" (as in Tob. 13:6 [LXX 8]; *Jub.* 23:23–24; *Pss. Sol.* 1:1; 2:1–2; 17:22–25; Matt. 5:47 with Luke 6:33; Gal 2:15). Not surprisingly this desire to live within the law and be marked off from the lawless and sinner became a dominant concern in the factionalism which was a feature of Judaism in the period from the Maccabeans to the emergence of rabbinic Judaism as the most powerful faction within post-C.E. 70 Judaism. It was expressed in the frequent complaints of "the righteous" and "devout" over against those (within Israel) whom they characterized as "sinners" (as in Wisd. Sol. 2–5; *Jub.* 6.32–35; 23.16, 26; *1 Enoch* 1.1, 7–9; 5.6–7; 82.4–7; 1QS 2.4–5; 1QH 2.8–19; CD 1.13–21; *Pss. Sol.* 3.3–12; 4.8; 13.5–12; 15.1–13; Pharisees probably = "separated ones"); see also on 3:7; 4:5, 7–8; and 9:6.

3.2 A natural and more or less inevitable converse of this sense of distinctiveness was the sense of *privilege,* precisely in being the nation specially chosen by the one God and favored by gift of covenant and law. This comes out particularly clearly in writings which could not simply ignore and dismiss Gentiles as sinners, but which had to attempt some sort of apologetic for the claims of Israel in the face of a much more powerful Gentile world. Thus both Philo and Josephus speak with understandable if exaggerated pride of the widespread desire among Greek and barbarian to adopt Jewish customs and laws (Philo, *Mos.* 2.17–25—"they attract and win the attention of all . . . the sanctity of our legislation has been a source of wonder not only to Jews and to all others also;" Josephus, *Against Apion* 2.277–286—"The masses have long since shown a keen desire to adopt our religious observances. . . . Were we not ourselves aware of the excellence of our laws, assuredly we should have been impelled to pride [*mega phronein*] ourselves upon them by the multitude of their admirers"). Expressive of the same pride in the law of Moses is what seems to have been a fairly sustained attempt in Jewish apologetic to present Moses as "the first wise man," who was teacher of Orpheus and from whose writings Plato and Pythagoras learned much of their wisdom (Eupolemus, frag. 1; Artapanus, frag. 3; Aristobulus, frag. 3–4; from Eusebius, *Praep. Evang.* 9.26.1; 9.27.3–6; and 13.12.1–4; texts in Charlesworth).

Pride in the law as the mark of God's special favor to Israel is also well illustrated in the identification of divine Wisdom with the law, the assertion that the universally desirable Wisdom, immanent within creation but hidden from human eyes, was embodied within "the book of the covenant of the Most High God, the law which Moses commanded us as an inheritance for the congregations of Jacob" (Sir. 24:23). The same claim is expressed more forcefully in Bar. 3:36–4:4:

[36] . . . (He) gave her to Jacob his servant and to Israel whom he loved

. . . .

[1]She is the book of the commandments of God,
and the law which endures for ever.

All who hold her fast will live,
  but those who forsake her will die.
²Turn, O Jacob, and take her;
  walk towards the shining of her light.
³Do not give your glory [tēn doxan sou] to another;
  or your advantages [ta sympheronta] to an alien people.
⁴Blessed are we, O Israel,
  for what is pleasing to God is known [gnōsta] to us.

For those confronted by the crushing power of Rome within Palestine
this sense of privilege was difficult to maintain. *Psalms of Solomon* found
a solution in pressing the older distinction between discipline and punishment (particularly *Pss. Sol.* 3, 10, and 13)—thus 13:6–11.

The destruction of the sinner is terrible
  but nothing shall harm the righteous, of all these things,
For the discipline of the righteous (for things done) in ignorance
  is not the same as the destruction of the sinners
. . . .
For the Lord will spare his devout,
  and he will wipe away their mistakes with discipline.
For the life of the righteous (goes on) for ever,
  but sinners shall be taken away to destruction. . . .

Less easy to satisfy was the writer of *4 Ezra*, who in common with his
fellow Jews saw the law given to Israel as a mark of divine favor (3:19;
9:31), but who could not understand how God could spare the sinful nations and yet allow his law-keeping people to be so harshly treated (3:28–
36; 4:23–24; 5:23–30; 6:55–59).

3.3 A sociological perspective also helps us to see how the conviction
of privileged election and the practice of covenantal nomism almost inevitably come to expression in focal points of distinctiveness, particular
laws and especially ritual practices which reinforced the sense of distinctive identity and marked Israel off most clearly from the other nations.
In this case three of Israel's laws gained particular prominence as being
especially distinctive—circumcision, food laws, and sabbath (cf. Limbeck,
Ordnung, 34; Meeks, *First Urban Christians*, 36–37, 97; Sanders, *Law*, 102).
These were not the only beliefs and practices which marked out Jews, but
from the Maccabean period onward they gained increasing significance
for their boundary-defining character and were widely recognized both
within and without Judaism as particularly and distinctively characteristic
of Jews. Not that they were intrinsically more important than other laws;
they simply had become points of particular sensitivity in Jewish national
understanding and were test cases of covenant loyalty. Since I will provide sufficiently full documentation later, I need say no more here (see
Dunn, *Romans 1–8, 9–16*, on 2:25 and 14:2, 5).

III. Paul and the Law in Romans

This, then, is the context within which and against which we must set Paul's treatment of the law in Romans. The Jews, proselytes, and God-worshiping Gentiles among his readership would read what Paul says about the law in the light of this close interconnection in Jewish theology of Israel's election, covenant, and law. They would, I believe, recognize that what Paul was concerned about was the fact that covenant promise and law had become too inextricably identified with ethnic Israel as such, with the Jewish people marked out in their national distinctiveness by the practices of circumcision, food laws, and sabbath in particular (Wright, *Messiah*, ch. 2, appropriately coins the phrase "national righteousness"). They would recognize that what Paul was endeavoring to do was to free both promise and law for a wider range of recipients, freed from the ethnic constraints which he saw to be narrowing the grace of God and diverting the saving purpose of God out of its main channel—Christ.

Not least in importance, by setting Paul's treatment of the law into this matrix we are enabled to offer a solution to the sequence of exegetical problems and disputes outlined earlier (I. above = Dunn, *Romans 1–8*, §5.2). Thus it should occasion no surprise that ch. 2 turns out to be a developing critique of precisely these features of Jewish covenant theology which were sketched out above (II. above = Dunn, *Romans 1–8*, §5.3)—the law as dividing Jew from non-Jew, the haves from the have-nots, those within from those without (2:12–14); the law as a source of ethnic pride for the typical devout Jew (2:17–23); and circumcision as the focal point for this sense of privileged distinctiveness (2:25–29) [Hartman draws attention to the consistent strand of "covenant ideology" in and behind these chapters]. Paul regularly warns against "the works of the law," not as "good works" in general or as any attempt by the individual to amass merit for himself, but rather as that pattern of obedience by which "the righteous" maintain their status within the people of the covenant, as evidenced not least by their dedication on such sensitive "test" issues as sabbath and food laws (see Dunn, *Romans 1–8, 9–16*, on 3:20 and 14:2, 5).

Likewise I will be arguing that an important hermeneutical key to such crucial passages as 3:27–31, 7:14–25, and 9:30–10:4 is precisely the recognition that Paul's negative thrust against the law is against the law taken over too completely by Israel, the law misunderstood by a misplaced emphasis on boundary-marking ritual, the law become a tool of sin in its too close identification with matters of the flesh, the law sidetracked into a focus for nationalistic zeal. Freed from that too narrowly Jewish perspective, the law still has an important part to play in "the obedience of faith." And the parenetic section (12:1–15:6) can then be seen as Paul's attempt to provide a basic guideline for social living, the law redefined for the eschatological people of God in place of the law misunderstood in too distinctively Jewish terms, with the climax understandably focused on a treatment of the two older test-cases, food laws and sabbath. It is my contention that only with such an understanding can we do adequate justice to both the positive and the negative thrusts of Paul's treatment of the law in Romans, and that failure to appreciate "the social function" of the law (as outlined above) is a fatal weakness both of alternative attempts (e.g., Cranfield, Hahn, and Hübner) and of Räisänen's critique.

In short, properly understood, Paul's treatment of the law, which has seemed so confused and incoherent to many commentators, actually becomes one of the chief integrating strands which binds the whole letter into a cohesive and powerful restatement of Jewish covenant theology in the light of Christ.

With the letter thus situated within the contexts of its author, of those for whom he wrote, and of the issues with which he engaged, we can now turn to the task of exegesis.

21

ISRAEL'S MISSTEP IN THE EYES OF PAUL

Lloyd Gaston

Christian theologians have often in the past developed a theology of Judaism on the basis of the Pauline epistles. Judaism was whatever Paul opposed or even the opposite of everything Paul said positively. Only in recent times have the scholarly maxim *ad fontes* and the religious injunction not to bear false witness been combined in the ideal of writing about Judaism solely from Jewish sources, read from the perspective of those sources. After the work especially of E. P. Sanders,[1] it will never be possible to return to old habits. Whatever positions Paul was opposing, none of them could be called Judaism as such. Nevertheless, he does have something against his fellow Jews, and I will discuss those passages where he speaks about them. First, however, I want to look briefly at some passages which ought not to be included in such a discussion.

Since every one of Paul's letters is addressed explicitly to Gentile Christians, it is not known what he would have said to Jews. That he would have had occasion to do so is clear from 2 Cor. 11:24, where he says that he was punished in synagogues five times. Since that could only happen if he voluntarily put himself under their jurisdiction, it means that Paul went to synagogues, presumably to worship. If Acts is put rigorously to one side, as methodologically must be done, there is no evidence from Paul's own hand that he ever preached to Jews, in synagogues or anywhere else.[2] From the account of the Jerusalem council in Galatians 2, it would appear that Paul was at one time in favour of Peter's preaching to Jews and that he acknowledged Peter's gospel and apostolate. In Romans, on the other hand, there is not a hint even of this.

Can statements about Paul's own past prove anything about what he thought of other Jews or even of Judaism? Did his prophetic commission-

---

[1]Cf. Sanders, *Paul.*
[2]The best description I know of Paul's missionary practice is found in Sanders, *Law,* 179–90.

ing as Apostle to the Gentiles also mean for him personally an advantage, a liberation from law perhaps, or a new hope for salvation? He does not say so. There is no indication that "making progress more than many contemporaries in my people, being to a greater degree zealous for the [oral] traditions of my fathers" (Gal. 1:14) was a bad thing to do. To be "circumcised on the eighth day, from the people of Israel, of the tribe of Benjamin, a Hebrew of the Hebrews, with respect to the law a Pharisee . . . with respect to righteousness in the law blameless" (Phil. 3:5–6) is said by Paul to be an advantage (*kerdos* 3:7) and to give that up a distinct loss (*zēmia* 3:7, 8). What he regrets about his past is not his "Judaism" but his persecution of the church (3:6; Gal. 1:13; 1 Cor. 15:9). But apart from that his advantages were real advantages, which he deliberately gave up. "Indeed, I count all things as loss for the superiority of the knowledge of Christ Jesus my Lord, for whose sake I have lost all things and count them as excrement, in order that I might gain Christ and be found in him, having my righteousness not from the law but through the faithfulness of Christ, the righteousness from God which [leads] to the faith of knowing him" (Phil. 3:8–10). It seems that it is possible to have a status of righteousness from either of two sources, from the law (in the sense of covenant) or from the faithfulness of Christ. Paul once had the former (cf. v. 6) and has shifted to the latter. He does not say that he wishes other Jews to do the same. Knowing Jesus Christ as Lord he says is superior (*hyperechon*, v. 8), but he does not deny at all the validity of life in Torah. Since Romans 7 is not autobiographical,[3] it seems that no critique of Judaism can be drawn from Paul's statements about himself.[4]

Galatians ought not to be included in this summary. Whoever the troublemakers are who are causing the Galatians to Judaize, and I am convinced that they are Gentile Christians, what Paul opposes is not what they have to say about *Judaism*. Even if the troublemakers should be Jews, they are Jewish Christians,[5] and the debate concerns what *Gentiles* ought to do to be faithful Christians (circumcision or not).[6] I have dealt elsewhere (Gaston, *Paul and Torah*) with some problem texts in Galatians,[7] and their conclusions do not need to be repeated here.

Second Corinthians ought not to be included in this survey. Paul's rivals are here clearly to be identified as Jewish Christians, and their views can be more clearly established than is the case in Galatians. Judaizing appears not to be an issue at all, and the word "law" is found nowhere in the whole epistle. If Georgi is even partly right in his characterization of

---

[3]This has been generally recognized since Kümmel, *Römer* 7, ix–160.

[4]This is the conclusion, for somewhat different reasons, also of Lüdemann, *Paulus und das Judentum*, 20–22.

[5]This is emphasized by F. Mussner, *Der Galaterbrief* and idem, *Tractate*.

[6]Cf. Sanders, *Law*, 17–29.

[7]Gaston, *Paul and Torah*, chs. 2, 4, and 5.

the opponents,[8] had Paul the Pharisee encountered them before Damascus, his rejection of them would have been just as sharp. Second Corinthians 3, however, is a different matter and deserves a separate discussion.[9]

Philippians also ought not to be included. The opponents in the fragment in chapter 3 seem so much like those of 2 Corinthians 10–13 that nothing more need be said about them.[10] It has been suggested that here Paul is referring not to Jewish Christians but to local Jews,[11] but even so, it is doubtful if one could infer very much from such intemperate language about his attitude to Jews in general, to say nothing of Judaism as such. His vicious invectives in Phil. 3:2 and Gal. 5:12 are hardly to be regarded as serious responses to the question "what is the value of circumcision?" (Rom. 3:1)!

First Thessalonians 2:13–16 ought to be included in the survey and discussed at some length, but it will not be. In the first place, I am firmly convinced that at least the relevant parts are an interpolation and would have difficulty imagining them to be otherwise. In the second place, they have been much discussed lately, and I have nothing to add to the arguments already adduced against Pauline authorship.[12] Nevertheless, something can be said. The best discussion of the tradition of the killing of the prophets lying behind these verses is by O. H. Steck,[13] and he points out the one phrase least derivable from the tradition: "hindering us from speaking to the Gentiles that they might be saved" (v. 16a). The interpolator may have included this phrase as a memory of the Pauline situation.

In sum: Paul had real opponents who caused real difficulties for his apostolate to the Gentiles. Many of them were Jewish Christians, and some may have been non-Christian Jews. Paul's sometimes violent disagreements with them, however, were not about the importance of Torah in the life of a Jew but about how Gentiles ought to relate to the law (Galatians) or about how Jewish apostles ought to relate to Gentiles (2 Corinthians). There presumably was also Jewish opposition to Paul not reflected in these inner Christian discussions. There is the charge in Acts 21:21 that some Jews (or Jewish Christians) said that Paul "teaches all the Jews who are among the Gentiles to forsake Moses, telling them not to circumcise their children or observe the customs." If the charge were true, then Paul really

---

[8]Georgi, *Die Gegner.* See also Collange, *Enigmes.*

[9]See Gaston, *Paul and Torah,* ch. 10. Nothing need be said at all about 1 Corinthians except to note with Weiss, *Korintherbrief,* and Moffatt, *First Corinthians,* 268–69, that 1 Cor. 15:56 is a gloss.

[10]Cf. Koester, "Pauline Fragment," 317–32.

[11]Beare, *Philippians,* 102–12, who incorrectly entitles the section "Renunciation of Judaism."

[12]Two recent thorough reviews of the literature on the question are Collins, "Integrity of 1 Thess," 96–135, and Baarda, "Maar de toorn is over hen gekomen," 15–74. Both authors conclude that the passage is authentic.

[13]Steck, *Israel,* 274–78. To be sure, he treats the passage as Pauline.

would have a fundamental quarrel with Jews in general and Judaism as such. I believe the charge to be false, but if even some believed it, it could have been a hindrance to Paul in carrying out his apostolic task for the Gentiles.[14] One could imagine an inner Jewish debate between Paul and Gamaliel,[15] even though I seriously doubt if either had in fact even heard of the other. Such a debate would not have been about the central concerns of Judaism but about the somewhat peripheral "Jewish theology of Gentiles," if I may use a very non-Jewish expression. It would have been about how Gentiles relate to Torah and election and the timing of their entry into God's people. But if that is true, those same issues might very well be on the agenda of a debate between Paul and James. What is at issue between Paul and Judaism is not the Torah of Israel but Paul as Apostle to the Gentiles.

I turn now to one of the two passages where Paul expresses himself at greater length. Romans 2:17–29 is a section which is in many ways puzzling. Even if its function were to show that Jews are as bad or even worse than Gentiles, which I doubt, it is difficult to understand it as a universal indictment of all Jews. The emphasis on doing as a prerequisite for salvation, with no reference to covenant or grace, would seem to make Paul into the supreme legalist. The identity of the uncircumcised is the despair of commentators. And there are many other problems. Perhaps one should cease to assume that what Paul ought to be saying can be derived from 3:9 and 19 and first look at the section apart from its context.

Three recent interpreters have done so and come to conclusions surprising for traditional law-gospel exegesis. J. C. O'Neill says, "This is a fine appeal to a Jew from a fellow Jew to keep the law which they both profess."[16] H. Räisänen says that the conclusion of Paul's argument is "that circumcision is of no avail to a Jew who is guilty of serious transgressions of the law, and that a true Jew is one who behaves like one (whether circumcised or not)."[17] E. P. Sanders describes the intent of the passage this way: "What one should do is to examine one's motives to make sure they are pure, to be sure that observance of the law is not merely external, and to act in such a way as not to bring disgrace on the synagogue; in short to repent and to mend one's ways."[18] These seem to me to be rather sensible readings of the text, but they are achieved only at a cost. For O'Neill the section is a later interpolation into the letter, for Sanders it is part of a virtually unchanged synagogue sermon incorporated by Paul, and for Räisänen it is an example of Paul's complete inconsistency in deal-

---

[14]We have seen no evidence in the epistles that it was in fact such a hindrance, even if the charge did lead to Paul's arrest.
[15]Werfel has in fact imagined such a debate in his *Paul among the Jews.*
[16]O'Neill, *Romans,* 52.
[17]Räisänen, *Paul and the Law,* 99.
[18]Sanders, *Law,* 129.

ing with the question whether the law can be fulfilled. But keeping their conclusions that Paul is here urging Jews (not Gentiles) to keep the law better, it is possible to make more sense of why he would want to say that.

In Rom. 9:4–5 Paul gives a list of what characterizes Israelites, a list with which Jews could agree. His list here, however, is quite different: "You bear the name of Jew and trust in the Torah and boast in God and know his will and discern what is excellent, being instructed from the Torah, and are confident of being a guide of the blind, a light for those in darkness, an instructor of the foolish, a teacher of the immature, having in the Torah the embodiment of knowledge and truth." That is not a description of a Jew as such but specifically of a Jewish missionary to Gentiles.[19] The section is then not about Jews as such nor about the law as such, and it is certainly not about soteriology; it centres on the accusation that "because of you the name of God is blasphemed among the Gentiles" (2:24). The description of the ideal is one in which such missionaries could recognize themselves, and it is not at all meant ironically. What then is the meaning of the three accusations of theft, adultery, and robbing temples? The strange last case is the most absurd if one is thinking of a universal indictment; as Sanders says,[20] "Did they all rob temples?" No, but four did, and it may be that Paul even has that specific case in mind.[21] The scandal of swindling the proselyte Fulvia of gifts she was sending to the Jerusalem temple in 19 C.E. was great enough to have at least four thousand Jews expelled from Rome, something serious enough to be long remembered. It was also a great setback to the missionary enterprise.[22] Even occasional scandals like that are enough to warrant the statement that "the name of God because of you is blasphemed among the Gentiles."

That, after all, is the point. Paul is accusing not all Jews but Jewish missionaries, and he is accusing not all missionaries but only some (cf. 3:3) of flagrant violations of Torah. But most important he does so not to speak of Jewish "theology" but of the bad effect such activity has for attracting proselytes. Even Josephus's "complete scoundrel," if he repented and restored the money, if he circumcised his heart, would be justified at the judgment, but the harm will still have been done. What follows in verses 25–29 is not directed against Torah and circumcision, even if some of the rhetoric about the latter is quite strong and will be corrected in 3:1. On

---

[19]Although the terminology is not quite accurate, what is meant can be seen in Dalbert, *Missionsliteratur.*

[20]Sanders, *Law,* 125.

[21]The story is told in Jos., *Ant.* 18.81–84. He uses the *hierosyl-* root to refer to robbery from the temple contributions of Jews from Asia in *Ant.* 16.45, 164, 168; to describe robbery from the Jerusalem temple itself in *War* 1.654 (= *Ant.* 17.163), 5.562, and *Ant.* 12.359; and in referring to Manetho's accusation that Jews robbed Egyptian temples before the Exodus (*Ag. Ap.* 1.249, 318f.).

[22]Cf. L. H. Feldman's note on Josephus, *Ant.* 18.83 (LCL), and Leon, *Jews of Ancient Rome,* 17–20.

the contrary, it is in favour of doing Torah and circumcision of the heart. But why does Paul go on after having made his point? Is it true, as some have maintained, that he himself had been such a missionary before Damascus and that therefore he got carried away? Does he hope that other Jews, in faithfulness to Torah, will help him, at least passively, in his new Gentile mission?

I now return to the question of why this rhetorical aside is placed where it is in the midst of Paul's indictment of the Gentile world (1:18–3:20). Its function in that context may be to say that one possible solution to the Gentile problem, that they become proselytes, has not worked well in the past (and is not necessary in the present, after 3:21). In any case, it is an aside and not part of an evenhanded invective against Jews as well as Gentiles. The larger context speaks of all Gentiles in relation to God, but the aside speaks of some Jews in relation to Gentiles. What then is the significance of the language of "the Jew and also the Greek"? That needs to be discussed in another context.[23]

I will now state a kind of preliminary summary, which needs to be tested in Romans 11. The oft-quoted conclusion of one of the most important books on Paul in this generation is this: "That is what Paul finds wrong with Judaism: it is not Christianity."[24] That is, of course, provocatively overstated, and its author also rightly says that Paul hardly ever speaks of Judaism.[25] But taking it as it stands, in the same spirit I will formulate my alternative thesis: "This is what Paul finds wrong with other Jews: that they did not share his revelation in Damascus."

Romans 11 is not a good chapter on which to base a Christian theology of Israel, if only because of the many tensions it contains.[26] There is something in the chapter which makes interpreters answer Paul's question, "Has God repudiated his people" by saying, "Well, yes, he did repudiate almost all of them, but only (!) for the period between Paul and Parousia," which is hardly the same as Paul's vehement *mē genoito*. The word "election" in verse 7 is a very small number contrasted with "the rest," while in verse 28 it refers to "all Israel." Although they tripped, Israel did not fall in verse 11, and yet they do seem to be fallen in verse 22. The chapter emphasizes God's action: it is God who blinds (vv. 7, 25), trips (v. 11), stupefies (v. 8), imprisons in disobedience (v. 32), and yet Jews are said to be broken off because of *their* unbelief (v. 20). Paul speaks of God's mercy

---

[23]See *Paul and Torah*, ch. 8.
[24]Sanders, *Paul*, 552.
[25]Sanders, *Law*, 19f.
[26]Thus Eckardt, *Elder and Younger Brothers*, 56, says that only a "strained exegesis" can deny that in Romans 11 Israel has not been displaced by the church in "the present dispensation"; Davies, A. T., *Anti-Semitism*, 104, speaks of "the inadequacy of Romans 9–11" in allowing Jewish self-definition; and Ruether, *Faith and Fratricide*, 106, says "contemporary ecumenists who use Romans 11 to argue that Paul does not believe that God has rejected the people of the Mosaic covenant speak out of good intentions, but inaccurate exegesis."

and grace (vv. 5, 32), a grace not from works (v. 6), and yet in verses 22–23 everything seems to be conditional on the human work of believing. In 10:19 and 11:11 God makes Israel jealous, and at the end the Redeemer will save all of them, while in 11:14 Paul makes Israel jealous, to save some of them. Most of the problems seem to centre on the olive tree section, verses 13–24, and I shall put it to one side on the first glance through the chapter.

If my reading of Romans 9 is correct,[27] Paul says nothing there whatsoever which is critical of Israel. On the contrary, these chapters must be understood "nicht als primär israelkritisch—sondern als primär kirchenkritisch."[28] It is important that the Roman Christians understand that God's election of Israel, which is not based on works or faith, still stands, and that Gentiles who were not chosen in the past had no valid ground for complaint. It is however also important that they understand that God, in a new act of righteousness, has now called also a new people, the Gentiles (9:25–26), who share the same advantages of election (8:28–39). I would now be even more positive about the election of Israel. Dinter has shown how later generations (for example, LXX) understood such remnant language as Isa. 10:20–23 as an act of salvation for all Israel who survived the Assyrian crisis.[29] There is no "only" in the Isaiah text,[30] and it seems that what was a threat in the original situation was later understood as a promise. The "remnant" which is to be saved in 9:27 is the same as the "all Israel" which is to be saved in 11:26, even "though the number of the children of Israel be as the sand of the sea." YHWH Sabaoth *has* left Israel "seed," and Israel did *not* become like Sodom and Gomorrah. Romans 9 ends like Romans 11 with the proclamation of God's mercy on both Gentiles and Israel.

There is another clue to interpretation from the end of the discussion when it becomes clear what specifically Jews have been hostile to (11:28): it is the gospel, Paul's gospel, the gospel that God would justify the Gentiles by faithfulness (Gal. 3:8). I would also now like to be less tentative about "the instruments of mercy . . . whom God called, even us, not only from the Jews but also from the Gentiles." They are quite specifically those whom God has called to the mission to the Gentiles, Paul and some Jews and some Gentiles. There is then both continuity and discontinuity be-

---

[27]See *Paul and Torah*, ch. 5.

[28]Eichholz, *Theologie*, 296.

[29]Dinter, "Remnant of Israel." According to Sanders, *Paul*, 242–57, this is true also of Qumran. Cf. "We the remnant of thy people shall praise thy name, O God of mercies, who has kept the covenant with our fathers. In all our generations thou hast bestowed thy wonderful favours on this remnant of thy people" (1QM 14.8–9), and "He raised up for himself men called by name, that a remnant might be left to the Lord, and that the face of the earth might be filled with their seed" (CD 2.11–12).

[30]As is assumed by most translations, which want Paul to distinguish between Israel as a whole and the small number of Jewish Christians who are to be saved.

tween the end of Romans 9 and the beginning of Romans 11, continuity in concept and discontinuity in language. But before taking up the continuation of this thread, there are passages in 9:30–10:20 which also bear on an interpretation of Romans 11.

In another context I looked at the race toward the goal from the perspective of what Gentiles obtained.[31] Now what Paul says there about Israel and what he does not say must be noted. First of all, he speaks about Israel as a whole and not only about some Jews. Paul, of course, knows that some Jews responded to "the gospel to the circumcised" (Galatians 2), but faith in Christ is not an issue in Rom. 9:30–10:4; it is rather openness to Gentiles. Paul would have said, for example, that the Jew who transmitted the saying of Jesus "Go nowhere among the Gentiles and enter no town of the Samaritans, but go rather to the lost sheep of the house of Israel" (Matt. 10:5–6) had stumbled just as much on the stone as did the non-Christian Jew. Israel was right to pursue the Torah of righteousness and was wrong only in not realizing that the goal of that Torah, in which God's righteousness would be extended also to the Gentiles, was now at hand. Being distracted by works (which of course should be done), Israel was faithful to Torah as it relates to Israel, but with respect to the goal of that Torah as it relates to Gentiles, they stumbled and were unfaithful. But even so it is doubtful if one should speak of the "guilt and responsibility of Israel," since they stumbled on a stone which was providentially put there by God precisely to make them stumble. Paul praises Israel's zeal but not Israel's knowledge (10:2). They did not subordinate themselves to the righteousness of God because they were ignorant of it (10:3). Nevertheless, Paul prays for their salvation, knowing that it stands firm in the purpose of God (that is, from a literary perspective the function of 10:1 is to prepare for 11:26f.).

In spite of its popularity, I believe it is simply wrongheaded to try to read these verses as a definition of "justification by faith." It is also not legitimate to appeal to Phil. 3:9, about which F. W. Beare comments, "If we did not possess Romans and Galatians, we would find his words [here] all but incomprehensible."[32] Besides, as I have shown, it is possible to understand Phil. 3:9 in a way that does not deny the righteousness of God given to Israel through Torah when it affirms that righteousness now given to Gentiles (and Paul!) through Christ. Rom. 10:3 is not about an individual righteousness or self-righteousness but about Israel's righteousness which, while it comes from God, is not enough, according to Paul. The righteousness of God for Gentiles, which is the goal of the Torah, has now been manifested, and it is the failure of Israel to acknowledge this, which is what Paul holds against them.

---

[31]Gaston, *Paul and Torah*, ch. 8.
[32]Beare, *Philippians*, 117.

Paul has a very strong opinion on how to answer the question, "Has God repudiated his people" (11:1).[33] Not only does he indignantly reject the question but he also states positively, "God has not repudiated his people, whom he previously chose."[34] Paul's first witness to this fact is astounding: since he himself is an Israelite and God has not repudiated him, therefore God has not repudiated Israel. As if Israel's rejection is not total but only 99.99999 per cent, since God has spared one out of ten million! If Paul were tempted to say with Elijah, "I alone am left," then he would deserve the same rebuke. In any case, the second witness is not Elijah but what the divine revelation says to him. "I have left for myself seven thousand men who have not bowed the knee to Baal." Because of the seven thousand all Israel was spared. Paul, who pleads to God not against Israel but for Israel (9:1–3; 10:1), hears in these words the answer to his prayer, the answer expressed most clearly in 11:26. How is this so?

"So then also in the present time there has been a remnant according to the election of grace. . . . What then? What Israel seeks, that it did not obtain. But the election obtained it, while the rest were blinded" (11:5, 7). The identity of the remnant, the election, has seemed so obvious to most as to not need discussion; it must be Jewish Christians in general, those Jews who responded favourably to Cephas's "apostolate to the circumcised" (Gal. 2:7). I believe that cannot be the case for the following reasons: If that is what Paul had meant, it would have been so easy for him to refer in verse 1 to "the saints in Jerusalem" (15:26). Instead, he refers only to himself, surely not as an example of a Jewish Christian but as the Apostle to the Gentiles. Had he gone on to name others, they would have included such fellow Jews from chapter 16 as Andronicus and Junia, Herodion, and Lucius and Jason and Sosipater, but not Jewish Christians as such. When he speaks of Israel seeking but not obtaining, there is a clear reference back to 9:31, where as I have argued the goal of the Torah is the inclusion of Gentiles.[35] The election, the remnant, refers to those Jews who like Paul are engaged in the Gentile mission. They are the "instruments of mercy" (9:23) whom God called in order to express his righteousness now for Gentiles.[36]

The remnant is "according to the election of grace. But if by grace then not from works, since [in that case] grace would not be grace" (11:5–6). Just as in chapter 9, Paul must emphasize that he is speaking of God's action in accomplishing his own purposes and that it is not a matter of any human achievement whatsoever, whether believing or doing. If the

---

[33]It is not necessary to think of a deliberate citation of either Ps. 94:14 or 1 Sam. 12:22.

[34]To which one could perhaps add from 8:30: "and predestined and called and justified and glorified."

[35]See Gaston, *Paul and Torah*, ch. 8.

[36]The "remnant" (*leima*) of 11:5 is then quite different from the "remnant" (*hypoleima*) of 9:27.

remnant were a remnant of achievers, then the vast majority could be blamed, but that is not the case. The vast majority were blinded[37] but blinded by God,[38] to fulfil his purposes, both for Israel and for Gentiles. The rest are not repudiated, and their blinding is not a punishment but part of God's action for salvation. It has been a longstanding assumption that Paul uses the remnant concept in order to disinherit Israel. That is not the case.[39]

Paul returns to his original question and comes to a preliminary conclusion. "I ask then, have they stumbled so as to fall? By no means! But by their misstep salvation [will come] to the Gentiles, in order to make them jealous. But if their misstep [means] riches for the world and their deficit riches for the Gentiles, how much more [will mean] their fullness?" (11:11–12). Israel has stumbled over the rock God put in Zion (9:32f.), but Israel has not fallen, and there is the prospect of their "fullness." For reasons that are not spelled out, this stumbling means salvation and riches for Gentiles, riches from God (10:12; 11:33). There is a brief reference to the jealousy motif, which must refer to Israel, as in 10:19. That too seems to be a promise, parallel to the fullness, so that somehow Israel's deficit and misstep will be overcome. The language is rhetorically artful but tantalizingly vague.

I pass over for now a certain digression and pick up the argument again in verse 25b, beginning with a recapitulation of 11–12: "a partial blindness has come on Israel until the fullness of the Gentiles comes in." Since Israel stumbled but did not fall, and since there were only some things that Israel did not understand, it seems best to understand *apo merous* to refer to a partial blindness[40] rather than to a division between the majority and the minority. It also follows better the first half of the sentence, where the Gentiles understand many things but perhaps not the "mystery." Since the fullness of Israel in verse 12 seems to be the same as all Israel in verse 26, the fullness of the Gentiles should probably be understood in the same way, but it must be remembered that Paul is speaking of groups and not individuals. As many have noted, the "coming in" refers to the eschatological pilgrimage of the Gentiles.

---

[37]*Pōroō* is not the same word as that translated "hardened" (*sklērynō*) in 9:18 and not quite so sclerotic. The substitution of "spirit of stupor" for the "heart" of the Deut. text also ameliorates the accusation. As Paul said in 10:2, their heart is in the right place, but they do not see what he sees. It should also be noted that Paul does not make use of Isa. 6:9f., the passage which is so important for the displacement theology of the Gospels and Acts.

[38]Note the addition of "for myself" to the 1 Kgs. 19:18 citation.

[39]There are problems with the citation of Ps. 69:23–24, added because of the catchword "eyes not to see." I personally believe with Lipsius that it is a post 70 C.E. scribal interpolation, similar to 1 Thess. 2:14–17. It is very suspect because it follows immediately on v. 22, which is used in all the passion accounts, a fact known to Christian scribes but not to Paul. The problem is not just the ununderstandable "table," but also the harshness of "bow down their backs forever" just before v. 11. Thus even if it were written by Paul, which I seriously doubt, he immediately corrects it.

[40]Cf. Mussner, "Ganz Israel," 242.

I come now to the mystery proper, found I believe not in the recapitulation but in the new statement only hinted at earlier: "and thus all
Israel will be saved, as it is written: There will come from Zion the Redeemer; he will turn impieties from Jacob; and this is my covenant with
them, when I take away their sins" (Isa. 59:20–21a; 27:9).[41] This means
to understand the disputed *kai houtōs* with the following,[42] for the mystery is contained in the Scripture cited.[43] Stendahl has recently advanced
the idea that the Redeemer is God as in Isa. 59:20 rather than the returning Christ as in 1 Thess. 1:10,[44] and in terms of the discussion up to now
he is surely right.[45] The key word is "covenant," a concept that applies
only to Israel for Paul,[46] and the covenant is, of course, the Sinai covenant,[47] according to which God in his covenant loyalty forgives Israel's
sins. The reason for Paul's change of "to Zion" (MT) or "on account of Zion"
(LXX) to "from Zion" is not clear. It probably would be too subtle to refer
back to the stone "in Zion" which God is about to remove by the entry
of the Gentiles, and for Paul, writing before 70 C.E., God now dwells *in*
Zion. It is more likely that the concept of the eschatological pilgrimage
of the Gentiles "coming in" (v. 25) has influenced the wording here, perhaps even specifically by the "from Zion" of Isa. 2:3.[48] The general contours of Paul's mystery are I think clear. They and the rest of the whole
discussion in Romans 9–11 are summed up in the conclusion.

Like most of what precedes, the summary deals with two global entities, Israel and Gentiles, seen from the perspective of God's purposes and
not their own responses.[49] As Stendahl has emphasized, Paul is dealing
in these chapters not with theological anthropology but with Jews and
Gentiles. "With respect to the gospel, to be sure, they are hostile for your
sake, but with respect to the election they are beloved for the sake of the

---

[41]Michel, *Der Brief an die Römer*, 249, has misled later interpreters by speaking of a
three-line prophetic oracle in vv. 25b–26a; so Müller, *Prophetie und Predigt*, 225–32; and
Aune, *Prophecy in Early Christianity*, 280–81.

[42]As does P. Stuhlmacher, "Römer 11:25–32," 555–70. Jeremias, "Römer 11,25–36," 193–
205, objects that *kathōs gegraptai* is otherwise not preceded by a *houtōs* in Paul. But then
this texts is prophetically understood to contain a mystery, and here as otherwise (1 Thess.
4:15 before 16–17) Paul gives his own paraphrase before citing the text.

[43]And not in the so-called threefold oracle, of which lines 1 and 2 are recapitulation and
line 3 is a commonplace of all "Palestinian Judaism."

[44]Stendahl, *Paul among Jews and Gentiles.*

[45]There is a good discussion in Davies, "Paul and Israel," 4–39, who finally cannot come
to a decision. Note also Scroggs, "Paul as Rhetorician," 276, "One of the striking features
throughout chapters 1–4, 9–11 (and in distinction from chapters 5–8) is the sparseness of explicit Christian language and content. It is God who is emphasized in these chapters, one
might even say 'the Jewish God,' while the figure of Christ remains in the background."

[46]Richardson, *Israel*, 128–29, notes that Paul does not go on to cite Isa. 59:21b, which
might misleadingly be understood to refer to Christians.

[47]There is no reference to Jer. 31:33 here or elsewhere in Paul; see Wolff, *Jeremia*, 134–
42. NEB is completely wrong to insert "I will grant," as pointed out by Davies, "Paul and Israel."

[48]So Hübner, *Gottes Ich und Israel*, 115–16.

[49]For the neat rhetorical balance, see Richardson, *Israel*, 127–28, from whom I have to
depart somewhat.

fathers" (11:28). Israel, all Israel in the context of these statements, is hostile[50] to the gospel, Paul's gospel to the Gentiles, and at the same time beloved as the elect Israel. Both of these statements are important for the Roman Christians to ponder. Without the first, the gospel would not have been preached to them, and without the second, their own election (8:28–39) would be doubtful. "For irrevocable are the gracious gifts and calling of God" (11:29). Here is a clear restatement of what was said concerning Israel's "advantages" and election in chapter 9 and support for 11:28b. Verses 30–31 comprise a beautiful chiastic construction, which conceals the fact that the two halves do not really balance. It goes without saying that not only the mercy but also the disobedience are seen from the perspective of their source in God.[51] "For as you were once disobedient to God but now have received mercy because of their disobedience, so they also now have become disobedient with respect to the mercy [shown] to you, in order that they too may now receive mercy" (30–31). For the disobedience of Gentiles and the mercy shown to them I could refer back to Romans 1–3, but the relationship between Gentile mercy and Israelite disobedience, referred to also in 11:11, is not at all clear and must be reserved for a further discussion below. The dative in verse 31 is different from that in verse 30 and must mean something like "with respect to," which shows the real disproportion in the two statements. Differing from that of the Gentiles, Israel's disobedience is only partial, it is caused by God, and it has two good outcomes, both in order that the Gentiles might receive mercy *and* in order that Israel too may now receive mercy. It is doubtful whether Paul noted this discrepancy, as the evenhanded conclusion in verse 33 shows. The final doxology is not a cry of despair that only God and not Paul can understand such things, but on the contrary a prayer of deep thanksgiving that Paul *has* been given understanding and that his prayers of intercession in 9:1–3 and 10:1 have been answered. I return now to material skipped over before.

It has been important for Paul throughout Romans 9–11 to make the point to his Roman readers that God has chosen Israel by grace alone and will save Israel by grace alone. The Roman Christians must understand themselves as being in no worse but also in no better a position than that. Beginning in Rom. 11:1, he speaks *to* Gentiles *about* Jews. There is then a significant shift in 11:13–24, where Paul turns to the Gentiles with explicitly paraenetic intentions. This new address begins with a personal note and rather than biblical material as in the surrounding sections it uses an analogy, a mode of rhetoric not the most successful in Paul's hands.[52] The

---

[50]*Echthros* in the NT is always active and never passive (hated, i.e., by God). That breaks a certain parallelism in the two halves of the verse, but so do the two different senses of *dia* ("for your benefit" and "because of"); see Jeremias, "Römer 11,25–26," 202.

[51]Sanders, *Law*, 196, reads into these verses what is not there when he says that "It is God's intent to have mercy on all, but mercy has faith as its condition."

[52]Cf., e.g., Rom 7:1–6. In general see Gale, *Analogy*.

paraenetic point is especially clear: "do not boast over the branches" (17); "it is not you who support the root but the root [supports] you" (18); "do not think haughty thoughts but fear [God]" (20); "consider then the goodness and severity of God" (22a); "you too might be cut off" (22b); "if you have been cut off from [your] native wild olive tree and against all nature grafted onto the cultivated olive tree" (24); and finally in the solemn transition to the next paragraph "I do not want you to be ignorant, brothers, of this mystery, lest you be wise for yourselves [in your own eyes]" (25). W. D. Davies has made the very interesting suggestion that the image of the olive tree was chosen because for Greek Gentiles "the olive tree could serve as a symbol as powerful as was the vine among the Jews." The Roman Christians are then provocatively told that they are only wild olive trees, that they "had nothing to contribute. To be fruitful they had to be grafted on to the cultivated olive tree which had [not Athena but] Abraham, the father of Israel, as its root."[53] In retrospect it is even possible to wonder if the jealousy motif was chosen not so much because of Israel but because it makes Gentiles recognize that without Christ they are "not a nation" and "a foolish nation" (10:19). It seems that the statement "branches were broken off so that I might be grafted in" is not only hypothetical. Roman Christians were boasting triumphantly that God preferred them to Jews, and Paul's explicit rebukes here are consonant with the implicit ones throughout Romans 9–11. All this is clear enough, but the problems come with the details.

"Now I speak to you, the Gentiles. Inasmuch as I am Apostle to the Gentiles, I glorify my ministry in the hope that I may make my flesh jealous and I will save some of them" (11:13–14). Already there is a subtle rebuke. Important as Paul's commissioning is to him otherwise (15:16), here it is only a means to an end. Gentile Christians, far from feeling superior, should understand that what is happening with them is in the service of the salvation of Israel. That here Paul makes Israel jealous can probably be understood as his participation in God's act of doing so (10:19), but it is not at all clear why he thereby saves "some." Is it really only "diplomatic caution which does not yet lay the cards on the table,"[54] whereby Paul really expects that God will save all when he brings the collection? Or is the expression merely a careless one because Paul's attention is now directed toward the Gentiles? This is not the only problematic statement in this section.

Verse 15 is in many ways a restatement of verse 12. Israel, or more precisely the vast majority, the "rest," have rejected Paul's gospel, or better the missionary task (presumably that is what is meant and not the rejection of Israel by God),[55] and that opens the way for the reconciliation

---

[53]Davies, "Romans 11:13–24," 140, 141.
[54]Käsemann, *Romans*, 306.
[55]Cf. 11:1–2; Fitzmyer, "Romans," 324; and Thyen, "Das Heil," 175, who interpret both as subjective genitives.

of the world (cf. 2 Cor. 5:18f.). Because Israel did not accept the task of being "the light for the Gentiles" that has opened the way for Christ to be that light. Their acceptance (of the task? of the fear of the Lord?[56] their acknowledgment of the truth of the reconciliation?) means then the consummation of all things, life from the dead. It is again rather vague, but suggestive of promise, and it makes the Gentiles understand themselves in relation to Israel.

Are the two metaphors in verse 16 to be understood in the same way, so that both first fruit and root refer back to the remnant (11:5) or forward to the patriarchs (11:28)? While that would be the most natural way of interpreting them, there are good reasons for dividing them.[57] "If the first fruit is holy, so also the lump." Because the Jewish-Christian missionaries to the Gentiles, like the seven thousand in Elijah's time, have been faithful to God's calling, therefore all Israel is holy and will be spared. "If the root is holy, so also the branches." Because of election, or in the Jewish way of putting it, on account of the fathers (*bzkwt 'bwt*), all Israel is beloved and will be spared. Both metaphors encourage the Roman Christians to look on Israel as holy.

The second metaphor is then expanded into the confused and confusing figure of the olive tree. It does not seem possible to sustain the idea of missionaries, so that the branches broken off might represent people like the false "super apostles" in Corinth. Indeed, it does not seem possible to read the figure allegorically in any consistent way. The branches broken off, for example, are not burned or the like but continue to live; and what about the tree trunk? Paul's entire interest is with the branches grafted in, who must be warned that they are only wild olive branches, that the root supports them, and that they must not boast over the branches broken off. Paul's concern is not at all with the broken-off branches as such, and the statement that "God is able to graft them in again" (23) is not a prediction about Jews as much as it is a warning to Gentiles, comparable to John the Baptist's statement that "God is able from these stones to raise up children to Abraham."[58] Even the more explicit "how much more shall those who naturally [belong to it] be grafted onto their own olive tree" (24) functions primarily to underline the unnatural and miraculous grafting of the wild olive branches. Paul also shows no interest at all in the cultivated branches not broken off;[59] it is not Jewish Christians but Roman Gentile Christians and their relationship to Israel which are his concern. It is only because the Roman Christians stand by faith and not by

---

[56]Cf. Sir. 10:21 for a comparable use of this word pair: "The fear of the Lord is the beginning of acceptance; obduracy and pride are the beginning of rejection."

[57]Cf. Leenhardt, *Romans*, 161–62; Dahl, "Future," 151; Fitzmyer, "Romans," 323; Johnson, "Romans 11," 98f.

[58]That statement is, of course, a warning to Israel and not a prediction of the Gentile mission.

[59]Cf. the lack of antecedent for "among them" in v. 17.

boasting that the branches are said to be broken off "by unbelief" (20, 23). It is only because of the injunction to remain in God's goodness that being cut off becomes a threat of punishment (22) or of being "not spared" (21). The olive tree, and particularly the branches broken off, is then not to be interpreted allegorically, and it is the paraenetic nature of this direct address which makes this section 11:13–24 (+25a) inconsistent with the rest of the chapter.[60]

C. Plag has noticed tensions in Romans 11, tensions so great that he felt forced to treat 11:25–27 as an interpolation taken from another letter from Paul.[61] While one can agree with him concerning the tension, I believe that he has isolated the wrong section and that it is verses 13 to 24 which are most out of line.[62] Not that I think it an interpolation nor that I think all the difficulties are confined to that section. Part of the problem with Romans 11 is that Paul gives too many answers to his own questions. I will review the chapter one more time, now from the perspective of what it says about Israel and to Gentiles.

Taking up the question of 9:6, whether "the word of God has lapsed," Paul asks, "Has God repudiated his people" (11:1) and responds very firmly: No, because "all Israel will be saved" (11:26). This is quite clear and surely the most important thing Paul wants to say on the subject. It is only when he goes on to ask the secondary question "Why?" that there are a number of answers, any one of which would suffice, but which are not completely consistent in their plurality.

Why will all Israel be saved? The first answer is that God is faithful to his covenant and forgives (26). Or, to say the same thing in slightly different words, "irrevocable are the gracious gifts and calling of God" (29; cf. 9:6). Another way to put the very same thing is to say that Israel is "beloved for the sake of the fathers" (28).[63] All of these variants were known to Paul from the biblical tradition, and they would continue in the later Jewish tradition, to support what E. P. Sanders calls the very centre of the Rabbinic "pattern of religion," *Sanh.* 10:1, "All Israel has a part in the age to come."[64]

Why will all Israel be saved? The second answer is that "there will come from Zion the Redeemer." I believe this to be only a variant of the first answer, but it deserves special treatment because most interpreters have seen here a reference to the parousia of Christ. It could be asked whether Paul could ever think of God apart from Christ,[65] but this ques-

---

[60]Thus Luz, *Geschichtsverständnis*, 34, speaks of a "paränetischen Exkurs." See also Zeller, *Juden und Heiden*, 217; Williams, S. K., "Righteousness of God," 252; Mussner, "Ganz Israel," 252; Hübner, *Gottes Ich und Israel*, 108–9.

[61]Plag, *Israels Wege zum Heil.*

[62]Also Mayer, *Prädestination*, 275, argues against Plag that the paraenetic section, which might imply Israel's conversion, is not characteristic of Romans 11.

[63]Marmorstein, *Doctrine of Merits*, and Sanders, *Paul.*

[64]See Sanders, "Patterns," 455–78.

[65]Sanders, *Law*, 194.

tion can be answered if at all only in connection with an exegesis of 1 Cor. 15:28. It may be that Christ was in Paul's mind, but even so it would be completely wrong to speak of an end-time conversion.[66] If Christ is meant, then it is Christ in a different role, Christ as the agent of the "Sonderweg"[67] of Israel's salvation. Some Jews have thought that eschatologically Gentiles would be absorbed into Israel, and most Christians have thought that eschatologically Jews would be absorbed into the church, but Paul's conviction is God's righteousness for salvation for both, without changing one into the other.

Why will all Israel be saved? Because a remnant of Jews, Paul and his Jewish co-workers, responded to the missionary task, therefore God will act graciously toward all Israel. That is how the concept of the representative righteous has functioned from Genesis 18 down to the later Jewish concept of the *Lamedvovniks* (thirty-six righteous).[68] This third answer, with which the chapter begins, is not mentioned again after verse 16a at the latest. While it is consonant with the first answer, it is not really the same, and so it is quietly dropped to be subsumed under the first.

Why will all Israel be saved? Because God will make them jealous of the salvation that has come to Gentiles. It is not said that God will provoke them to faith in Christ, although this is usually assumed without discussion. Paul certainly does not share Luke's concept of the jealousy of Jews (Acts 5:17; 13:45; 17:5), although it shows that "conversion" is not the most natural way to think about it. It has happened again and again in genuine Jewish-Christian dialogue that a nominal Jew became jealous of a faithful Christian and so became a more faithful Jew[69] or that a nominal Christian became jealous of a faithful Jew and so became a more faithful Christian. While Paul does not have individuals as such in mind, surely a good way to understand the jealousy motif (as in Deut. 32:21) is that Israel would become more faithful to Torah. Of course, for Paul that means also acknowledging the goal of Torah, the expression of the righteousness of God for Gentiles, but it does not mean abandoning the Torah by making themselves Gentiles. That Paul himself hopes to make some Jews jealous (11:14) need not mean anything very different, if we understand it in terms of the collection and the eschaton.[70] Here is then a fourth answer.

Why will all Israel be saved? *Not* by individual Jews converting to faith in Christ. The one place where this was happening in Paul's time, in the

---

[66]Among those who insist strongly on this point are Davies, "Paul and Israel"; Mussner, "Ganz Israel"; Klappert, "Traktat," 58–137. See also Luz, *Geschichtsverständnis*, 294; Mayer, *Prädestination*, 289f.; and Wilckens, *Römer*, 252.

[67]The phrase is usually associated with Mussner, who, however, now seems to want to partially retract it: "Gesetz," 200–220. Better would be perhaps the "Partizipationsmodell" proposed by Klappert, *Israel und die Kirche*.

[68]On this see b. *Sanh.* 97b and Scholem, *Messianic Idea*, 251–56.

[69]One classic example is the relationship between F. Rosenzweig and Rosenstock–Huessy.

[70]Cf. Munck, *Paul and the Salvation of Mankind.* Aus, "Paul's Travel Plans," 232–62.

preaching of the gospel to the circumcised by the Jerusalem church, is completely ignored in this chapter. This observation is, I believe, fatal to any attempt to understand Paul as blaming Jews for refusing to believe in Christ and hoping for Jews that they will come to such a belief in the future. Nowhere in these chapters does Paul refer to Jewish Christians as such.[71] When a distinction is made within Israel, it is between those few like Paul engaged in the Gentile mission and the "rest" who do not acknowledge it. Usually, however, he speaks about Israel as a whole in an undifferentiated manner. All Israel stumbled on the stone and all Israel will be saved.

Why will the fullness of the Gentiles come in? Here there are two answers, whose relationship one to the other is not at all clear. One answer is that it is by the preaching of Paul and his associates (10:14–18), by the activity of "the remnant according to the election of grace" (11:5). One could apply here Eckardt's concept of the "bridge generation," which he defines as a "vocational remnant of Jews serving as instruments for the salvation of the world within a relatively faithful Israel."[72] It is for this reason that Gentile Christians owe a debt of love, not just to the Jerusalem "saints" but to all Israel: "for if the Gentiles have shared in their spiritual things, they are obliged to serve them in material things" (15:27). Here is the Pauline version of "salvation is from the Jews" (John 4:22), and it seems to be his normal way of thinking about the matter.

Why will the fullness of the Gentiles come in? The second answer is found only in Romans 9–11 and is harder to understand. It is because Israel has stumbled on the stone, not to fall, but nevertheless stumbled, that salvation will come to the Gentiles (9:30–33; 11:11–12, 15). It appears that to make this point Paul needs to say "all Israel," without differentiation. This line of thought makes no use of the idea of the remnant and certainly not of "Jewish Christianity." Here again Gentile salvation is from the Jews, but now not just a few Jews but all Jews, who as a whole have stumbled. Why this is so is not at all clear, but also from this perspective Gentile Christians owe a debt of love to all Israel. It would be a mistake to read into Paul the Lukan concept that Gentile mission presupposes the failure of Jewish mission. It would be an even greater mistake to suppose that the Lukan portrait represents Paul's actual practice. From his own account, Paul never tried to convert Jews, and apostolate to the Gentiles was never for him a second best. It must also be emphasized that Paul does not speak of stumbling in order to attach any blame to Israel at all. The emphasis is always on God, who blinds and trips Israel in order to save Gentiles. The starting point is, of course, the rock placed in Zion with its double function: stumbling for Israel, inclusion for Gentiles, but why did Paul choose Isa. 8:14 as a starting point? Why did Paul think God had to

---

[71]The term is used for convenience' sake, with full knowledge that it is an anachronism.
[72]Eckardt, *Elder and Younger Brothers*, 138.

trip Israel in order to make manifest his new act of righteousness for Gentiles? Since Paul does not give an answer one can only speculate. Perhaps it goes back to the parallel apostolates described in Gal. 2:7–8 and Paul's reflection that if Peter succeeded then Paul would be unnecessary.[73] If Peter was right then in the normal pattern of centripetal mission of the eschatology not only of the prophets but also of Jesus, the Gentiles would join Israel in the end times. Paul, on the other hand, wanted a Gentile church now as an equal co-partner alongside Israel. That would account for the silence of these chapters on the Jerusalem church and Jewish Christianity as such. Of course, if something like this is what Paul thought, the "blindness" was necessary only for a generation or so until the Gentile church became established. But he does not reflect on this.

What do Gentiles need to learn from what Paul says about Israel? First of all, that God is faithful to his promises to Israel, that the word of God has not lapsed, that all Israel will be saved, and that all this has to do not with human doing or believing but with the grace and mercy of God.[74] They should know this because they have been called into the people of God on exactly the same basis. That is what Paul has to say *about* Israel (and Gentiles). What he has to say *to* Gentiles is related to this but expressed in the quite different mode of paraenesis (11:13–25a). There Gentiles are told that they ought not to think that they have supplanted Jews in God's favour or that the election of Israel, on which their own depends, has in any way been abrogated. That is an important consequence to be drawn from what is said overall in these chapters, but there is a difference between speaking of Israel in God's eyes and speaking of Israel in Gentile eyes, between mystery and exhortation. Failure to recognize this difference and failure to recognize the different mode of address in the olive tree digression has led, I believe, to a distorted understanding of the main point of what Paul was endeavouring to express in Romans 9–11.

[73]The reverse is also true and is in fact what happened.
[74]Again, see especially Eichholz, *Theologie*; Davies, "Paul and Israel"; and Klappert, "Traktat."

22

THE FAITHFULNESS OF GOD AND THE PRIORITY OF ISRAEL IN PAUL'S LETTER TO THE ROMANS*

J. C. Beker

I have contended for some time that Paul is a hermeneutic theologian rather than a systematic theologian. Paul must be viewed primarily as an interpreter of the early Christian tradition and not as a builder of Christian doctrine. The texture of his hermeneutic calls for special attention. Paul is able to translate the abiding Word of the gospel in such a manner that it becomes word on target for his congregations. And so his hermeneutic is characterized by the reciprocal interaction between the constant of the gospel and the variables of historical circumstance. I call this interaction the dialectical relation between the coherence of the gospel and the contingency of the situations to which the gospel is addressed.

This dialectical hermeneutic applies as well to Paul's most systematic letter, the letter to the Romans. Although the tendency persists to view Romans as a dogmatics in outline, or as a version of a *compendium doctrinae Christianae* (Melanchthon), Romans is actually a profoundly occasional letter. And the challenge to the interpreter of Romans is to clarify—in this, Paul's most systematic letter—the peculiar interaction between coherence and contingency, that is, between universality and particularity.

I. The Occasion of Romans

A. This challenge pertains especially to the "Jewish question" in Romans 9–11. The relation between universality and particularity has frequently been distorted with respect to these chapters. Romans 1–8 was considered to be the systematic-universal core of Romans, whereas Romans 9–11 was relegated to a Pauline afterthought, too particular and awk-

*This essay originally appeared in a volume dedicated to Krister Stendahl. Two paragraphs acknowledging this were deleted.

ward to be awarded any theological weight. Rudolf Bultmann,[1] C. H. Dodd,[2] William Sanday and A. C. Headlam,[3] and Robin Scroggs[4] all essentially concur in their own way with F. W. Beare's judgment:

> We have left out of consideration three chapters (9–11) of this letter, chiefly because they do not form an integral part of the main argument. They are a kind of supplement in which Paul struggles with the problem of the failure of his own nation. We cannot feel that the apostle is at his best here, and we are inclined to ask if he has not got himself into inextricable (and needless) difficulties by attempting to salvage some remnant of racial privilege for the historic Israel—Israel "according to the flesh"—in spite of his own fundamental position that all men are in the same position before God.[5]

This statement contains two fundamental errors: (1) it disturbs the unique texture of Paul's hermeneutic by simply disjoining the coherent-universal elements of his thought from their contingent-occasional counterparts; and (2) it misconstrues the purpose and theological thrust of Paul's letter to the Romans.

B. Although the two issues are closely related, I will concentrate my remarks on the last one because it will also unmask the first mentioned error.

The occasion for Paul's letter to the Romans is a convergence of several factors, which explains its occasional, yet "systematic" form. There are at least four such factors:

(1) When Paul writes Romans, he finds himself in a new situation. Since the mission work in the East has been accomplished, he is eager to go to Spain and to be supported in this endeavor by Rome (Rom. 15:24).

(2) Paul's forthcoming visit to Jerusalem with the collection from the Gentile churches preoccupies him. Indeed, the collection visit occupies center stage in Romans 15, especially vv. 30–32. The Jerusalem visit focuses on the "Jewish question" because it expresses symbolically the eschatological unity of the church of "Jews" and "Gentiles" in the purpose of God as the fulfillment of Paul's apostolic mission.

(3) Paul had written Galatians just prior to Romans. Again the "Jewish question" had troubled him there in the form of the judaizing opposition. And it is likely that Paul had lost his case with the Galatian churches. Moreover, the repercussion of his letter to the Galatians could only have worsened his relations with Jerusalem, for in Galatians, Paul had created the impression that the place of the Jew in salvation history was a purely negative one and had in fact become obsolete with the coming of Christ. And so Romans attempts to discuss the "Jewish question" within the context of the special situation in Rome.

---

[1]Bultmann, *Theology of the New Testament*, 2.132.
[2]Dodd, *Romans*.
[3]Sanday–Headlam, *Romans*.
[4]Scroggs, "Paul as Rhetorician," 271–98.
[5]Beare, *St. Paul and His Letters*, 103–4.

(4) The situation in Rome—although quite unlike that in Galatia—necessitates as well a solution to the "Jewish question," for in Rome there is the threat of disunity caused by the tension between the weak and the strong, between a minority of Jewish-Christians and a majority of Gentile Christians (Rom. 14:15).

C. Romans then is directed to a particular church with particular problems by an apostle who is faced by particular historical challenges. However, the occasionality of the letter does not deprive it of universal importance. Indeed, the contingency of its motivation and address is radically interwoven with the coherent structure of Paul's gospel, that is, the continuity of the gospel with God's promises to his covenant people Israel. In other words, the "Jewish question" in Paul's former missionary territories, heightened both by his forthcoming visit to Jerusalem and by the threat of disunity in the church at Rome, compels him to reflect on the relationship of Judaism to Christianity, on its continuous and discontinuous dimensions.

II. The Theme of Romans

The theme of the letter (Rom. 1:16–17) revolves around four interrelated issues: (1) the gospel reveals the righteousness of God; (2) the righteousness of God is apprehended by faith; (3) the gospel is the "power of God for salvation to everyone who believes, to the Jew first and also to the Greek"; (4) the righteousness of faith in the gospel is the confirmation and fulfillment of the Old Testament promise of Hab. 2:4.

Tracing Paul's development of the theme, we notice that, notwithstanding preliminary climactic statements along the way (4:24–25; 5:9–11; 5:20–21; 8:38–39), the basic climax is reached prior to the paraenesis of Romans 12–15 in 11:32: "For God has consigned all people to disobedience, that he may have mercy upon all," followed by a hymnic conclusion in 11:33–36. The climax of the letter seems to suggest that the *pas* argument carries the day so that the universal pitch of the gospel ("to everyone") seems to drown out the emphasis on the particularity or the priority of the Jew in the thematic statement of Rom. 1:16.

However, the first impression is quite mistaken. Why? How is Paul able to maintain both the priority of Israel and the equality of Jew and Gentile in Christ on the basis of justification by faith alone (cf. Rom. 3:28–31)?

A. In the first place, it is important to recognize that although Paul uses the terminology of *anthrōpos* (3:28) and *pas/pantes* (11:32), he never loses sight of the fact that Jews and Gentiles are two distinct peoples who even in Christ cannot be fused into one general category of *homo universalis*. Just as Paul's notion of the body of Christ is characterized by "many members in one body" (Rom. 12:3), this same concept of unity amidst diversity applies to his discussion of Jew and Gentile. In other words, Paul's emphasis on equality of Jew and Greek in the body of Christ does not nullify the distinctiveness of both peoples. Therefore, there is no contradiction for Paul when he juxtaposes the universal equality of the believer and the particular priority of the Jew in Rom. 1:16. Just as Karl Barth and Ernst Käsemann are wrong in characterizing the Jew in Romans as the *homo religiosus* in general, so it is wrong to suppose that the emphasis on *pas* or *anthrōpos* blots out the ethnic specificity of two different peoples, Jews and Gentiles.

Paul intends to stress not uniformity, but unity in diversity. The pluralistic diversity of peoples in their ethnic and cultural variety is maintained, although in Christ this pluralism becomes nevertheless a unity.

B. It is essential for Paul to maintain the priority of the Jew in the gospel, not only for the sake of the Jew, but especially for the sake of the Christian. What is at stake is nothing less than the faithfulness of God. If it could be argued that God has rejected the people of the election, Israel, and that therefore God's promises to Israel have become null and void, how are the Gentiles to trust the confirmation of these promises to them through God's righteousness in Christ? Could it not be said in that case that there is arbitrariness on God's part (Rom. 9:14) and that God is not to be trusted—even the God who justifies us in Christ? In other words, the gospel cannot have any authentic validity or legitimation apart from the people of Israel because the theological issue of God's faithfulness (Rom. 3:3) and righteousness determines the truth of the gospel.

Moreover, such a rejection of Israel by God would simply cut the connection of the gospel to its foundation in the Hebrew Scriptures and degrade the God of Jesus Christ into the God of Marcion—a "new God" who has no relation either to creation or to Israel's salvation history.

Therefore, it is crucial for Paul to confirm the faithfulness of God as an inalienable dimension of the righteousness of God and to emphasize that the protological election of Israel in the Old Testament will be confirmed by the eschatological priority of Israel at the time of the parousia and the establishment of the triumph of God.

Paul's struggle with this issue comes to a climax in Rom. 11:26–32. If, as I have argued, Rom. 11:32 is the climax and crown of Paul's argument, its emphasis on the universal embrace of God's mercy ("that he may have mercy upon all") occurs in a context which affirms the particularity of Israel's eschatological priority (Rom. 11:25–26). Thus Rom. 11:26–32 confirms the thesis of the theme of Rom. 1:16–17 where both the equality of Jew and Gentile and the priority of Israel are accepted. In other words, the total sweep of the argument of Romans is held together by the theme of the peculiar interaction between Israel's particularity and the universality of the gospel for the Gentiles.

C. In the third place, as is well known, Paul uses the phrase *dikaiosynē theou* (righteousness of God), with the exception of 2 Cor. 5:21, only in

Romans and here in such a central way that it must be characterized as the key term for the letter as a whole (cf. Rom. 1:17; 3:5, 21, 22, 25, 26; 10:3). According to Käsemann, the "righteousness of God" has a consistent apocalyptic meaning. As God's eschatological salvation power, it claims the creation for God's lordship and sovereignty which the Christ-event has proleptically manifested. It denotes the victory of God and his cosmic act of redemption. As such, it not only acquits the sinner but also abolishes the power of sin by transferring us to the dominion of the lordship of Christ. Within the context of the theme of Romans the *dikaiosynē theou* must be understood in terms of its theocentric focus and in its overarching significance as connoting the full range of God's soteriological activity.

The theocentric focus of the phrase *dikaiosynē theou* points to the hermeneutical field in which it functions. The term gathers up in itself the rich connotations of Israel's covenant terminology: *hesed* (steadfast love), *emet* (truth), and *zedakah* (righteousness), especially in its eschatological dimensions as documented, for instance, in 2 Isaiah and the Psalms.

In other words, in Romans the *dikaiosynē theou* comprises a hermeneutical field in which it is correlated with terms like *pistis theou* (faithfulness of God, Rom. 3:3), *alētheia theou* (truth of God, Rom. 3:7; 15:8; cf. 3:4), and *eleos theou* (mercy of God, cf. Rom. 11:31–32; 15:9).

In this function the *dikaiosynē theou* must be understood both as God's faithfulness to himself and as his redemptive activity in accordance with his faithfulness.

Concretely speaking, the *dikaiosynē theou*—now manifested in Christ— points backward to God's promises to Israel and forward to God's full realization of his promises in the apocalyptic hour when Israel, along with the Gentiles and the whole created order, shall "live" in the *gloria dei*, when God will triumph over everything that resists his will—the moment in which the promise of "life" according to Hab. 2:4 (Rom. 1:17) will be fully realized and the *dikaiosynē theou* will be synonymous with the order of cosmic peace (*shālôm*), salvation (*sōtēria*), and life (*zōē*) that has been proleptically manifested in Christ.

D. As we have seen, the priority of Israel is the necessary consequence of God's character as being faithful to himself and as manifesting this faithfulness in his saving actions. This fundamental-coherent dimension of Paul's gospel has direct contingent relevance both for his audience in Rome and for his own immediate plans.

1. Paul is about to travel to Jerusalem to deliver the collection of his Gentile churches to the Jerusalem church. And as he reports, the Gentile churches "were pleased to do it, and indeed they are in debt to them (i.e., the saints in Jerusalem), for if the Gentiles have come to share in their spiritual blessings, they ought also to be of service to them in material blessings" (Rom. 15:27). In other words, the Roman church is asked to acknowledge the priority of the Jew in the gospel by the apostle to the Gentiles, Paul.

2. The situation in the Roman congregation demands an urgent solution (Rom. 14–15). "To a church that seems split between a Gentile majority and a Jewish minority, Paul argues for the unity of that community. Paul stresses the salvation-historical priority of the Jew while also arguing for the right of the Gentiles to belong to the people of God."[6] It is in this context that the prevalent theme of "boasting" in Romans must be heard. In Romans 11 Paul explicitly condemns the Gentile majority in Rome for its boasting which is directed at the Jewish minority (Rom. 11:17–18; cf. 11:25).

Earlier in the letter Paul had likewise castigated Jewish boasting which served as a fundamental reminder to Jewish Christians in Rome of what constitutes the true and the false claim to the priority of the Jew in the gospel (Rom. 2:17–23; 3:27; 4:2). Indeed, true boasting can only be an act of gratitude for God's gift of grace in Christ (Rom. 5:2, 3, 11).

The Christ-event makes clear the true nature of Israel's priority. It does not lie in Israel's "boasting," that is, in its empirical achievement of "covenant keeping" or in Israel's elitist awareness of its exclusive status before God, but solely in God's faithfulness to his promises, that is, in God's grace. But the Christ-event also makes clear that the Gentiles cannot boast to have supplanted Israel simply because they represent the majority in the Christian church.

3. In this context the Gentiles must hear that the Gentile church has no authenticity or identity unless it realizes that it "is grafted, contrary to nature, into a cultivated olive tree," that is, into Israel, "beloved for the sake of their forefathers" (Rom. 11:24–28). Therefore Paul is careful in Romans to argue the unity of two distinct peoples in the gospel. Contrary to Galatians 3, Romans 4 maintains the distinctiveness of Jew and Gentile as Abraham's seed (4:12–16). Moreover, Paul corrects in Romans 9–11 the argument of Galatians 3 (and even Romans 4?), where Israel seems simply absorbed into the church. Thus Paul argues in Romans against any conception of the church as the "true Israel." By so doing he protects not only the priority and separate identity of Israel in the gospel, but also the full range of his conception of the faithfulness of God.

[6]Myers, "Romans 5:1–11," 234.

23

THE THEME OF ROMANS

Peter Stuhlmacher

Paul worked laboriously, as he dictated the letter to the Romans to his amanuensis, Tertius; in Rom. 16:22 Tertius gives his own greetings to the Christians in Rome.[1] The work of dictation turned out to be especially difficult for the apostle, because he had to weigh painstakingly every word as well as the overall composition of his letter. As I have attempted to demonstrate elsewhere in more detail,[2] with this letter Paul wanted to prepare for his visit in Rome and to win the support of the Roman Christians for his mission plans of reaching as far as Spain (Rom. 15:14–24). But this was not easy, for he had discovered from friends and acquaintances like Aquila and Prisca (Rom. 16:3) that in Rome there was not only agreement with, but also criticism of the preaching and mission of the apostle. In all likelihood, this criticism derived from Jewish Christian sources and was the result of disputes which Paul had to fight out in Galatia, Philippi, and Corinth with the "counter-missionaries" who had appeared against him there. The voice of these critics had hurried on ahead of the apostle to Rome, and, in view of such opposition, the letter to the Romans represents the attempt to convince the Christians in Rome of the superior content and legitimacy of the Pauline gospel.

According to the model developed by Hans Lietzmann,[3] Peter Lampe, in his book concerning *Die stadtrömischen Christen in den ersten beiden Jahrhunderten*,[4] has analyzed sociologically the names of the friends and acquaintances of Paul listed in chapter 16. For the most part, the names

---

[1]The basic outline of this essay was delivered in October, 1983 by invitation of Fuller Theological Seminary in Pasadena (California, U.S.A.) as part of the Payton Lectures. I dedicate it to Eric Osborn with grateful memories of our long standing discussions over the years in Tübingen of Paul and theology. For the translation I thank my former assistant Dr. Scott Hafemann.

[2]Stuhlmacher, "Abfassungszweck," 180–93 (= ch. 15 in this vol.).

[3]Lietzmann, *Römer*, 125–27.

[4]Lampe, *Die stadtrömischen*.

represent women and men who have come to the city from other parts
of the Roman Empire. Moreover, the names betray in most cases that they
were not aristocratic and educated people, but instead simple folks: slaves,
freedmen, and small-time craftsmen. And if this is the case for the friends
and acquaintances of Paul, how much more would it be characteristic for
the Christians in Rome as a whole! Hence, as Paul dictated the letter to
the Romans, he stood before the twofold task of having to express himself
in writing as persuasively as possible in regard to his subject matter and
as understandably as possible to women and men whom we would designate today as "lower middle class" and (at the most) "middle class."

When we pose the question concerning the theme of the letter to the
Romans, we must therefore take these circumstances into consideration.
If there is one central theme in the letter at all, then it must be evident
for the reader on the basis of the text of the letter itself. Formulations of
the theme which only suggest themselves after a long period of reflection, or only after many years of having used the letter to the Romans
in the church have their justification, but they are not suitable for an historical determination of the letter's content. In the time of the Reformation and since then one has gladly considered Romans to be a compendium
of the doctrine of justification by faith. This appraisal is not to be considered simply false, and in any case it corresponds to the predominant,
dogmatic use of our letter in the sixteenth century and in Protestant
orthodoxy. But we must still ascertain whether this view of the theme of
Romans is also of use to us historically.

I

The letter to the Romans was read aloud in the various house-churches
of the city. If we follow this example there can hardly be any doubt concerning the theme of the letter: it is about the Pauline gospel; or even
more precisely: it is about the gospel of the divine righteousness in and
through Christ testified to by Paul.

Right at the beginning of the so-called "Epistolary Prescript" (=Rom.
1:1–7), which has been formulated with unusual care, the catch-word
"gospel" appears: "Paul, servant (slave) of Christ Jesus, called to be an
apostle, set apart for the gospel of God. . . . " Then, after this introductory
sentence, Paul goes on to explain in a series of subordinate and relative
clauses what the significance of the gospel and the ministry of Paul is:
God already announced the gospel in advance through his prophets in the
Holy Scriptures (of the Old Testament). The gospel is about Jesus Christ,
the Son of God. He was born as a member of the tribe of David (in accordance with the messianic promises) and, by virtue of his resurrection,
was installed in power to the authority and dignity of the messianic Son
of God. It was this glorified Christ who called Paul to be the apostle to

the Gentiles, and it is in this character as one called to be an apostle that
Paul now greets the Christians in Rome with the Christian salutation of
peace.

After the prescript there follows in Rom. 1:8–17 a *prooemium* or
"epistolary introduction," which once again is very carefully formulated.
Paul assures the Roman Christians of his prayers of thanksgiving and intercession. He praises their standing in the faith and declares how much he
has desired for a long time to visit Rome. If his visit should one day come
to pass, Paul would like to strengthen the Romans in their faith and experience from them the encouragement that comes through the mutual
exchange of faith. The *prooemium* closes with two sentences that refer
back to the prescript and at the same time introduce a new and, in scholarship, highly controversial catch-word, namely, the righteousness of God.
The concluding sentences read: "For I am not ashamed of the gospel for
it is the power of God for salvation to every one who believes, to the Jew
first and also to the Greek. For in it the righteousness of God is revealed
from faith to faith; as it is written, 'But the righteous shall live by faith' "
(Hab. 2:4). The gospel, which God caused to be announced through the
prophets and which concerns the sending and exaltation of the messianic
Son of God, Jesus Christ (1:3f.), is now characterized by Paul as the power
of God, since in it the righteousness of God is being revealed, which in
turn procures life for those who believe from among both Jews and Gentiles. The two definitions of the gospel from the letter's prescript and the
closing of the *prooemium* thus supplement and interpret one another: the
gospel is the saving power of God, because it contains the declaration of
Jesus Christ as the revelation and realization of the righteousness of God,
which bestows life on those who believe.

*If there is an overall theme in the letter to the Romans, then according
to Romans 1:1–17 this theme must be the gospel carried by Paul, i.e., the
gospel of the divine righteousness in and through Christ, by virtue of which
those who believe from among the Jews and Gentiles (according to the
promise from Hab. 2:4) obtain life.* Moreover, the concordance demonstrates
that in speaking of the gospel we are, in fact, dealing with the formulation
of a theme. For the two catch-words "gospel" (or "my gospel") and the
"righteousness of God," together with the related verbs "to preach the gospel" and "to justify," traverse the entire letter to the Romans.[5] Finally, in
Rom. 3:21–31 Paul returns to his densely formulated statements from the
introduction of the letter and explains to his readers more exactly what
is the significance of the divine righteousness, as manifested in the sending of Christ, and how those who believe obtain eternal life by virtue of
this righteousness.

[5]Cf. for "gospel" and "to preach the gospel," Rom. 2:16; 10:15f.; 11:28; 15:16–20; 16:25.
For "the righteousness of God," "righteousness," and "to justify," Rom. 2:13; 3:4f.; 3:21–31;
4:1–25; 5:1–21; 6:1–23; 8:10, 30, 33; 9:30–10:10; 14:17.

But what does the pointed formulation: "I am not ashamed of the gospel" actually mean? Otto Michel[6] and Charles Kingsley Barrett[7] call attention in their commentaries on Rom. 1:16 to the fact that this expression "I am not ashamed" belongs to the language of the early Christian confession. It corresponds to "I acknowledge (the gospel)," a declaration to be uttered in a difficult situation (cf. Mark 8:38 par. and 2 Tim. 1:8). Walter Schmithals[8] is right in thinking that this confessional language points to an historically concrete situation. In the light of our overall view of Romans as dialogical in nature, we do not need to ponder long what situation Paul has in mind. It is the situation in Rome itself, where certain people are attacking Paul and his gospel and are seeking to pervert the authentic doctrine of faith already believed in Rome (cf. Rom. 3:8 and 16:17ff.). The short remark "I am not ashamed of the gospel" thus signals Paul's intention, in spite of all the criticism which is being levelled against him, to remain true in Rome as well to the gospel entrusted to him by Christ. Indeed, Paul is ready to explain his controversial gospel in detail and to take up in an argumentative manner the critical questions most often brought into the field of battle against him. But he is not prepared to alter the gospel of the divine righteousness in Christ, nor to place it entirely at their disposal. Were he to do so, he would be renouncing Christ and his apostolic mandate (cf. Gal. 1:6ff.; 1 Cor. 9:16).

II

Before we go further, we must take into account two warnings. The first comes from Krister Stendahl. In his well-known article, "The Apostle Paul and the Introspective Conscience of the West,"[9] Stendahl warned us against reading, without further reflection, Luther's famous search for the gracious God into the historical Paul and his statements about justification and the law. Moreover, in the epilogue to his book, *Paul among Jews and Gentiles*, Stendahl resists the attempt to understand the view of justification represented in Romans fundamentally in an abstract and dogmatic manner (for example, with E. Käsemann) as "a fighting doctrine, directed against Judaism" (German: as an *"antijudaistische Kampfeslehre"*). In Stendahl's words, "Its place and function, especially in Romans, are not primarily polemic but apologetic, as he defends the rights of Gentile converts to be full members of the people of God."[10] Thus, according to Sten-

[6]Michel, *Römer*, 86.
[7]Barrett, *Romans*, 27.
[8]Schmithals, *Der Römerbrief als historisches Problem*, 91–93.
[9]The essay, which first appeared in 1963 in *HTR*, has been reprinted in Stendahl, *Paul Among Jews and Gentiles*, 78–96. At the end of this volume Stendahl responds to Ernst Käsemann's objections against his essay which Käsemann presented in his *Perspectives*, 60–78. For a debate with Stendahl, cf. also Espy, "Paul's Conscience," 161–88.
[10]Stendahl, *Paul Among Jews and Gentiles*, 130.

dahl, Paul's so-called doctrine of justification has its place only where the apostle defends "the rights of the Gentiles to participate in God's promises."[11] The Pauline doctrine of justification, according to Stendahl, may in no way be perverted into a "triumphalist doctrine," which then justifies a religious imperialism of Christendom over against "the Jew or the Jews."[12] In view of Stendahl's warning and critique, we must ask ourselves whether we are on the right path.

I dare to say, yes. According to our understanding of the purpose for which it was written, the letter to the Romans as a whole is precisely not a fundamental abstract *"dialogus cum Judaeis"* (J. Jeremias), but rather an apologetic, comprehensive description of the Pauline gospel in the face of Jewish-Christian objections to the preaching of Paul. In my opinion, Stendahl has understood correctly the apologetic motive in Paul's presentation in Romans. The warning against a Christian imperialism over against "the Jews" based on the doctrine of justification is also warranted. But this warning cannot be a ground for diminishing the fundamental meaning of the Pauline gospel of justification! Even with the apologetic accentuation of the writing, the theme of the letter to the Romans remains the gospel of the divine righteousness in Christ for those who believe from among the Jews and Gentiles. According to Paul, this gospel is not simply a message which proclaims the acceptance by God of the Gentiles as well, without having to be circumcised. Instead, the gospel is the only saving revelation of the end-times salvation "for everyone who believes." Indeed, according to Rom. 1:16, it even holds true that the gospel of the divine righteousness in Christ is addressed "first to the Jews," since God chose Israel and promised his people deliverance through the Messiah. The gospel turns "also to the Greek (Gentiles)" because God desires, in a wonderful way, to allow the Gentiles also to take part in the deliverance promised to Israel. From Paul's perspective, therefore, there is only one way of salvation and only one single gospel. The heart of this one gospel is the divine righteousness in and through Christ available for everyone who believes. Not only in Galatians (Gal. 1:8f.), but also in Second Corinthians (2 Cor. 11:3f.), Paul rejects, without compromise, those who preach another gospel. He himself or others have no right to alter God's own revelation according to human discretion. This inability to compromise is also the basis for his statement, "I am not ashamed of the gospel" in Rom. 1:16. Stendahl's warning should not hinder us, therefore, from expounding the fundamental meaning of the gospel of justification which Paul stands up for in Romans. What this means theologically will become evident.

Now to the second warning. We have already indicated earlier that in the letter to the Romans Paul is writing to Christians without an advanced education and that he is attempting to make himself understand-

---

[11]Ibid., 131.
[12]Ibid., 132.

able to them. Hence, before we penetrate even deeper into the theological discussion, we must ask ourselves whether our determination of the theme of the letter to the Romans is really appropriate in view of the intellectual background of the Roman Christians, or have we already read too much of the (Western European) theological tradition of interpretation into this theme?

Again I dare to answer that our delineation of the theme is historically correct. For although to this day we still find Paul's conceptual language and mode of argumentation just as difficult as 2 Peter did (cf. 2 Pet. 3:16), we ought not to forget one important thing. The majority of Paul's technical expressions, which today we must first painstakingly work out for ourselves, were already familiar to the (Gentile) Christians of the first century from their worship services, since they, for the most part, came from the synagogue. The Holy Scriptures of the Old Testament were read aloud in the worship services, and the essential texts were memorized in the Christian schools. The identity of the prophets of God was known from the Scripture. That the Messiah would come from the seed of David was familiar from 2 Sam. 7:14 and Isa. 11:1ff. The word "gospel" was the technical term for the missionary message of the Christian teachers and missionaries (who had already come to Rome before Paul). Even the expression "the righteousness of God," which is so difficult for us to understand, need not have been unknown to those whom Paul addressed. Again and again in the Psalms, in (Deutero-) Isaiah, and in Israelite prayers of repentance God's salvific righteousness is mentioned, and the concept of the "righteousness of God" is also used in the Gospels (cf. Matt. 6:33) and in James (cf. Jas. 1:20). This famous concept was in no way unintelligible. The question was only how Paul wanted to nuance it. But this could only be determined for his readers from the further reading of the letter itself. It is to the letter then that we must now return.

III

The way in which the gospel from Rom. 1:11ff. fits together with 1:16f., i.e., the gospel of Christ with the revelation of the righteousness of God, can be seen in a formulation used by the apostle in 1 Corinthians. There in 1 Cor. 1:30 he writes, "(by God's doing) you are in Christ Jesus, who became to us wisdom from God, i.e., righteousness as well as sanctification and redemption." First Corinthians 1:30 allows the sending of Christ (in accordance with Rom. 1:3f.) and the revelation of the divine righteousness (in accordance with Rom. 1:16f.) to be brought together conceptually in the sense Paul intended in the way we have already indicated. God's salvific will for Jews and Gentiles becomes a reality in the sending, sacrifice, and exaltation of Christ in such a way that those who believe find all the righteousness, sanctification, and redemption necessary to live before God realized and embodied in Christ.

Evidently, however, Paul himself detected the need to interpret further his compact formulations in Rom. 1:1ff., 16f. Thus, in Rom. 3:21f. he returns to his thematic introductory statements and presents to his readers in detail how these concepts relate to the righteousness of God. This famous text only becomes understandable, however, if we proceed with Paul and his readers from the Old Testament and Jewish perspective that there can be fellowship with God in this life (and in the world to come) only for the righteous, i.e., the saints. On the other hand, according to the biblical understanding, the godless live separated from God and must fear the verdict of destruction in the coming judgment. The opposite is true for the repentant righteous. God accompanies them already in this life through every good fortune and misfortune that comes their way, and he also graciously remains faithful to them in the final judgment (e.g., see Ps. 51 for this entire concept). The question of how one shares in God's faithfulness and righteousness is thus the key to true life here on earth and in the world which belongs to God.

According to Rom. 3:21ff., the following is true concerning the divine righteousness which is revealed in the gospel: the righteousness of God is the gift of God for all those who believe, inaugurated by God as a result of his free grace and without the assistance of the law (v. 22). For since Adam's fall into sin and the expulsion of the first human couple out of paradise, the original glory and with it also the original righteousness of the sinless creation of God are lacking in all people, whether Jews or Gentiles (v. 23). No human sinner can bring himself back into the paradise of God's presence on the basis of his own strength or with the help of the Mosaic law (cf. Rom. 7:7ff.). He can only allow himself to be given the righteousness necessary for life through the justification for which God laid the foundation by means of the sacrifice of Jesus in (an atonement-) death. Because God effected an atonement for all sinners through Jesus Christ on the cross on Golgotha, he is able to bestow as a gift the result of this atonement in the form of the divine righteousness given to every sinner who believes in Jesus Christ as his redeemer and Lord. The divine righteousness which is granted to the sinner who believes is thus, according to Rom. 3:25f., the result and effect of the righteousness which God himself demonstrated in the surrender of his Son. Consequently it follows that God himself is just and at the same time justifies the one who lives on the basis of faith in Jesus (v. 26). Hence, Paul can signify (in a typically Jewish manner) both poles of the event of justification with the one concept "the righteousness of God": the gracious activity of God himself and the end result of the divine work in the form of the righteousness granted to the sinner.

Paul writes concerning this divine righteousness in Rom. 3:21 that it has been revealed "apart from the assistance of the law." What does that mean? In reality, the sending of Jesus and his sacrifice were not forced by the law, but are grounded in God's free grace. The gospel does not depend on a prior revelation and acknowledgement of the law. However, according to Rom. 3:21, the revelation of the righteousness of God is certainly witnessed to by the law and the prophets (i.e., by the Scripture) as a valid activity of God. As a matter of fact, we read already in the Septuagint version of Exod. 34:6f. that God is gracious, compassionate, long-suffering, and rich in grace and faithfulness and that he exercises his righteousness and his mercy on thousands, in that he forgives their debts, wickedness, and sin. In exactly the same way it then says in Isa. 43:25 and 45:7f. that God forgives sin on the basis of his free grace and causes righteousness to extend to his people. God fulfills and surpasses the instructions for the ritual from Leviticus 16 with the appointment of Jesus as the *hilastērion*. Thus, both the "law" (Exod. 34:6f. LXX; Lev. 16) and the prophets (Isa. 43:25; 45:7f.) speak with great clarity concerning the activity of God that is designated by Paul with the expression "the righteousness of God." Paul adopts this language in order to explain with its help the heart of the gospel entrusted to him. The apostle could choose this Old Testament mode of expression without having to fear misunderstandings because he knew that the women and men in Rome were familiar with the witness of the law, with the prophets, and with the language of the Psalms and the (Antiochian) tradition of the faith which was the foundation of his argumentation in 3:25f. (cf. Rom. 6:17; 7:1; 16:17).[13]

IV

Ever since Adolf Schlatter's major commentary appeared in 1935,[14] the "righteousness of God" has been gladly seen in German research to be the main theme of the letter to the Romans. The important commentaries of Ernst Käsemann,[15] Heinrich Schlier,[16] and Ulrich Wilckens[17] have followed Schlatter's example. Is this delineation of the theme just another example of a typical German propensity for systematizing, or has something correct been seen here?

The answer is entirely dependent upon how much breadth one gives to the expression "the righteousness of God," so important for Paul (and then for Luther and the reformers). If what is meant by this notion is merely the salvation of the individual sinner—or to put it in Luther's words, *"die*

[13]See my article, "Romans 3:24–26," 94–109.
[14]Schlatter, *Gottes Gerechtigkeit*.
[15]Käsemann, *Romans*.
[16]Schlier, *Der Römerbrief*.
[17]Wilckens, *Römer*.

Gerechtigkeit, die vor Gott gilt" (i.e., "the righteousness which is valid before God")—then the letter to the Romans actually extends beyond this individual perspective from perhaps as early as 5:12 (the contrast between Adam and Christ), but without a doubt from chapter 9 on. But if what is meant by the expression derived from the Old Testament, "the righteousness of God," is the entire redemptive activity of God in Christ from creation to redemption, then the theme "the righteousness of God" holds the letter to the Romans together, both from the standpoint of the history of salvation and christologically, while at the same time giving to the gospel of Jesus Christ a world-wide dimension. In my opinion, Rom. 3:21–31 shows convincingly that historically we ought not confine the biblical idea of "divine righteousness" in Paul to "the righteousness which is valid before God," but that we must allow the word the breadth which is inherent in it from the Old Testament: according to Paul, the one God acts in and through his one Son, Christ, on behalf of the entire world. Christ is his righteousness in person. The work of salvation begun by God in Christ will thus only be completed when the world must no longer sigh under death and transitoriness (Rom. 8:18ff.) and when God's chosen possession, Israel, will have experienced the redemption and fulfillment of the irrevocable promises of God concerning his people in the Parousia of Christ Jesus (cf. Rom. 11:25ff.). In this way the arc of tension is drawn tightly from Romans 1 through Romans 11.

But chapters 12–16 are also to be classified under the theme "the righteousness of God" for two reasons. First, and above all, because God in Christ does not just declare those who believe to be righteous on the basis of grace, but at the same time, in doing so, lays hold of them anew in obedience. The new life that the justified obtain is thus called, according to Rom. 6:15ff., a "slavery to righteousness" and finds its God-pleasing expression in the new way of life which the Christians lead. Second, chapters 12–16 belong inextricably to the letter to the Romans because the apostle nowhere (and certainly also not in Romans) expounds abstract theology, but always only concrete exhortation. Whether the Romans really believe in Christ as their redeemer and Lord will be evident, according to Paul, by how they (as Gentile and Jewish Christians) deal with one another and how they resolve the tensions among one another in Rome (cf. ch. 14). Whether the Christians are actually living from and in God's righteousness is demonstrated in the life of the community within and without. Romans 12–15 are thus the practical test case for the justification which Paul teaches.

When it concerns this test, Paul can speak in a manner as simple and as readily understandable for everyone as the Gospels do (cf. Luke 15:2 and the parables concerning the lost collected in Luke 15). In Rom. 15:7 he calls upon the Jewish and Gentile Christians who are simultaneously making life difficult for one another in Rome, "Accept one another, just as Christ also accepted you to the glory of God." The expression, "Christ has accepted you," which is readily understandable to everyone, encompasses the entire act of justification. On the other hand, the admonishment "accept one another" is a result of justification because, according to Paul, Christ is not only the Reconciler and Saviour, but also the example and Lord of the church. If the small groups and house churches really listened to the public reading of the letter to the Romans to the end, then even the simple people knew in Romans 15 where they stood in relationship to Paul's gospel, for the Pauline gospel confronts them with Jesus as the Christ of God in his sacrificial goodness and sovereign demand.

V

Thus, the letter to the Romans has as its theme the Pauline gospel of the divine righteousness in Christ or, for short, the righteousness of God (in and through Christ). Finally, the idea that this theme was not first forced upon Paul through the situation of discussion and struggle in Rome, but is the theme of his Christian life as an apostle as such, must still be explicitly dealt with, since this understanding of the focus of Paul's gospel has repeatedly been disputed in recent times. The fact, namely, that Paul does not speak about justification in 1 Thessalonians but only in Galatians, in 1 Corinthians 1–2, in Philippians 3, and then in Romans seems to suggest from the standpoint of the history of tradition that Paul first formulated his gospel of justification in the debate with the Judaizers in Galatia and the "Counter-missionaries" in Philippi, Corinth, and Rome.[18]

In order to gain some clarity in this regard, we must turn our attention briefly to the Pauline testimonies concerning his revelation on the Damascus road and then to his testimony in 2 Cor. 11:21ff. The pertinent statements with reference to the revelation on the road to Damascus are Gal. 1:13–16; 2 Cor. 4:4–6; and Phil. 3:4–11 (all of which, naturally, are formulated by Paul himself only in reflection on an event which already lies almost twenty years in the past). In Gal. 1:13ff. the apostle writes that it pleased God to reveal "his Son" to him, the persecutor of the church of Christ and the zealot for the ancestral-Pharisaic traditions of the law. Whether one should translate *en emoi* in v. 16 with "in" or "to" me is disputed. But the following evidence is clearly a result of the presentation in Galatians: as a persecutor of the church and a zealot for the law, Paul was surprised by the Damascus road revelation. Its essential content was the appearance of Jesus as the "Son of God." On the basis of Rom. 1:3; 1 Cor. 9:1, and Phil. 2:6–11, one can add to this that Paul beheld Christ as the divine Son exalted to the right hand of God (in accordance with Ps. 110:1) and installed in the dignity of the "Lord." It was precisely this

---

[18]See for example, Strecker, "Das Evangelium Jesu Christi," 183–338, 205, 208f.; Räisänen, *Paul and the Law*, 229–69.

sight which transformed the persecutor of the church and advocate of the law into the apostle and preacher of the gospel among the Gentiles. For Paul, therefore, the revelation of Christ on the road to Damascus brought about the turning away from his Pharisaic zeal for the law and his embracing of the revealed Christ. The knowledge implied by this revelation can be even more precisely determined from 2 Cor. 4:4ff., for 2 Cor. 4:1–6 is also written from the line of defence against Jewish Christian opponents of Paul's preaching and refers to the call of the apostle on the road to Damascus. Thus, under these circumstances, Gal. 1:13–16 and 2 Cor. 4:4–6 are comparable and interpret one another.

According to 2 Cor. 4:4, the gospel bestows *photismos*, i.e., knowledge which enlightens, to those who are willing and able to hear. It bestows this knowledge as the *euangelion tēs doxēs tou Christou, hos estin eikōn tou theou*. The gospel bestows the enlightening knowledge of the glory of Christ, who, like wisdom in the Old Testament and Jewish tradition, is the image of God being revealed and effective for the world. According to 2 Cor. 3:7–11, the glory of Christ and his ministry far outshines the glory of the Torah and its ministry. Second Corinthians 4:5f. then shows how Paul himself came to the knowledge of the gospel: God, the creator of light, enlightened Paul in his heart and did so through the shining of the knowledge of the glory of God on the face of the living Christ. Thus, on the road to Damascus Paul beheld and learned to see God's power and glory in the face of the crucified Son of God, whom God raised and exalted to his right hand. It was this knowledge of Christ which transformed him into the apostle to the Gentiles and a servant of Jesus Christ because, by virtue of this knowledge, he learned to abandon his activity as a persecutor and his zeal for the law.

The persecution was motivated, as 2 Cor. 5:16 demonstrates, by a view of Christ recognized by Paul after his call to be erroneous and false. Paul writes, "even though we have once known Christ according to the flesh, yet from now on we no longer know him in this way." As a persecutor of the church, Paul could have seen in Christ a messianic seducer of the people . . . who quite rightfully died cursed on the cross. Therefore one could confess him as the resurrected Lord and Messiah only as an act of blasphemy.[19] Paul was enlightened on the way to Damascus by the knowledge that Christ is not a messianic seducer and false prophet but rather, in accordance with God's will, the "end" (*telos*) of the law, which Paul had defended against the Christians as the way to salvation (cf. Rom. 10:4), for the glory on the face of Christ cuts off and outshines the law in glory. Seized by this knowledge, he set out on the mission and was promptly entangled in strenuous debates with his former Jewish colleagues in the faith (see below).

[19]See for this view, Strobel, *Die Sünde der Wahrheit*.

When one adds to these statements Phil. 3:4ff., the picture rounds itself out. In view of and on the basis of the knowledge of Christ imparted to him, Paul deprived himself of all those prerogatives of Jewish birth, education, and righteousness based on the law which, up until his call, seemed to him to be gain and a deposit toward his future deliverance. From now on he considers them unimportant and to be merely "dung" (*skybala*). The change in his life and in Paul's conception of righteousness is clear and complete. Righteousness on the basis of one's own fulfilment of the commandments and the righteousness of faith received as a gift from Christ stand over against one another as alternatives, specifically so that the apostle who has built his life since Damascus on the righteousness of faith might not be misled into a false security (cf. the *ei pos* in Phil. 3:11 and, moreover, 1 Cor. 4:4f.)!

In view of all of this, it follows that the essential content of his gospel was already given to Paul, from his call on, in the form of his knowledge of Christ, a knowledge which was critical of the law, and that he gave expression to this knowledge from the beginning of his mission. The Pauline gospel does not become a gospel of reconciliation and justification critical of the law only after the mix-up in Galatia! We may thus take the apostle by his word in every regard in Gal. 1:12, 16.

The check-test for this interpretation can be conducted on the basis of 2 Cor. 11:24–33. Here Paul reports about his beginnings as a missionary and about the afflictions suffered during them. Besides other miseries, in the course of the years he suffered from the Jews the "forty-minus-one" five times, i.e., the punishment of whipping given in the synagogue, and once he even suffered the punishment of being stoned (v. 24f.). As we find explicitly codified later in the Mishnah, tractate *Mak.* 3.10, whipping was inflicted by the synagogue court against Jews who were guilty either of sexual transgression (according to the criteria of Leviticus 18–21), of transgression against the prohibition concerning unclean food (e.g., the eating of blood) or of desecrating the great day of atonement by working, etc. If one keeps in mind that table fellowship with Gentiles (on the occasion of the celebration of the Lord's Supper) outside of Palestine almost inevitably necessitated breaking the Jewish food laws and purity regulations and that during Paul's missionary journeys in the Diaspora there was not always time nor opportunity to keep the Jewish order of feasts and holidays, then it becomes understandable that Paul was easily and hastily made liable for transgressions, as listed in the Mishnah *Mak.* 3.10, wherever he (as a Jew) dared to appear in a synagogue as a missionary. Thus, 2 Cor. 11:24f. demonstrates that offences against the law were connected with the Pauline approach to missions from the beginning. The stoning mentioned by Paul in v. 25 took place in Lystra (cf. Acts 14:19). According to Mishnah *Sanh.* 7.4, stoning was inflicted on those who blasphemed God and those who led the people into heresy (in conformity with Deut. 13:2ff.).

According to all of this, the critique of the law as a way of salvation was essentially connected with the Pauline understanding of Christ on the road to Damascus rather than first being joined to it by way of later inferences. This does not exclude the idea that the arguments in which Paul was entangled in Jerusalem (at the Apostolic council), in Antioch (in his conflict with Peter and the Jewish Christians), in Galatia (with the Judaizers), in Philippi and in Corinth (with counter-missionaries orientated toward Peter) forced him to develop his critique of the law with a consistency that was not yet necessary at the beginning of his missionary journeys.

When all of this is taken together as a whole, it can thus be said that the Pauline proclamation of justification was not merely the late fruit of Paul's reflection, but was an initial implication of his understanding of Christ on the way to Damascus. In accordance with the way the apostle repeatedly cites pre-Pauline Christian tradition concerning justification in the Corinthian correspondence and in Romans (cf., for example, 1 Cor. 6:11; 2 Cor. 5:21; Rom. 3:25f. and 4:25), the same thing may also be formulated in the following way: *On the basis of his experience of being called, Paul had every reason to concur with the perceptions of justification of those who already belonged to the Christian community before him; he had learned to affirm their understanding of faith and taught others to see the divine righteousness in and through Christ as the center of the gospel. It is precisely this righteousness that the letter to the Romans is about.*

INDEX OF MODERN AUTHORS

Davies, A. T., 314
Davies, W. D., 68, 257, 260, 262, 319, 321, 324, 326
Davis, J. J., 276
Debrunner, A., 223
Dederen, R., 69, 77
De Lacy, P. H., 153, 155, 157
De Wette, W. M., 96
Deissmann, A., 122
Dennison, J. D., 159
Dibelius, M., 81, 83, 111, 247
Dietzfelbinger, C., 242
Dillon, J., 284
Dinter, P. E., 315
Dittenberger, G., 198
Dodd, C. H., lxx, 12–13, 32, 176, 180, 212, 247, 269, 272, 275, 294, 302, 328, 261
Donfried, K. P., xliii–xliv, xlvi, l, lxi, 103, 105, 116, 118–20, 124–32, 144, 175, 202, 208, 232, 235–36, 245, 253, 289
Doty, W. G., 122, 130, 245
Drane, J. W., 203
Driver, G. R., 159, 276
Dunn, J. D. G., lv–lvi, lxii–lxiv, lxx, lxii, 192, 246–49, 266, 269, 295, 299–300, 303–4, 306–7
Dupont, J., 72, 79, 82, 258–59, 265
Düring, I., 166, 281–82, 287, 293
Du Toit, A. B., 269–70

Eckardt, A. R., 314, 325
Ehrhardt, A. A. T., 189–90
Eichholz, G. 253, 315, 326
Einarson, B., 153, 155, 157
Eisler, R., 179
Erbes, K. 94–95
Espy, J. M., 336

Fábrega, V., 223, 225
Faw, C. E., 168
Feldman, L. H., 313
Festugière, A. J., 283
Feuillet, A., 68, 78–80, 83, 265
Fischel, H. A., 144
Fitzmyer, J., lxii, lxv, 71, 321–22
Focke, F., 284, 291
Fraiken, D., 246
Frankemölle, H., 261
Franklin, E., 201
Frey, J.-G., 89, 91
Friedrich, G., 32, 39–40, 199
Fuchs, E., 46, 48, 58, 62, 103, 124, 192
Fuhrmann, M., 121
Fuller, R. H., liv, 66
Funk, R. W., 121, 223
Furnish, V. P., 71, 73, 75, 78, 81–82, 107, 111, 140, 143–44, 203

Gaiser, K., 282

Gale, H. M., 320
Gamble, H., Jr., 120, 176, 181–82, 252
Garlington, D., 300
Gaston, L., lxii–lxiv, lxviii, lxx, 299, 310–11, 316–17
Georgi, D., 33, 146, 200–201, 207, 215, 310–11
Gerhäusser, W., 281, 291
Gielen, M., 229
Gilbert, M., 285
Godet, F., 86
Gommel, J., 146
Goppelt, L., 252
Grafe, E., 86, 96
Graves, R., 179
Grayston, K., 266
Grube, G. M. A., 169
Grundmann, W., 80
Guerra, A., 288
Guterman, S. L., 88
Guthrie, W. K. C., 283
Güttgemanns, E., 131

Hadot, I., 111
Haenchen, E., 93
Hafemann, S., lxviii–lxix, 333
Hahn, F., 31, 200, 301, 308
Hanson, A. T., 145
Harder, G., 35, 39, 66, 86
Harnack, A. v., 10, 93, 179, 181
Harrisville, R. A., 275
Hartlich, P., 284–85
Haufe, G., 86
Headlam, A. C., lxx, A. C., 29, 37, 71, 74, 77, 208, 211, 213–14, 247, 272, 328
Heil, J. P., 269
Helmbold, F. W. C., 152, 155–56, 167–68
Hengel, M., 278, 286
Herbert, C. C., 155
Hercher, R., 151, 156, 169
Hester, J. D., 130–31
Hicks, R. D., 149, 155, 157
Hild, A., 100
Hock, R. F., 270
Hoennicke, G., 92
Holland, L., 216
Hooker, M. D., 301
Hübner, H., 205, 207, 210, 214, 299, 301, 308, 319, 323
Hughes, F., lvii, lix
Hyldahl, N., 285

Jacoby, A., 100
Jaeger, W., 278, 282
Janne, H., 92
Jaubert, A., 300
Jeremias, J., 93, 97, 256, 258–59, 265, 319–20, 337
Jervell, J., xlv, 54, 56, 59, 63, 65, 69, 103, 124, 192, 199, 232

INDEX OF ANCIENT SOURCES

Pelagius
Expositions 5

Pseudo-Clementines
Recognitions 10.71 (GCS 51, 371) 95

Tertullian
Apologeticum
16.2 100

E. DEAD SEA SCROLLS

CD (*Damascus Document*)
1.4–5 303
1.13–21 305
1.15–18 303
1.20 303
2.11–12 315
3.2–4 303
3.10–16 303
4.7–10 303
6.2–5 303

1QH (*Hodayot*)
2.8–19 305

1QM (*War Scroll*)
14.8–9 315

1QS (*Manual of Discipline*)
1.7–8 303
2.4–5 305
5.1–3 303
5.24 303
8.16–9.2 303

F. RABBINICAL LITERATURE

Mishnah
Makkot 3.10 344
Sanhedrin
7:4 344
10:1 323

Tosefta
Meg. 4.14 89

Babylonian Talmud
Meg. 3.3 89

Mekhilta
Exod. 20:6 304

Sifre
Deut. 53b–75b 304

G. CLASSICAL AND HELLENISTIC AUTHORS

Antisthenes [Diogenes Laertius, *Vitae philosophorom* 6.16] 284

Apollodorus Mechanicus
Poliorcetica 137.1 155

Archytas
ep. 1 169

Aristides
Fragmenta
121–71 288
181–294 285

Aristobulus
Fragmenta 3–4 305

Ariston of Ceos [Diogenes Laertius, *Vitae philosophorom* 7.163] 284

Aristotle
Ars rhetorica
1.3.4 lxi
3.13.4 267
Protrepticus 283
B29–32 281
B34 293
B38 293
B43 293
Rhetoric 116
1.9 (1368A) 291

Artapanus
Fragmenta 3 305

Athenaeus Mechanicus
De machinis 155

Cato, M. Porcius (1)
De Agri Cultura 115

Cicero
Pro Flacco 67–69 87
Hortensius 281, 283
De inventione
1.19 267
1.31–33 268
Orator 14.45–46 115
De partitione oratoria 27 267